MW00855997

THE ROUTLEDGE COMPANION TO SCENOGRAPHY

The Routledge Companion to Scenography is the largest and most comprehensive collection of original essays to survey the historical, conceptual, critical, and theoretical aspects of this increasingly important aspect of theatre and performance studies.

Editor and leading scholar Arnold Aronson brings together a uniquely valuable anthology of texts especially commissioned from across the discipline of theatre and performance studies.

Establishing a stable terminology for a deeply contested term, this volume looks at scenography as the totality of all the visual, spatial, and sensory aspects of performance. Tracing a line from Aristotle's *Poetics* down to Brecht and Artaud and into contemporary immersive theatre and digital media, *The Routledge Companion to Scenography* is a vital addition to every theatre library.

Arnold Aronson, a theatre historian and professor of theatre at Columbia University in New York City, writes on scenography as well as modern and contemporary theatre. Books include *Ming Cho Lee: A Life in Design*; *The Disappearing Stage: Reflections on the 2011 Prague Quadrennial*; *Looking into the Abyss: Essays on Scenography*; *American Avant-Garde Theatre: A History*; *American Set Design*; and *The History and Theory of Environmental Scenography*. He is a former editor of *Theatre Design & Technology* and is currently co-editor of the journal *Theatre and Performance Design*. He has a long history with the Prague Quadrennial, the international exhibition of theatre and performance design and architecture, serving as President of the Jury in 1991 and 1999, curator of the US exhibit in 1995 and General Commissioner in 2007.

THE ROUTLEDGE COMPANION TO SCENOGRAPHY

Edited by Arnold Aronson

LONDON AND NEW YORK

First published 2018
by Routledge
2 Park Square, Milton Park, Abingdon, Oxon, OX14 4RN

and by Routledge
711 Third Avenue, New York, NY 10017

Routledge is an imprint of the Taylor & Francis Group, an informa business

British Library Cataloguing in Publication Data
A catalogue record for this book is available from the British Library

Library of Congress Cataloging in Publication Data
A catalog record for this book has been requested

ISBN: 978-1-138-91780-4 (hbk)
ISBN: 978-1-315-68881-7 (ebk)

Typeset in Sabon
by Swales & Willis Ltd, Exeter, Devon, UK

For Max Edward Aronson

CONTENTS

FIGURES

CONTRIBUTORS

Arnold Aronson is Co-Editor of the journal *Theatre and Performance Design*. He is author of *Ming Cho Lee: A Life in Design*, as well as several books and articles on scenography. He served as General Commissioner of the 2007 Prague Quadrennial. Professor Aronson teaches theatre at Columbia University in New York.

Evan Baker (PhD, 1993, New York University) is an independent scholar specializing in the history of opera and theatrical production and staging, theatre architecture and technology, and opera iconography. His most recent publication, *From the Score to the Stage: An Illustrated History of Continental Opera Production and Staging* (University of Chicago Press, 2013), was recognized in 2014 by the Association of American Publishers as the best publication in Music and the Performing Arts. Presently, Baker is preparing a study on Gustav Mahler and Viennese stage designer Alfred Roller, and their influences on opera production at the Vienna Court Opera, 1897–1907.

Christopher Baugh is Emeritus Professor of Performance and Technology at the University of Leeds. As scenographer he has worked in the USA, Dublin, and extensively in the United Kingdom. His writing on scenography includes *Garrick and Loutherbourg* (Chadwyck-Healey, 1990), *Brecht and Stage Design: The Bühnenbildner and the Bühnenbauer* (Cambridge, 1994 and 2006), and the second edition of *Theatre, Performance and Technology: The Development and Transformation of Scenography* (Palgrave, 2013). In 1975 he was one of the founding members of the SBTD (Society of British Theatre Designers).

David Bisaha is an Assistant Professor of Theatre History and Theory at Binghamton University, State University of New York. His research focuses on the studio and collaborative practices of theatrical designers and their relationship to performance institutions and technologies. He is writing a history of scenic design praxis in interwar New York City, currently entitled 'American Scenic Design and Freelance Professionalism.'

Stephen Bottoms is Professor of Contemporary Theatre and Performance at the University of Manchester, UK. His books include *Playing Underground: A Critical History of the 1960s Off-Off-Broadway Movement* (Michigan, 2004), *Small Acts of Repair: Performance, Ecology and Goat Island* (with Matthew Goulish; Routledge, 2007), and *Sex, Drag and Male Roles: Investigating Gender as Performance* (with Diane Torr; Michigan, 2010). He is also a practicing theatre-maker, whose recent work has been concerned with the use of site-specific performance in areas of environmental change: see www.performancefootprint.co.uk and www.multi-story-shipley.co.uk.

Thea Brejzek is Professor for Spatial Theory at the University of Technology Sydney and has a background in opera stage directing and theatre studies; in 2007–2012 she was a Professor at Zurich University of the Arts (ZHdK) and the Director of the practice-informed PhD program of Scenography. She publishes and lectures widely on the history and theory of scenography and performative environments with a particular interest in transdisciplinary practices and the politics of space in performance. Thea is a member of the scientific advisory board of the Bauhausfoundation Dessau and an Associate Editor of the journal *Theatre and Performance Design* (Routledge).

Kate Burnett, Reader in Theatre Design at Nottingham Trent University, is an award-winning theatre designer working with a wide range of contexts and audiences. Since 1994 she has curated and co-curated five national exhibitions of design for performance for the Society of British Theatre Designers. Selections from these have been exhibited at the international Prague Quadrennial (winning a Gold Medal in 1995, Golden Triga in 2003 and Special Jury Award in 2015) and also in regional UK galleries and the Victoria & Albert Museum, London. For World Stage Design 2013, held in Cardiff, Kate was editor of the print catalogue.

Pannill Camp is Associate Professor of Drama at Washington University in St Louis. His book, *The First Frame: Theatre Space in Enlightenment France*, examines theatre architecture reform in the second half of the eighteenth century. It received the honorable mention for the ATHE Outstanding Book Prize and was a finalist for the Kenshur Prize in eighteenth-century studies.

Marvin Carlson is the Sidney E. Cohn Professor of Theatre, Comparative Literature and Middle Eastern Studies at the Graduate Center of the City University of New York. He has received an honorary doctorate from the University of Athens, the ATHE Career Achievement Award, the ASTR Distinguished Scholarship Award, the George Jean Nathan Award for Dramatic Criticism, and the Calloway Prize for writing in theatre. He is the founding editor of the journals *Western European Stages* and *Arab Stages*. He is the author of 23 books, the most recent of which is *Shattering Hamlet's Mirror* (Michigan, 2016).

Michelle Liu Carriger is an Assistant Professor of Critical Studies in the Theater Department of UCLA, with a PhD from Brown University. Her work concerns clothing, historiography, reenactment, and the performance of self in everyday life with special focus on gender, race, and sexuality in Britain and Japan.

Jane Collins is Professor of Theatre and Performance, University of the Arts, London. She is a writer, director, and theatre-maker who works all over the UK and internationally. She has written extensively on scenography and in 2010 co-edited *Theatre and Performance Design: A Reader in Scenography*. She is one of the founders of the Routledge journal *Theatre and Performance Design* which she currently co-edits with Arnold Aronson. Jane lives in Brighton on the Sussex coast.

Matt Cornish is Assistant Professor of Theater History at Ohio University. He is the author of *Performing Unification: History and Nation in German Theater after 1989* (University of Michigan Press) and the editor of *Everything and Other Performance Texts from Contemporary Germany* (Seagull Books – In Performance, forthcoming spring 2018). Matt held a Fulbright Research Fellowship and a DAAD Postdoctoral Research Fellowship, both at the Freie Universität Berlin, and he received his Doctor of Fine Arts from Yale School of Drama.

Amanda Culp is a PhD candidate in theatre at Columbia University, where she studies classical Sanskrit drama, Indian theater, and intercultural performance. As a dramaturg, Amanda is a frequent collaborator with New Delhi-based director Nikhil Mehta, and a founding member of The Living Room, a collective of female theater artists from New York. She holds an MAR in Asian Religion from Yale Divinity School and a BA in drama and Asian studies from Vassar College.

Arnaud Dechelle is an architect and scenographer specializing in the design of narrative exhibitions. Recent works include the House of European History in Brussels and the award-winning POLIN, Museum of the History of Polish Jews in Warsaw. He holds a Master of Arts in Scenography from Central St Martins in London and was an Associate Lecturer there. Arnaud is currently a Senior Lecturer in Design for Exhibition and Museums at the University of Lincoln. He has presented papers at various international conferences and wrote a chapter in the book *Amy Winehouse, a Family Portrait*, published by the Jewish Museum London.

Stephen Di Benedetto is Chairman of the Department of Theatre Arts, Executive Director of the Jerry Herman Ring Theatre and Associate Professor of Theatre History at the University of Miami, USA. He is an associate editor of the journals *Scene* and *ASAP/Journal* and publications include *The Provocation of the Senses in Contemporary Theatre* (2010), *An Introduction to Theatre Design* (2012), and *Designer's Shakespeare* (2016).

Kathy Foley is a Professor of Theatre Arts at University of California, Santa Cruz, and editor of *Asian Theatre Journal* (2005–2017). She is a dalang (puppet master) of Sundanese wayang golek rod puppetry of West Java, Indonesia, with recent performances at the Smithsonian Freer Gallery and she curates exhibitions of Asian masks and puppets.

Mel Gordon is Professor Emeritus of Theatre at University of California, Berkeley. He is the author of numerous books on Weimar Berlin, including *Expressionist Texts* (Performing Arts Journal Books, 1986).

Andrew Gurr, a New Zealander, is Professor Emeritus at the University of Reading and former Director of Research at the Shakespeare Globe Centre, London. He has written more than 20 academic books and hundreds of articles. His books on theatre history include *The Shakespearean Stage 1574–1642*; *Playgoing in Shakespeare's London*; *The Shakespearian Playing Companies*; *The Shakespeare Company 1594–1642*; *Staging in Shakespeare's Theatres* (in collaboration with Mariko Ichikawa); and *Shakespeare's Opposites: The Admiral's Men 1594–1625*. He has also edited Shakespeare's *Richard II* and *Henry V*, and three plays by Beaumont and Fletcher.

Dorita M. Hannah is Research Professor of Interdisciplinary Architecture, Art & Design at the University of Tasmania (Australia) and Adjunct Professor of Stage & Space with Aalto University (Finland). Her practice-led research focuses on live events, installations and exhibitions, as well as specializing in theatre architecture. She co-chairs the Performance+Design Working Group for PSi (Performance Studies international), sits on several editorial boards, and has created exhibitions and events for the Prague Quadrennial as design director, architectural commissioner and theory curator. Focusing on spatial performativity, Dr Hannah is completing *Event-Space: Theatre Architecture & the Historical Avant-Garde*, to be published by Routledge Press (2017).

Franklin J. Hildy (PhD Northwestern University) is Professor of Theatre History and Director of Graduate Studies at the University of Maryland. He is a Fellow of the College of Fellows of the American Theatre and a Senior Research Fellow at Shakespeare's Globe, London. He is co-author, with Oscar G. Brockett, of five editions of *History of the Theatre* (now translated into Chinese, Czech, Fārsī, Greek, Korean and Ukrainian) and author of *Shakespeare at the Maddermarket* and over 60 articles on theatre architecture and Shakespearean staging. He edited *New Issues in the Reconstruction of Shakespeare's Theatre*, and is General Editor for theatre-finder.org.

Amy Holzapfel is Associate Professor of Theatre at Williams College. She is author of *Art, Vision & Nineteenth-Century Realist Drama: Acts of Seeing* (Routledge, 2014). Her new monograph-in-progress, *The Commons of Tragedy: Re-finding the Chorus in Performance After the Millennium* (University of Michigan Press), charts the aesthetic and political impact of the tragic chorus in contemporary forms of theatre and performance. She received her MFA (2001) and DFA (2006) in Dramaturgy & Dramatic Criticism from the Yale School of Drama.

Ewa Kara received her PhD in Theatre from Columbia University in New York. Her research investigates contemporary scenography, in particular the emergence of new visual paradigms and their challenge to earlier staging conventions. She previously studied theatre and art history at the Jagiellonian University in Krakow, Poland, and taught at Columbia University and the Johannes Gutenberg University in Mainz, Germany. Her interests focus on scenography and the visual culture, modern and contemporary theatre, as well as the history of the theatrical avant-garde and Polish drama and theatre.

Dennis Kennedy is Samuel Beckett Professor of Drama Emeritus at Trinity College Dublin. He is the author or editor of many award-winning books, including *The Spectator and the Spectacle*; *Looking at Shakespeare*; *Foreign Shakespeare*; *Shakespeare* *in Asia* (with Yong Li Lan); *The Oxford Encyclopedia of Theatre and Performance*; *The Oxford Companion to Theatre and Performance*; and *Granville Barker and the Dream of Theatre*. He has also worked as a playwright and director in London, Dublin, New York and Beijing, and his short stories have appeared in numerous literary magazines.

Gordon Kipling, Professor of English Emeritus at UCLA, has published widely on the literature and culture of late Middle Ages and the early Renaissance, particularly on topics concerned with the period's various forms of theatrical spectacle. His book, *Enter the King: Theatre, Liturgy, and Ritual in the Medieval Civic Triumph* (Clarendon Press, 1998), won both the Otto Gründler Prize for Medieval Studies and the David Bevington Prize for Early Drama Studies. His next book, 'Jean Fouquet's Martyrdom of St Apollonia: The Art of the Miniature and the History of the Theatre,' is forthcoming from Brepols.

David Kornhaber is Associate Professor of English and Comparative Literature at the University of Texas at Austin. He is the author of *The Birth of Theater from the Spirit of Philosophy: Nietzsche and the Modern Drama* (Northwestern University Press, 2016), and his work has appeared in *PMLA*, *Modern Drama*, *Theatre Journal* and *Theatre Research International*, among various other journals and edited collections. He has served as guest editor of *Modern Drama*, as an affiliated writer with *American Theatre*, and as a contributor to the theatre sections of *The New York Times* and *The Village Voice*.

Lidia Kosovski, an award-winning set designer, lives and works in Rio de Janeiro, Brazil. She studied architecture and urbanism and has a PhD in Communication and Culture from the Universidade Federal do Rio de Janeiro. She is an Associate Professor in the Scenography Department of the Theater School and of the PhD Program of Performing Arts (PPGAC-UNIRIO-RJ). Professor Kosovski is a member of the Editorial Board of *O Percevejo*, an online journal, and was formerly Director of Performing Arts at RIO-ARTE Foundation, Rio de Janeiro's city hall, and Artistic Manager of Sergio Porto Theater in Rio de Janeiro (2001–2002).

Dominika Łarionow, PhD, is a lecturer at the Department of Art History, University of Łódź, and Head of the Department of Theatre at the Polish Institute of World Art Studies in Warsaw. She was a convener of Scenography Working Group FIRT/IFTR (2006–2013) and a member of the editorial boards of *Theatre and Performance Design* and *Theatre Arts Journal*. Professor Łarionow is author of *Przestrzenie obrazów Leszka Mądzika* [*Spaces of Images by Leszek Mądzik*], Lublin 2008, and *"Wystarczy tylko otworzyć drzwi . . .": Przedmioty w twórczości Tadeusza Kantora ["You only need to open the door . . .": Items in the works of Tadeusz Kantor*], Łódź 2015.

Julia Listengarten is Professor of Theatre and Director of Graduate Studies at University of Central Florida. She has written on avant-garde and contemporary theatre, scenographic practices and performances of national identity. Her translation of Vvedensky's *Christmas at the Ivanovs*' premiered Off-Broadway at Classic Stage Company. She is the author of *Russian Tragifarce: Its Cultural and Political Roots* (2000), co-author of *Modern American Playwriting: 2000–2009* (with Cindy Rosenthal, 2017), and co-editor of *Theater of the Avant-Garde, 1950–2000* (2011) and *Playing with Theory in Theatre Practice* (2012). She is currently editing 'Decades of Modern American Playwriting: 1930–2009' (with Brenda Murphy).

Kevin Lotery is a scholar of modern and contemporary art. His research focuses on the development of cross-disciplinary aesthetic strategies from 1945 to the present. Lotery is co-editor of *Artists Design Exhibitions*, a special issue of *October* magazine tracking the medium of exhibition design from the interwar avant-gardes to the end of the twentieth century. His current book project, *The Long Front of Culture: The Independent Group and Exhibition Design*, examines the exhibition designs of Richard Hamilton, Nigel Henderson, Lawrence Alloway, Alison and Peter Smithson and other members of the research collaborative known as the Independent Group in 1950s London. He is currently Visiting Assistant Professor of Modern and Contemporary Art at Sarah Lawrence College.

Joslin McKinney is an Associate Professor in Scenography at the University of Leeds, UK. She leads the Performance Design MA program and researches into the materiality and agency of scenography. In 2015 she was chair of the international jury for the Prague Quadrennial of Performance Design and Space. She is the lead author of *The Cambridge Introduction to Scenography* (2009). She has published articles and chapters on scenographic research methods, scenographic spectacle and embodied spectatorship, phenomenology, kinaesthetic empathy, and material agency. With Scott Palmer, she is the co-editor of *Scenography Expanded: An Introduction to Contemporary Performance Design* (Bloomsbury Methuen, 2017).

C. W. Marshall is Professor of Greek at the University of British Columbia in Vancouver, Canada.

Scott Palmer, University of Leeds, UK, was co-convenor (2013–2016) of the International Federation of Theatre Research Scenography Working Group and an associate editor of the *Theatre and Performance Design* journal. His publications include *Light* (2013), articles on new ways of thinking about lighting as a creative performance practice, and he has recently co-edited *Scenography Expanded: An Introduction to Contemporary Performance Design* (2017).

Mike Pearson is Emeritus Professor of Performance Studies at Aberystwyth University. He creates theatre as a solo artist; with artist/designer Mike Brookes in Pearson/Brookes; for National Theatre Wales; and with senior performers' group Good News From The Future. He is co-author with Michael Shanks of *Theatre/Archaeology* (2001) and author of *In Comes I: Performance, Memory and Landscape* (2006), *Site-specific Performance* (2010), *Mickery Theater: An Imperfect Archaeology* (2011), and *Marking Time: Performance, Archaeology and the City* (2013).

Barbora Příhodová received her PhD in theatre history and theory at Masaryk University in Brno, Czech Republic. Her research interests include contemporary and historical forms of design and space in performance, and theatre and scenography in post-war Czechoslovakia. Among her publications are the co-authored book *Czech Theatre Costume* (2011) and edited book *Scenography Speaks: Conversations* *of Jarka Burian with Josef Svoboda* (2014, in Czech). She is one of the curators of the exhibition Shakespeare in Prague: Imagining the Bard in the Heart of Europe (Columbus Museum of Art, Ohio, 2017). She teaches at Villanova University.

Austin E. Quigley is the Brander Matthews Professor of Dramatic Literature at Columbia University, where he teaches courses on theatre and drama. From 1995 to 2009 he was Dean of Columbia College. He is the author of *The Pinter Problem* (Princeton, 1975), *The Modern Stage and Other Worlds* (Methuen, 1985), *Theoretical Inquiry: Language, Linguistics, and Literature* (Yale, 2004), and many related articles. He has served on the editorial boards of *Modern Drama*, *The Pinter Review*, and *New Literary History*. He has also served a term as President of the Association of Literary Scholars, Critics, and Writers.

David Roesner is Professor for Theatre and Music-Theatre at the LMU Munich. He previously worked at the universities of Hildesheim, Exeter, and Kent. In 2003 he published his first monograph on *Theatre as Music*, followed by major publications on Theatre Noise. *The Sound of Performance* (with Lynne Kendrick, CSP, 2011), *Composed Theatre: Aesthetics, Practices, Processes* (with Matthias Rebstock, Intellect, 2012), and his latest monograph *Musicality in Theatre: Music as Model, Method and Metaphor in Theatre-Making* (Ashgate, 2014). David has also worked as a theatre musician and sound designer. For a full list of publications and projects see: http://mhn.academia.edu/DavidRoesner.

Luiz Henrique Sá has a PhD in Performing Arts (UNIRIO – Universidade Federal do Estado do Rio de Janeiro) and MA in History of Brazilian Design (Escola Superior de Desenho Industrial). He was a Fulbright visiting scholar at Columbia University in New York (2014/2015). He is a Professor in the Scenography Department and Director of the traditional School of Theater of UNIRIO. Professor Sá also works as photographer, graphic artist, and set designer for theatrical productions, concerts, cinema, and exhibitions. He is a collaborator with designer Helio Eichbauer, and is partner in the design studio Bigodes.

Chris Salter is an artist, University Research Chair in New Media, Technology and the Senses at Concordia University, Professor of Computation Arts, and Co-Director of the Hexagram network for Research-Creation in Media Arts, Design, Technology and Digital Culture. Salter's performances, installations, research, and publications have been presented at numerous festivals, exhibitions, and conferences around the world. He is the author of *Entangled: Technology and the Transformation of Performance* (MIT Press, 2010) and *Alien Agency: Experimental Encounters with Art in the Making* (MIT Press, 2015).

Jesse Weaver Shipley, Professor of African and African American Studies at Dartmouth University, is an ethnographer, filmmaker, and artist. His work explores the links between aesthetics and politics by focusing on performances and popular cultures in the midst of changing economic regimes and forms of sovereignty. He is the author of two books – *Living the Hiplife: Celebrity and Entrepreneurship in Ghanaian Popular Music* and *Trickster Theatre: The Poetics of Freedom in Urban Africa*.

Amy Skinner is Lecturer in Drama and Theatre Practice in the School Arts at the University of Hull. Her research interests include Russian and Early Soviet theatre, theatre direction and scenography, and interdisciplinary connections between theatre, fine art, and early twentieth century physics. She is also a theatre director and designer, specializing in contemporary stagings of multi-lingual texts and plays in translation. She is a member of the executive committee of the Standing Conference of University Drama Departments (SCUDD) and the founder and coordinator of the Russian Theatre Research Network UK.

Melissa Trimingham is a Senior Lecturer in Drama at the University of Kent. She has published widely on scenography, the Bauhaus stage, and the use of puppetry, masks and costume with autistic children. As a researcher on the Arts and Humanities Research Council-funded project 'Imagining Autism: Drama, Performance and Intermediality as Interventions for Autistic Spectrum Conditions' she developed scenographies for working with children on the autistic spectrum using puppetry, masks, costumes, sound, light, and projection in immersive environments. Her monograph *The Theatre of the Bauhaus: the Modern and Postmodern Stage of Oskar Schlemmer* was published in 2011.

Beth Weinstein is an Associate Professor of Architecture at the University of Arizona and PhD candidate at the University of Tasmania. Her research and practice explore architecture in relation to performance, through writing, drawing, event-making and intervening in urban and landscape spaces. She co-edited *Ground|Water: the Art, Design and Science of a Dry River* (2012), curated the Collaborative Legacy of Merce Cunningham exhibition (2011) and is writing a book on collaborations between architects and choreographers.

W. B. Worthen, Alice Brady Pels Professor in the Arts, is Chair of the Department of Theatre at Barnard College, Columbia University; he is also Professor in the faculty of Theatre in the School of the Arts, in the Department of English and Comparative Literature, and co-chair of the PhD in Theatre at Columbia. He has written widely on drama and performance theory, most recently in *Shakespeare Performance Studies* (2014), *Drama: Between Poetry and Performance* (2010), and *Print and the Poetics of Modern Drama* (2005), and is currently writing a book on theatre as technology.

Yi Tianfu is Dean of the Stage Design Department of the Shanghai Theatre Academy; Vice Director of the lighting committee of the China Institute of Stage Design; Vice Director of the stage, film, and television lighting committee of China Illuminating Engineering Society; and Executive Director of the lighting committee of the China Association of Performing Arts.

INTRODUCTION

Scenography or design

Arnold Aronson

Most "Companions" have a clearly defined subject such as a discipline, a genre, or a person that is reflected in the title. A "Companion to Shakespeare," say, or a "Companion to Greek Tragedy" tells you immediately what will be inside, even if the individual essays might challenge or contradict accepted approaches or understandings. But, for this volume, even the title was a contested subject. Should this be a "Companion to Theatre Design" or to "Stage Design," or a "Companion to Scenography"? I have opted for the latter for reasons I will explain. On one level, the problem is essentially a linguistic one. Scenography and design have different connotations and are understood by different people in different contexts to mean different things. The English language has several words or phrases that address the visual aspects of theatre, some related to specific fields (lighting, costume, etc.) and some, more broadly, a factor of the language's tendency to absorb and borrow from many other languages, giving us words such as "decor" and "scenery," for example. Considerations ranging from shifts in disciplinary thinking – theatre studies has been challenged by performance studies which has significantly expanded the range of activities and practices beyond traditional Western concepts of theatre – to economic models and modes of training also play a role in nomenclature. In the United States in particular, graduate programs and conservatories tend to train designers in specific disciplines; and the United Scenic Artists – the professional union for designers – administers examinations in separate design categories.

Until the latter part of the twentieth century, the word "scenography" was rarely found in reference to theatre within the English-speaking world, although it was an established term in the field of architecture, referring to the use of perspective in rendering three-dimensional objects. In 1975 the Nordic Theatre Union published the first edition of *Theatre Words* – a lexicon of theatre and technical terms in English with their equivalents in five Scandinavian languages; subsequent editions over the next decade added more languages. It included illustrations but no definitions; it was intended as a reference manual so that theatre artists could communicate across linguistic divides – something increasingly important as opera designers in particular began to work ever more frequently on the international circuit. Through all these early editions, the word "scenography" did not appear in English. One could find "decor," "scenery," and "scenic designer" as well as "lighting designer" (though, interestingly, not costume designer).

The word "scenografia" was listed as the Italian equivalent of scenery, and in Spanish one could find "escenógrafo" for scenic designer. The 1995 edition, however, retitled *New Theatre Words*,[1] retained "decor" and "scenery," but now included, for the first time in English, a separate entry for "scenography."

What led to the change? Part of the answer may lie with the emergence in the 1960s of Czech designer Josef Svoboda as arguably the most famous, and certainly one of the most influential, theatre artists in the world. Working across theatrical genres from classical drama, to opera, to dance, to World's Fair expositions, to his own theatre of wonders, the Laterna Magika, Svoboda redefined the art of stage design. Following in the footsteps of Adolphe Appia and Edward Gordon Craig, he shaped the stage as much with light as with scenery, often developing innovative technologies in his workshop. His artistry was so powerful that he was occasionally accused – at least by some critics – of overwhelming the productions. His creations came as close as anything in the modern era to the Wagnerian *Gesamtkunstwerk*, the total work of art. In Czech the word for scenic design is, in fact, *scénografie*. In 1971, theatre historian Jarka Burian, picking up on this linguistic turn, published his highly influential and widely-read book, *The Scenography of Josef Svoboda*. A quote from the book even makes it into the *Oxford English Dictionary* as a modern source.[2] Burian did not create a neologism out of Czech any more than Svoboda invented a new field. As other examples in the *OED* make clear, it was not a new word – there are theatrical references dating back to the eighteenth century – but at the time it was rare, and its usage was generally vague, imprecise, and ambiguous. The international reputation of Svoboda, however, gave it a hitherto unprecedented prominence. Here was someone who was not merely a designer, a designation that still was redolent of craft rather than art, he was a *scenographer*; and he did not merely create set designs or lighting designs for the stage, he created something more comprehensive and central to the conception of theatre: he created *scenography*.

Also, in 1968, a new organization emerged: The International Organization of Scenographers and Theatre Technicians (OISTT in its French acronym – in 1985 architecture was added so that it became the International Organization of Scenographers Theatre Architects and Technicians, or OISTAT).[3] The membership consisted of national centers (including the above-named Nordic Theatre Union) rather than individuals, and it was structured around working groups or commissions – one of which was Scenography. While the working group nominally incorporated all aspects of design, it was really focused on set design. Tellingly, over the years, other design disciplines broke off to found their own working groups.[4] The organization was, originally, based in Prague where the Prague Quadrennial (PQ) had debuted in 1967 – an international exhibition and competition of stage design and theatre architecture. With the steady growth of OISTAT and the PQ, the term scenography became increasingly understood as an international designator of design.

By the beginning of the millennium the term was widely, if still ambiguously, employed and British designer Pamela Howard wrote a seminal study entitled *What Is Scenography?* While much of the book was taken up with a discussion of her own practice, it began with brief responses to the titular question from some 50 theatre practitioners from around the world – most of whom were active in OISTAT, many of whom had exhibited at the PQ. Not surprisingly, no two answers were identical; some were blatantly – and delightfully – contradictory.

As the term gained wider usage in the English-language theatre, however, it often became little more than a synonym – one is tempted to say a pretentious synonym – for set design, and set designers were increasingly referred to (or occasionally referred to themselves) as scenographers, though costume and lighting designers retained their more pedestrian titles.

The identification of scenography solely with scenery is reinforced in the second definition of scenography in the *Oxford English Dictionary*:[5] "The art of painting theatrical scenery according to the rules of stage perspective; the scenery thus created," with a citation dating to 1738. Implied in that definition, of course, is the concept of the pictorial and the painterly, organized along perspectival principles. It suggests that scenery is a visual theatrical element akin to easel painting; it is something to be looked at. Embedded in such a definition are notions of both background and, especially, illusion. But as the concept and practice of design expanded, such a definition was limiting and old fashioned. Svoboda expressed his "great fear . . . of becoming a mere 'décorateur.' What irritates me most," he complained, "are such terms as 'Bühnenbildner' or 'décorateur' because they imply two-dimensional pictures or superficial decoration" (Burian 1971: 15). In fact, within the history of Western theatre, at least from the development of the proscenium arch in the seventeenth century until the late nineteenth century, this was largely true. But most forms of classical theatre – ancient Greek, Roman, Sanskrit, Noh, Yuan, early modern English, French, and Spanish, to name but a few – occurred on architectural stages that privileged the spatial over the pictorial and foregrounded the actor.

Beginning around the turn of the twentieth century, however, thanks to attempts at recreating the Shakespearean stage, and especially because of the theories and practices of Appia and Craig, space began to re-emerge as a dominant element of theatrical design in Western theatre. This, too, contributed to a conceptual shift from design – understood as painted decor – to scenography, which implied the three-dimensional environment of the stage. It emerged, not coincidentally, as electric light replaced gas, thus allowing not merely a greater intensity and brightness, but greater control. The space of the stage could be sculpted through light, and mood could be evoked through ephemeral shifts in lighting – what Appia called active light (as Scott Palmer discusses in his chapter). For perhaps the first time in history, light was being considered as an integral artistic component of theatre, not merely a necessary source of illumination or special effect. It made sense that, since light, space, and atmosphere were so integrally related, they might all be created by a single, unifying artist. Since the actors – historically the focal point of theatre – wore costumes with their own color, shape, texture, and rhythms and moved through the scenic environment, shouldn't the costumes, too, be part of the larger scenographic event and, together with scenery and light, fall under the auspices of a single artist?

Perhaps it is the root word "scene" that sows confusion. It seems almost implicit that scen(ography) = scen(ery). But following that logic, why didn't related arts such as light, costume, and sound develop analogous terminology? As the theories of Appia and Craig made clear, and the practice of Svoboda and several others demonstrated, there is something more inclusive and comprehensive within the notion of scenography that goes well beyond the mere arrangement of the visual elements. Svoboda himself declared that "True scenography is what happens when the curtain opens and can't be judged in any other way" (Burian 1971: 15). The *OED*'s third definition of scenography delineates a roster of component elements: "scenery, costume, lighting, etc." Within that definition it may, in fact, be the "etc." that is the most significant word. Svoboda himself noted that "scenography also implies a handling of total production space, which means not only the space of the stage but also the auditorium" (ibid.: 16).

This multidisciplinary concept of scenography, together with the emphasis on spatiality and the unity of creation, is crucial to understanding the difference between design and scenography. Scenography, as I have written elsewhere, is the "all-encompassing visual spatial construct" of the theatrical event and embodies "the process of change and transformation that is an inherent part of the physical vocabulary of the stage" (Aronson 2005: 7). As a means of understanding performance, scenography should, in fact, lie at the heart of any analysis of theatrical and performance art. Hans-Thies Lehmann, in *Postdramatic Theatre*, identifies a "visual dramaturgy" that "activates the dynamic capacity of the gaze to produce processes, combinations and rhythms on the basis of the data provided by the stage" (Lehmann 2006: 157). Similarly, Elinor Fuchs and Una Chaudhuri have noted that "a pervasive new spatiality, of which scenography is the most obvious site, has turned the Aristotelian hierarchy on its head: now spectacle may be the 'soul' of the dramatic enterprise" (Fuchs and Chaudhuri 2002: 2). As has been proposed elsewhere, we are experiencing a "scenographic turn" (see Collins and Aronson 2015). As with its obvious model, the linguistic turn that posited language and its structures as key to the understanding of philosophy and history, so too can we posit the vocabulary of scenography as fundamental to an understanding of the performative act. It is perhaps time that "scenographic studies" emerges as a fully developed discipline to stand beside performance studies.

Etymological history

To further examine the centrality of scenography to theatre it is useful to return to the origin of the word scenography, which is first found in Aristotle's *Poetics* in which he claims that Sophocles invented *skenographia* (along with introducing the third actor) (*Poetics* 1449a: 18). The word derives from *skene*, which refers to the stage building at the rear of the orchestra, but also means tent or hut, suggesting the humble origins of that structure; and *graphia*, meaning writing, from *graphein*, meaning to write. Thus, *skenographia* may be translated literally as scenic writing. But what Aristotle, lecturing several decades after the death of Sophocles, meant is unclear. As C. W. Marshall points out in his chapter in this volume, it is highly unlikely, for both practical and aesthetic reasons, that Aristotle was referring to illusionistic scenery,[6] although by the mid-fourth century BCE it is conceivable that there may have been some sort of emblematic if not illusionistic scenery and it is possible that Aristotle mistakenly attributed contemporary practice to fifth-century production. Perhaps Aristotle meant simply that Sophocles introduced the *skene*, a very real possibility. The legendary Thespis performed in the agora and, until the turn of the fifth century BCE, that is where the tragic contests were presented, perhaps on a trestle stage of some kind. All we know for certain is that the audience sat on banks of wooden risers (*ikria*) that collapsed in 498 BCE, an event that no doubt hastened the move from the agora. When the festival relocated to the southwest slope of the Acropolis by the temple of Dionysus, an orchestra – an open space for the chorus and actors – was leveled out near the base of the gentle hillside. But the *skene* was probably not introduced until around 460 BCE. We can make this supposition because the first extant play to require a structure of any kind is Aeschylus's *Oresteia* of 458. All prior extant plays take place on an open space. Whoever was responsible for this innovation, we can assume that it was employed simply at first. We can also imagine the aging Aeschylus, wanting to prove himself in light of the successes of his younger rival Sophocles, realizing the potential of this new structure and brilliantly grasping that he now had the option to employ multiple levels, to create dramatic entrances and exits, for hiding and revealing – for creating the fundamental theatrical notion of onstage and offstage. The murder of Agamemnon and Cassandra, for example, visually hidden but horrifically audible, could occur within the mimetic time of an ongoing scene precisely because of the possibilities offered by this structure (see Aronson 2004). The *Oresteia* is literally impossible without scenography. But we should not think of the *skene* as background, let alone backdrop. Whatever it looked like at the time – and we have absolutely no conclusive visual evidence[7] – it was not an illusionistic image. It was a simple and unchanging structure that was designated as a particular locale or edifice through the words and actions of the characters, just as the actors of the classical Yuan drama of China, using little more than a table and two chairs, announce the locale of each scene as they arrive; just as the Chorus of *Henry V* asks us to image this "wooden O" as the "vasty fields of France," and just as the Prologue of Plautus's *Menaechmi* tells us that, "This is the city of Epidamnus while this play is acting; when another shall be acted, it will become another town."

Because Aristotle, in the *Poetics*, was providing an analysis of the genre of tragedy – not a discourse on staging practices – he concentrated on the component elements of the tragic form, with plot as foremost, even going so far as to say that it should be possible to experience catharsis, the desired goal of tragedy, simply by hearing the text. He relegated *opseon* – the visuals (sometimes translated as spectacular elements) – to the bottom of his hierarchy of components. But the Greeks nonetheless understood theatre, at least in part, as a visual art. The very word "theatre" comes from the Greek *theasthai* "to see," which is the root of the word *theatron* – the place where the spectators (those who see) gathered: the seeing place. Centuries later the Romans substituted a different vocabulary. The Latinate word for the equivalent location is, of course, *auditorium*, which might be rendered as hearing place. While the term auditorium has come to dominate English as the locale for the audience (hearers), we do not say, "I'm going to *hear* a play," but rather, "I'm going to *see* a play." Of course just to confuse matters, English, drawing from both Latin and Greek, also uses the word spectators – those who see. Thus, we have spectators in an auditorium.

Neoclassical theorists, notably Ludovico Castelvetro, seizing upon Aristotle's emphasis on the literary, in combination with the Latin foregrounding of the aural, embedded Western drama deeply within the realm of literature, while largely rejecting its visual and physical constituents. It was precisely this attitude that led some scholars, well into the twentieth century, to attempt to embrace drama as a literary form, not merely ignoring the physical and production aspects of theatre but even rejecting them – arguing, for instance, that Shakespeare, like a variant of a well-behaved child, should only be read and not seen. Even the Symbolist playwright Maurice Maeterlinck argued that "most of the great poems of humanity are not fit for the stage. Lear, Hamlet, Othello, Macbeth, Anthony and Cleopatra cannot be represented, and it is dangerous to see them on the stage" (Maeterlinck [1890] 1995: 145). Even down to the present, very few theatre critics, even the most astute among them, are comfortable discussing the scenographic aspects of a production.

The word scenography occurs a few more times over the next centuries after Aristotle. In the second century BCE, Polybius, paraphrasing Timaeus, explained that the difference between history and declamatory writing "is as great as that between real buildings or furniture and the views and compositions we see in scene-paintings [*skenographia*]" (quoted in Small 2013: 112). For the Romans, certainly by the first century BCE, *skenographia* seems to have taken on the meaning of painted backdrops as suggested by Strabo's use of the term to describe the topography and monuments of the Campus Martius (Small 2013). Vitruvius is the Roman architect whose writings would have the greatest impact on Renaissance theory and practice. Writing in the late first century BCE, in *De Architectura*, he employs the term *scaenographia*, but significantly applies it only in relation to perspective drawing for architecture as "a method of sketching a front with the sides withdrawing into the background."[8] When Vitruvius discusses theatre (Vitruvius 1960: Book 5, 3–8), he refers to the decoration of the *scaena* but the word *scaenographia* never appears.[9] Nonetheless, some theatre historians mistakenly cite him as a source for the theatrical use of *scaenographia*.

Italian architect Sebastiano Serlio was the first person to situate the work of Vitruvius in the context of Renaissance practice. Book II of his *Architettura*, published in 1545, is devoted to perspective, which, he notes, "Vitruvius calleth Scenographie"[10] but the brief section at the end of the chapter that deals with theatre architecture and scenic design refers only to perspective (*perspettiva*), not scenographia. He notes that "mong all things made by hand of man few in my opinion bring greater contentment to the eye and satisfaction to the spirit than the unveiling to our view of a stage setting" ["*una scena*" in the original] (Hewitt 1958: 24). He goes on to enumerate the various wonders that can be revealed, including lights "like so many sparkling jewels" and costumes that "delight . . . the wonder of the spectators" (Hewitt 1958: 25). So, at least from Roman times, the term scenography was used almost exclusively for architecture but not for theatre.

Whatever Aristotle meant by *skenographia*, the notion of "scenic writing" is appealing: scenography as the creation and telling of a story through scenic means rather than linguistic narrative.

How the *skene* creates scenography

When we go to the theatre today we usually expect to find some form of scenery but, as I suggest above, this was not a Greek expectation until the middle of the fifth century. The ancient Greek audience, sitting at the Theatre of Dionysus, or later at Epidaurus or any of the dozens of other theatres around the Greek world, saw the performers on the orchestra set against the surrounding countryside that stretched to the horizon. When the *skene* was introduced and even when it grew larger and more elaborate it would not have been large enough to block out the world beyond the theatre (that would have to wait for the elaborate *frons scaenae* of the architecturally unified and enclosed Roman theatres). Thus, the Greek spectator viewed the performance, appropriately enough, in the larger context of the Greek cosmos. In the pre-scenic theatre actors entered onto the orchestra from some offstage space, always in full view of the audience; in the post-scenic theatre, characters, entering from the *skene*, emerged, as it were, from other times and other places, and as they did so they transformed the neutral space of the orchestra into an extension of that world. So, within the topographical space of the Greek world, the *skene* sat literally at the center of the spectator's field of view – an emblematic structure representing another time and place.

Almost half a century ago, Christian Norberg-Schulz defined architectural space "as a concretization of man's existential space" (Norberg-Schulz 1971: 12) and in a sense that is precisely what the introduction of an architectural structure onto the ancient Greek orchestra did. It became a site for the gods, mythological beings, and historical foundation of the society; a locus for the fears and anxieties, as well as hopes and affirmations, of the world in which the theatre was situated. It also functioned analogously to architectural negative space, a kind of hollowing out of the existing environment. The *skene* existed as a scenic rupture that shaped and defined the world of the spectators. I would like to suggest further that the *skene*, as well as later scenic units within architectural stages, function not unlike a wormhole – those devices popularized in science fiction, and known in physics as an Einstein-Rosen bridge – that operate as a sort of trap door within the space-time continuum that allow passage into parallel universes or as a shortcut on a journey through the vastness of space. In Richard Foreman's classic avant-garde play, *Rhoda in Potatoland*, a voice says, "Certain spaces suddenly appear in the center of the audience. Find them. Find them." While Foreman was concerned with the metaphysical aspects of reception, it is nonetheless a useful metaphor for thinking about the experience of theatre made possible by scenography. The scenic structure now introduced onto the stage created a gap – perhaps more accurately, ripped a hole – in the visual field and thus introduced a separate reality to invade the world of the spectators.

If we take the notion of *skenographia* as deriving directly from the introduction of the *skene* onto the stage of the ancient Greek theatre, and if we understand this "scenic writing" – quite literally inscribing a scenic structure on the stage (the orchestra) – as creating a world within a world, then *skenographia* can be understood *not* as the creation of scenery, *nor* the creation of a backdrop, but as the creation of an atmosphere as described by Gernot Böhme. Citing Hermann Schmitz, Böhme defines "atmosphere" as that which is "experienced in bodily presence in relation to persons and things or in spaces" (Böhme 1993: 119), and elsewhere as "the common reality of the perceiver and the perceived" (ibid.: 122). The *skene* – and by extension, scenography – creates a web of relationships. It has a physical shape and the properties of its constituent materials and architectural structures, but it is understood in the context of the particular performance. It signifies on at least two levels: the structure itself signifies a theatrical event (keeping in mind that architecturally it resembles other civic structures and will thus possess a certain familiarity), while contextually suggesting a locus separate from its site. It is an almost infinitely malleable presence that is in constant dialogue with the spectators on one side, and the Greek cosmos behind (and, in reality) all around.

The scenographic turn

Because the dramatic text was, historically, almost the only aspect of performance to survive through time, and because of the neoclassical emphasis on drama as literature, it has come to dominate Western theatre. But what if the structure of a performance, particularly its primary means of communicating with the spectators, was not – or not merely – the written text as spoken by actors (or the libretto sung by opera singers) but rather the visual, spatial, aural, and sensorial elements that comprise live performance? Herbert Blau recognized this when he described "the distance of looking and the distance of listening, both of which are determined largely by the material arrangement of theatre space, the architecture of perception" (Blau [1990] 2010: 53). Gertrude Stein, recalling her earliest memories of theatre stated that "nothing is more interesting to know about the theatre than the relation of sight and sound" (Stein [1935] 1985: 113). Both Stein and Blau are resituating the performative experience in the realm of the scenographic. We may think of the production "merely" as a vessel for a literary text, but in fact the opposite is true. The text is merely one component within the larger theatrical framework that is conveyed through scenography. This is not a new idea, of course. As Edward Gordon Craig wrote in 1911,

> the Art of the Theatre is neither acting nor the play, it is not scene nor dance, but consists of all the elements of which these things are composed: action, which is the very spirit of acting, words, which are the body of the play; line and colour, which are the very heart of the scene; rhythm, which is the very essence of dance.
>
> *(Craig 1911: 138)*

Pamela Howard's definition of scenography goes so far in its Craig-like expansiveness that it practically colonizes all theatre practice: "the seamless synthesis of space, text, research, art, actors, directors and spectators that contributes to an original creation" (Howard 2002: 130). For Howard, then, virtually everything that comprises the creation and production of theatre is scenography.[11]

Theatre, in fact all art, requires a frame – explicit or implicit – in order to exist. A frame distinguishes the quotidian from the extraordinary, what the Sanskrit treatise on theatre, the *Nāṭyaśāstra* , called *lokadharmi* and *natyadharmi* (everyday behavior versus performance behavior).[12] Patrice Pavis rightly explained that the notion of a frame goes beyond any physical theatre space to encompass "the set of the spectators' experiences and *expectations*, the contextualization of the fiction represented. *Frame* is to be taken both literally (as a 'boxing in' of the *performance*) and abstractly (as a contextualization and foregrounding of the action)" (Pavis 1998: 155). Thus, the frame can be understood as a scenographic creation, and the existence of a frame is essential to create the spectator – someone who exists outside the frame as observer.

In the theatre, the observer and the thing observed exist in time and space. Thus, a performance must take place somewhere. This immediately necessitates space – a space in which the performance occurs and one in which the spectators reside. These can, of course, be shared spaces or architecturally unified spaces; they can be found or transformed, they can be elaborately constructed and embellished. But, regardless of the specifics of the space, the performance occurs and is seen in some sort of environment. Once we have acknowledged that, then we are faced with the question of what the space looks like and how it is read by the spectator. The designer Ming Cho Lee had a question for any student who suggested staging a production in a "void." "OK," he would respond, "what color is the void?" Despite Peter Brook's famous proposition, there is no such thing as an empty space. Every space has a quality, texture, color, shape, and history and any decision about that space is an act of design. To leave a stage bare is a design decision; to place a single chair on that stage is a bold decision (and where is the chair placed?). To stage something in a "non-theatrical" space is a design decision. As David Roesner points out in Chapter 5, there is really no easy separation of the scenographic elements. Sound affects our perception of space; the textures of costumes affect movement which affects rhythm which affects our understanding of a performance. Every possible element of a theatrical production affects every other one. This is scenography.

Artaud

Antonin Artaud, more than anyone, grasped the notion of scenography. (See Austin E. Quigley's "Theatrical Languages: The Scenographic Turn and the Linguistic Turn" in this volume.) In his essay, "The Theater and Cruelty," Artaud declared his desire to "attack the spectator's sensibility on all sides," and advocated "a revolving spectacle which, instead of making the stage and auditorium two closed worlds, without possible communication, spreads its visual and sonorous outbursts over the entire mass of the spectators" (Artaud 1958: 86). He elaborated on this idea in "The Theater of Cruelty (First Manifesto)," in which he called for "dynamic expression in space" (ibid.: 89) and declared,

> Here too intervenes (besides the auditory language of sounds) the visual language of objects, movements, attitudes, and gestures, but on condition that their meanings, their physiognomies, their combinations be carried to the point of becoming signs, making a kind of alphabet out of these signs. Once aware of this language in space, language of sounds, cries, lights, onomatopoeia, the theater must organize it into veritable hieroglyphs, with the help of characters and objects, and make use of their symbolism and interconnections in relation to all organs and on all levels.
>
> *(Artaud 1958: 90)*

Artaud clearly recognized the complexity of the theatrical vocabulary embodied in the scenographic. Theatre is perhaps the most complicated art form to analyze because of its multiple and dynamic constituent elements, and because it is a live time-based artform usually observed from multiple points of view. While recognizing that there are genres and variants that may not possess all elements, and that the nature of the elements may vary, most traditional forms of theatre in most parts of the world, throughout most of history, have contained language, music, actors, a stage, and an audience (the latter being an irreducible requisite of theatre; without a spectator there may be performative activity, but not theatre). An actor implies voice, movement, costume (which may include makeup, mask, and ornament); stage implies spatial organization and visual elements including color and light; audience usually implies an organized and contained viewing space, but at the very least implies a spectator who exists in a spatial and temporal relation to the performance. Many of these elements, but especially light, move and transform during the course of the performance. For light this has been especially true since the introduction of electric light, and especially since the introduction of computerized control systems. (One could argue that set and costume design have existed ever since the birth of theatre, even if not always recognized as such, but lighting design is essentially a twentieth-century phenomenon, dependent as it is on the ability to focus light and control its levels and movement – something that was limited prior to electricity.)

It is true that our response to any work of art is shaped by a multitude of factors. When we read a novel, for instance, everything from the size and style of the typeface to the texture of the paper (or the quality of the e-reader), to the lighting and temperature in the locale in which we are reading will have an impact on our reception, but the novel itself remains unchanged. Something similar may be said of painting. Yet a theatre performance (as opposed to a dramatic text) exists only in the moment of its presentation and, because it is a temporal art, it changes moment to moment throughout the duration of the performance. Simply by being present in a performance venue (which could be anything from an opera house, to a post-industrial space, to a street, to an open field) the spectator is aware of the surrounding space and the relationship of the stage to the auditorium. As I have noted elsewhere,

> We are spatial creatures; we respond instinctively to space. Our arrival into the world, the moment of birth, is a spatial experience as we emerge from a safe, enclosed environment into the vastness of an unknown expanse. Every time we confront a stage we are, in a sense, confronting the space – the abyss – we first confronted at birth. The stage, regardless of its configuration, functions as an optical focal point and creates the impression that we are looking through this lens into a boundless space beyond. In fact, for most spectators, it is the apprehension of space that may be the most profound and powerful experience of live theatre although, admittedly, it is one that is most often felt subconsciously.
>
> *(Aronson 2005: 1)*

Our awareness of space extends to a sensibility of the presence of other spectators and perhaps even aspects of touch and smell. (I am reminded of the line from David Bowie's song "Candidate": "We'll pretend we're walking home . . . / My set is amazing, it even smells like a street.") Thus, a spectator at a theatrical performance in a conventional theatre space will be responding to the ambience of the auditorium, including space and volume, light, decor, acoustic ambience, the qualities of the seats, the number and density of other spectators; the size of the stage (which entails depth and height, framing, relation to the spectators); the nature of scenic elements, ranging from a bare stage with the walls of the theatre exposed, to elaborate illusionistic scenery; the arrangement of the scenic elements on the stage; color and texture of these elements; acoustical qualities of the stage; light (color, intensity, movement); costumes (again, color and texture as well as indexical signs of gender, class, historical period, and geographic locale, etc.); music (live or recorded) and sound; and much more.

Who is the scenographer?

Scenography, therefore, is all of this. It is the total visual, spatial, and aural organization of the overall theatrical event; it potentially involves all the senses; and it incorporates the temporal aspect of theatre, meaning that any definition of scenography must allow for the dynamic process of change that occurs throughout the course of a performance. In *The Semiotics of Theater*, Erika Fischer-Lichte posits multiple systems for decoding the complex vocabulary of theatre. She quotes Y. M. Lotman in this regard: "All of its elements bear meaning" (Fischer-Lichte 1992: 220). As she notes, "no element of a theatrical text . . . can be regarded as redundant" (ibid.). In other words, if the theatrical text – the totality of the performance – is to be understood, then the entire signifying system must be understood. To ignore any part of the complex vocabulary of performance can result in an imperfect understanding or even a misunderstanding. This complex vocabulary might be understood as scenography.[13]

In more conventional forms of theatre, where each scenographic element is isolated and sub-contracted, as it were, to specialists, each contributor is easily identified (costume designer, lighting designer, etc.). If, however, scenography is the total visual–spatial–aural–sensorial creation, it raises an interesting question: who is the scenographer?[14] Even in a *Gesamtkunstwerk* it is rare for a single individual to be responsible for everything. Gordon Craig argued that if theatre were to be an art it had to answer to a single artist. But in the phenomenologically complex world of theatre, this is a difficult proposition. In addition to Svoboda, the term has been applied correctly to some of the more visually-oriented contemporary directors such as Robert

Wilson, who generally conceives and supervises all the scenographic elements of a production, even if discipline-specific designers create some of the actual component elements such as costumes. Richard Foreman certainly fits the role, and Robert Lepage might as well, though he works with an array of designers. But even in Germany where scenography is often a major aspect of theatrical production, the work is often a joint venture between directors and designers such as it was with Frank Castorf and Bert Neumann at the Berlin Volksbühne, or the various collaborations of Christoph Marthaler and Anna Viebrock. Thus, unless scenographer is used solely as a synonym for set designer – a designation I am rejecting – it is very hard, with rare exceptions, to designate a single individual as scenographer.

So we are left with a conundrum. As Joslin McKinney and Philip Butterworth have stated, "scenography defines an active role for the audience" (McKinney and Butterworth 2009: 7), by which they mean that the scenography is completed by the spectator; scenography's performative role requires what is called, in reader-response criticism, interpretive communities. While multiple interpretations may certainly be possible in response to any given theatrical performance, there is usually an underlying assumption that all the component elements are working together to create a unified aesthetic whole.[15] Yet I am suggesting that a scenographer – someone who might in fact create this unity – is a rare creature. One might argue that directors often fulfill the role of unifying artist, but usually they do so as head of a creative team including multiple scenographic artists.

The notion of scenographer is also being challenged by the disintegration of the stage in the wake of the increasing use of digital media. Video and projection are increasingly fragmenting the stage, combining live and pre-recorded imagery, eliding onstage and offstage space, challenging notions of two- and three-dimensional space, and subverting temporal and even geographic structures and limitations. The "worm hole" of the ancient *skene* has now been replaced by the screen and its associated video technology. Sound has emerged as an art form in its own right. The sound score of effects that Stanislavski devised for his productions at the Moscow Art Theatre, and that famously made Chekhov distraught, have morphed into the complex digital sonorities of music, effects, and vocal amplification and transformation. The auditory is beginning to achieve the same pervasive power as light. Scenography remains at the heart of performance and production, but the identity of the scenographer is under pressure.

The Prague Quadrennial

The disintegrating or disappearing stage, as I have called it (Aronson 2012), actually provides a segue to the Prague Quadrennial (PQ). The PQ comes up frequently in the various chapters in this book. While many readers will have at least a passing familiarity with this exhibition – the largest of its kind – it does need a brief introduction. The event was inaugurated in 1967 in the midst of the "Prague Spring," inspired by the success of scenographic exhibits that were a component of the *Bienal de São Paulo* in Brazil (for more information see: www.pq.cz/en/). The first Quadrennial showcased work from 20 countries; its most recent edition (2015) included more than 60. Over the first two decades of its existence it functioned in part as a meeting place for theatre artists from east and west, and during the most repressive years of the Cold War it was a significant site for the exchange of ideas and information. It is organized by country and until recently it exhibited primarily artifacts of the design and the design process (set models, sketches, costumes, props, etc.) along with documentation of performances. More recently it has become as much a performative festival as an exhibition, reflecting the inherent contradiction in a theatre exhibition: how do you exhibit something that truly exists only in the moment of performance? Looking at the catalogues of the exhibitions over the past half century provides a window onto the development and trends of scenography across the globe. (Because it was, for so long, tied to geopolitics, not to mention economics, it provides a glimpse of the world beyond theatre as well.)

The exact title of the PQ altered in minor ways over the years, but at least in English it was generally referred to as the Prague Quadrennial of Theatre Design and Architecture. In 2011, however, a very conscious decision was made to change the name to the Prague Quadrennial of Performance Design and Space. As artistic director Sodja Zupanc Lotker explained, the change in nomenclature was a response to radical shifts in theatre itself. "In recent decades with found theatre, site-specific theatre, devised theatre, applied theatre, media theatre, interventions, installations and so on, the term 'stage design' become too limiting" (Lotker 2015: 8). With PQ 2015, whose theme was "Shared Space: Music Weather Politics," the goal was "to look at scenography not only as the 'visual' aspect of performance but also as something invisible, something that is a force as strong as music, weather and politics" (ibid.: 13). While traditional displays of scenographic artifacts continued to be exhibited, a significant number of exhibits were given over to installations, and enhanced or even replaced by performances, along with lectures, workshops, and peripheral events. Most radically, the architecture section – traditionally an exhibition of models and plans – was replaced by "Performing Space or Ephemeral Section of Architecture." It truly was ephemeral, consisting largely of events in the streets and on the river, in installations, and performances. As curator Serge von Arx declared, "Architecture is a time-based art form, experienced with all our senses as we progress through space, and it inheres within it the same performativity of a work's intrinsic evolution in time as scenography" (von Arx 2016: 82). If the PQ is seen as a barometer of world scenography, then the purely visual, concrete, and semiotic aspects of scenography are being replaced by the spatial, the temporal, and the intangible.

Notes on this volume

As with the title itself, determining the contents of this volume presented its own set of issues. I did not want an encyclopedia-like compendium of names, genres, movements, and the like, nor did I want a straightforward history (which would have been a large undertaking in its own right). At the same time, I did not want this to be a purely theoretical volume in which the historical and empirical elements were overlooked. So, wisely or not, this book is an amalgam of all the above. Almost inevitably, it is incomplete. There are, to borrow Richard Foreman's locution, "spaces." Some were inadvertent, and some were unavoidable for a whole host of reasons, both prosaic and subjective, in an undertaking of this size.

The chapters are divided into three broad categories. Part I deals with the basic elements of scenography. Whether we are discussing a complex opera or street theatre, a Broadway musical or a ritual in an open field, all the scenographic elements are present in every imaginable performance. Broadly speaking these concern the senses on the one hand, and the relationship of spectators to the performance on the other. Modern Western – and Western-influenced – theatre has tended to categorize and isolate these elements, even building them, as I've noted, into the economic structures of producing and the teaching of the craft: typically these consist of sets and props, costumes, lights and projection, and sound. Theatre institutions tend to reify the separation of stage and auditorium, one venue overseen by creative and technical personnel, the other by administrative staff. But in many forms of theatre and performance, both historical and contemporary, such neat distinctions do not exist. Increasingly, such categories are being intentionally elided. Technology certainly plays a part. When costumes include technology that allow for projection mapping or the creation of a sound score, when actors are also videographers for live video projection, when sets are created by digital or holographic means, when a performance can occur in multiple locations, literally around the world, linked electronically, etc., then such precise definitions, categories, and distinctions rapidly disintegrate. Nonetheless, I thought it useful to begin this volume with an examination of the broad traditional scenographic components of performance. One might almost think of them as analogous to Aristotle's six parts of tragedy as enumerated in Book VI of the *Poetics*, though without any hierarchical ordering. I simply asked the authors within this section to write on the given subject and they have responded in their own ways, from their own viewpoints.

Part II looks at scenography from several theoretical and critical perspectives. Included in this section are chapters that examine the scenographic outside the traditional performative settings. Scenography, meaning the organization and arrangement of the spatial and visual, has increasingly been applied across a broad spectrum of disciplines. The École Nationale Supérieure d'Architecture de Paris-La Villette, to take but one example, offers a seminar on scenography that includes "visual arts, installations, performance art, public art, exhibition spaces and other artistic 'showcases', dance video, hybrid, theatre productions" and claims that it touches upon cultural politics, Tanztheater, video, public art, museography, and exhibitions (La Villette website). Art reviews, when discussing the spatial arrangement on a canvas or within an installation, will often refer to the scenography of the work. The scenographic has now become a descriptor applicable to any work that engages in the visual and spatial, including those well beyond the traditional confines of either theatre or architecture. The essays here look at scenography from the perspective of literary drama, the scopic regime, the event space, and the technological, as well as scenography in the visual arts, and in museum exhibition design.

Finally, Part III deals with history and practice subdivided into thematic sections. I felt that a companion to scenography could not ignore certain artists, historical developments, or countries with significant scenographic traditions, yet, at the same time, this could not be a comprehensive history. While I can make a case for every chapter in this section, I am well aware that there are gaps and omissions.

***

In "Metaphysics and the Mise en Scène" Artaud declares, "the stage is a concrete physical place which asks to be filled, and to be given its own concrete language to speak" (Artaud 1958: 37). Although as this introduction, as well as several chapters in the volume, suggest theatre is not limited to the stage, and the stage itself is dematerializing, Artaud's insistence that the theatre must move beyond verbal language remains valid. I would suggest that scenography provides the concrete language that addresses the enormous perceptual complexities of the performative event.

Acknowledgements

I would like to thank Talia Rodgers for asking me to edit this volume, and the editors at Routledge, Stacey Walker and Meredith Darnell, who guided the process. Thanks to my assistant, Ned Moore. My conversations with Austin Quigley helped me shape many of my ideas as I began this project, and my ongoing conversation with Jane Collins, my co-editor at *Theatre and Performance Design*, continues to expand my understanding of scenography. I could not have undertaken this project without the knowledge of scenography gained over decades through the Prague Quadrennial. Among the many individuals associated with the PQ I must single out Joel E. Rubin, Jaroslav Malina, Jarmilla Gabrielova, Daniela Pařízková, and Sodja Lotker. I owe a debt of gratitude to my late teachers Brooks McNamara and Michael Kirby who started me on this path, as well as my late friend and colleague John Russell Brown. This book, of course, would not have been possible without the generous contribution of all those who wrote for this volume, taking the time to expand the study of scenography with their wisdom and insight. I am most especially grateful to Lorie Novak for her help and support throughout.

Notes

1 1010 words in 3 volumes in 23 languages.
2 I became aware of the book in the mid-1970s when I was working on my PhD dissertation on environmental theatre and my advisor, Brooks McNamara, suggested I look at the book and possibly use the term "scenography" – which I did.
3 See www.oistat.org/Item/list.asp?id=1162 for a detailed history of the organization.
4 Currently the commissions include performance design, costume design, lighting design, sound design, and space design. The latter "provides a forum for performance designers interested in spatial thinking as it relates to place, body, object, light, sound and media" (see www.oistat.org/).
5 The *OED* offers three definitions. The first refers to architectural drawing, the next two to theatre.
6 Some scholars even believe that the line about the third actor and scene design is actually a later interpolation.
7 The foundations that survive today, and the vase paintings that may depict theatrical performance, date almost exclusively from the fourth century BCE or later.
8 It appears in this way for the first time in Book 1.2.2.
9 In the Roman theatre buildings that developed in the late first century BCE there is an elaborate architectural façade behind the narrow raised stage. It is called the *frons scaenae* – literally, the front of the stage, but actually meaning the front of the *skene* which is now part of the larger structure of the architecturally unified theatre. The raised stage becomes the *proskene* – in front of the skene – from whence we derive the English word "proscenium."
10 "*e qila cosa che Vitruvio domáda scenographia*."
11 McKinney and Butterworth make a useful distinction between scenography and *mise en scène*. The latter "refers to the process of realizing a theatrical text on stage and the particular aesthetic and conceptual frames that have been adopted as part of that process" (McKinney and Butterworth 2009: 4).
12 The *Nāṭyaśāstra* is one of the few such texts to deal extensively with scenography. It includes chapters on how and where to build a theatre, with details on all aspects of the stage, chapters on music, and a chapter (XXIII) devoted to costume, ornament, make-up, hair, and props.
13 It is noteworthy in this regard that theatre productions done within totalitarian regimes, such as those in the Soviet Union and its client states in Eastern Europe, often employed scenographic means to convey critiques of the government since these would often evade the watchful eyes of censors.
14 This question was raised by artist Lorie Novak at the conference Monitoring Scenography 3: Space and Desire/Raum und Begehren at the Zurich University of the Arts, Switzerland, 2009.

15 Brecht may have reacted against the modern attempt at the unification of theatrical, particularly scenographic, elements, but one could argue that there is an overarching aesthetic unity to his foregrounding of difference.

References

Aristotle 1987. *The Poetics of Aristotle*. Translated by Stephen Halliwell. Chapel Hill: University of North Carolina Press.

Aronson, Arnold 2004. "Their Exits and Their Entrances: Getting a Handle on Doors." *New Theatre Quarterly* 20 (4): 331–40.

Aronson, Arnold 2005. *Looking into the Abyss: Essays on Scenography*. Ann Arbor: University of Michigan Press.

Aronson, Arnold 2012. "The Dematerialization of the Stage." In *The Disappearing Stage: Reflections of the 2011 Prague Quadrennial*, edited by Arnold Aronson, 86–95. Prague: Arts and Theatre Institute.

Artaud, Antonin 1958. *The Theater and Its Double*. Translated by Mary Caroline Richards. New York: Grove Press.

Blau, Herbert [1990] 2010. "The Most Concealed Object." In *Theatre and Performance Design: A Reader in Scenography*, edited by Jane Collins and Andrew Nisbet, 51–5. London: Routledge.

Böhme, Gernot 1993. "Atmosphere as the Fundamental Concept of a New Aesthetics." *Thesis Eleven* 36: 113–26, doi: 10.1177/072551369303600107.

Burian, Jarka 1971. *The Scenography of Josef Svoboda*. Middletown, CT: Wesleyan University Press.

Collins, Jane and Arnold Aronson 2015. "Editors Introduction." *Theatre and Performance Design* 1 (1–2): 1–6.

Craig, Edward Gordon 1911. *On the Art of the Theatre*. London: William Heinemann.

Fischer-Lichte 1992. *The Semiotics of Theater*. Bloomington and Indianapolis: Indiana University Press.

Fuchs, Elinor and Una Chaudhuri 2002. *Land/Scape/Theater*. Ann Arbor: University of Michigan Press.

Hewitt, Barnard (Ed.) 1958. *The Renaissance Stage: Documents of Serlio, Sabbattini and Furttenbach*. Translated by Allardyce Nicoll, John H. McDowell, and George R. Kernodle. Coral Gables, FL: University of Miami Press.

Howard, Pamela 2002. *What Is Scenography?* London: Routledge.

La Villette. Available online at: www.paris-lavillette.archi.fr/uploads/international/anglaisprog/2016-2017/M74-S701B.pdf (accessed 10 December 2016).

Lehmann, Hans-Thies 2006. *Postdramatic Theatre*. New York: Routledge.

Lotker, S. Zupanc 2015. "Expanding Scenography: Notes on the Curatorial Developments of the Prague Quadrennial." *Theatre and Performance Design* 1 (1–2): 7–16

Maeterlinck, Maurice [1890] 1995. "Menus propos—le théâtre." In *Symbolist Art Theories: A Critical Anthology*, edited by Henri Dorra, 143–6. Berkeley: University of California Press.

McKinney, Joslin and Philip Butterworth 2009. *The Cambridge Introduction to Scenography*. Cambridge: Cambridge University Press.

Nāṭyaśāstra 2007. Translated by Adya Rangacharya. New Delhi: Munshiram Manoharlal Publishers.

Norberg-Schulz, Christian 1971. *Existence, Space and Architecture*. New York: Praeger Publishers.

Pavis, Patrice 1998. *Dictionary of the Theatre: Terms, Concepts, and Analysis*. Translated by Christine Shantz. Toronto: University of Toronto Press.

Serlio, Sebastiano 1982. *The Five Books of Architecture*. New York: Dover.

Small, Jocelyn Penny 2013. "Skenographia in Brief." In *Performance in Greek and Roman Theatre*, edited by George W. M. Harrison and Vayos Liapis, 111–28. Leiden, the Netherlands, and Boston, MA: Brill.

Stein, Gertrude [1935] 1985. *Lectures in America*. Boston, MA: Beacon Press.

Vitruvius 1960. *The Ten Books of Architecture*. New York: Dover.

von Arx, Serge 2016. "Unfolding the Public Space: Performing Space or Ephemeral Section of Architecture, PQ 2015." *Theatre and Performance Design* 2 (1–2): 82–94.

PART I

Scenographic elements

1
STAGE AND AUDIENCE
Constructing relations and opportunities

Beth Weinstein

You head to a place designed for performance in order to attend an event. After crossing a threshold, you enter the space of the event – an amphitheatre in a landscape, the horseshoe-shaped balconies of an opera house, a black box. The architecture of this place conditions relations between *you*, as a member of an audience, and the *action*, in relation to *others* in the audience, and in relation to itself as *spatial construct*. This space constructs, contains, and controls relations between the audience and action, between audience member and audience member, and it may also suggest alternative inhabitations, and afford the shifting of these relations over time.

How does this theatre architecture *construct relations* through the siting of the audience in space in relation to action and to other audience members? How does this theatre architecture, and its construction of relations, condition the seeing and sensing of the performed event? How do the designed spatial relations of the theatre prescribe, suggest, or perhaps inadvertently offer alternative staging opportunities and, through that, contribute to the experience of the event?

As an architect interested in the performance in and of space, I come to understand performances of a given space through the analytic drawing out, literally and conceptually, of the spatial and relational, or formal, structure of the architecture and its link to an architectural type and the performance-event type with which it is affiliated. As a designer, rather than historian, I am interested in *potentials* latent within space, and therefore the purpose of my analysis is to identify and understand the conventions of relations between space and event in order to go beyond that to uncover potentials for other spatial performances that the theatre architecture affords.

What follows is a discussion of stage and audience space, first through the lens of theatre architecture and the conventions that are associated with dominant types, and second through alternative propositions to the conventions of stage–audience relations through both unbuilt speculative works and built works. The chapter concludes with several examples in which conventions of stage, auditorium, or the relation between them, were critically re-interpreted through designs for theatre buildings or the contribution of the architecture to particular performances.[1] As such this chapter is concerned with how the architecture of stage and auditorium contributes in a leading or supporting role to the event. It is concerned with scenographic designing that consciously works *with* and pushes up *against* the conventions of theatre architecture types. It is concerned with taking advantage of what a work of theatre architecture has to offer to augmenting consciousness of the performance with the aim of creating a truly eventful spatial experience.

In architectural terms, buildings may be categorized and discussed through the framework of *program* – the uses and activities intended to occur there. For instance, we might discuss performing arts buildings in terms of programs such as opera houses, play houses, chamber music halls, and so on. As a counterpoint to *program* one may examine works of architecture according to *type* described as "a group of objects characterized by the same formal structure . . . It is neither a spatial diagram nor the average of a serial list." (Moneo 1978, 23).

Within the programmatic subcategory of theatre we commonly group these architectural objects according to the qualities of stage or stage–audience relations, such as arena, proscenium or thrust, or by the absence of a structured relationship within a spatial container as found in black box spaces. In discussing theatre architecture, many authors of theatre histories intertwine specific performance genres (programs) with their affiliated formal structures (types), such as associating Shakespearian drama with a thrust stage (particularly in a circular courtyard) (see Brewster and Shafer 2011; Mitchley and Spalding 1982). While this approach is useful for identifying conventional links of performance type to architectural type, it may obscure other performances latent within spatial relations. Another model for discussing theatre architecture is through conceptual frameworks such as the *cave* (for projection and illusion) and *cosmic circle* (participatory ritual) (Wiles 2003).[2] Still others focus in on the details of space that are of pragmatic concern to scenographers, such as viewing distance and intimacy,[3] while others focus attention on ambiance or the symbolism of theatre décor. At a level more diagrammatic than architectural type as defined above, Ned Bowman, in his article "The Ideal Theatre: Emerging Tendencies in Its Architecture" (Bowman 1964), homed in on the topic of "Space Relationships" – proscenium, central, peripheral, thrust and

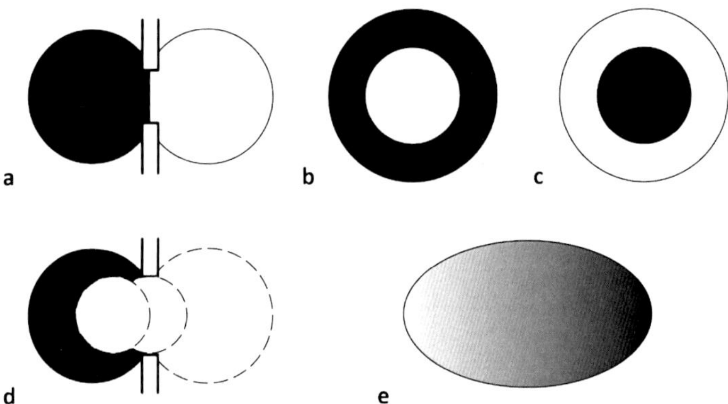

Figure 1.1 "Space Relationships," after Bowman. Above, left to right: (a) proscenium, (b) central, (c) peripheral. Below: (d) thrust and (e) open. (Drawings: Beth Weinstein.)

open – captured in a diagram redrawn here (Figure 1.1). We may gain a more critical perspective on constructed-relations by adopting theatre-neutral language such as *split*, *surrounding*, *surrounded*, *projecting*, and *interspersed*.

Conventions

How do these space-relationships control, contain and construct the event and the audience experience? While the theatre, the *theatron* as the spectator area was called in ancient Greece, is literally a viewing place, the space and what it contains is not necessarily limited to a singular sense (vision) perceiving a singular action (on a stage behind a frame) within a narrow perceptual field. The stage–audience relationship can be shaped and inhabited so that it is focused or it can be a multi-sensory experience. It may construct focused attention or facilitate distraction; it may offer comfortable relaxation or oblige energetic engagement.

Each theatre architecture type carries with it assumed conventions about the site for the action, scenographic contribution to the performance, and the place of the audience; as well as the audience members' sensory and spatial awareness of the action, other audience members and the building itself. By unpacking the conventional and specific relationships through case studies we can speculate about the audience experience – whether audience members experience the work as a distant image; as visual environment, or through an embodied, multi-sensory experience; as a static and isolated body, a dynamic or mobile body, or as a body within a collective; or as an observer or a participant with agency.

To start we must first analyze the relationship of stage to audience. These generally fall into two categories – those in which the audience and performers share an undivided volume of space and those in which performers and audience occupy a space cleft, by the proscenium arch, into performatively and architectonically separate spaces. All conventionally contain a single stage, either split off from the audience, projecting into the audience (thrust) or surrounded by the audience (arena). A second level of relationships that we must consider is the three-dimensional organization of the audience in the house – in plan (horizontal) and in section (vertical). One should ask how the scene will be seen and sensed. Is the audience clustered in one place as a singular body? Or are they split or distributed, either along the horizontal plane or vertically within the theatre volume? If in a single horizontal plane, is the arrangement of audience members in parallel rows facing forward, or in a fanning shape that allows sideward, oblique glances? If divided into balconies, or "circles," are these parallel to the stage front or wrapping, affording views across to other audience members? Or is there no view anywhere but to one's box-neighbors? How different is the view from balconies, which privileges the planimetric experience of movement patterns on the stage floor, to the view from the orchestra, privileging the elevation, or vertical surfaces, and perspective? Are balconies a continuous space or divided into private boxes? Do audience members sit on individual fixed seats or mobile chairs, shared benches, or in a recumbent position on pillows? Depending upon the spatial arrangement of the audience and audience member's situation (seated, standing or reclining), the design may assist in focusing the audience attention on the action occurring on stage or may draw awareness towards other members of the audience seated across the house or stage, to the company within one's box, the shared bench beneath one's behind or the room that holds all of this in tension.

I want to examine stage–audience relationships in a few examples of well-known theatre architecture types in order to reveal the conventional assumptions about space relationships that we might overlook out of familiarity, drawing from both first-hand, embodied experiences of performances in theatres as well as understanding of spaces through drawings. After addressing a number of dominant space-relationship types, I will consider experiments that took on or deviated from these conventional space relationships, exploiting plan, section, and volume in ways that yielded new arrangements of audiences in relationship to stage(s). I will consider the impact of theatre architecture space on the audience experience, how spaces construct intimate engagement or distanced overview, establish potentials for participation, and shape perception as image-dominated or multisensory and immersive. To convey the relations between performer-spaces and audience-spaces, the case studies are presented in parallel projection drawings, a form that communicates overall volumetric relations rather than an embodied view from a singular vantage point.

The first example is an amphitheatre in a landscape, in which the audience, along a single, sloped and fanning surface, nearly surrounds a stage.[4] Some obvious points: this space is outdoors, unconditioned, and thus without the controlled environments to which we are generally accustomed today. The physical comfort of audience members is contingent on physical wellbeing and garments worn in relation to constantly changing weather conditions, and contingent on the cushioning (or lack thereof) beneath one's seat. Wind and rain, daylight and darkness, heat of day and cool of night all inform who and what performs, detracts, and distracts attention, or adds to and augments the experience. We, the audience, are undeniably bodies exposed to elements of time and weather, tempo and tempus, while following the unfolding events on stage before us. Within this open space, the fan-shaped configuration of the audience space points us towards the orchestra and stage while keeping the collective audience within view. The scale of physical and visual gestures on stage aim to overcome the distance that may lie between us. The continuity between the environment as image and context for the action, and that which envelops us as audience members, assists in bridging between the time and space of theatre and life. Beyond the *skene* we perceive the connection to and distance between ourselves in this theatre space and the city where we conduct our lives. Does this bring to our attention this moment dis-placed from our habitual space of action? These exterior spaces, due to their siting and unconditioned environments, augment, rather than suppress, the embodied full-sensory attendance at the event. The shifting time and tempos call attention to fleetingness. The containing or continuity of space connects or severs this moment from the space-time around us.

Attending an event in the reconstructed Globe in London today situates the audience in a relationship that is slightly more focused and protected from natural elements than the amphitheatre. Standing in the yard one is exposed to rain and jostling by fellow theatre-goers. The circular courtyard and wrapping galleries in section set up an intimate and contained space, and unavoidable gazes across from one side of the yard to the other. The galleries, each one gently cantilevering out over the level below, bring audience members closer to the action on the raised stage that projects into the courtyard. The sense of proximity is furthered by actors crossing the yard, literally rubbing elbows with the audience, blurring the lines of division between the audience's space and performers' space. The heavy timber structure that contains the yard and holds the balconies flexes with the audience movement; wooden bleachers register and dissipate vibrations of laugher between those seated in the gallery. Though hierarchy of place in society is articulated through the distinction between yard and gallery, the collective experience is inscribed and contained in the space relationships of the architecture.

How different are the space relationships in these exterior theatres from those of fully enclosed, interior theatres? The proscenium theatre, with its picture frame, supported the construction of illusory images of city streets or pastoral landscapes beyond, within a controlled setting. Parallel flats or forced perspectives of converging street facades leveraged what were then new understandings of optics and geometrically constructed perspectives, and new concepts of the viewing subject. The perspectival illusion was constructed from and for a singular, privileged point in space, creating a hierarchy and gradient of experiences from an illusion of "truth" from one central point to undeniable distortion from all other audience locations. Yet at times illusion and reality were at play in ways other than the position of the audience member within the house. Margarete Baur-Heinhold suggests that the Schlosstheater at Schwetzingen, Germany (1753), not only presented perspectives of formal gardens on its painted flats, but also overlooked a formal garden lying just beyond the rear wall of the theatre (Baur-Heinhold 1967, 182–3). Plans of the theatre reveal the stage as having an even greater depth than the house, which must have been useful in blurring lines between painted sets and reality off in the distance. Entangled with the development of the proscenium or picture frame is the fly tower and other stage machinery, facilitating the hoisting away and lowering of design elements and performers. The traps and pit allow the emerging of performers from below. The proscenium frame frames the perspectival image beyond; borders crop the image. The illusion depends on the directionality of our looking through the aperture in the wall that divides audience from where the action occurs. In traversing the fourth wall performers break and call attention to this illusion. The architecture of the stage has its own construction and logic, and the architectural volume and spatial arrangement of the audience in the house is separate yet in correspondence to the apparatus of view through this picture frame into the depth of the stage.

Taking the specific example of the house of Garnier's Paris Opera, we acknowledge that these environs are constructed, contained and controlled, including lighting, cooling and heating, and cushioned seats in boxes to offer individual comfort. Partitioning of the boxes and balconies and parterre seating have been developed to support our attentiveness to events, be they ones occurring in our box or ones on stage. The horseshoe shape of the balconies constructs opportunities for lateral glances across the house. The balcony experience is distinct from that in the more frontally focused seats in the orchestra. A still more restricted visual access is offered to those in the rear of the boxes. Audience members glimpse what happens on stage over the heads of others, but their perceptual realm is predominantly contained within the private space of the box. The house holds heterogeneous audience–audience and audience–action relations. This house is a spatial structure constructed to make evident the distinction of privilege and social class through the space relationships.

The undifferentiated space of the black box as type wipes the slate clean of such hierarchies and scripted relations. These unified spaces are intended to be flexible laboratories, neutral canvases, into which diverse space relationships can be inserted and onto which other visions may be projected. Audience may surround or be surrounded, face and confront or intermingle with the performance. In theory, the black box can contain the most formal, frontal and visually oriented experience, or afford informal, multiple, distributed performances and an embodied, multi-sensory experience. The alternatives to formal, frontal space-relationships between stage and audience that we now take for granted in black box spaces have their origins in the early twentieth century, as structures and hierarchies outside of theatre were being challenged and overturned.

Works challenging the conventions

Architects, artists, performers, and theatre directors in the early twentieth century sought to question these spatial conventions, hierarchies, and divisions between audience and action, integrating new modes of presentation, interaction, and engagement. Heinrich Tessenau and Adolphe Appia in Hellerau, Walter Gropius with Erwin Piscator, El Lissitzky with Vsevolod Meyerhold, as well as Frederick Kiesler and many others proposed radically different configurations of stage and audience from those found in historical amphitheatre, thrust, and proscenium types. In their proposed (and occasionally built) theatres, stages mechanically rotated causing audience and performer to switch places during the course of the performance. Stages developed vertically on multiple levels linked by elevator platforms. Stages multiplied and publics were divided; screens and performer action surrounded the audience.[5] Under the heading of the *Spatial Stage* there was an

> effort of modern theatre directors and architects to reunite the auditorium and stage constructionally and spatially into a single whole, . . . free of circle and gallery levels, that overcome the directional nature of the proscenium-arch form and that avoided the tiers of boxes of the Baroque theatres . . . 'Open forms of stage performance call for open forms of theatre construction,' and 'variability instead of monumentality.'
>
> (*Wimmer and Schelle 2009, 248*)

One such built work is the *Festspielhaus* in the garden city of Hellerau designed by Heinrich Tessenau (1911–12, Dresden, Germany) (Figure 1.2). The venue originally served as home for Émile Jaques-Dalcroze's dance explorations of Eurythmics in conjunction with Adolphe Appia's scenographic experiments (Tallon 1984 and Jaques-Dalcroze 1933). The performance space, an elongated rectangular volume, had no proscenium subdivision. The design of the stage–auditorium continuum unified public and performers in a perceivably undifferentiated space. Audience members experienced the same view from parallel rows of seating that could be retracted. An imperceptible separation between audience and action is the small orchestra pit that can be made to disappear into the floor of the space, leaving a fairly neutral volume. As a counterpoint to the design of Bayreuth's orchestra pit and repetitive parallel framing in service to the creation of mysteries emerging from darkness, Hellerau was designed as a light-box. A dense array of lamps in the grid above was used to explore the play of light upon the fabric scrims that originally wrapped the entire ceiling and walls of the space, around both audience and action. The abstract, almost featureless white volume of space in many ways anticipated the flexibility and laboratory quality of contemporary black box spaces. Today, although Hellerau's array of lights and scrims are gone, the space still serves as a white-box lab for contemporary companies.

Walter Gropius's design for Erwin Piscator is an important, unbuilt theatre building that proposed to overturn stage–audience relations. Their *Total Theater* (1926) sought to

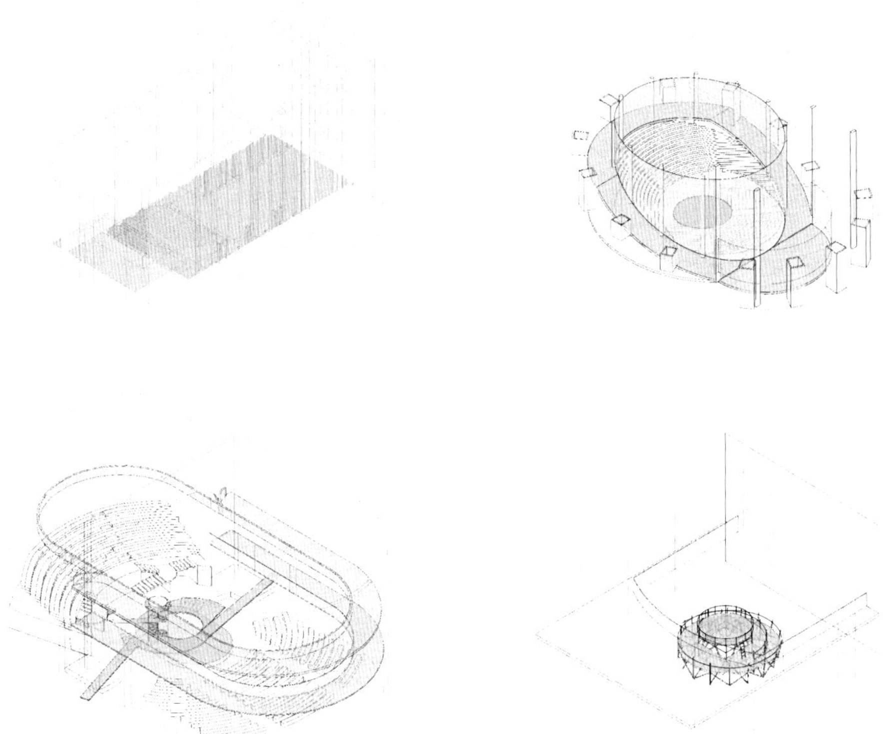

Figure 1.2 Above, left to right: Heinrich Tessenow, Hellerau; Walter Gropius, Total Theatre. Below, left to right: El Lissitzky set for Meyerhold Theatre, Kiesler Space Stage. (Drawings: Beth Weinstein with Masoud Sharikzadeh.)

surround the audience with action and projection and through all spatial means available "rouse the spectator from his intellectual apathy, . . . (and) coerce him into participation in the play" (Gropius quoted in Moholy-Nagy 1969, 53). Actors would be able to perform along an outer ring of the oval-shaped space; here screens for film projections would have been stretched between the columns. During the course of a performance, the architecture of stage–audience relations transformed through the mechanical revolving of a disc platform. This disc contained a small circular performing area (similar to the orchestra of ancient Greek theatres) and a sloping section of seating. Revolving this disc would have allowed the orchestra to move from a position directly in front of the elevated stage platform at one end (if a frontal theatre arrangement was needed) to a location embedding this stage between the main expanse of seating and the rise of seats that share this same revolving disc. When rotated into this position, Gropius' design created an undivided space animated by live, human action in the center, two groups of audience members each perceived as background or "extras" in the performance for the other and projected film surrounding stage and audience.

Frederick Kiesler's Endless Theater (1923–5) also proposed a unified space with action in the round. His drawings show a massive ellipsoidal volume choreographing an "interplay of ramp, platform and elevator, . . . a continuous intertwining of vast ramps, (where) the players and the audience can intertwine anywhere in space" (Aronson 1981, 60). Where ramps spiraled around the edges of the theatre volume, at the center actors moved vertically from platform to platform within elevator towers. Although unbuilt, many spatial qualities and relations were realized through the *Raumbühne* or Space Stage that Kiesler presented within the exhibition of the Music and Theater Festival (1924, Vienna). Intended to be seen and approached by the audience from all sides, the Space Stage ultimately was installed on the orchestra floor of the Vienna Konzerthaus, with seats removed, well away from the existing stage which was hidden behind a projection screen. Audience members viewed performances on this construction – including ramps, platforms and an elevator cage vertically linking levels – from the existing concert hall balconies that offered views from 300° around the Space Stage. It modeled new opportunities for actors in the vertical dimension, revealing what traps and rigging hide on conventional stages, celebrating the dynamics of performance. It situated audience members surrounding the action and in visual dialogue with each other.

El Lissitzky proposed a similar re-ordering of relations within the Vsevolod Meyerhold Theatre for the intended production (1926–8) of Sergei Tretyakov's *I Want a Child*. Action was to be displaced from the conventional location on the elevated stage at one end of the theatre to a space mounted in the center of the auditorium. In this central location action was to be distributed vertically, spiraling along a double ramp from floor to elevated platforms and branching out to connect with an even higher elliptical balcony – a suspended running track for performers. The new stage that El Lissitzky proposed inserting within the theatre, similar to that of Lyubov Popova's 1922 set for *Magnanimous Cuckold*, drew more from the language of *agitprop* pavilions in public squares. It was "not a set, but a construction . . . not intended to decorate anything" [it was] separate . . . that could exist anywhere – on the street, on a square" (Marcadé and Petrova 2005, 63).

On the platform normally intended as the stage Lissitzky introduced a second area of seating, creating a split audience. The combination of these interventions would have resulted in a performance environment in which the architecture created opportunities for performers to both surround the audience, with action on the track above, and to divide, by their actions on the ramps and platforms mid-space, the audience into two sections – one section on the parterre and, facing them, the other seated on the stage. While respecting territories of actor and audience, this proposal would have resulted in a spatially immersive environment akin to urban life.

In relation to the upheavals taking place politically and socially in these early decades of the twentieth century, all four of these proposed theatre architectures aspired to overturn the class stratification physically manifest in stage–audience relations of the past. As Chris Salter reflects,

> Theatre artists problematized the cultural divide between stage and street, audience and event, with stage action invading the sacredness of audience space, suspending the passive role usually attributed to spectators and placing them in an oscillating position between observer and performer.
>
> *(Salter 2010, 16)*

In the above unrealized and partially realized projects, stage and audience shared the same volume and a continuous or connected ground (no hierarchical tiers). The arrangement of the audience (surrounding the action or split by it and facing each other) would have constructed relations such that a spectator would always be aware of participating in a collective event, witnessing fellow audience members sharing the experience all around. Despite the interest at the time in developing immersive theatre architectures, such experimental works were rarely implemented. The theatre architectures of the avant-garde proposed space relationships of immersion and participation, blurring boundaries between action and audience by shifting physical and visual relations to the action and to each other. These unbuilt visionary theatre architectures modeled aspirations for new relationships that would be realized in other ways decades later.

What the spatial container affords

In more recent times, several theatre spaces have been realized that re-imagined stage–audience relations by adapting existing buildings or building types into places of performance. I will discuss just two examples briefly before turning to projects that critically play upon and push against conventions of purpose-built theatre buildings. In the two following works, the volumetric container of space deformed and thereby questioned and afforded new relations between audience and action.

The Spiral Theatre (1991, Prague) at first glance fools us (Figure 1.3). The drum-shape of its building form, its structure and material logic all suggest that it is a repurposed gasholder tank. Yet it is a purpose-built theatre that upsets expectations. Jindrich Smetana's *Laterna Animata* uses the "principle of continuous film projection from above the stage onto a stage floor/projection surface" as the generator of the theatre architecture and scenographic starting point (Firman 1992, 44). The audience, after descending a cut into the earth to enter the building from below, would have ascended two spiral ramps to reach viewing balconies around the full height of a cylinder of scaffolding. This cylinder performs as a vertically stretched arena, a well of space gathering flickering images at its base, a drum across which to view one's fellow theatre-goers. The original 1991 stage, perforated with traps, was a shallow convex surface acting as both screen for cinema and stage for live action. It recalls the early courtyard theatres, yet shielded from the elements, light and sound controlled, and with all of the audience arrayed around the cylindrical space, clearing the entire ground for the spectacle.

As intently as this theatre building sought to keep the exterior world out and create a new incarnation of the cave, a new theatre of projection, the architecture of the

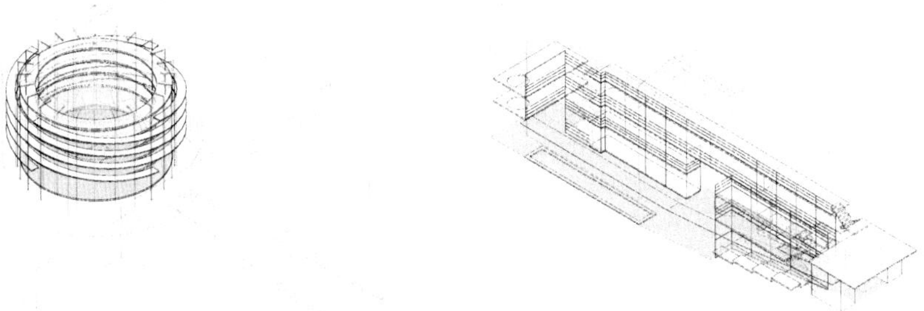

Figure 1.3 Left to right: Spiral Theatre, Teatro Oficina. (Drawings: Beth Weinstein with Masoud Sharikzadeh.)

Teatro Oficina invites in the interruption of nature and the complexity, mutability, and chaos of life and creative process. The *Teatro Oficina* (1991, Sao Paulo, Brazil), developed between Director Ze Celso and architects Lina Bo Bardi and Edson Elito, works within the constraints of an existing structure of narrow and tall proportions. The combination of site constraints and of the philosophical positions of both director and architect lead to nearly all theatre conventions being questioned, if not outright discarded. Similar to other works with which Bardi was involved, the fit-out of the theatre manifests a social and creative position of incompleteness, open-endedness, inviting ongoing experimentation. A scaffolding – a building system that in itself is intended to be impermanent and transformed – runs the length of the main wall. The audience could sit here, or not. No front or back of house is evident; in fact, it is the top of house that holds most of the actor support functions. No frame. No curtains. No enclosure: natural light and night sky enter through an expanse of glass that runs nearly the length of the space. This skylight slides open to connect interior to the stars. Nature invades with the kind of force that is unavoidable in Brazil; a tree, tropical plants and water interrupt the space. Action runs the length and height of this theatre workshop. After participating in a collective danced and sung procession taking one from a pre-show gathering in the garden outside, audience members enter the theatre through an opening in the rear wall. Everyone present is invited to move around throughout the performance, and is explicitly invited to join in at times. Action moves from one end to another, from ground to air, and down into habitable cuts in the ground. It is not a cave of illusions; it is a space for collective transformation akin to carnival time and space.[6]

What stage and house afford

Several performances and performance spaces in recent years have explored the blurring of interior and exterior. Contemporary concert halls in particular, and OMA's *Casa da Musica* (2005, Porto, Portugal) as one example, make use of landscape or sky as live backdrop.[7] Another space, the OMA-Rex-designed *Wyly Theatre* (2009, Dallas, TX), although conceived as a hyper-versatile black-box with a "superfly" tower, is glazed on three of the four elevations of the theatre, allowing the interior performance space to connect to the developing urban context around it. Sky or landscape are invited into spaces that are normally contained and controlled interiors.

Noh Performance, however, originated in open fields and, in modernizing during the Meiji period, moved indoors, taking with it its exterior architecture – roof, handrails, and (images of) trees. Kengo Kuma returned Noh to its space under the sky in his *Noh Theatre in the Forest* (Miyagi, Japan, 1996). Here he gathers around a stepping exterior courtyard a traditional stage structure and bridge for the performers and a minimalist loggia from which the audience can enjoy the event as well as the forest beyond. Kuma's theatre opens up to and co-exists with its environs with grace and discretion, being a building that is *of*, *in* and *representing* the forest all at once.

Yet regardless of whether one has occasion to work in exceptional theatres such as these or a seemingly neutral theatre architecture, one can critically reflect upon the spatial container as constructor of relations or opportunities and for the potential of this to contribute to the performed event. One of the most eventful spatial performances I recall occurred during a dance performance at the Opera de Paris. All of a sudden the wall at the rear of the stage opened up to reveal the ornate rehearsal room behind the stage where dancers were performing another section of the work. Literally, a window opened up, resituating the event onstage that we had been experiencing up until that point as just a fragment of a larger phenomenon. Here the specific theatre conditions created opportunities.

This play of disorientation is one of the ways in which Diller Scofidio + Renfro, as architects and as designers for performance, problematize conditions, of both the specifics of place and the conventions of type. In one of their earliest designs for stage, *The Rotary Notary and his Hotplate* (1988, La Mama, NYC), Diller + Scofidio explored an interrupting and reflecting plane, a hinge, a contingent condition; in this instance a reflective surface, hinged 45° from the vertical, revealed what was hidden behind another concealing plane. Though set in a space without proscenium or curtain, the set constructed a wall-curtain to be subverted. This idea, of rotating/re-orienting reality through the device of concealing/revealing planes, reappeared almost a decade later as the *inter-scenium* they designed for *Moving Target* (Charleroi 1996). This dance performance, created with Frédéric Flamand, employed a gigantic reflective surface that descended into the stage space similar to a garage-door stuck mid-way. The depth of field of the stage was interrupted. The spectators' vision of performers' actions was reflected and redirected by the inclined plane. Action occurring in plan (on the ground), through the reflecting plane, was rotated 90° into an elevated, floating image. In both conditions the audience faced directly forwards, to look into this reflecting surface (Weinstein 2008). In their Institute of Contemporary Art (2006, Boston, MA), the building as a whole, as well as performance space, draws from these earlier explorations of theatre as viewing machine. The architects describe the project: "A choreographed passage through the building dispenses the visual context in small doses. Upon entry the view is compressed, . . . (the view is) used as a variable backdrop in the theatre" (DS+R). The architects seat the audience in this theatre, facing forward, on a folded surface (set of bleachers) that flattens to create the performance area before extending, through a glass curtain-wall, down another two stories of steps, to form the grandstand overlooking the waterfront. Whereas earlier designs for performance interrupted the view of the on-stage action, in this architectural space for performance the performance interrupted the view. The ICA theatre also plays to the public outside, as vitrine at the top of the grandstand that the public can approach but not enter.

An opportunistic experiment with the specifics of a theatre building and stage as site, and with pushing the conventions of the stage, occurred in the production of *DQ in Barcelona* (2000, Liceu, Barcelona) (Figure 1.4). The architecture of the performance took advantage of the sophisticated stage machinery and its space within the Liceu Theatre. Although the hall itself and proscenium arch reveal nothing out of the ordinary, the theatre, rebuilt and significantly modernized after a fire in 1994, includes a mobile platform that descends five stories below stage level and also includes vast lateral subterranean spaces, fly tower and wing space. In this collaboration with La Fura dels Baus, architects Enric Miralles and Benedetta Tagliabue took advantage of these spaces. The stage platform was lowered to the bottom of this well, an abyss of space below the stage level. The extension upward into the height of the fly tower and laterally into wings was integral to performance and its perception. Performance action and space was at times evident, and at others invisible or distorted. The opera's events took place in three times and places: "now," the thirty-first century, and the near future; Geneva,

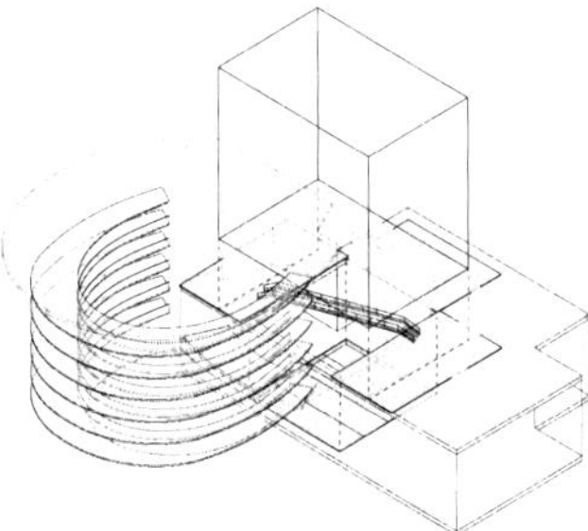

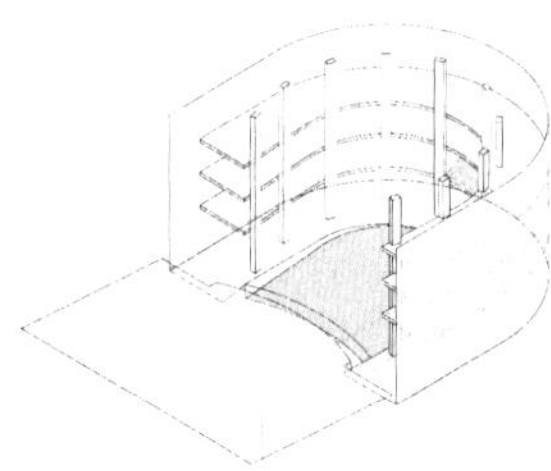

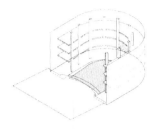

Figure 1.4 Left to right: DQ at the Liceu; Le Balcon at the Odeon. (Drawings: Beth Weinstein with Masoud Sharikzadeh.)

Hong Kong, and "here." Thus displacement and distortion were integral to the work. Drawing parallels to the mythic chasm of the Bayreuth orchestra pit, the scenographic concept located the chorus of singers at the bottom of this five-story pit. Above this pit floated a slew of physical constructions (a bridge, a zeppelin), and immaterial images (projection screens and reflective surfaces), that confound understandings of what was real versus illusion. The specific architecture of the Liceu stage undeniably gave rise to these decisions, making for a work specific to its theatre architecture.

When the architecture of the hall encourages us to turn our heads away from the picture frame and stage, across the house, our gaze might preferentially fall upon our co-spectators and all that is between and separates us. What are the opportunities for experimentation that these afford? How might this space shift our experience of the action? As mentioned earlier, Friederich Kiesler made use of the house in the Vienna Konzerthaus to test the stage–audience relations for his Endless Theater. The orchestra floor became the ground for his new *Spatial Stage*, while the audience overlooked from balconies. El Lissitzky proposed placing the audience on stage, and stage, as agit-prop, in the center of the orchestra. Spatial performance and relations between proscenium, thrust and arena intermingled in ambiguous ways. Similar to Kiesler and El Lissitzky, Lluis Pasqual sought to critically reimagine the stage–audience space relationships within the conventional, purpose-built Odeon Theatre in Paris, calling into question who and what performs. Jean Genet's *Le Balcon* demanded breaking conventions, leading Lluis Pasqual in his production of *Le Balcon* (1991) to shift the performance from stage to the orchestra floor of this horseshoe theatre. The audience was also shifted out of their conventional place in the house; they slipped in through the curtains and found their place on the stage platform. The boxes and balconies of the house, draped in scarlet and gold fabric, served as stage and scenery for the performance. The inhabitation of existing space-relationships was inverted, creating a backwards world that reflected onto itself, down to the gestures of actors who applied their makeup as if the audience was their mirror (Antle 1992). Though not seeing themselves or their fellow spectators across the horseshoe, the shift of audience from balcony to stage and performers from stage to orchestra floor and balcony, in its strange reversal of places, augmented the perceived relation, spatial and conceptual, to the event taking place.

Conclusion

Without opening up Pandora's box – of stage–audience relations in site-specific performance or the recognized flexibility and opportunity to critically re-imagine stage–audience relations in a black box space – these presented case studies of built and unbuilt theatres of the early twentieth century and more recent purpose-built and adapted buildings for theatre, such as the Spiral Theatre and Teatro Oficina, are important examples of rethinking stage–audience relations in support of new ways of performing *in* and *with* space. These spaces were conceived as critical reflections upon and opportunities to perform new social, spatial and technological relations as a parallel to the contemporaneous dynamics taking place just beyond the theatre walls. The space-relationships of these theatres re-configured relations between audience and action, and between audience members, between interior and exterior. Space and the redistribution of action within space aligned with more physically dynamic performances and demanded new modalities of attentiveness from the audience. The last series of examples call attention to conventions and opportunities to rethink the performative possibilities of stage and of audience space and the relations between them within existing structures. The questions posed at the outset of the chapter can be tools for becoming more aware of that which we take for granted, the relations and inhabitations that have become habit, convention. Asking these questions is a first step towards interrogating a space in terms of its performances and uncovering others latent in the space-relationships. Drawing and diagramming can also serve as means to reveal the space-relationships, and a means to ask, "What if . . .?" What if this traded places with that? What if this element within the space-relationship was split and re-distributed, or elongated, or moved from the horizontal surface to a vertical relationship? Conventional inhabitations arise from habit and are also habits than may be broken or critically reconsidered. We should not assume; rather we should ask, "What other space-relationships are possible within this and any other space?"

Notes

1 The design of performance spaces within buildings originally intended for other uses (such as factories, warehouses, slaughterhouses, and so on) is an extensive topic on its own that I will not elaborate upon. One could view such projects as durational scenographies of site. Similarly, I will not discuss ephemeral site-specific designs within non-purpose-built theatre buildings, as these too are a genre of their own.
2 In addition to the chapters referred to, Wiles' book discusses Sacred Space, Processional Space, Public Space, and Sympotic Space.
3 See Howard 2009. She addresses issues such as light, costume, sound scape, intimacy and distance, viewing-sound relation.
4 I refer to my own experiences in the Gallo-Roman theatre (15 BCE) on the slopes of Lyon and the modern Theatre Grec (1929) in Barcelona.
5 Arnold Aronson's *The History And Theory of Environmental Scenography* was instrumental to identifying both the conventions of theatre space and both built and unbuilt theatre architectures challenging those conventions (Aronson 1981).
6 These observations are based upon my experience of a performance in the Teatro Oficina and my conversation with Marcelo Suzuki in August 2014 and Sara Rachel (2013) "Citadels of Freedom: Lina Bo Bardi's SESC Pompéia Factory Leisure Centre and Teatro Oficina, São Paulo." *Architectural Design* 83 (6): 52–7; and the lectures affiliated with the exhibition, *Lina Bo Bardi:Together* (available online at: http://linabobarditogether.com/2012/06/08/lectures/ [accessed 20 March 2014]).

7 Ryan Center for the Musical Arts at Northwestern University by Goettsch Partners, and DS+R's Granoff Center for the Creative Arts at RISD (Providence, RI) are but two more recent performance spaces that extend the stage or the auditorium into the landscape through a glazed building wall.

References

Antle, Martine 1992. "L'année Théâtrale 1991." *The French Review* 65 (6): 941–8.

Aronson, Arnold 1981. *The History And Theory of Environmental Scenography*. Ann Arbor, MI: UMI Research Press.

Baur-Heinhold, Margarete 1967. *The Baroque Theatre: A Cultural History of the 17th and 18th Centuries*. New York: McGraw-Hill.

Bowman, Ned A. 1964. "The Ideal Theatre: Emerging Tendencies in Its Architecture." *Educational Theatre Journal* 16 (3): 220–9.

Brewster, Karen and Melissa Shafer 2011. *Fundamentals of Theatrical Design*. New York: Allworth Press.

DS+R (Diller Scofidio + Renfro). "Institute of Contemporary Art." Available online at: www.dsrny.com/projects/ica (accessed 12 December 2015).

Firman, Ron 1992. "The Spiral Theatre in Prague." *Theatre Design & Technology* 28 (5): 43–6. Available online at: http://tdt.usitt.org/GetPDF.aspx?PDF=28-5fall92-5spiraltheatre (accessed 13 October 2014).

Howard, Pamela 2009. *What is Scenography?* (2nd ed.). London: Routledge.

Jaques-Dalcroze, E. 1933. "Remarks on Arrhythmy." *Music and Letters* 14 (2): 138–48, doi: 10.1093/ml/XIV.2.138.

Marcadé, Jean-Claude and E. N. Petrova 2005. *The Avant-garde Before and After*. Bad Breisig: Palace Editions.

Mitchley, Jack and Peter Spalding 1982. *Five Thousand Years of Theatre*. London: Batsford Academic and Educational.

Moholy Nagy, Sybil 1969. *Moholy Nagy: Experiments in Totality*. Cambridge, MA: MIT Press.

Moneo, Rafael 1978. "On Typology." *Oppositions* 13: 23–45.

Salter, Chris 2010. *Entangled: Technology and the Transformation of Performance*. Cambridge, MA: MIT Press.

Tallon, M. E. 1984. "Appia's Theatre at Hellerau." *Theatre Journal* 36 (4): 495–504.

Weinstein, B. 2008. "Flamand and his Architectural Entourage." *Journal of Architectural Education* 61 (4): 25–33.

Wiles, David 2003. *A Short History of Western Performance Space*. New York: Cambridge University Press.

Wimmer, Franz and Barbara Schelle 2009. "Auditoriums for the arts: typology of theatre buildings with examples." *Detail* (English ed.) 3: 243–9.

2
SCENERY

Thea Brejzek

In a general understanding, scenery locates the dramatic action on the stage in time and space and provides a physical and symbolic framing of events, thus operating as the driving visual force of the overall performance. Scenery may attempt to replicate reality through landscape elements, architectural structures, and interiors, or it can be comprised entirely of abstract configurations or immaterial elements such as projections.

Scenery has functioned in widely different ways throughout theatre history. Extended towards heaven and the underworld in the Baroque, excessively detailed during nineteenth-century naturalism, and generally held in contempt by the historical avant-garde, scenery has had a recent comeback. The resurgence of practicable rooms, functional detail, and found objects on the stage warrants a new look at the history and present of scenery, its functions and potentialities, its varying relationship to reality and to the spectator, and at the different approaches developed to "read" scenery.

The question of the treatment of reality in the theatre, namely through mimesis or artistic representation, has been heatedly discussed since Plato's denigration of mimetic practices as imitations of reality that are far removed from knowledge and thus inferior (*Republic*, Book 10) and Aristotle's subsequent defense, in his *Poetics*, of mimesis as an inherent human desire enabling catharsis. The attribution of relevance, function, and merit of mimetic realism over abstract expressive or symbolist scenery has moved through several shifts throughout theatre history and can be seen to be one of the leitmotifs of scenographic practice, thought, and innovation.

Scenery and the representation of reality

In the history of scenery in Western theatre, the desire to expand the physical limits of the stage has been and continues to be instrumental for its technological development and artistic innovation. With the rediscovery of Vitruvius's fundamental work, *De Architectura*, in the Cinquecento, the antique Greek stage machinery and scenic elements described by the Roman architect remained seminal well into the nineteenth century. Vitruvius described the painted wooden flats of the theatre (*pinakes*), the three-sided wooden prism with different scenes painted on each side and allowing for rapid scene changes when revolved (*periaktoi*), and the *mechane*, a wooden crane and pulley-system for apparitions and flying actions, all of which comprised practicable technical solutions in the production of special effects and the sequencing of space and time. Following the Renaissance treatises on perspective by Baldasare Peruzzi and Sebastiano Serlio, the first raked stages in Ferrara and Vicenza were built, exploiting the vanishing point and enhancing the illusion of depth through (usually) three sets of wings in three generic sets each for tragedy, comedy, and satyr play. With the subsequent development of the *telari* system in the late sixteenth century and the invention of machines and lighting systems for diverse effects (foremost Buontalenti, Bernini, Torelli, Servandoni, and Sabbatini), the potentials of the stage began to be explored systematically, allowing for the theatrical space to gain both depth and a multitude of transformations. The high point of the baroque illusionist stage was reached with the development and European-wide dissemination of Ferdinando Galli-Bibiena's *scena ad angolo*, the so-called angled stage (1690), and, subsequently, Giuseppe Galli-Bibiena's polygonal, bird's-eye views and perspectives of curvature reimagined for the stage. The illusionist and, later, naturalist stage of the nineteenth century strived to copy real forms and materials and to perfect optical illusions and functional details (André Antoine, Otto Brahm, and the early Stanislavsky, Meiningen Court Theatre).

In a refusal of nineteenth-century naturalism and psychologism, stage reformers such as Adolphe Appia and Edward Gordon Craig understood the stage to be foremost an abstracted space for acting. This new stage did not require the imitation of landscape, exteriors or interior spaces and neither did it require props to support the production's distinct, yet abstract setting. Appia and Craig had developed specific abstracted objects (stairs, platforms, screens) to foreground the actors on a stage devoid of the usual scenery. Appia's rhythmic spaces (from 1908) and Craig's patented screens (1910) represent the development from set design as image and background to the notion of theatre as *Gesamtkunstwerk* and the stage as an autonomous space that is not reliant on realistic scenic detail. Futurist, constructivist, and expressionist scenery equally refused to copy reality in their elaborate and utopic, often architectural, constructions that resulted in subjective worlds and distinct atmospheres on the stage. In 1920s and 1930s Russia, Vsevolod Meyerhold emphatically refused scenery overall in favor of kinetic stage constructions and an extension of his acting theory of biomechanics onto the stage. The socially engaged and political theatre of Bertolt Brecht required constructed scenery that was both functional and "real"[1] and Erwin Piscator's multi-tiered "Theatre of Totality" aimed at the dissemination of the revolutionary concepts of Marxism through the extensive use of technological innovation on the stage.[2]

The critical realism of Brecht and Piscator and their scenographer-collaborators[3] refused decoration and subordinated all scenic elements to functionality, as in the scaffolded acting areas and mechanical and image technologies. Significantly, with the increasing use of technology on the stage and the intentional visibility of stage machinery and constructive elements, together with a heightened realistic mode of representation in 1920s and 1930s political theatre, scenery acquired a completely new function, namely to become an integral part of a scenography operating as an ideological instrument. From the 1960s onwards, postmodernism and postdramatic theatre set into motion a departure from modernist coherent and unified scenographic and architectonic concepts and constructions such as Appia's and Craig's highly symmetrical and abstracted space stages that seemed in no need of the actor's bodily presence anymore (Aronson 2005).

Scenery and the politicized domestic

While the notion of scenery retained negative connotations throughout the twentieth century, recent scenographic practice has seen its resurgence in the form of detailed built structures complete with floors and ceilings, windows, doors, and skylights based on found architectures and objects, as well as diverse built-in media configurations on the stage. Fully furnished and practicable rooms or labyrinthine, multi-story environments suggest the critical reestablishment of the fourth wall, operating now as an isolating and confrontational instrument in the representation of a hybridized, expanded domesticity and its inherent politics, a design approach I identify, with recourse to Brecht's and Piscator's "critical realism," as a "new critical realism."

If one is to describe the works of individual scenographers and collectives such as Bert Neumann, Anna Viebrock, Reinhard von der Thannen, or The Builder's Association, questions as to the function and impact of both "scenery" and "object" come to the fore. In their detailed scenographic re-articulations of private dwellings, these scenographers portray the domestic with its attributes, objects, and behaviors not as a counterpart of the political, but rather as closely linked to it. The scenographic trend toward a politicized domestic cannot be grasped by the typical categories of describing scenery's relationship to reality, namely imitative (mimetic), symbolic, or abstract. The hyperrealist and highly detailed sceneries of Viebrock's *Ariadne on Naxos*, Neumann's *The Insulted and Humiliated*, and The Builder's Association's *House/Divided* (designed by John Cleater and Neal Wilkinson), for example, spatialize

Figure 2.1 Bert Neumann, *The Insulted and Humiliated* (after Dostoyevsky), Vienna 2001. (Photo courtesy of Thomas Aurin.)

the political dimension underlying all domestic structures and behavior through a kind of "reality-hacking" approach. The process and method of reality-hacking takes existing elements and objects and appropriates and recombines these in such a way as to provoke new perceptions of the external reality on the stage. In new critical realism, scenery, the domestic object, and the architectural element operate as the material manifestation of the inventory of a neoliberal society. Media, in the form of a multitude of large-scale projections of soap-opera-type images, has become an integral part of many "domestic" productions, realized as visually overwhelming trashy collages intended to portray the popular iconography of commercial television and (social) media. Linked to the portrayal of the domestic as both consequence and symptom of the political is the emergence of the many standardized "non-spaces" (Augé 1995) of the postfordist period of capitalism on the stage such as airports, subway stations, and hotel lobbies, as well as generic, standardized apartment blocks and courtyards designed with disturbing detail. Richard Strauss' *Ariadne* has been set in a shabby hotel lobby (Viebrock 2001), Dostoyevsky's *The Insulted and Humiliated* in a fully functional prefabricated bungalow with slightly dysfunctional surveillance technologies (Neumann 2001), a repurposed original single dwelling has operated as acting area and projection surface for the cynical proclamations of US-American mortgage lenders (The Builders Association's *House/Divided* 2013) and Verdi's monumental *Aida* has turned into a reflection on war victims and perpetrators when set in a twentieth-century petit bourgeois living room by scenographer Reinhard von der Thannen, yet these new and possibly unlikely settings are never completely what they seem to be at first sight. Instead, fragmented and collaged, found or appropriated real facades, architectural elements, interiors, and objects have been meticulously appropriated in such a way as to render the spectator both complicit and critical of the present-time society in which the narrative takes place. With a generation of scenographers focused on social critique through making visible the politics of space, new critical realism has departed from the safe aesthetics of symbolic representation and embraced the conflicted domestic scene as a political arena. Such renewed and politicized material realism demands a new understanding of objects and an awareness of their "agency" (Latour 2005). Adapted from a school of thought in the philosophy of science and social science and pointing back to Brecht's "critical" or "socialist" realism, the concept of "critical realism" (Bhaskar 1975) acknowledges that there is no single (or unified) truth but only fragments. New critical realist scenery supports the postmodern and postdramatic skepticism of the unified modernist stage while at the same time maintaining "material" to be the foundation of reality, and staging a hybridized, compacted, and dense material reality with a distinct social and political agenda.

Scenery and lived space

Outside the theatre, scenery operates as an active agent and co-player in site-specific theatre and performance practices by constructing a dual layer of architectures, histories, and temporalities between site and performance. With an increased activation of public space as theatrical space since the 1960s, performance artists and theatre practitioners began to participate in urban discourses by leaving the physical confines of the theatre building and the bourgeois conventions of the proscenium stage behind, and entering the spatial and political territory of the city. The physical body of the city became a desired playing field where scenery operated on the scale of the city, comprising both large-scale theatrical objects and the urban fabric itself. Urban interventions utilize the dynamic and unstable scenery comprised of architecture, infrastructure, and people to disrupt the capitalist efficiency of the city and to shift the audience's focus onto specific, often urbanistic issues. Actionist art performances, happenings, and street theatre such as Peter Schumann's *Bread and Puppet Theatre* in the US, Colombia's *Mapa Teatro*, or Berlin's theatre collective *Rimini Protokoll* look upon the urban fabric as providing a rich contemporary and historical scenery and enabling a highly immersive and often interactive audience experience.

Typically, scenery adheres to the spatial organization between the space of action and the space of observation, immersion, or participation. Even where scenery resists or transgresses the boundaries of the stage by spilling out into the auditorium or taking over the entire theatre building and thus creating an immersive, performative environment (for example, Okhlopkov's *The Iron Flood*, Moscow 1934; Castorf and Neumann's *Hotel Neustadt*, Berlin 2001), it invariably defines, frames, and envelops what is seen and experienced by the spectator. As rhythm, visuality, perspective, scale, and materiality of the scenic, supported by light and sound, are in constant flux during a performance, and closely linked to the dramatic action, these are chiefly responsible for the audience's individual and subjective overall perception of the live event. The world created between the totality of the scenic composition and the spectator's experience becomes what Otto Friedrich Bollnow, in regard to differing spatial experiences and atmospheres depending on one's subjective perception and feelings, calls a "lived" and "inclined" space[4] (Bollnow 1961: 38–9), and one that is able to invoke the imagination of the spectator. Gernot Böhme extends Bollnow's notion of the "inclined space" as atmospheric space to stage design as a model or blueprint for an aesthetics of atmosphere overall.[5] While acknowledging the role of lighting as a "generator" of atmosphere (Böhme 2013: 4), Böhme significantly revaluates the object or "thing" in the making of atmospheres, and attributes to the "thing" the potential of "ekstasis," through its specific form, volume, color, and smell. Ekstasis, the Greek term for "displacement" or a "standing outside oneself," as applied by Böhme to the conditions of atmosphere, describes the presence that is felt between the subject (spectator) and the object (understood here both as single object and scenery). To put it precisely: the object/scenery emits its presence into the space and the resultant atmospheric space is a finely tuned space, "tuned as ecstasies" (Böhme 1993: 121) and always thought of with lighting in mind. Appia, whose abstracted, minimal stage objects located and orientated a space yet only created a specific world in conjunction with lighting, is recognized as one of the early scenographers passionately arguing for, what we now, with Bollnow and Böhme, call a "tuned" or "inclined" space on the stage.

When writing on the staging of Richard Wagner's *Siegfried* in his 1902 *Ideas on a Reform of our Mise en Scène,* Appia succinctly highlighted the importance of the creation of scenic atmosphere and the necessary failure of naturalistic representation. "We need not try to represent a *forest*; what we must give the spectator is *man* in the atmosphere of a forest" (Appia 1902 in Beacham 1994: 118). Significantly, it was in the scenographies of the stage reformers of the turn of the century that scenery was for the first time recognized not anymore simply as a machine for special effects[6] but as instrumental in the creation of specific atmospheres with the aim to affect the audience's senses and emotions.

Scenery and the agency of the object

With the cultural and performative turns of the 1950s and 1990s respectively, and an increased understanding of "culture as performance" rather than as text (Fischer-Lichte 1999: 168), classical semiotic theories in the reception and understanding of theatrical signs have shifted considerably to include previously marginalized issues of context and perspective (Dolan 1998), and more recently been complemented by phenomenological and affect studies into the theatrical experience (Hurley and Warner 2012; Bleeker *et al.* 2015). Following Saussurian semiology, theatre had initially been understood as a decodable system of signs (Prague Linguistic Circle 1928–1939; McAuley 2010; Elam 1980) and stage space, scenery, and objects were seen as communicating specific sets of related and contextual meanings. In a critique of the potential rigidity of semiotic analysis, Patrice Pavis has indicated the "mobility" of the sign in both directions, that of the signified and that of the signifier (Pavis 1998: 335). Erika Fischer-Lichte, equally critical, speaks of the emergent processes of making meaning during a live performance, which require a constant contextual reframing by the spectator (Fischer-Lichte 2008). The phenomenological approach informed by Husserl's notion of the unity of self and body, and Maurice Merleau-Ponty's concept of the inseparability of sensorial perception into singular units, takes into account the individual spectator's constitution, frame of mind, and experience and can thus be understood as the most personal of performance analysis approaches. Bert States posits phenomenological analysis against "the radical skepticism of deconstruction and postmodernism" (States 2010: 27) and puts forward the phenomenological analysis of scenery as particularly evident and simple when compared with the analysis of, say, character. Referring to Merleau-Ponty's definition of the phenomenological approach as looking at "how the world becomes world" (States 2010: 29), States declares that performance phenomenology should ask "how the theatre becomes theatre" (ibid.), particularly in asking how scenery has been intentionally designed and manufactured so as to create its own reality.[7] Applying Husserl's systematic phenomenological reduction (*epoché* or *bracketing*) to the process of scenic analysis, as States does, reveals the presence of scenery as the presence of illusion, even by its very absence.

Such a "reading" of scenery aims at the Husserlian suspension of judgment through a phenomenological stripping-away of layers of meaning perpetrated due to a general belief-system that holds us captive, and proposes the experience and perception of phenomena as they originally appear in our consciousness. The appeal of Husserl's *epoché* for theatre and performance studies is evident, as this figure or operation, as seen from today, seems to suggest an inherent critical impetus and a refusal to adhere to codified models of theatrical reception. From the mid-1980s onwards, and with the influence of French poststructuralism, a merging of semiotic and phenomenological approaches occurred with a dual focus on the spectator's subjective experience of the live event as well as on questions of meaning and representation, and their exploration through semiotic analysis.[8] In addition, the notion of an "agency of objects" (Latour 2005) was brought forward by sociological, semiotic, and phenomenologically-based research into the making of objects and their relationship to both maker and spectator (Ingold 2011; Bennett 2010; McKinney 2015). This promises to be a rich research area for scenography in its emphasis on the action potential of objects, especially in regard to the perceived increase in detailed scenery, objects, and assemblages on the stage. Studies in material culture relating to scenery will thus take into account both an object's making and its individual and collective history, looking at the traces of both and its role in the make-up and theatrical representation of the spaces of a specific society. In the context of describing non-human objects as actors who have agency, Bruno Latour writes: "In addition to 'determining' and serving as a 'backdrop for human action,' things might authorize, allow, afford, encourage, permit, suggest, influence, block, render possible, forbid, and so on" (Latour 2005: 72).

In contrast to a phenomenological understanding of the agency of objects that is limited to the analysis of the function and symbolic value of objects, Latour's Actor-Network-Theory (ANT) is based around the concept that social, technical, and natural objects are able to explain society and thus make valid and critical statements regarding the social, cultural, and political makeup of a given society. Stage objects and scenery, following Latour's ANT, can thus speak of spatial politics and hegemonies, of social identity and inequalities. Both a politicized method, such as Latour's, and a more internal argument focused on processes of making and the maker such as Ingold's, are particularly suited to close readings of new critical realist scenery and its emphasis on articulating a different reality by designing a kind of "relentless naturalism" and a "rehabilitation of the fourth wall" (Bert Neumann as cited in Nioduschewski 2001: 33).

From the modest *skene* in the antique Greek amphitheatre to contemporary fully mechanized proscenium stages and urban outdoor locations, scenery has strived to act as a visual, dramaturgical structuring tool that locates the performance in time and space. Throughout theatre history, scenery's relationship to reality has oscillated between a mimetic or critical realism, abstraction, and symbolic representation. Since the 1990s, the aim to portray the condition of the postmodern subject in a globalized and mediatized world has seen a resurgence of detailed construction and functional objects, resulting in what is defined here as a new critical realism on the stage. Independent of its mode of representation, scenery and lighting are instrumental in the creation of distinct atmospheres through a set of intermediate relations between stage, actor, and spectator. Diverse approaches based on semiotic and/or phenomenological analysis have helped to "read" scenery while recent theoretical positions that acknowledge the action potential of the object shift the focus from spectator to object. As an active agent, the object (and scenery) is not "read" but rather "speaks" beyond its singular existence on the stage of social, cultural and political realities.

Notes

1 "A picture is never realistic, the stage is always realistic. That's why I maintain that the 'realistic stage picture' is nonsense." Neher to Brecht, *c.* 1951 (cited in Willett, *Caspar Neher*, p. 75 as cited in Baugh [1994] 2002: 239).

2 Piscator's production of *The Merchant of Berlin* in 1929 showed a three-tiered stage with treadmills on a rotating disc and four simultaneous projections by Laszlo Maholy-Nagy.

3 Brecht's most significant scenographer-collaborators were Caspar Neher, Teo Otto, and Karl von Appen. Piscator worked closely together with Traugott R. Müller, John Heartfield, and László Moholy-Nagy.

4 O. F. Bollnow, German philosopher and teacher (1903–1991). The term "inclined space" goes back to Swiss psychiatrist and psychoanalyst Ludwig Binswanger (1881–1966). German philosopher Gernot Böhme developed the concept of atmosphere as a central category of aesthetics.

5 Atmosphere, to Böhme, is an "intermediate phenomenon, something between subject and object" (Böhme 2013: 10), and he regards stage design as a paradigm for the making of atmospheres in a postmodern theatricalized world where all areas of life are staged before an ever-changing scenery.

6 With an acute view to the creation of spectacle through special effects, painter and scenographer Philippe de Loutherbourg wrote in 1772 about the need to develop specific scenery and stage machinery in order to extend and heighten the audience's perception of the scene:

> I must invent scenery, which will have the effect of creating a new sensation upon the public. To this end, I must change the manner of lighting the stage so as to serve the effects of the painting. I must also change the method of pulling off simultaneously an entire scene – and generally, alter such machinery as might be necessary to the aspiration of my talents.
>
> *(De Loutherbourg 1772 as cited in Baugh 2005: 14)*

7 States' position is reminiscent of Brecht in *Set Design for the Epic Theatre*: "It's more important nowadays for the set to tell the spectator he's in a theatre than to tell him he's in say, Aulis" (Brecht-Archive 331/173, as cited in Brecht [1964] 1974: 233), and "He [the spectator] sees that arrangements have been made to show something" (ibid.: 141).

8 See Marvin Carlson's extensive overview of the history and development of semiotics (Carlson 2010: 13–25).

References

Aronson, Arnold [2005] 2008. "Postmodern Design." In *Looking Into the Abyss: Essays on Scenography*, 13–29. Ann Arbor: University of Michigan Press.

Augé, Marc 1995. *Non-Places: Introduction to an Anthropology of Supermodernity*, translated by John Howe. London/New York: Verso.

Baugh, Christopher [1994] 2002. "Brecht and Stage Design." In *The Cambridge Companion to Brecht*, edited by Peter Thomson and Glenyr Sachs, 235–53. Oxford: Oxford University Press.

Baugh, Christopher 2005. *Theatre, Performance and Technology: The Development of Scenography in the Twentieth Century*. London: Palgrave Macmillan.

Beacham, Richard C. 1994. *Adolphe Appia: Artist and Visionary of the Modern Theatre*. London: Routledge.

Bennett, Jane 2010. *Vibrant Matter*. Durham, NC: Duke University Press.

Bhaskar, Roy 1975 [1997]. *A Realist Theory of Science* (2nd ed.). London: Verso.

Bleeker, Maaike, Jon Foley Sherman and Eirini Nedelkopopulou (Eds) 2015. *Performance and Phenomenology: Traditions and Transformations*. London: Routledge.

Böhme, Gernot 1993. "Atmosphere as the Fundamental Concept of a New Aesthetics." *Thesis Eleven* August, 36: 113–26, doi: 10.1177/072551369303600107.

Böhme, Gernot 2013. "The art of the stage set as paradigm for an aesthetics of atmospheres." Paper delivered in the University of Aarhus, 16–17 March 2012. Available online at: http://conferences.au.dk/fileadmin/conferences/Understanding_Atmospheres/abstracts.pdf (accessed 10 February 2016).

Bollnow, O. F. 1961. "Lived Space." Translated by Dominic Gerlach. *Philosophy Today* 5: 31–9.

Brecht, Bertolt [1964] 1974. *Brecht on Theatre: The Development of an Aesthetic*. Translated and edited by John Willett. London: Eyre Methuen.

Brockett, Oscar, Margaret Mitchell and Linda Hardberger 2010. *Making the Scene: A History of Stage Design and Technology in Europe and the United States*. San Antonio, TX: Tobin Theatre Arts Fund.

Carlson, Marvin 2010. "Semiotics and its Heritage." In *Critical Theory and Performance*, edited by Janelle Reinelt and Joseph Roach, 13–25. Ann Arbor: University of Michigan Press, revised and enlarged edition.

Di Benedetto, Stephen 2012. *An Introduction to Theatre Design*. London: Routledge.

Dolan, Jill 1998. *The Feminist Spectator as Critic*. Ann Arbor: University of Michigan Press.

Elam, Keir 1980. *The Semiotics of Theatre and Drama*. Hove, UK: Psychology Press.

Fischer-Lichte, Erika 1999. "From Text to Performance: The Rise of Theatre Studies as an Academic Discipline in Germany." *Theatre Research International* 24/ 2: 168–78.

Fischer-Lichte, Erika 2008. *The Transformative Power of Performance: A New Aesthetics*. London and New York: Routledge.

Foucault, Michel 1986. "Of Other Spaces." *Diacritics* 16/1: 22–7.
Hurley, Erin 2010. *Theatre & Feeling*. Basingstoke, Hampshire: Palgrave Macmillan.
Hurley, Erin and Sara Warner 2012. "Special Section: Affect/Peformance/Politics." *Journal of Dramatic Theory and Criticism* 26/2 2: 99–107.
Ingold, Tim 2011. *Being Alive: Essays on Movement, Knowledge and Description*. London and New York: Routledge.
Latour, Bruno 2005. *Reassembling the Social: An Introduction to Actor-Network-Theory*. Oxford: Oxford University Press.
McAuley, Gay 2010. *Space in Performance: Making Meaning in the Theatre*. Ann Arbor: University of Michigan Press.
McKinney, Joslin 2015. "Vibrant Materials: The Agency of Things in the Context of Scenography." In *Performance and Phenomenology: Traditions and Transformations*, edited by Maaike Bleeker, Jon Foley Sherman and Eirini Nedelkopoulou, 121–39. New York: Routledge.
Nioduschewski, Anja 2001. "Imitation of Life. Interview with Bert Neumann." *Theater der Zeit*, 10: 31–5.
Pavis, Patrick 1998. *Dictionary of the Theatre: Terms, Concepts and Analysis*. Toronto and Buffalo: University of Toronto Press.
States, Bert O. 2010. "The Phenomenological Attitude." In *Critical Theory and Performance*, edited by Janelle Reinelt and Joseph Roach, 26–36. Ann Arbor: University of Michigan Press, revised and enlarged edition.

3
COSTUME

Michelle Liu Carriger

"The simplest, and most theatrical, way of thinking about how many characters there are in any one play is to ask how many costumes the play requires," declare the authors of an important book on early modern English clothing and costume (Jones and Stallybrass 2000: 197). This statement is at first straightforward and concrete – if you're making a play, count the costumes required and you know how to proceed. However, this "simple" statement betrays complex issues about the role costume plays in the alchemy of turning actors into characters, the stage into a story.

Costume is the element of the theatre that integrates the performer into the scenography; it constitutes the margin between the performer's body and all the other material factors that make up the performance. As such, costume occupies a complicated position – is a costume part of the actor or the character or the material context of the performance? In the theatre, costumes perform many functions: they establish facts about the character, participate in and communicate the overall production scheme, they must function well no matter what the actors do while wearing them, and they provide visual appeal, calibrated to interest the viewer. Meanwhile, audiences "read" costumes on many levels too, looking to them to signify dramaturgically and semiotically, aesthetically, and as "real" material goods. Aoife Monks describes an "essential perceptual indistinguishability between the actor and their costume," which not only makes analyzing costume complicated but can also verge on the affective and uncanny. "Costume," Monks writes, "is a body that can be taken off" (Monks 2010: 11).

Definitions

Costumes are complicated, not just in the way they need to mediate between moving, performing bodies and the rest of the *mise-en-scène*, but also because of costume's continuities with the equally fraught realm of clothing "in real life." Today the word "costume" in English usually has a very clear meaning: clothing put on in order to appear like someone or something one is not. A costume's theatricality is supposed to be evident – that is, the person in the costume should be recognizable as double, both signifying the thing to which the costume refers *and* signifying that she or he is not *really* that thing.

This theatrical doubleness can be articulated in comparison with other terms for clothing. For example, a *disguise* is also "false" like a costume, but in a successful disguise those who see the disguised person do not recognize that the wearer is not what they appear to be. The word "fashion" meanwhile does not immediately suggest a doubleness of identity in the same way that "costume" and "disguise" do, but if we think through some of the common critiques of fashion – that teenagers dress too sexily or sloppily or that women should dress to disguise their bodily "flaws" – we realize that anxieties about fakery, doubleness, or theatricality seem to cling to virtually all forms of clothing.

In some sense, all clothing always maintains some danger of theatricality (that the person wearing the clothes may not be what she or he seems) – a quality that can provoke intense anxieties as well as pleasure. Indeed, many people rely on clothing to help outwardly create (perform) and fix the identities they feel are essentially true. For example, a transgender person may use clothing to display the gender that they feel is true for them. A motorcycle gang member may wear biker boots and leather jackets to establish herself as a member of a subcultural identity. On the other hand, biker boots and jackets have also been adopted as fashionable items in their own right, and so may be worn not to identify with motorcycle culture, but as simply "cool."

Today then, "costume" is one of the more unambiguous words denoting clothing, however the meaning of the word "costume" was not always so evident. Just a hundred years ago, the word costume could refer to all kinds of ordinary everyday clothing: fashion magazines presented images of "walking costumes," "morning costumes," "riding costumes," "children's costumes," and so on. This more ambiguous sense of costume is still present in terms like "folk costume" or "traditional costume," which ostensibly do not indicate that their wearers are somehow dressed other than they truly are (although this is debatable – a careful history of folk costume reveals that these "traditions" are carefully calibrated productions, often made at the behest of colonial or elite powers, not the "natural" outgrowths of folk culture they are often fantasized to be [Maxwell 2014]). Costume could also have the meaning we ascribe to it today, but just as often the Victorians used the word "get-up," or "fancy dress" (the latter is still in use today in Britain) to refer to stage and special occasion outfits meant to present a person in the guise of some other identity.

Thus, costume both adds *and* subtracts a layer of uncertainty. On the stage, an additional layer is added to interpretation because the person in the costume is at least two personas at once – the actor and the character (and sometimes more, as when characters disguise themselves). However, other uncertainties that accrue to clothing off the stage are assuaged because we can be certain that costume was planned, was meant to be seen, and meant to be read semiotically as indicative of the character, or the stage setting, or the artistic vision of the production. That is, a "costume" is less ambiguous than everyday clothing, precisely because it explicitly acknowledges its theatricality. In contrast, on the street, it can be unclear whether a sartorial statement is ironic or sincere, what the wearer intends as his or her sartorial message, or *if* they intended to send a message at all. Of course, costume, just like other clothing, remains susceptible to "failures" of communication – sometimes leaving audiences wondering *who* someone is, what kind of character was meant to be portrayed, or oblivious to intended semiotic messages.

Costume as *mise-en-scène*

Costume is one of the earliest scenographic elements – it could even constitute the entire *mise-en-scène*. For example, a performer in costume can transform an ordinary public space into a performance space simply by entering it, even before beginning to "perform." That is, costume functions as portable scenography, the *mise-en-scène* inextricable from the body of the performer herself. To be more provocative we could say that at times the actor is secondary to the costume in presenting character or story: in much ancient Greek and Roman theatre character types were created by masks and costumes, brought to life by the voice and movement of the actors within. In Japanese noh theatre, a male actor plays every main role (*shite*), be it a demon, a young woman, a warrior, behind the appropriate mask and huge, symbol-laden costume. The mask and the costume do the majority of the establishment of character; the actor doesn't even modulate his voice to approximate the character's voice – verisimilitude is not the point of the actor's performance. The sumptuous brocade and silk costumes contrast with the spare, never-altered stage, presenting the main actors as ghosts, gods, demons, and other supernatural beings, not because the costumes make the actor look how a ghost, god, or demon would "really" look, but through highly conventionalized semiotic codes of fabric pattern, costume style, and mask.

Like noh, early modern English theatre invested heavily in costume as their primary scenographic expenditure: historians speculate that with relatively simple and unchanging stage designs, the establishment of place and time was most often left to costumes and text. Costume holdings of an early modern theatre company were so important that S. P. Cerasano calculated that the costume collection of the Rose Theatre was worth more than the entire playhouse itself (Cerasano 1994: 51).

In part this is because, before the Industrial Revolution, the manufacture of fabrics was a time-intensive process, raw materials often came from distant sources, and therefore clothing was much more expensive and precious than it is today. Philip Henslowe, who invested in more than one company of players, was also a pawn broker who often took in noblemen's clothes, and noble patrons of companies were known to donate their old clothes to the troupes, so that an actor playing a nobleman may very well have been attired in an actual nobleman's garments (Jones and Stallybrass 2000: 189).

Because fabrics and clothing were so valuable, they circulated across boundaries, accruing meaning and value as they traveled between nobles and commoners, on- and off-stage. Plays also consistently dramatized the emotional and memorial value of clothing – as when *Twelfth Night*'s Viola dresses in her (seemingly) dead brother's clothes or when a misplaced handkerchief serves as a precipitating event to Othello killing his wife.

Shakespearean actors were occasionally disciplined for wearing their valuable costumes out into the city as if they were their own clothes. Indeed, in many other theatres over history actors were responsible for providing their own costumes. The contents of a nineteenth-century actress's costume trunk, for example, needed to prepare her for comic and serious roles, with attractive, eye-catching costumes that would enable her to stand out. Tracy C. Davis declares, "while black velvet and white lace were the marks of artistry, gauze and spangles were the key to mass appeal and commercial success" (Davis 1991: 111). Some costumes in the nineteenth and early twentieth century were even meant to double as fashion advertisements to encourage audience members to buy what they saw on stage (Kaplan and Stowell 1994; Schweitzer 2009).

Beauty and realism

Oftentimes, as costume-as-advertisement might suggest, the primary function of the costume has been not so much to convey information as to impress the spectator through its sheer beauty or magnificence. Many traditional and popular performance forms such as noh and kabuki, Chinese opera, kuttiyattam and kathakali, west African egungun masquerade, and Las Vegas showgirl revues prominently feature elaborate and beautiful costumes. Garments that emphasize spectacle over functionality highlight the visuality of theatre – put another way, we might declare that an audience member's visual experience of a costume is ultimately the *real* function of costume, trumping the garment's practicality for daily activities or approximation of offstage norms. These performance genres often feature wildly oversize costumes that render the performer more monumental and easier to see from afar – literally larger than life. Other forms emphasize beauty in other ways through sumptuous fabrics and decoration as in Indonesian legong, or ballet, where the "skirt" of most tutus has become so stylized it no longer even fulfills the ostensible function of the skirt: to cover the lower half of the wearer's body. For many of these monumental costumes, such spectacularity isn't intended only to impress spectators but to *impress upon them* the spiritual or metaphysical connections performers have beyond the realm of ordinary human existence, as is the case of the ceremonial garments of Catholic and Orthodox clergy members.

While visually spectacular or beautiful costume remains a constant in many contemporary performance forms (think of pop singers' concert outfits or Mardi Gras and Mummers parade costumes), for more than a century Anglophone and European theatre has most often been costumed under a different rubric: realism. Realistic costume cannot be thought of as opposite to spectacular or aesthetic costume – realism is itself a stylized aesthetic, one that guides a viewer to evaluate and appreciate costumes on the basis of their indistinguishability from "real life" or how one imagines "real life" was in the time and place depicted on the stage. Within realism's appeal to verisimilitude, costumers still regularly balance measures of historical "accuracy" with contemporary audience tastes and storytelling; for example, plays set in the medieval period often eschew stocking-like hose for men in favor of trousers because modern audiences find hose unattractive, dampening the aesthetic appeal of a medieval hero like Romeo or Robin Hood. Indeed, sometimes realistic costumes are themselves presented as spectacular – perhaps through jaw-dropping luxury, as one might see in a magnificent period Shakespeare production, or perhaps through painstaking recreations of worn and patched clothes, suggesting a long life before and after the production itself.

Trends and tastes for realistic costume index modern concerns with "theatricality" and modern and postmodern theatres' navigations of the "fourth wall," and theatrical illusion. Modern and contemporary theatre makers have gone ever farther in pushing the boundaries between realistic illusory costumes and the "real itself" onstage by using strategies of neutral costume (plain black turtlenecks and trousers for example) or an aesthetic of "rehearsal clothes" – as if the actors had simply walked onstage from their everyday lives or continued to wear for the performance the clothes they would choose for rehearsals. Costume choices like these that present themselves as *not choosing* may be thought of as the triumph of the "real" over illusion on the stage; they take the notion of realism so far as to break open the fourth wall and introduce onto the stage the "real" of performers physically working – ballet dancers in legwarmers and sweatshirts, actors in mismatched contemporary garments. The apparent non-costume of neutral clothing or of rehearsal clothes semiotically suggest that performing is *labor*, and that actors or dancers are in their "work uniform." These costumes seem to suggest, a couple thousand years after Aristotle, that scenographic "spectacle" is the least important element of the performance. On the other hand, the performance of apparently untheatrical "reality" on the stage remains highly illusory in its careful disavowal of the fact that the bodies on stage remain self-consciously presented before the audience.

What about cases where costume is entirely absent – when performers appear without clothes at all? Certainly, many performance forms exploit the tensions costume can evoke through revealing and concealing the performer's body. Because the naked human body is often considered taboo or transgressive in contemporary Western society, nudity tends to punctuate theatrical illusion by breaking audiences' absorption; audience attention splits between the theatrical presentation and the phenomenological experience of being live with someone else's unclothed body. However, these audience encounters with non-costume are entirely encoded with the effects of clothing and costume's ubiquity. It is precisely because, as writer and journalist Karl Kraus put it back in 1906, "Nakedness is still indissolubly bound to the idea of clothing. We perceive a clothed state as the natural condition and nakedness for us, is primarily a state of being undressed and appears to us as bareness, as nudity" (Kraus 2004: 242).

Far from seeming natural or neutral, the shock of the nude performer demonstrates how powerfully costume and clothing works to normalize the human body. For example, in Young Jean Lee's 2012 *Untitled Feminist Show*, the six performers were naked throughout the wordless one hour show until appearing clothed for the curtain call. One of the performers, Becca Blackwell, described how complicated it was for them,[1] as a non-gender-conforming individual who has never identified with the label "female" (Cruz 2012), to perform themself without clothes. Blackwell's example reveals that, far from being neutral, the body itself can be as much a vehicle of illusion as a costume can be.

Conclusion

Like so many elements of scenography, costumes are often judged most successful when they are not noticed at all, but blend seamlessly into a general impression. Yet, the position of costume is perhaps the most complicated element of scenography, mediating between audience and actor, stage and "real life," reality and illusion, inextricable from any of those spheres. Just as psychologists have demonstrated that the concept of "dress for success" has real psychological impact, actors frequently acknowledge the power of the costume to prepare them for the emotional and psychological work of portraying a character (Adam and Galinsky 2012). Far from being "mere" superficial spectacle that Aristotle deemed least important to tragedy, costume has deep and broad import, across the apparent boundaries of stage, street, audience, actors, real, and theatrical.

Note

1 Blackwell uses the singular pronoun "they/them."

References

Adam, Hajo and Adam D. Galinsky 2012. "Enclothed Cognition." *Journal of Experimental Social Psychology* 48.4: 918–25. ScienceDirect.

Cerasano, S. P. 1994. "'Borrowed Robes,' Costume Prices, and the Drawing of Titus Andronicus." *Shakespeare Studies* 22: 45–57.

Cruz, Araceli 2012. "Becca Blackwell, Performer, On Being Naked in the Untitled Feminist Show." *The Village Voice*, 26 Jan. Available online at: www.villagevoice.com/news/becca-blackwell-performer-on-being-naked-in-the-untitled-feminist-show-6725005 (accessed 12 November 2015).

Davis, Tracy C. 1991. *Actresses as Working Women: Their Social Identity in Victorian Culture.* London and New York: Routledge.
Fisher, Will 2006. *Materializing Gender in Early Modern English Literature and Culture.* Cambridge, UK, and New York: Cambridge University Press.
Hunt, Alan 1996. *Governance of the Consuming Passions: History of Sumptuary Law.* Basingstoke, UK, and New York: Palgrave Macmillan.
Jones, Ann Rosalind and Peter Stallybrass 2000. *Renaissance Clothing and the Materials of Memory.* Cambridge, UK, and New York: Cambridge University Press.
Kaplan, Joel H. and Sheila Stowell 1994. *Theatre and Fashion: Oscar Wilde to the Suffragettes.* Cambridge, UK, and New York: Cambridge University Press.
Kraus, Karl 2004. "The Eroticism of Clothes." In *The Rise of Fashion: A Reader*, edited by Daniel L. Purdy, 239–44. Minneapolis: University of Minnesota Press.
Maxwell, Alexander 2014. *Patriots Against Fashion.* Basingstoke, UK, and New York: Palgrave Macmillan.
Monks, Aoife 2010. *The Actor in Costume.* Basingstoke, UK, and New York: Palgrave Macmillan
Schlueter, June 1999. "Rereading the Peacham Drawing." *Shakespeare Quarterly* 50(2): 171–84.
Schweitzer, Marlis 2009. *When Broadway Was the Runway: Theater, Fashion, and American Culture.* Philadelphia: University of Pennsylvania Press.
Zola, Emile 1974. "Naturalism on the Stage." In *Dramatic Theory and Criticism: Greeks to Grotowski*, edited by Bernard F. Dukore, 692–719. New York: Holt, Rinehart and Winston.

4
LIGHT AND PROJECTION

Scott Palmer

Light has long been acknowledged as a scenographic material that plays a critical role in the reception of the theatrical event. However, in comparison with other areas of performance studies it has received surprisingly little critical attention.

Light is a material that has the ability to make a profound impact on audiences – it is not simply an illuminant but has meaning in and of itself. The role of stage lighting, however, has historically often been dominated by concerns with the practical – the need to be able to see the performers and the scenery, and the technological means by which light might be created and delivered to the stage. As I will show, the historic demands of illuminating the theatre with the technologies that were available created a range of aesthetic issues that were to have a far-reaching impact on the audience's experience of the theatre and the way in which we have come to think about the role of light in performance.

For much of the twentieth century it was commonly accepted that good theatre lighting was that which did not draw attention to itself and went largely unnoticed by an audience. In the naturalistic theatre of illusion with its "brightness that pretends to be another brightness . . . light that pretends to be another light" (Handke 2002: 30), lighting's main task, often, was to replicate the conditions of the natural world – most usually "pretending" to be sunlight or the light reflected from the moon. Interior spaces may have appeared to have been lit by visible practical lights but, in fact, their light was usually "cheated" by the hidden stage lighting pretending to be "another brightness."

There were two key pioneers of theatre design whose writings at the turn of the twentieth century had a profound influence on the development of the modern theatre and the role of light. Both Adolphe Appia (1862–1928) and Edward Gordon Craig (1872–1966) envisaged new possibilities for light on the stage, and their respective manifestos – in essays and through drawings and detailed imagined scenarios – have been fundamental to the development of the thinking about the scenographic potential of light. It is notable that their individual fascination with light as a new expressive material for the stage can be traced back to formative embodied experiences of bright light and darkness that each experienced while backstage in the theatre.

The phenomenal impact of theatrical light on the human body has been largely underestimated, but both Appia and Craig were acutely aware of the effects of light.

Each witnessed advanced lighting technologies – the electric carbon-arc, gas lighting, and limelight – from the wings of two remarkable theatres in which new aesthetics of light were being developed. Appia was working as an intern with the German lighting pioneer Hugo Bähr at the Dresden Hoftheater between 1889–1890 and recognized the power of light and shadow created by electric arc-lights.[1] Craig first experienced Irving's innovative lighting at the Lyceum in London when, as an eight year old, he was taken backstage during a performance of *The Corsican Brothers* in the autumn of 1880. His experience, like Appia's, was a profound one and he "could think of nothing else for days and wanted desperately to go back to the theatre."[2] Craig's experience of the light piercing the dark stage was later acknowledged formally through "my debts to the limelight men of the Lyceum, and to Rembrandt" (Craig 1913: xi).

In recognizing both the power and the potential for light to transform our experience of theatrical space, their individual responses and fascination led directly to the emergence of light as a scenographic phenomenon of the modern theatre. Through their theorizations and advocacy for light's agency and potential to liberate the theatre from dated traditions, Craig and Appia can be seen to be jointly responsible for what Christopher Baugh terms "A Century of Light" (2005; 2013). Throughout the twentieth century, practitioners from Max Reinhardt to Antonin Artaud to Robert Wilson experimented with the scenographic possibilities of light – not principally as a technique of illumination but rather as a central, integral, and active element of their productions.

The first to realize the potential of light on the modern stage was Swiss scenographer Adolphe Appia who recognized the need to light the stage in a "natural" way (Aronson 2005: 30–1), but crucially also advocated the requirement for light to be employed as an expressive and unifying force in the theatre. Appia identified three types of lighting that will form the basis for this chapter and to which I will return: *diffused light* that is unspecific and used to achieve general visibility; *active light* used for specific visual impact through the creation of shadow; and *projected light* created by specialized instruments to allow the creation of specific images that reflect the natural world (for example, clouds, fire) as well as the potential for more abstract, dappled, and moving light effects.

Appia's ambition for a new role for light on the late nineteenth- and early twentieth-century stage, like Craig's in the decades after, was initially treated with suspicion and not immediately adopted. However, key technological advancements and a gradual reappraisal of the role of theatre beyond naturalism contributed to the growing recognition of light in the modern and post-dramatic theatre as a critical, creative material in the processes of performance and meaning-making. Both Appia's and Craig's advocacy for light therefore opened new possibilities for the stage and are widely regarded as the origins of modern lighting practice. They articulated a bold new ambition for the role and contribution of light to dramatic art and, it could be argued, led subsequently to the emergence of the specialist role of the theatre lighting designer.[3]

The problem with light

Given the history of theatrical presentation, it is perhaps surprising that light and lighting practices have been so frequently ignored by critics and reviewers and that it has largely been overlooked as an area of legitimate academic study (Bergman 1977: 11). Even in contemporary publications that have focused primarily on scenography surprisingly little attention has been paid to the role of light as a fundamental scenographic material or its impact on the overall audience experience of performance. There is barely a mention of light in publications that focus specifically on scenography such as Howard (2002), Collins and Nisbet (2010), or Lotker and Gough (2013). Patrice Pavis (2013), for example, acknowledges the essential importance of light to the emergence of the *mise en scène* but without analyzing its role or precise contribution. In relation to naturalistic staging at the end of the nineteenth century he argues that, "The use of gas from 1820 and electricity from 1880 led to the ability of light to sculpt an entire stage universe that appeared autonomous and coherent"[4] (2013: 6). Pavis suggests that changes in production practice mark a rebirth of modern theatre, through a new scenography, with light at its heart – but he is unable to develop this theme and only defines the contribution of light in terms of the technologies involved to produce it. This represents a key and recurrent issue in discussing the impact of light, which has so often resorted to a description of the tools or a focus on describing the spectacular effect. Commentators such as Christopher Baugh (2005; 2013) and Arnold Aronson (2005) have sought to address this lacuna through their writing and in recent years there is evidence of an increasing body of published work by those with an expertise in lighting design practice that have made significant contributions to the way that light can be thought about as a creative force in performance (for example, Crisafulli 2013; Palmer 2013; Abulafia 2015; Moran 2017).

Given the acknowledged importance of light to the presentation and reception of theatrical work, highlighted in Pavis' observation above, why has detailed consideration of light been so largely absent in writings on theatre and performance studies? Partially this might be explained by its ephemeral nature and the difficulties in putting into words our experience of light. It is something that we take for granted. We do not "see" light, although we need it to see, and can only see when light hits a surface and we perceive the effect it has upon objects and spaces through shadow. Maurice Merleau-Ponty explains the importance of this phenomenon through an analysis of Rembrandt's painting *The Nightwatch*:

> We see that the hand pointing to us . . . is truly there only when we see that its shadow on the captain's body presents it simultaneously in profile. The spatiality of the captain lies at the meeting place of two lines of sight which are incompossible and yet together. Everyone with eyes has at some time or other witnessed this play of shadows, or something like it, and has been made by it to see a space and the things included therein. But it works in us without us; it hides itself in making the object visible. To see the object, it is necessary *not* to see the play of shadows and light around it.
>
> *(1964: 167; emphasis in original)*

Merleau-Ponty's observations can be translated to the stage space where the relationship between light and shadow, as Appia and Craig had recognized, was fundamental to both our experience of the theatre and for the future creative contribution of light to dramatic art.

Recent scientific studies have shown that the human body responds in multiple ways to the impact of light: light has a profound psychological and physiological affect which conditions our entire experience of the world and the way in which we think and feel (de Kort and Veitch 2014). Light is therefore of primary importance in shaping our experience of performance. Stephen Di Benedetto has outlined the way in which light impacts upon the human body in the act of engaging with theatre (Di Benedetto 2010) whilst Martin Welton has explored the phenomenological impact of light in relation to darkness for the audience experience (Welton 2012). Emerging scholars are beginning to articulate the issues inherent in analyzing light (for example, Graham 2016) and attempting to establish new frameworks to analyze how light both impacts and makes meaning on the audience.

A key reason for the relative paucity of material that analyses the scenographic contribution that light has made to past performances can also in part be attributed to the lack of physical evidence. Documents such as eye-witness accounts, press reviews, engravings and artists' black and white impressions need to be treated with caution – especially since they tend to focus upon spectacular theatrical moments that are recorded because they provided exceptional experiences. These accounts are best regarded as impressions rather than accurate documentation of the event. Even more recent contemporary photographs of performances have tended to be monochrome and primarily focused on shots of actors for publicity purposes rather than providing a fuller sense of what the whole stage might look like under lighting. A single image can of course never hope to provide us with a sense of the overall lighting design – we cannot understand the contribution of light without being able to experience it in time and space – in fact its temporal qualities may even be the aspect of light that has the most profound influence on an audience (Aronson 2005: 35). Even filmed recordings of performances are unhelpful, as they are usually re-lit for the camera, which can't tolerate the same range of contrast as the human eye, and these documents can never provide the same experience of light as that experienced by the live audience in the space of the performance.

It is therefore important to acknowledge the difficulties inherent in attempting to represent in writing ideas concerned with the use of light – especially for performances that have not been witnessed at first hand – and we need to be as cautious of historical graphic illustrations and photographs as of written sources in providing definitive evidence of how lighting in the theatre may have appeared at a particular moment in performance.

Technologies of light

The history of lighting in the theatre can be traced through key technological developments that each resulted in brighter light sources and the possibility of new artistic effects. The mechanisms of lighting technology before the era of electricity have been documented in some detail (for example, Fuchs 1929; Rees 1978; Penzel 1978), while associated issues are evident in volumes focusing on the consequent impact on staging practices and scenographic affect (for example, Bergman 1977; Baugh 2013; Palmer 2013).

Although the development of technologies of light, from the wax candle to the oil lamp, from gas-light to electric light, were each significant in their own way, they do not represent distinct historical periods or separate practices. Candles and oil lamps, for example, were used in tandem from antiquity and each also underwent specific technological advancements that provided whiter and brighter illumination. These included refinement in the making and sources of wax, technologies of the braided and self-trimming wicks, and the evolution of the Argand burner, for example, which significantly increased the amount of light from the oil lamp.[5] Key developments in the last two hundred years center on the advent of gas lighting, introduced to the stage in 1816 (and still in use a century later) and electric lighting that began to be installed in theatres from 1881 onwards. Histories of the theatre tend to ignore the fact that new lighting technologies were rarely used in isolation but often overlapped in their use on the stage.[6] Drawings from early-twentieth-century Broadway theatres, for example, show both the gas "table" and the new electrical switchboard that were operated side-by-side and in tandem. What is more important to note in the history of stage lighting is that each new source of light, together with further equipment refinements (for example, developments in lenses, lamps, color media, dimmer and control technologies), offered new creative possibilities as a consequence of an ever-expanding palette through a greater choice and control over the four key aspects of light: brightness, color, direction/shape, and movement (in space and through time).

In the twentieth century, the development of electric light and the technologies associated with electronics and the micro-processor significantly extended the potential of light to make a key contribution to the drama. As a consequence, the specialist role of the theatre lighting designer emerged mid-century in order to coordinate the new complexities involved in lighting that had become too time-consuming for the director, producer, or stage manager (who had previously usually taken responsibility for coordinating the lighting). For the first time it was possible to resolve historic issues related to levels of illumination of the stage and, once liberated from the problems associated with achieving sufficient visibility, stage lighting practices were able to become more ambitious and to begin to realize Appia's vision of active light. The new job title and artistic credit both recognized the importance of light to the experience of modern theatre and also suggested the potential for new ways of thinking about the role of light and darkness in the theatre.

Diffused light: achieving visibility

Appia's thinking about light was in response to what he termed "*lumière diffuse*" – the general lighting of stage space that was prevalent in order to ensure visibility. This diffused illumination added little to the drama beyond the ability to see the faces of the actors and the painted settings from the auditorium. How this should be achieved had its own technical problems that were at the heart of key debates about the role of light in drama since the Renaissance.[7]

Once theatrical performances moved into indoor spaces in the early-modern era, light immediately became a key consideration. The potential to use light as a creative force in the presentation of drama, however, created a tension between the illuminated audience space and that of the stage. Limitations in lighting technology (candles and oil lamps) dictated the overall levels of light and, until the advent of electric light, significantly restricted which areas of the stage could actually be used by performers.

Renaissance architect/designers such as Peruzzi, Serlio, Di Somi, and Ingegneri, who were responsible for creating performances in the Italian court theatres, attempted to solve two fundamental issues: how should the auditorium be lit to view the illuminated stage and how might light be used as a creative material in dramatic presentations? They produced a series of treatises that discussed the problematics inherent in theatrical production and advocated principles of dramatic illumination, such as the lowering of house lights and the dimming of stage lighting to accentuate the impact of tragic scenes. This mix of practical guidance and aesthetic concerns in relation to the sixteenth-century stage established the key principles and the origins of theatre lighting practice. Nonetheless, the darkened auditorium coupled with a brightly lit stage became a typical feature of theatre experience only from the late nineteenth century.

Until this point the upstage scenic stage remained dimly lit and actors were restricted largely to performing downstage center where the footlights ensured that their faces could be seen. The illuminated auditorium with its chandeliers and candle sconces assisted in the general levels of illumination but, because the house and stage shared the same light, the potential for a distinctly different use of light on stage was reduced. The diffused general light of the eighteenth- and nineteenth-century playhouse therefore provided a conundrum that revealed a philosophical question about the role and purpose of the theatre. Should it be, as its derivation "*theatron*" suggested, a place to "see," or a social space where it was as important to be seen as to attend to the action on stage? The scenographic potential of light was therefore largely restricted by the need to retain the illuminated auditorium, and by lighting technologies that, certainly until the advent of gas, struggled to illuminate the whole stage space adequately.

Appia termed this general diffused illumination of the stage as "passive" light (*éclairage passif* or *Helligkeit*). In the late-nineteenth-century theatre this was created by gas footlights, battens, and border lights that were fixed in position around the periphery of the stage space. With the advent of electric light the even illumination of the stage was often the fundamental underlying rationale and starting point for the design of light. This was exemplified in key lighting manuals and textbooks from the methods of Stanley McCandless (1932) to Frederick Bentham (1950) and Richard Pilbrow (1970; 1997). The emphasis on an evenly-lit stage without shadows often relegated light to a supporting role in the performance that should remain unobtrusive. Although these approaches offered ways of achieving technically competent illumination of the stage, they also revealed an inherently conservative view and ambition for light in theatrical performance. This is exemplified in Richard Pilbrow's assertion that "it is clearly the lighting designer's duty never to try to achieve an attractive visual picture at the expense of visibility" (1997: 8). Despite citing Appia's view that "shade and shadow are of equal importance" (ibid.), Pilbrow's philosophy, emerging from McCandless, reveals a pre-occupation of twentieth-century practitioners to prioritize visibility (Appia's *éclairage passif*) over a more active role for light.

Bertolt Brecht, in contrast, employed bright diffused lighting as a deliberate strategy to assist his own epic form of dialectical theatre. His poem *The Lighting* (*Die Beleuchtung*), written in 1948, represents the epitome of the modernist attitude towards light on the twentieth-century stage that, through the employment of the technology of electricity and the associated developments of lamp, dimmer, and control technologies, allowed for the first time the ability to illuminate the whole area of the stage and in an even, controlled fashion.

> Give us some light on the stage, electrician . . .
> we need the audience's
> Wakeful-, even watchfulness. Let them
> Do their dreaming in the light.
>
> *(Brecht 1987: 426)*

The modernist urge to make everything visible was exemplified on Brecht's stage for a clear aesthetic and social purpose – that the audience must not be allowed to hide in the darkened auditorium, and the bright lighting encouraged a critical distancing or *verfremdung*. Brecht's poetics of a non-realist light was an essential component of a radical new dramaturgy that aimed to provoke a debate rather than immerse the audience within the world of the drama.

To avoid any sense of illusion Brecht also advocated that the lighting equipment itself should be visible to the audience and not concealed behind masking as was customary in what he termed "the old-fashioned theatre" (Brecht in Willett 1964: 141). Light in Brecht's theatre was not "pretending to be another light" but instead was intended to provide a kind of diffused light like that found in sports stadia – a bright light of even illumination in which the sources of the light themselves were integral to the scenography. Although it was based on a diffused all-embracing light, it cannot be considered "passive" in the way that Appia critiqued the prevailing illumination of the nineteenth-century stage. Brecht's advocacy of a non-naturalistic role of light together with the acceptance that lighting fixtures could be mounted in full view of the audience – even in theatre buildings that had been constructed before the advent of electricity and didn't easily accommodate lighting positions downstage of the proscenium – opened up new aesthetic possibilities and creative potential. This radical new lighting aesthetic liberated designers from the need to subsume the lighting to other elements of the production, and the new approach to the role and function of light in performance was to have a profound impact on subsequent lighting practice in Western theatre, promulgated in large part through the international tours of Brecht's Berliner Ensemble.

In many ways this dissemination of new lighting ideas in the mid twentieth century followed similar historic trans-national traditions; the lighting practices of the Italian Renaissance courts had gradually spread to France, England and areas north of the Alps by acting troupes in the seventeenth and eighteenth centuries; and in the nineteenth century the gas and arc-lighting innovations of the Meiningen Ensemble were widely admired and adopted by others as the company toured across Europe.

Active light

Lumière actif (or *Gestaltendes Licht*) was the second type of light that Appia identified. In contrast to the passive general light, it offered the potential to transform the stage space with individual beams of light. Appia's concept of "active light" envisaged light as an expressive force rather than the illuminating agent of the diffused general light. Crucially, active light created shadow and emphasized the three-dimensional form of the actor and scene rather than the tendency of diffused light to flatten. Furthermore, active light could contribute to the drama as an expressive force and should be modulated like music in a "choréographie"[8] of scenographic elements: "[t]he art of staging is the art of projecting in space what the playwright could not project in Time . . . Light, just like the actor, must become active; . . . it can create shadows, make them living, and spread the harmony of their vibrations in space just as music does" (Appia [1910] 1954: 3).

Whereas diffused light tended to throw incongruous shadows (for example, from footlights) onto the painted backcloths, which immediately destroyed the theatrical illusion, active light offered the potential for a liberation of the stage space from the tyranny of the two-dimensional scenery. Light, Appia argued, is a unifying, poetic, and active agent that through its revelation of shadow could transform the stage space and become a co-player in the drama. Appia's "active light" was, therefore, in direct opposition to the notion of general diffused light; it placed light and shadow – and its movement over time – as central to the dramatic experience and the audience's immersion in the world on stage. This new vision of a "choréographie" of scenographic elements heralded a new genealogy of performance practice in which light might be modulated like music and "will in the future become an integral part of the score" (Appia [1891– 1892] 1983: 109–110, my translation).

Appia had first-hand experience of the lighting techniques of the Meiningen Ensemble and the work of lighting engineer Hugo Bähr in Dresden in the late 1880s and this experience was seminal in the evolution of a new lighting aesthetic that was to revolutionize thinking about the way light and shadow might be used scenographically (see Palmer 2015).

Light, darkness, and spectacle

The principles of "active light" can be seen to underpin all contemporary lighting for performance where the importance of shadow to the visual image has been recognized and the McCandless method of illumination has at last become less relevant.

Spectacular lighting moments on stage often rely upon the contrast between light and darkness and the ability to perceive the materiality of light. This occurs, for example, when light hits a surface or individual beams of light are defined as they interact with haze in the stage space. Appia had already recognized the importance of adding steam – "*vapeur*" – to the stage space and noted the impact that this had on the definition of light. The bright shafts of light that so impressed observers of the nineteenth-century stage, for example,[9] were perceived as they cut through the dust in the air of the theatre, while Svoboda's famous "cylinder of light" – the central image for his *Tristan and Isolde* – failed to materialize when the production toured in 1967 because of the absence of dust and smoke in the clean air of the Wiesbaden theatre (Svoboda 1993: 58–60).[10] This particular scenario led to the development of a haze machine – an engineering solution designed to allow Svoboda's creative vision to be realized. The impact of this device can be seen in countless rock concerts, television music spectaculars, and stage shows where the air above the stage space becomes a three-dimensional canvas for the play of continually moving light beams that become prominent because of the haze. Devices such as smoke machines and hazers have therefore transformed our perception of light on (and above) the stage. Light in these instances is no longer simply regarded as an illuminant but an active, tangible material that has agency and can, at times, be allowed to be foregrounded.

The development of the automated, remote moving light fixtures – so-called "intelligent lights" that first emerged in the 1980s but are now ubiquitous – have also revolutionized the way in which light might be controlled and modulated. Appia advocated moving lights but not in the same way as we currently understand the term. In reacting to theatre practices where light sources were fixed, Appia recognized the need to rig lanterns for specific creative effect – what we might term a "special" in today's theatre. Appia's concept of "active light" has frequently been interpreted as "mobile" or "moving light," and the term has been widely misunderstood and misused in both academic and stage lighting textbooks.[11] The type of automated lanterns that can be controlled remotely could only have been a distant dream for Appia, but their impact on contemporary performance, with their high-temperature beams that stand out above other stage lighting and through dynamic color and movement of beams across the space of both the stage and auditorium, and often in haze, can certainly be seen as generating light that is truly "active" in all senses of the word.

Appia recognized that the positioning of light sources provided control over the direction and that volume, color, and intensity also needed to be considered in order to achieve a fluid plasticity in which light could be modulated like music. Automated ("intelligent") lights provide the logical extension of Appia's vision, each providing a remotely controllable source of active light. When these lights are used in combination, for example at a rock concert, we perceive these instruments and their beams, visible in haze in the air above the stage space and in their robotic movements, moving in time with the music creating spectacular choreographies of light and space.

The modern black box theatre, without its separation of audience and stage areas, has become a ubiquitous, homogenized trope that has its detractors,[12] but its dark, abstract space demands a lighting contribution. Audiences enter under carefully controlled lighting conditions that at once establish it as a space that is distinct from the world outside – the light sources experienced here are rarely of the ubiquitous fluorescent tube, but of tungsten, xenon arc lamps, and increasingly LED lamps that provide a quality of illumination that demark the space. The audience witness the performance as it emerges from the darkness of the blackout, and stage space is conjured from the void through light. Czech scenographer Josef Svoboda remarks: "Darkness is my raw material. Just as the sculptor needs his clay, the carver his wood, I carve my theatre out of darkness" (Svoboda 2011). This is a useful metaphor for thinking about the contemporary role of the lighting designer, whose work is brought forth and literally emerges out of the dark void of the theatre space.

The control of darkness that is central to the creative contribution of light in the theatre is also fundamental to the realization of the projected image. The evolution of the modern darkened auditorium can be attributed to the aesthetic concerns of the naturalist theatre of illusion but its advent was also hastened by the arrival of cinema and the need for dark spaces in which to experience the projected light of the film.

Projection

Appia identified "*La projection*" as a distinct third type in his taxonomy of light that should also be thought of as "active":

> Projection . . . is without doubt one of the most powerful scenic devices; as a union between lighting and setting it dematerializes everything it touches. It is helpful as it offers the potential for all kind of effects.
>
> *([1891–1892] 1983: 113; my translation)*

Projection offers the potential to render representations of volume onto a flat surface through the medium of light. Although all light emitted from a theatre lantern can be thought of as "projected," the term as used in the theatre is usually associated with light that is controlled and focused through a lens onto a surface such as a screen or scenic items such as gauze (scrim) or the stage floor. Projected light has a long history that dates back at least to experiments described by Athanasius Kircher in *Ars Magna Lucis et Umbrae* (1646). These magic lanterns created simple projected images such as a clock face or hand using rectangular glass slides that could use either sunlight or candles as a source and a convex lens to focus them onto a projection surface such as a wall. There is a long history of projected shadows, magic lanterns, phantasmagoria, and projected lighting effects realized in darkened spaces that often provided popular spectacular entertainments such as those by Étienne-Gaspard Robert (1763–1837) long before the advent of the cinema (see Jones 2011). Importantly, these spaces needed to control ambient light levels in order to prioritize the visual effect, a convention that the theatre later widely adopted.

In witnessing the power of projected light from magic lanterns – and related specialist lighting equipment powered by intense carbon-arc sources – Appia recognized the artistic potential of projection but also its potential flaw. Appia's advocacy for active light was in response to the prevalent tendency to use two-dimensional painted scenery and he saw light as a way of liberating the stage space in the service of the actor. While the strength of the light source in magic lanterns enabled painted and photo-realistic images to be projected into the stage space, Appia was concerned that this ran the risk of simply replicating the aesthetic issues inherent in the images created through pigment on canvas. "A realistic image will always be ridiculous," he observed, "because of the spectators' literal-mindedness . . . no matter what projection is shown" (Appia 1892 in Palmer 2013: 83).

In his essay "Can theater and media speak the same language?" Aronson observes that in the contemporary theatre "the use of projections and moving images is disconcerting, even confusing to spectators; and it rarely functions as its users intend" (Aronson 2005: 86). This statement responds to a genre of theatrical practice where projection is frequently used primarily as a substitute for scenery – either as an economic short-cut or for spectacular technological effect such as the digital projections created for the first staging of the musical *The Woman in White* (2004). This use of projection as a two-dimensional backdrop is fundamentally incompatible in the theatre as it fails to address the aesthetic issues with paint and canvas that Appia identified over a hundred years earlier. The "instability" of the two-dimensional, projected image (Aronson 2005: 93) creates an unintentional dislocation of stage space with associated issues of volume, scale, proportion, perspective, and – if the image is moving – fundamental questions relating to temporality. However, as Steve Dixon established in his comprehensive volume *Digital Performance* (Dixon 2007), the potential disjunction between the two-dimensional actor and the projected image has developed through the twentieth century into a form of "intermedia performance" with a host of new creative possibilities.

One important example of this can be seen in Josef Svoboda's hybrid theatre space of the Laterna Magika in Prague,[13] which was established specifically to experiment with the potential of live theatre and the projected image. In the comedy *The Magical Circus*, for example, first presented in 1977, live actors appear on stage and through a playful interaction with the projected film, comic moments ensue as a direct result of a combination of the live and the recorded image. In this example the audience are delighted rather than confused by the deliberate interplay between projected light and the three-dimensional settings and performers. Svoboda had experimented with the potential of theatre and film, the live and the recorded image, as a central concern of his contributions to the Czech pavilions at several World's Fairs and he used this experience to develop work on the stages of theatres and opera houses of central Europe. Rather than using projection as a scenic backdrop, Svoboda typically presented a montage of abstract and expressionist images simultaneously on multiple screens and surfaces – using projection as an extension of the possibilities of the stage – as an active scenographic tool. The use of projection contributed significantly to his vision of the stage as a "psycho-plastic space" (Burian 1971: 126) – a fluid and malleable environment that can offer a "polyphonic spectacle" of contrapuntal elements and that enables key ideas of the drama to be expressed through shifting textures of light and the intangible forces of time, space, and movement.

There has been a long tradition of the use of the screen on stage, from the incorporation of film and projected image in Piscator's theatre to contemporary post-dramatic performance by companies such as The Wooster Group, Station House Opera, and the Builder's Association. The screen has become a productive medium for exploration and offers the potential for multiple narratives to emerge. Whereas early cinema borrowed consciously from the theatre, recently there has been a coalescence of art forms and the theatre has re-appropriated the projected image for its own ends.

Robert Lepage, a director of film as well as the stage, has worked with his own experimental laboratory Ex Machina to develop multi-media and mixed-reality performances that often have projection at their heart. In *Elsinore* (1996), his one-man version of *Hamlet*, projection offered a solution to how the culminating duel between the protagonists might be presented. The dynamic finale was relayed to the audience on a screen through live projection from cameras located at the end of each sword. In *The Andersen Project* (2006) Lepage used the screen both as a backdrop to the live action – and memorably also as a separate stage area that he was also able to step into, thus becoming part of the projected image, reminiscent of Svoboda's playful experiments at Laterna Magika.

The projection of feature films has also been incorporated as a centerpiece of so-called immersive theatre experiences in which the audience are invited to enter a theatricalized rendition of the world of the Hollywood film. Secret Cinema, a company specializing in live cinema events, has offered the opportunity to become a part of the futuristic worlds of *Star Wars* and *Back to the Future* or to enter other recreated spaces such as a correctional facility as part of experiencing the world of *The Shawshank Redemption*. Each performance involves a blurring of the real and the mediatized. In the latter example audience members were instructed in advance what they should wear and where they should attend. On arrival they were made to change out of their clothes into prison uniforms before being transported into a simulated world of the film. During the performance familiar moments derived directly from the film's narrative are experienced and later, as part of the communal viewing of the entire projected film, they are invited as prisoners to share a can of beer in synchronization with the characters on screen.

Projection and the digital

The live manipulation of projected image with the assistance of digital technologies has also offered new potential for interplay between the human performer and projected light. This is evident in the work of director Katie Mitchell where, for example, in *Waves* (2006), performers worked as creative technicians to produce a sequence of beautiful filmic images that were projected onto a screen above the stage action in real time. These carefully crafted moments created with bodies, light, and a selective use of props, costume, and sound were captured live through the roaming video camera. The whole process both deconstructed and witnessed by the audience to provide a "psycho-plastic" space through which new insight into the internal torments of Woolf's characters emerged.

Contemporary dance has often been at the forefront in the use of projection as scenographic tool, although this has often been at the expense of the performers who, rather like the actors on the historic perspective stage, have been limited as to how they might use the stage space. Merce Cunningham's *Biped* (2001) and DV8's *To Be Straight with You* (2007–2008), for example, both emerged from research in computer animation and projection and offered spectacular, engaging visual imagery, but in final presentation before a live audience required the dancers to work in strict synchronization with the pre-determined, pre-recorded projected images to achieve the creation of a simulation of live inter-action.[14]

The blurring of theatrical world and the projected image has been a rich source of artistic endeavor that has increased significantly with the development of the computer and digital projection technologies (see Dixon 2007). The computer has liberated the scenographic potential of the projected image beyond the simple re-presentation of filmed material. The digitally-created image and the potential to transmit this wirelessly in real time has opened up a host of new scenographic possibilities from the telematic environments of Paul Sermon to interactive spaces for urban street games (see below).

Dorita Hannah argues that scenographic screen space has become an essential part of contemporary performance practice and that its importance extends well beyond a scenic theatrical backdrop. In projecting images onto structures beyond the theatre building projection offers

> a spatial, social and politicized element for practicing artists, designers and performance-makers to critique and engage with the pervasive geo-cultural, geo-mythical and geo-political issues of our time. No longer the planar surface upon which light, still and moving images are 'thrown,' the screen has become an extension of the body and lived space as well as a contemporary site for reiterating and/or challenging world views.
>
> *(Hannah in McKinney and Palmer 2017: 40)*

Projection design intervenes beyond the theatre space to make us reconsider our world. Hannah reveals how it has been used to challenge the political status quo such as with the live footage projected onto the West Bank wall that momentarily transformed the barrier through making it appear to be transparent and bringing divided communities together (ibid.). Projection can also be used to transform our experience of city space through morphing digital spectacles projection-mapped onto buildings. It has also facilitated theatrical interventions into the urban environment in order to disrupt established political narratives and to make us re-think both world events and our place in relation to them. Famously Krzysztof Wodiczko's guerilla intervention through the projection of a swastika symbol onto the South African Embassy made a brief but lasting impression:

> My projections are a series of individual acts, however complex they are in terms of engaging institutions and groups, of gaining access to the city. But this does not mean that on occasion even a single act cannot be remembered for years. In London, a year and a half after I did the South African Embassy projection, it was listed in a popular magazine as one of the most important events of 1985. I was encouraged to learn that even a short-lived (in this case two hours) individual act, if exercised against a strategic urban site at a precise moment, can carve itself into the memory of the city.
>
> *(Wodiczko 1990: 273)*

On a more prosaic level the impact of large-scale projection has been taken up in commercial advertising stunts that have, often illegally, appropriated buildings such as the Houses of Parliament as a projection surface. Projection using the surface of the ground as a screen has also offered a new urban scenography through a disruption of everyday space. Frieder Weiss and Emily Fernandez's beguiling *Schlamp* (2003), for example, surprised Dresden residents with an interactive virtual body that responded as you walked past. KMA's large-scale interactive abstract kinetic light installations such as *Dancing in the Streets* (2005) and *Congregation* (2010) offered interactive experiences in public squares for communal engagement through a playful immersion in projected light (Palmer and Popat 2007). Interactive projection has also offered new artistic possibilities on the stage. Weiss' work with Australian dance company Chunky Move on performances such as *Glow* (2006) and companies such as Troika Ranch, have explored the new potential of real-time interactive light when harnessed to new software and digital algorithms.

Projection mapping (spatial augmented reality) has also more recently allowed the simulation of three-dimensional images that can be made to shift our perception of space. This technique, when used to animate familiar buildings within our city spaces, has become a familiar trope of contemporary light festivals. In simulating a plasticity of space, projection mapping seems to offer new potential for scenographic environments in the theatre that are only just being explored. However, when this technology is harnessed within controlled environments our entire perception of the world is challenged through the manipulation of light. The convergence of technologies such as that of the lamp and the projector and research projects (for example, MIT's Luminous Room [1999]), have facilitated exploration into how dynamic projection can affect a pervasive transformation of architectural space where every surface is capable of both illumination and interaction.

We are therefore in an era where the projection screen is an inherent part of our experience of the world. We no longer need to enter a darkened auditorium to experience the delight of the projected image. Beyond the theatre space we encounter projected light through television broadcasts of talent shows, at the rock concert, the sporting event and on the macro-scale of the city-space. We have come some way from Appia's third type of light, which has truly escaped the world of the theatrical backdrop. In tandem with the power of the computer we are entering a new era of the projected image realized both in public space but also on a more intimate scale on micro-screens. The creation of new worlds through virtual reality and their projection via the VR headset offers new scenographic potential that places the participant at the heart of the experience. This collision between the world of the stage and that of the world of computer-gaming offers a future *Gesamtkunstwerk* – a total experience in which individual spectators become immersed entirely within a world of projected light.

Notes

1 See Palmer 2015 for a fuller account of this period and its significance.
2 This account is from *Ellen Terry's Memoirs*, London: Victor Gollancz, (cited in Craig, Edward A. 1968: 54).
3 See Morgan 2005 and Palmer 2013 for details on the way this role emerged.
4 There is evidence to suggest that gas was first introduced to theatres at least as early as 1816 (see Penzel 1978: 36; Palmer 2013: 175) and was only gradually superseded by electric stage lighting from 1881 onwards.

5 Baugh suggests that the circular wick of the Argand burner "more than trebled the output of light" whilst "the glass chimney steadied the flame" and "further intensified the light" (2013: 248n). Bergman recounts an experiment that suggests the Argand lamp was twelve times brighter than a good quality candle (1977: 199).
6 Oil and candles were still used on the stage well into the nineteenth century. Gaslight introduced to the stage in the UK in 1816 was still in use in the twentieth century. Electric lighting introduced in 1881 was still not in widespread use until the second decade of the twentieth century.
7 See Bergman 1977; Palmer 2013.
8 Appia uses this archaic term, not at the time attributed or used in connection with dance, to express the need for a coordination of light as an integral part of the scenography. See Palmer 2015.
9 For example, see accounts of Kean's "The Vision of Queen Katherine" in *Henry VIII* (1855) in Finkel 1996: 34; and Rees' accounts of lighting, 1978: 72–5.
10 Also reproduced in Palmer 2013: 113–4.
11 For further discussion of the widespread misunderstanding of Appia's notion of "moving light" and its prosaic origins, see Palmer 2015.
12 See Hannah 2011: 54–63; Wiles 2003.
13 Currently known as the New Stage at the Czech National Theatre it still presents work combining projection and live action.
14 For further thinking about the relationship between the live performer, the projected image and the operator of the technology, see Popat and Palmer 2008.

References

Abulafia, Yaron 2015. *The Art of Light on Stage*. Abingdon, Oxon: Routledge.

Appia, Adolphe [1891–1892] 1983. "Notes de mise en scène für Den Ring des Nibelungen." In *Œuvres Complètes, Vol. 1, 1880–1894*. Socièté Suisse du théâtre. Lausanne: L'Age d'Homme, 109–117.

Appia, Adolphe [1910] 1954. "Acteur, espace, lumière, peinture" ["Actor, Space, Light, Painting"]. *Journal de Genève*, 23 (4) January. Available online at: www.letempsarchives.ch/page/JDG_1954_01_23/2 (accessed 12 December 2016).

Aronson, Arnold 2005. *Looking into the Abyss: Essays on Scenography*. Ann Arbor: University of Michigan Press.

Baugh, Christopher 2005. *Theatre, Performance and Technology: The Development of Scenography in the Twentieth Century*. Basingstoke: Palgrave Macmillan.

Baugh, Christopher 2013. *Theatre, Performance and Technology: The Development and Transformation of Scenography* (2nd ed.). Basingstoke: Palgrave Macmillan.

Bentham, Frederick 1950. *Stage Lighting*. London: Sir Isaac Pitman & Son.

Bergman, Gösta, M. 1977. *Lighting in the Theatre*. Stockholm/Totowa, NJ: Almqvist & Wiksell International/Rowman & Littlefield.

Brecht, Bertolt 1987. *Poems 1913–1956* (2nd Rev. ed.), Willett, J. and Manheim, R. (Eds). London and New York: Methuen.

Burian, Jarka 1971. *The Scenography of Josef Svoboda*. Middletown, CT: Wesleyan University Press.

Collins, Jane and Andrew Nisbet (Eds) 2010. *Theatre and Performance Design: A Reader in Scenography*. London: Routledge.

Craig, Edward Gordon 1913. *Towards a New Theatre*. London and Toronto: J. M. Dent & Sons.

Craig, Edward A. 1968. *Gordon Craig: The Story of His Life*. London: Victor Gollancz.

Crisafulli, Fabrizio 2013. *Active Light: Issues of Light in Contemporary Theatre*. Dublin: Artdigiland.

de Kort, Yvonne A. W. and Jennifer A .Veitch 2014. "Introduction: From Blind Spot into the Spotlight," Introduction to the special issue "Light, Lighting, and Human Behaviour." *Journal of Environmental Psychology* 39 (September): 1–4.

Di Benedetto, Stephen 2010. *The Provocation of the Senses in Contemporary Theatre*. London: Routledge.

Dixon, Steve 2007. *Digital Performance: A History of New Media in Theater, Dance, Performance Art, and Installation*. Cambridge, MA: MIT Press.

Finkel, Alicia 1996. *Romantic Stages: Set and Costume Design in Victorian England*. Jefferson, NC, and London: McFarland & Company.
Fuchs, Theodore 1929. *Stage Lighting*. New York: Benjamin Blom.
Graham, Katherine 2016. "Active Roles of Light in Performance Design." *Theatre and Performance Design* 2 (1–2): 73–81.
Handke, Peter 2002. "Offending the Audience," translated by Michael Roloff. In *Contemporary German Plays II*, edited by Margaret-Herzfeld Sander. New York: Continuum.
Hannah, Dorita 2011. "Event-space: performance space and spatial performativity." In *Performance Perspectives: A Critical Introduction*, edited by J. Pitches and S. Popat, 54–63. Basingstoke: Palgrave Macmillan.
Howard, Pamela 2002. *What Is Scenography?* London: Routledge.
Jones, David J. 2011. *Gothic Machine: Textualities, Pre-Cinematic Media and Film in Popular Visual Culture 1670–1910*. Cardiff: University of Wales Press.
Kircher, Athanasius 1646. *Ars Magna Lucis et Umbrae* [The Great Art of Light and Shadow] Hermanni Scheus, Rome. Available online at: http://echo.mpiwg-berlin.mpg.de/MPIWG:9WZNM3XV (accessed 12 December 2016).
Lotker, Sodja and Richard Gough 2013. On Scenography edition of *Performance Research* 18 (3).
McCandless, Stanley 1932. *A Method of Lighting the Stage*. New York: Theatre Arts Books.
McKinney, Joslin and Scott Palmer 2017. *Scenography Expanded: An Introduction to Contemporary Performance Design*. London: Bloomsbury Methuen.
Merleau-Ponty, Maurice 1964. *The Primacy of Perception: And Other Essays on Phenomenological Psychology, the Philosophy of Art, History and Politics*, edited by James M. Edie. Evanston, IL: Northwestern University Press.
Moran, Nick 2017. *The Right Light: Interviews with Contemporary Lighting Designers*. London: Palgrave Macmillan.
Morgan, Nigel 2005. *Stage Lighting Design in Britain: The Emergence of the Lighting Designer 1881–1950*. Great Shelford, Cambridge: Entertainment Technology Press.
Palmer, Scott 2013. *Light: Readings in Theatre Practice*. Basingstoke: Palgrave Macmillan.
Palmer, Scott 2015. "A 'Choréographie' of Light and Space: Adolphe Appia and the First Scenographic Turn." *Theatre and Performance Design* 1 (1–2): 31–47, doi: 10.1080/23322551.2015.1024975.
Palmer Scott and Sita Popat 2007. "Dancing in the Streets: The Sensuous Manifold as a Concept for Designing Experience." *International Journal of Performance Art and Digital Media* 2 (3): 297–314. Available online at: 10.1386/padm.2.3.297_1.
Pavis, Patrice 2013. *Contemporary Mise en Scène: Staging Theatre Today*. London: Routledge
Penzel, Frederick I. 1978. *Theatre Lighting Before Electricity*. Middletown, CT: Wesleyan University Press.
Pilbrow, Richard 1970. *Stage Lighting*. London: Cassell and Co.
Pilbrow, Richard 1997. *Stage Lighting Design: The Art, The Craft, The Life*. London: Nick Hern.
Popat, Sita and Scott Palmer 2008. "Embodied Interfaces: Dancing with Digital Sprites." *Digital Creativity* 19(2): 125–37, doi:10.1080/14626260802037478.
Rees, Terence 1978. *Theatre Lighting in the Age of Gas*. London: The Society of Theatre Research.
Svoboda, Josef 1993. *The Secret of Theatrical Space: The Memoirs of Josef Svoboda*, edited and translated by J. M. Burian. New York, Tonbridge: Applause Theatre Books.
Svoboda, Josef 2011. In *Theatre Svoboda (Divadlo Svoboda)* [Film]. Directed by Jakub Hejna Endorfilm, Czech Republic.
Welton, Martin 2012. *Feeling Theatre*. Basingstoke: Palgrave Macmillan.
Wiles, David 2003. *A Short History of Performance Space*. Cambridge: Cambridge University Press.
Willett, John (Ed. and Trans.) 1964. *Brecht on Theatre: The Development of an Aesthetic*. London: Eyre Methuen.
Wodiczko, Krzysztof 1990. "Projections." *Perspecta* 26: 273–87. Available online at: www.jstor.org/stable/1567168 (accessed 12 December 2016).

5
SOUND (DESIGN)

David Roesner

Attention to sound

The notion of sound design in theatre includes sound effects, ambiences, music, and amplification and is used both for the *process* of crafting sonic events – and thus directing and manipulating an audience's attention – and for the *finished design*. The design as a *result* consists of a mixture of material and immaterial settings (such as speaker positions, microphone choices, mixing board settings, sound files, MIDI cues or live music) and consequently in the unfolding of the designed sonic events over the course of a theatre performance.

Unfortunately, sound design tends to be overheard and overlooked. It has long been considered a subsidiary craft, mainly designed to serve a higher purpose, be it the creation of convincing illusions of site, situation or action, be it as a kind of atmospheric "glutamate," enhancing and reinforcing the audience's senses for a protagonist's character traits or the general mood. If we take theatre reviews and critical acclaim through awards as an indication, sound design in theatre is indeed quite marginalized, seldom mentioned, and rarely validated through proper recognition.

At the same time, sound design and, as part of this, original musical composition for theatrical performances, flourish in theatres from London to Paris, from Berlin to New York. The UK Association for Sound Designers, for example, lists more than 230 sound designers[1] and the German annual theatre directory for 2015 lists more than 350 theatre musicians/theatre composers[2] for the major 13 theatres alone (out of 715 theatres in total). Intricate sound design has developed into a ubiquitous phenomenon in theatre productions, and sound cues or live music have become more significant both in quantity and quality. In many cases, sound has shifted from being treated as an afterthought and merely an illustrative "final touch" to becoming a major conceptual and dramaturgical tool, both in developing new work or re-interpreting texts from the dramatic canon. As Peter Sellars puts it: "[w]e are beyond the era of sound 'effects'. Sound is no longer an effect, an extra, a garni supplied from time to time to mask a scene change or ease a transition" (cit. in Kaye and LeBrecht 2009: loc. 70).

What has led to this renewed proliferation and significance of designing the auditory events of a theatrical production? For Western theatre traditions, which are my main focus, I would credit four predominant (but not exclusive) contributing factors:

1. The avant-garde in theatre showed great interest in all things sonic both by embracing noise, loudness and the material textures of sounds from voices to machines, and by rejecting what Michel Chion calls "semantic listening" (1994: 25) – paying attention mostly to the signals and discourses conveyed by sounds or language. Artaud's skepticism of putting the "logos" above all other elements of theatre and his interest in sound as pure vibration may serve as an example for this rejection.[3]
2. The advent of film and the quick development of more and more refined techniques of accompanying film with music and sound effects initiated an iterative relationship with theatre sound, on the one hand borrowing from established aesthetics of nineteenth-century melodrama while, on the other, acting as an impulse and challenge to theatrical practice. It is quite telling that the advent of the sound film around 1927 coincides with Jack Foley's development of what we now know as "Foley effects": sounds created in the studio to match the film image but often generated by imaginatively different means.
3. The invention and development of electronic sound recording, playback and amplification from the 1890s[4] and its – surprisingly slow – integration into theatres from the 1950s,[5] which allowed for the creation and inclusion of all manner of sound and music, not just what could be created live in the theatre.
4. The introduction of digital audio from the early 1970s and subsequently the development of affordable and mobile digital audio synthesizers, samplers, interfaces and playback devices. In particular the advent of the sampler and of MIDI (Musical Instrument Digital Interface) meant that sound could not only be stored and played back, but manipulated along a wide range of parameters in real time and with intuitive ease, and that audio triggers and events could be interconnected with instruments, cameras, light sensors, etc. This not only caused a quantum leap in terms of versatility and tempo of production for the sound designer but has also had a significant impact on the economics of sound design and the compositional flexibility of the actual design: rather than being a series of fixed recordings, which is played against a live performance, played-back sound can now retain a greater degree of "liveness," keeping cues open to real-time manipulation, be it by a sound operator or by the performers on stage themselves.[6]

These developments have also led to a re-emergence of sound on the horizon of academic thinking on theatre; Jonathan Sterne even speaks of a "boom in writings on sound" (Sterne 2012: 1). When looking at these publications (listed in the references), it is striking how much the themes and proposition differ from what we read in some of the seminal manuals and handbooks for the sound design practitioner. I'd like to explore some of these discursive threads, which have emerged from contrasting contributions to the aesthetics of sound and sound design.

Looking at sound design manuals first, it becomes evident how intimately techniques, aesthetics and understandings of the role of sound (design) are linked to theatrical modes of performance. These handbooks are predominantly based on a model of production in which theatre is based on a playtext, which in turn is interpreted by a director in the context of a hierarchically organized institution with an economic *raison d'être.*

The theatrical paradigm here is a naturalistic one – anecdotally this may be evidenced by the fact that the sound effect of a dog barking (something I have not heard being used in a theatre for at least two decades!) is cited more than 25 times in Kaye and LeBrecht 2009. It is as if the world of sound design had never heard of postdramatic theatre, devised theatre, live art, performance art, applied theatre, *Regietheater*, etc., in all of which those fundamental assumptions about "the theatre" have continuously been called into question. As soon as the framework shifts – due to theatre makers embracing new modes of production, new paradigms of representation, new relationships to text and so forth as we have seen it over the last 20–30 years – many of the certainties of what constitutes good practice in sound design are up for renegotiation. The potential of sound to contribute to or actively create theatrical illusion, to take a prominent example, and to thus aid an audience's suspension of disbelief, has seen a bifurcated development: in some theatre forms efforts towards immersivity have redoubled, leading to spatio-sonic concepts that envelop the audience and suspend the separation of stage and auditorium. The fact that we perceive sound at a 360° angle around us, in what P. Sven Arvidson calls a "sphere of attention" (2006), compared with our more limited visual field, contributes significantly to this – such as in the complex fictional worlds of theatre company Punch Drunk,[7] which the audience explores freely, cocooned by a permeating sound-track.

In other forms of theatre, designers consciously turn their backs on any attempt to create a sense of illusion: here, the fabrication of all theatrical elements is made explicit and transparent and the creation of sound and music often deliberately displayed and highlighted self-referentially, sometimes even ironically, such as in theatre company Filter's[8] playful takes on Shakespeare. In their *Midsummer Night's Dream* (2012) in which the wood of Athens, for example, is invoked exclusively by chirping a *guiro* in front of a microphone, a sound that is then visibly looped, multiplied and spread across different speakers to place us in the wood. We enjoy watching the creation of an imaginary forestial soundscape with croaking frogs and chirping insects and the tongue-in-cheek theatrical performance that goes with it.

The academic discourse is characterized by different preoccupations: here the dominant question is less about how sound design enables, modifies and inflects our semiotic and emotional understanding of the theatrical narrative, but concentrates more on the kind of experience sound provides in the specific medial circumstance of *live* performance. "Meaning," in this context, is not limited to decoding sonic signs by which we navigate a plot or judge a character, but often emerges from specific ways of perceiving and attending a theatrical performance. Sound contributes particularly strongly to the phenomenological process of exposing oneself to the specific and unique circumstances of seeing and hearing, which performances provide and shape. It is therefore no coincidence that academic writing on sound (design), draws less on the acoustic and psychoacoustic properties of theatre sound, and more on philosophical and cultural aspects, which have been developed in neighboring disciplines as part of a proclaimed "sonic turn" (Drobnick 2004: 10) or "acoustic turn" (Meyer 2008). On the one hand, this concentration on sound is often part and parcel of an interrogation of the still dominant visual culture or ocularcentrism in Western societies, but, on the other, also acknowledges the intricate and inseparable relationship between our senses of hearing and seeing and investigates how intimately both influence and configure each other.[9]

For the sake of clarity, this is a somewhat simplified categorization, creating a binary between a naturalist aesthetic, which attributes a certain semiotic and dramaturgical functionality to sound design (I will come back to these functions later, as they are obviously still relevant in many theatre performances to this day) and emphasizes its role in producing "meaning" for the spectator,[10] and a performative aesthetic, within which phenomenological, somatic, or cognitive aspects are foregrounded to explore how theatre sound affects our experience. In reality, things are not as clear-cut and both aspects constantly intermingle, creating a complex oscillation between different listening modes, different kinds of engagement and degrees of distraction.[11]

Taxonomies of listening, as they have been suggested numerous times (see, for example, Barthes 1985, Chion 1994 or Truax 1999), are similarly helpful to distinguish and map out *normative* forms of reception with an *ideal* recipient in mind, but are hardly useful as defining labels for the plethora of modes of attention actually at play in live performance.[12] Here, auditory attention is, as Katharina Rost puts it, "plural, diverse, differentiated, incoherent and paradoxical" (2017: 382).

A particularly interesting and salient point is the phenomenon of "silence," which can be a very deliberate part of the *designed* sound rather than its mere absence.[13] As John Cage has famously discussed and demonstrated,[14] there is no absolute silence. Indeed, as Salomé Voegelin puts it, "when there is nothing to hear, so much starts to sound" (2010: 83). Furthermore, silence is a phenomenon that is experienced particularly subjectively, affects listeners in very different ways and is prone to being "filled" individually by a wide range of internal echoes of previous sounds and foreshadowings of anticipated sounds to come. Silence thus pinpoints two general challenges both for any attempt of a general aesthetics of sound and for any specific decision of a sound designer. First, the difficulty to generalize how sound affects listeners, since "no two people will hear a sound in exactly the same way" (Leonard 2001: loc. 375). What we actually hear in the theatre is highly contingent on our physiological and psychological abilities and attunements as well as our fluctuating attention.[15] Second, that sound is not a thing, but a process with many variables, which are difficult to account for completely.

This more nuanced sense of sound design corresponds with the complex developments in the actual design practice, which has seen a range of rapid changes that I will outline as a widening purview and a shift in function.

A widening purview

Historically, the notion of sound design (before it would have been called by this name)[16] focused on sound effects – predominantly thunder and gunshots, it would seem, if we look at Collison's *The Sound of Theatre: A History* (2008). Now it also covers the above-mentioned areas of soundscapes, music and amplification. The development of music in the twentieth century has further contributed to the fact that "sound/noise" and "music" are no longer clearly separate aesthetic categories (see Kahn 1999; Ross 2007; and again Cage 1961). As a consequence, they also do not necessarily fall into different practitioners' responsibilities.[17] Furthermore, the human voice as an important aural element of the theatrical event has increasingly become part of the purview of sound design: microphones, both visible and hidden, are frequently used in theatrical productions and subject the human voice not only to amplification but also to being "designed," i.e. modified in its characteristic, distorted, pitched up or down, or placed in virtual acoustic spaces. Finally, the acoustic sphere in general and the acoustic characteristic of the theatrical space, which used to depend largely on the architecture and material design of the theatre building or site, have also become "designable" through the possibilities afforded by modern sound systems to create and emulate infinite acoustic properties and sonic atmospheres. A vast array of artificial environmental sounds – concrete or abstract, subtle or overwhelming – can thus be created or reproduced, immersing the audience in an aural sphere of the sound designer's choice.

There are, however, limits to the reach of sound design as an intentional, purposeful artistic and technical endeavor. To begin with, sound design starts with theatre architecture and/or outdoor venue (see Smith 1999; Tkaczyk 2014) and anything a subsequent designer does within a given space is already framed by a specific constellation of acoustic properties and listening situations. Sound design is thus determined by place as much as it can create or evoke place. Furthermore it is not only the place that has an impact on sound design, but also the space as a "practiced place" in its realization and use (following de Certeau's distinction of space and place [1984: 117]). There is consequently an intrinsic "noisiness" of theatre: no theatre venue, from the amphitheatre to the contemporary proscenium arch or black box building, is sound proof and the sound sphere in each case will consist of a mixture of designed sounds and those leaking into the venue from outside or from within, such as audience gasps, laughter, rustlings or mobile phones as well as the noises of clanging set design structures, ticking lights, or creaking floorboards. "Sound in the theatre . . . can never be fully contained, controlled, or conceived, and is always (and necessarily) susceptible to material, as well as perceptual, manipulation and alteration" (Home-Cook 2015: 167). The "sonic" in theatre is thus always a combination of designed sounds, composed or adapted music and other, un-designed, audible events. Separating these "noisy" aspects out and declaring them irrelevant for the sonic experience of the audience would be as problematic as if we were to try to separate out and disregard "private" features of an actor, such as jug ears or a lisp, from their "intentional" and crafted acting appearance.

Despite these caveats, sound in theatre is still often devised with certain dramaturgical strategies in mind, many of which also work predictably well, especially in the realm of theatrical realism. Here, sound design can often rely on certain intersubjectively shared reactions and interpretations of the sonic within a given cultural context. In Western Europe, for example, playing a few bars of Mendelssohn's "Wedding March" from his incidental music to Shakespeare's *Midsummer Night's Dream* (composed in 1842) will signal the idea of a wedding to most adult Western audiences, and the sound of crickets will in all likelihood conjure up an evening in a place with a warm climate.

From sound effect to sound affect

A sound design for a narrative/psychological production will potentially have certain effects on the audience, which can be categorized in the following way, bearing in mind that in reality these categories will blur and overlap.[18]

- Meta-function: here, sound design functions more in relation to the theatre event as such than to the performance and/or narrative. Sonic signatures, or even sonic "branding," may aid in attracting certain segments of the audience, masking transitions, shifting our attention, attunement and listening, or heightening the feel-good factor during applause and exit of the audience, etc.
- Narrative function: sound design can (help to) establish time, location, situation, character and narrative mode (flashbacks, dream sequences, monologues) and thus play a significant part in giving the audience information and orientation in a story or performative situation.

- Dramaturgical function: sound design will have a significant influence in supporting and/or creating the structure of a theatrical event: shaping hard or soft transitions, highlighting climaxes or turning points, establishing a sense of pace or energy. In (post)-Brechtian theatre dramaturgies, sound and music may also work as a device of defamiliarization (*Verfremdung*).
- Mood/atmosphere: sound design contributes particularly strongly to our sense of mood and atmosphere. This may happen both consciously and subconsciously, and by either tapping into our collective knowledge about sonic markers for certain moods and atmospheres, or somatically by causing us comfort or distress. Certain bass frequencies, for example, have been known to cause nausea and vomiting in audiences (Kaye and LeBrecht 2009: loc. 558). In other words, the sonic works on our brains *and* our guts and our responses to it are influenced both by nature and nurture.
- Perception: sound design can shape and guide our attention and can prompt different modes of listening, different ways of appreciation to the audience.

Having said all this, I would still argue that on a level of meaning-production and sense-making sound is often more elusive and obscure than, for example, language or set design[19] and tends to *modify* perception and meaning in conjunction with texts, bodies, gesture, images, etc. rather than *creating* it by itself from scratch.

Its potential is also clearly not exhausted by the above framework of functions. If we thus move from the question of sound as *effect* – both in the sense of a sound cue, which provides a very concrete and often illustrative sonic piece of information such as a door bell, a roll of thunder or a dog bark, and in the sense of the functional narrative effect attributed to this cue – to the noteworthy capacity of sounds to *affect* the audience, I would suggest that on this phenomenological level sound affects us physically, emotionally and subconsciously more than other expressive elements of the theatre.[20]

From function to friction

The above model of functionality is further rendered problematic, if not obsolete, particularly in forms of theatre that abandon psychological characters, stringent plot lines and Aristotelian rules of dramaturgy. Here, sound design may, for example, emphasize the performativity of the given situation, heighten the sense of rhythm and/or musicality as a key aesthetic quality, contribute to a strong sense of intertextuality by creating a web of musical citations, organize or counterpoint a choreography of bodies, images, objects or words, or raise what Hans-Thies Lehmann called the "politics of perception" (2006: 184): i.e. rendering problematic and thus pointing us to our habits and tacit hierarchies of hearing and seeing.

In causing friction between the audible and the visual and by rejecting the often redundant relationship between the sonic and other elements of the theatre, which the handbooks still strongly suggest (if a character mentions an airplane passing over, we need to hear that very airplane),[21] postdramatic sound design can often no longer be reduced to serving a specific *purpose* in relation to a performance, but becomes an aesthetic category in its own right.

As such, sound design has gained significantly in terms of its importance and creative versatility in recent developments of theatrical aesthetics, namely the emergence of what has been called director's theatre (or "Regietheater") since the 1970s and in the development of forms of postdramatic or devised theatre. In both cases, sound design often plays a crucial part in the development process from the very beginning in relation to the production's conceptual and performative layout and dramaturgy. Moving from a tradition of providing illustrative sound effects and relatively interchangeable overtures and entr'acte compositions to the tailored, layered and integral designs of today has been an astonishing process for sound design.

At the risk of stating the obvious, we should point out that while it is highly commendable to devote a space for a chapter on sound as a discreet design category in a volume on scenography, one should be aware that we cannot talk about the aesthetics, impact or meaning of the sonic in theatre if we don't consider it *in relation to* the other elements of the theatre.

Recent theatre forms have often interrogated the idea of sound and music as distinct elements in theatrical performance: their entanglement with aspects of site, set design, performers' movements and voices, technologies of amplification, props, etc. suggest thinking of sound design as a rather pervasive and intermedial phenomenon, not merely a technical activity controlled from the sound booth – which, ironically, is probably the least suited place in the auditorium to experience the sounds and sights of a theatrical performance.

This physical separation, which still exists in many theatres, is, however, symptomatic for a lingering impression, which Peter Sellars addresses when he claims: "It is time for artists working in sound . . . not to be second-class citizens in the theatre, not to be afterthoughts, not to be utilitarian drudges, but to assume that place of inspiration and centrality that their medium demands" (cit. in Kaye and LeBrecht 2009: loc. 81). He wrote this in 1992 – and there is still some way to go in the theatres, the institutions of theatre training, the drama courses and in theatre criticism to give sound design the consideration it deserves.

Notes

1 See www.associationofsounddesigners.com/directory/ (accessed 16 October 2015). By comparison, the Society of British Stage Designers lists approx. 300 designers (see www.theatredesign.org.uk/designers/full-list-of-designers/ [accessed 16 October 2015]).
2 In German theatre it has become an exception to have dedicated sound designers for theatre productions: music and sound are usually both created by a theatre musician, who is part of the creative team of the production, and subsequently operated by a specialist member of the technical team (i.e. sound engineer) employed permanently by the theatre.
3 See Curtin 2014 and Ovadija 2013 for a more detailed discussion.
4 See Collison's informative history of sound in the theatre for more detail (2008).
5 Jean-Marc Larrue describes this in his chapter on the "mediatic resistance" of theatre in the case of sound amplification (2011).
6 Jörg U. Lensing's chapter on the work of his company Theater der Klänge (Theatre of sounds) is a good example for this (2012).
7 See http://punchdrunk.com/ (accessed 1 February 2016).
8 See www.filtertheatre.com/page/home/ (accessed 1 February 2016).
9 The famous McGurk effect is demonstrated in a limited and controlled cognitive experiment, which highlights with regard to certain phonemes how what we see influences what we hear (and vice versa). See, for example, www.youtube.com/watch?v=G-lN8vWm3m0 (accessed 20 October 2015).
10 Madeleine-Marie Mervant-Roux (in Kendrick and Roesner 2011, 189–97) and others discuss the telling nomenclature for audience members and actors/characters, which either highlight the visual (spectator [Eng.], *spectateur* [Fr.], *Zuschauer and Schauspieler* [Ger.], *spettaore* [Ital.]) or aural (audience [Eng.], *auditeur* [Fr.]) persona (from Lat. *personare*) aspects of perception.

11 Ross Brown refers to sound design as the "scenography of engagement and distraction" (2010a).
12 See, for example, Rost who critiques the underlying normative ideals of listening, which are fundamental for the handbooks: *concentrated listening* (for example in speech perception), *structural listening* (for example in music reception) and *listening-to-signals* (for example in noticing significant sounds and noises) (2017: 117; 199; 293). These notions privilege forms of listening based on an awake and investigative focus with an aim of understanding over the many ways in which our auditory attention is distracted, drifting, unconscious and unfocused.
13 Home-Cook discusses this in more detail in his chapter "Sounding Silence" (2015: 99–130).
14 See Cage's seminal work *4'33* (1952) and his collection of essays/lectures *Silence* (1961).
15 George Home-Cook investigates this process in more detail to find out "what 'happens' when we pay attention to sound in the theatre" (Home-Cook 2015: 2). He suggests that to "be *in* sound is not to be straightforwardly, spherically and passively 'immersed', but rather consists of an ongoing, dynamic and *intersensorial* bodily engagement with the affordances of a given *environment*" (Home-Cook 2015: 3, original emphasis).
16 Kaye and LeBrecht claim that Dan Dugan was the first to be credited as "sound designer" in 1968 for his work at the American Conservatory Theatre in San Francisco.
17 To my knowledge, this differs across various theatre cultures, genres and institutions: in German theatres there are hardly ever designated "sound designers" for (straight) theatre productions – this is usually part of the theatre musician's job in collaboration with the in-house sound engineer. In the US and UK, however, sound design is more commonly listed as a distinct creative task from that of the show's composer. Some of the seminal handbooks of sound design, however, list music as part of the sound designer's tasks (see, for example, Kaye and LeBrecht 2009).
18 The following owes great debt to the discourse on film-music, see in particular Bullerjahn 2001.
19 Ross Brown puts it like this: "Sound design rarely 'says' anything unequivocal, in the way that a set and costume design might within one consistent, visual concept" (2010a: 131).
20 Cf. in the realm of film the seminal study of Claudia Gorbman, *Unheard Melodies: Narrative Film Music* (1987).
21 In contrast, see, for example, Heiner Goebbels' aesthetic philosophy, which is expressed in the preface of his book on the "aesthetics of absence": "When you mention a tree, you don't also have to show it" (2015: xxiii).

References

Arvidson, P. Sven 2006. *The Sphere of Attention: Context and Margin*. Dordrecht: Springer Press.

Augoyard, Jean-François 2005. *Sonic Experience: A Guide to Everyday Sounds*. Montreal: McGill Queens University Press.

Barker, Paul 2002. "Music and Composition." In *Devised and Collaborative Theatre: A Practical Guide*, edited by Tina Bicât and Chris Baldwin, 75–87. Ramsbury, Marlborough: Crowood Press.

Barthes, Roland 1985. "Listening." In *The Responsibility of Forms: Essays on Music, Art, Representation*, trans. by Richard Howard, 245–66. Los Angeles: University of California Press.

Bracewell, John L. 1993. *Sound Design in the Theatre*. Englewood Cliffs, NJ: Prentice Hall.

Brown, Ross 2010a. "Sound Design: The Scenography of Engagement and Distraction." In *Theatre and Performance Design: A Reader in Scenography*, edited by Jane Collins and Andrew Nisbet, 342–7. London: Routledge.

Brown, Ross 2010b. *Sound: A Reader in Theatre Practice*. Basingtoke: Palgrave.

Bullerjahn, Claudia 2001. *Grundlagen der Wirkung von Filmmusik*. Augsburg: Wißner.

Cage, John 1961. *Silence*. Middletown, CT: Wesleyan University Press.

Certeau, Michel de 1984. *The Practice of Everyday Life*. Berkeley: University of California Press.

Chion, Michel 1994. *Audio-Vision: Sounds on Screen*. New York: Columbia University Press.

Collison, David 2008. *The Sound of Theatre: A History*. Eastbourne: Plasa.

Crook, Tim 2012. *The Sound Handbook*. Abingdon, Oxon: Routledge.

Curtin, Adrian 2010. "Cruel Vibrations: Sounding Out Antonin Artaud's Production of Les Cenci." *Theatre Research International* 35: 250–62.

Curtin, Adrian 2014. *Avant-Garde Theatre Sound: Staging Sonic Modernity*. New York: Palgrave.
Drobnick, Jim (Ed.) 2004. *Aural Cultures*. Toronto: YYZ Books.
Finelli, Patrick 1989. *Sound for the Stage: A Technical Handbook*. New York: Drama Book Publishers.
Goebbels, Heiner 2015. *Aesthetics of Absence*. London & New York: Routledge.
Gorbman, Claudia 1987. *Unheard Melodies: Narrative Film Music*. London: BFI Publishing.
Home-Cook, George 2015. *Theatre and Aural Attention*. Basingstoke: Palgrave.
Kahn, Douglas 1999. *Noise Water Meat: A History of Sound in the Arts*. Cambridge, MA: The MIT Press.
Kaye, Deena and James LeBrecht 2009. *Sound and Music for the Theatre: The Art and Technique of Design* (3rd ed., Kindle). Oxford: Focal Press.
Kendrick, Lynne and David Roesner 2011. *Theatre Noise: The Sound of Performance*. Newcastle upon Tyne: Cambridge Scholars Publishing.
Larruc, Jean-Marc 2011. "Sound Reproduction Techniques in Theatre: A Case of Mediatic Resistance." In *Theatre Noise: The Sound of Performance*, edited by Lynne Kendrick and David Roesner, 14–22. Newcastle upon Tyne: Cambridge Scholars Publishing.
Lehmann, Hans-Thies 2006. *Postdramatic Theatre*. London & New York: Routledge.
Lensing, Jörg U. 2012. "From Interdisciplinary Improvisation to Integrative Composition: Working Processes at the Theater der Klänge." In *Composed Theatre: Aesthetics, Practices & Processes*, edited by Matthias Rebstock and David Roesner, 155–68. Bristol: Intellect.
Leonard, John A. 2001. *Theatre Sound*, (Kindle ed. 2011). New York & London: Routledge.
Meyer, Petra Maria 2008. *Acoustic Turn*. Tübingen: Fink.
Ovadija, Mladen 2013. *Dramaturgy of Sound in the Avant-Garde and Postdramatic Theatre*. Montreal: McGill Queens University Press.
Roesner, David 2010. "Musicking as *Mise en scene*." *Studies in Musical Theatre, Special Issue: Music on Stage* 4: 89–102.
Roesner, David 2014. "Theaterrauschen – Spielarten der performativen Hervorbringung von Geräusch." In *Sound und Performance: Positionen, Methoden, Analysen*, edited by Wolf-Dieter Ernst, *et al.* Würzburg: Königshausen & Neumann.
Roesner, David 2015. "No more 'unheard melodies' – Zwölf Thesen zur Schauspielmusik im zeitgenössischen Theater." *etum – E-Journal for Theatre and Media* 3/2. Available online at: http://ejournal.theaterforschung.de/index.php?journal=ausgabe1&page=article&op=view&path[]=42 (accessed 29 January 2016).
Ross, Alex 2007. *The Rest is Noise: Listening to the Twentieth Century*. New York: Farrar, Straus and Giroux.
Rost, Katharina 2017. *Sounds that Matter. Dynamiken des Hörens in Theater und Performance*. Bielefeld: transcript.
Schafer, R. Murray 1994. *The Soundscape: Our Sonic Environment and the Tuning of the World*. Rochester, VT: Destiny Books.
Schulze, Holger 2008. *Sound Studies: Traditionen – Methoden – Desiderate. Eine Einführung*. Bielefeld: transcript.
Smith, Bruce R. 1999. *The Acoustic World of Early Modern England: Attending the O-factor*. Chicago, IL: University of Chicago Press.
Sterne, Jonathan 2012. *The Sound Studies Reader*. New York: Routledge.
Tkaczyk, Viktoria 2014. "Listening in Circles: Spoken Drama and the Architects of Sound, 1750–1830." *Annals of Science* 71/3, 299–334.
Truax, Barry 1999. *Handbook for Acoustic Ecology*. Burnaby, BC, Canada: A.R.C. Publications.
Voegelin, Salomé 2010. *Listening to Noise and Silence: Towards a Philosophy of Sound Art*. New York & London: Continuum.
Walne, Graham 1990. *Sound for the Theatre*. London & New York: Black.

6

SCENOGRAPHY AND THE SENSES

Engaging the tactile, olfactory, and gustatory senses

Stephen Di Benedetto

A scenography of the senses consists of the conception of a design and the elements and principles used to create the material environment for performance, and also an audience's response to that material performance environment. It is a sensual engagement experienced through a body's response to and within the theatrical event. This chapter explores how the senses, particularly those other than sight and sound, fit into the theatrical event and audience experience. The audience's engagement with the designed experience begins with a theory of embodied cognition describing that an onlooker's apprehension is situated; a perceiver uses the tools of observation deployed in everyday existence as a frame to understand the communitarian accessibility of the performative experience. Theories of embodied cognition describe the ways that we scan the environment for situational clues about how and to what we ought to respond. Even when decoupled from the environment, the activity of the mind is grounded in mechanisms that evolved for interaction with the environment – that is, mechanisms of sensory processing and motor control. We look for moving lights, bright colors and actions to see how we ought to negotiate the environment and look for clues of how to engage within it. It is in this mode of engagement that audiences explore what the theatrical event offers.

This active sensory-rich exploration of the environment is contrasted with the fallacy of the passive audience in a theatre. Jacques Rancière explains, "The spectator must be removed from the position of observer calmly examining the spectacle offered to her" (Rancière 2009: 4). Instead the onlooker trades this rational illusionary control for sensory rich embodiment. This openness to the experience of the world in which we are situated, regardless of whether it is crafted or natural, is seen as the ideal viewing state, where we make use of our sensory faculties to understand the constructed world around us. From our perspective the mechanics of encouraging involvement with the event through design is what is important – the elements entice onlookers to become immersed within the theatrical event using his or her senses to navigate the constructed experiences. In this conception of an event we start not only with the analysis of what it is but with the analysis of what it is perceived to be.

What is a scenography of the senses?

Being a spectator is not some passive condition that we should transform into activity. It is our normal situation. According to the neuroscientist Michael Anderson, embodied cognition treats cognition as a set of tools evolved by organisms for coping with their environments. Evolutionary history believes cognition evolved because it was adaptive – that is, it enhanced survival and reproductive success primarily by *allowing more effective coping* with the environment. Anderson argues, "Cognition evolved in specific environments, and its solutions to survival challenges can be expected to *take advantage of the concrete structure or enduring features of those environments*" (Anderson 2007: 65). An onlooker's cognitive activity takes place in the context of a constructed performance environment, purpose-built for the challenges of the action. Understanding how cognitive activity functions under the pressures of real-time interaction with the environment helps us understand the ways in which our audiences engage with the designed environments of performance.

In the conception of the production design a scenography of the senses foregrounds potential stimuli to actively engage taste, touch, hearing, smell, and sight. Much the same way that line, shape, color and movement are used to create textures, moods, emotions and other emotional aesthetic responses, the principles and tools of design are used to create tastes, smells, vibrations and sights to stimulate the audience's natural sensory responses to the world as they might in everyday interactions. In other words, there are a range of communication channels open to exploit for the purpose of engaging audiences in the experience of the theatrical event and, by understanding some of the basic physiological and neurological principles underpinning our responses to these type of stimuli, a scenographer has a means to create a more nuanced audience response to the event's material world. It is irrelevant whether we accept a theatrical environment as fact or fiction because our immediate sensory experience cannot distinguish the difference. It is only through subsequent cognitive processes where we analyze and parse out the meaning or significance of what occurred that we make a conscious assessment of the stakes of what was experienced.

Taste, smell, and sight encountered in the theatre make us feel something because they work the same way as any other situation we encounter. The sounds of the actors moving through their space, sound effects, and doors shutting all create a mood and energy in the space. A theatrical event uses a stimulus to capture our attention and then distracts us with another to create a new sensation to entice us to follow along. Once immersed within a design the audience's focus becomes limited and the event captures our attention, leading it moment to moment. We keep following the stimuli down the different paths hoping to make sense of the action and piece together what the whole experience means as an event.

Tactile communication

Touch as a component in the theatrical event is incorporated in two dominant modalities: haptic stimulation and visual stimulation. As the philosopher Yi-Fu Tuan explains,

> Most tactile sensations reach us indirectly, through the eyes. Our physical environment feels ineluctably tactile even when we touch only a small part of it. Reddish fluffy surfaces are warm, light-blue glittering ones cool . . . seeing and the tactile sensation are so closely wed that even when we are looking at a painting it is not clear that we are attending solely to its visual qualities.
>
> *(Tuan 2005: 77)*

It is this approach that is most commonly thought of in traditional theatre-making, where the audience is expected to understand, say, the gray blocks of color on the stage of the opening of *Hamlet* as cold stone, or the *tromp-l'œil* painted surface as a cobbled street in a Victorian melodrama. It is through attending to these indicators that we perceive the feel of the environment and the physical conditions of the action. We also read physical interaction between actors as tactile, interpreting different types of body contact in relation to our own experiences. From a cognitive perspective our minds access the stimuli through a mirror neuron response and access memory to determine and manifest the tactile stimulation as meaningful. Haptic stimulation, however, is a far more direct communicator. As we move through the world we are able to access the size and textures around us based on our experience of differing materials, volumes and conditions. An echo in a cavernous empty stone cathedral sounds and feels different from that of an echo in a cozy cottage. The blend of aural and tactile informs us of the conditions of the space.

Popular entertainments use haptic elements in their most basic application; a 4D theme park amusement will spray you with water to simulate passing through a cloud or a rainstorm, a circus will sell you cotton candy to consume, or an arcade will have you hold a joystick simulating a pilot's yoke to steer. The act of feeling the cold water, holding the food and masticating, or grasping the yoke are access points to fill in environmental details to engage attention. More nuanced touch interactions used in live art have included interactions between the performer and audience; a performer grasping the hands of the audience as they move them to a position within a space, a performer dancing with or on the lap of a character, objects left within a performance space for audience members to pick up to explore, or objects used in a magic act handed over to convince others that a card or a box is without secret compartments. Each of these tactics is integrated for a particular function used to actuate sensory experience.

Other common forms of touch are related to the temperature of the space – if the temperature changes by two degrees our bodies note the change. While watching the Disney theme park 4D movie *Mickey's PhilharMagic* you feel a sudden drop in temperature and you may perceive the wind on your skin as you gain altitude on Aladdin's carpet in a more immediate manner since you cannot feel the carpet flying. Vibrations from sounds that can be heard can also be felt. If a sound vibrates the seat you sit in or vibrates the floor you are able to perceive size or proximity. Societas Raffaello Sanzio's *Thumbkin* (1995) simulates the presence of a giant by the trembling of the earth that the audience could feel as he walked closer to Thumbkin's house. The intensity of the vibrations provided sensory clues establishing his size and weight. The type and style of the seats the audience sit in can also signify. If we join This Is Not A Theatre Company's production of *A Serious Banquet* (2014) the texture of the seat and the act of drawing a dinner plate inform you about the experience you are having, and you are able to imagine you are attending the party that Pablo Picasso threw for the painter Henri Rousseau in 1908 as recorded by Gertrude Stein. The close proximity of the performers' interactions helps actuate our embodied reception and interpretation of the event.

Olfaction and gustation

The chemical senses are often considered as integrally related, though recent concepts of the perceptions of the senses demonstrate that the five senses all influence what each sense experience is. Both olfaction and gustation are tied to the body's processing of chemicals that come in contact with the sense receptors. The stimulation of tastes and smells in the theatre is often a byproduct of other production choices. However, both sensory pathways have rich potential for affecting an audience's physical and emotional response to the environment's stimulation. Contemporary marketing agencies have been experimenting with chemical ads to entice buyers to purchase their products. For example, there were widespread press reports in 2006 of cookie odors piped into San Francisco bus shelters next to the print advertisements "Got Milk" by the Milk Processor Board to influence desire for the product. Theatrical producers have tried to incorporate food and smell into performance to try and influence emotional responses to a performance. At the more radical end food becomes the theatrical event and smell activates the chemical receptors in the mouth. The sensations of taste and smell work together to produce feelings from those perceiving the stimuli. Whether tasting popcorn and cotton candy at the circus or tasting a butterbeer at the Three Broomsticks restaurant at the Wizarding World of Harry Potter theme park, the theatrical event has worked as a sensory-rich supplement to the action performed on stage.

Smell has been used as a means to stimulate associative responses from audiences such as with David Cromer's production of *Our Town* (2009), where the smell of bacon wafts into the audience a few minutes before a curtain opens at the rear revealing Myrtle Web cooking sizzling and crackling bacon the morning of Emily's twelfth birthday. The audience's immersion within the setting of play and the contemporary costuming of the characters blurs the line between actor and audience and the audience is primed to experience the action as if they are a part of it. The smells of the cooking food permeating the house create naturalistic objectivity to their response to the action. As smell is intimately tied to our early memories the smells of cooking breakfast and our own memories of childhood accentuate the potency of the image. More recently in Universal Orlando's Halloween Horror Nights *Walking Dead: Dead Inside* (2012) visitors worked their way through a maze of locations depicting the journey the character Rick Grimes took during the television show's first season. Designers meticulously endeavored to immerse attendees in the macabre post-apocalyptic setting, from the sound of buzzing flies to the smell of corpses. To create the odors of the rotting flesh the design team used a technique similar to that of a perfumer, selecting notes of scents to take the nose through an olfactory journey. They sampled a kit of individual notes to create the scent that they wanted, choosing, for example, whether to add garbage notes to evoke rotting flesh. The designers wanted to impart an idea or sensation or emotion that accompanied Grimes as he explored his new world. A corpse's putrid scent accompanies the embodied responses generated by the sights, sounds and actions of the setting of the immersive adventure. We have innate aversions to putrid smells and attractions to sweet smells. Olfaction is the sense most directly related to memory recall and scents are the longest-lasting sensation stored in our memories. Therefore, any activation of the olfactory sense can evoke emotional associations for audiences, and most easily triggers our reptilian responses in the natural world.

Gustation is the most difficult stimulus to incorporate into traditional scenographic practice. Some productions may make use of the act of eating – and the implication of taste – as visual cues to evoke a visceral response from observers. An extreme example is Mark Ravenhill's *Over There* (2009) at London's Royal Court Theatre, which depicted twin brothers who had been separated by the Berlin Wall covered in a lurid goo of smeared custard, Nutella and ketchup which one brother then licked off the other's semi-clothed body. Ravenhill evokes successive meetings between the brothers over the five years spanning the buildup and then fall of the Berlin Wall. In its penultimate sequence the West German brother metaphorically and literally consumes his East German twin. Imagining the taste of the noxious mess as it is licked off triggers a shocking physical unease that mirrors the play's larger themes of the excitement and incestuous revulsion felt by the brother who is transplanted to the West after the fall of the Wall. Ingestion by the audience as an effective tactic has been limited to date in traditional dramaturgy, but is used extensively in live art or other performative theatrical landscapes. Take, for example, the Blind Cafe, a touring company that has taken so-called "Dark Dining" experiences into the theatrical. Dark dining is an eating experience where diners experience a meal in total darkness to encourage sensitivity to gustatory and olfactory stimulation. Blind Cafe is intended to make people more aware of the experience of blindness and they host events in cities around the country that include eating, lecturers, and music to create an overall experience bringing awareness to issues facing the blind. They find that the immersion in the experience where participants must rely on other senses evokes powerful reactions, "Be warned, you will be in the pitch dark and uncomfortable feelings may come up for you. We find that if you stay present, breathe and bring attention to letting go of control, any anxiety you have will let up and you may find this event to be a life changing experience" (Blind café n.d.). Similar to *A Serious Banquet*, the action of eating becomes an act of embodied theatrical perception. When designers destabilize our natural embodied processes for perceiving the world our neural networks shift the brain's attention to the novel experiences. This attention imbues the incoming stimulus with added importance as we attempt to understand the environmental context.

Foregrounding sensation

Cognitive scientists have begun to examine the ways in which the simultaneous processing of multiple sensations affects the qualities of what is being experienced. Charles Spence posits that at least half of our experience of food and drink is filtered through vision, sound, and touch and not determined solely through smell and taste. He performed a test with Pringles chips, handing subjects two hundred chips to sample while listening to modified amplified crunching noises. Even though all the chips were identical, participants rated chips as different, some fresh while others stale. What he found was "participants rated the potato chips as tasting both significantly crisper and significantly fresher when the overall sound level was increased and/or when just the high-frequency sounds were boosted" (Spence 2015). The experiment demonstrates that food can taste differently through the addition or subtraction of sound alone. A scenography of the senses has the potential to modulate experience by adding or subtracting stimuli to the experience.

The effect of a century of photographs, television, cinema, and internet viewing created a sensory dynamic that privileged seeing at the expense of other more traditional forms of sensory engagement (Howes 2014: 15). A scenography of the senses makes use of all the senses adding the sensations of touch, taste and smell to grab the attention of the audience and further their experience of the performance unfolding in front of them. The social function of live theatre necessitates contact between audience members and the performers and taste, touch, and smell can be significant triggers in our conscious perception and interpretation of the events transpiring in our proximity.

References

Anderson, Michael 2007. "How to Study the Mind." In *Brain Development in Learning Environments: Embodied and Perceptual Advancements*, edited by Flavia Santoianni and Claudia Sabatano, 65–82. Newcastle, UK: Cambridge Scholars Publishing.

Blind Cafe, "Seattle Blind café." Available online at: www.theblindcafe.com/seattle/ (accessed 5 July 2017).

Howes, David 2014. *A Cultural History of the Senses in The Modern Age, 1920–2000*. New York: Bloomsbury.

Rancière, Jacques 2009. *The Emancipated Spectator*, translated by Gregory Elliott. London: Verso.

Spence, Charles 2015. "Eating with our ears: assessing the importance of the sounds of consumption on our perception and enjoyment of multisensory flavour experiences." *Flavour* 4: 3. Available online at: https://flavourjournal.biomedcentral.com/articles/10.1186/2044-7248-4-3 (accessed 5 July 2017).

Tuan, Yi-Fu 2005. "The Pleasures of Touch." In *The Book of Touch*, edited by Constance Classen, 74–9. Oxford: Berg.

PART II

Scenographic theory and criticism

7
THEATRICAL LANGUAGES
The scenographic turn and the linguistic turn

Austin E. Quigley

Like many of the concepts we use to guide our theatre thinking and theatre practice, scenography is a term with a range of implications. The word "scene," to which it is related, sometimes designates the visual background of a situation and sometimes the whole situation. Scenography is thus sometimes used minimally, to cover only the design of the set, and sometimes maximally, to cover every functioning element of theatre structures. This variability responds to the recognition that, over the years, successful designers have included painters as well as architects, craftsmen as well as playwrights. These uncertainties about the scope of scenography register persisting uncertainty about its nature that have long been complicated by the unclear relationship between scenography and play scripts, and that complexity is grounded in centuries-old debate about the relationship between, and relative priority of, the visual and the verbal in the theatre. This relationship has become even more critical at a time when many involved in theatre and theatre studies conceive of a "scenographic turn," one that echoes the "linguistic turn" taken by many modes of inquiry in the twentieth century.[1] Should we view these as analogous or as alternative turns and might they usefully inform each other? To anyone working in the theatre, these are all related issues that might well benefit from being considered together, as we weigh the appropriate scale and scope of scenography.

The uncertain scope of scenographic responsibility and consequence has a long history that can be traced back to the origins of theatre and the earliest discussions of it. The etymology of the word "theatre" takes us back to Greek roots suggesting that theatre is primarily a place to see or view. Aristotle, by contrast, famously remarked that the "spectacle" in the theatre is the "least artistic of all the parts," has "least connection with the art of poetry," and is "more a matter for the costumier than the poet" (Aristotle 1963: 15). He was, of course, writing primarily about the performance of a particular kind of tragedy in a particular era, but his views have been, to say the least, influential. His separation of the activities of the writer from those of the designer, his subordination of the latter to the former, and his claim that "the tragic effect is possible without a public performance" are all early versions of dichotomies that have haunted theatre practice and theatre theory to this day (Aristotle 1963: 15). Their recurring and continuing impact, even as terminology has evolved, is registered in the persisting uncertainty today about the scale, scope, and consequence of scenographic activity.

Once invited to take sides in debates about the relative standing of the poet/writer versus that of the designer/director, theatre commentators, over the centuries, have been more than happy to oblige. Two of the most well-known examples map out the dimensions of the contested terrain. Samuel Johnson, in his eighteenth-century "Preface to Shakespeare," was ready to assert that "A play read affects the mind like a play acted," effectively reducing theatre performance to a neutral and optional background (Johnson 1957: 503). Antonin Artaud, on the other hand, insisted, early in the twentieth century, that theatre is distinctively grounded in its visual "*mise en scène*," and that what was, in fact, optional was a play script.

> It is simply a matter of changing the point of departure of artistic creation and of overturning the customary laws of the theatre. It is a matter of substituting for the spoken language a different language of nature, whose expressive possibilities will be equal to verbal language . . . the language of words may have to give way before a language of *signs*.
>
> *(Artaud 1958: 107, 110)*

With consequences to be considered later, Artaud was not always consistent in his arguments, but he was not inconsistent on the importance of what was at stake here: "to break through [verbal] language in order to touch life is to create or recreate the theatre" (Artaud 1958: 13).

The distant historical provenance of these contrasting assertions by Johnson and Artaud should not prevent us from considering, rather than which side to take, whether this verbal/visual dichotomy largely involves a battle over two sides of the same coin. This possibility is evident, for example, in Artaud's own oscillations between arguing that we need to banish language entirely from the theatre and arguing that we need to replace its verbal language with a different kind of language. Instead of borrowing the verbal language of the world outside, theatre should ground itself, he suggests, in a visual language generated entirely inside the theatrical domain: "this language of the *mise en scène* [is] the pure theatrical language" (Artaud 1958: 69).

Artaud's radical reformulation of the visual/verbal debate hinges less on the (modernist) conundrum of what is inside or outside the art world, than upon the notion that there might be a linguistic complementarity rather than an inside/outside competition between the verbal and visual elements of theatre, one that would have evident implications for the field of scenography. This is not just a matter of their complementarity but of a particular kind of complementarity. Much is at stake in Artaud's notion that the visual elements of theatre might be considered as a language, as he, himself, was at pains to emphasize. We have all been much constrained, he argues, in our thinking about theatre and in our theatre practices by an Occidental tradition that

> recognizes as language, assigns the faculties and powers of a language, permits to be called language (with that particular intellectual dignity generally ascribed to this word) only articulated language, grammatically articulated language, i.e., the language of speech, and of written speech.
>
> *(Artaud 1958: 117)*

The potential importance to scenography of this reformulation only escalates when Artaud goes on to consider whether the language of the "*mise en scène*" is a single language or a set of languages. But the conceptual realignment he suggests requires us to consider a series of questions about how we conceive of verbal languages, why they have acquired the status (dignity) Artaud refers to, what an equivalent visual language would be like, and how different kinds of languages, if we use several, might be assumed to relate to each other.

One of the historical voices that anticipated Artaud's position was that of Schiller. His belief in the importance of theatricality to theatre was based in some part on his conviction that the eye is much more powerful than the ear (Schiller 1902b: 340). Responding appropriately to the power of the eye provides one of the grounds for his early nineteenth-century argument in favor of a visual theatricality inspired by the imagination rather than a more limited visual realism grounded in the material world.[2] But the historical authority that might have been most sympathetic to the notion that the visual in the theatre effectively constitutes a language was Bharata. Though he did not invoke the term himself, he was more than ready to catalogue extensively the visual signs of the theatre and their related significations. Indeed, he was prepared to do this at every scale, from the smallest to the largest, including the "thirty-six looks" that can be achieved with the eyes:

> Raised brows, side glances, distended eyes, unwinking look, closed and half-closed eyelids, looking down the nose, drooping brows, contracted eye-corners, laughing look, contemptuous look, thoughtful look – these are the looks which give us the different thirty-six looks. Roving pupils . . . contracted eyelids, raised eyebrows, lowered eyebrows, contracted eyebrows and knitted eyebrows – all these change the look. In this way, the author had described a total of thirty-six looks and given a name to each of them.
>
> *(Bharata 1999: 80)*

In Bharata's theatre, the actor's and the designer's roles overlap, with the body painted "according to the region, custom and age of the character," while "snakes and the other animals, mountains, rivers, some weapons . . . are treated as living human beings for the sake of drama"(Bharata 1999: 178). As costumes, gestures, and movement are similarly incorporated into the visual design, there is little that the visual language cannot (in principle) accommodate: "[t]here is no art, no knowledge, no yoga, no action that is not found in natya" (Bharata 1999: 4).

Bharata's description of comprehensive reach, fixed rules, and stable signs might well serve to elevate the visual in the theatre to the status of a language, as Artaud later wished, but we must first consider whether this claim would rely upon a misleading picture of how verbal languages work. Signs are here reduced to signals with fixed meanings, thus overstating the stability and understating the flexibility of verbal signs that typically have a capacity to change their function.

Inhabiting Bharata's largely visual perspective is the same tension that inhabits Aristotle's largely verbal perspective. The aspiration to achieve coherence and comprehensiveness through a single and stable set of unifying categories and rules inevitably inclines the description toward the permanent and prescriptive, rather than towards the temporary and contingent, effectively precluding future change. This has historically been a recurring issue in the reception of Aristotle's work. Instead of these documents being positioned as descriptions of particular theatres in particular eras, instead of being positioned in the flow of history and change, they came to be seen as a prescriptive source of required rules, of what theatre ought to be and do. This is particularly evident in Bharata's widespread use of exhortations and admonitions. The creativity of the past is codified in these documents in such a way that it approaches the status of a template, so that the creativity of the future is as much constrained as enabled. Wherever we might seek to position scenography along the visual/verbal divide, it is not well served by pictures of theatrical or linguistic traditions conceived as unified systems with fixed sets of categories and rules. An alternative understanding of how languages and categories work is needed, and the renaissance views opposing Aristotle's began to move in an instructive direction.

Though renaissance arguments on these matters focused extensively on the unnecessarily restrictive requirements of unities of time, place, and action, the claims for variety rather than unity were increasingly directed at the restrictiveness of the very notion of unity itself. De Vega's invocation of nature's counter example serves both to echo and to appropriate the underpinnings of Aristotle's mode of thinking. Aristotle was (among many other things) a botanist, and a botanist whose mode of classifying depended on consistent parts and unified wholes. De Vega, however, is at pains to make us aware of what might be lost, as well as gained, by such tidiness: "varied mixtures lead to much delight / For this let nature our example be / Gaining much beauty in variety" (De Vega 2000: 140). The point here is not just variety across categories, but variety within categories, like those of tragedy and comedy, a variety put at risk if classification depends upon fixed components and required rules. De Vega recognizes the impending collision between such prescriptive unifying descriptions and the creativity of subsequent artists. Speaking not just of an alternative picture of nature, but also of an alternative national heritage, De Vega invokes both a different theatrical tradition and a different notion of tradition more broadly:

> Playwriting here began in such a way / That he who would artistic rules obey / Will perish without glory or resource, / For custom is more powerful a force / Than reason or coercion.
>
> *(De Vega 2000: 136–7)*

Variety entirely unregulated would, of course, serve only to dissolve all categories, so De Vega invokes instead the controlling, but presumably more flexible, power of "custom," without defining it in more detail. Custom seems potentially poised between the liberating and the constraining, but it is escape from the latter rather than clarification of the former that comes across most forcefully: "sometimes something charms the taste because / It is in fact contrary to the laws" (De Vega 2000: 145).

Though De Vega is largely making the case for comedy, he does not do so by identifying its parts and establishing its rules, but by suggesting another kind of regularity, one emerging from an interplay between custom and variety. The regulative "power" of custom is not, however, clarified further. His fear that rules, social, linguistic, and theatrical might constrain us more than liberate us is a concern that has long persisted, being shared and extended in Marinetti's repeated invocation of the same word, "variety," to celebrate the importance of another kind of theatre three hundred years later. As for many others in the modernist avant-garde, the response to tradition was still, as in the renaissance, to a tradition viewed as prescriptive and deterministic. He thus positioned a reconstituted, "futurist," version of popular variety theatre as a mode of creative destruction, a theatre not only refusing to follow rules, but bent on destroying them. So committed was he to this project that he refused to contemplate creating new traditions or conventions to replace the older ones.

> The Variety Theatre destroys all our conceptions of perspective, proportion, time, and space . . . It cooperates in the Futurist destruction of immortal masterworks . . . One must completely destroy all logic in Variety Theatre performances . . . [and] prevent a set of traditions from establishing itself in the Variety Theatre.
>
> *(Marinetti 1972: 119–20)*

Such is Marinetti's determination to be free from the constraint of inherited rules that he ends up apparently cutting the ground from under his own feet. The creative dimension of his program for creative destruction seems oddly out of balance with the scale and scope of the destruction – until he begins to contradict himself:

> Today the Variety Theatre is the crucible in which the elements of an emergent new sensibility are seething. Here you find an ironic decomposition of all the worn-out prototypes . . . and also the abstract elaboration of the new prototypes that will succeed these.
>
> *(Marinetti 1972: 117)*

The old prototypes are sometimes denounced because they are prototypes and sometimes, more narrowly, because they are old. The recurring question, once unity is replaced with variety, is what to use to replace rules in the deployment of prototypes so that they liberate and don't just constrain.

Marinetti's inconsistent arguments, first that old traditions not be replaced by new traditions, and second that old prototypes should be replaced with new ones, is an inconsistency shared with both Artaud and De Vega. Artaud sometimes argues that linguistic order be banished from the theatre and sometimes that it be replaced with another kind of linguistic order. De Vega is unclear whether variety is an alternative to inherited custom or a continuation of it. The recurring desire to enable current creativity to escape past conformity is haunted by a tendency to overstate the prescriptive unity of the past. What has so often been lost is the force of Pascal's astute observation that "those whom we call ancients were really new in all things" (Pascal 1859: 550).

Resistance to what is perceived as a past of prescriptive constraint has complicated the theatrical conceptual terrain to this day, in ways that need some adjustment if scenography is to find its way forward. The recurring desire to be "free from" a certain kind of past always leaves its mark on attempts to be "free to" do something else. What is so often being reacted to is not so much an actual cultural heritage as a misleading picture of that heritage. The attribution of comprehensive rules and consistent categories, whether in theatre history, linguistic history, or cultural history, distorts the relationship between the creativity of the past and that of the present and future. As Hillis Miller once remarked, "Periods differ from one another because there are different forms of heterogeneity, not because each period held a single coherent 'view of the world'" (Miller 1975: 31). We are, however, far from recognizing the larger implications of this shift in thinking. What makes Artaud so important is that he was caught up in the process of working his way out of the former way of thinking and into the latter. His inconsistencies are thus instructive, rather than just confusing, as we consider how best to relate the linguistic turn in Artaud's work to the scenographic turn that would follow from it.

The tension in Aristotle's work between his descriptive inclination and its prescriptive implication is well known, but its larger consequences now become clearer. The desire for tidy categorizations and comprehensive rules not only leads to a mistaken separation of theatre's verbal from its visual elements, but also to a misleading description of its verbal elements. Scenography, of course, has a stake in the correction of both, not just for how it views the various elements of theatre and their relationships, but also for how it conceives of theatre's social function and of scenography's role in it. Aristotle's commitment to a vocabulary of parts and wholes, of unity and uniformity, of distinctive rather than evolving species, leads not only to the prescriptive in the theatre but also, as Boal in particular has pointed out, to theatre's effective endorsement of the social status quo (Boal 1985: 47). It logically involves the cathartic disposal of any emotion that might be subversive, of anything that might challenge established rules and social orthodoxies, indeed, of anything that could promote social change. For Boal, this cathartic disposal of subversive responses constitutes Aristotle's best defense of the poet against Plato's assertion that there is no room for the poet in an ideal society if the poet is an agent of change. But this does little, Boal argues, to address the role of an agent of change in the non-ideal societies we all inhabit. For Boal, as for Brecht: "the world is revealed as subject to change, and the change starts in the theatre itself" (Boal 1985: 155).

A key question, however, is whether the notion of theatre that Boal attributes to Aristotle is an accurate version of Aristotle's sense of theatre history or, indeed, of theatre's actual history. When Boal, like De Vega, Marinetti, and Artaud, describes the past as a serial set of orthodoxies that preclude, rather than promote, theatrical, linguistic, and social change, is his sense of how to be "free to" do something new still much influenced by a misleading conception of what it is necessary to be "free from"? Whether theatre has supported or should support the social status quo by illustrating and reinforcing orthodox views is a matter of some debate. Indeed, as Barish has traced in exhaustive detail in *The Anti-Theatrical Prejudice*, theatre's counter-cultural inclinations have long been visible in its readiness to exemplify and incite unorthodox behavior. But what has not been so well traced is what Artaud invites us to trace, the relationship between our understanding of the history and function of theatre and our understanding of the history and function of its languages. From Artaud's struggles to generate a different picture of the nature of language there emerges a very different conception, central to the nature of scenography, of how the verbal relates to the visual in the theatre and how the past relates to the present. Key matters in this reorientation are the status of unity in any kind of language, uniformity in its rules, and consistency in its categories – issues about to become central to linguistics and philosophy of language in the twentieth century. Ironically, at a time when a "linguistic turn" was being taken by many modes of inquiry, linguistics itself was contemplating a major shift in its understanding of language.

When Wittgenstein famously asserted that the way to describe a category (like tragedy) is not to list its (supposed) common features but to note some typical examples and explain that these "*and similar things*" constitute the category, he provided a different notion of categorization that accompanied a similarly flexible notion of the nature of rules (Wittgenstein 1969: 33). Signs in this context become, as Haas has put it, evolving "souvenirs" to be adapted, not, as Bharata describes them, fixed signals to be replicated (Haas 1962: 223). To the extent that languages provide regularities to guide us, they emerge from a varied history of use, not from an ahistorical set of rules – a point confirmed by consulting any serious dictionary. Halliday usefully summarizes this alternative linguistic terrain:

> [A] linguistic system . . . is a system of variation . . . [It is] not . . . a system of invariants, the way the layman (or the philosopher of language) tends to see it, but . . . a system with a great deal of flexibility in it.
>
> *(Halliday 1978: 155)*

Fuzzy categories, flexible rules, and inherent variety provide only the beginnings of a picture of language that allows it to provide adaptable resources for the future, rather than fixed rules from the past. These are mechanisms that make past and present complementary, as the past is just a varied history of other present moments. The order of language is not that of an overall or underlying unity, but an order containing a great deal of disorder, or, to put it more helpfully, verbal language records and exhibits many kinds of not always consistent ordering principles. In Halliday's terms and those of fellow linguist J. R. Firth, language is polysystemic, not monosystemic (Firth 1957: 137).

This picture of language, by no means universally accepted but by now widely recognized, returns us to what Artaud was reaching toward in his claims about the centrality of its languages to the history and function of theatre. It is possible, in the light of this alternative picture, both to clarify the inconsistencies in Artaud's arguments and to indicate the importance of what he was guiding us toward for the status and scope of scenography. A picture of the past more continuous with the present does not just help us understand how theatre might more readily pursue change, but also raises a key question about why change, as in the modernist mantra of creative destruction, has so often been pictured as inconsistent with continuity. Rather than focusing upon how to free the creative present from the constraining past, we might seek, instead, how best to connect the history of theatrical, linguistic, and cultural change to their current and future changes. In effect, we would seek to enable the creativity of the past to inform the creativity of the present and future – a goal variously advocated and pursued by Zeami as far back as the fifteenth century (Zeami 1984: 52–3).

Artaud's shift from picturing language as unified and constraining to picturing it as various and enabling is registered in his sudden swerve from treating verbal language as the villain in the theatre to treating it as one of its fellow victims. "Theatre," he suddenly argues, "like speech, needs to be set free" (Artaud 1958: 118). Both need to be liberated from false pictures that inhibit our use of them, not least our scenographic use of them. It is not that verbal language is inherently constraining but that theatre has come to use it in constraining ways. So treated on the stage, "speech becomes ossified and . . . words, all words, are frozen and cramped in their meanings, in a restricted schematic terminology" (Artaud 1958: 117). Verbal language, it seems, is not going to constrain us unless we first constrain and debase it. The implications for other scenographic languages and for the nature of the scenographic turn are clear.

Artaud's shift of focus underpins one of his most famous inconsistencies. At one point he argues that

> if . . . a contemporary public does not understand Oedipus Rex . . . it is the fault of Oedipus Rex and not of the public . . . Sophocles speaks grandly perhaps, but in a style that is no longer timely. His language is too refined for this age, it is as if he were speaking beside the point.
>
> *(Artaud 1958: 74–5)*

This is emphatic enough and clearly exemplifies a dichotomy between past and present. But at another point, Artaud argues the opposite case, and, in doing so, uses a phrase of considerable consequence to our understanding of theatre, linguistics, culture, and the role of scenography:

> if we are clearly so incapable today of giving an idea of Aeschylus, Sophocles, Shakespeare that is worthy of them, it is probably because we have lost the sense of their theatre's physics . . . their way of speaking and moving, their whole scenic rhythm, escapes us.
>
> *(Artaud 1958: 108)*

There is no division in this conception of a theatre's physics between the verbal and the visual, between the pictorial and the kinetic, or between the past and present. Different they may be, but related, and it is the nature of that relatedness, with evident scenographic implications, that Artaud continues to pursue.

It is against this background that we can begin to grasp what Artaud is after when he takes on the centuries-old issue of how the verbal and the visual are related in the theatre. If both are to be set free, it is in interacting, as languages, with each other. Their freedoms are complementary, rather than contrasting. What provides them with the flexibility to interact is the recognition that languages are much more variously constituted than is often assumed. Extending De Vega's insistence upon the importance of variety rather than unity, Artaud, in characteristic style, takes matters even further: "where simplicity and order reign, there can be no theatre nor drama, and the true theatre, like poetry as well, though by other means, is born out of a kind of organized anarchy" (Artaud 1958: 51). The intellectual journey from unity to variety to organized anarchy is a long one historically, but not necessarily so long conceptually. Once variety is introduced, so are elements of what might earlier have been described as disorder; once change is valued, fixity becomes problematic rather than normative. The key issue is not to oppose order to disorder, but to consider how they are related. In effect, we are contemplating other kinds of order within, and other kinds of relationships among, variously ordering languages.

Instead of resting content with one of the positions he took, that of simply reversing Aristotle's view of the primacy of the verbal over the visual in the theatre, Artaud now argues that "it is not a matter of suppressing speech in the theatre but of changing its role" (Artaud 1958: 72). Intriguingly, what will change its role will be realigning verbal language with visual language so that they interact fruitfully with each other. Instead of replacing one language with another, instead of "substituting," as he had earlier recommended, verbal language with visual language, he now announces that

> I am adding another language to the spoken language, and I am trying to restore to the language of speech its old magic, its essential spell binding power, for its mysterious possibilities have been forgotten.
>
> *(Artaud 1958: 110–11)*

Artaud's version of what is to be recovered from the history of languages is idiosyncratically his own. What matters is what others would also be able to recover if the visual and verbal elements of the theatre were to be repositioned as interacting and mutually informing languages. Artaud's picture of a theatre's physics is an inclusive one and his principle of order as "organized anarchy" creates a lot of space for creativity and change, but not at the necessary expense of the creativity that has gone before or of the creativity that might succeed his. There can be no programmatic version of where this might or should lead, or of how the languages of theatre might interact – a point made even more important when Artaud begins to multiply the number of non-verbal languages in the theatre. To replace the misleading linguistic picture of homogeneous order, prescriptive rules, and autonomous languages, Artaud offers a picture of more limited order, of more flexible rules, and of complementary languages. This leads him to make a remarkable shift from viewing the predominance of verbal language as what disables theatre to arguing that what disables theatre is giving generalized priority to any one of its languages. The latter step, he suggests, not only disables the assumed secondary languages, but also the one viewed as primary.

> The theatre, which is in no thing, but makes use of everything – gestures, sounds, words, screams, light, darkness – rediscovers itself at precisely the point where the mind requires a language to express its manifestations. And the fixation of the theatre in one language – written words, music, lights, noises – betokens its imminent ruin, the choice of any one language betraying a taste for the special effects of that language; and the desiccation of the language accompanies its limitation.
>
> *(Artaud 1958: 12)*

The awkward translation of that final clause does not obscure its implication. What allows any language to "ossify" in the theatre is its inadequate interaction with other languages. Unchallenged by other modes of ordering, its own ordering principles begin to congeal into a privileged and limiting order. Furthermore, in claiming that "theatre . . . is in no thing, but makes use of everything," Artaud parts company, simultaneously, with a set of (avant-garde) orthodoxies, to which we will return, that are bound up in inherited pictures he is trying to transcend. But just as important is the recognition that theatre is not a fixed category to be described in terms of parts and wholes, and certainly not an autonomous aesthetic domain with a "pure" language of its own (Artaud 1958: 69). Rather, it is a site of interaction of all the languages we care to bring to it – a conclusion that goes right to the heart of any conception of the scenographic enterprise. Should we be concerned that Artaud's governing picture of organized anarchy might be excessively fluid, it is important to note how much of what he says falls directly in line with that other picture of language variously invoked by Wittgenstein and many others in the twentieth century.

This alternative picture of the linguistic terrain, and reaction to it, directly informs the way in which we might now picture the several languages of the scenographic terrain. A particularly pertinent set of remarks was provided by linguist Firth, who not only provides a variant on Artaud's phrase "organized anarchy," but also begins to address the key issue of how such flexibility is nevertheless "organized."

> Unity is the last concept that should be applied to language. Unity of language is the most fugitive of all unities, whether it be historical, geographical, national, or personal . . . We must not expect to find one closed system. But we may apply systematic categories to the statement of the facts.
>
> *(Firth 1957: 29, 187)*

The question, of course, is how systematic? For Firth, the notion of a "language as a whole" is highly misleading as it understates the inherited heterogeneity and familiar diversity of ever-changing languages (Firth 1957: 71). It is widely recognized that individual languages vary by region (dialect), by social group (register), and by historical era (however roughly the boundaries are drawn). Furthermore, these and other variables continually overlap and interact in ways that keep a language in a process of turbulent change, a process only accelerated by the ways in which verbal languages interact with other kinds of, also changing, languages. From this emerges the recognition, as Bakhtin has put it, that "language is never unitary . . . at any given moment of its historical existence, language is heteroglot from top to bottom" (Bakhtin 1981: 288–91). The Aristotelian picture of order with which we began, with all its unifying principles and implications, becomes, in this context, more of a hindrance to scenographic activity than a help.

Though heroic attempts have been made in linguistics to establish an underlying order to linguistic disorder, these attempts betray more of a nostalgia for the principle of unity than a readiness to deal with the need for some other ordering principles. They offer a useful cautionary tale for those in theatre studies inclined to do the same with the several languages of theatre. Though the work of Chomsky in linguistics is relevant in this regard, the more informative case is that of the widespread misuse of the work of Saussure.[3] From his attempts to locate a highly ordered underlying linguistic system and his suggestion that success here would provide the basis for a more comprehensive science of semiotics, structuralism emerged as an explanatory mode from which much was anticipated. A comprehensive survey of all of a society's semiotic systems might, it was suggested, effectively describe how a society, as a whole, organized itself. In the words of one of its key proponents, Umberto Eco, we might envisage "a possible global semiotic system (that is, a representation of a culture in its totality)" (Eco 1976: 26) and this would include:

> zoosemiotics, olfactory signs, tactile communication, codes of taste, paralinguistics, medical semiotics, kinesics and proxemics, musical codes, formalized languages, written languages, natural languages, visual communication, systems of objects, plot structure, text theory, cultural codes, aesthetic texts, mass communication, and rhetoric.
>
> *(Ibid.: 9–13)*

It is immediately clear from Eco's puzzling list that these semiotic categories are not mutually exclusive, they are not exhaustive, they are not based on any consistent principles of classification, and they do not exemplify a privileged way of distinguishing and relating semiotic systems. Indeed, rather than make the case for a single global semiotic system, they suggest the likelihood of its endless iteration. The familiar hopes in this linguistic turn toward unity, consistency, and comprehensiveness produce familiarly unfortunate results. Nevertheless, attempts have been made to view the many languages of theatre in just such terms.

Elam's version of theatre semiotics is particularly instructive, as he recognizes some of the challenges to be confronted, and those recognitions guide us toward a different scenographic view of multi-linguistic theatrical terrain.

> The present state of our knowledge regarding the internal laws of scenic, costumic, cosmetic and most other systems is too scanty and impressionistic to

> allow anything resembling formalization. This is undoubtedly one of the more interesting and important tasks awaiting theatrical semiotics, as is, still more, the investigation of the global or trans-systemic syntax of the overall theatrical system (what constraints, if any, govern the combination in a given performance text of kinesic with linguistic and scenic signs?).
>
> *(Elam 1980: 51)*

While Elam rightly acknowledges the fuzziness of some of these semiotic systems and the flexibility of their interaction, he is inclined to treat our current inability to systematize their internal laws and external relationships as a temporary state of affairs, reflecting the limitations of "the present state of our knowledge." In time, he hopes, unifying success can be envisaged. Here and there, however, he wonders whether the problems may lie deeper and be more permanent, whether "some systems . . . are more stable and better articulated than others" and whether "boundaries between systems . . . are not always . . . well marked" (Elam 1980: 51). Indeed so, but the implications of this fuzziness are considerable, as we have noted.

The semiotic approach to theatre languages is governed by expectations of future unified categories and comprehensive rules that would not be unfamiliar to Aristotle. Just as Aristotle's work slid from the descriptive to the prescriptive, so also did the structuralist approach to language and other semiotic systems. It was soon unable to defend itself against criticism that, once we had established a global semiotic system of all we did, it would become a description of all we could do. A unified and comprehensive set of rules, whatever its anticipated explanatory power, would leave no room for individual agency, personal responsibility, or human creativity, and it would be unable to explain how social change occurs. The individual is effectively dissolved into the social codes, as are all the concepts at society's disposal. As a consequence, theatre, viewed in such terms, would become a place where conventional and avant-garde artists alike would imagine "that they have got hold of an apparatus which in fact has got hold of them." The phrase, of course, is Brecht's, who voiced this fear for different, but related reasons (Brecht 1964: 34). But the appeal of unified concepts and comprehensive sets of rules are intellectual ghosts that refuse to go away. Even today, performance studies finds itself pursuing the chimera of "performativity," a concept informed by J. L. Austin's attempts to establish the rules for felicitous performance of speech acts. The widespread linguistic turn toward underlying order so conceived has led only to the twin dilemmas of structuralism and post-structuralism, exemplifying not the error of a linguistic turn but the error of taking the wrong linguistic turn when another was available.[4] To the extent that theatre activities and theatre studies are exploring an analogous scenographic turn, it is important that the cautionary tale of this linguistic turn be widely recognized.

It is thus noteworthy that three of the most influential scenographic figures in the modern theatre (including Brecht) took as their point of departure, not the unity of the theatre, but its non-unitary nature, its inherently composite character. Wagner, Artaud, and Brecht all regarded this recognition as essential to artistic creativity in the theatre and to its capacity to generate social change. If we are to develop for scenography an alternative view of multi-linguistic interaction in the theatre than that provided by semiotics, we should try to grasp how we might accommodate versions of them all. For the key question, after the cautionary tale supplied by semiotics, is how scenography might suitably picture this heterogeneous scene, which displays a composite and interactive conception of theatre, rather than a unified and stable one.

For Wagner, theatre is where all forms of art meet and interact – not just poetry, music, and dance, but also painting, sculpture, and architecture (Wagner 1892: 184, 190). For Artaud, as we have noted, it is the various verbal, visual, and aural languages of the theatre. For Brecht, it is the "words, music, and setting" (Brecht 1964: 38). Each, having assumed the composite character of theatre, adopts a different view of the interaction of the disparate parts. Where Wagner was inclined to favor the transporting synthesis of the separate elements in transcendent performance, Brecht thought it important that their separateness be preserved throughout, not generating a coordinated effect for the audience, but demanding of it an attitude of "complex seeing" – a balancing of perspectives that effectively avoids what he saw as an often unproductive competition among the elements for supremacy in the theatre (Brecht 1964: 44).

> The great struggle for supremacy between words, music and production – which always brings up the question 'which is the pretext for what?': is the music the pretext for the events on the stage, or are these the pretext for the music? etc. – can simply be by-passed by radically separating the elements . . . *Words, music and setting must become more independent of one another* . . . Once the content becomes, technically speaking, an independent component, to which text, music and setting 'adopt attitudes' . . . then a change has been launched which goes far beyond formal matters and begins . . . to affect the theatre's social function.
> *(Brecht 1964: 37–9)*

The shared recognition of Wagner, Artaud, and Brecht that theatre is inherently composite is more important to scenography than the different ways that they deal with it. But by invoking the word "language" to describe the various components, Artaud opens up perspectives on their nature and the nature of their interaction that is less clear with the terminology used by Wagner and Brecht. For example, when Brecht speaks of the various "elements" adopting different "attitudes" to the "content," he makes it difficult to grasp what the language of the content is, once words, music, and setting have been set to one side. Artaud's terminology makes it clearer that the "content" derives from all of the languages and that their interaction includes differing versions of whatever we might consider the content to be. Complex seeing, in the theatre worlds Artaud depicts, is more radical than that in the worlds of Wagner and Brecht. For the key issue in elevating the visual elements of theatre to the status of languages is to recognize all that this implies, once an informative picture of verbal language is adopted. Verbal language does not offer us a picture of the world as it really is. Nor does it offer us a single picture of the world. Rather it offers us an inherited set of resources for picturing the world and participating in it. As recent brain research confirms, we continually cross-reference the various modes of patterning that are generated by all of our senses. To think of visual languages in these terms is to recognize how high the stakes are for scenography in assembling an informative picture of how the various languages of irreducibly composite theatre interact. As Brecht remarked, such reconceptions do, indeed, "affect the theatre's social function" – and, of course, the function of each of its elements (languages). Artaud's description of what is needed to set speech free, thus informatively applies to the other languages of the theatre, too.

As Artaud pointed out, an impoverished picture of verbal language leads to its impoverished use. This is no small matter, for reasons he illuminatingly describes. If verbal language does, indeed, become "ossified" and "words . . . are frozen and cramped in their meanings, in a restricted schematic terminology," then each "word is used only to sidestep thought; it encircles it, but terminates it; it is only a conclusion" (Artaud 1958: 117–18). A conclusion, in effect, that serves only to illustrate a presupposition, not just about theatre, but also about everything that the language impinges upon:

> we have become too well accustomed . . . especially in France, to employing words in the theatre in a single defined sense. We have made the action turn too exclusively on psychological themes whose essential combinations are not infinite . . . We have overaccustomed the theatre to a lack of curiosity and above all of imagination.
>
> *(Artaud 1958: 118)*

In effect, the "withering of words" results in a withering of the worlds we engage through them (Artaud 1958: 118). This is the important sense in which Brecht's "content" is not readily separable from the languages by which we compose it. What Artaud is grasping here is that in a world of many facets and perspectives, in a world of various kinds of inherited and emerging order, misused words do not just ossify, they do not just restrict the imagination, they effectively "congeal" into reality. The phrase is Genet's, from *The Balcony* (Genet 1966: 96). To the extent that we use languages to order the worlds we live in, keeping their elements fluid is essential if their capacity to change offers us access to individual agency and degrees of social freedom. Genet pictures the brothel in the play as more "real" than the "falser" world outside it because clients can bring their own scripts and images to studios where cultural icons, the establishment "nomenclature," can be transgressively engaged (Genet 1966: 36, 86, 96). It is also the place where new icons can be added to the cultural archive. Genet calls the brothel, so conceived, a theatre, a place where the visual and verbal signs and scenarios are, like the studios spinning around on stage, in constant motion. Outside, the world of the ostensible revolution fails, because, in adopting the conventional images of a banner, an iconic woman, and an anthem, it congeals into the orthodox emblems of the world it is trying to rebel against. For Genet, there is no escaping the world of emblems and icons. What matters to the writer whose autobiography is called *The Thief's Journal* is the possibility of reviving the malleability of congealed signs, whether verbal, visual, or aural, so that they can be appropriated and adapted to new uses. It is in this sense that the brothel/theatre becomes more real than the world outside, because the composite theatre of interacting languages is the place where we are reminded of the malleability of signs that, if otherwise pictured, can congeal into an ossified, constraining, and false reality.

The recognition that languages, individually and collectively, shape and reshape the worlds we inhabit is not a new one. What matters is not just our remembering this, but our assigning it to its proper place. That is not off in the margins as an interesting eccentricity, but right at the center of our understanding of what we do when we talk, look, and listen. Languages can not only shape and reshape the worlds we live in, they can also shape and reshape each other – but we have to take responsibility for guiding the process and theatre is one of our key instruments for doing so. When we unthinkingly adopt the prevailing impoverished picture of verbal language, we tend to see it primarily as a means of expression and communication. We then overlook the extent to which it is a means of configuring the very situations and circumstances of which we speak, about which we express opinions, and within which we seek to communicate with each other.

As Halliday phrases it, languages provide "ways of organizing experience," including our experience of the material world and of each other, so that "the context plays a part in determining what we say; and what we say plays a part in determining the context" (Halliday 1978: 26, 3).[5]

In an important sense, languages do not just confront situations, they help make them what they are, and they do so in cooperation with and/or in conflict with the other languages at our disposal. Remembering the heterogeneous history of our languages is an indispensable resource if we are, individually and collectively, to contribute to their and our future. Artaud's recognition that a linguistic turn in scenography might be helpful is particularly helpful when he displays the initial appeal of the wrong linguistic turn before adopting the better one. By extension, the analogous scenographic turn would be informed by the recognition that theatre characteristically serves cultural inquiry by reminding us of the malleability of our modes of understanding. It is this malleability that enables them to serve as our instruments of exploration, discovery, and change. Rules can be both restraints and resources, but only if we can learn (in a non-trivial sense) to play with them as well as by them. Rather than allowing any one of our languages to achieve unchallenged supremacy, to congeal into a reductive reality, scenography can help reveal and deploy, through the interaction of several languages, the contingency that inheres within each and all of them. This clearly echoes what Brecht was pursuing with his exhortations to defamiliarize and historicize, but doing so in Artaud's realm of interacting languages makes the issues of even larger consequence.[6]

These observations about interacting languages and their implications for scenography are given informative visual exemplification, for example, in Fjelde's attempts to describe the unexpectedly complicated nature of Ibsen's highly detailed and apparently realistic sets. He noted with both wonderment and approval,

> the degree to which Ibsen . . . succeeded in transforming the apparently neutral trappings of the realistic stage into highly charged ingredients in a spiritual action, to which no element of the *mise en scène* is finally unrelated . . . Thus the costumes, properties, lighting and décor become the diction of a new kind of dramatic poetry, the vocabulary of a vision of the human situation.
>
> *(Fjelde 2006: xvi)*

Ibsen would doubtless be wary of any attempt to summarize the human situation, but what is illuminating is Fjelde's attempt to grapple with the interactions among Ibsen's verbal and visual languages and with the ways in which Ibsen's sets acquire a voice. He acknowledges his debt to Northam for these recognitions, including the key one that we both see and see by means of the visual elements that Ibsen lays out in such scrupulous detail. There is no clear line here between what is rendered verbally and visually, and we can anticipate, in a playwright's interest in design, the scenographer's complementary interest in configuring the contingent components of a play script. Rather than being coordinated into Wagner's grand syntheses or frozen into Brecht's unchanging separateness, the languages of irreducibly composite theatre are open to any range of relationships to serve an open set of purposes. The gains of creative flexibility thus achieved far outweigh the risk that this "organized anarchy" might become more anarchistic than organized. But for scenography, both the range of the responsibility and the character of the responsibility are clarified by Artaud's informative swerve from viewing verbal language as the villain in the theatre to viewing it as one of theatre's fellow victims, and, indeed, one of all the other theatre languages' fellow victims. The consequences of this shift, however, continue to extend in ways that return us to the opening question about the pertinent scale and scope of the scenographic turn.

The key change in perspective, as we have noted, is from viewing verbal language as unified, ossified, and coercive to recognizing that its heterogeneity makes it compatible with and constitutive of a theatre that, in its reliance on many languages, is inherently composite. In Artaud's terms, theatre "is in no thing, but makes use of everything." That modern sense of the inherently composite nature of theatrical material is, by now, widely evident, but the challenge of locating the ordering principles that inhabit the disorder is not so widely met. So far have we traveled, however, from the unifying mind-set of Aristotle, that plays, as well as theatre, are now often viewed as productively composite.

Shaw, for example, praises modern comedy as a "higher form" than tragedy because of the contesting perspectives it deploys (Shaw 2000: 431–2) – a point taken several steps further by Littlewood:

> The old pigeon-holes will no longer serve . . . Polonius did not know the half of it: a modern play can, if it wishes, be tragical-comical-historical-pastoral-farcical-satirical-operatical-musical-music hall, in any combination or all at the same time.
>
> *(Littlewood 2006: xxxvi)*

The widespread emergence of improvisational workshop productions displays this interest in mingling the composite character of plays with the composite character of theatre more broadly, along with the composite character of the worlds we live in. The work of the Wooster Group has focused not just upon mingling the languages of the theatre, but also on expanding their range, by incorporating the resources of modern media. In contrast to the dated orthodoxies of the modernist avant-garde, this process of adding languages to the theatre is not based on the assumption that new languages earn their place by replacing old ones, but upon Artaud's recognition that adding new languages adjusts the role of older ones. Just as important, as Artaud has again pointed out, is the recovery of the physics of older theatrical modes. The most productive through line of theatrical creativity from Artaud to post modernism has been that of adopting, adapting, recovering, and extending whatever languages and conventions that are capable of serving as useful resources. As Suzan-Lori Parks has put it:

> Most playwrights who consider themselves avant-garde spend a lot of time badmouthing the more traditional forms. The naturalism of, say, Lorraine Hansberry is beautiful and should not be dismissed simply because it's naturalism. We should understand that realism, like other movements in other art forms, is a specific response to a certain historical climate.
>
> *(Parks 1995: 8)*

It is in this context that we can recognize that Artaud's insistence upon recovering the "physics" of earlier forms of theatre is important in two informative ways. First, if theatre is, as he says, "in no thing, but makes use of everything," theatre has no Aristotelian common core or fixed boundary. Like the typifying categories Wittgenstein describes, theatre has neither required nor prohibited features. Instead of definitive rules to be followed it has a regulative history of uses to be explored, adapted, and extended, and the better we know that history, the better we are able to make use of its past and future resources. Without that varied history, conceptually and practically for theatre, there is no there there. Stipulative definitions of theatre, like stipulative definitions of performance, offer only confirmation that people have lost their way. The second point, however, is just as important. In recovering any historical theatre's physics, we are not setting out to replicate it. As in the case of the text of *Hamlet*, where there is no definitive version, there is also no definitive version of, say, Shakespeare's theatre. Instead of modernism's creative destruction, we rely upon a process of creative reconstruction. But the key issue here is how theatre organizes this process. With the responsibilities of playwright, director, and designer often more distributed than related, the organization part of organized anarchy is not always well arranged. Because of a reliance upon inherited and impoverished pictures of theatrical terrain, scenography's capacity to relate all of the moving parts has been clear neither in principle nor in practice.

To move forward scenographically from and with Artaud, we should note the other linguistic dimension that Parks adds to the scenographic scene. As she puts it, the informative concept here is that of conversation. Any form of theatre is, in her words, a "response to a certain historical climate" (Parks 1995: 8). It is part of a cultural conversation of an era and a continuation of theatre's cultural conversations with the past. Dialogue in the present and dialogue with the past are complementary parts of any theatre's physics, however imprecise the regulative concepts and practices invoked. Indeed, it is precisely because languages are so imprecise that they can provide sufficient clarity, but no more than that, to conversations that would grind to a halt if excessive clarity, in an interactive and changing world, is inappropriately demanded. As Wittgenstein famously remarked about verbal concepts, "'inexact' . . . does not mean 'unusable'" (Wittgenstein 1969: 41). Indeed, for many of the uses we seek to make of them, their inexactness, variously deployed, is a key element of their usability. So often it is, indeed, the case that "an indistinct picture" is "exactly what we need" (Wittgenstein 1969: 34).

The importance to scenography of this historical perspective on cultural conversations is exemplified in the much-overlooked role of revivals in the theatre. While new shows and new perspectives are all vital to the creativity of the present, so also is the renewal of our conversations with the past, as notably exemplified in revivals. An obvious factor here, no less important for being obvious, is that when we perform or attend a revival of *Hamlet*, it is not to see again what we saw before, but to see the play renewed in its revival. A new production that largely replicates the play's performance history will not stir us or earn our approbation. The bogus attempt to recover Shakespeare's authentic voice will ring hollow. An alternative kind of revival that seems indifferent to performance history will (usually) dismay us, as the voice of the director will, disappointingly, drown out the voice of Shakespeare. But a historically informed revival that registers a convincing conversation between past and present voices, with actors, directors, and designers engaged in and extending the cultural conversation, travels on the tides of history. It fruitfully enlarges our understanding of Shakespeare, the theatre, and ourselves – all of which are evolving. It is in the tradition of revivals, however radical, that theatre displays the ever-evolving historicity of its interacting languages. Signs, as Haas put it, are souvenirs, and new signs, as Genet has depicted them, have to earn their place in the cultural conversation. Social changes, as Ibsen so astutely indicated in *Ghosts*, are inescapably grounded in the continuities that both restrict and enable them. But the key responsibility and opportunity for scenographers is to integrate the overall performance perspective by deploying and displaying the conversation between the variously related signs of the variously related languages. It is in this interactive sense that audiences are enabled to see and see by means of them, so that their historicity and malleability are displayed together.

The transformative reach of such a scenographic turn is illuminatingly described by Parks. Having refused the avant-garde readiness to short circuit the process of theatrical and social change, she offers a version of change whose reach is just as extensive, as is the implied scale of the scenographic impact. Theatre's deployment of the malleability of its many resources has the capacity to take our conversations with the past to unexpected places, no matter how remote they may initially seem.

> A play is a blueprint of an event: a way of creating and rewriting history . . . Since history is a recorded or remembered event, theatre, for me, is the perfect place to 'make' history . . . [and] one of my tasks as playwright is to . . . locate the ancestral burial ground, dig for bones, find bones, hear the bones sing, write it down . . . I'm re-membering and staging historical events which, through their happening on stage, are ripe for inclusion in the canon of history. Theatre is an incubator for the creation of historical events – and, as in the case of artificial insemination, the baby is no less human.
>
> *(Parks 1995: 4–5)*

Parks acknowledges the particular challenge she faces in reconstituting history when "so much of African-American history has been unrecorded, dismembered, washed out," but with history always so variously and selectively recorded and represented, her approach is widely applicable (Parks 1995: 4). The effort involved in "putting the body back together" is an effort requiring a creative exchange between archeological research and teleological imagination, an activity she engages in herself, depicts in her characters, expects of her designers, and demands of her audiences (Parks 1995: 5). In *The America Play*, she deploys a picture, in the larger context of cultural theme parks, of a black Abraham Lincoln. As history records and reiterates, Lincoln is depicted in her play in the endlessly repeated process of being assassinated – but, of course, always resisting any final death. Raiding the archive of our cultural iconography, she, like Genet in *The Balcony*, appropriates and adapts our collective memories, effectively renewing and revising our cultural conversations. But the fact that it is the playwright, the writer of the verbal script, who is deploying the subversive visual images takes us one step further down the road of informative reminders about collective responsibility for interacting theatrical languages. Images and narratives do not distribute themselves so neatly into the separate Aristotelian domains of the costumier and the poet. In a complementary manner, Robert Wilson's extended images in *the CIVIL warS* invoke and adapt the narratives of our collective memory, while exhibiting a visual vocabulary that evolved across his career.

Artaud's shift in perspective, from seeing verbal language as the villain in the theatre to seeing it as one of theatre's fellow victims, led him to view all of theatre through the lens of language, but through a very different picture of language than the impoverished one with which he began. As a result, he noted,

> far from restricting the possibilities of theatre and language, on the pretext that I will not perform written plays, I extend the language of the stage and multiply its possibilities . . . It is not a matter of suppressing speech in the theatre but of changing its role.
>
> *(Artaud 1958: 111, 72)*

That change in role is brought about by discarding the impoverished theatrical picture of a single, unified, ossified, and dominant language and replacing it with a picture of several, multiform, evolving, and interactive theatre languages that are guided but not governed by their histories of continuity and change. No longer dominated by a misconception of what he needed to be "free from," Artaud was "free to" follow his own route forward in pursuing the scenographic "possibilities" he could now envision.

There is nothing privileged about Artaud's chosen route forward. Like all good theatre, it is exploratory, and the several languages of the theatre can be otherwise aligned in various kinds of production. There is ample room for the "total theatre" he intermittently envisaged and for the grand artistic syntheses pursued by Wagner, but there is also room for Beckett's minimalism, for Grotowski's Poor Theatre, and for everything in between, including Robert Wilson's intense focus on a visual language, the Wooster Group's exploration of the impact of technological languages, and the widespread appeal of various kinds of musical theatre, including Joan Littlewood's *Oh What a Lovely War*, that provides the otherwise unconsulted soldiers of World War I with a collective, contentious, and continuing voice in the historical songs they once sang together, adopting popular melodies but revising the words. The only potentially inhibiting factor would be that of an avant-garde tradition that values novelty primarily on the basis of what it can claim to have superseded and displaced. Unlike the poets who, in Aristotle's theatre, could hope to achieve their goals as much by being read as being performed, the characteristically post-Artaud playwrights compose specifically for the theatre, aware of the demands and possibilities of a scenographically informed theatre in which plays and performances alike incorporate the interaction of a variety of languages – an interaction that reminds us that theatrical divisions between them and between responsibilities for them are based on misleading premises.

Elam is thus right to point out that "[i]t is often less than easy to distinguish prop from set, just as 'movement', 'gesture', and 'facial mime' are in practice intimately connected and complementary aspects of the general kinesic continuum" (Elam 1980: 51). The intricate interaction of ostensibly separable elements once generated Pinter's concern that "the lifting of a coffee cup at the wrong moment can damage the next five minutes. As for the *sipping* of coffee, that can ruin the act" (Gussow 1996: 33). It would be no small thing if today's directors, rather than coming up prematurely with a governing "concept," and besides working closely with the actors, assumed extended responsibility for convening and coordinating scenographic conversations among all the interested parties. Without such practical implementation, the scenographic turn may not become productive or prolonged. Creative conversations and shared practices would need, however, to be informed by a scenographic turn that conceptually and practically facilitates, and does not just encourage, collective engagement.

The complementarity of the visual and the verbal in the theatre, misleadingly set apart by Aristotle, is, in these terms, much clarified. It is an old adage that every picture tells a story, but, like many an old adage, it captures a persisting element of truth. In the case of theatre, each of the pictures drawn by the set designer, costume designer, and lighting designer has the capacity to tell a story that interacts both with those generated by the verbal languages and with those generated by the rest of the performance space. This narrative employment of the visual is not necessarily its primary use, but it echoes a long tradition exemplified, for example, in medieval iconography and in the popular nineteenth-century theatrical tableau. In complementary ways, the verbal languages of theatre, as Shakespeare's plays (among many others) so regularly indicate, also contribute to the visual images that help constitute performance. This complementarity of narrative and image speaks directly against inclinations to treat them separately or in parallel, as the verbal and the visual so often help constitute each other. Pinter probably speaks for a great many other playwrights when he reminds everyone who will listen of the centrality of "images," both "visual" and "verbal," to his process of composition (Gussow 1996: 106). Together, and in overlapping ways, the collectively generated scenic and verbal images provide one of the theatre's key resources for picturing our world and our (often contested) participation in it. What Artaud so helpfully recognized was not just the complementary nature of verbal and visual languages, but also the mutually illuminating character of their interaction, an interaction that brings the linguistic turn and the scenographic turn into similarly illuminating alignment. As a result, the scenographic turn becomes of more comprehensive scale, scope, and consequence than could otherwise have been envisaged.

Samuel Johnson noted many years ago that "[i]mitations produce pain or pleasure, not because they are mistaken for realities, but because they bring realities to mind" (Johnson 1957: 503). That process of "bringing realities to mind" is, in these terms, more complicated than Johnson ever envisaged. Those realities may be social, psychological, political, spiritual, material, and a great deal more, including historical and/or emergent, as Johnson's use of the plural word "realities" might suggest to us today. For scenography now, the notion that theatre enables us both to see and see by means of what is presented on stage requires Aristotle's famed word "imitation" to cover a wider cognitive spectrum than hitherto: from replication, through representation, to exemplification. The notion that a play, specifically a "tragedy" for Aristotle, is an "imitation of an action" would have to include the notion that a show can also be an exemplification of an interaction: between characters, languages, genres, audiences, and eras (Aristotle 1963: 15). Theatre's peculiar capacity to be "in no one thing, but make use of everything" positions it as an historical site of many kinds of interaction, thus rendering malleable whatever it borrows and invents. Scenography, in these terms, can align itself not just with Artaud's picture of theatre as interacting languages, but also with his sense of its liberating function, as an historically informed instrument of exploration and change. For theatre in general, and for each of its visual, verbal, and aural languages, it is possible to "wonder . . . whether it has the power, not to define thoughts but to cause thinking" (Artaud 1958: 69).

Notes

1 Rorty attributes the phrase "linguistic turn" to Gustav Bergmann. Richard Rorty, *Consequences of Pragmatism* (Minneapolis, MN: University of Minnesota Press, 1982), xxi.
2 Friedrich von Schiller, "On the Use of the Chorus in Tragedy." In *Complete Works of Friedrich Schiller, V* (New York: P. F. Collier and Son, 1902), 241–5.
3 Ferdinand de Saussure, *Course in General Linguistics*, edited by Charles Bally and Albert Sechehaye, translated by Roy Harris (London: Gerald Duckworth & Co., 1990).

4 Rorty describes the linguistic turn as a turn toward "necessity." *Consequences of Pragmatism*, 27. For further discussion of contrasting linguistic turns, see my *Theoretical Inquiry: Language, Linguistics, and Literature* (New Haven, CT, and London: Yale University Press, 2004).
5 The gap between everyday assumptions about how language works and how it actually works can be considerable. See, for example, Halliday's remarks on the polysystemic and polyphonic nature of the sentences we produce and understand, which typically have "a number of threads of meaning running simultaneously." For Halliday, "all speech . . . is polyphonic; different melodies are kept going side by side, and each element in the sentence is like a chord which contributes something to all of them." *Language as Social Semiotic* (Baltimore, MD: University Park Press, 1978), 31.
6 Thus the larger implications of Brecht's insistence that we constantly be shown that we are being shown something: "he who is showing should himself be shown." *Brecht on Theatre* (New York: Hill and Wang, 1964), 45.

References

Aristotle 1963. *Poetics*, translated by John Warrington. London: J. M. Dent and Sons.
Artaud, Antonin 1958. *The Theater and its Double*, translated by Mary Caroline Richards. New York: Grove Press.
Austin, J. L. 1970. "Performative Utterances." In *Philosophical Papers*, 233–52. London: Oxford University Press. See also 1962, *How to Do Things with Words*, edited by J. O. Urmson. New York: Oxford University Press.
Bakhtin, Mikhail M. 1981. *The Dialogic Imagination*, edited by Michael Holquist, translated by Caryl Emerson and Michael Holquist. Austin: University of Texas Press.
Barish, Jonas 1981. *The Anti-Theatrical Prejudice*. Berkeley and Los Angeles: University of California Press.
Bharata, Muni 1999. *The Nāṭyaśāstra* , translated by Adya Rangacharya. New Delhi: Munshiram Manoharlal.
Boal, Augusto 1985. *Theatre of the Oppressed*, translated by Charles A. and Maria-Odilia Leal McBride. New York: Theatre Communications Group.
Brecht, Bertolt 1964. *Brecht on Theatre*, edited and translated by John Willett. New York: Hill and Wang.
Eco, Umberto 1976. *A Theory of Semiotics*. Bloomington: Indiana University Press.
Elam, Keir 1980. *The Semiotics of Theatre and Drama*. London and New York: Methuen.
Firth, J. R. 1957. *Papers in Linguistics, 1934–51*. London: Oxford University Press.
Fjelde, Rolf 2006. Foreword to *Ibsen: Four Major Plays, 1*, translated by Rolf Fjelde. New York: Signet.
Genet, Jean 1966. *The Balcony*, translated by Bernard Frechtman. New York: Grove Press.
Gussow, Mel 1996. *Conversations with Pinter*. New York: Grove Press.
Haas, W. 1962. "The Theory of Translation." *Philosophy* 37: 208–28.
Halliday, M. A. K. 1978. *Language as Social Semiotic: The Social Interpretation of Language and Meaning*. Baltimore, MD: University Park Press.
Johnson, Samuel 1957. "Preface to Shakespeare." In *Dr. Johnson: Prose and Poetry*, edited by Mona Wilson, 489–529. London: Rupert Hart-Davis.
Littlewood, Joan 2006. Quoted in introductory commentary to *Oh What a Lovely War*, edited by Joan Littlewood, commentary and notes by Steve Lewis. London: Methuen.
Marinetti, Filippo Tommaso 1972. "Variety Theatre." In *Marinetti: Selected Writings*, edited and translated by R. W. Flint, 116–22. New York: Farrar, Straus and Giroux.
Miller, J. Hillis 1975. "Deconstructing the Deconstructers." *Diacritics* 5 [2]: 24–31.
Northam, John 1973. *Ibsen: A Critical Study*. London: Cambridge University Press.
Parks, Suzan-Lori 1995. *The America Play and Other Works*. New York: Theatre Communications.
Pascal, Blaise 1859. *The Thoughts, Letters and Opuscules of Blaise Pascal*, translated by O. W. Wright. New York: Derby and Jackson.
Quigley, Austin E. 2004. *Theoretical Inquiry: Language, Linguistics, and Literature*. New Haven, CT, and London: Yale University Press.
Rorty, Richard 1982. *Consequences of Pragmatism*. Minneapolis: University of Minnesota Press.

Saussure, Ferdinand de 1990. *Course in General Linguistics*, edited by Charles Bally and Albert Sechehaye, translated by Roy Harris. London: Gerald Duckworth & Co.
Schiller, Friedrich von 1902a. "On the Use of the Chorus in Tragedy." In *Complete Works of Friedrich Schiller*, V, 241–5. New York: P. F. Collier and Son.
Schiller, Friedrich von 1902b. "The Stage as a Moral Institution." In *Complete Works*, V111, 339–45. New York: P. F. Collier and Son.
Shaw, George Bernard 2000. "Tolstoy: Tragedian or Comedian?" In *Theatre/Theory/Theatre: The Major Critical Texts*, edited by Daniel Gerould, 430–2. New York: Applause Theatre and Cinema Books.
Vega, Lope De 2000. "The New Art of Writing Plays." In *Theatre/Theory/Theatre: The Major Critical Texts*, edited by Daniel Gerould, translated by Marvin Carlson, 136–45. New York: Applause Theatre and Cinema Books.
Wagner, Richard 1892. "The Art-Work of the Future." In *Richard Wagner's Prose Works*, 1, translated by William Ashton Ellis, 67–213. London: K. Paul, Trench, Trubner & Co.
Wittgenstein, Ludwig 1969. *Philosophical Investigations*, translated by G. E. M. Anscombe. New York: Macmillan.
Zeami 1984. "Teachings on Style and the Flower." In *On the Art of the No Drama: The Major Treatises of Zeami*, translated by J. Thomas Rimer and Yamazaki Masakasu, 3–63. Princeton, NJ: Princeton University Press.

8
SEEING SCENOGRAPHY
Scopic regimes and the body of the spectator

Joslin McKinney

Given the designation of theatre as "the seeing place" (Aronson 2005: 2) and the strongly visual nature of scenography, we might wonder at how little consideration has been given so far to the act of looking, whether in scenographic studies or in theatre scholarship more generally. Yet concerns within wider cultural discourse about a dominance of the visual that "has its end in rapt, mindless fascination" (Jameson 1990: 1) have certainly influenced the way we conceptualize the visual dimension of theatre experience as "a medium of optical illusion" (Rancière 2007: 272) and have marginalized scenography as mere decoration or as a distraction. But there are, to borrow from John Berger (1972), different ways of seeing scenography that reveal themselves in the act of looking. In this chapter I challenge dominant interpretations of the act of seeing in theatre by arguing for the explanatory power of a dynamic, embodied conceptualization of scenographic spectatorship centered on co-construction.

In the theatre, visual spectacle has been denigrated as idealized, as superficial or as excessive. Jen Harvie and Paul Allain identify common concern among "many observers" that the visual is "trivial" and distracts audiences "from more important issues" (Allain and Harvie 2014: 194). "The paradox of the spectator," as Jacques Rancière points out, is that "there is no theatre without spectators" but being a spectator is "a bad thing"; it implies looking, which is "the opposite of knowing." Theatrical spectacle, it is claimed, conceals its means of production and produces a passive spectator (Rancière 2007: 271–2). But Rancière has proposed that spectators are "emancipated" from the disabling grip of spectacle by virtue of "the power to translate in their own way what they are looking at" (Rancière 2007: 278). His solution to the paradox is to emphasize the intellectual freedom of the spectators to make their own "story" of the story in front of them; to translate images into words. But he is nonetheless wary of the visual itself and the recent blurring of boundaries between art and theatre and a proliferation of visual hybrids have led, he says, to stultification and "hyperactive consumerism" (Rancière 2007: 280).

Rancière's suspicion of visual excess is familiar within a broader critique of visual culture and it helps explain why scenography has rarely been considered as offering something more than seductive or dazzling effects to the experience of viewing theatre.

Part of the problem seems to be the dominance of one model of vision, that of the disembodied and passive viewer associated with the development of Renaissance perspective that continues to have some influence even now. In the late 1980s the Dia Art Foundation organized a symposium to explore plural modes of vision and the different ways we see or are enabled to see. Of particular interest to scenography is Martin Jay's contribution that addresses "scopic regimes"[1] of modernity as applied to the viewing of paintings. In it he reviews the hegemonic visual model of modernity that unites Renaissance perspective with Cartesian ideas of subjective rationality (Jay 1988: 4) and then identifies two alternatives to this model; the Baconian "world of objects" and the "baroque." But how do the scopic regimes that Jay proposes apply to scenography? In particular, how might different models of seeing in the theatre dislodge the persistent notion of the disinterested, disembodied and passive spectator? What does thinking about the relationship of the viewer to the visual tell us about the scenographic ways of seeing? Jay's models focus on the visual dimension of seeing, but I will also explore embodied vision and ask: what role does the body of the spectator assume within the realm of the scopic?

Theatre, scenography, and the visual

Scenography is now established as an integral component of theatrical performance and its reception. No longer considered simply as background, scenography has been shown to shape performance and to exert dramaturgical and poetic effects.[2] Within this, the role of the spectator is also beginning to be considered. Authors including Benedetto (2010), McKinney (2013), and Trimingham (2013) have investigated how scenography contributes to audience experience in many contemporary forms of performance and how its multisensorial nature invites active and co-creative spectatorship. But there are gaps in relation to the wider and historical practice of scenography where we have tended to think about visual experience as synonymous with the aims and approaches of individual designers and accept that the intentions of scenographers and directors are sufficient to explain the experience of seeing. Rancière proposes emancipation from the spectacle through cognitive subjectivity rather than considering different ways of seeing spectacle itself. However, the expansion of scenographic practices, both on stage and beyond (Lotker and Gough 2013) require us to engage with scenographic spectacle directly and theorize the act of looking at scenography.

In one of the very few books that addresses visuality in the theatre, Maaike Bleeker identifies the importance of the "institution of perspective" in helping us understand how "our senses are cultured to perceive certain privileged modes of representation as more natural, real, objective or convincing than others, and to relate these effects to the discourses which mediate in what we think we see" (Bleeker 2008: 13). For Bleeker, perspective is a way of seeing the world that is based on a kind of deception, a promise of authenticity or direct access to reality, that can never be fulfilled:

> The institution of perspective theatricalizes the field of vision. It creates a scenographic space in which all that is seen is staged for a viewer. Paradoxically, despite the high degree of scenic manipulation required to successfully integrate the rules of perspective into a painted or otherwise constructed scene, the promise of perspective is that of immediacy.
>
> *(Bleeker 2008: 15)*

Dominic Johnson adds to this by observing that in the dramatic theatre narrative has often presented a linguistic equivalent of visual perspective, one where spectatorship is an attempt "to second-guess the supposedly singular, orthodox vision of the dramatist" (Johnson 2014: 28). Bleeker also considers how contemporary theatre positions the spectator, and includes some consideration of the "spectator as body perceiving" (Bleeker 2008: 6) as part of her analysis of the subjectivity of vision. In this chapter I build on Bleeker's idea of "the body seeing" (Bleeker 2008: 16) by focusing specifically on scenography and consider how the idea of a perceiving body modifies notions of the spectator rendered compliant and passive by the spectacle. But first I need to say more about the idea of scopic regimes and the regulatory structures of the visual.

Vision, visuality, and scopic regimes

For the field of visual studies the Dia Art Foundation symposium marked an important contribution to the academic discourse on modern vision. In the preface to the published papers, Hal Foster points out that vision, or the physical operation of seeing, might be distinguished from visuality, or the historical, discursive and social dimensions within which any act of vision is located. A "scopic regime" accounts for the complex operation and intertwining of vision and visuality in a given time or place. Between these two aspects of the visual a whole host of differences in "how we see, how we are able, allowed, or made to see, and how we might see this seeing or the unseeing therein" might reside (Foster 1988: ix). But it is always the tendency of every scopic regime to "close out these differences" and make it seem that there is just "one essential vision." In the same publication, Jay says that while "it is difficult to deny that the visual has been dominant in modern Western culture" (Jay 1988: 3), there is not one scopic regime or single model of vision that pertains throughout this period and that there are "subcultures" of the visual that we have only come to appreciate from a postmodern vantage point (Jay 1988: 4).

Johnson has suggested that thinking about scopic regimes helps us understand "how historical developments have intruded upon visual experience in the theatre" (Johnson 2014: 23) and he uses the examples of Renaissance perspective in the fifteenth century and the introduction of gas and electricity in the nineteenth century. He quite rightly points out that these technological innovations go beyond enhancing visibility. They also change the process of seeing and understanding and scenography might come to have dramaturgical meaning that is equivalent to or may even exceed the text (Johnson 2014: 32). But there is more to consider regarding the way scenography positions the spectator within competing, and sometimes overlapping, scopic regimes and the extent to which the spectator is complicit with or resistant to spectacle.

Perspective and disembodied looking

The origins of Western scenography are bound up with scenic verisimilitude and techniques of perspective have been instrumental in that development. Vitruvius, a Roman architect who recorded his studies of Greek theatre in *De Architectura* in 27 BCE describes scene painting practices that used the idea of lines radiating from a fixed point to make painted buildings seem to have three dimensions; "what is figured upon vertical and plane surfaces can seem to recede in one part and project in another" (Vitruvius 1914). However, it is in the (re)invention[3] of perspective in fifteenth-century Italy, where the use of perspective in the theatre developed into elaborate painted scenery and perspectival scenic constructions that perspective emerges as a scopic regime. Renaissance perspective was not simply a technique of verisimilitude but a demonstration of the "modern scientific world view" (Bleeker 2008: 12) after the "religious underpinnings" (Jay 1988: 6) of the medieval world had been displaced. Alberti's theorization of perspective in painting, *Di Pittura*, 1435, offered a new approach to the representation of space that drew on geometrical and scientific understanding:

> The basic device was the idea of symmetrical visual pyramids or cones with one of their apexes the receding vanishing or centric point in the painting, the other the eye of the painter or the beholder. The transparent window that was the canvas, in Alberti's famous metaphor, could be understood as a flat mirror reflecting the geometricalized space radiating out from the viewing eye.
>
> *(Jay 1988: 6–7)*

Importantly, this rationalized and objectified view of space reflects the view from a single eye, fixed and unblinking, and does not replicate our physiological, binocular vision that moves in jumps between focal points.[4] This abstracted and disembodied viewpoint has been widely associated with Rene Descartes's ideas about the dominance of the mind in determining the nature of things and this "Cartesian" perspective has been taken by many to be the determining concept of vision in the modern era (Jay 1988: 3–5). Cartesian perspectivalism has seemed to offer an objective and truthful view of the world. Even though there is a "fundamental discrepancy" (Panofsky 1991 [1927]: 31) between our actual experience of seeing and the way that vision is constructed in Cartesian perspectivalism, this model has "pervaded our conception of the visible world" and explains how "our senses are cultured to perceive certain privileged modes of representation as more natural, real, objective, or convincing than others" (Bleeker 2008: 13).

It has been pointed out by several theatre scholars that a particular problem with the realization of a perspective effect in the theatre is the physical placement of viewer in theatre. Richard Southern notes that there is only one place where the view completes the effect of perspective scenery as a "real" structure and not just a painting (Southern 1962: 231). Marvin Carlson says this place was located as the position from which the "sponsoring prince" was seated (Carlson 1993: 137). From his elevated central position[5] the prince was provided with a clear view of the stage and his subjects at the same time as he himself became the "visual anchor for the stage perspective." The less privileged spectators, meanwhile, had "imaginatively to correct their distorted view of that city by calculating their spatial (and thus social) distance from the duke's perfect view" (Carlson 1993: 140). Perspective scenery (and the theatres that were built to house it) can be seen to act as endorsement of the dominant social order. Idealized and elegantly abstracted, the spectator in this model of vision is disciplined to perceive the artifice as rational, objective and natural.

In other ways, too, perspective scenery fits well with readings of Cartesian perspectivalism, especially those that see it as complicit with commodification of art and enabling capitalist exchange (Jay 1988: 9). Renaissance practice signals a commodification of the scenographic and its capacity to demonstrate wealth and power through the costly material and labor it required. The many publications that circulated across Europe showing theatre designs by artists such as Sebastiano Serlio and Nicola Sabbattini meant that the practice of perspective scenery could be replicated and adopted by those who possessed the considerable capital resource that it required (see Baugh 2017: 24–29).

Perspectivalism in the theatre is associated not just with the way scenery is conceived but with the whole apparatus of the auditorium. Richard Wagner's Festspielhaus at Bayreuth is a renowned example that sought to structure and control the audience's vision so that their full attention was given to the work on stage. The fan shape of the steeply-raked, single-sweep auditorium with no balconies or boxes combined with a double proscenium was aimed at achieving an unimpeded view of a scene that separates the stage. The darkness of the auditorium and the orchestra hidden from view, by means of a curved canopy over the pit, further enhanced the effect of the brightly lit stage as the sole focus of the audience's attention. The arrangement and positioning of the viewer was calculated in such a way that "the spectator would be exclusively preoccupied with the spectacle" (Crary 2001: 252). Wagner aimed to create the illusion of a stage that was distant while the people appearing on it "are of superhuman stature" (ibid.: 251 f.n. 249). The spectators in this arrangement are absorbed and dominated by the stage scene and by the single vision of the director to which the scenography is subordinated.

Looking in Wagner's theatre seems to be the epitome of a perspectival model where the spectator is disciplined to defer to the transcendental image. This reinforces the idea of scenography operating within a scopic regime based on disembodied deception. Yet even in the Renaissance period there is evidence that looking at scenography has the potential to play on the relationship between an idealized depiction and quotidian experience. Fabio Finotti, who has studied eye-witness accounts from the Italian Renaissance, says the appeal of perspective scenery lay in the way it connected the daily lives of spectators with the idealized and fictionalized scene. The combination of architectonic and painted scenery meant the loss of an imaginary boundary between the theatrical space and reality. As a consequence, "the scene becomes the center for interplay between reality and fiction that fuses the space occupied by the spectators with that of the actors" (Finotti 2010: 27).

Bernadino Prosperi, a contemporary witness of a 1508 performance of *Cassaria* at Ferrara says "the best part" of the performance were the scenes (by Pellegrino da Udine) which

> consisted of a street and perspectival view of land with houses, churches, bell towers, and gardens, rendered with such diversity as to leave the viewer unsatiated; all this contrived with such ingenuity and skill that I doubt it will be discarded, but rather preserved for later use.
>
> *(Cited in Finotti 2010: 30)*

Another eye witness is Baldassar Castiglione who saw a performance of Bibbiena's *Calandria* in Urbino in 1513. He writes:

> Moreover, the scene gave the illusion of a beautiful city with streets, palaces, churches, towers, and real streets, each of which appeared in relief, being enhanced further by fine painting and well-rendered perspective . . . Certain areas were adorned with illusive glass of precious stones that looked absolutely genuine, freestanding illusive marble figures.
>
> *(Cited in Finotti 2010: 37)*

Prosperi says he is left "unsatiated," which suggests that he has been "captured by images" in the negative sense that spectacle is said to produce (Rancière 2007: 272). Castiglione, though, makes it clear that he is knowingly complicit in the scenic illusion. These contrasting accounts seem to be evidence of a complex interaction between vision and visuality that complicate the regime of Cartesian perspectivalism; rather than a single and totalizing image working on a passive and disembodied spectator, the scene here is registered as "a fluid network of interrelationships between relief and profundity, architectonic mass and pictorial vertigo, order and motion, centrality and centrifugal explosion, reality and scenic fiction" (Finotti 2010: 32–3). In this reading, the visual experience appears to anticipate other models of vision, particularly, as we shall see, what Jay calls the baroque. So, while the craft and skill of scenographers might have been harnessed to reinforce the illusion of a "natural" order, we need to be cautious about the extent to which Cartesian perspectivalism was predominant in the theatre either in the Renaissance period or since.

A world of objects

Considering alternative scopic regimes, Jay draws from Svetlana Alpers' book, *The Art of Describing: Dutch Art in the Seventeenth Century*. In contrast to the religious and classical themes seen in Italian art, Dutch painting featured landscapes, domestic interior scenes and still lives. In doing so, it drew attention to a proliferation of objects, their textures and surfaces and the way that light was reflected by them (see Alpers 1983: 44). Furthermore, the worlds that are depicted in Dutch painting are "not contained entirely within the frame" (Jay 1988: 12). In Italian perspective painting the frame positions the viewer in the place that the painter stood, but in Dutch seventeenth-century paintings there is "no clearly situated viewer" (Alpers 1983: 44) and their frames are "arbitrary and without the totalizing function they serve in Southern art":

> Rejecting the privileged, constitutive role of the monocular subject, it emphasizes instead the prior existence of a world of objects depicted on the flat canvas, a world indifferent to the beholder's position in front of it.
>
> *(Jay 1988: 12)*

The model of looking in Dutch painting is underpinned by empiricism rather than the rationalism of Cartesian perspectivalism[6] and correlates, Jay says, with the philosophy of Francis Bacon rather than that of Descartes. Dutch painting lingers, and encourages the viewer to linger, on the "fragmentary, detailed, and richly articulated surface" of its content in a way that suggests that a combination of sense experience and visual interrogation are key to understanding the depicted world (Jay 1988: 13).

In the theatre, too, there are indications that a scopic regime based on the deployment of objects and on attention to the surface and texture of things were in operation, although not necessarily concurrent with that of Dutch painting.[7] The system of organizing and changing perspective scenery established in Renaissance Italy (see Mohler 2008) and which was subsequently adopted and perpetuated across court theatres in Europe was generally speaking an ordered, symmetrical arrangement of wings leading the viewer's eye to a backdrop in a manner that echoes the principles of Cartesian perspectivalism. There were some notable refinements of this basic approach, though, that offer further evidence of competing models of vision and an increasing interest in "the world of objects" in scenography. Philippe de Loutherbourg's scenes in late-eighteenth-century London required asymmetric, heavily profiled wings to accommodate depictions of actual places and the detail of objects that might be found in them. A description of his design for *Omai; or, A Trip Around the World* (Covent Garden, London, 1785) runs as follows:

> The scenery is infinitely beyond any designs or paintings the stage has ever displayed. To the rational mind, what can be more entertaining than to contemplate prospects or countries in their natural colorings and tints – to bring into living action, the customs and manners of different nations! To see exact representations of their buildings, marine vessels, arms, manufactures, sacrifices and dresses?
>
> *(Cited in Baugh 1990: 47)*

Loutherbourg, a renowned landscape artist as well as a scenographer, was known to have recorded the natural sites from first-hand observation and translated this into his stage productions using both painted and actual light to accentuate the effect of the surface detail of the painting. Productions such as *The Wonders of Derbyshire* (1779) at Drury Lane, London, mark, in England at least, a shift away from idealized scenes towards a capturing of the material qualities of the real world. However, it is only at the very end of the nineteenth century that a "world of objects" becomes a significant model of vision in the theatre.

In his preface to *Miss Julie* (1888), August Strindberg registers his dissatisfaction with the gap between representation and actuality exemplified by stage doors that "are made of canvas and sway at the slightest touch." He is calling for a new approach to design that is drawn from empirical experience:

> nothing is more difficult than making a room on stage resemble a real room, no matter how easy the scene painter finds it to create erupting volcanoes and waterfalls. Even if the walls have to be of canvas, it is surely time to stop painting shelves and kitchen utensils on them. There are so many other stage conventions in which we are asked to believe that we might be spared the effort of believing in painted saucepans.
>
> *(Strindberg 1888)*

Alongside a desire that scenography should pay more attention to the characteristics and behaviors of the material world, Strindberg, like the Dutch painters before him, also recognizes, the effect of using "asymmetry and cropped framing" in order to leave the viewer "free to conjecture." Strindberg, though, credits Impressionist painting, not Dutch seventeenth-century art, as his inspiration. What is significant here is the way the spectator is given room to reflect on what is left out of the scene as well as what is included. Strindberg doesn't advocate the reconstruction of real rooms, simply sufficient attention to actual experience of the material world so as engage and activate the imagination of the audience.

Konstantin Stanislavsky's use of authentic objects[8] in his productions might also be considered as part of an empirical approach to seeing. For the 1901 production of Chekhov's *Three Sisters* at the Moscow Art Theatre, the designer Viktor Simov located commonplace objects to reflect "the ponderous pettiness of provincial life" (Senelick 1999: 60). These objects included

> a damask tablecloth, provincial wallpaper, yellowed painted floors, a threadbare Turkoman carpet, a cuckoo clock that was slow to strike and then counted out the time hurriedly, as if embarrassed.
>
> *(Senelick 1999: 61)*

The scenography evoked the daily life of the middle classes through particular details of the color and texture and the wear and tear of real objects. It was intended to appeal directly to audiences who, through the medium of the objects, would be able recognize their own lives in the one that was being depicted on the stage. The bedroom in Act 3 was "cluttered with furniture, and [had] little apparent architectural harmony" (Gottlieb 1984: 25). The wealth of surface details and the apparent lack of pictorial organization is reminiscent of Jay's Baconian model of vision. The effect is not simply to illustrate the type of house that the Prozorov family are living in, but to draw attention to the way that objects are conceived as part of the fabric of their lives. Laurence Senelick says that the Art Theatre's aim was "quotidian materiality" rather than "self-sufficient displays of painterly technique" (Senelick 1999: 80) but this overlooks the potential of objects to evoke feeling as well as simply describe. These particular objects were considered by Simov to be capable of evoking a particular milieu where "colors fade, thoughts become debased, energy gets smothered in a dressing-gown, ardour is stifled by a housecoat, talent dries up like a plant without water" (Simov quoted in Gottlieb 1984: 24). The affective potential of real objects and materials marks a significant point in the development of western scenography and the fascination with the agentic capacity of apparently inanimate things has been a persistent feature of practice since then.

Nonetheless, the appeal of a "world of objects" can seem superficial. The delight in objects and the "valorization of material surfaces" in Dutch painting is a representation of the "fetishism of commodities" that serves a market economy (Jay 1988: 15). The enthusiasm for Loutherbourg's scenographies, for example, coincides with a period of increasing leisure travel and cultural consumption for an expanding bourgeoisie. The appeal of the accurate realization of designs that make reference to actual places, existing architectures, and the objects and materials that belong with them, is still evident in contemporary practice. Bunny Christie's designs for *The White Guard* (2010) and *The Cherry Orchard* (2011) for the National Theatre, UK, both took inspiration from paintings of evocative interiors and from existing buildings and were realized using subtlety and variation in color, texture, and translucency to produce an ultra-realistic effect of surface texture. However, the discussion of these designs on the National Theatre website focuses on the skills of recreation, fetishizing the surface detail and the lifelike replication of it rather than exploring their affective potential.

But scenic naturalism has been influential, in Western theatre at least, in establishing a more profound connection between the look and the action of the environment. Raymond Williams explains that

> in high naturalism the lives of the characters have soaked into their environment . . . Moreover, the environment has soaked into the lives. The relations between men and things are at a deep level interactive, because what is there physically, as a space or means for living, is a whole shaped and shaping social history.
>
> *(Williams 1973: 140)*

As far as scenography is concerned, high naturalism goes beyond simply noting the inventory of objects on stage and comparing them with real rooms, real places, and begins to implicate the spectators' embodied experience of the material world. In order to appreciate the reciprocal way in which fictional lives and their environments are intertwined, the spectator is asked to call on their own spatial and tactile memories of the experience of objects and of how particular materials and surfaces feel to the touch. Seeing the movement of materials, for example in a costume, can trigger embodied understanding of the weight of fabric or the effect on the wearer's posture; noting the marks of wear on a piece of furniture can evoke a spectator's tactile memory. In this way an intellectual appreciation of the characters in their environment is supplemented, enriched and possibly even supplanted by visual observation and embodied understanding. So, while a "world of objects" approach to scenographic seeing is sometimes too bound up with the appearance of authentic artifacts, it also contains the possibility of a more profound and embodied connection between theatre and the material world.

Palpable visions

Jay's third model of vision is the "baroque." This he associates with the architecture and painting of the Catholic Counter Reformation of the seventeenth century. "In opposition to the lucid, linear, fixed, planimetric, closed form of the Renaissance . . . the baroque was painterly, recessional, soft-focused, multiple and open" (Jay 1988: 16). Jay refers to Christine Buci-Glucksmann's analysis of the baroque as a "dazzling, disorientating, ecstatic surplus of images" that rejects both the idealized space of the Cartesian tradition and the "faith in the material solidity of the world" demonstrated in the Baconian model. The baroque model of vision has no single guiding philosophy and, moreover, seems to eschew the idea of "intellectual clarity" in favor of "an irreducibly imagistic" approach (ibid.: 16–17).

This fits well with the idea of scenography as collage of images and effects aimed at blending reality and fantasy. Baroque tendencies in scenography might be traced back to the end of the Renaissance period and to scenographers such as Inigo Jones who combined perspective scenery together with a variety of complex stage machinery and opulent costume. Although Jones was influenced and inspired by Renaissance design of the kind practiced by Serlio, he departed from a strict adherence to Serlian principles, "flouting the scientific orderliness of the method in order to achieve something more humane and expressive" (Orrell 1988: 239). But, at the same time, the management of the visual experience in Jones' design for court masques, as in other such masques and ceremonies, was shaped quite specifically in the service of the wealthy patrons. The extravagance of costumes, ingenious changes of scene and astounding effects were a celebration and affirmation of the wealth and power of the court (Sawday 2007: 185). Court masques such as these harness the dazzling display of the baroque as a metaphor for the magnificence and ultimate authority of the court.

Later, in the English theatre of the mid-nineteenth century, when the patrons were the theatre-going public rather than the nobility, Victorian spectacle offers perhaps a more compelling example of the "ecstatic" baroque. This vivid description of a pantomime transformation scene serves as an example of the dazzling imagery that scenography can produce:

> First the 'gauzes' lift slowly one behind the other – perhaps the most pleasing of all scenic effects – giving glimpses of 'the Realms of Bliss,' seen beyond in a tantalizing fashion. Then is revealed a kind of half-glorified country, clouds and banks, evidently concealing much. Always a sort of pathetic and at the same time exultant strain rises, and it repeated as the changes go on . . . Now some more of the banks begin to part slowly showing realms of light, with a few divine beings – fairies – rising slowly here and there . . . Thus it goes on, the lights streaming on full, in every color and from every quarter, in the richest effulgence.
>
> *(Fitzgerald 1881: 89)*

As with the eye-witness accounts from the fifteenth century, there is a complicity in the illusion; the writer combines his understanding of the technologies being deployed with a desire to be transported by the effects. The orientation towards metaphysical and erotic desire chimes with the baroque model where "the body returns to dethrone the disinterested gaze of the disincarnated Cartesian spectator" (Jay 1988: 18).

This "theatre of pure diversion" (Gilder cited in Bratton 2003: 9) is exactly the kind of theatre experience that was seen to undermine theatre's more cerebral aims and to attract a new kind of spectator, "gluttonous . . . clamorous, ill-bred, uncouth" (Filon cited in Bratton 2003: 13). Alongside the cultural and class-based prejudice displayed here, the implication is that spectacular scenography crowds out the more edifying experience of attending to dramatic literature. This sentiment is reinforced by William Bodham Donne, journalist and theatre censor ("Examiner of Plays" 1857–1874) who mocked the popular Victorian taste for "palpable" visions:

> To touch our emotions we need not the imaginatively true but the physically real: the visions which our ancestors saw with the mind's eye, must be embodied for us in palpable forms . . . All must be made palpable to sight, no less than to feeling: and this lack of imagination affects equally both those who enact and those who construct the scene.
>
> *(Cited in Booth 2005: 7)*

Donne suggests that spectacular scenography inhibits the spectators' imaginative engagement with the drama and implies that the arousal of emotion and feeling through the visual elements is a distraction from theatre's proper purpose. Donne's views belong to a longstanding line of criticism of the visual in Western theatre where the text is privileged over the visual (Kennedy 1993: 5). The popular taste for spectacular scenography has also been seen as evidence of its lack of artistic worth (Bratton 2003: 14–15) and the sensuous appeal that the baroque makes to the whole body further compounds this idea of popular spectacle as vulgar or decadent and quite distinct from the values claimed by the dramatic theatre.

However, contemporary postmodernist and postdramatic theatre exhibits a much more favorable view of the scenographic baroque. Hans-Thies Lehmann, in recognizing the importance of Robert Wilson's work, says it is part of a tradition of that which includes "baroque theatre effects," "Jacobean masques," and "Victorian spectacle" where "the phenomenon has priority over the narrative, the effect of the image precedence over the individual actor, and contemplation over interpretation." In Wilson's theatre it is not just static images that are the focus for spectators, but the metamorphosis of images, often accentuated by the slow speed at which they occur. This creates a space of visual "transitions, ambiguities and correspondences" (Lehmann 2006: 80). Wilson's work, like Jay's designation of the baroque is "irreducibly imagistic." It requires the spectator to experience what is actually happening on the stage and frustrates attempts to offer clear readings or narrative unties. Wilson's scenography, along with the scenographies created by artists such as Richard Foreman, Heiner Goebbels, and Societas Raffaello Sanzio (and many others besides) employ an abundance of visual images that expect spectators to "postpone" meaning while they attend to a conglomeration of "sensory impressions" (ibid.: 87). Lehmann gestures towards a phenomenological basis of postdramatic theatrical perception, but he does not pursue this; his focus, instead, is on the forms and compositional structures of postdramatic work where spatial, temporal, and material structures displace dramatic texts. However, he does make it clear that the sensory impressions of postdramatic "visual dramaturgy" has turned the stage into "the arena of reflection on the spectators' act of seeing." Rather than "abandoning oneself to the flow of narration," spectators are invited to involve themselves in a dynamic and "constructive co-producing of the total audio-visual complex of the theatre" (ibid.: 157).

This co-construction is an active engagement with the visual and is at odds with Jay's claims that the baroque "generates only allegories of obscurity and opacity" (Jay 1988: 18). While an active reflection on the process of viewing in postdramatic performance does not necessarily lead to clear-cut messages, the material phenomena of the stage are, nonetheless, the means by which spectators are able to access potential meanings or "concrete, sensuously intensified *perceptibility*" (Lehmann 2008: 99). The spectator's body is significant as part of the way in which scenography might be understood; not simply as a representation of the world, but as a material and spatial environment within which awareness and understanding can be triggered. In order to pursue the idea of the spectator's body as part of the process of visual perception I want to propose a further model: one of embodied spectatorship.

Embodied spectatorship

Each of Jay's three models figures the body of the spectator differently. In Cartesian perspectivalism the spectator's actual body is dismissed and replaced with a disembodied monocular view; in the Baconian "world of objects" model the sensory, tactile experience of the viewing body is summoned up through the detailed observation of visual surfaces; in the baroque model the body of spectator is stimulated or disorientated by an abundance of visual material. With each model the engagement of body and "the carnal density of the observer" (Crary 1988: 43) becomes more apparent. But none of them encompass the idea of a fully "embodied" spectator, that is, a spectator that is positioned as Maurice Merleau-Ponty says, within "the weight, the thickness, the flesh of each color, of each sound, of each tactile texture" (Merleau-Ponty 1968: 114). Furthermore, Jay's three models are predicated on the idea that the act of spectatorship is determined by the artwork and the historical, discursive and social conditions within which it was produced and this tends to assume a passive spectator. Even though there are appeals to the spectator's body that begin to admit the possibility of a more reflective and interactive response to an artwork, Jay's models do not account for the kind of co-constructive experience of contemporary theatre that Lehmann describes.

In film studies, however, Vivian Sobchack has articulated an embodied and phenomenological approach to spectatorship that extends Merleau-Ponty's idea that the body is a material object among all the other objects in the world (Merleau-Ponty 2001: 236). Sobchack proposes that what filmmaker, viewer and the film itself have in common is an "embodied existence [that] inflects and reflects the world as always already significant" (Sobchack 1992: 12). This position recognizes the physiological nature of incarnated vision and the interconnection of visual and other senses[9] and it reinforces the idea of vision as an active interplay of a seeing body and material world within which it is placed (Sobchack 1992: 25). Merleau-Ponty proposes that a "strange system" of exchanges occurs through the correspondences between things looking and the thing being looked at. In the case of paintings, for example, "Quality, light, color, depth, which are there before us, are there only because they awaken an echo in our bodies and because the body welcomes them" (Merleau-Ponty 1993: 125).

This is different from the scopic regimes reviewed so far, where the artwork and the materialist conditions of its production are taken to shape the act of viewing. Here the act of seeing is co-constructive with the thing being seen; the embodied spectator is positioned in a dialogic exchange with the artwork. Like Rancière's emancipated spectator, the embodied spectator is engaged in a process of making sense of the performance "through an unpredictable and irreducible play of associations and disassociations" (Rancière 2007: 279). But the process of "making sense" through embodied understanding needs to be understood in a very different way than Rancière suggests. Rancière's spectators are translators who appropriate the material they can associate with and turn it into their own story; images are understood by being turned into words (Rancière 2007: 280) whereas an embodied model of spectatorship engages with the materials themselves. It proceeds from Merleau-Ponty's philosophy that our contact with the world is "pre-reflective" and is "a function of all our sensory, motor, and affective capacities" as well as our intellectual capacity (Crowther 1993: 102–3) and this accounts for the "sensuously intensified perceptibility" that Lehmann describes (Lehmann 2008: 99). Like film spectatorship, scenographic spectatorship that takes account of the sensory and material dimension offers a model of embodied seeing and an actively engaged spectator. A phenomenological and embodied account of seeing explains how the palpability of vision is the basis of aesthetic experience.

It also opens up the possibility that scenographic materials might have agentic capacity in themselves. In the historical examples of scenography I have referred to so far, the assumption might be that the scenography is activated, given purpose, by human agents, principally the performers; stage objects are mere "props" for actors, stage environments are illustrative fictional spaces for characters who are agents. But as I hope is clear by now, scenographic materials always have the capacity to act on us directly and bodily as well as to signify social and cultural meaning. Embodied spectatorship brings this capacity to the fore and allows that, within an emergent, co-creative process of perception, scenography itself has agency.

Erika Fischer-Lichte says that contemporary performance does not try to control and discipline audiences in the way that it once seemed to do. Instead it pursues an aesthetic of "autopoiesis" (Fischer-Lichte 2008: 39) that operates through the "feedback loop" (Fischer-Lichte 2008: 38) between the performer and spectator. This is particularly apparent where traditional relationships between performers and audience are set aside and roles become blurred, for example in found spaces or "socially-integrated locations" (Fischer-Lichte 2008: 53). In these instances it is apparent that the space itself is an active part of the "self-generating and ever-changing autopoietic feedback loop" (Fischer-Lichte 2008: 50). But autopoiesis is activated not only inter-subjectively, but between human spectators and the performance environment. Between the space of performance, the performers and the spectator the "atmosphere" of the performance is formed (Fischer-Lichte 2008: 116). According to Gernot Böhme, atmospheres establish the basis of aesthetic and perceptual experience and they come about due to the "ecstasy of things." The properties of things (form, extension, volume color, smell, sound) don't just simply define the parameters of things as objects but radiate outwards. A property such as the form of a thing can exert "an external effect. It radiates as it were into the environment, takes away the homogeneity of the surrounding space and fills it with tensions and suggestions of movement" (Böhme 1993: 121). On a bodily level, the ecstasy of things provokes sensual impressions that are "ultimately incommensurable with linguistic expression and only very inadequately describable" yet they form the basis of understanding where the perceived object triggers associations and becomes "interlinked with ideas, memories, sensations and emotions" (Fischer-Lichte 2008: 142).

Since the publication of "Scopic Regimes of Modernity," Martin Jay has lamented what he sees as the displacement of spectatorial distance with the titillating and vertiginous pleasure of sensorial overload. In contemporary culture (films, performance art, fairground rides and exhibitions) he sees a "kinesthetic regime based on rapturous stimulation and participatory immediacy" (Jay 2003: 110) that robs us of a capacity for judgment. Where Fischer-Lichte sees sensual impressions leading to some form of understanding, Jay sees only superficial stimulation. However, Renee van de Vall questions Jay's supposition of critical judgment resting on the achievement of distance between spectator and spectacle. A "phenomenological aesthetics" of contemporary spectatorship doesn't place experiential involvement in opposition to critical reflection. Instead, she says, reflection emerges from within experience (Van de Vall 2008: 109). The "experiential openness" that can be staged by works of art might initiate moments of "reflexive awareness" that might counteract the anaesthetizing tendencies of spectacle that Jay and many others fear (Van de Vall 2008: 131). Vall proposes a "reflexivity in the sphere of the senses" that is continuous with reflexivity in thinking (Van de Vall 2008: 119), and this serves to extend Fischer-Lichte's notion of autopoiesis. In addition to this, an openness to the spectator's experience of scenography should also include an acknowledgement of the agentic capacity of non-human materials.

In a model of embodied vision in the theatre, material elements such as light, volumetric space, smell and sound take on a particular significance. The postdramatic work that Lehmann discusses and contemporary site-specific and immersive theatre more widely (Punchdrunk, Pearson/Brookes, La Fura dels Baus, Teatro da Vertigem) has served to highlight this mode of spectatorship, but it might equally be applied to work such as that made by those pioneers of contemporary scenography such as Adolphe Appia and his idea of rhythmic space, Edward Gordon Craig and architectonic space, or Josef Svoboda's psycho-plastic space. This embodied model underlines the active role that materials can play; the spectator is an active part of the emergence of meaning but so too are the scenographic materials themselves. In that sense, embodied spectatorship not only acknowledges the co-creative capacity that contemporary performance often invites; it also flattens the ontological distinction between subjects and objects so that the act of seeing scenography can be understood as a discursive practice that is rooted in what Karen Barad calls a "posthuman performative" approach (Barad 2007: 135). Following Barad's account, the body of the spectator is not "the fixed dividing line" (ibid.: 136) between itself and other things, human and non-human, and the emerging perceptibility (or autopoiesis) of performance comes about through the iterative "intra-actions" of "matter-in-the-process-of-becoming" (ibid.: 179). Embodied spectatorship recognizes that the event of experiencing scenography is a dynamic and iterative process of intra-action between the materiality of human and non-human where "knowing and being . . . are mutually implicated" (ibid.: 185).

Conclusion

Applying Jay's regimes to scenography reveals some tension between models of vision and the actual experience of viewing. It also reminds us that what we think we see in the theatre is staged and always being challenged because "the scopic drive is always being subverted and displaced" (McAuley 2000: 239). But models of vision assist in thinking through the relationship between the scenography and the spectator and the basis of spectacle as a "bad thing" (Rancière 2007) is revealed in different ways. Cartesian perspectivalism configures the spectator as disembodied and docile, disciplined to accept an idealized image; a "world of things" dwells in commodities and surfaces; and the baroque offers a dazzling and distracting display of excess. But at the same time there are indications that within these broad models other possibilities might be at work, and that rather than vision and action always being in opposition, they might be brought closer together or even merge in a model of embodied spectatorship.

There are some overlaps between embodied spectatorship and other models. The Baconian or "world of objects" that I have associated with scenographic naturalism also draws on embodied experience. The baroque provokes and stimulates embodied looking that might be active and co-constructive and not simply distracting or disorientating. In offering embodied spectatorship as a model of vision for scenography, I am not suggesting we should abandon the others (as Jay and Foster point out, there is merit in considering a plurality of models), but I do want to argue for the need to overhaul and revise entrenched ideas about the passive nature of looking in the theatre and, in particular, the act of looking at scenography. By insisting on the bodily basis of seeing in the theatre we can appreciate the full extent of how scenography activates perception and emergent understanding.

Looking in the theatre is not a purely visual experience. To look at scenography is to apprehend not only illustrations or depictions, but to notice the composition and orchestration of materials and feel the way they work on us at a bodily level. This is a way of knowing and a kind of action because it connects us to our own experience of the world, our memories and imaginations and our experiential understanding of daily life. The effects of theatrical spectacle need not overwhelm us or disable our capacity for reflexive looking. Rather, acknowledging the bodily dimension of looking in the theatre might stir us to an awareness of the processes of spectatorship and point towards the dynamic, co-constructive, and intra-active potential of seeing scenography.

Notes

1 "Scopic regime" is a term coined by Christian Metz. See Metz, Christian 1982. *Psychoanalysis and Cinema: The Imaginary Signifier*, trans. Celia Britton, Annwyl Williams, Ben Brewster and Alfred Guzzetti. London: Macmillan.

2 I am thinking here of recent volumes that include Aronson 2005, Baugh 2013, Hannah and Harsløf 2008 listed above and also Collins, Jane and Nisbet, Andrew 2010, *Theatre and*

Performance Design: A Reader in Scenography. London: Routledge; and Palmer, Scott 2013 *Light*. Basingstoke: Palgrave.

3 There is some debate about the precise nature of the contribution of Vitruvius' ideas to the Renaissance adoption of perspective on the Italian stage and this sits within a broader literature and debate on the history and "discovery, rediscovery or invention" of Renaissance perspective (Jay 1988: 5).

4 Jonathan Crary says that by the 1850s scientists had established that vision is not the result of "an instantaneous intake of an image" but "a complex aggregate of processes of eye movements that provisionally built up the appearance of a stable image" (2001: 290).

5 Orrell points out that this commonplace observation might be challenged by evidence from Sebastiano Serlio's designs (Orrell 1988: 218).

6 *The Stanford Encyclopedia of Philosophy* explains: "The dispute between rationalism and empiricism concerns the extent to which we are dependent upon sense experience in our effort to gain knowledge. Rationalists claim that there are significant ways in which our concepts and knowledge are gained independently of sense experience. Empiricists claim that sense experience is the ultimate source of all our concepts and knowledge." Available online at: http://plato.stanford.edu/entries/rationalism-empiricism/ (accessed 6 April 2016).

7 Although Martin Jay's scopic regimes are each associated with a particular period in painting, he sees them as models that operate throughout the period of modernism and beyond.

8 Stanislavski's approach was criticised by Meyerhold for being obsessively over-elaborate (see McKinney and Butterworth 2009: 38) and by Chekhov for trivialising the text (see McKinney and Butterworth, 2009: 91).

9 Jonathan Crary (1990) has written extensively about the discoveries of "subjective vision" and the implications for art in the nineteenth century, when scientists discovered the operation of vision was not separate and objective like a camera but located in the body and influenced by the other senses.

References

Alberti, Leon Battista 1972 [1435]. *On Painting and On Sculpture: The Latin Texts of "De Pittura" and "De Statua,"* trans. Cecil Grayson. London: Phaidon.

Allain, Paul and Harvie, Jen 2014. *The Routledge Companion to Theatre and Performance* (2nd ed.). London: Routledge.

Alpers, Svetlana 1983. *The Art of Describing: Dutch Art in the Seventeenth Century*. Chicago, IL: University of Chicago Press.

Aronson, Arnold 2005. *Looking into the Abyss: Essays on Scenography*. Ann Arbor: University of Michigan Press.

Bablet, Denis 1977. *The Revolutions of Stage Design in the 20th Century*. New York: L. Amiel.

Barad, Karen 2007. *Meeting the Universe Halfway: Quantum Physics and the Entanglement of Matter and Meaning*. Durham, NC: Duke University Press.

Baugh, Christopher 1990. *Garrick and Loutherbourg*. Cambridge: Chadwyck-Healey.

Baugh, Christopher 2009. "Scenography and Technology." In *The Cambridge Companion to British Theatre, 1730–1830*, edited by Jane Moody and Daniel O'Quinn, 43–56. Cambridge: Cambridge University Press.

Baugh, Christopher 2013. *Theatre, Performance and Technology: The Development and Transformation of Scenography* (2nd ed.). Basingstoke: Palgrave.

Baugh, Christopher 2017. "'Devices of Wonder': Globalizing Technologies in the Process of scenography." In *Scenography Expanded: An Introduction to Contemporary Performance Design*, edited by Joslin McKinney and Scott Palmer. London: Bloomsbury Methuen.

Benedetto, Stephen di 2010. *The Provocation of the Senses in Contemporary Theatre*. London: Routledge.

Berger, John 1972. *Ways of Seeing*. London: British Broadcasting Corporation and Penguin Books.

Bleeker, Maaike 2008. *Visuality in the Theatre*. London: Routledge.

Böhme, Gernot 1993. "Atmosphere as the Fundamental Concept of a New Aesthetics." *Thesis Eleven* 36: 113–26.

Booth, Michael 2005. "Public Patronage and Pictorial Taste: Victorian Scenery." In *Patronage, Spectacle and the Stage*, edited by Irene Eynat-Confino and Eva Sormova. Prague: Theatre Institute Prague.
Bratton, Jacky 2003. *New Readings in Theatre History*. Cambridge: Cambridge University Press.
Carlson, Marvin 1993. *Places of Performance: The Semiotics of Theatre Architecture*. Ithaca: Cornell University Press.
Crary, Jonathan 1988. "Modernizing Vision." In *Vision and Visuality*, edited by Hal Foster, 29–44. New York: The New Press.
Crary, Jonathan 1990. *Techniques of the Observer: On Vision and Modernity in the Nineteenth Century*. Cambridge, MA: MIT Press.
Crary, Jonathan 2001. *Suspensions of Perception: Attention, Spectacle, and Modern Culture*. Cambridge, MA: MIT Press.
Crowther, Paul 1993. *Art and Embodiment: From Aesthetics to Self-Consciousness*. Oxford: Oxford University Press.
Edgerton, Samuel 1975. *The Renaissance Rediscovery of Linear Perspective*. New York: Harper and Rowe.
Finotti, Fabio 2010. "Perspective and Stage Design, Fiction and Reality in the Italian Renaissance Theater of the Fifteenth Century." *Renaissance Drama*, 36/37: 21–42.
Fischer-Lichte, Erika 2008. *The Transformative Power of Performance*. Abingdon: Routledge.
Fitzgerald, Percy 1881. *The World Behind the Scenes*. London: Chatto and Windus.
Foster, Hal (Ed.) 1988. *Vision and Visuality*. New York: The New Press.
Gottlieb, Vera 1984. *Chekhov in Performance in Russia and Soviet Russia*. Cambridge: Chadwyck-Healey.
Hannah, Dorita and Olav Harsløf 2008. *Performance Design*. Copenhagen: Museum Tusculanum Press.
Jameson, Frederic 1990. *Signatures of the Visible*. London: Routledge.
Jay, Martin 1988. "Scopic Regimes of Modernity." In *Vision and Visuality*, edited by Hal Foster, 3–23. New York: The New Press.
Jay, Martin 2003. *Refractions of Violence*. London: Routledge.
Johnson, Dominic 2014. *Theatre and the Visual*. Basingstoke: Palgrave.
Kennedy, Dennis 1993. *Looking at Shakespeare: A Visual History of Twentieth Century Performance*. Cambridge: Cambridge University Press.
Lehmann, Hans-Thies 2006. *Postdramatic Theatre*, trans. Karen Jürs-Munby. London: Routledge.
Lotker, Sodja and Richard Gough 2013. "On Scenography" editorial. *Performance Research* 18(3): 3–6.
McAuley, Gay 2000. *Space in Performance: Making Meaning in the Theatre*. Ann Arbor: University of Michigan Press.
McKinney, Joslin 2013. "Scenography, spectacle and the body of the spectator." *Performance Research* 18 (3): 63–74.
McKinney, Joslin and Butterworth, Philip 2009. *Cambridge Companion to Scenography*. Cambridge: Cambridge University Press.
Merleau-Ponty, Maurice 1968 [1964]. *The Visible and the Invisible*, translated by Alphonso Lingis. Evanston, IL: Northwestern University Press.
Merleau-Ponty, Maurice 1993 [1961]. "Eye and Mind." In *The Merleau-Ponty Aesthetics Reader: Philosophy and Painting*, translated by Michael. B. Smith, edited by Galen A. Johnson, 121–49. Evanston, IL: Northwestern University Press.
Merleau-Ponty, Maurice 2001 [1945]. *Phenomenology of Perception*, translated by Colin Smith. London: Routledge.
Mohler, Frank 2008. "Medici Wings: The Scenic Wing Change in Renaissance Florence." *Theatre Design and Technology*, Fall 2008: 58–64.
Orrell, John 1988. *The Human Stage: English Theatre Design, 1567–1640*. Cambridge: Cambridge University Press.
Panofsky, Erwin 1991 [1927]. *Perspective as a Symbolic Form*, translated by Christopher Wood. New York: Zone Books.
Rancière, Jacques 2007. "The Emancipated Spectator." *Artforum* 45 (7): 270–81
Sawday, Jonathan 2007. *Engines of the Imagination: Renaissance Culture and the Rise of the Machine*. Abingdon: Routledge.

Senelick, Laurence 1999. *The Chekhov Theatre*. Cambridge: Cambridge University Press
Sobchack, Vivian Carol 1992. *The Address of the Eye: A Phenomenology of Film Experience*. Oxford: Princeton University Press.
Southern, Richard 1962. *The Seven Ages of the Theatre*. London: Faber and Faber
Strindberg, August 1888. *Miss Julie* [play].
Trimingham, Melissa 2013. "Touched By Meaning." In *Affective Performance and Cognitive Science*, edited by Nicola Shaughnessy. London: Bloomsbury.
Vall, Renée van de 2008. *At the Edges of Vision: A Phenomenological Aesthetics of Contemporary Spectatorship*. Aldershot: Ashgate.
Vitruvius 1914. *The Ten Books on Architecture*, translated by Morris Hicky Morgan. Cambridge: Harvard University Press.
Williams, Raymond 1973. *Drama from Ibsen to Brecht*. London: Penguin.

9

ABSOLUTE, ABSTRACT, AND ABJECT

Learning from the event-space of the historical avant-garde

Dorita M. Hannah

> Have you not heard of the madman who lit a lantern in the bright morning hours, ran to the market place, and cried incessantly, "I seek God! I seek God!" . . .
>
> "Wither is God" he cried. "I shall tell you. We have killed him – you and I. All of us are his murderers . . . Who gave us the sponge to wipe away the entire horizon? . . . Is there any up or down left? Are we not straying through an infinite nothing? Do we not feel the breath of empty space? . . . God is dead. God remains dead. And we have killed him.
>
> *(Friedrich Nietzsche,* The Gay Science *[1882])*

The nineteenth century was brought to a close with the echoes of Nietzsche's declaration that "God is dead" (1974: 95; [1882] 1961: 12), an announcement foreshadowing the approaching existential crisis of the twentieth century and signaling the end of a perspectivally constructed view of space, the body's central position within that construction, and – critical to this essay – the end of *scenography*; a word that belonged to "art," "architecture," and "theatre," spatially and representationally, for over 300 years. Published in 1882, the philosopher's statement also followed the recent completion of two significant theater buildings: Garnier's Paris Opéra (1875) and Wagner's Bayreuth Festspielhaus (1876) – monuments directly associated with male titans of architecture and music – which bridged the end of one era and the beginning of another, yet neither addressing scenography's increasing inability, along with live performance, to be encapsulated within a framed stage.

However, Nietzsche's philosophy didn't advocate ends, but rather eternal returns, where the iterable is never the same. Nor did he believe in the resounding "great event" but in shifts that created new values (Nietzsche 1966: 131). Gilles Deleuze acknowledges the philosopher's proclamation, first outlined in *Gay Science* (Nietzsche 1882), as "*the* dramatic proposition *par excellence*" through its denial of an identifiable unity from which all the differences of the world emanate and to which they return (Deleuze 2006: 152). Reflecting the general intensification of doubt in the eternal, in order to place more faith in the present, God's death could also be considered *the* decisive modern event; "an event with a multiple sense" (ibid.: 4) fracturing that entity which was previously considered singular, including our spatial perception. As architect, Daniel Libeskind, wrote over a century later, "Space is not one, but space is plural, space is a heterogeneity, a difference" (Libeskind 2000: 68).

Considering the impact of *evental* thinking as *spacing*, this chapter focuses on the influence of Europe's historical avant-garde on theatre architecture: whereby sceno-*graphy* as spatial scripting[1] – initially predicated on a centralized view of the Monarch's immobile all-seeing-I standing in for the all-seeing-eye of God – could no longer be contained within geometrically constructed vistas on the prescribed stage, resulting in new spatial models that undermined architecture's will to fixity, stability, and endurance. In concentrating on modernism's philosophical, political, and perceptual revolutions I identify three distinctive attitudes to performance space – loosely cohering around the avant-garde movements of symbolism, constructivism, and surrealism – that emerged between 1872 and 1947.

Termed *absolute*, *abstract*, and *abject* these revolutionary spatial models challenged the nineteenth-century auditorium, which could no longer house the theatrical and technological upheavals that were occurring. While reflecting the modernist "crisis" of representation and the emergence of a spatial dis-ease, the models also propose alternative architectural strategies for facilitating performance and return us to contemporary discussions around the "scenographic turn" – integrating the visual, spatial, and performing arts – or what Thea Brejzek calls "(re-)turns" that emerge from crises as significant spatial "shifts": one of which is the early twentieth-century's "passage into modernity" that produced Europe's historical avant-garde (Brejzek 2015: 17).

This critical avant-garde period includes late nineteenth-century symbolism and political revolution as well as the repercussions of two world wars. The first date of 1872 coincides with the start of construction of Richard Wagner's Festspielhaus in Bayreuth and the publication of Nietzsche's *Birth of Tragedy*, while 1947 marks Antonin Artaud's un-broadcast performance of *To Have Done with the Judgment of God* and the publication of Sigfried Giedion's *Mechanization Takes Command*. The 75-year time-span, which indicates a trajectory between two declamations of modernism's loss of faith,[2] also takes us between the technological innovations of the industrial revolution to the technological slaughter of the Second World War.

The setting for this chapter's discussion is therefore characterized by modernism's preoccupation with the metropolis, new technologies, and a rejection of tradition. "Shocks" elicited by the mechanization of transport, communication, and war led to the collapse of Cartesian perspectivalism, which defined and stabilized the spatial image of stage and architecture, resulting in a tendency toward fragmentation, ambiguity, and irrationality. The revolutions of Lenin combined with the dreams of Freud to create implosions and explosions of socio-politics and psychoanalysis that undermined both the theatrical *conventions* and the material *walls* of the melodramatic realistic theatre. The well-constructed playhouse seemed as meaningless as the well-made bourgeois play; principally challenged by the avant-garde's writing and unbuilt proposals, out of which the absolute, abstract and abject spatiotemporal models emerged, which not only illuminate theatre history but also, hopefully, inspire new approaches to contemporary performance space.

Before outlining these spatio-temporal models, it's necessary to establish a general theory of event-space in which the event, actualized in architectural space, transforms the built environments – in this case the theatre's auditorium – through the element of time from passive, homogeneous container/object into something more uneven, contracting, and expanding. Space, saturated with spaces, becomes a continual unfolding defined by time and multiplied by an "accelerated succession of actions" (de Certeau 1988: 118). Buildings, no longer perceived as works of architecture, are experienced as and through "spacing": preceding action . . . as action.

Avant-garde event-space

> The tendency of twentieth-century art is to revolve around the act rather than the work, because the act, as the intense power of beginning, can only be thought in the present.
>
> *(Badiou 2007: 136)*

Referring to its many avant-gardes, Alain Badiou suggests that the twentieth century "managed – through its artists, scientists, militants and lovers – to be Action itself" (Badiou 2007: 147). But amid the commotion created by these riotous movements dedicated to deploying various artistic genres for radical acts, political agitation, and social activism, resides a relative silence from architecture's so-called vanguard, especially in the first half of the century when the term avant-garde was most resistant, adamant, and potent. It would appear that, whereas artists were fixated on the fleeting act, architecture maintained its focus on the enduring work through a new classical modernism. While theatre addressed the pervading psychosis and revolutionary fervor by literally playing it out, architecture reacted by attempting to make whole that which was shattered and establishing utopian ideals that had little place for the ideals of the theatrical avant-garde. Yet even as the Modern Movement sought to industrialize, control, and harmonize space, the avant-garde wished to radically undermine it, celebrating the sacrificial body dancing amid the debris. Their theatrical will-to-destruction stood in direct opposition to modern architecture's will-to-creation.

Last century's relationship between architecture and theatre was therefore a troubled one, with the architectural rejected by theatre and the theatrical negated by architecture. However, although revolutions of the historical avant-garde did not always coincide with the architectural reforms of modernism, the gaps and overlaps between the two discourses provide new ways of perceiving and producing theatre architecture, here discussed more broadly as *event-space*: a term attributed to Swiss "neo avant-garde" architect Bernard Tschumi and developed more fully in my book, *Event-Space: Theater Architecture and the Historical Avant-garde*, as the intersection between architectural theory (as the discourse of space) and performance theory (as the discourse of events).[3]

As a compound term, event-space combines the disciplines of performance and architecture through the hyphen – a punctuation mark that simultaneously separates and joins while enacting a break or interruption. In *Of Grammatology*, Jacques Derrida aligns this dynamic action in punctuation to "spacing" that "speaks the articulation of space and time, the becoming-space of time and the becoming-time of space" (Derrida 1997: 68).[4] The hyphen provides a necessary performative membrane holding the fluid from the solid, the dynamic from the static – event from space. As an expressive interval, the simple dash adopts a performative gesture reflecting the creative and conflicting relationship between the fields of performance and architecture, forming an-other space for productive expression.

In *Architectures of Time*, Sanford Kwinter insists that architecture confront its character as "an *illocutionary event*, or at the very least as an element inseparable from and in constant interface with the world of force, will, action and history" (Kwinter 2001: 14). He notes that this idea of the evental signaled a break with architectural history in which past epochs expressed their "will to form" (ibid.: 13). Through last century's spatiotemporal revolutions in science, arts, and communication, architecture is now perceived as an intimate system of forces giving shape and rhythm to everyday life via "micro-architectures" and "macro-architectures" derived from spatial practices (as in specific embodied actions of occupation) that are both private and political.[5] Kwinter outlines how these modernist revolutions shifted the static *spatialization of time* to a more dynamic *temporalization of space* through an emphasis on movement, relativity, and duration.[6] Architecture, no longer recognized as a fixed, eternal entity, is rendered performative, realigning it as active *becoming* rather than passive *being*.

Approaching space by way of the transitory event – whether *historic* (epic incidents), *aesthetic* (theatrical displays), or *banal* (daily occurrences) – exposes a complex system of active forces that undermine architecture's traditional role as a fixed, durable object designed to order space and those who inhabit it. As a multiplicitous *event* in motion, space (both actual and virtual) is an intricate and active player in our everyday lives: most profoundly experienced in theatre's concentrated event, which negotiates the site of lived reality with the more inventive territories of myth and the imagination.

As a contemporary lens for re-viewing the twentieth-century crisis in theatre architecture, where the built form was negated in favor of more non-representational spaces, event-space facilitates the consideration of architectural performativity generally and performance space specifically; establishing not what architecture-as-object *passively is*, but what as dynamic-space it *actively does*. This general theory of spatial performativity, emerging from the specificity of performance space, establishes the built environment housing the event as an event itself and an integral driver of experience. By virtue of its "taking place," theatre architecture becomes Derrida's "event of spacing" (Derrida 1986)[7] *par excellence*: a two-fold act of both the scenographer/architect (designing) and the performer/participant (inhabiting).[8]

A definitive twentieth-century model for performance space remains elusive, although, despite experimentation with varying flexible formats in the latter half of last century (thrust, arena, transverse, and promenade), the persistent form of a rationally planned fan-shaped or shoe-box theatre – in which all seats face the proscenium/end stage in an auditorium focusing on clear sight lines, comfort, and acoustics – tends to dominate, alongside the ubiquitous black box studio that replicates the stage itself as a spatial void within which theatrical images are manufactured. This was a direct legacy of Richard Wagner's Festspielhaus at Bayreuth, a coherent model that opened in 1876 and was embraced by architecture's Modern Movement. Yet as David Wiles suggests, "Theatre architecture turned out to be one of modernism's greatest failures, flexible, versatile theatres stripped of social messages proving a conceptual impossibility. The *machine a jouer* proved as chimeric as Le Corbusier's *machines á vivre*" (Wiles 2003: 22).

Garnier and Wagner's late nineteenth-century glory machines[9] – the former a spatial feast of spectatorial distraction to which the latter reacted by establishing a so-called democratic model that focused the audience on a reinforced proscenium – both privileged the framed perspectival stage construction; simultaneously distancing and centralizing the viewer in the event while integrating the monumental architecture of the house with the pictorial architectonics of scenery. The plane of the proscenium forms both window and mirror, beyond which a perspectival world is artificially constructed through spatial collapse and distortion. This apprehension of a spatial continuum via geometric projection is dependent on a horizon line and vanishing point where "infinity, aesthetics, mathematics, and theology meet on a unified plane whose grandeur and perfection symbolizes God himself" (Weiss 1995: 59). However, as Nietzsche's madman claimed, the horizon had been wiped away and the vanishing point had opened up to reveal the "infinite nothing" of a gaping void; undermining hitherto rational, stable, and homogenous space, which assumed the sovereignty of vision through a single immobile eye and the mathematization of psychophysiological space (Panofsky 1991: 29–30).[10] The proscenium's spatial scripting – dividing audience and stage action – was being challenged and, as Max Herrmann has discussed, the idea of theatre as a "festival" and therefore "event" had already begun to take hold.[11]

Asserting the avant-garde as modernism's volatile edges working to destabilize the fixity of architecture and bring it more in line with the flux of performance, what follows is the isolation and exploration of three distinctive spatial models that were seldom brought to fruition in built form: *Absolute Space*, as exemplified by the atmospheric, universal landscapes of Edward Gordon Craig and Adolphe Appia, the latter who managed to build such an environment in the Hellerau Festspielhaus; *Abstract Space*, condensed in the technology-focused propositions of constructivist architects, such as Walter Gropius' design of the Total Theater for Erwin Piscator that proffers an architectural machine; and *Abject Space*, called upon by Antonin Artaud and Georges Bataille to enact a physical revolt against architecture's denial of the visceral and uncontainable body, encapsulated in Frederick Kiesler's Endless Theater, signaling a failure in the early twentieth-century utopian projects of both architecture and theatre. These revolutionary spatial models challenged the nineteenth-century auditorium that could no longer house the theatrical, socio-political and technological upheavals that were occurring. Each of the three spatial models (invariably containing spatialities of the other two) forms an archetype that is haunted by yet an-*other* event-space, emerging from it to develop over the century as the black box, industrial site and found space.

Absolute space: dark landscapes and the constructed void

Posited as a spatial paradigm that emerged from French symbolist theatre, absolute space is much more than a radically simplified stage. Borrowing Henri Lefebvre's term "absolute space," as a dimensionless space of "invisible fullness" (Lefebvre 1991: 49), this immersive and mobile spatiality that resisted containment and an ocularcentric focus was taken up by the European Symbolists based in Paris during the 1890s and reinforced further by the scenographic visions of Edward Gordon Craig and Adolphe Appia, who were influenced by the rhythmic movement explorations of Isadora Duncan and Émile Jaques-Dalcroze.

While naturalist drama contained the pictorial scene via the fourth wall (transparent to audience and opaque to performer), the symbolists acknowledged the impossibility of sealing off the flowing and fluctuating forces emanating from the abyssal space of the stage, which Wagner had established for "scenic pictures that seem to rise from an ideal world of dreams" (Wagner 1896: 328). No longer part of a multi-leveled audience, wrapped around and within its own distracted gaze, the maestro had disciplined spectators by arranging them in rows on the steeply raked plane, eradicating side galleries and suspending them in an immersive darkness where the dominance of the contained image is troubled and released through the uncontainable element of sound. The ensuing symbolists revealed (and reveled in) the absolute space of the theatrical void, previously marked by the infinitesimal signification of perspective's vanishing point, which was no longer centered on a contained horizon within the unified spatiality of a proscenium stage.[12]

Resisting realism and naturalism, the nineteenth-century symbolists sacralized the stage in an attempt to recuperate the unrepresentable absolute through a negation of traditional theatrical representation. Inhabiting a vertiginous no-man's land, they delighted in a Nietzschean "breath of empty space" where the senses were deliberately disordered. The stage became a nonrepresentational psychic landscape; the drama of the abyss that opens out to infinity. As Daniel Gerould points out, they seemed intent on retelling and revising the parable of Plato's Cave, one of the earliest "landscapes of the mind" (Gerould 2001: 318), where the internal darkness resonates with and is dependent on its counterpart, the external expanse of light.

For these artists the empty space was not simply a stripping bare to make way for innumerable fabricated worlds, but a means of both expressing and facing the breach that had opened up toward the end of the nineteenth century. Predicated on movement, openness, and flexibility, architecture and scenography are folded into universal landscapes, which presage the abstract spaces of the Modern Movement and infuse them with performative qualities that challenge their static rationality.

The symbolists aimed to render the stage itself a suspended site out of which symbolic worlds emerge. The stage provided an empty space to be filled and emptied, akin to the space of the imagination. As an abyssal realm, the stage is a place for imaginary voyages between the *horror vacui* of the void's emptiness and the pleasure of submitting to a space without coordinates or gravity.

It would be easy to defer to the archetype of the black box studio, which came to represent experimental theatre space in the second half of the twentieth century, as the definitive empty space without coordinates and horizon: described by Marvin Carlson as "a featureless box filled with light and abstract figures" (Carlson 1996: 196–7) and by George C. Izenour as an "uncommitted space" that refuses architecture entirely in favor of an experimental "of-the-moment" approach by the artist aided by kinetic systems for altering formats (Izenour 1977: 103). Built as an instrumentalized theatrical void that suspends notions of time and place, the black box – associated with the second-wave theatrical avant-garde – presents a symbolic location cut off from the concrete world. Complemented by its visual arts counterpart – the white cube gallery – it has sought to construct emptiness, silence, and lack through an apparent dematerialization of form facilitated by the simple absence of color and detail.

While the symbolist notion of a placeless, timeless site, which evades location and exceeds borders, resists the emphatic presence of typologically fixed auditorium architecture, it tends to distil the multiple spatialities of the work into performative architectonics that worked with an audience's imagination to complete the places it evoked. Merging mysticism, exile, and an interest in rhythmic movement, their integration of scenography and architecture establishes the "universal landscape," reflected in Isadora and Raymond Duncan's Kopanos Temple (Athens, 1903), Appia's Festspielhaus Hellerau (Dresden, 1913), and Copeau's Théâtre du Vieux-Colombier (Paris, 1920). The performance landscapes built on stage by Appia and Craig were ideal countries[13] – universal to place and time and presaging the utopias of the modernist movement – yet as sacred-secular spaces, they were also cast adrift within the imagination of those occupying the performances for a limited time. Like Sir Thomas More's original utopia, these non-existent island spaces re-presented an ideal: "Considered in itself – absolutely – absolute space is located nowhere. It has no place because it embodies all places, and has a strictly symbolic existence" (Lefebvre 1991: 236).

Absolute Spaces, as atmospheric settings, defy containment, especially on the stage where they leak, drift, and hover, resisting the frame that binds the image. Like the vibratory ether that spreads around us so do these environments, which suggest an unlimited spatiality as they meld and dissolve into an infinity of blinding light, confounding mist or deep shadows. This is reinforced by the visual representations of Craig's "Architectonic Scene" and Appia's "Rhythmic Spaces" that tend to ignore, and therefore deemphasize, the proscenium arch. Their ambient drawings – seeking to capture light's musicality through movement – imply the frame of the image was only established to hold in the scene on the page, the atmospheres of which are designed to envelop spectators and performers alike. Such theatrical atmospherics also trouble the theatre architecture by surrounding, clinging, and seeming to emanate from its physical form; extending the dramatic setting and binding the stage with the auditorium, which itself becomes indistinct as a material container. No longer scenery or setting these evocative environments become an indeterminate architecture, eradicating the proscenium boundary and including all in a unified theatrical ambit. This is best encapsulated in Craig's proposal for *The St. Matthew Passion* (1914), which occupied him for many years and was never realized in built form, and Appia's contribution to the Hellerau Festspielhaus, a fruitful collaboration between Heinrich Tessenow (architect), Alexander von Salzmann (light artist), and Jacques-Dalcroze (choreographer). *The St. Matthew Passion* proposed a complex, multilevel, permanent structure of stairways, bridges, platforms, and receding arches, all in a unified architectural setting beyond which lay a limitless field of light. This glowing arena was artfully achieved in the short-lived dreamscape of Hellerau (itself meaning "shining meadow") with its pale, backlit, linen-covered walls and "practicables": a kit of mobile architectonic parts for creating "terrains," which, not "merely the part of the stage walked upon by the actor" (Appia and Beacham 1993: 49), enfolded audience and performers in a rhythmic atmosphere of shifting, diffuse, and formative light, operated from Salzmann's "light organ."

The absolute space of late Romanticism was an attempt to stay the accelerating interruptions of modernity by seeking a space from which to escape its continuing alienation. This came together most profoundly with the architecture of the Deutscher Werkbund in Hellerau, a briefly lived attempt at Utopia that resisted industrialization's totalizing force through an emphasis on the intersection of arts and crafts, at the center of which was staged the joyous rhythmic body. As architectural historian and theorist Manfredo Tafuri writes, "The city and the industrial universe were not considered as effects or causes of the destruction of values or of the advent of an anguished chaos but as premises for a new totality, for the conservation of culture brought about by absorbing its antithesis, civilization" (Tafuri and Dal Co 1986: 84). However, by the time Hellerau's Festspielhaus had been built, this notion of an integrated industrialized metropolis with self-contained forms had been fragmented, and the cubist movement exploded the European art world profoundly affecting architecture and its will to a synthesized spatial object. The new type of spacing that emerged to shatter and desacralize the absolute space of artistic unity was that of interruption rather than suspension, with its attendant move from *poesis* to *techne*, as both architecture and theatre took on the scientific age.

Abstract space: impossible machines + an architecture of alienation

> The contemporary theater architect should set himself the aim to create a great keyboard for light and space, so objective and adaptable in character that it would respond to any imaginable vision of a stage director; a flexible building, capable of transforming and refreshing the mind by its spatial impact alone.
>
> *(Walter Gropius,* Theater of the Bauhaus*)*

The avant-garde that emerged after World War I replaced the earlier quest for an unalienated space with a desire to harness the chaotic nature of an increasingly alienating world and its inherent qualities of defamiliarization and interruption. The symbolist stage, as a rhythmic landscape out-of-time, was too internal and ethereal for a more politically motivated avant-garde, which demanded an activist stage to operate as a mobile and open network. The shift was therefore from a focus on absolute space to that of abstract space posited by Henri Lefebvre as the "space of modernity" – "at once homogeneous and divided, at once unified and fragmented" – which provokes a dialectic spacing to be played out (Lefebvre 1991: 306–8). This was evidenced in the utopian move toward constructivism; celebrating art, life, and history itself as a construction, where the city was acknowledged, in the words of Sergei Eisenstein, as a "montage of attractions" (Eisenstein 1991: 87) in which incidents can be isolated amid its distracted complexity.

While architecture's Modern Movement reinforced abstract space as a *tabula rasa* from which to build a brave new world, the constructivists played with contradictions and divisions in abstract space, exposing its inherent theatricality. The theatre entered the street scene and the street scene entered the theatre. However, the theatrical, artistic, and architectural avant-garde operating between last century's two world wars productively utilized the disruptive techniques of modernity's estrangement to explore alternative event spaces that begin to articulate an *architecture of alienation*. This was particularly played out by the Russian constructivists and within the Bauhaus of the Weimar Republic. Architecture provided a fertile laboratory within which to test their ideas, utilizing "construction" as their "favorite theoretical instrument" (Michaud 2000: 310–11). They were architects not only of the stage but also of new social relationships, discovering a means of mastering the new "Machine Age" in an attempt to create harmony and unity within the industrial environment.

Emerging out of the industrial revolution are the proposed theatres of avant-garde directors, Vsevolod Meyerhold (who worked with architects, Sergei Vakhtangov and Mikhail Barkhin) and Erwin Piscator (who collaborated with ex-Bauhaus director, Walter Gropius) that aimed to transform the auditorium into a machine-for-action. Meyerhold's 1932 collaboration – completely eliminating the proscenium and exposing the back of the stage with a balcony of doors to dressing rooms – was realized as a steeply raked amphitheatre wrapping a highly mechanized stage comprised of two turntables. This was clearly influenced by Gropius' unrealized *Total Theater* (1927) for Piscator, in which the audience could directly face, partially embrace, or fully surround an acting zone defined by a fixed stage and a double-revolve, comprised of a small turntable offset within a larger one. Revolutionary in its ability to create multiple stages and flexible formats, the Total Theater's radicality lies in an extensive scenic environment facilitated by mobile stage wagons within an encircling aisle defined by columns between which screens could be stretched for projection, as well as the domed ceiling, which expanded the stage cyclorama into the entire auditorium as an enveloping surface for moving images. This three-dimensionality, reinforced by vertical stages at variable heights, created by lowering scaffolding structures from above, would transform the theatre into a space in which performance is totally enfolding: "the projection surface (cinema) is superseded by the projection space . . . and this space, filled with illusions created by the projectors, itself becomes the scene of events" (Gropius 1963: 183).

In 1924, Frederick Kiesler had managed to build his Space Stage (Raumbühne) via curation of Vienna's "International Exhibition of New Theater Techniques"; an ellipsoid multilevel construction of curving ramps, stairs, ladders, and elevator that wrapped a spiral tower, the dynamics of which was similarly explored by Meyherhold and Lissitzsky as a radical integration of staging and auditorium architecture in their unrealized proposal for *I Want a Child* (1928–9). These stage machines as scenographic architectures, which utilized techniques of collage and assemblage, shared a mutual fascination with the anti-institutional spaces of the circus, fairground, and variety hall. They exploited the industrialized metropolis to incorporate the anti-mechanical, the revolt of the object, spatial fragmentation, disruptive techniques, and a disordering of the senses – all incompatible with architecture's inherent objective to build a safe, new world.

The eventual legacy of Europe's constructivists for theatre architecture was not new theatrical machines but the eventual adaptation of historic industrial sites by grafting new technology into an existing fabric. These conversions proliferated in the latter half of the twentieth century. Those who adapted such buildings – invariably warehouses, power stations, army sheds, and factories – were not only fascinated with industrial architecture as a space of performance or exhibition, but also saw them as technological icons. This equated the machines of the Victorian Industrial Age with those that followed them, referred to by Reyner Banham as the "machines of the First Machine Age" (Banham 1962: 11). No longer "light, subtle, clean" (ibid.) these buildings figure in the collective awareness of a mechanized past and a failed utopian dream; constituting a threat of estrangement that both haunts and delights exiled postmodern subjects, bringing them home through the *unhomely*. As an outmoded machine the industrial building reawakens us to the failed dream of the apparatus and a lost time when artists and engineers sang the praises of an industrialized utopia.

Abject space: un-containable bodies and an architecture of cruelty

It is on the limit where the avant-garde sited themselves in the years between the two world wars, and it was at the limits where they wished to physically place their performances. As the Modern Movement progressed, Bataille and Artaud, with their theatrical tendencies to abjection and excess, were at the forefront of those challenging architecture's imperative to construct unified, stable edifices. Their preoccupation with intoxication, the Sacred, the Plague, and hallucinatory performance, conjures up an abject theatre that defies containment and propriety, proposing an *architecture of cruelty* that resists representation.

The scatological and infantile cries of the Surrealists (echoing Alfred Jarry's anarchic *Ubu Roi* of 1896) were employed as "a mode of disorganization by means of excess, waste, and irrationality" (Weiss 1989: 22), destabilizing theatre practices and the spaces designed to house them. If the limit of architecture lies in its dissolution – where it is no longer, static, secure, or durable – then abjection transforms the object from stable entity to unstable action. Through an "act of exclusion," the abject becomes the outcast contaminant capable of infecting and affecting those within its ambit (Bataille 2005: 11). This contaminating physical presence, which leaks, deforms, decays, and erupts, indexes the "fluid states of structures" that are political, social, cultural, psychological, and physical (Kristeva 2005: 16). Asserting the paradoxical condition of *in-betweeness*, the abject creates hybrid conditions that indicate "a non-respect of structure" (ibid.: 18). Oscillating between the sacral indeterminacy of the absolute, and the material forces of the abstract, abject space provides a subversive site where things are done and undone: "the space of the bounding and undoing of the identities which constitute it" (Grosz 2001: 93). Through performance at the limits, which calls forth the virtual other, this spatial model answers Elizabeth Grosz's desire to "make architecture tremble" (ibid.: 6).

The *abject* – whether erotic, primitive, infantile, feminine, degenerate, or excremental – confronts us with the limits of our bodies and the buildings housed to contain them, revealing both as contaminants. Matter is no longer static and invariant but always in motion, evading classification and meaning, eluding both the frame and form. As something mobile and fluid, the abject indexes the instability and reality of that which is covered and held in by an ostensibly smooth skin, exposing the organism's vulnerability to contamination.

Echoing Artaud's insistence on "no more masterpieces" (Artaud 1958: 74), Bataille wished to eradicate architectural monuments, which (as static, dominant, and authoritarian forms) "impose silence on the multitudes" and "inspire socially acceptable behavior, and often a very real fear" (Bataille 1997: 21): a consideration of the disciplinary nature of built form eventually proposed by Michel Foucault and Henri Lefebvre. Foucault aligned the history of *powers* with the history of *spaces* (Foucault 1980: 149), in which architecture can be understood as an embodiment of abstract, discursive forms of power, permeating the material realm of flesh, activity, and desire by defining, regulating, and limiting our quotidian practices. For Lefebvre, the "logic of space" conceals an authoritarian and brutal force that conditions the competence and performance of the subject who can experience it as an obstacle of "resistant 'objectality' at times as implacably hard as a concrete wall" (Lefebvre 1991: 57). Lefebvre's *objectality*, as a silent oppositional force, stands in contrast to Delueze's *objectile*, where the continuous and explosive phenomenon of form and matter mobilizing the built environment is perceived as an object-event. Rather than a contained event, the object contains the event of its own annihilation.[14] This transformation of architecture from a disciplinary machine to an open-ended volatile form of space-in-action was what Artaud sought in his quest for a Theatre of Cruelty, not just as art form but also as built form. Bataille's notion of the *informe* (formless) – "a term that serves to bring things down in the world" – further challenges the built form and architecture's will to make the world safe and sound (Bataille 1985: 31).

For Artaud, the body of the building, like the physical body it houses, doubles as the social body, which is neither whole nor clean, nor ever at a standstill. Gathered for the event, this collective body is actively complicit within a culture-in-action. Dis-eased, the audience is no longer composed of passive witnesses, but, as a communal body-in-peril, becomes implicated in the force of the event. Architecture, as inert matter, is disturbed, weakened, and thrown into convulsions. This feverish space then vibrates to the point of explosion, as an event triggered by the burning need to place the body at risk.

Like the dis-eased and de-centered body, the *architecture of cruelty* is neither comfortable nor yielding, neither safe nor sound. As a material embodiment of Artaud's spatial speech, it is fractured, without boundaries, discontinuous, open to fluidity of motion, and accessible to the carnality of the spectacle. The illusions of the scenographic theatre have been dissipated in favor of an architecture apprehended directly for what it is rather than what it represents.

Two specific historical avant-garde schemes attempted to build an abject and performative dis-ease through material propositions – Kurt Schwitters' Merzbau installations, also referred to as his *Cathedral of Erotic Misery* (1923–1943), and Kiesler's Endless Space proposals, which began with the Endless Theater (1924–1925). Although art works rather than performance venues, Schwitters' *Merzbau* projects speak to abject spatiality as fragmented, archival assemblages grafted into various existing buildings. Always in the process of being made and remade but never completed, these feverish "spatial growths" were constructed of found materials – flowers in urine, death masks, fetish altars, recycled partial objects – taking on their own life as dripping parasitical matter, accumulating and decomposing over time, while thickening and temporalizing the surfaces to which they adhered. Such organic spatiality is also found in Kiesler's Endless Theater, unveiled in 1926 at the New York International Theater Exposition, which combined the immersive qualities of Craig's dramatic space with the mediatized architecture found a year later in Gropius's Total Theater. Kiesler proposed a mobile-flexible architecture suspended within the double skin of an egg-shaped shell structure. As an open space designed to respond to the theatrical event as well as the crowd in motion, his theatre comprised of intersecting platforms, bridges, and spiraling ramps, dedicated to an "elasticity of building adequate to the elasticity of living" (Kiesler 1930: 49). From this responsive environment Kiesler developed his theories of "Correalism" and "Biotechnique," played out as forms contiguous with both body and cosmos. As an expanding and contracting material dream-space, his architecture evokes Plato's impressionable model of *chora*, outlined in *Timaeus* as an all-embracing "receptacle of becoming" (Plato 1965: 67). This mutable space-matter is also aligned to the ancient theatre's *choros*, which Nietzsche referred to as the "womb" that gave birth to drama; a "primal ground" melding dream into communal being by presenting "itself to our eyes in continual rebirths" (Nietzsche 2000: 65–6).

The move 'against architecture' sought to express an art of excess in an environment that no longer resists the imperative to be representational and whole. Such an anti-architecture un-houses and re-houses performance predating the 'found-space' of Tadeusz Kantor and Mike Person's site-specific performances, more ubiquitous in the late twentieth and early twenty-first centuries. Far from being liquid or porous, auditorium architecture persists as an unyielding spatial predictability and homogeneity, which compels many contemporary performance makers to flee its hermetically sealed and highly controlled interior: escaping the dead air of the theatre for the *plein air* of found spaces and the multiple and fragmenting stories they harbor. These performances in found spaces tend to seek and work with dis-easy, de-centered, and ex-plosive spatialities, articulated in the spatial speech of Artaud: embracing the specific multiplicity of site, not only as objectile, but as *abjectile* – vibrant matter in perpetual motion.

Conclusion: void, machine, and organism

Nietzsche, who dedicated *The Birth of Tragedy* to Wagner, had hoped the composer would create drama that was no longer considered a work of art as art, but something that "acts" on the spectator "corporeally and empirically" (Nietzsche 2000: 57). Instead of reimagining the ancient choric space, where Nietzsche saw theatre's re-birth, Wagner reworked the ancient theatron to hold the spectators' attention within a darkened auditorium that focused their gaze onto a newly strengthened picture frame into which they could project themselves. The philosopher's proclamation of God's death coincided with his deep disappointment in the composer. Nietzsche's challenge to the perspectival scene was followed by the symbolists, whose productions aimed to loosen performance from its framed confines by utilizing darkness on stage as well as in the auditorium. As scenographers, Adolphe Appia and Edward Gordon Craig proposed an alternative architecture through a "new monumentality," which folded the scenic in on the architectural through architectonic landscapes that created a more ambiguous spatiality (Appia and Beacham 1993: 136).[15] Oscillating between the material and immaterial their universal sites are akin to Ignaci Solà-Morales's concept of "weak architecture" (Solà-Morales 1997: 56) – a utilization of the fleeting, vestigial, and ephemeral – with clear boundaries undermined by rhythmic atmospherics, activating space via sound, light, and gesture, which integrated viewers and viewed within a more immersive site.

The socialist agenda of the constructivists, and others advocating a radical utopia, wished to return theatre space to the dazzling reality of the industrialized marketplace in which they established a new cathedral to dramatic mechanization and cultural production. However, that secular temple elicited its most potent theatrical charge when exposing the impossible and failing nature of the machine it purported to be; heightening the pervading sense of alienation in a spectacular form. Attempting to construct new environments, regimes, and identities, the socialist avant-garde was caught between the rigidity of utopia's idealism and the fragmentation and complex layering of a relative existence in which body and machine had become ensnared. Their shocks and montage techniques played with the fragmented theatricality of cubist cinematics, which architecture's Modern Movement futilely wished to orchestrate and discipline.

Modernism's disciplinary desire was critiqued by the anarchic gestures of the post–World War I Dadaists and surrealists whose shock effects recognized the devastation wreaked by technological warfare, dismembering the body and disenchanting the eye. This catastrophe returned the "agonistic sacrifice" to the avant-garde theatre "as the fatal obligation of the individual artist" (Poggioli 1968: 68). Artists such as Artaud sought to match history's volatility with an equally explosive space that rendered form formless, annihilating the commanding overview of the Enlightenment in favor of a more sensorial and labyrinthine space in which performance could assail a public enwrapped in its chaotic embrace. However, while this spatiality was vertiginous and disordered, it was also porous, contingent, and emergent. The activism, antagonism, and agonism of the theatrical avant-garde, coupled with a return to Nietzschean nihilism, undermined the unified global image of a purified and rational monumentality that architectural modernism strove to create by deliberately destabilizing its foundations.[16]

A move against the faux constructions of mimetic representation is a defining feature of the absolute, abstract, and abject event-spaces outlined in this chapter; encapsulated in the symbolist refutation of illusionistic scenery, the constructivist move toward machinic abstractions, and the surrealist belief in hallucinatory territories that spatialized the unconscious. In storming mimetic representation the avant-garde was also laying siege to the structures that housed and constructed dissimulating worlds, insisting on a more integrated relationship between theatricality's enchantment and the socio-political reality of everyday.

Nietzsche's alter ego, the madman, who declares God's death and therefore the end of mimetic representation, occupies what Derrida names "the space of dis-traction" (Derrida 1986: 336). As "*the one who is spacy, or spaced out*," he cannot be housed and is obliged to wander (ibid.). Carrying a lantern like a failed prop in the blinding light of day, this madman appears in the chaotic marketplace; a theatrical figure calling to account those who gather around him as implicated in great events. His declaration (of God's death) is also a demand that the public (as God's murderers) realize their complicity in the creation of history. Like Dionysus, Nietzsche came to shatter form. Replacing perspectival construction with the multiplicity of perspectivism, he wished to transform the "herd" into a reflective community that is no longer dominated by a singular totalizing reality but could occupy and create multiple realities with varying interpretations of existence. This (re-)turns us to scenography - even more than the postdramatic "visual dramaturgy" advocated by Hans-Thies Lehmann (2006: 93) – as an evental integration of "art," "architecture," and "theatre," capable of proposing and working with new environments for performance that recognize the vertigo of the void, the impossibility of the machine and the fleshiness of the organism.

Notes

1 For a further discussion of scenography see the introduction to this volume.

2 Nietzsche's claim that we have killed God to Artaud's repudiation of His judgment.

3 Although Tschumi's specific mention of this term is not prevalent in his texts, K. Michael Hays has cited him as its progenitor in *Architecture Theory Since 1968*, 216 (Hays 2000). In an interview with *Manifold Magazine*, Hays states that "the term 'event-space' belongs to Tschumi" (Hays and Gass 2007).

4 Derrida's reference to spacing as the "provocation of an event" through spatial performativity specifically references the "performative" outlined by language philosopher, J. L. Austin, in his seminal lecture, *How to Do Things with Words* (Austin 1975), where – separating the *constative* (descriptive) from the *performative* (active) – the dynamic nature of "speech acts" are expanded beyond language into action itself. Translating this to architecture and scenography we can consider not only *How to Do Things with Spaces and Things* but *How Spaces and Things Do*.

5 Kwinter (2001: 14) defines "micro-architectures" as the relations that saturate and compose the architectural object, whereas in "macro-architectures" the relations envelop and exceed the object.

6 This is discussed by Kwinter who describes "evental," with its alliance to time, as "concrete, plastic and active," in *Architectures of Time: Toward a Theory of the Event in Modernist Culture*, (Kwinter 2001: 69 n. 29). Peter Hallward's translation of *événementielle* is something akin to "of the event," or that which constitutes the event as new and irruptive of the old, discussed in his introduction to Badiou's *Ethics: An Understanding of Evil* (Badiou 2001).

7 Originally published in Bernard Tschumi, *La Case Vide: La Villette*. Derrida, who was introduced "into" architectural discourse by Tschumi, saw an application of his philosophy of deconstruction to architecture within the project of the Parc de la Villette. As the philosopher noted, this invitation to participate in the project threw him "into the space of architecture, rather than architectural space" exposing him to a new discipline. See Wigley 1992.

8 In dance, "spacing" is movement relating to the dancers' spatial organization, plotting their moves and orienting themselves to the existing environment and each other.

9 "The Glory Machine" refers to one of Villiers de L'Isle-Adam's *Cruel Tales* (Villiers de L'Isle-Adam 1985), in which the French playwright creates an *archi-textual* event that exposes late nineteenth-century theaters as monumental bourgeois systems (social and instrumental) against which the theatrical avant-garde was on the verge of rebelling.

10 In his essay on *Las Meninas*, Michel Foucault refers to the vanishing point as the "essential void" (Foucault 1970: 16). It is worth noting that the aristocratic gaze was first undermined in the eighteenth century with the introduction of two-point perspective (also referred to as *scene ad angolo* or *vedute per angolo*), which was no longer predicated on the sovereign view of an ideal single-point perspective. Although still constructed around a centralized viewer, the new location of vanishing points in the wings outside the stage picture withheld the power and scrutiny of a monocular view, weakening the central position of the royal box and the all-seeing I of the Monarch that had replaced the all-seeing eye of a medieval God.
11 Discussed at length by Erika Fischer-Lichte (2005).
12 Both god and his omnipotent representative, the Monarch, had been displaced from their central position in society and the theatre. The center no longer held sway.
13 This recalls W. B. Yeats' remark (1902), upon seeing Craig's production of *Dido and Aeneas* at the turn of the new century, that the designer had "created an ideal country where everything was possible, even speaking in verse or in music, or the expression of the whole of life in a dance."
14 Peter Eisenman (1992: 17) discussed this as the "catastrophe fold."
15 In his seminal essay, "Monumentality," Appia advocated a new monumentality that promoted a flexible environment capable of anticipating changes: the walls would open out onto the lobbies or adjacent gardens; the proscenium could change its width and discretely disappear; the orchestra pit could be covered over; and the floor would be systematized into hydraulic units for staging and seating. As an adaptable building it could open to the sunlight during the day and at night concealed lighting would create the ambience. The interior decor would minimize detail but, "beautiful in design and colour," would have a presence that played a role in the events it houses.
16 Renato Poggioli establishes and outlines *activism*, *antagonism*, *agonism* and *nihilism* as defining features of the historical avant-garde in Chapters 2 and 4 of *The Theory of the Avant-Garde* (Poggioli 1968).

References

Appia, Adolphe and Richard C. Beacham 1993. *Adolphe Appia: Texts on Theater*. London and New York: Routledge.

Artaud, Antonin 1958. *The Theatre and its Double*, translated by C. M. Richards. New York: Grove Press.

Austin, J. L. 1975. *How to Do Things with Words*. Cambridge, MA: Harvard University Press.

Badiou, Alain 2001. *Ethics: An Understanding of Evil*, translated by Peter Hallward. London and New York: Verso.

Badiou, Alain 2007. *The Century*, translated by Alberto Toscano. Cambridge, UK: Polity Press.

Banham, Reyner 1962. *Theory and Design in the First Machine Age* (2nd ed.). Cambridge, MA: MIT Press.

Bataille, Georges 1985. *Visions of Excess: Selected Writings, 1927–1939*, edited by Allen Stoekl. Minneapolis: University of Minnesota Press.

Bataille, Georges 1997. "Architecture." In *Rethinking Architecture*, edited by Neil Leach, 21. London: Routledge.

Bataille, Georges 2005. "Abjection and Miserable Forms." In *More and Less*, edited by Sylvère Lotringer, translated by Yvonne Shafir, 3–13. Cambridge, MA: MIT Press.

Brejzek, Thea 2015. "The Scenographic (Re-)turn: Figures of Surface, Space and Spectator in Theatre and Architecture Theory 1680–1980." *Theater and Performance Design* 1 (1–2): 17–30.

Carlson, Marvin 1996. *Performance: A Critical Introduction*. London and New York: Routledge.

de Certeau, Michel 1988. *The Practice of Everyday Life*. Los Angeles: University of California Press.

Deleuze, Gilles 2006. *Nietzsche and Philosophy*, translated by Hugh Tomlinson. New York: Columbia University Press.

Derrida, Jacques 1986. "*Point de Folie – Maintenant l'Architecture*." In *Rethinking Architecture: A Reader in Cultural Theory*, edited by Neil Leach, 324–36. Originally published in Bernard Tschumi, *La Case Vide: La Villette*. London: Architectural Association.

Derrida, Jacques 1997. *Of Grammatology*, translated by Gayatri Chakravorty Spivak. Baltimore, MD: John Hopkins University Press.
Eisenman, Peter 1992. "Unfolding Events." In *Incorporations*, edited by Jonathan Crary and Sanford Kwinter, 422–27. New York: Zone.
Eisenstein, Serge 1991. "Montage and Architecture." In *Eisenstein: Vol. 2 – Towards a Theory of Montage*, edited by Michael Glenny and Richard Taylor, 58–81. London: BFI.
Fischer-Lichte, Erika 2005. *Theater, Sacrifice, Ritual: Exploring Forms of Political Theater*. London and New York: Routledge Press.
Foucault, Michel 1970. "Las Meninas." In *The Order of Things: An Archaeology of the Human Sciences*, 3–16. New York: Vintage Books.
Foucault, Michel 1980. *Power/Knowledge: Selected Interviews and Other Writings, 1972–1977*, edited by Colin Gordon. New York: Pantheon Books.
Gerould, Daniel 2001. "Landscapes of the Unseen: Turn-of-the-Century Symbolism from Paris to Petersburg." In *Land/Scape/Theater*, edited by Elinor Fuchs and Una Chaudhuri, 303–21. Ann Arbor: University of Michigan Press.
Giedion, Sigfried 1948. *Mechanization Takes Command: A Contribution to Anonymous History*. New York: Oxford University Press.
Gropius, Walter 1963. "On the Construction of the Modern Theater, with Particular Reference to the Building of the New Piscator Theater in Berlin." In Erwin Piscator, *The Political Theater: A History, 1914–1929*, translated by Hugh Rorrison, 180–5. London: Avon Publishers.
Grosz, Elizabeth 2001. *Architecture from the Outside: Essays on Virtual and Real Spaces*. Cambridge, MA: MIT Press.
Hays, K. Michael (Ed.) 2000. *Architecture Theory Since 1968*. Cambridge, MA: MIT Press.
Hays, K. Michael with Izabel Gass 2007. "Postcriticality," *Manifold Magazine*, May 6. Available online at: www.manifoldmagazine.com/index.php/2007/05/06/k-michael-hays/.
Izenour, George C. 1977. *Theater Design*. New York: McGraw Hill
Kiesler, Frederick 1930. "Manifesto of Tensionism." In *Contemporary Art Applied to the Store and its Display*. New York: Brentano.
Kristeva, Julia 2005. "Fetishizing the Abject" In *More and Less*, edited by Sylvère Lotringer, translated by Yvonne Shafir, 15–35. Cambridge, MA: MIT Press.
Kwinter, Sanford 2001. *Architectures of Time: Toward a Theory of the Event in Modernist Culture*. Cambridge, MA: MIT Press.
Lefebvre, Henri 1991. *The Production of Space*, translated by Donald Nicholson-Smith. Oxford: Blackwell.
Lehmann, Hans-Thies 2006. *Postdramatic Theater*, translated by Karen Jürs-Munby. Abingdon, UK: Routledge.
Libeskind, Daniel 2000. *The Space of Encounter*. New York: Universe.
Michaud, Eric 2000. "Social Criticism and Utopian Experiments." In *Painters in the Theater of the European Avant-Garde*, edited by Margaret Paz, 309–55. Sofia: Museo Nacional Sofia.
Nietzsche, Friedrich 1961. *Thus Spoke Zarathustra: A Book for Everyone and No One*, translated by R. J. Hollingdale. London: Penguin.
Nietzsche, Friedrich 1966. "On Great Events." In *Thus Spoke Zarathustra: A Book for All and None*, 129–33. New York: Penguin Books.
Nietzsche, Friedrich [1882] 1974. *The Gay Science*, translated by Walter Kaufmann. New York: Vintage.
Nietzsche, Friedrich 2000. "The Birth of Tragedy out of the Spirit of Music." In *Basic Writings of Nietzsche*, translated by Walter Kaufman, 15–144. New York and Toronto: Random House.
Panofsky, Erwin 1991. *Perspective as Symbolic Form*, translated by Christopher S. Wood. New York: Zone.
Plato 1965. *Timaeus and Critias*. London: Penguin Books.
Poggioli, Renato 1968. *The Theory of the Avant-Garde*, translated by Gerald Fitzgerald. Cambridge, MA: Belknap Press of Harvard University Press.
Solà-Morales, Rubió Ignasi 1997. *Differences: Topographies of Contemporary Architecture*, edited by Sarah Whiting, translated by Graham Thompson. Cambridge, MA: MIT Press.
Tafuri, Manfredo and Francesco Dal Co 1986. *Modern Architecture*. New York: Electra/Rizzoli.

Wagner, Richard 1896. "Bayreuth (The Playhouse)." In *Richard Wagner's Prose Works*, Vol. 5, translated by William Ashton Ellis, 320–40. New York: Broude Brothers.
Weiss, Allen S. 1989. *The Aesthetics of Excess*. Albany: State University of New York Press.
Weiss, Allen S. 1995. *Mirrors of Infinity: The French Formal Garden and 17th-Century Metaphysics*. New York: Princeton Architectural Press.
Wigley, Mark 1992. "Jacques Derrida: Invitation to a Discussion." In *Columbia Documents of Architecture and Theory* 1: 7–27.
Wiles, David 2003. *A Short History of Western Performance Space*. Cambridge, UK: Cambridge University Press.
Villiers de l'Isle-Adam 1985. "The Glory Machine." In *Cruel Tales*, translated by Robert Baldick, 48–63. New York: Oxford University Press.
Yeats, W. B. 1902. *The Saturday Review*, March 8: 299.

10
"WHAT IS HAPPENING"
Notes on the scenographic impulse in modern and contemporary art

Kevin Lotery

A scenographic impulse has been bound up with modern art from its earliest days. Its history, however, remains elusive. While scenographic conditions of spectatorship in the visual arts are often immediately recognizable, the set of formal maneuvers required to produce them are notoriously difficult to define. Some key aspects can be identified: a dependence on a community of viewers, the use of the effects of the stage (lighting and sound among them), the deployment of prop-like objects calling out for human users, or a tableau-like frontality. But none of these operations – and many more could be named here – guarantee the affective conditions of a scenographic environment.

The editor of the present volume has made some important headway in formulating what might be called a scenographic aesthetic in the visual arts, finding a key precedent in the looping self-reflexivity of Diego Velázquez's *Las Meninas* (1656) (Aronson 2005). Following Michel Foucault's ([1966] 1970) analysis of the painting, he shows how the work presents a scenography of painterly production in order to lay its operations bare for spectators, who are, and forever will be, drawn into the painting's "system of feints" (Foucault [1966] 1970: 3). Like the ambiguous mirror reflection in *Las Meninas*, art, in this reading, becomes scenographic when it organizes itself around the spectator's gaze such that vision is transformed by the aesthetic world of the image. A parallel, though somewhat more pessimistic, analysis can be located in the work of Michael Fried (1980), who has spent many pages theorizing the condition of "theatricality" – the image's self-reflexive acknowledgment of its own conditions of spectatorship – alongside its twin, an "absorptive" turning away from the social world of the spectator.

The present chapter examines some strains in modern and contemporary scenographic practices. It assumes that these traditions represent special cases, dependent on particular spatial and technical transformations constitutive of modernity at large. Something has changed by the time of the founding works of modernist painting like Mary Cassatt's *In the Loge* (1878) or Édouard Manet's *A Bar at the Folies-Bergère* (1882). In both, the viewer is beckoned into a world of performed pleasures in which she might be reflected too. What differentiates such pictures from their predecessors is, among many other things, their more developed awareness of the penetration of theatrical, scenographic forms of spectatorship by modern forms of technologically-mediated visual experience, from the reflective surfaces of the city to new apparatuses of image making and image reception, like photography. They also recognized – and puzzled over – a crisis of collectivity taking shape within the fantastical new scenographies of modern, everyday life. What type of collective subject, they asked, could serve as an alternative to the alienated audiences of individual subjects required by the new forms of spectacular entertainment and commodity objects?

No one charted the technological and biological bases of this new collective more subtly than Georges Seurat, particularly in the scenographies of late paintings like the mysterious *Parade de Cirque* (1887–8). All the components of a scenographic environment are present here (Figure 10.1). In the foreground, a crowd has gathered to watch a sideshow and cavort among themselves. The circus master to their right, whip in hand, indicates the setting. On a platform in the center of the composition, a hooded, nymph-like horn player faces the crowd with one knee bent, his (or her? or its?) demonic face occluded by Seurat's particular technique of paint application. Stiffened back-up musicians stand behind and to the left of the central figure, positioned within some kind of carnival stage set. This backdrop is demarcated at top by a row of stage lights that also delimit the top framing edge of the canvas itself, aligning painterly representation with depicted theatrical performance. This is only one of Seurat's many tactics for joining the surface of his canvas with the imagined plane of the theatrical proscenium. Another is the way in which Seurat, in a common tactic of his, bounds his image with a thin painted frame, which he connects up with the lights, as if to construct a hinge between the simulated world of the image (and the performance therein) and the material presence of the painted surface.

Seurat sets up this rigorous self-reflexivity only to surgically dissect its spatial order. For as soon as we accept his painterly scenography, we can't help but notice that it

Figure 10.1 Georges Seurat, *Parade de Cirque* (1887–8). (Metropolitan Museum of Art.)

simply does not hold together. First, Seurat places us, as spectators, within an ambiguous, impossible space. We seem to be positioned both within the depicted crowd *and* above and behind it such that our eyes meet those of the elven horn player at the same elevated position. The spectator is poised, impossibly, both within the space of the depicted performance and outside of it, within the space of the painting's exhibition. Along with this spatial – and temporal – disjunction comes a blurring of the spectator's place within a presumed collective of viewers; she takes on a twofold life, oscillating between gallery visitor and member of the mysterious collective in the picture itself. Gallery space links up with the topsy-turvy world of the circus.

In an important analysis of the painting, Jonathan Crary (1999) has described further formal discrepancies, focusing on the peculiar background. This "scenic space," Crary indicates, collapses on itself, flattened into so many planar fragments that do not add up to a believable illusionistic space (Crary 1999: 214). Stairways lead nowhere, doorways give way to abstract patterns. In place of a vanishing point, we are given twinned zeroes, a doubled, flattened nothingness. Here, in short, is an alluring "spectacle to which we are emphatically denied visual access" (Crary 1999: 200).

But it is a spectacle to which we are biologically linked, a result of Seurat's divisionist technique. The basic operation of the technique is simple: colors are, at least in principle, left unmixed on the canvas, isolated into touches of pigment dispersed across the surface. No longer mixed by the painter, pigment gives itself over to "optical mixture": color is mixed in the eye of the beholder whose vision is now responsible for making points of color cohere into recognizable figures and objects.[1] Transformed from passive contemplation into productive act of spectatorship, the viewer's visual apparatus fuses, theoretically at least, with the painterly process itself, now physically dependent on its public. Crary details how Seurat learned to manipulate this dynamic spectatorship within sinister scenographies like that of *Parade de Cirque*. Seurat's demonic pied piper presides here over an unknown rite in which we can't help but partake. Our role in this sideshow is, however, forever withheld, despite the fact that our visual, even physiological, participation is crucial to its constitution.

It is in this sense, Crary writes, that the work might effect a painterly performance of "the inescapable universality of modern exchange and circulation" (Crary 1999: 223). An economic system promising, even requiring, universal bodily access to the spectacular pleasures of the commodity, this spectacle was, and continues to be, at pains to conceal the secret absence at its core, symbolized, in Crary's logic, by the double zeroes in the center of the painting: the very emblem of an equivalence of nothingness. Muted music tempts us forward, beckoning us into a spectacle whose questions refuse to be answered: who are these figures before us? Into what sinister scenography do they lure us and for what purpose? What transformation are they effecting within our bodies? In short, what is happening to us?

Rather than attempt a canonical history of the scenographic impulse, I trace in the following text a loose lineage of immersive scenographic environments that extend from these questions, so presciently posed by Seurat in the early decades of modern art. This is a story that will intersect at various points with the vicissitudes of related aesthetic practices, such as installation art, theorized most forcefully by Rosalind Krauss (2000), and especially Claire Bishop (2005), whose meditations on the "dream scenes" of installation art have been crucial to our understanding of immersive aesthetic environments. What distinguishes the scenographic impulse from such practices is, as Seurat's example shows, its peculiar attention to the economic and technological transformations conditioning spectatorial experience. Certain scenographic practices have proven particularly sensitive to the possibility – and sometimes impossibility – of constructing collective forms of subjectivity to act out, and even rescript, specific historical conflicts. To this end, scenographic environments often function by constructing tenuous collectives and placing them within some form of narrative structure. Sometimes, as we will see, such narratives seek to braid themselves into the temporal unfolding of life outside of "art" spaces, that is, as it is lived on the street, in communal spaces, or in natural ecologies. In these cases, the production of life and the production of theatre merge in uncanny fashion. At other times, as in Seurat's early example, scenographies seek to splice themselves into sensory or organic processes or even, in certain cases, into the internal wiring of cognition itself, the very seat of subjectivity.

I begin with key precedents of the interwar avant-garde and the postwar period in order to set the stage for the expanded scenographic techniques of the immediate present.[2] Throughout I dwell on the enigmatic core of scenography in the visual arts: its ability to disorient and unground collectives of subjects by weaving bodies into a world of fantasy in which the realities of space, time, and history seem momentarily upstaged, as it were, by the new rules of a fantastical, scenographic realm. The practitioners that we will examine here – from Marcel Duchamp to Walid Raad – worked within the bewildering, and sometimes paranoiac, multiple life they saw conjured in scenography's hybrid spatial order: a life that made actors out of flesh and blood bodies, dreamlike gestures out of everyday movements.

Street-store-bedroom-stage

It seemed to many in the interwar avant-gardes, the Dadaists and Surrealists foremost among them, that a new spatial order had come into being under the regime of the commodity. Formerly partitioned spaces – public and private alike – now seemed united by the dreams and desires harbored within the magical objects of capitalism. The shop window, that original habitat of the commodity linking, via the act of consumption, street, store, and domestic space, became for many avant-gardists a site of aesthetic research and experimentation. Duchamp for one took note of "the question of shop windows" and wrote cryptically of some mysterious gambit they posed: "[t]o undergo the interrogation of shop windows" (Duchamp [1913] 1999: 5). Frederick Kiesler, who along with Duchamp would become one of the avant-garde's key exhibition designers, devoted whole texts and projects to the "new art" of the "store window," which he likened to "the stage" (Kiesler 1930: 110). But there were key differences. Grimly illustrating the ways in which the commodity fetish's thingly life had come to replace human relationships, Kiesler writes that "actors are speaking plastics in motion, whereas the merchandise is a silent, static object" (Kiesler 1930: 110).

The "interrogation of shop windows" haunted the infamous Exposition Internationale du Surréalisme, held in 1938 at the Galérie Beaux-Arts, Paris. An elaborate dreamscape housing various installations and paintings, the exhibition involved many collaborators, including Duchamp, the "*générateur-arbitre*" of the exhibition, and the Surrealist photographer Man Ray, brought on as lighting expert (Kachur 2003). At the entrance to the main exhibition space, many of the participating artists (Duchamp included) installed actual store mannequins that they dressed up, creating a kind of red-light district street scene visitors had to navigate. For them, the figure of the mannequin represented a regime of equivalence, in which objects of sexual, commercial, and artistic consumption had taken on the same hardened physiology.

The exhibition's scenography charted this all-encompassing dreamworld of the commodity, where carnal fantasy meets deathly fetish. A bed installed in one corner of the main exhibition space made this dreaming life explicit. But the nightmare was best exemplified by the dozens of coal sacks Duchamp collected from a site outside Paris and attached to the full surface area of the ceiling (Figure 10.2). Though filled with newspapers, the hanging sacks leached actual coal dust into the air, conjuring a hellish cloudscape raining down agitating filth rather than refreshing rain. As Benjamin Buchloh (2014) and T. J. Demos (2007) have noted, this thickened atmosphere quickly did away with any hope for the comfortable, optical experience of art normally proffered by exhibition spaces, substituting instead a tactile cloud that literally got in the eyes. The sacks also, according to Brian O'Doherty's important observations, overturned the architectural frame of display space itself, flipping floor and ceiling in a "topsy-turvy" anti-architecture (O'Doherty [1976/1980] 1986: 69). This was accentuated further by the presence of freestanding revolving doors. Denied, like the architecture itself, of their primary function, the doors instead sported paintings. But all this was, at least implicitly, under threat of destruction. Not only did, as Demos has described, the coal sacks threaten visitors' heads, but thanks to a coal-burning brazier placed on the floor, there

Figure 10.2 Marcel Duchamp's *1200 Coal Sacks* in the Exposition Internationale du Surréalisme, Galérie Beaux-Arts, Paris, 1938.

was also a "genuine danger of explosion" (Demos 2007: 177). To navigate this dark scenography of aerial bombardment, Man Ray provided flashlights to visitors on opening night. Here, then, was a multivalent site, linking street and store, bedroom and stage in some kind of enigmatic theatrical event. Though it might all go up in smoke, this hybrid space was freely explorable by visitors who, like coal miners, might dig out their own pathways and narratives through it, flashlight in hand.

A key aspect of the scenographic impulse is put to the test here. A space of fantasy in which different sites and settings might temporarily blend together, immersive scenographies like this one possess a demonic charge too, as Seurat recognized early on. In Duchamp's shifting environment, all spaces (and all viewers as well) faced the risk of violent disintegration, becoming so many particles of color or points of light in a darkened space. No revolutionary collectivity in this theatre space; only individual viewers remain, alienated from one another and wandering in a darkened landscape evacuated of any decipherable meaning or unifying purpose. Kept at bay by the separation of coal sacks from brazier, only total destruction might bring about a terrible collectivity here, one that promised the most sinister form of universal equivalence.

In the postwar period, artists took the disorienting hybridity of immersive scenographic space in a number of different directions. One of the most fruitful lay in the New York-based Happenings of Allan Kaprow or Claes Oldenburg, both of whom found ways to, in often disturbing fashion, bleed theatrical space into the routine spaces of life outside the gallery (think only of Oldenburg's related *The Store* [1961]). The story gets a bit more complicated in the hands of the London-based Independent Group, whose members, Richard Hamilton in particular, looked for ways to merge interwar avant-garde scenographies with the environments of a burgeoning pop world of mass culture and throw-away technological marvels. A close friend and admirer of Duchamp, Hamilton reversed the master's course, however, foregoing the violence of his anti-aesthetic scenography for spaces that rejoiced in the possibility of blending as many types of aesthetic spaces and as many types of aesthetic products as possible. With John McHale and John Voelcker, Hamilton was behind the "Fun House," a foundational Pop structure made for the interdisciplinary *This is Tomorrow* exhibition at London's Whitechapel Art Gallery in 1956. The "Fun House" was one of many "display stands" (Alloway 1956) making up the exhibition, which was geared towards staging a future in which, as organizer Theo Crosby stated, "the integration of the arts" will have eliminated discrete disciplines (Crosby 1956: 356). For this reason, many of the structures took on features of scenographic environments, which have often been propped up, for better or worse, as models for an integrated approach to the arts.[3]

The "Fun House" was carnivalesque, a pop version of Seurat's circus side-show that scrambled the senses – sight, touch, hearing, smell – within a hall-of-mirrors set-up. A collage Hamilton installed at the entrance announced this intention from the outset. On a blow-up image of a man's face, diagrammatic arrows pointed to each sensory input: eyes, nose, mouth, ears, and forehead. "Feel!" read an arrow adhered at cheek level. "Smell!" read another at the tip of the nose. Inside, magazine images wallpapered canted surfaces, film clips projected across the space, hypnotic optical illusions borrowed from Duchamp's rotoscope machines rotated endlessly. In the rear, a linoleum floor adorned with a Jackson Pollock-like motif emitted a strawberry scent when stepped on; nearby, visitors spoke into an open microphone hooked up to speakers at the other end of the structure. Outside, a working jukebox stood near a painted replica of the billboard for the film *Forbidden Planet* (1956), featuring the famous Robby the Robot cradling an unconscious Anne Francis, his eyes flashing. The cyborg and its machinic life, it seems, had replaced the mannequin in this bright post-war world in which the dream of consumption commingled with the nightmare of total atomic destruction.

An expanded scenographic impulse takes hold here, extending the sensory assault that lay at the core of Seurat and Duchamp's work. Requiring full sensory attention, the "Fun House" removed the senses from their physiological domain, approaching them as always already mediated by, even dispersed into, various technological apparatus – microphone, jukebox, film projection. More than just inputs for consuming popular culture, however, Hamilton and Co. made sure to frame the senses as technical implements too: apparatus for producing the sounds, sights, and smells of a thoroughly pop world of ephemeral fantasies. Here again was a scenographic space in which the materiality of the senses mixed with the immateriality of fantasy, a hybrid order requiring a new conception of space.

For other artists in Duchamp's wake, Louise Bourgeois in particular, scenographic environments had to look beyond fantasy to the unconscious drives guiding it. For Bourgeois, scenographic space – its props, its frontality, and its dependence on, if only implied, a backing drama – could invest the neutrality of the white cube interior with the messiness of the subject's psychosexual interiority. At least one of her tasks, as Mignon Nixon has argued, was to draw out the counter-scenes of psychosexual encounter that have been relegated to the shadows of those other "primal scenes" – the encounter with female genitalia, for example – that Sigmund Freud saw as construction sites of patriarchy itself.

"This piece is basically a table," Bourgeois stated of *The Destruction of the Father* (1974), "the awful, terrifying family dinner table headed by the father who sits and gloats" (Bourgeois 1997: 142). Based on Bourgeois's own childhood fantasies, this little domestic scene quickly turns against the father, however, and a grim "oral drama" unfolds (Bourgeois, in Nixon 2005: 258). The children grow tired of the ranting "tyrant," and so, Bourgeois recounts, they "dismembered him and proceeded to devour him" (Bourgeois 1997: 142). The work does not explicitly depict the event, of course, but signals it via abstracted bodily masses splayed out horizontally across a table and hanging from above, like Duchamp's coal sacks. Made of synthetic materials, these brown accumulations are bathed in dark red light and set against black curtains; the whole tableau is sunk into a gallery wall, a theatrical womb-space burrowed into neutral gallery architecture (Figure 10.3).

In one sense, Bourgeois' diorama-like installation offers a riposte to other patently scenographic aesthetic practices, James Turrell's foremost among them, which also dissect neutral gallery architecture into theatrical events. In important early works like *Afrum I* and *Prado (White)* (both 1967), darkened gallery walls are carefully, even surgically, illuminated by projected light, which seems to, thanks to a trick of optics, either carve out or insert new spaces within existing architecture. These spaces are, of course, purely optical phenomena, immaterial zones that cannot be inhabited by the body, but succeed in tripping it up nonetheless. If the tactility of Duchamp's environments or Bourgeois' projects enters in here, it is a purified one. Turrell's spectator is, in the main, a physiological being, separated from psychosexual desire or from historical conditions of production and consumption. An almost spiritual affirmation of the immateriality of optical experience often takes hold in his works. Adamantly scenographic in their use of sometimes colored lighting effects, Turrell's optical interventions often end up dramatizing, rather than mounting a critical attack on, the existing architectural conditions

Figure 10.3 Louise Bourgeois, *The Destruction of the Father*, 1974: latex, plaster, wood, fabric and red light. Installation at Museum of Modern Art, New York. (Photo: Rafael Lobato, © The Easton Foundation//Licensed by VAGA, New York.)

of space (even of Euclidean space in general). In so doing, they risk spectacularizing the very neutral institutional spaces that Bourgeois, and Duchamp before her, viewed as maintaining bourgeois conditions of spectatorship, with their masculinist allegiance to the controlled separability and ahistorical purity of optical, bodily, and psychological experience. Indeed, Turrell's work would only become grander and more spectacular as the artist gained institutional support, in some cases bathing whole spaces in heaven-directed portals of light.[4]

In place of the masculinist fantasy of control and the purifying architectures supporting it, Bourgeois' *The Destruction of the Father* presents a humble domestic scenography given over to the messy violence of disintegration, dispersal, and ultimately, "dangerous incorporation" (Nixon 2005: 260). This fantastical stage-set refuses to shield spectators from psychosexual desire and violence nor cloak them in purely optical aesthetic experiences. Instead, the very process of bodily constitution and deconstitution makes up the core of Bourgeois' scenography. Like Duchamp's leaching coal sacks, the threat of bodily disintegration commingles with the prospect of a dangerous oral re-incorporation of foreign bodies. We might also recognize Seurat's precedent as well. His divisionist technique was fundamentally a critique of the bodily constitution of the subject too, inserting spectators into a scenographic spectacle in which they had to assemble dispersed particles of color into cohesive, bounded figures and objects, a constant shuttling between violent dispersal and transformative re-organization.

Communities of paranoia

"Former Midland/HSBC Bank and Hauser & Wirth's Piccadilly gallery is currently being transformed into a fully functioning Community Centre" (Hauser and Wirth 2011). So reads the press release announcing *Piccadilly Community Centre* (2011), with nary a word of the person responsible for the aforementioned transformation, the Swiss artist Christoph Büchel. The release was true to its word: during its run, the Centre completely erased the commercial conditions of its own exhibition (and the artist responsible), occupying the newly minted London gallery – itself recently transformed from a bank – with several stories of actually functioning community services, leisure activities, educational programs, computer labs, and a pub. On one floor, visitors might pick up a flyer from a display stand for the Conservative Party; on another, they might spy senior members of the community partaking in dance classes or knitting circles, or emoting in a "Laughter Network," encouraging "positive thinking" through laughter. A fully functioning website (still live) allows the public to volunteer, sign up for courses, or view pictures of activities. One uncredited statement on the homepage reads, perhaps a bit ominously: "Piccadilly Community Centre gave me the opportunities, encouragement and support that helped me to make a new life for myself" (piccadillycommunitycentre.org). Who, however, is the "me" that speaks in this statement? Is this a real or fantastical person? Whose lives are being "encouraged" in this mysterious space and what type of "community" is being constituted here? What, to repeat an earlier question, is happening?

Reviewers were quick to pick up on the uncanny quality of Büchel's intervention. Adrian Searle described "a trompe l'oeil political artwork where the fault lines in reality are subtly amplified." Are we, he continued, in the midst of "a kind of immersive theatre in which we are the unwitting actors?" (Searle 2011). Though no trace of the gallery nor the former financial institution was detectable, the work clearly banked on the history of its site; it was a scenography haunted, we might say, by unseen spaces, functions, and institutions as well as by the grim societal transformations conditioning each one. Critic Helena Reckitt (2012) and others (Farquharson 2011) recognized "the language of Prime Minister David Cameron's Big Society in which acts of communal goodwill are claimed to replace public funding" (Reckitt 2012: 103). One of the questions posed by the work, Reckitt continues, was "the state of public funding and communal resources" (Reckitt 2012: 103) in a Britain increasingly giving itself over to the financial sector. The specter of global capital, deregulation, and the neoliberal faith in the individual over and against the collective, haunted this short-lived communal space. In a way not so distant from Seurat before him, Büchel seemed to recognize that an absence was endemic to this universalizing system, which he hinted at in the attic level of the Centre, where an evacuated squat presents the visitor with trash, food, graffiti, and mattresses.

A crisis of collectivity was clearly at stake here and, as we have seen in earlier examples, scenographic techniques again provided the tools for gathering a troubled community together and interrogating its individual members on the level of the body in space. Unlike Duchamp's coal sacks or the Happenings at midcentury, Büchel's environment, like a waking daydream, had literally no division between its scenography and the production of life itself. All participants – gallery visitors and local inhabitants – became productive participants in the same "Community," and yet, at least for this writer, divisions proliferated everywhere. Part of the difficulty of this work requires, I think, being honest about these frightening encounters. Who were all these people and what sinister game were they playing? Was this all an elaborate ruse and, if so, at whose expense? Whose activities could be trusted as genuine and whose were theatrical, merely part of this smiling charade? The "Big Society" quickly gave way here to a community of paranoia and fear. The myth of neoliberalism seemed exposed for a moment, a myth that has only just recently been tragically preyed upon by reactionary forces in Britain. With its urge to unite all individuals under the sign of exchange, international capital, the Centre implied, could only create a community of enemies, a paranoid world in which all things become touched by the anxious delusions of the adversary.

Other projects have mapped this paranoid scenography of fantasy and madness, in which institutional spaces haunt one another. Lebanese artist Walid Raad has long dwelt in the realm where historical narratives – of war, trauma, imperialism – are forged, and he recognized from the beginning, as the head of the semi-fictitious collective The Atlas Group, that its terrain is comprised of both the visceral facts of suffering and the fictions of institutional memory. More recently, he has begun to probe the structure of paranoia, which seems most able to grasp the spatial logic of an increasingly global economy of images. This is the terrain of *Walkthrough* (2016), a roughly hour-long performance Raad inaugurated at his 2015 retrospective at The Museum of Modern Art.

Set within a hybrid stage-like structure, the work resists categorization, let alone formal description. Like a manic TED talk, it begins as a lecture cum media experience, transitions into a mad monologue before shifting into a zone of collective delusion, where as Eva Diaz has written, a "lattice of paranoia" takes over (Diaz 2016). In the first part, Raad stands in front of a seated audience, a mural-sized diagram of names, places, and faces behind him. Spectators wear headphones isolating Raad's voice from the ambient noise of the museum. Importantly, they also isolate each viewer from one another: While primed for the simultaneous collective reception so central to the stage, Raad's headphoned spectators are instead isolated bodily and cognitively, an internal monologue piped into their ears via a linked, technical apparatus. What they hear are Raad's attempts to unravel, via a personal story, a global economic system in which perpetual war and cultural imperialism, financial speculation and aesthetic production have merged, dangerously. He soon admits failure, inviting his audience to follow him behind the mural, where he delivers a fantastical narrative against a bizarre trompe l'oeil scenography of gallery architecture. In a future that has already happened, Raad explains, a man cannot enter a museum currently being constructed in the Middle East under the auspices of an American art institution. The audience is then taken to the other side of the stage set, where the temporal and spatial coordinates of *Walkthrough* begin to reconstellate themselves wildly. An increasingly frenetic narrator describes patches of pigment on an architectural fragment that had been sent to a pre-cog chef. This pigment will no longer exist in the future, Raad explains, and so it has found refuge in financial contracts and documents, hung salon-style nearby. Beckoning individual audience members to inspect such props, Raad draws his spectators into an increasingly paranoid infrastructure conditioned by fearful fantasy.

Much could be said of Raad's extraordinary work and the cognitive disorientation it engenders. Here, we might simply mention *Walkthrough*'s peculiar ability to traffic in specifically scenographic codes of spectatorship only to radically invert them. As the performance unfolds, the scenographies of conventional performance spaces (lecture hall, stage) devolve into a scenography of the intimate, internal structures of the mind. *Walkthrough*, I think, attempts to organize its public there, within the mental plane of fantasy. It is within the cognitive space of subjects, Raad seems to claim, where the contradictions of our present are being performed – not in the vagaries of military–financial transaction, but in the feeling of paranoia that they produce. Any critical public of the future must, *Walkthrough* implies, learn how to intervene within the sphere of fantasy as much as in the material world itself.

In an exhibition running virtually simultaneously with Raad's, German sculptor Isa Genzken explored similar terrain.[5] The main performers were Genzken's *Schauspieler (Actors)* (2012–), a series of mannequins (adult- and child-sized) that the artist dressed and adorned with prop-like accessories: sunglasses, wigs, police gear, textiles, hula hoops. Grouped throughout the gallery in different positions, the figures mingled visually with visitors as well as passersby, thanks to the glass street-facing wall of the gallery (occasionally rolled up so that spaces physically merged too). The result was a cheeky, uncanny scenography of figures: plastic bodies blurred with fleshy ones, art's public merged, if only momentarily, with a public of lifeless showroom dummies.

Benjamin Buchloh has described a formal "psychosis" at play in Genzken's works, a "psychotic state" that the "sculptor of the future" cannot help but articulate now that an all-encompassing financial order of "universal equivalence and exchangeability" (Buchloh 2005; 2014: 97) governs bodies and things alike (exemplified, it should be noted, by the Chelsea gallery system of which Genzken's show was a part). Elsewhere, Buchloh has noted similarities between Genzken's work and the mannequins of the Surrealists we discussed earlier (Buchloh 2014). In both cases, publics had to be organized around a zone of collective delirium. Once the stage is set, new critical tools might be found for navigating a world increasingly given over to a logic less rational than paranoiac.

Scenographies of nature and history

By now it should be clear that radically immersive scenographic environments tend to actively resist verbal description, let alone formal analysis. Each spectator's unique encounter must be considered an absolutely singular aesthetic unit, opening up potentially infinite formal variations. Such parameters define French artist Pierre Huyghe's *Untilled* (2011–12), first installed in Kassel's Karlsaue Park during Documenta 13. Arrival at the work's site was indicated by a label. "Alive entities and inanimate things," read the medium line, "made and not made." This poetical language revealed little, however, being so all-encompassing that it might describe the ingredients of any aesthetic encounter, even of any encounter at all. Paths led past patches of wild plants and stacks of cement blocks. Visitors strolled along, gazes were exchanged. A man (in this writer's encounter) rested on a pile of soil and rubble, his white hound patiently at his side, but something was awry; the dog's left front leg appeared to have been dipped in hot pink paint. At a clearing, a low hum became audible. In the center of a large patch of mud rested a reclining nude sculpture. The gaze of this odalisque, however, was many-eyed, not human. Transfigured into an active beehive, her head dispersed itself out into the world, its buzzing messengers establishing a perimeter, a sort of no-fly zone that onlookers smartly did not enter. Instead, they gazed at the scene from a distance. A scenographic space asserted itself, but it was one that remained elusive, something felt but not locatable in any specific aesthetic maneuver.

Huyghe's project has already become a locus classicus of contemporary art for its attention to ecological systems and nonhuman forms of life, but it is probably the experiential dimension of *Untilled*'s peculiar *mise-en-scène* that has lent the work its enigmatic appeal. Like any theatrical environment, *Untilled* gathers together various communities of "alive entities" – actors, audience – with collectives of "inanimate things" – props, sets. Only now, both these normally partitioned collectives interpenetrate, as in the fantastical worldscapes of Hieronymus Bosch. In his works too – think only of Bosch's *The Garden of Earthly Delights* (*ca.* 1490–1500) – the living and the thingly act out sinister proverbs or mysterious narratives.[6] Wandering through such a landscape, as *Untilled* reveals, is to wander into a space in which the materiality of life and the immateriality of fantasy have been bred together.

In Huyghe's environment, it is also never clear when the time of the work is to begin, or whether its narrative is eternally ongoing. The work seems to present itself to each "entity" differently, renewed by each wanderer's absolutely unique pathway through the space. One thinks of John Cage's chance-determined scores or the mysterious "zone" in Andrei Tarkovsky's film *Stalker* (1982), which follows wanderers in search of a ruined, depopulated area where every space presents new mysteries to characters and audience alike. In this sense, Huyghe's environment takes a cinematic shape given over to what Gilles Deleuze might have called the "time-image" (Deleuze 2007); here is a zone in which space bows to the logic of time, extinguishing and remaking itself with each moment. No person or thing – artist least of all – knows any better what shape the work will take next.

But Huyghe's is also a theatrical space, replete with actors and props; it is, in short, *live*, in all senses of the word. What purely ecological analyses of Huyghe's work miss, I think, is this uncanny, even terrifying, quality of liveness. Biological life does not pre-exist the dreaming life of the theatre here, as if motored by some vital force; rather, what animates it is the fantasy-creating energy of the theatre itself: the scenographic spectacle makes life move. The sinister question remains: is this a utopian aesthetic space open to new types of life and new forms of interspecies communication, as the curator of Documenta hoped for, or is it an ecology of control, now widened to include all forms of life in its fluid, adaptive net?[7] In microcosm, Huyghe's environment might describe what Deleuze has elsewhere termed the society of "control" (Deleuze 1992). In this zone, distinctions between living and non-living matter, animal, and human subjects are leveled, equalized under a logic expansive enough to modulate all things, regardless of species or material difference. Huyghe's work remains crucial for posing this frightful question. With the apocalyptic fears and fantasies of climate change quickly becoming realities, nature, as well as the dreaming life of subjects, must be transformed into a site of collective political struggle.

Perhaps no project of the last 20 years has explored this problematic more subtly than Paul Chan's 2007 production of Samuel Beckett's *Waiting for Godot* (Figure 10.4). Staged in two outdoor locations in New Orleans amid the devastation of Hurricane Katrina, the play almost uncomfortably mirrored the political reality of waiting – for governmental relief, recognition – that persisted two years after the disaster.[8] Here, the sadness, anxiety, and absurdity performed by Beckett's tramps must have struck the audience as both timely and timeless, even endless. For Beckett's, as Stanley Cavell has written, is a story of eternal waiting which must not, even cannot, end, "otherwise waiting would stop" (Cavell [1969] 1976: 139).

It is important from the outset to note some crucial differences between Chan's project and the previous works discussed here. *Waiting for Godot in New Orleans*, as it is now called, connects up with a history of site-specific productions – and of previous

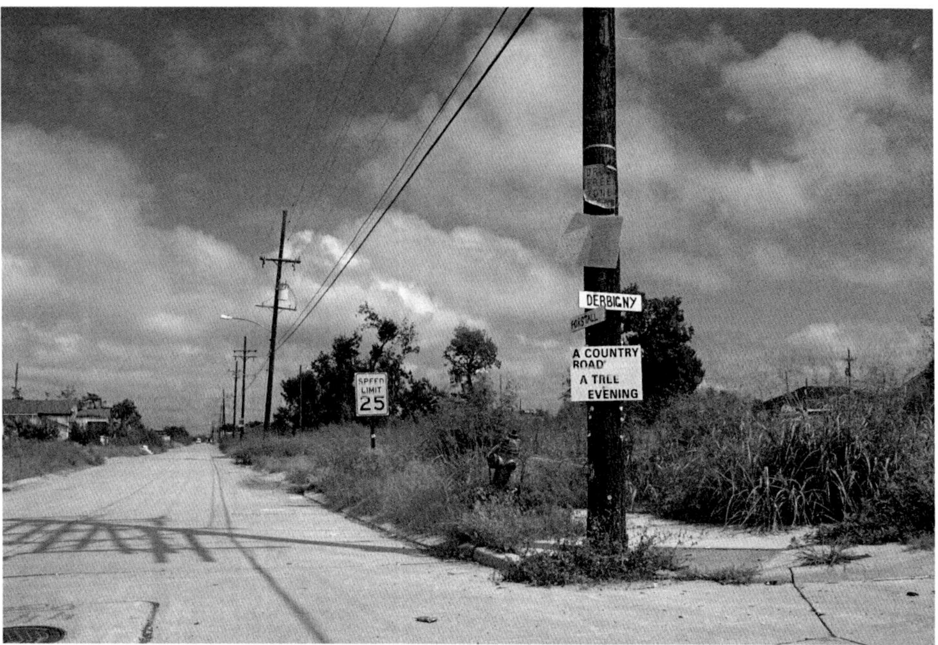

Figure 10.4 *Untitled* (sign for *Waiting for Godot* in New Orleans, Lower Ninth Ward, 2007) by Paul Chan. (Courtesy of the artist and Badlands Unlimited.)

productions of this particular play – that sought, through their staging, to intervene in the specific historical conflicts of a given site.[9] Mike Pearson's contribution to the present volume deals more explicitly with the practice of site-specific theatre, and Chan's work should at least partially be seen within this rubric, though, of course, the scenographic works traced here, beginning with Duchamp's, also maintained a degree of site-specificity. In different ways, they were all conscious of the specific contexts or infrastructures within which they had to be staged (think only of Büchel's or Raad's works, for instance). But, unlike these works, Chan's project maintained the theatre's conventional conditions of spectatorship: separation of audience and stage, professional actors, a pre-existing script, rehearsals, to name only a few.

Many different types of producers were involved in the staging process too. It would, in short, be unethical, not to mention patently false, to frame Chan as the sole author of the project. He did not write the play, nor did he direct it. Instead, he might be seen as one of many authorial nodal points making up this sprawling, adamantly collaborative project. Other nodes included key sponsor Creative Time as well as the Classical Theatre of Harlem, the two primary institutions that administered the execution of the project. Chan invited Christopher McElroen, who had staged the play at the Classical Theatre of Harlem a year prior, to direct. Professional actors – including New Orleans-born Wendell Pierce – were brought on as well. Many other New Orleans-based organizations and institutions were vital to the project too, and Chan's (2010) edited volume records many of them.

Intrinsic to Chan's conception was the integration of all aspects of the production with the existing infrastructure and rebuilding efforts of the community; it would not have been ethical, in his view, to simply helicopter in, stage the play, and leave, having made his artistic statement. Thus, Chan and others organized several non-theatrical branches to the project, including a shadow fund to finance related efforts after the performance and an educational program in which Chan participated.[10] Each arm of the project would demand extensive analysis, but we might briefly take stock here of some elements of the staging itself, particularly those that connect up with the scenographic tactics we have developed thus far.

Indeed, Duchamp haunted Chan's staging. At least one goal of the project was to see if Duchamp's infamous readymade paradigm could be put back to work. For his staging, Chan designed props to be used by the three actors, one of which directly referenced, and inverted, the formal structure of the first "readymade aided," Duchamp's *Bicycle Wheel* (1913). Replacing the handlebars of a junked bike with a white stool like the one Duchamp used as a sculptural "base," Chan turned Duchamp's project on its head: the very thing that had aestheticized and thereby defunctioned the bicycle wheel in 1913 had now been refunctioned as a usable prop for stage actors. Such props illustrate the staging's uncanny core, the way in which art objects might function both in the realm of the illusion (the scenography of a play) as well as in the realm of lived experience (the desolated backdrop of the city). This double life was prepared via publicity leading up to the performance. Before the staging, Chan designed and posted a series of posters around the city with Beckett's minimal stage direction – "A country road. A tree. Evening." – as if to transform any 'readymade' lamppost or street corner into a possible hinge-point between the space of theatre and the routines of life. It will be important, as a conclusion, to briefly take stock of this enigmatic scenographic cue.

As Cavell has written of Beckett's *Endgame*, a strange "feeling" materializes in the language and structure of the play (Cavell [1969] 1976: 145). It is conjured, he writes, by the fact that Beckett endows all subjects, whether "on the stage or in the house," with the same degree of knowledge and power regarding the unfolding of the play's narrative: no one "knows better than anyone else what is happening, no one has a better right to speak than anyone else" (Cavell [1969] 1976: 145). The same might be said of *Waiting for Godot*, particularly in Chan's production, for at that particular historical moment, everyone gathered to watch or perform in the play did not in fact know what was to come or whether waiting would actually cease. Real time and dramatic time fuse here, like some kind of horrific, ongoing epiphany. Signs auguring the future might be searched for but none are to be found. Faced with such a terrifying scenography where fantasy and history merge, what is open to subjects – whether character, stage actor, or audience member – but to find collective forms of production amidst absurd injustice? The future of the scenographic impulse will, I think, have to occupy this terrain, one that Duchamp's coal dust and Seurat's touches of color had already, in their own way, begun to chart in the early stages of the avant-garde.

Notes

1 For more on the theory of "optical mixture," see Félix Fénéon's key early analysis (Fénéon [1886/1887] 1978).

2 In this short study, major strains will of course have to be left out, including the Soviet and Futurist avant-gardes. For a recent treatment of both, see Claire Bishop's (2012: 41–75) excellent chapter.

3 The original modern attempt to synthesize the individual artistic disciplines under the rubric of the theatre was, of course, Richard Wagner's model of the *Gesamtkunstwerk*. See Theodor W. Adorno's ([1952] 2005) classic, and deeply critical, take on this model.

4 See, for example, Turrell's recent site-specific *Aten Reign* (2013) constructed for the Solomon R. Guggenheim Museum in New York.
5 The exhibition was at David Zwirner Gallery from Sept. 26–Oct. 31, 2015.
6 For more on the enmity-filled worlds of Bosch, see Joseph Koerner's (2006) recent work.
7 Director Carolyn Christov-Bakargiev (2012) describes her theoretical approach to the exhibition at large: "The attempt is not to put human thought hierarchically above the ability of other species and things to think or produce knowledge" (p. 31).
8 There were two showings in each location. The first two took place in the Lower Ninth Ward (November 2–3) and the second two in Gentilly (November 9–10).
9 *Waiting for Godot* has been restaged several times for sites undergoing various political crises. Susan Sontag, for example, famously staged the play in Sarajevo in 1993. Chan (2010) includes her important essay on the experience in his edited volume.
10 For more on these other aspects of the project, see Bishop, "Pedagogic Projects" (2012).

References

Adorno, Theodor W. [1952] 2005. *In Search of Wagner*, translated by Rodney Livingstone. London: Verso.

Alloway, Lawrence 1956. "Introduction 1: Design as a Human Activity." In *This is Tomorrow*, exhibition catalogue. London: Whitechapel Art Gallery.

Aronson, Arnold 2005. "Looking into the Abyss." In *Looking into the Abyss: Essays on Scenography*, 97–113. Ann Arbor: University of Michigan.

Bishop, Claire 2005. *Installation Art*. London: Tate.

Bishop, Claire 2012. "Artificial Hells: The Historic Avant-Garde" and "Pedagogic Projects." In *Artificial Hells: Participatory Art and the Politics of Spectatorship*, 41–75 and 241–74. London: Verso.

Bourgeois, Louise 1997. "Untitled statement." In *Louise Bourgeois: Blue Days and Pink Days*, edited by Jerry Gorovoy and Pandora Tabatabai Asbaghi, 142. Milan: Fondazione Prada.

Buchloh, Benjamin H. D. 2005. "All Things Being Equal." In *Isa Genzken*, edited by Lisa Lee, 93–7. Cambridge, MA: MIT Press.

Buchloh, Benjamin H. D. 2014. "The Dialectics of Design and Destruction: The *Degenerate Art* Exhibition (1937) and the *Exposition international du Surréalisme* (1938)." *October* 150 (Fall): 49–62.

Cavell, Stanley [1969] 1976. "Ending the Waiting Game: A Reading of Beckett's *Endgame*." In *Must We Mean What We Say?*, 107–50. Cambridge University Press.

Chan, Paul (Ed.) 2010. *Waiting for Godot in New Orleans: A Field Guide*. New York: Creative Time.

Christov-Bakargiev, Carolyn 2012. "The dance was very frenetic . . . ." In *DOCUMENTA (13), The Book of Books*, 30–45. Ostfildern: Hatje Cantz.

Crary, Jonathan 1999. *Suspensions of Perception: Attention, Spectacle, and Modern Culture*. Cambridge, MA: MIT Press.

Crosby, Theo 1956. "This is Tomorrow." *Architectural Design* 26 (October): 334.

Deleuze, Gilles 1992. "Postscript on the Societies of Control." *October* 59 (Winter): 3–7.

Deleuze, Gilles 2007. *Cinema 2: The Time-Image*. London: Continuum.

Demos, T. J. 2007. *The Exiles of Marcel Duchamp*. Cambridge, MA: MIT Press.

Diaz, Eva 2016. "In a Performance, Walid Raad Playfully Probes His MoMA Survey," *Hyperallergic*, January 22. Available online at: https://hyperallergic.com/269091/in-a-performance-walid-raad-playfully-probes-his-moma-survey.

Duchamp, Marcel [1913] 1999. *à l'infinitif: A Typotranslation by Richard Hamilton and Ecke Bonk of Marcel Duchamp's* White Box, translated by Jackie Matisse, Richard Hamilton and Ecke Bonk. Paris: Succession Marcel Duchamp.

Farquharson, Alex 2011. "The Double Club." *Artforum* (October): 117.

Fénéon, Félix [1886/1887] 1978. "Excerpts from *Some Critical Writings*." In *Seurat in Perspective*, 36–41. Englewood Cliffs, NJ: Prentice Hall.

Foucault, Michel [1966] 1970. "Las Meninas." In *The Order of Things: An Archaeology of the Human Sciences*, 3–16. London: Random House.

Fried, Michael 1980. *Absorption and Theatricality*. Chicago, IL: University of Chicago Press.
Hauser & Wirth Gallery 2011. Press release, "Piccadilly Community Centre." Available online at: http://cloud.hauserwirth.com/documents/o57koGt144Sz6fGyO3xJ752B25S5wDzz681zV4i79lXATyGHGl/piccadilly-community-centre-RMZORt.pdf.
Kachur, Lewis 2003. *Displaying the Marvelous: Marcel Duchamp, Salvador Dalí, and Surrealist Exhibition Installations*. Cambridge, MA: MIT Press.
Kiesler, Frederick 1930. *Contemporary Art Applied to the Store and its Display*. New York: Brentano's.
Koerner, Joseph 2006. "Bosch's Enmity." In *Tributes in Honor of James H. Marrow*, edited by Jeffrey Hamburger and Anne Korteweg, 285–300. London: Harvey Miller.
Krauss, Rosalind 2000. *"A Voyage on the North Sea": Art in the Age of the Post-Medium Condition*. New York: Thames & Hudson.
Nixon, Mignon 2005. *Fantastic Reality: Louise Bourgeois and a Story of Modern Art*. Cambridge, MA: MIT Press.
O'Doherty, Brian [1976/1980] 1986. *Inside the White Cube: The Ideology of the Gallery Space*, Exp. Ed. Berkeley: University of California.
Reckitt, Helena 2012. "Christoph Büchel, *Piccadilly Community Centre*." *Journal of Curatorial Studies* 1 (1): 101–4.
Searle, Adrian 2011. "Piccadilly Community Centre: Broken Britain Invades Westminster." *Guardian*, May 30. Available online at: www.theguardian.com/artanddesign/2011/may/30/piccadilly-community-centre-christoph-buchel.

11

SCENOGRAPHY BEYOND THEATRE

Designing POLIN, the Museum of the History of Polish Jews

Arnaud Dechelle

The British newspaper, the *Evening Standard*, presents annual theatre awards covering most of the usual categories. But in 2015 it presented an award in the category "Beyond Theatre" to *Savage Beauty*, an exhibition of the work of fashion designer Alexander McQueen at the Victoria and Albert Museum. In its explanation of the award, the paper referred to the show's "staging" (*Evening Standard* 2015). The curator, Claire Wilcox, was also the curator of an exhibition I designed at the V&A in 2001, *Radical Fashion*. In her introduction to the catalogue for that exhibition Wilcox highlighted the crucial role of narrative exhibitions in museums. "The history of any museum is as much made up of its exhibitions as by the sum of its permanent collections. These events mark moments in time, and changes in attitudes" (Wilcox 2001: 1).

The main concept for *Radical Fashion* provides an example of what scenography could do in museums. The aim was to create an environment that would make visitors feel as if they had fallen into the pages of a fashion magazine of the future, only in three dimensions. The striking and varied fashion collections to be presented inspired totally different environments, making the design for the entrance to such a radical and diverse group exhibition a real challenge. The inspiration came from the expression "beauty is in the eye of the beholder." Embracing this idea quite literally, we invited visitors to step into a giant eye as if entering the creative minds of the designers. Visitors could then explore a series of spaces dedicated to each of them, all connected by totally black corridors, "non-spaces" devoid of artifacts. A soundtrack and audio-visual projections further enhanced the daydream atmosphere.

To me this exhibition still presents today a successful example of a total scenography outside of theatre. Space, color, images, lighting, sound, and projections all contributed to create an environment that is hard to label. Was it a fashion exhibition, an art installation, a promenade theatre, or a multimedia and multisensory immersive journey? Probably a little bit of all of them, and that is the point; it is beyond the now blurred boundaries between disciplines. It exists within the shared territories of narrative environments that we may call scenography beyond theatre.

In conventional forms of theatre, scenography is usually employed to support a narrative that is primarily conveyed through words. But in exhibition design, as in architecture

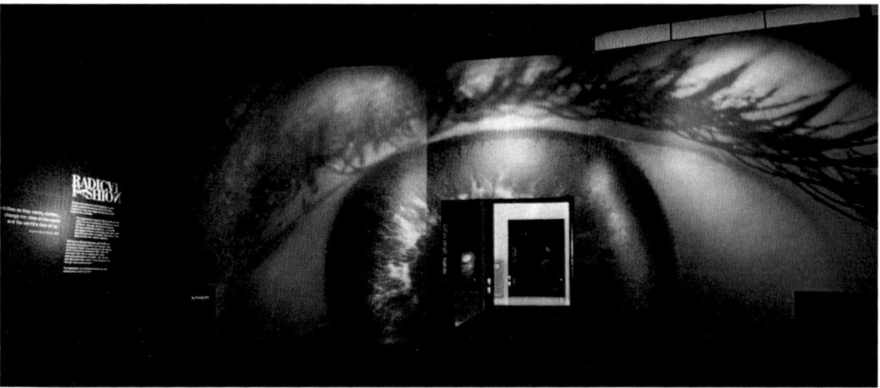

Figure 11.1 *Radical Fashion*. (Photo: Arnaud Dechelle.)

and some forms of installation art, one is creating narrative space: narrative conveyed through scenography. As a Narrative Exhibition Designer, I create environments specifically designed to support or express a narrative, and it is my view that exhibition design combines aspects of all disciplines that aim to deliver meaning in time and space. But, unlike theatre or film, in which a narrative unfolds sequentially in front of a spectator, an exhibition is a story being told as the spectator moves through the environment. As such, it is the linear narrative format that built scenography is able to challenge. As French filmmaker Jean-Luc Godard famously said, "[a] story should have a beginning, a middle and an end, but not necessarily in that order." Narrative exhibitions and themed environments have the ability to create spatial constructs that could be experienced in a random sequence as chosen by the viewer. This freedom of movement through the narrative is at the heart of narrative exhibitions. They can provide the suspension of disbelief that theatre was born to convey, but that architecture alone does not provide, and at the same time embrace the freedom of movement that a built environment offers, hence allowing the spectators to step onto the stage and explore different scenes in a sequence of their own choosing.

Architecture and narrative

In Sergei M. Eisenstein's seminal work, *Montage and Architecture*, he uses the example of the Acropolis complex in Athens to demonstrate how architecture can be experienced as a kind of narrative sequence, not unlike a film, with constructed perspectives unraveling as scenes would in a movie:

> [When talking about cinema], the word *path* is not used by chance . . . Nowadays it may also be the path followed by the mind across a multiplicity of phenomena, far apart in time and space, gathered in a certain sequence into a single meaningful concept; and these diverse impressions pass in front of an immobile spectator . . . In the past, however, the opposite was the case: the spectator moved between [a series of] carefully disposed phenomena that he absorbed sequentially with his visual sense.
>
> *(Eisenstein 1989: 116)*

Eisenstein reveals the deep paradox that lies at the heart of any attempt to consider architecture as a true "narrative" environment. On the one hand, architectural environments reflect the millennia-old tradition of creating monuments and buildings along processional paths, primarily to stage religious events, a tradition well established and recorded in antiquity in places like Mesopotamia and Egypt, and all the way back to prehistory with monuments such as Stonehenge. Some examples of medieval processions also remain in existence today, in various forms, such as the Semana Santa in Spain, or the various Carnivals around the world, such as those in Venice or Rio de Janeiro.

All the above examples could easily be classified as performances that use architectural and urban environments as backdrops in order to set the scene, either for religious or cultural events. The temporary narratives that are constructed during these processions, and witnessed by the crowds gathered along them, are nevertheless totally dependent on the events, the performers and the routes they take. They will not leave any permanent meaningful traces once the streets are cleared. When the people, costumes, music, and floats have disappeared, the city and its facades will return to their silent state. It is my view that architectural environments cannot perform as scenography in stone alone. It is only through a constructed point of view applied over them, such as processions, scenic routes, or even guided tours, that one can analyze buildings and cities through a scenographic lens. That said, the power of heavily decorated classical and medieval buildings, built and used as "books of stone," cannot be denied.

From writings carved on walls, such as Egyptian hieroglyphs, to decorative elements, frescos, and sculptures integrated into ancient temples and cathedrals, it is fair to say that architecture was a true scenographic art. However, as Victor Hugo astutely observed in *Notre Dame de Paris*, publishing (and one could include theatre as well), gradually robbed architecture of its narrative mantle:

> This will destroy That. The Book will destroy the Edifice . . . It signified that one great power was to supplant another great power. It meant, The Printing-Press will destroy the Church . . . the book of stone, so solid and so enduring, was to give way to the book of paper, more solid and more enduring still . . . Architecture began like all writing. It was first an alphabet . . . Presently they constructed words. Stone was laid upon stone, these granite syllables were coupled together, the word essayed some combinations . . . Occasionally, when there were many stones and a vast expanse of ground, they wrote a sentence.
>
> *(Hugo 1917)*

This account of buildings and architectural ensembles as "books of stone," built with their own stylistic alphabet, is a rather romantic notion. But the first point about the loss of architecture's supremacy over the book, in a world suddenly flooded by the written word, still resonates today. Hugo already highlights in his time a crucial phenomenon that still defines the tensions between architecture and scenography today: the power of fiction over reality, books over monuments, paper over stone, scenography over architecture. While stones may crumble, stories will remain. Religious and cultural practices will always require ceremonial or performance environments. But these can be endlessly rebuilt and reinvented, as long as the stories they are meant to stage are still known and willingly told. Ultimately no temple or theatre, or set or scenography, can justify its existence or make sense without a story to tell and an audience to observe it.

Another phenomenon that contributed to the demise of architecture as the primary narrative space was the impact of modernism. The war against decorative art and "ornaments" waged by the modernists still echoes today through the bare concrete and glass walls of our cities. However, the advance and spread of visual media in post-modern times, as Victor Hugo had in a way predicted, has brought unexpected ways for architectural environments to reclaim a narrative role. On The Las Vegas Strip, in Times Square in New York, Piccadilly Circus in London, or the futuristic city center of many Asian metropolises, lighting, billboards, and huge LED screens are reclaiming the urban realm as open-air theatres. The modernist status quo is also challenged by the rise of urban graffiti and its now established status as an art form. For example, Banksy, one of the most famous urban artist of our times, created a pop-up theme park in Weston-super-Mare in the UK, a dystopian version of Disneyland called 'Dismaland' (2015), in collaboration with 58 other artists. It embraced and perverted all medias associated with themed attractions. Theme parks, of course, are another form of narrative space that, though often denigrated for their commercialism and appeal to pop culture tastes, are nevertheless prime examples of scenography on an architectural and urban scale.

Staging history

The French philosopher Pierre Nora once gave comparative definitions of memory and history in *Les Lieux de Mémoire* (Nora 1989: 6) that can help understand the nature of the appeal for more open historical narratives in museums today:

> Memory is a perpetually actual phenomenon, a bond tying us to the eternal present; history is a representation of the past . . . memory is by nature multiple and yet specific; collective, plural and yet individual. History, on the other hand, belongs to everyone and to no one.
>
> *(Nora 1989: 8–9)*

Memory, as both "made up" or a constant "phenomenon" are both key to the role played by narrative exhibitions in historical exhibitions. One of the most recent and compelling examples of this approach is the permanent exhibition in POLIN Museum of the History of Polish Jews that opened in Warsaw in 2013 on the site of the former Jewish ghetto (and which won the 2016 European Museum of the Year Award). I had the privilege to be lead exhibition designer for the permanent exhibition.

The ethos for the museum was from the start inscribed in a postmodern conception of history, where no single curatorial voice alone can claim to hold the truth. The best historians in their field were invited to collaborate for many years on eight loosely chronological galleries, conceived as "chapters" in a story that would span more than one thousand years. Their curatorial voices would therefore be multiple and rarely appear as direct statements. Primary historical sources were used instead to create the main narrative, with comments from the historians only provided to add to or frame difficult topics, and presented as an anonymous "museum voice."

The main challenges on this project were set from the very start when, on one hand, no collection was yet available and, on another hand, years of academic research was gradually being distilled in a clear narrative sequence for the content of the exhibition. The answer to the lack of artifacts was the historical narrative. This remained the guiding principle all along. This museum would be a "narrative" museum, with a permanent exhibition that would embrace scenography and theatrical devices to present the rich culture of Polish Jewish life over one thousand years. The lack of objects, that was in itself a testament of the extent of the destruction, would be faced head on through a design that based itself on the story and its "key messages." Fortunately, over the years, the momentum of the project helped a collection to grow so that some object-rich displays could ultimately be introduced. In realizing this vision, all variety of scenographic treatments were borrowed from the fields of theatre, film, and art installation, with digital media and interactivity allowing for the folding in of rich textual and visual content into the narrative spaces. Professor Barbara Kirshenblatt-Gimblett, who led the academic team on the project and worked closely with the design team, clearly summarizes the overall scenographic approach:

> Enter a theatre of history, a story told in four dimensions – time is the fourth dimension. Only as the visitor moves does the story unfold . . . They may not be used to making their way through a continuous visual narrative that is organized in acts and scenes, much like a play. They may be surprised to find themselves on the stage, and in the scenography, not on the other side of the proscenium.
> *(Kirshenblatt-Gimblett 2015: 58)*

The following examples exemplify the theatrical approach adopted as a way to place visitors within the story, especially when artifacts were sparse.

In the gallery entitled Paradisus Judaeorum, which is the second gallery of the exhibition, and presents the "Golden Age" of Polish Jewish history, the aim was to create an open-plan gallery around a large white model of the towns of Krakow and Kazimierz, animated with projections and interactive screens, from which a series of thematic areas would radiate. The challenge was therefore to create a coherent and period-relevant design language for the whole gallery, while at the same time defining distinct themed areas. The solution came in a striking theatrical structure, a series of large illuminated "rings" inscribed with glowing historical quotes and suspended above each area. While the rings communicate no more than a title would do, their theatricality makes good use of the generous height in this part of the exhibition while adding drama. A meta-architecture in the space, the 'rings' instantly frame the themed areas below them and help to give the gallery an impactful and memorable visual and spatial identity.

Another example of the "walk-in set" approach can be found in the nineteenth-century gallery, "Encounters with Modernity," an installation that the team liked to refer to as the "Royal Cake." The scenography is inspired by a cartoon of the time depicting the partitions of Poland between the Prussian, Austro-Hungarian and Russian empires, as if Poland were a cake and all three powers were cutting a slice of it for themselves. The "Royal Cake" is in effect an empty set that visitors can explore at will. It makes full use of the space and height to communicate in one visual statement the key message about the partitions. Three grand portraits of the rulers of the three powers that divided Poland are suspended above a table onto which an animated partitions' map is projected. Three throne-like chairs sit below the portraits while opposite stands an empty and transparent throne, a symbol of the dissolution of the Polish-Lithuanian Commonwealth.

A final example of this approach is in the Postwar gallery where a Jewish 'Klub' is depicted as a walk-in set seemingly cut in half by a glass wall. The glass wall is in fact

Figure 11.2 The "Royal Cake" installation depicting the partitions of Poland. (© M. Starowieyska D. Golik/POLIN Museum of the History of Polish Jews.)

a one-way mirror allowing the first half of the space to appear visually complete, if duplicated, through its own reflection. On the other side, an almost identical half set is discovered. Looking back, the glass wall is now transparent allowing visitors to compare one half of the Klub with the other for their striking similarities and few differences – a television replaces a radio, signs of popular culture invade what used to be a rather traditional and dogmatic environment. This approach could not be more representative of the way scenography can be used in exhibitions to emulate a narrative experience more often associated with theatre. If this gallery was a play, spectators would have witnessed a temporary black-out of the stage to allow for props to be changed, while the setting would remain the same. In the exhibition, the same effect is created by doubling the set and using the trick of a one-way mirror to hide and then reveal the connection between the two spaces, only in the exhibition the change happens through the movement of the visitors, not the set or props. This inversion of the static and mobile conditions between set and audience is in fact the one and only real difference between this scenographic environment as an exhibition space and a theatrical set.

Some examples within POLIN illustrate further the use of even larger architectural environments in a narrative way, playing with scale, symbolism, and a freedom of movement that allows for a truly individual and immersive experience. The Synagogue Roof, for example, was a large suspended recreation of a wooden synagogue roof, reconstructed and painted to resemble the original, which was sadly destroyed with all other examples of this type of wooden architecture in Poland. It was built at a slightly smaller size than the original, in order to fit the architectural space available.

The Synagogue Roof is surrounded by more three-dimensional, yet incomplete structures, that together create a metaphorical "Jewish Town," an environment devised to

Figure 11.3 The "Klub" with the "mirrored" set depicting the slight changes within Jewish Klubs. (© M. Starowieyska D. Golik/POLIN Museum of the History of Polish Jews.)

frame sub-themes within the general narrative of the gallery. The strong conceptual scenography used in the 2003 film *Dogville* by Lars von Trier was the inspiration. The film was shot as a filmed play, within an incomplete set defined by ground plans of dwellings and other buildings along the main street of a small town taped out on the floor. We translated this approach by creating deconstructed buildings that would define a market place surrounded by a home, a tavern and a church, with the larger synagogue roof reconstruction looming behind. Animated large projections of historical illustrations featuring people populate the space. The "sets" are further enriched by low-tech interactive elements such as wooden models of goods on the market stalls, playing cards in the tavern, an open book in the home; all incorporated as "props" within the exhibition furniture but always inspired by period styles.

Perhaps the most powerful example in the POLIN museum of a narrative space at an architectural scale is the "Street" gallery. It was conceived as a full-height white set, inspired by real streets of the interwar period in Poland, but never meant as a literal

Figure 11.4 The market place in the Jewish Town gallery. (© M. Starowieyska D. Golik/POLIN Museum of the History of Polish Jews.)

Figure 11.5 The "Street," a full-height three-dimensional white set installation with full length projections. (© M. Starowieyska D. Golik/POLIN Museum of the History of Polish Jews.)

Figure 11.6 Concept visual: the Wall of Forms in the Postwar gallery. (© Event Communications Ltd.)

reconstruction, hence the all-white treatment of the facades. The street supports its own content through large projections on the facades, but also leads to thematic areas on each side and on two levels. These thematic "rooms" are also sometimes, but not necessarily always, inspired by specific period interiors such as a cinema, a café, a school, or an urban courtyard.

Finally, as an example of exhibit as art installation, there is the Postwar gallery that starts with the "Wall of Forms" (Figure 11.6), a display designed like an art installation, even though it was inspired by historical documents; forms used to register survivors of the Holocaust and reconnect them with relatives and friends. The installation spans the full height and width of the opening wall of the gallery. Identical white tiles, embossed with a relief based on an empty registration form, cover the entire wall. A few showcases and graphics with original colorful completed forms are integrated within the white tiles. The proportion between the many empty forms and the few original filled-in forms simply convey the scale of destruction of Jewish life in Poland during the Holocaust; white tiles for the people that were killed, and the few colored forms for the very small number of survivors. Museum text is kept to a very short introductory statement printed directly on the wall as the scenography speaks for itself.

All these examples from the POLIN museum show in various ways how scenography within narrative exhibitions is able to use all the basic elements of theatrical scenography, while also borrowing from film, multimedia technology, and, of course, architecture. All these disciplines are combined to fully immerse the audience in a total and holistically designed environment. This type of narrative space eventually functions most closely to immersive theatre environments, where meticulously recreated interiors can be explored at will, randomly encountering "performers" – a role played here by the artifacts and associated people and stories within the exhibition narrative. One can only imagine the possibilities when the audience will also be asked to participate, and become performers themselves, like "extras" in this "staging of history."

Museums have already begun to embrace the power of "role play," usually associated with themed environments, especially to appeal to younger audiences. These participatory approaches will without doubt open further doors on the endless possibilities offered by scenography outside of theatres. However, when dealing with history it is important that the curation and design still help to convey a clear line between reality, the sources, the artifacts, and fiction, the scenography.

Into the eye of the beholder

To conclude, it is important to remember that even if architectural and urban environments may never again reach the same level of artistic symbiosis and expression that they arguably attained in different periods and cultures in the past, they will always offer a dimension that time-based theatre cannot provide. Spectators witnessing a staged or screened performance are ultimately passive viewers. They cannot control the sequence of the drama unfolding in front of them. Visitors to a three-dimensional outdoor or indoor space may still be provided with a general narrative to follow should they wish to, but ultimately they can choose their own path and pace of visit.

This fundamental difference is why scenography outside of theatres can offer new forms of expression in what is now described as "narrative environments," not only in immersive forms of theatre and exhibitions in museums, but also in commercial venues and themed attractions. All of these environments may continue to look to architecture and other artistic disciplines as models as they devise ever more complex, fluid, and participative forms of narrative immersion.

References

Eisenstein, Sergei M. 1989. "Montage and Architecture (*c.* 1937 to 1940)," translated by Michael Glenny. *Assemblage*, issue 41, December.

Evening Standard 2015. "Evening Standard Theatre Awards 2015: Who Won and Why." 23 November. Available online at: www.standard.co.uk/goingout/theatre/evening-standard-theatre-awards-who-won-and-why-a3120701.html (accessed 19 July 2016).

Hugo, Victor 1917. *Notre Dame de Paris*, Book V, Chapter 2. The Harvard Classics Shelf of Fiction, Vol. 12. Available online at: www.bartleby.com/312/0502.html (accessed 20 July 2016).

Kirshenblatt-Gimblett, Barbara 2015. "A Theatre of History: 12 Principles." *The Drama Revue*, 59 (3): 49–59.

Nora, Pierre 1989. "Between Memory and History: Les Lieux De Mémoire." *Representations*, 26: 7–24.

Wilcox, Claire (Ed.) 2001. *Radical Fashion*. London: Victoria and Albert Museum.

12

PARTICIPATION, INTERACTION, ATMOSPHERE, PROJECTION

New forms of technological agency and behavior in recent scenographic practice

Chris Salter

In his article "The Future of Scenography," Arnold Aronson observes a shift in the theoretical and practical boundaries of the scenographic so momentous that it "call(s) into question the very notion of theatre and performance as it has been understood for over 2,500 years." The theatre faces (as usual) a crisis, "albeit an exciting one – brought about by digital technology" (Hannah and Harsløf 2008: 23–4).

With this radical alteration of scenographic *knowing* through the digital, we might first expect what Jonathan Sterne calls the "impact" narrative to hold – the idea (perpetrated mainly by Silicon Valley ideology) that technology appears from nowhere and carries with it the total transformation of the world. Of course, as Sterne argues, "such narratives cast technologies themselves as primary agents of historical change: technological deification is the religion behind claims like 'the telephone changed the way we do business,'" or the iPod changed the way we listen to music (Sterne 2002: 7).

Yet, at the same time, it is undeniable that *something* is going on within the theory and practice of scenography that is deeply tied to the social–technical upheavals wrought by the introduction of new technologies. If, as Aronson writes, the late theatre historian Denis Bablet claimed that the impulse of twentieth-century scenography was constituted by the "battle with space" (with Aronson concatenating image to this as well), I want to argue here that our "computational" technological moment realigns this battle to a new one between space and participation, atmospheric temporality and behavior. Indeed, if there is a cornerstone to the shift scenographic practice is undergoing with digital technologies, it is the *agency* increasingly attributed to invisible processes and procedures operating within the machine: the algorithms or set of instructions that govern, control, and instruct the computer on what it should *do*.

Riffing off Foucault's notion of the episteme, media theorist Alexander Galloway articulates the notion of periodization; namely, that history can be divided into certain broad phases "that allow us to gain access to history and historical differences" (Galloway 2004: 3). Foucault's own sense of the episteme comes about in his understanding of the historical shifts between what he terms sovereign and disciplinary societies. In expanding on Foucault's notions, Gilles Deleuze demonstrates yet another epistemic shift: that of moving from the enclosures of the disciplinary society to the algorithms and databases of the control society (Deleuze 1992).

What is interesting about such notions of periodization is that they bypass chronology as a determining factor for history and, instead, attempt to examine practices across a wide range of political-social-technical-aesthetic-ethical contexts within specific temporal periods. Likewise, according to Foucault, each episteme is also associated with a particular set of techniques and technologies. As Manuel De Landa has written, each technological episteme and its associated "machinic paradigms" is easily superseded or replaced by the next: the clockwork by the motor, the motor by the computer (De Landa 1991: 225).

From the point of view of twentieth- and twenty-first-century stage performance history, the traditional site of the scenographic, we can witness a similar set of epistemic ruptures and transformations: the re-imagining of the stage as a kinetic machine in the utopian theatres of the Constructivists and the Bauhaus with the backdrop of the machine age; the introduction of the medium of filmic languages and techniques in the 1920s with Robert Edmond Jones' proclamations of a screenal future; the re-imagining of kinetics in the post-war optical experimentation of Svoboda; the introduction of live electronic images in the work of Jacques Polieri; and, finally, the shift towards real-time interaction and feedback between performers and the stage environment, facilitated by new forms of technological materiality at the end of the twentieth century.

The digital and its relationship to the theatre has recently become the subject of a growing array of literature (Giannachi 2004; Kaye 2007; Salter 2010; Broadhurst and Machon 2012; Parker-Starbuck 2011; Klich and Scheer 2011). But the digital's impact on scenography has been largely conflated with models and methods that already predate the computer, for example, the use of projected images. In fact, the often-used term "digital scenography" is usually a misnomer, referring mainly to the use of computers to pre-render or project real-time images onto screens or surfaces using digital projection technology. Ironically, this "digital" exists only in the machine itself, since the forms of projected light that these surfaces, and eventually our retinas, capture are resolutely in the analog world because they are still constituted as light waves.

A second aspect of the digital's impact on the scenographic is the use of the computer to *model*, that is, to calculate and fabricate the weight, size, shape, forces, and interdependencies of different materials used in the construction of scenographic environments. Here, a whole range of digital fabrication technologies such as 3D modeling and printing, rapid prototyping and CNC fall under this kind of category. But there is another sense of the digital that is usually ignored in many accounts of theatre and technology and it is one, which I will subsequently argue, that has led to a more radical transformation: that is, the digital as a specific type of numerically-based *process* that enables an unheard of degree of control and precision of operation on electronic signals. Part of this precision comes from the discretized representations and consequent algorithmic manipulations of analog data that the computer makes possible – for example, being able to operate at the micro-sonic level on a sound or performing complex mathematical processes like convolution or edge detection on a live (analog) video signal that then becomes digitized, all in real time. This notion is articulated extremely well by the electronic composer Trevor Wishart when he states, "[c]omputer technology, offering us the most detailed control of the internal parameters of sounds, . . . fulfills the original dream of electronic music – to be able to sculpt all aspects of sound" (Wishart 1996: 5).

What this suggests through such terms as interaction, feedback and modulation is the inherent possibility of the machine to perceive (in a very limited sense), react and respond, thereby altering the material conditions of the world. In other words, the computer is *performative* itself, in the sense that the sociologist of science Andrew Pickering uses and defines the term: "as a field of powers and capacities situated in machinic captures of material agency" (Pickering 1995: 7).

But why, through its algorithmic, interactive and performative contexts laid out above, has the digital been so embraced? The American director Peter Sellars states that

> the high tech interface has been appealing to artists because it does have the potential to fragment and diversify the master narrative, offering simultaneous multiple perspectives, freshly negotiated independent vocabularies and the direct experience of ambiguity, the ineffable and a sensory and mental landscape that lies above, below and beyond ideology.
>
> *(Salter 2010: x)*

In other words, instead of mere representations, the digital does something else. It offers the possibility of capturing the world; abstracting, manipulating and shaping it in a wholly other form and then sending it back out in a newly altered state.

The question of whether the digital then has radically altered and, in the process, destabilized the ontology of the scenographic is thus more complex than it would first appear. Aronson, for example, states there is a need to distinguish between scenography, which, regardless of its visual and spatial approach, continues to be a part of an "historical continuum of theatrical design," and scenography that finds itself not only outside of the "architecture of theatre," but "denies the presence of the stage," and escapes the traditional conventions of "spectator and performer" (Aronson 2011: 87)

If we look back over the last 50 years, it is clear that scenography long left the context of the global stage, settling into lofts, museums, galleries, streets, stadiums, and the urban landscape. What instead I want to examine here therefore is less the question of genre (whether the scenographic is in the theatre or not) or site (theatre versus visual arts) but rather four core epistemic shifts that mark an evolutionary (rather than revolutionary) impact of new technologies on scenographic thinking and making. These include:

1 The shift to scenography that is inhabited and shaped by an intertwining of both human (performers or, more increasingly, spectators) and nonhuman (machines, algorithms) forces.
2 The move from scenography as the site of the visible in the guise/image of the machine to the invisible, in the form of hidden sensing and control systems.
3 A shift from space, image, and object to temporality, atmosphere, and behavior.
4 An increasing interest in senses beyond vision and an embrace of the acoustic, the tactile, the olfactory, the gustatory, and the proprioceptive.

In other words, what I want to claim is that the roots of these shifts already lay in the twentieth century but their impact has been accelerated, amplified, and also problematized by recent digital technological developments. What new technologies, both in direct use (forms of computer generated interaction between performers/spectators/audiences) and within a general cultural mindset bring to scenographic practice are new senses of interaction and participation within a total environment that invokes and enrolls all of the senses (Salter 2015).

I identify four core thematic arenas where I see the issues discussed above increasingly played out: *participation*, which examines a wide range of established but also emerging practices in the theatre, the visual and media arts, live role-playing games, architectural environments, and location-based entertainment that deploy the audience within (rather than outside of) the scenographic surround; *interaction*, which involves direct *feedback* and *response* (through digital technologies such as sensors/actuators) as models; *atmospheres*, in which the built solidity of "scenic design" is replaced by ephemeral elements such as light, fog, sound, water, heat, smell, and similar that operate across all of the senses; and finally, *projection*, which encompasses historical but also contemporary attempts to turn urban space into a dramaturgical–scenographic arena through the use of large-scale images integrated within architecture and the global city.

With this thematic, I explore the dramatic epistemic shifts that are in process due to the "digital" impact on scenographic practices across a wide range of territories and histories without falling prey to a method of historiography that is strictly chronological or an ideology that insists on a narrative of technical determinism and "progress" to explain socio-technical transformation. My aim here is thus to flesh out trends that are happening cross-laterally in order to develop and enlarge a continuity between the history of scenographic experimentation within its traditionally understood context (the stage) and the possibilities of new technologies and new sites of knowing and experience that continually transform our understanding and experience of interaction, participation and even representation.

Participation

The British born, American-based art historian Claire Bishop defines installation art as

> a type of art that the viewer physically enters and which is often described as 'theatrical,' 'immersive' or 'experiential.' What the term installation particularly focuses on is 'a desire to heighten the viewer's awareness of how objects are positioned (installed) in a space and our bodily response to this . . . installation art creates a situation in which the viewer physically enters and insists that you regard this as a singular totality.
>
> *(Bishop 2005: 1)*

Bishop's work attempts to instantiate a lineage of visual arts practices that have their origins in Duchamp's installations the *Large Glass* and the late *Étant donnés*, carrying through to Allan Kaprow's Happenings and Cage's participatory environments of the 1960s as well as the full-scale Land Art of Robert Smithson, Michael Heizer, Jean Claude and Christo, and others in the 1960s–1970s and, finally, coming full circle with the "immersive" environmental practices of artists such as Ilya Kabakov, Mary Kelley, Christian Boltanksi, Gregor Schneider, Carsten Höller, Yayoi Kusama, and others.

What the term installation does is not only re-situate the traditionally distanced "viewer" of artworks into active participants in the work itself but also (and more importantly for our purposes) transform the artistic work from a self-sufficient object to a situation or environment that is wholly dependent on the viewer's sense of their own (and others) embodiment, perception and time. The partial aim of such a strategy was and is to make the viewers become reflexively aware of their role as actors within what we can term a scenographic unfolding.

For example, in the 1970s, Brazilian artists like Lygia Clark and Hélio Oiticica designed multi-sensorial environments and "wearable architectures" that aimed to envelop and, simultaneously, involve spectators in the work's creation. While Clark focused on the manipulation and wearing of objects to heighten sense perception by spectators, Oiticica developed temporary makeshift spaces inspired by Brazilian favelas (slum towns) in which a kind of "total lived experience" (*vivencia*) would take place through a vivid use of color, labyrinthine architectures, and other sensorially provocative techniques. With both Clark and Oiticica's work, the visitors themselves could never be passive onlookers but instead became simultaneously subjects as well as objects of the environment.

Yet, the role of technological agency, of what these environments do and the impact of their material actions, is curiously absent from the installation art analysis. For example, in the case of artists such as Bruce Nauman, Dan Graham, Höller, Schneider, Olafur Eliasson, and others that Bishop describes, there is little to no mention at all about the complex entanglements between their artificially constructed environments made possible through advanced technologies (in Nauman or Graham's case, real time CCTV, or, in Eliasson's, complex logistical and mechanical systems that distribute natural elements such as fog, light, heat, haze, steam, and others) and the experiences of viewers that are shaped by such technical systems.

Instead, participation is chiefly seen as a social strategy. The aim to turn the viewer into an active social participant and actant within an environment itself is principally a social–political motivation – a context famously described by curator Nicolas Bourriaud as "relational aesthetics": artistic practices that examine "the realm of human interactions and its social context, rather than the assertion of an independent and private symbolic space" (Bourriaud 2002: 114). Tracing his genealogy in Joseph Beuys' notion of "social sculpture" and anchored in the practices of artists such as Rirkrit Tiravanija, Philippe Pareno, Höller and others, Bourriaud's interest stems less from the environment in which such social interactions take place and more in the fact that such actions can be collectively articulated.

At first, the emphasis on the viewer becoming actors/participants within highly designed environments appears to have a similar resonance within the history of stage-based scenography, where calls from Frederick Kiesler, El Lissitsky, Moholy-Nagy, Lybov Popova, and others in the 1920s sought to destroy the idea that scenography amounted to 2D painting – a call that was brilliantly captured by Kiesler's argument in his 1924 manifesto "The Scenery Explodes" that "the stage is not a buttonhole that should be decorated" (Lesák 1988: 42).

Designing a range of kinetic environments in which audiences would pop up, slide through, dance, and, in general be physically displaced by all manner of hydraulic, mechanical, ballistic, and other kinetic systems (most of which were imagined in sketches and diagrams but never built), stage designers in the 1920s incorporated techniques and technologies from the visual arts, cinema, architecture and design in order to fuse engineering progress with aesthetic daring do while chipping away at the artificial distance between stage environment and spectator.

This attempt to break what Richard Schechner famously called "the great divide," the split between audience and stage, would thus reach its culmination in theatrical experiments in the 1960s and onwards, dubbed by Schechner as "environmental theatre." Interestingly close to Bourriaud's argument, Schechner's description of environment chiefly involved the notion of a scenographic context emerging from and expressing the *social* dynamics of participation between performers, spectators and the space itself. Such a scenographic "environment" emerges as a transaction between different social forces and, in the spirit of the 1960s, even transcends the borders of the theatre by entering into non-theatrical "performances" or "events" such as demonstrations and happenings as well as more environmentally based performances such as the work of The Performance Group, Schechner's own company at the time (Schechner 1968).

Examining a lineage that includes The Living Theatre, Robert Wilson, Peter Brook, Jerzy Grotowski, Joseph Chaikin, Ariane Mnouchkine, and Luca Ronconi, to the later work of European and American theatre makers like Klaus Michael Grüber, Peter Stein, Deborah Warner, Reza Abdoh, Michael Simon, and many others, leading up to more contemporary practitioners like the early work of dumb type, La Fura dels Baus, rimini protokoll or Punchdrunk, there has been a long history of specific scenographic experiments that have evolved in relationship to Schechner's criteria in the predominantly European, American, and Asian experimental theatre scenes from the 1960s to the 1990s.[1] Yet, despite Schechner's call for "living spaces," there is a key ontological difference between a scenographic environment that is developed based on the social relationship between performers, text, and audience, and one that removes entirely a focus on the human performer and, instead, shifts the locus of performative agency towards the (non-human) actions of the environment. While this might invoke Bishop's understanding of installation, the fact that there is either witnessing, interplay or, in the case of computationally mediated environments, direct interaction between the spectator and the space suggests a different entanglement between human and technical agency.

To be more specific, we might see three different types of participatory scenographic agencies at work: (1) machine-like environments that function as performers and in which the viewer remains either relatively passive (in the case of there being the traditional cut between the stage and the audience) or active in so far as they are physically moving or moved through the environment; (2) environments in which spectators role-play characters or actions that advance a narrative or sequence of actions in the environment, or physically react off and inside the space with their bodies; and (3) environments in which technologically-driven forms of electronic or computer-augmented interaction enable direct feedback between the spectators and the scenography itself.

This first case is exemplified by a range of recent works that harken back to the early automata performances of the eighteenth century. While such machine *mise en scène* have constituted a continuing tradition in late-twentieth-century experimental performance, many of the most well-known works from groups such as Survival Research Labs have focused on the almost anthropomorphic acts of the machines themselves, rather than conceiving of the machine as a total environment in which spectators become literal components. According to German director/composer Heiner Goebbels, whose 2007 "performance without performers" or "no man show" *Stifters Dinge* featured a machinic mass of five piano-like instruments performing a music-theatre work inspired by the nineteenth-century German romantic writer Adalbert Stifter, such a machine environment "sets human bodies into a relationship with non-human machinery" (Goebbels 2008).

In *Stifters Dinge*, the public becomes witness to a strange automaton environment that performs itself: a scenic areal replete with a gigantic mechanical–electrical moving assemblage consisting of piano elements merged with electrically driven robotic components, a series of rails that disclose a long channel of water that undergoes various state changes from dry ice to liquid, and a range of other scenic paraphernalia such as winch-driven white traveler-like screens that descend and ascend, a series of bare trees, light boxes and other apparatus that constitute the event.

A similar type of machine witnessing takes place in South African-born artist and filmmaker William Kentridge's 2012 sculptural-filmic walk-in environment *The Refusal of Time*, realized for the 2012 Documenta 13. Consisting of five video channels of projected drawings that appear to continually redraw themselves over the course of 30 minutes, *The Refusal of Time*'s main performer was a gigantic mechanical "elephant" – an accordion-like "breathing machine" occupying the physical center of the installation space. Exploring concepts of the relativity of time and developed in dialogue with Harvard historian of science Peter Galison, Kentridge's mechanical elephant, inspired by Charles Dickens' description of factory machines in the nineteenth century in *Hard Times*, acted as both a metaphoric generator of energy for the work as well as a visual and acoustic enactment of a foregone machine age.

While Goebbels and Kentridge's machines are automata in the true sense of the word, literally wind-up figures or contrivances that seem to act on their own volition or power, a different kind of automata-like environment can be found in the room-scale works of the Canadian artist pair Janet Cardiff and George Burris Miller. In mixed media installations like *Storm Room* (2009), *The Killing Machine* (2007), *Opera for a Small Room* (2005), and *Pandemonium* (2005), Cardiff and Miller construct site-specific, room-within-room works in which architectural elements behave in strange, ironic, and playful ways.

In *Storm Room*, an installation built inside an abandoned dentist office in Japan, Cardiff and Miller created a 10-minute artificial storm replete with rain inside and outside of the space's windows, strobe-generated lighting, and multi-channel audio, all of which conveyed the sense of a real storm passing in and out of the space. This kind of narrative autonomous scenography without actors, however, reaches its apex in the pair's 2005 work *Opera for a Small Room*. Telling the story of a deceased record collector from a small Canadian town, an antique-strewn 1950s-style room is built inside a room-sized wooden crate in which visitors peer through holes and cracks in the walls but which they cannot enter. The cluttered space narrates a kind of ghost opera as it comes alive through synchronized lighting and robotically-controlled gramophones, which proceed to autonomously "compose" the installation's soundtrack by playing hundreds of records whose sounds are broadcast through 24 antique speakers.

Perhaps the most colossal example of a kind of machinic autonomous scenography, however, is the warehouse-scale contraption built by industrial sculptors/musicians Nicolas Baginski and Barry Schwartz for their 1995 "orchestrated sculpture" *I-Beam Music*, at the Kampnagel Theatre in Hamburg. With the spectators witness to its actions, roaming inside and around the hulking machine, Baginski and Schwartz's computer-actuated string instrument was constructed from a 4-meter-long steel I-beam, strung with stretched piano wire and "plucked" by solenoid actuators. Traveling down the length of the vast former industrial hall, the entire scenic space was "played" by an environment of dry ice "fingers" (chemicals such as liquid nitrogen, water, electric current, and machine parts) as well as by acoustic information gathered and analyzed from the environment and transduced back to the instrument to affect its performance.

What such a work like *I-Beam Music* contributes to this history of automata scenography is the possibility of feedback between machine and environment within the scenographic setup itself, creating (even if limited) improvisational behavior outside of direct human orchestration. The manner in which an environment can "play itself" and evolve based on such actions differs significantly from the recent scenographic machines found in director Robert Lepage's *Ka* Las Vegas spectacle for Cirque du Soleil or Carl Fillion's monstrous 40-ton machine designed for Lepage's 2010 *Ring* cycle at the Metropolitan Opera in New York, both of which, while featuring spectacular hydraulic, robotic maneuvers, were essentially pre-programmed *a priori* by stage technicians, with no possibility of improvisation (for perhaps good reasons in terms of safety).

A second form of non-human scenographic performance involves situations in which the audience becomes a willing (or unwilling) partner by becoming either the focus or target of the environment's actions or role-playing directly within it. The spectator thus shifts roles, functioning as a substitute actor and evolving the dramaturgical development of the environment. Some well-known works from groups such as Blast Theory or the "post-dramaturgical theatre" (Lehmann) of the German–English collective Gob Squad have created successful role-playing events in which audiences morph from their usual role as passive spectators into active characters within projected virtual game spaces (*Desert Rain*), and are thrown into direct action by observing characters who are being filmed and becoming "co stars" in a running film (*Super Night Shot*), or moving through the real-time scenography of a cityscape that is overlaid or mixed together with various forms of augmented reality information (*Can You See Me Now?*, *Uncle Roy All Around You*).

A much more imaginative example of this kind of work, however, involves spectators who literally play roles directly within an unfinished scenic scape. In a clever inversion of the gaming movement called larping (live action role playing), the Montreal-based interactive design agency Daily Tous les Jours' 2012 *Kit Operette* created an environment from props, costumes, sensor-driven interactive furniture and projections in which visitors follow sets of instructions and advance the *mise en scène* by "dancing and singing their way through a dynamic décor that is virtually and physically reminiscent of a period operetta" (Daily Tous les Jours 2012).

While these works operate on the assumption that visitors will engage in direct interaction with a pre-determined but not yet finished scenic scenario, large-scale installation projects operating on the boundaries of theatre, visual art, sound installation and new media from the Linz Austria-based collective Time's Up, Japanese artists Towata and Matsumoto, and the author of this chapter have experimented in a more extreme manner with the audience's role as experimental subjects within environments that are specifically designed to provoke perceptual and emotional disorientation by directly implicating and impacting spectator's bodies.

Active principally in the 1990s, the Austrian-based collective Time's Up – Laboratory for the Construction of Experimental Situations created game-like environments of objects and projections in which participants would interact with immersive media environments through the use of body-based interfaces, demanding intense physical exertion (Boykett 1996). In *Hyperfitness Studio*, also known as *Hypercompetition for Beginners* (1996–9), for example, participants encountering a science-fiction-themed fitness studio outfitted with bizarre workout devices, and engage in a hybrid of game, sporting competition and mock psychological experiment as they attempt to compete against each other.

SPIN (Spherical Projection Interface) and *Body Spin* (1999–) attempted to "close the gap between physical and virtual environments," integrating the spectator's body into a complex and disorienting physical feedback loop. By placing spectators into gigantic rolling spheres and using their psychophysical data such as pulse rate, breath, and stress levels gathered from worn body sensors to generate game-like situations with projection-based environments, passive visitors became active sensing forms within a gigantic pinball machine (Salter 2010: 334).

More extreme, almost Artaudian, forms of such sensory scenographies were explored by Japanese artists in the early 1990s. Beginning with their 1991 group installation performance *Divina Commedia: Practices for Death* and continuing with *Trobar Clus* (1992–3), a similar installation albeit for one visitor, the artist duo Masayuki Towata and Yasuakai Matsumoto designed participatory light, sound, and architectural environments that at times invoked near-death experiences and aimed to push participants into altered states of bodily sensation and consciousness.

In *Divina Commedia*, originally staged at Xebec Hall in Kobe, Japan, five audience members who donned specially designed dust-proof clothing lay inside a five-meter pool filled with three tons of edible gel. After a period of time in total darkness, the group underwent an intense acoustic and visual experience: a choreographed sequence of flashing lights, generated from an array of computer-controlled Dataflash strobes hung directly above. Aiming to "loosen their sensory-motor connections," Towata and Matsumoto's work was inspired by the float tanks of John Lilly as well as research into near-death experiences (Iwaki 2013: 219). Exploring the "grey zone between death and life," the artists utilized audio-visual–architectural scenography to both calm and imperil visitors' bodies through a fully immersive limit experience.

In a different manner, my own "performative sensory environments," such as *JND* (2010), *Displace* (2011–14) and *Ilinx* (2014–15), also explore the intimate entangling of felt sensations between spectators' bodies and performance spaces whose sense of shape, size and dimensions are continually altered by composed sequences of light, sound and tactile vibration operating at varying perceptual thresholds. In *Ilinx*, a performative installation developed in collaboration with the Italian audio-visual artist TeZ, wearables designer Valerie Lamontagne, and a team of music technology researchers from McGill University, a small group of spectators wear wirelessly-enabled full-body haptic clothing and navigate with extremely reduced vision inside a large space continually altered by way of a carefully composed sequence of light and acoustic cues.

Generating what might be labeled a *synesthetic* (the crossing over of one sense into another) experience in which sounds, light, and the thickness of space are blurred together, the artificial caresses, strokes, and vibrations felt on and over the spectators' bodies shape both their sense of space and perceived sense of time, resulting in a panoply of sensory impressions that blur distinctions between bodies and space through simultaneous proprioceptive, haptic, acoustic, (semi)-visual, and equilibrioceptive sensations.

Akin to what choreographer Steve Paxton labeled "participatory environments," (referring to his famous *9 Evenings: Theatre and Engineering* installation *Physical*

Things in 1966) in which a performance environment exclusively comes into being through the public's co-presence and direct physical interaction, a range of recent artists, architects and choreographers have designed massive architectural–scenographic setups that present challenging physical affordances to visitors. With some of these projects enabled through the complex material calculations made possible by digital systems, most explore a physically-driven system of feedback between the participants and carefully engineered spaces in which experiences of friction, dislocation, and precarious, yet simultaneously playful, states of bodily experience occur.

Examples of this approach are the elaborate installation projects from the Argentinian artist-architect Tomás Saraceno. Inspired by the material and biological sciences, cosmology, philosophy, and visionary architects like Archigram, Paulo Solieri, and Yona Friedman, Saraceno's works include inflatable mylar clouds and bubble-like forms (*In Orbit*, *Cloud City*), rooms strung with spiderweb-like filigree (*Galaxies Forming Along Filaments*) that ensnare, encircle and transform visitors' quotidian movement patterns, or mass inflatable sculptures constructed of industrial plastic sheeting and other materials functioning as trampolines that suspend jumping and rolling visitors hundreds of feet in the air (*On Space Time Foam*). Described by philosopher Bruno Latour as "visual experiences that are not situated in any fixed ontological domain" (Latour 2011) since they work across different scales (from the nano-scale of molecules to the dimensions of flying cities), Saraceno's scenographies present the conditions for visitors to experience such physical sensations as weightlessness, the sense of flying, falling in space, and other almost utopian corporeal experiences within spectacularly engineered structures.

Another interesting example of scenography re-imagined as highly engineered, physically interactive playscapes comes from the Belgian artist Carsten Höller who, over a long career starting in the 1980s, has constructed environments and installations that the artist labels "large scale experiments with people." Trained as an agricultural entomologist and described by *The Guardian* in 2015 as "the Willy Wonka of conceptual art," Höller's works, which range from pitch-black labyrinths that end in blinding light to out-of-proportion, almost psychotically designed corkscrew-shaped spiral "isomeric" slides, seek to blur the line between art and spectacle, amusement-park entertainment and philosophical–perceptual conundrums.

Many of Höller's installations and objects function as hallucinatory scenescapes in which the visitor's normal perceptual habits are thwarted, most particularly in *Flying Machine*, where visitors are strapped into a harness and flung around in the air through a machine that resembles a centrifuge. Most radically and in a scenography worthy of '60s artists like Cage who sought to destroy the lines between art and life, Höller's *Double Club* was a six-month nightclub-dancefloor-bar and restaurant produced by the Fondazione Prada and set up inside an abandoned West London warehouse. Called "Studio 54 for the flash mob generation," the Club itself presented visitors with a typical Höller schizophrenic environment, literally divided and designed in two split parts juxtaposed next to each other spatially and temporally: a "Western" side and a "Congolese" side.

In a different manner, the "choreographic objects" of choreographer William Forsythe comprise spatial–sonic–architectural interventions sited in museums, government buildings, shopping centers, abandoned warehouses and other public spaces, which function as "an alternative site for the understanding of potential instigation and organization of action to reside" (Forsythe 2011). Long known for his deconstruction of classical ballet and the modes of perception and attention that have sustained choreographic practice, Forsythe's interest with "choreographic objects" lies in a broader public "self-choreographing" themselves and experiencing their own physical limits.

From a distance, works such as *White Bouncy Castle* (1997), a gigantic inflatable structure in which jumping visitors vicariously experience the ballistic actions and "physical destabilization" undergone by dancers; *Scattered Crowd* (2001), where visitors navigate a space filled with thousands of white helium balloons and washes of composer Ekkehard Ehler's sampled walls of sound; or *The Fact of Matter* (2009), which is built from a setup of hanging Olympic-style gymnast rings on textile bands that the audience has to jump through and hang on to in order to move through a space, appear to be benign objects positioned in space, without clear instructions for use or context. Yet, what the balloons, inflatable structures, rings, or swinging pendulums in many of Forsythe's choreographic objects seem to offer to spectators is more than purely visual (or sonic) pleasure from a distance. Instead, in attempting to navigate through such a highly constructed space like *Fact of Matter*, participants are offered up a kind of profound kinesthetic vertigo, in which one needs to rely completely and totally on their own weight and coordination skills to navigate the spaces.

Interaction

Forsythe's interest in the "body of the spectator" entering into a kind of temporally altering experience also plays out in his *City of Abstracts* (2000): a real-time video installation deployed in public spaces utilizing techniques developed by the Icelandic-American video artist Steina Vasulka. In the installation, a passer-by's movements are captured by a camera in real time and fed into a digital process that removes scan lines from the image, thus temporally delaying and distorting any movement and making bodies appear as a kind of spiraling liquid. While similar to many real-time video works (including Steina's own *Bent Scans*) of the 1990s, *City of Abstracts* suggests yet a fourth connection concerning participatory and performative scenography – one that brings the moving body of the audience in direct feedback with computational processes that are perceptually inaccessible to the participant since they happen within the confines of the computer.

Traced back to the 1960s where cybernetic techniques and paradigms aimed to reimagine audience participation as part of a feedback and response loop, the histories of computationally augmented interactive spaces have since evolved across a diverse set of genres and practices including the visual arts, games, theatre and stage performance, architecture, and other forms of intermedia, cross-media, multi-media, and intramedia art and design (Paul 2003; Grau 2003; Brouwer *et al.* 2007; Graham and Cook 2010; Kwastek 2013).

Historically the term "interactive," unlike participatory, immediately suggests the presence of the computer (whether through analog electronics, like earlier works in the 1950s and 1960s or the later use of digital processes), the use of time as a process and some form of feedback that serves to alter parameters of a system (hardware and software) in *real time* – meaning that the speed of input matches or is close to the speed of output. Defining interaction, however, is somewhat of a mammoth task given the enormous literature around the term in media art history, STS, anthropology of science, sociology and other fields. One classic definition from German art historian Söke Dinkla is that "interactive art serves as a category-specific designation for computer-supported works in which an interaction takes place between digital computer systems and users" (Kwastek 2013: 4).

The socio-technical-aesthetic history of interactive art, design, performance, games, and architecture works have been well documented across the sources listed above whose geneaologies and specific works we will not re-rehearse here. What is more pertinent in relation to the question of the impact of interaction modalities on scenography is the historical context that such interaction in the present takes and *will take* in the future. In other words, the potential impact of the digital in scenographic practice still remains to be seen but will doubtlessly go beyond command and control (programming cues and watching the results) as new kinds of self-organization and algorithmic reasoning within the context of what sociologist Marc Andrejevic has called the "sensory society" take over.

If, as Andrejevic argues, the sensor society refers "to a world in which the interactive devices and applications that populate the digital information environment come to double as sensors" and "to emerging practices of data collection and use that complicate and reconfigure received categories of privacy, surveillance, and even sense-making," then the traditional mechanisms of the visual-spatial understanding of the scenographic will start to erode, replaced by computational logics that yield continually reconfigured environments and experiences (Andrejevic and Burdon 2014).

It is the possibility of real-time transformation of the environment in which present and future scenographic practice must come face to face with a radically different paradigm of interaction. On the one hand, we have the model of the performer holding (or acting) like an interface – influencing and shaping pre-existing (usually) audio-visual content through sensing and output. This has mainly happened in numerous works in the last 20 or so years, in which an audio-visual environment is controlled by dancers, performers or, most recently, visitors by being "sensed" from some kind of input device (camera, motion sensor, etc.). This was already articulated by computer scientist Myron Kruger who famously argued that *interaction itself* was the medium in creating relationships between human performers and the audio-visual environment: the paradigmatic image of digital scenography of the performer standing before the screen and affecting some kind of change in the display (Kruger 1996).

But current software paradigms in computer science such as supervised and unsupervised machine learning, deep-learning networks and other contemporary AI processes all propose a radically different model of imagining mapping, control and interaction, which, as historian of science Orit Halpern writes, involves "the disavowal of the present in the interest of prediction" (Halpern 2005: 293). In other words, what the future of scenography might have in store will have more to do with how such algorithms function to predict and produce future actions than what appears at present to us.

From the smallest-scale Arduino microcontrollers to large-scale "smart dust" networks that include thousands of independently operating sensor/actuator nodes, the use of mass distributed wireless sensor network infrastructures and smart objects/things have only slowly begun to enter the scenographic arena but, if Andrejevic's arguments suggest anything, it is that the socio-technical ground is quickly being laid for a transition from scenography as a visual battle between space and image to an invisible one in which the real processes of prediction and production and agency will be held by algorithms.

Indeed, if cognitive science increasingly sees the brain itself as a kind of self-organizing network (Varela *et al.* 2001; Kohonen 1990), what then would (near) future self-organized scenographic models *act* (rather than look) like? For example, with new protocols, standards and interoperable form, motion control, lighting and sound (specifically Skelton and Tipton lighting ideologies) as cue based and fixed in time are soon to be replaced by complex multi-layered, network-based systems already being introduced in the location-based entertainment industry such as ACN (Architecture for Control Networks), which present a fundamentally different paradigm of interaction between scenographic entities in contrast to limited bandwidth systems like DMX and MIDI. In addition to somewhat arcane technical breakthroughs like time synchrony between different manufacturer's devices, and multi-cast transport protocols, the ability to handle "intelligent" (i.e., sensor-based) control at each lighting instrument, object, or human body in a space suggests a mass of semi-sentient "agents" that communicate among each other over some spatio-temporal distance. Is swarm-based scenography in the near future?

There are (only) a few scenographically based works at the moment that deploy such distributed sensor-based intelligence or at least suggest this direction. For example, the urban projects of Rafael Lozano-Hemmer, which develop a host of sophisticated technologies for capturing user actions (pulse, body motion, breath, etc.), making decisions and controlling temporal patterns in robotically controlled lighting and video systems, create critical comments on participation and interaction in the city.

In architectural contexts, works exploring these directions include architecture collectives like the Japanese group Double Negatives Architecture (dNA) who, with the installation *Corpora in Si(gh)te*, turned the environmental data around the Hungarian pavilion during the 2008 Venice Architecture Biennale into large-scale images and sounds; the architectural–media environments of designer Usman Haque, whose 2012 mass public action *Another Life* staged in the public square of Bradford, UK, also made use of a mass of sensor-networked controlled lighting, sound, lasers, water fountains, misters, and pyrotechnics; or architect Philip Beesley whose dense forests of filigreed tendrils composed from intricately laser-cut materials come alive in motion through a battery of distributed sensors, actuators and other electronics. Exploring the link between architecture, visual art, sound and new forms of emergence and self-organization, this author's own work *N-Polytope* (2012), a re-imagining of Iannis Xenakis' large-scale scenographic *Polytope* installations from the 1960s–1970s, utilizes real-time machine learning and a distributed wireless sensor network to create an emergent composition of lighting and sonic behaviors within a huge architectural structure. Indeed, with these and other projects on the horizon, it is clear that the notion of participation–interaction will become one of the defining features of future scenographic practice, shifting the earlier question of how participants interact with a scenographic arrangement to a more complex question: what does the scenography do to itself and to its environment?

Atmospheres

As we have seen, one would think that the long-standing concept of scenography as something solid and built, a weighty object or *thing*, would have been challenged principally by digital systems' trends towards the invisible, the simulated, the predictive and the distributed. But there is another shift that Josef Svoboda already announced in the 1960s when he argued that a scenography could consist of "a stage filled with vapor and a beam of light cutting a path" (Burian 1971: 15): that is, the idea of *atmosphere* as scenography.

The architectural theorist Mark Wigley has defined atmosphere as "some kind of sensuous emission of sound, light, heat, smell and moisture; a swirling climate of intangible effects generated by a stationary object [building]" (Wigley 2009). As architect Peter Zumthor has argued, atmosphere brings together a range of elements we would tend to call ephemeral: sound, temperature, emotional affect, a surround of objects, the flow of movement, luminosity, a blur between interior and exteriority (Zumthor 2006). More specifically, atmosphere amounts to the idea of architecture (or scenography) as "surrounding" – as something that envelops, encircles, demarcates, and resonates as the inhabited environment without having any specific point of focus or origin. Scenography thus becomes about temporal, spatial, architectural, corporal diffusion; something that is both everywhere (delocalized) and, at the same time, operating on the skin, the eyes, the ears, the tongue, the nose, and sensing bodies in general, all at different spatio-temporal scales.

The shift to a concentration on atmosphere in a range of contemporary artist and architects' practices perhaps not only points to advanced digital technologies of control that enable the fine control of layering of mist in a room, the artificial production of standing waves in a space that vibrate in the air or the injection of scents into the paint on a wall of gallery. It also points to a general level of what Félix Guattari called *ecosophic* crises that are economic, environmental, and socio-technical. Atmospheres are ontologically puzzling: a surplus, a not really there, an in-between state, a feeling that is somehow nowhere. But what is it about something that philosopher Gernot Böhme calls "in a certain sense indeterminate, diffuse but precisely not indeterminate in relation to its character" (Böhme 2009: 28), that speaks so strongly to us in our current historical moment or that encourages new forms of scenographic thinking where all that is solid melts into air, to ironically quote Marx and Engels.

Ever since the so-called California Light and Space artists like James Turrell, Robert Irwin, Larry Bell, Doug Wheeler, Maria Nordman, and others in the 1960s began to focus on light as an architectural and perceptual material, the idea that art could consist of experiences conditioned by spaces and environments that were bereft of objects has become second nature in art historical terms.[2] But the same could be said for architecture as well. Already British critic Reyner Banham, who argued in this 1969 manifesto *Architecture of the Well-tempered Environment* that the history of architecture should consist as much of studies of the creation and management of *environmental conditions*, the flow of heat and cold, the manufacture of artificial ventilation systems, the critically important acoustic properties of spaces that go unseen but not unheard as its focus on objects, was preparing scenographic history and practice for what was to come: a conception of the scenographic as an interlocking between a temporal dramaturgy of gradients of atmospheric phenomena like light, heat, vibrations, smells, and air currents and the human inhabitants of these conditions.

Artist James Turrell, perhaps the most celebrated of the California group, had already established, as early as the mid-1960s, a kind of performative scenography based on a perceptual loop between the inhabitant and a shifting, almost threshold environment of shapes and forms produced solely from light. Not detailed in any history of scenography or theatre lighting book, the famous *Mendota Stoppages* (1967–74), in which Turrell cut slits of varying sizes into the walls of his Santa Monica studio (a disused hotel) and led spectators through a durational experience from the brightness of daylight into the blurring of vision in the twilight of evening and, finally, absolute darkness, already provides a way of thinking of scenography as Georges Didi-Huberman labeled Turrell's own work – "the submission of a disquieted vision to a field of perception void of objects or plane" (Didi-Huberman 2001: 46).

One might say that Turrell's interest in the manner in which light constructs atmospheres through what Gilles Deleuze called "haptic vision," producing palpable perceptual and physiological experience but never making direct contact with the skin, reaches its apex in his colossal 2013 installation *Aten Reign*, premiered within a completed redesigned Guggenheim rotunda in New York. Visitors to the museum lay underneath a massive upside-down, five-story-tall "stack of lampshades viewed from the inside": a physical structure consisting of a series of concentric circles outfitted with 1,000 LED strips that cycle through a gradation of complementary colors over a continuously changing 45-minute cycle (Turrell 2013).

Turrell's choice of creating a dynamic time profile for the light (fading it up and down) used in the installation contrasts with many of his earlier indoor (and outdoor) works in which the environment itself remains static and time is given over to human perception through the eye of the viewer that gradually reveals the space itself. In *Aten Reign*, however, the room saturates in extreme colors that are continually modulating, causing the space of the rotunda itself to undergo transformation together with the visitor's temporal-spatial sensibility.

If Turrell aims to use light as something that opens up our experience of time and space while simultaneously suspending it, other contemporary artists are interested in the transformative potential of atmospheres to increase perceptual obscurity. The fog sculptures of the great Japanese artist Fujiko Nakaya, whose principal scenographic material since the 1960s has been condensed water droplets, sprayed and scattered at high pressure into rivers, parks, the undersides of bridges, fountains, theatres (a fog environment for Trisha Brown's *Set and Reset*), the tops of mountains, Philip Johnson's Glass House, the moat around Gehry's Bilbao Guggenheim and a host of other spaces, form masses of undulating, kinetically behaving and enveloping air subject to dissipation by way of changing meteorological conditions. For example, Nakaya described her "Fog sculpture" for the 1970 Pepsico Pavilion at Expo 70 in Osaka as "a fog to walk into, to feel and smell, and disappear in" (Nakaya 1972: 207).

Riffing off Nakaya's work at perhaps an even larger scale, architects Diller + Scofidio's spectacular *Blur Building* for the 2002 Swiss Expo produced an atmosphere of acoustic, visual and tactile wet white noise through the spraying of water from some 31,710 computer-controlled Mee fog nozzles (the same developed in collaboration with Nakaya by physicist Thomas Mee in the 1960s) generating a mass of scattered light and water over the border of Lake Neuchatel.

In a more intensive, mediated manner, in artist Kurt Hentschlaeger's works *Feed* (2004) and *Zee* (2008), dense fog and flicker-based stroboscopic light become a palpable and powerful scenic apparatus for generating hallucinogenic experiences in the visitor. In *Feed*, premiered at the Venice Theatre Biennale in 2004, a seated audience is first exposed for 20 minutes to a large projected video image depicting the spatial contortions of 3D animated characters' bodies afloat in a gravity-less space. As the images fade, the space grows dark, subsonic sound increases in amplitude and a mass of dense smoke suddenly engulfs the entire room, simultaneously cutting off vision and proprioceptive orientation. The atmosphere transitions to a chaotic turbulence of eddies and whorls, finally giving way to extreme retinal afterimages, produced through a battery of ten high-powered stroboscopes, each tuned to a different frequency, which illuminate and reflect off the surging fog.

But atmosphere does not just constitute rooms or planes of light, haze, and fog that mainly appeal to the eye. Instead, we can examine events that cut across all of the senses, particularly those that we would be hard pressed to call scenographic: touching, standing in space, temperature, etc. For instance, in the earlier "physiological architecture" projects from architect Philippe Rahm and Jean-Gilles Décosterd such as *Melatonin Room* (2000) and *Hormonorium* (2002), the architects explored how architectural environments are constituted through the inter-relations among chemical, thermal, biological and electromechanical interactions explored at room and environmental scale. *Hormonorium*, for example, creates what we might call a *physiochemical scenography* where a massive Plexiglas floor of white florescent fixtures simulating the UV basis of the solar spectrum and specifically regulated room temperatures and chemical compositions (i.e., nitrogen/oxygen combinations) were engineered to induce hormonal shifts in visitors. In this way, Décosterd and Rahm present a future scenario for scenography that "creates a synthesis of the organic, of mood and space, by establishing a continuity between architecture and human metabolism, between space, light and the endocrine and neurological systems" (Rahm 2015).

From the atmospheric point of view, we only have to look at several editions of the Venice Architecture Biennale since 2008 to see the way such environmental thinking has entered into the practice of architects and designers, who have increasingly begun to perceive and shape space through temporal media. In Aaron Betsky's 2008 "Architecture Beyond Building"-themed Biennale, the group show in the Arsenale was filled with, among others, environments that consisted of white light (Asymptote), pulse-sensor driven flashes of light within a gigantic inflatable sphere (Coop Himmelb(l)au), enormous, luminous interactive display surfaces that tracked visitors (M-A-D and the Rockwell Group) and a "meteorological space" in which different hot and cold convection currents circulated (Rahm 2015). Two years later, SAANA's Kazuyo Sejima's 2010 "People in Architecture" Biennale continued the thematic exploration of habitation within changing environments by featuring architecturally born, walk-through scenographies such as a spiraling ramp into the clouds (Tetsuo Kondo and the German climate engineering firm Transolar) or a stroll through environments of stroboscopic-lit water spray (Olafar Eliasson, whose much hailed 2003 *Weather Project* at the TATE Modern also operated between inhabited event, environment and atmosphere).

Perhaps most radical in forcing us to rethink the scenographic is work from the Norwegian artist Sissel Tolaas, whose confrontational smell-based installations provoke us to question whether scenography should be focused at all on space and image. Certainly, olfactory elements have been an overlooked aspect of the history of theatre set design; witness David Belasco's naturalist obsession with having real pancakes cooked in his hyperrealistic recreation of a Child's Restaurant in *The Governor's Lady* (1912) or his adding pine needles on the stage floor to generate the smell of a forest in *Tiger Rose* (1917) (Banes and Lepecki 2012: 31). Yet, Belasco's and many other directors' and designers' use of smell was and is to add value to already dense visual spaces. In contrast, in Tolaas' works like *The Smell of Fear/The Fear of Smell* (2006), visitors encounter a room of empty numbered white walls. Scratching the wall (if one chooses to do so) releases scents of the sweat of returning PTSD war veterans or psychiatric patients with extreme phobia, thus making the stimuli and perception of smell itself the ultimate scenographic act. It is, in fact, this sense of the ultimate disappearance of image and space under the increasing forces of the molecular and the invisible that contemporary and future scenographic practice faces its greatest challenge.

Conclusion: projectionscapes

From examining the transformation of space through electro-mechanical-molecular-chemical means, we might finally ask what role that emblematic scenographic element – the projected moving image – can still play within current epistemes of smartness, the climatic and the corporeal–participatory? As stated in the introduction, most writing on so-called "digital scenography" encompasses the projected screen-based image. In point of fact, for most historians and thinkers of the digital, the digital image *is* the new scenography, replacing the three-dimensionality of real space with its polygon-driven doppelganger.

It would be an understatement to claim that, in all its variations, the screen has become a ubiquitous element of twenty-first century life. This emphasis on the screenal spans multiple scales, from the screen of monitors alone or embedded into *mise en scène* that have become ubiquitous on the stage (of course, already coupled with the development of technologies such as the Portapak and the CCTV camera at the end of the 1950s), to the wrap around "expanded cinema" environments of 1960s artists like Stan Van der Beek and Eventstructure Research Group, to the current moment where the screen is no longer fastened to a structure but floats, as Villem Flusser called it, as so many disembodied surfaces and "technical images," across our tablets, mobile phones, cameras, and micro-monitors. Within another context and scale, all it takes is a trip to any contemporary Asian city to get a glimpse of the screen as architectural image, projecting a constantly running audio-visual narrative of late capitalism, which has become a central element of the so-called "smart urbanscape."

Just as we cannot divorce the perceptual shifts that accompany the invention, distribution and reception of a new cultural technology, we also cannot separate the emerging "surface thought," as Flusser called it, of the screen from an ad infinitum list of technological advances that power it: LED, OLED, DLP, DLA, UHD 4K, 8K, HD, QXGA, WHUXGA, and on. It is, of course, these shifts in resolution and frame rate, microcontrolled optics and CMOS-enabled sensing technologies that even make possible such kinds of colossal urban-scale motion pictures that meld with the architecture of the cityscape, like photographer David Michalek's astounding 2007 *Slow Dancing*, which comprises a series of video portraits shot at 1,000 frames/second of living dancers and choreographers whose movements in time are slowed down to infinitesimal, almost subatomic, levels. Michalek's journey into the temporal limits of the moving image, however, could only be made possible by the techniques and site of their deployment – enormous resolution forms enabled by industrial digital projection technology that allows an entire urban plaza at Lincoln Centre or the building surface of Opera Bastille to be transformed into a scenographic event.

Such works, like Michalek's, the politically charged projection pieces of artist-activist Krzysztof Wodiczko or video artist Doug Aitken's *Sleepwalkers* projected onto the MoMA's outside walls in 2007, however, pale in comparison to theatre maker Robert Lepage's more than immense *Image Mill* for a cluster of grain silos during Quebec City's 450 years celebration in 2008. Exploring the history of the city in still and moving images and sound, the *Image Mill* resulted in the largest projected image ever produced: a 600-meter-long by 30-meter-high film that was the equivalent of 25 IMAX screens. Lepage's work, which transfixed audiences who watched and listened to the intricately assembled work from blocks away was no less a technological feat, created through custom precision-edge blending and projection-mapping virtuosity from local Quebec-based engineers and image-processing experts.

Despite the continual reinforcement of what sound artist Bruce Odland calls "the seduction of the glowing rectangle," through the work of countless artists and designers the screen is slowly on its way to leaving the square-aspect ratio, carving out new urban topologies and turning the cityscape into a moving event or, according to some critics, a "scenographic syrup" (Payne 2007: 56). Starting in the late 1990s with the first deployment of high-resolution LED technology that turned building surfaces like Renzo Piano's KPN Rotterdam headquarters or non-descript office towers in Qatar, Dubai, Singapore and Seoul into gargantuan pixel displays, the so-called "urban screen" movement has exemplified this new scenographic condition.

The term urban screen refers to a conglomeration of different public art projects in the 2000s aiming to develop and display "content" on gigantic LED screens in urban public spaces. For example, the Hong Kong-based ICC, the ninth tallest building internationally, has become a new display surface for artist's works with its white LED façade of "77,000 square meters of display space," suggesting that artistically motivated scenographs of moving images now compete with advertising real estate for "eyes." Similarly, the recent "Connecting Cities" project, a group of 14 cultural institutions in Europe and Canada, has developed a consortium that seeks "to open these urban media facades as networked communication platforms to circulate artistic and socio-cultural content" (Connecting Cities).

The concept that audiences of the LED-fueled spectacles playing out in malls and public squares around the world would simply sit back passively, as in the once-heralded form of the drive-in or the billboard is also a thing of the past. Instead, the location-based interactive entertainment industry in partnership with artists and designers is rushing to develop interactive portals through smart phone apps and other user-centered interfaces where the public can achieve the long-time dream of direct engagement with the filmic narratives and non-narratives of such "content." Nowadays, in fact, such urban-art works have become almost a routine element of the crowd-based "sharing economy" – the economic model that announces all consumers as producers and providers of commercial services through some form of mediating interface application, from giving people a lift (Uber) and the offering of cheap labor (Amazon Mechanical Turk) to the creation of collective artworks.

Witness sculptor Janet Echelmann's *Skies Painted with Unmarked Sparks* which hung a massive tensile net over the city of Vancouver during a 2014 TED innovation conference. Echelmann's net, consisting of 860,000 hand- and machine-made knots and 145 miles of braided fiber, was clearly not enough. Instead, the sculptor engaged the collaboration of data artist Aaron Koblin, creative head of Google Creative Lab's Data Art division, who enabled viewers to interact with the flying net through touch gestures on a mobile phone app, thus creating the possibility of the visitors' gestures being turned into streaks of light, projected onto the surface of the structure.

Although Echelmann's interest in allowing visitors to feel "connected to those around them – to neighbors and strangers" sounds like a radically new form of public participation in the scenographic evolution of the battle between image and space, it too has historical precedents in the dreams of countless works that have sought, as architect Toyo Ito once claimed, "to make air convert into light" (Ito 1994: 87). Yet, it may be that it is in this vision of the public as no longer mere observer from the outside, but a creator from within environments under transmutation from technologies of the digital, the biological and the chemical that a future historian tracking the evolution of scenographic agency and behavior will ultimately have to search.

Notes

1 This is not a purely random list but rather points out that, despite a range of traditional theatrical proscenium-based productions, many of these theatre makers also relied on techniques of audience participation (in the case of the 1960s works), the design of specific scenographic environments outside of the realm of the theatre (Grüber's famous "installation" works of the Schaubühne in the 1970s such as the *Winterreise im Olympiastadion* or *Rudi* in the abandoned Hotel Esplanade, both in Berlin, or Stein's *As You Like It* and *Shakespeare's Memory* in the closed CCC Film Studios in Spandau, or works in unusual spaces like Deborah Warner's staging of *The Wasteland* in an abandoned Brussels department store or Reza Abdoh's *Father Was a Peculiar Man*, held in the now beyond gentrified Chelsea Meatpacking District.
2 See, for example, *The New York Times* article on Robert Irwin.

References

Adams, Tim 2015. "Carsten Höller: It is Impossible to Travel Down a Slide Without Smiling." Available online at: www.theguardian.com/artanddesign/2015/may/17/carsten-holler-travel-down-a-slide-without-smiling-decision (accessed 4 January 2016).

Andrejevic, Mark, and Mark Burdon 2014. "Defining the sensor society." *Television & New Media*, July 11.

Aronson, Arnold 2005. *Looking Into the Abyss: Essays on Scenography*. Ann Arbor: University of Michigan Press.

Aronson, Arnold 2010. "The Future of Scenography." *Theatre Design & Technology*. Winter.

Aronson, Arnold 2011. "Dematerialization of the Stage." In *The Disappearing Stage: Reflections on the PQ 2011 Prague Quadrennial*, edited by Arnold Aronson, 84–95. Prague: Arts and Theatre Institute.

Banes, Sally and André Lepecki (Eds) 2012. *The Senses in Performance*. New York: Routledge

Banham, Reyner 1984. *Architecture of the Well-tempered Environment*. Chicago, IL: University of Chicago Press.

Bishop, Claire 2005. *Installation Art: A Critical History*. London: Routledge.

Böhme, Gernot 2009. "Atmosphere as the Fundamental Concept of a New Aesthetics." In *Breathable*, edited by Cristina Diaz Moreno, 28–55. Madrid: Rueda.

Bourriaud, Nicolas, *et al.* 2002. *Relational Aesthetics*, translated by Simon Pleasance and Fronza Woods. Dijon: Les presses du reel.

Boykett, Tim 1996. "Theory of Hypercompetition." *Time's Up*, available online at: www.timesup.org/thinktank/hypercompetition.html (accessed 12 June 2017).

Broadhurst, Susan and Josephine Machon (Eds) 2012. *Identity, Performance and Technology: Practices of Empowerment, Embodiment and Technicity*. London: Palgrave Macmillan.

Brouwer, J., *et al.* 2007. *Interact or Die*. Rotterdam: V2_ publishing.

Burian, Jarka 1971. *The Scenography of Josef Svoboda*. Middletown, CT: Wesleyan University Press.

Connecting Cities (n.d.). Available online at: www.connectingcities.net (accessed on 4 January 2016).

De Landa, Manuel 1991. *War in the Age of Intelligent Machines*. New York: Swerve/Zone Books.

Deleuze, Gilles 1992. "Postscript on Control Societies," *OCTOBER* 59, Winter, 3–7. Cambridge, MA: MIT Press.

Didi-Huberman, Georges 2001. "The Fable of the Place." In *James Turrell: The Other Horizon*, edited by Peter Noever. Ostfildern-Ruit: Hatje-Cantz.

Flusser, Vilém 2002. *Writings*, edited by Andreas Ströhl, translated by Erik Eisel. Minneapolis: University of Minnesota Press.
Galloway, Alexander 2004. *Protocol: How Control Exists After Decentralization*. Cambridge, MA: MIT Press.
Giannachi, Gabriella 2004. *Virtual Theatres: An Introduction*. London: Routledge.
Goebbels, Heiner 2008. "Why I Made *Stifters Dinge*." Artangel. Available online at: www.artangel.org.uk/projects/2008/stifter_s_dinge/heiner_goebbels_on_stifter_s_dinge/heiner_goebbels_on_stifter_s_dinge (accessed 4 January 2016).
Graham, Beryl and Sarah Cook 2010. *Rethinking Curating: Art After New Media*. Cambridge, MA: MIT Press.
Grau, Oliver 2003. *Virtual Art*. Cambridge, MA: MIT Press.
Halpern, Orit 2005. "Dreams for our Perceptual Present: Temporality, Storage, and Interactivity in Cybernetics." *Configurations* 13.2: 283–319.
Hannah, Dorita and Olav Harsløf 2008. *Performance Design*. Copenhagen: Museum Tusculanum Press.
Ito, Toyo 1994. "Architecture and the Simulated City." Available online at: http://newprairiepress.org/cgi/viewcontent.cgi?article=1237&context=oz (accessed 2 January 2016).
Iwaki, Akihisa 2013. "The Body as an Image Processor." In *Diversities in Aesthetics: Selected Papers of the 18th Congress of International Aesthetics*, edited by Peng, Gao Jian Ping and Peng Feng, 213–23. Beijing: China Social Sciences Press.
Kaye, Nick 2007. *Multi-Media: Video–Installation–Performance*. London: Routledge.
Klich, Rosemary and Edward Scheer 2011. *Multimedia Performance*. London: Palgrave.
Kohonen, Teuvo 1990. "The Self-organizing Map." *Proceedings of the IEEE* 78.9: 1464–80.
Krueger, Myron W. 1996. "Responsive Environments." In *Theories and Documents of Contemporary Art: A Sourcebook of Artists' Writings*, edited by Kristine Stiles and Peter Selz, 473–86. Berkeley: University of California Press.
Kwastek, Katja 2013. *Aesthetics of Interaction in Digital Art*. Cambridge, MA: MIT Press.
Latour, Bruno 2011. "Some Experiments in Art and Politics." Available online at: www.e-flux.com/journal/some-experiments-in-art-and-politics (accessed 4 January 2016).
Lesák, Barbara 1988. *Die Kullisse Explodiert: Frederich Kieslers Theatreexperimente und Architekturprojekte 1923–1925*. Vienna: Löcker Verlag.
Nakaya, Fujiko 1972. "Making of 'Fog' or Low-Hanging Stratus Cloud." In *Pavilion*, edited by B. Kluver, J. Martin and B. Rose, 207–23. New York: E. P. Dutton.
Parker-Starbuck, Jennifer 2011. *Cyborg Theatre: Corporeal/Technological Intersections in Multimedia Performance*. London: Palgrave Macmillan.
Paul, Christiane 2003. *Digital Art*. London: Thames and Hudson.
Payne, Andrew 2007. "Between Art and Architecture, Structure and Sense." In *Hylozoic Soil: Geotextile Installations 1995/2007*, edited by Philip Beesley, Christine Macy and Andrew Payne, 51–8. Toronto: Riverside Architecture Press.
Pickering, Andrew 1995. *The Mangle of Practice: Time, Agency and Science*. Chicago, IL: University of Chicago Press.
Rahm, Philippe 2015. Available online at: www.philipperahm.com (accessed 3 January 2016)
Salter, Chris 2010. *Entangled: Technology and the Transformation of Performance*. Cambridge, MA: MIT Press.
Salter, Chris 2015. *Alien Agency: Experimental Encounters with Art in the Making*. Cambridge, MA: MIT Press.
Schechner, Richard 1968. "6 Axioms for Environmental Theatre." *The Drama Review* 12 (3) (Spring): 41–64.
Sterne, Jonathan 2002. *The Audible Past: The Cultural Origins of Sound Reproduction*. Durham, NC: Duke University Press.
Varela, Francisco, *et al.* 2001. "The Brainweb: Phase Synchronization and Large-scale Integration." *Nature Reviews: Neuroscience* 2.4: 229–39.
Wigley, Mark 2009. "The Architecture of Atmosphere." In *Breathable*, edited by Cristina Diaz Moreno, 86–99. Madrid: Rueda.
Wishart, Trevor 1996. *On Sonic Art*. London: Routledge.
Zumthor, Peter 2006. *Atmospheres: Architectural Environments-Surrounding Objects*. Zürich: Birkhäuser.

Works cited

Baginski, Nicolas and Barry Schwartz 1995. *I-Beam Music.*
Cardiff, Janet and George Burris Miller 2005. *Opera for a Small Room.*
Cardiff, Janet and George Burris Miller 2005. *Pandemonium.*
Cardiff, Janet and George Burris Miller 2007. *The Killing Machine.*
Cardiff, Janet and George Burris Miller 2009. *Storm Room.*
Daily Tous les Jours 2012. *Kit Operette.*
Décosterd, Jean-Gilles and Philippe Rahm 2002. *Hormonorium.*
Diller+Scofidio 2002. *Blur Building.*
Double Negative Architecture 2008. *Corpora in Si(gh)te.*
Duchamp, Marcel 1915. *The Large Glass.*
Duchamp, Marcel 1966. *Étant donnés.*
Echelmann, Janet and Aaron Koblin 2014. *Skies Painted with Unmarked Sparks.*
Forsythe, William 2001. *Scattered Crowd.*
Forsythe, William 2002. *City of Abstracts.*
Forsythe, William 2009. *The Fact of Matter.*
Forsythe, William, Dana Caspersen and Joel Ryan 1997. *White Bouncy Castle.*
Goebbels, Heiner 2007. *Stifters Dinge.*
Haque, Usman 2012. *Another Life.*
Hentschlager, Kurt 2004. *Feed.*
Hentschlager, Kurt 2007. *Zee.*
Höller, Carsten 1996. *Flying Machine.*
Höller, Carsten 2008. *Double Club.*
Kentridge, William 2012. *The Refusal of Time.*
Lepage, Robert 2010. *The Image Mill.*
Masayuki, Towata and Yasuakai Matsumoto 1991. *Divina Commedia: Practices for Death.*
Masayuki, Towata and Yasuakai Matsumoto 1992. *Trobar Clus.*
Michalek, David 2007. *Slow Dancing.*
Paxton, Steve 1966. *Physical Things.*
Salter, Chris 2010. *JND.*
Salter, Chris 2011– 2014. *Displace.*
Salter, Chris, TeZ and Valerie Lamontagne 2014–2015. *Ilinx.*
Saraceno, Tomás 2009. *Galaxies Forming Along Filaments.*
Saraceno, Tomás 2012. *On Space Time Foam.*
Time's Up 1996. *Hyperfitness Studio.*
Time's Up 1999. *Body Spin.*
Tolaas, Sissel 2006. *The Smell of FEAR/The FEAR of Smell.*
Turrell, James 2013. *Aten Reign.*
Turrell, James 1967. *Mendota Stoppages.*

PART III

History and practice

Architecture as design

Within purpose-built theatres there are essentially two kinds of scenic environments: one in which scenery is constructed to hide or transform the stage; and one in which the architecture of the stage itself or the theatre as a whole functions as the scenic locale – stage as stage. Many forms of classical and non-Western theatre fall into the latter category. We see this, for instance, in the Greek and Roman theatres, in the Sanskrit stage, and in the early modern English theatre. In a certain way, the classic example is the Japanese Noh theatre.

The Noh stage, made of polished cypress, is essentially square, and even though it has been an indoor theatre since the nineteenth century, it remains covered by a roof supported by four pillars, a holdover from its origins as an outdoor theatre. (Imagine it as if the awning above the Tudor–Stuart stage had become incorporated into the permanent structure of subsequent indoor English theatres.) As explained by Kunio Komparu, the roof, whose design derives from worship pavilions, "exists to define the Noh space as sacred, unified, and architecturally discrete" (Komparu 2005: 114). The stage is reached by an angled bridge that meets the rear stage at the up right corner. Based on a modular system, the stage was designated as three square *ken* (approximately 320 square feet) (ibid.: 113). The only permanent scenery is a painted pine tree on the upstage wall and, since the seventeenth century, a painting of bamboo on a panel in the up left wall. Each pillar has a name and function, and the stage itself is understood to be divided into nine square units. All movement and action is prescribed by the pillars and stage units. Benito Ortolani has remarked on the sacred nature of the Noh stage as a place of "meeting of our world with the other dimension . . . The bridge becomes the passage through which gods become visible, restless or angry ghosts appear to haunt, or to implore the prayers that can give them salvation" (Ortolani 1995: 145). Here was a stage whose features became inscribed on a particular mode of performance, whose very structure became intertwined with both the diegetic and spiritual meanings of the plays presented on it, and which determined the movement of the actors.

This could, in fact, be said of any architectural stage. When Sophocles, Kalidasa, Zeami, and Shakespeare wrote, they presumably had the shape and features of their respective stages in mind, knowing how these would affect entrances and exits and thus the rhythms of the play; they understood the architectural relationship of the stage to the spectators and how this might create intimacy or grandeur.

In the twentieth century, many directors were attracted to the architectural stage. Jacques Copeau and Louis Jouvet renovated the Théâtre du Vieux Colombier to strip it of all ornament and decor in order to create "le tréteau nu" – the bare stage – that would, in the words of Denis Bablet, restore "real majesty and purity to the stage" (Bablet 1977: 66). The second renovation of 1920, which eliminated the proscenium and added an apron projecting into the auditorium, "resembled the nave of a church, the frontal relationship linking the public to the dramatic action was modified from what it had been in the illusionist theater" (ibid.: 69). Émile Jaques-Dalcroze with Appia at Hellerau, and Max Reinhardt at the Circus Schumann, were among those seeking a modern version of the architectural stage.

The architectural stage does not seek to create illusion through design. Rather, it presents itself as site for performance, a platform for actors. It would seem to be the epitome of the stage-as-stage. Yet it is important to recognize that there is no such thing as neutral architecture. The structure, style, shape, materials, and texture of the architectural stage inevitably reflected the aesthetic and social world that created it. The *skene* of the fourth century BCE or the stage of Molière's theatre looked like other civic architecture of the time and would have presented a familiar face to the audience. When Peter Brook declared that he could take "any empty space and call it a bare stage" he was not acknowledging the fact that there is no such thing as an "empty space." All spaces have histories, contexts, atmospheres, and meanings. There is a well-known marble relief from Naples showing "new comedy" actors in front of an architectural facade (see Bieber 1961: 92), but behind a few of the actors is a loosely hung, wrinkled curtain covering part of the facade. Thus, the question for architectural design, from ancient times to the present, is, do you foreground these inherent qualities or attempt to hide them?

References

Bablet, Denis 1977. *Revolutions in Stage Design of the 20th Century*. Paris and New York: Leon Amiel.

Bieber, Margarete 1961. *The History of The Greek and Roman Theater*. Princeton: Princeton University Press.

Komparu, Kunio 2005. *The Noh Theater: Principles and Perspectives*. Warren, CT: Floating World Editions.

Ortolani, Benito 1995. *The Japanese Theatre: From Shamanistic Ritual to Contemporary Pluralism*, revised Ed. Princeton: Princeton University Press.

13

SCENOGRAPHY IN GREECE AND ROME

The first thousand years

C. W. Marshall

"Three and scene-painting Sophocles" (τρεῖς δὲ καὶ σκηνογραφίαν Σοφοκλῆς, Aristotle 1449a: 18): this enigmatic statement represents the earliest account of the origins of scenography. This phrasing in *Poetics* is notoriously terse, and claims made there often fudge actual knowledge into an artificial evolutionary model. Nevertheless, the short sentence appears to attribute to the fifth-century playwright Sophocles two significant innovations in Athenian stagecraft: the expansion of the number of permitted speaking actors from two (plus the chorus) to three, and the introduction of *skēnographia*. Both of these details are problematic.

The Rule of Three Actors, generally believed to apply to all tragedy in the fifth century (Pickard-Cambridge 1988: 134–56) and possibly comedy as well (Marshall 2013), is best explained in terms of creating a level playing field among competitors. Since all theatrical performance in Athens was typically part of dramatic competitions at festivals for Dionysus, providing notionally equal resources to competitors makes sense. Since Sophocles' earliest dramatic entry was in 467 BCE, and since three actors are used to startling effect in Aeschylus' *Oresteia* in 458 BCE, this innovation can be attributed to the period 467–58 BCE inclusive, assuming Aristotle is drawing on accurate information. What, then, does it mean to suggest that the practice originates with Sophocles (who would have been playwright, director, and one of the actors)? There are three likely possibilities: (1) Sophocles suggested that the number of permitted actors be increased in advance of his production, and it was agreed; (2) Sophocles convinced his *chorēgos* (producer) to pay for a third actor, and its use proved effective and was later institutionalized; or (3) another director requested the additional actor, it was allotted to all competitors, and Sophocles was victorious in the competition that year. Any of these is a reasonable explanation of the "fact," and it is not easy to choose between them.

Similar issues beset the issue of scene-painting. For one of the same three reasons Sophocles is attributed with the first (successful) use of *skēnographia*. What might that mean? The Theatre of Dionysus in Athens was a large outdoor venue, with the audience seated on wooden benches in the *theatron* around an *orchēstra*, a dancing-place, at the center of which was an altar (*thymēlē*; see Wiles 1997: 69–86). Most spectators looked down on the *orchēstra*; surviving examples from the fifth century display a range of possible shapes, including irregular trapezoids (see Wiles 1997: 23–62).

The *skēnē*, a temporary wooden building, erected anew for each festival (Csapo 2010a: 126), provided a backdrop for the actors. The Roman author Vitruvius (first century BCE) identifies Agatharchus of Samos as Aeschylus' scene-painter (7. *praef.* 11). Since a *skēnē* seems not to be required in Aeschylus' *Suppliant Women* (463 BCE) nor in earlier plays, but is required in the *Oresteia*, the introduction of the *skēnē* may be ascribed to the years 462–58 BCE inclusive (though see Bees 1995). A straightforward reading of Vitruvius would say *skēnographia* also emerged at this time: Agatharchus would have been young, contemporary with Sophocles. Because other sources have Agatharchus still active during the Peloponnesian War (Plut. *Alc.* 16.4; Andoc 4.17), it may be the association comes from an Aeschylean revival or is simply mistaken. Regardless, painting of the *skēnē* would have begun as soon as it was introduced, and was not tied to individual productions (a given director's entry in the dramatic competition), but was part of the festival and so would have been available to all of that year's competitors (see Rouveret 1989: 65–127): Vitruvius' association would be a relic of the Athenian desire to ascribe an individual "inventor" to any new technology.

Skēnographia is then best understood to refer to the painting of a temporary wooden *skēnē* to have the appearance of a stone building, generic enough to serve as the backdrop for any tragedy or comedy: "[t]he purpose of scene-painting was to create out of transient materials the illusion of a stone monument" (Wiles 1997: 161); while the term subsequently came to be used for a kind of perspective drawing, "we must abandon the idea of any kind of elaborate painted stage 'setting' in Greek or Roman theater" (Small 2013: 127–8, and see Padel 1990: 346–54). The generic background could easily represent a palace or temple, but representational sets providing individualized depictions keyed to a particular play or production were not typical.

This is not what we would normally think of as scenography. If scene-painting was not used to individuate dramatic settings in ancient theatre, then what elements of scenic realization were subject to the creative control of the director (*didaskalos*) and his team? To proceed, we can consider three periods, all BCE, for which plays survive: Athens 472–*c.* 388 (represented by the extant plays of Aeschylus, Sophocles, Euripides, and Aristophanes); Athens 321–*c.* 290 (represented by the extant fragments of Menander); and Rome *c.* 205–160 (represented by the comedies of Plautus and Terence). For each of these it is possible to say something about the visual, spatial, and sensory aspects of performance, with reference to the performance space, the stage building, the chorus, performers, costume, masks, props, music, and special visual effects. Following a discussion of these three periods we can consider the miserably attested seven centuries that followed.

It is the argument of this chapter that throughout Greek and Roman antiquity individual sets for plays were not typically used. The fact of performance, however, insists that these plays had scenography: even when presented on a neutral stage, an audience is presented with a *mise-en-scène* that demands interpretation. Visual and auditory elements were part of all performance, detailing a theatrical landscape that deepened the world depicted. Nor is it the case that these sensory components merely repeated what was indicated verbally. Visual and audible elements were central to the theatrical experience, and were not simply a means of illustrating the text. Stagecraft criticism cannot be restricted only to what was attested by the extant scripts (Taplin 1977: 28–39) and a less logocentric methodology adds richness to the theatrical event (Revermann 2006: 46–65). This nevertheless leaves an inevitable tension between the generic setting and the delivered verse, and that tension is resolved in part through the willing participation of the audience, and in part by the introduction of specific scenographic effects. This was a productive tension that generated the memorable visual effects throughout the first thousand years of the practice of scenography in Greece and Rome.

Athens, 472–*c.* 388

The playing space in the Theatre of Dionysus in Athens consisted of the *orchēstra*, the area immediately before the *skēnē*, and the *skēnē* roof. The three speaking actors and their attendants could occupy any of these locations. Chorus members tended to occupy only the *orchēstra*, but since they can emerge from and enter the *skēnē* building (see Euripides' *Helen* 385 and 515) travel between the two must be possible. Scholars are divided about the existence of a low platform distinguishing the area immediately before the *skēnē* as being separate from the *orchēstra* (Taplin 1977: 441–2). While not required for the staging of any extant scene, visual evidence from vase-painting seems to corroborate the existence of a low (1 m) wooden platform physically connected to the *skēnē* building and accessed from the *orchēstra* by a few steps (see Hughes 2006 for an Athenian vase *c.* 420; a fourth-century vase-painting from South Italy also presents a low platform). The existence of a demarcated area immediately before the *skēnē* allows for two distinct areas to be used in dynamic tension, as in Sophocles' *Oedipus Tyrannus* (Scully 1999: 68–74) or Aristophanes' *Frogs* when the *orchēstra* represents the Stygian lake and the platform represents the shore (lines 180–270). To call this platform "the stage" is mistaken, however: both platform and *orchēstra* are part of the actors' performance area, and speaking actors will regularly have occupied the dance-floor.

The *skēnē* building itself can represent whatever permanent building a play requires, be it a palace, a temple, or a soldier's tent (the word *skēnē* can also mean "tent"). If the central door is left open, it can represent a cave mouth (as in Sophocles' *Philoctetes* or Euripides' *Cyclops*; Arnott 1962: 91–106). The absence of any representational set allows locations to shift easily during a play: in Aeschylus' *Eumenides*, from Delphi to Athens; in Sophocles' *Ajax* from a military tent to a deserted shore; in Aristophanes' *Frogs*, from Heracles' house to the gates of Hades. This is not to deny that specific scenic effects were possible on the Athenian stage, only that when they occurred they were introduced by deliberate choice: the *skēnē* was not made to resemble the temple of Apollo at Delphi in Euripides' *Ion*, but references to a net blocking the door in Aristophanes' *Wasps* (131–2, 164, 367–8) and a chimney (143–51) are insistent enough that this could represent a rare attempt to add stage dressing. Similarly, Aristophanes' *Ecclesiazusae* 884–975 is the only place where it appears a second story is required for the *skēnē*: it is most straightforward to explain this as an attempted innovation for the particular play (a small superstructure placed on the *skēnē* roof?) rather than as a one-off innovation for that year's dramatic festival or a resource regularly present but not otherwise used in extant drama.

No play in this period requires more than a single *skēnē* door, if it is allowed that the same door can represent multiple locations over the course of a play (Thiercy 1986: 19–89; Padel 1990: 354–65). If more than that were regularly available, there would be a number of underexploited theatrical opportunities among surviving plays. A fragment of the comic playwright Eupolis (fr. 48) does make reference to three shacks, possibly onstage, but a bizarre suggestion from a later period (Pollux 4.124, tying individual speaking actors to individual doors) demonstrates the hazards of guessing. The *skēnē* roof was accessible by ladder from within or behind the *skēnē*: gods could appear here, "above" the action (whence the name *theologeion*), or it could simply be a palace roof, as at *Agamemnon* 1–39, Euripides' *Heracles* 815–74, or *Orestes* 1567–1690.

The altar of Dionysus in the *orchēstra*, the *thymelē*, could represent an altar or tomb within the dramatic setting: this block would become the tomb of Agamemnon in Aeschylus' *Libation Bearers* and the altar of Zeus in Euripides' *Children of Heracles* (Poe 1989; Ley 2007: 46–69). There is no real indication that the altar's sacred character prevented it assuming a dramatic function, and using this permanent feature seems preferable to erecting a temporary altar near this same location when required for a play (Rehm 1988; Scully 1996). Stage properties could be placed on or near it to help define its dramatic function: reference is made to a bed of reeds beside the tomb of Theoclymenus (*Helen* 798); painted depictions of Electra sitting at the tomb can show many grave offerings, and possibly this reflects stage practice. Euripides' *Iphigenia among the Taurians* 72–75 makes reference to the blood-stained surface of a barbarian altar and decorations from its previous human victims (skulls or captured weapons): possibly some stage dressing complemented this exceptional verbal description. Furniture is employed sparingly: a couch or litter is required in Euripides' *Alcestis* and *Hippolytus*, a chair in Aristophanes' *Frogs*. Generally, the outdoor setting means such objects can be avoided.

The Athenian theatre also had resources for special effects. From at least 458 the *ekkyklēma* (a low wheeled platform) was available to reveal interior scenes, as if the building represented by the *skēnē* were turned inside-out, as corpses killed in darkness are brought into the light: Euripides' *Heracles* reveals the hero tied to an interior column while the corpses of his wife and children lie around him. The *mēchanē* (the theatrical crane, using a mast-and-boom design) seems to have developed in the 430s as a means to allow heroes to fly (for example, Perseus on his winged sandals in Euripides' lost tragedy *Andromeda* in 412) or to allow a divinity to appear, typically at the conclusion of a play (whence the Latin phrase, *deus ex machina*). Both of these devices are parodied in Aristophanic comedies, showing the audience possessed a metatheatrical appreciation of stage devices. The *mēchanē* appears only to have been constructed as part of the *skēnē* at the Dionysia, but not at the Lenaia or smaller theatrical festivals (Russo 1994: 3). There are also indications of a thunder-machine in the fifth-century theatre (the *bronteion*, see Russo 1994: 118), providing rumbling from behind the *skēnē*, and this sound may have accompanied earthquakes or other natural disasters (for example, *Bacchae* 585–603).

The central axis of the performance area therefore notionally travelled from the audience through the *thymelē* to the central door of the *skēnē* to a hidden interior space that could be revealed with the *ekkyklēma*. Along this axis, two points offer an actor the opportunity for particular prominence with respect to the spectators: the *thymelē*, notionally at the center of the *orchēstra*, and the doorway, serving as a threshold to the darkness (Wiles 1997: 161–86). The left/right axis also conveyed meaning, and the *eisodos* (entryway) at either side of the performance area was employed consistently to help extend the dramatic world beyond what the audience saw. Messengers and other characters describe offstage locations and events. The physical geography of Athens meant that a move from stage right to stage left follows the direction of the sun from east to west (Wiles 1997: 133–60). This could be employed by playwrights to create meaning, associating different *eisodoi* with opposing values: at its simplest, this might create a tension between city and countryside (Pollux 4. 126–7, Vitruvius 5.6.8) or the city and the harbor, but such associations were not fixed and could be created as required for each play.

A number of environmental factors beyond the control of the *didaskalos* crucially shaped the theatrical experience. Plays were presented in the daytime, but individual productions (which typically were written to be presented in competition once, though some plays did get re-performed and toured to other city-states) were completely dependent on the weather. The outdoor venues used only natural light, but cold temperatures, clouds, rain, or burning sun would all change the fundamental experience of a given production. We do not know how the weather affected judges and audiences, but it must have done so. Shadows from the *skēnē* could darken any actor on the *ekkykēma* or standing in the doorway; references to the sun (for example, Aristophanes' *Clouds* 225) mean different things depending on whether the sun were visible (Revermann 2006: 111–13). *Rhesus*, the only Greek tragedy that may post-date this period but which survives among the plays of Euripides, is set entirely at night: this seems to defy an audience to incorporate the natural daylight with the dramatic setting. Athenian spectators always contribute to the creation of the fictional world though their imaginations, and the fundamentally minimalist stage setting encourages this. When the Pedagogue at Sophocles' *Electra* 4–9 identifies specific geographical landmarks for his fellow travelers, the words replace literal representation by a set. The audience is invited to be complicit in the reification of the setting. The primary resource available to fill this performance area was human bodies.

The chorus is perhaps the most distinctive feature of Greek drama, and its almost constant physical presence means it does more to shape the theatrical experience than anything else. Choruses numbered 12 or 15 for each tragic entry and 24 for each comedy. Choreographed movements through the orchestra, in and around other bodies on stage, meant that visual interest was continually being stimulated by choral dance. The chorus always assumes a dramatic identity within the play, and the range of these roles demonstrates the intense physical demands expected. In the *Oresteia*, the same choristers successively play old citizen men, young captive women, divine female embodiments of revenge, and (in the satyr play that was fourth in the tetralogy) half-animal hypermasculine satyrs. The dramatic range suggested by these roles, along with the presumed differences in movement, song, and tempo, point to the challenge of reconstructing choral experience. Comedies were presented singly, but choral identity could range just as far, including theriomorphic choruses of wasps, goats, or wild beasts. In Aristophanes' *Birds*, each chorus member has a distinct costume, and this was probably true also in Eupolis' *Cities* and *Demes* [*Local Villages*]. Aristophanes' *Frogs* presents two choral identities (first frogs, then religious initiates).

Greek theatre was musical theatre, and music, vocal pitch, mimetic dance, and verbal characterization would all make each chorus unique. Music was provided by an *aulētēs*, an instrumentalist playing a double pipe, the *aulos*, whose elaborate costume marked him as a professional, separate from the dramatic action (Wilson 1999): occasional metatheatrical jokes show that this distance can be removed, as when the pipe-player in Aristophanes' *Birds* is taken for the trilling nightingale (Romer 1983). Choral dance is poorly understood, and much must be inferred indirectly from the meter of the choral texts (Pickard-Cambridge 1988: 232–62; Ley 2007: 114–99). Many choral songs contain metrically corresponding stanzas (*strophē* and *antistrophē*), and this implies they were presented with identical music and parallel, or at least complimentary, choreography (Wiles 1997: 87–132). Regular geometrical formations could be interrupted: in Aristophanes' *Lysistrata* semi-choruses of men and women reify the play's gender conflict by creating two tragic-sized choruses of 12; in Aeschylus' *Agamemnon* 1346–71, the death of the king precipitates a shattered choral identity, as individuals respond in disunited voices.

Innovation and dynamism made the chorus the focus of the theatrical experience, and any Athenian chorus is simultaneously evoking ritual associations, affirming a social identity uniting the men performing, alluding to other choral performance genres, and serving a dramatic function within the play. Playwrights use the chorus to mislead the audience, as the emotional associations of the music often stood in ironic contrast with the narrative implications of the scene. Though chorus members are often costumed identically, the integration of costume and mask with the actors' physical bodies would allow individual choristers to emerge from the collective whole. Leading the chorus was the *koryphaios* ("head-speaker"), the chorus leader. In addition to leading the singing and dancing, the *koryphaios* also is the chorus's representative in dialogue with the other characters. The disposition of the bodies of the chorus around the stage was thus the primary means available for determining the stage picture: clustered, scattered, in formation, on the periphery, in small groups, responding to dramatic action, the chorus constantly change the weight and balance of the *mise-en-scène*.

Role doubling was institutionalized, and spectators were aware of multiple roles being played by individuals within a play and across multiple plays (Pickard-Cambridge 1988: 126–76). Helmet-masks covered the head and operated within a convention that expected the audience to be able to perceive a character's sex (with darker skin tones for men) and generational age (with hair color and style determining whether a character is young, mature, or old; see Marshall 1999). While more detail did exist than this, the basic information presented visually was therefore quite limited. Costume isolated other variables, including class and societal role. Vase-painting indicates that Sophocles exoticized the Ethiopian princess Andromeda in his play about her, presenting her in variegated barbarian trousers, while Euripides made her appear as the Greek princess she was destined to become. Euripides is mocked by Aristophanes for presenting his heroes as beggars in rags (*Acharnians* 412–34, *Frogs* 1063–64), part of a naturalizing tendency that developed over the second half of the fifth century. Though tragedies were typically set in the mythological past, all plays functionally used modern dress: characters wore clothing typical of fifth-century Athens (Pickard-Cambridge 1988: 177–231; Wyles 2011).

Athenians found considerable humor in the comic grotesque, and comic bodies were made malformed through the use of padded body suits that had distended bellies, breasts, and buttocks, and (for male characters) an oversized flaccid phallus visible beneath any other layers of costume. This would be true even for the presentation of the god Dionysus in *Frogs*, where the body suit was covered by an effeminate saffron robe, on top of which was placed a Heracles "disguise" of a lion-skin and club. While the audience perceives all three layers of costuming (and the actor beneath), characters in the dramatic world confuse anyone wearing a lion-skin for Heracles. The possibility of "portrait masks" in comedy may be indicated, but these too would be grotesque caricatures (presenting Socrates as an aged satyr, for example) and not lifelike portraits.

Stage properties and additional performers also allow the *didaskalos* to affect the stage picture. Tragedy typically employs few props, but imbues them with thematic significance that magnifies their narrative importance (Taplin 1978: 77–100; Segal 1980): the urn in Sophocles' *Electra* or the blood-purple tapestries in *Agamemnon* resonate far beyond their visual instantiation. The sparseness of tragic props can be overstated, however, since walking sticks, traveler's bags, swords, etc. all appeared regularly. Extremes of busy-ness are rare, but the initial appearance of Theoclymenus at *Helen* 1265–71, with hunting gear, attendants, nets, dogs, and captured animals, no doubt made a stunning visual impression. A greater number of props appeared on the comic stage (Tordoff 2013: 89–105), and though these were often ordinary everyday items, they could be bizarre scientific instruments, as at Aristophanes' *Clouds* 200–17. Even though the default aesthetic was minimalistic, characters and relationships were defined through the visual. Lit torches provide solemnity to the chorus' departure in Aeschylus' *Eumenides* or Bacchic fervor to the dance of Cassandra in Euripides' *Trojan Women* 308–52. Purifying incense infuses the performance space in Euripides' *Helen* 865–72, providing an olfactory experience for the spectators and evoking their personal knowledge of religious worship.

Occasionally, characters enter the *orchēstra* on horse-drawn chariot, as Agamemnon does with Cassandra in *Agamemnon*. The sensory experience of the moment is magnified, as the chorus makes way for the chariot and trailing attendants carrying victory spoils from Troy (Ley 2007: 69–85). Such a scene would resonate for an audience with the pre-play ceremonies performed at the Dionysia (where tribute from subject cities were later regularly displayed). The chariot remained throughout the tapestry scene, as the king despoils the wealth of his own house. When Tecmessa and her silent son Astyanax appear in a wagon in Euripides' *Trojan Women*, some spectators recall Agamemnon's much more magnificent entry. Such associations are inevitable, but difficult to isolate. This one example shows how the history of scenic representation in tragedy could draw on historical associations with earlier productions. In the same way, vase-painting demonstrates that comic parody of Euripidean tragedy involved the repetition of specific gestures and movements, in addition to verbal allusion: one scene shows a comic actor in a South Italian performance of Aristophanes' *Thesmophoriazusae* evoking the memory of the earlier performance of Euripides' *Telephus* (Csapo 1986).

Productions often introduce non-speaking performers to theatrical casts, in the form of attendants or children (Stanley-Porter 1973; Sifakis 1979). A king entering with armed guards gains stature, and the act of dismissing them (as at Euripides' *Hecuba* 978–81) can show a misplaced trust. In that same play, the silent presence of Polymestor's children make them surprising victims of Hecuba's revenge. A character can be defined by his relationship to an unspeaking character: the silent presence of Pylades throughout *Libation Bearers* goes unnoticed until he suddenly speaks (*LB* 900–02), the attendant having been substituted unexpectedly with a speaking actor wearing the same mask. As a result, an alert spectator is rightly wary of Pylades in Sophocles' *Electra*, since at any time dramaturgical sleight-of-hand may mean he too finds a voice. Nowhere is the use of silent extras more spectacular than in Euripides' *Children of Heracles*, where unnumbered children flock around the *thymelē* seeking sanctuary, surrounded by the chorus. Their movements, responding to the threatening presence of the herald Copreus or the supportive reassurances of the Athenian kings Demophon and Acamas (the latter also a silent character) physicalize the emotional contours of their desperate predicament.

Every play from this period offers unique opportunities for scenic presentation. The arrival of an unnamed messenger can interrupt the dramatic flow to allow the spoken delivery of a messenger speech that pauses the action for several minutes, while it deepens the audience's emotional connection to the event. Individual actors sing accompanied monodies, heightening their character's emotional expression, or enter into a lyric dialogue with the chorus. Further, there are moments of visual theatre that defy easy explanation, such as the suicides of Sophocles' Ajax and of Evadne in Euripides' *Suppliant Women* or the dog trial in Aristophanes' *Wasps*. Athenian plays achieved meaning in performance, and depended on music and scenic representation to communicate their richness. Beyond the initial presentation at a theatrical festival, plays could be exported to other theatres where they enjoyed a continued life on the stage. Little is understood about this ongoing performance tradition, though production records show the impact of these plays beyond their initial performance contexts.

Athens, 321–*c.* 290

There is no satisfactory account of the stagecraft of theatre in Athens following the death of Alexander the Great, a period represented primarily by the extant comedy of Menander. Dramatic competitions continued, and playwrights and actors participated in a continuing tradition of dramatic contests reaching back to the fifth century. Nevertheless, a number of interrelated changes in scenography can be isolated that demonstrate the development of Athenian theatre over this time.

Through the fourth century, the Theatre of Dionysus in Athens underwent substantial architectural expansion, often attributed to Lycurgus: changes in performance styles surely influenced this architectural change, which in turn affected performance. The Lycurgan theatre probably still had a wooden *skēnē*, though by now the foundations and the audience seating were stone, and the *orchēstra* was widened and was now circular. The performance area in front of the *skēnē* was raised, making travel between the door and the *orchēstra* more difficult. About a dozen Hellenistic theatres possess an underground tunnel connecting the *skēnē* to the center of the *orchēstra* (what Pollux 4.132 calls "the steps of Charon"), suggesting that the surprise appearance of actors, perhaps as part of a necromancy scene, was possible. The spatial division, however, between the *orchēstra* and what can now more properly be called the stage, affected the audience's visual understanding of the performance space. Because Menander's actors typically announce the initial appearance of the chorus and get out of its way (for example, Menander, *Dyskolos* 230–2), it is possible that comedies did not even consider the *orchēstra* available for performance: this might point to a greater division between the conventions of performance of tragedy and comedy than had been evident in the fifth century. It remains possible that the chorus did occupy the *orchēstra*, and the other performers clear the higher stage as dramatic focus shifts (Sifakis 1967: 126–30): this is suggested in a papyrus fragment of a fourth-century *Medea*, where Medea addresses the chorus after an act-dividing song (Sifakis 1967: 113). Since only meager fragments of Hellenistic tragedy survive, discussion here focuses on the extant remains of Menander (but see Kotlińska-Toma 2015: 243–80).

Three doors are certainly part of the standard *skēnē* by this time, and, even when not all are used, the possibility of new locations being identified during the dramatic action always remains. Again an undifferentiated background meant that the identity of stage locations was typically introduced in the play's prologue. When one of the buildings represents a temple, a prop altar would have been placed in front, on the *skēnē* platform. A common scene, preserved in terracotta figurines and papyrus fragments of Menander's *The Woman from Perinthos*, presented a disobedient slave seeking sanctuary at an altar to avoid punishment. There is no indication that the *mēchanē* was available for these plays, though the *ekkyklēma* is apparently used at *Dyskolos* 758–9. Given that plays now possessed a more international character, and might reasonably be toured to other smaller venues, dependence on local specific machinery naturally decreased.

Actors still accessed the performance area at the sides by *eisodoi*, but now could enter directly onto the platform. This shifted the basic axis of performance, which now crosses left to right. As a result, direct audience address is less frequent than it had been in Aristophanes and, when it occurs (as in *The Woman of Samos* 488), it is more startling. Plots generally concern the everyday realities of the love lives of young men and staging depends on parallels from Euripidean tragedy, drawing principally (we may presume) on fifth-century plays still in the performance repertoire. Comedies are articulated into five acts, and the appearance of the chorus represents both a disruption of the dramatic action and a narrative interlude. The music and lyrics of these choral pieces no longer survive, and the reduced performance area available may suggest a chorus diminished in numbers. It would be a mistake, however, to suggest that the chorus and music was less important to these productions. The theatrical experience still involved high-quality singing and dancing, and extant fragments suggest the *aulētēs* remained particularly active in the final act.

Menandrean masks now also depict whether characters are slave or free, and only two generations are typically represented, polarizing the generational conflict between old and young, fathers and sons. Padded bodysuits become less distended and grotesque over the fourth century, particularly for citizen characters, as costumes begin to cover the prop phallus. Stage properties continue to be used for comic effect (Tordoff 2013: 105–10).

As an example, we can consider a scene preserved on a Roman mosaic from Menander. Menandrean scenes were reproduced in elite dining halls throughout the empire, and their consistent presentation suggests they drew on Hellenistic models (Csapo 2010b: 140–67; Gutzwiller and Çelik 2012). One mosaic from the so-called House of Menander in Mytilene is labeled as coming from *The Woman of Samos*, Act 3. Stage right shows a *mageiros*, a butcher/cook hired for a feast. Dark skin demonstrates his African origin, a detail not mentioned in the surviving text, and there is hint of a pot-belly, perhaps resulting from the diminished padded bodysuit. In the center is Demeas, an elderly citizen man dressed in white and gesticulating wildly with his walking stick. He moves towards Chrysis, the title character, who is a non-citizen woman in a quasi-marital relationship with Demeas. She holds a child that he believes is the product of a sexual relationship between Chrysis and his son, a confusion that will be resolved by the end of Act 4. Chrysis' mask is pale, her hair ornate, and her modest clothes are a rich blue with yellow and red trim. She appears defiant and proud, since she knows the child's true parentage.

The theatre space continued to develop through the third and second centuries BCE, with the *skēnē* becoming tiered (Csapo 2010a: 131–3). Grooves and sockets in some excavated theatres suggest that adjustable "flats" could be introduced and could allow for painted backgrounds tied to individual productions (Moretti 1997). Greek theatre now becomes truly international, with professional touring companies such as the Artists of Dionysus taking plays across the Mediterranean and the Hellenistic world (Pickard-Cambridge 1988: 279–321). Scripts from this later period do not survive, but the evolution of theatre space through the Hellenistic period provided antecedents for the shape of Roman theatres that emerged in the early empire.

Rome, *c.* 205–160

The performance venues in Republican Rome were fundamentally different than those of Classical and Hellenistic Greece. While the Hellenistic world enjoyed permanent theatres of stone, there were no permanent performance venues in Rome before 55 BCE. Though attempts were sometimes made (Livy 40.51.3, 41.27.5), the Roman aristocracy was suspicious of theatre and regulated it strictly. As a result, transient venues were used, and playwrights could not know in advance for which performance space their plays were destined. Theatre was staged during festivals (*ludi*, "games"), at which point itinerant troupes would be hired along with other entertainments. A complex festival calendar began to emerge towards the end of the Hannibalic War (218–201), and it is at this time that the comedies of Plautus and Terence were initially performed. Theatrical troupes could also be hired for funeral games, as happened with the initial performance of Terence's *The Brothers* in 160.

The comedies purport to be adaptations of the Greek comedy of Menander and his contemporaries: prologues typically identify the source play and its author, but the playwrights were free to adapt as they saw fit. In doing so, they drew heavily on other performance traditions, such as Hellenistic mime (a kind of unmasked street theatre in which women could perform) and *fabulae Atellanae* (Atellan farce, a native Italian improvisatory theatre using repeated stock characters). The cosmopolitan hybrid produced was no mechanical translation but embodied a dynamic new genre that was thoroughly Roman.

The genre of Roman comedy was defined by its costume choices: extant plays are *fabulae palliatae*, "plays in Greek dress" (Marshall 2006: 56–66), while other genres without extant examples include *fabulae togatae*, "plays in Roman dress," and *fabulae tabernariae*, "plays set in pubs." *Palliatae* were performed with masks, which drew freely on the Hellenistic Greek tradition and the *Atellanae* tradition to produce a unique hybrid (Marshall 2006: 126–58). Stage properties in the Roman theatre could be invested with wider meaning, as had been the case with some fifth-century tragic props. This is particularly true of recognition tokens, a theatrical technique adapted from Euripidean tragedy and Menandrean comedy. Several Plautine plays have objects in their titles (*Cistellaria*, "the Casket Comedy," *Aulularia*, "the Pot of Gold," *Rudens*, "the Rope"; see Telò, forthcoming). In *Rudens*, a character enters pulling a fishing net that has captured a trunk from which is dragged a long rope; another character seeks to claim the chest by grabbing the rope, and a tug-of-war ensues until the two men agree to submit the question of ownership to an arbitrator (905–1044). Inside the chest is a small box, inside of which are recognition tokens that will identify the citizen status of one of the female characters; on these tokens are tiny letters identifying the young woman's parents by name, revealing that her father is none other than the man chosen to be the arbitrator (1045–1190)! The nesting-doll effect of props within props is drawn out for comic effect.

Roman troupes were contracted to perform by the magistrates or benefactors offering *ludi*. Actors no longer compete, and troupes of slave and free performers determine the financial viability of the venture themselves (Marshall 2006: 16–31). Roman plays consequently lack the Greek restrictions on speaking actors, and scenes with four- and five-speakers emerge (Lowe 1997; Franko 2004). Eavesdropping scenes (and other techniques that divide audience focus between two areas in the performance space) develop naturally in this context. Troupes might now typically contain 6–8 performers responsible for all roles, but the bulk of the plays appears still to fall on two or three "star" performers (Marshall 2006: 83–125). Music is provided by a *tibicen*, playing a double pipe (*tibia*). In the troupe that performed Terence's plays, this was a slave who adjusted the left and right pipes so that each play possessed a distinct musical character. Instead of Greek choral interludes, Roman comedy provided a highly musical continuous performance (act divisions identified in modern editions of Plautus and Terence come later, and are best ignored).

The flexibility of performance space represents the greatest difference for the scenography of Roman comedy. Without purpose-built theatres, magistrates offering *ludi scaenici* (theatrical games) would adapt whatever space was appropriate. For some *ludi*, this was the temple precinct of the god being honored. For others, it might be the forum itself. For example, the *ludi Megalenses* were performed on the Palatine hill by the Temple of the Great Mother, which was dedicated in 191 BCE, an event celebrated with a performance of Plautus' *Pseudolus*. The temple was raised and on its many steps the audience sat, looking down on the area immediately before the temple (Goldberg 1998). This crucial realization similarly suggests that the *ludi Apollinares* were performed in front of the Temple of Apollo on the Capitoline hill. In contrast, the *ludi Romani*, *ludi Plebeii*, and funeral games were evidently celebrated in the forum, where temple steps or wooden bleachers or even the seats of a wooden amphitheatre could be used for the audience (Marshall 2006: 31–48).

As a result, the available performance space was often quite constrained, and again it appears theatrical minimalism was the driving aesthetic. There was a temporary scene building with three doors, not all of which were used in every play, and again a prop altar could signify a temple door without needing any further distinguishing markers (Marshall 1999: 49–56). The same venue could be used for multiple performances in the same day: Terence's *Hecyra* 33–6 suggests that the promise of boxers and tightrope-walkers could distract potential theatre audiences. Depending on the nature of the contract, plays might enjoy a small run over successive days (*Pseudolus* 1335–6). Inclement weather or an interrupted performance could lead to an *instauratio*, a religious objection that authorized an additional performance. A series of manuscripts by Terence preserve rich illustrations documenting the performance of the plays scene-by-scene (Jones and Morey 1931). It is not clear whether these illustrations reflect an ongoing performance tradition for Terence's plays (and if they do, to when it might be dated), but the details of costume and mask suggest some genuine theatrical knowledge. In that light, the completely bare doorways reinforce the minimal representation within any stage setting.

The Roman performance space shows no distinction between platform and dance-floor, and it may be that the stage building was not even raised (this would then contrast with the temporary wooden stages seen in fourth-century South Italian vase-painting, which were still operating within the Greek theatrical milieu). The Roman space was smaller, and this may have helped foster the use of improvisation and the intimacy with the audience (Goldberg 1998: 16; Goldberg 2004; Marshall 2006: 245–79). Plautus' *Curculio* preserves an amazing scene in which the *choragus* ("costume-manager," ostensibly part of the play's backstage personnel) interrupts the dramatic action set in the Greek town of Epidaurus to make observations about people who loiter in the Roman forum (*Curc.* 462–86; see Moore 1991). Though the character speaks verse, in other respects he may appear completely unlike the other roles of the play, fully naturalized in the Roman setting and even appearing unmasked.

These transient performance spaces could still be marked off by sound (Plautus' *Asinaria* 4 refers to a herald), and awnings could provide an ambient fluttering sound, protection from the direct sun, and color to the natural light (Lucretius 4.72–84; see Marshall 2006: 45–7). It is also possible that Roman companies toured and might perform in a Greek stone theatre in South Italy. This would help explain the exceptionality of the only Roman mythological comedy, Plautus' *Amphitruo*, which uniquely needs only a single door and the use of the roof of a stage building.

Roman Empire

The three periods for which plays are extant represent only a small fraction of the thousand years promised in my title. Extant first-century CE tragedy has been excluded from this discussion (eight plays by Seneca the Younger, two by near contemporaries) because we lack any sense of the venues in which they were performed: some scholars have suggested these plays received full theatrical staging in the large theatres found across the empire, and others that they were never staged but were "closet drama," intended only for the theatre of the mind. Neither of these extremes is at all probable, and some intermediate position, with the plays staged in elite private venues (and so possibly indoors or in a domestic courtyard), would allow the texts to communicate clearly to an audience. The plays possess a theatrical power and they appear to presume a consistent use of dramatic space. Parts read (or memorized) by slaves or dinner guests would still constitute "performance" even if there was no fully realized *mise-en-scène*. Though some scholars insist on labeling such performance *recitatio* ("recitation," by one or several voices), there is little evidence to justify rigid divisions between this and other forms of theatrical realization: the plays will have been delivered by performers, and some degree of mimetic representation will have occurred (see Harrison 2000 for a range of informed views). Were performers masked? Was there accompanying music? Was there a delineated performance space? These are unknowns: nevertheless a consistent and meaningful performed realization will have occurred in order to justify the emergence of these texts in an imperial context. The existence of scenes that seem particularly challenging to stage, such as the notorious *extispicium* (entrail-examination) in *Oedipus* 299–402, may point to a more impressionistic representation (without naturalizing props), but by themselves do not mean the plays remained unperformed. Whatever the venue, the minimalism in scenography for which this chapter argues would typically still be practiced.

Romans did have theatres, however, in every major urban centre (Izenour 1992; Sear 2006). The Theatre of Pompey was the first permanent theatre in Rome, dedicated in 55 BCE, and remained in use until the sixth century CE (Gagliardo and Packer 2006). A typical Roman theatre could have a roof or awnings (*vela*) that could be drawn over spectators; it possessed a semicircular orchestra and a long, wide stage that was backed by the grandiose facade of the *scaenae frons*, which could be several stories high, providing spectators a greater sense of being enclosed than did Greek-built venues. Plays could be staged in such locations: Cicero, *ad Fam.* 7.1 (55 BCE) imagines opulent performances of tragedies with "600 mules in a *Clytemnestra* or 3000 drinking-jugs in a *Trojan Horse*" (both of these probably refer to revivals of earlier Roman tragedies); but there is no indication that such performances persisted into the empire.

Instead, theatres were primarily associated with the ill-understood genre of pantomime, a kind of mimetic ballet that became the most distinguished elite performance genre of the empire (see Hall and Wyles 2008: 378–419 for ancient sources on pantomime). In pantomime a solo dancer, supported by music and a chorus, would typically represent a mythological scene, employing a complex lexicon of movement and gesture, while wearing a distinctive close-mouthed mask. Indeed, pantomime may have been the primary referent for the audiences of Seneca (Zimmerann 2008; Zanobi 2008; Slaney 2013). It is possible that slots in the *scaenae frons* did allow for painted panels to function as flats, but this would require covering the elaborately carved *scaenae frons* at the lowest level, and there is no indication that this was a desired aesthetic. Pantomime was one performance genre that we know filled Roman theatres; another was *epideixis*, showcase display-speeches whereby a single travelling orator could engage an audience as a public intellectual.

Other genres flourished, but these have left little mark on the material or literary record. In the Classical, Hellenistic, and Roman periods there are indications of many venues for performance beyond the urban centers of Greece and Rome, and many types of performance, including street-theatre, mime, private performances in elite houses and royal courts, and (at Rome) gladiatorial contests and "fatal charades," staged executions that presented mythological stories (Coleman 1990). In different ways, all of these achieved their meaning through some form of scenography.

All of the genres discussed here demonstrate the importance to the Greeks and Romans of the public performance of verse, which, supplemented by music, characterized Mediterranean cultural display. The consistent picture that emerges is one in which most performance spaces were unmarked by the needs of an individual production, but established a space in which imaginative theatre could nevertheless emerge. Even neutral spaces were ideologically loaded (from the ritual context of the Theatre of Dionysus to the licensed space authorized by Roman magistrates), but such messages were functionally separate from the plays themselves. The consistent picture that emerges from this survey of Greek and Roman scenic design is that spectators were invited to focalize on specific objects or locations to which meaning could be ascribed over the course of the performance. It was through this minimalist aesthetic that ancient performance traditions achieved their rich flexibility and meaning.

References

Arnott, P. 1962. *Greek Scenic Conventions in the Fifth Century* BC. Oxford: Oxford University Press.

Bees, R. 1995. "Die Skene in Aischylos' *Persen, Sieben gegen Theben*, und *Hikitiden*." In *Studien zur Bühnendichtung und zum Theaterbau der Antike*, edited by E. Pöhlmann, 73–106. Frankfurt: Peter Lang.

Brown, A. L. 1984. "Three and Scene-Painting Sophocles." *PCPS* 110: 1–17.

Coleman, K. M. 1990. "Fatal Charades: Roman Executions Staged as Mythological Enactments." *JRS* 80: 44–73.

Csapo, E. 1986. "A Note on Würzburg Bell-Crater H5697 ('Telephus Travestitus')." *Phoenix* 40: 379–92.
Csapo, E. 2010a. "The Production and Performance of Comedy." In *Brill's Companion to the Study of Greek Comedy*, edited by G. W. Dobrov, 103–42. Leiden, The Netherlands: Brill.
Csapo, E. 2010b. *Actors and Icons of the Ancient Theatre*. Chichester: Wiley-Blackwell.
Franko, G. F. 2004. "Ensemble Scenes in Plautus." *AJP* 125: 27–59.
Gagliardo, M. C. and J. E. Packer 2006. "A New Look at Pompey's Theater: History, Documentation, and Recent Excavation." *AJA* 110: 93–122.
Goldberg, S. 1998. "Plautus on the Palatine." *JRS* 88: 1–20.
Goldberg, S. 2004. "Plautus and his Alternatives: Textual Doublets in *Cistellaria*." In *Studien zu Plautus' Cistellaria*, edited by R. Hartkamp and F. Hurka, 385–98. Tübingen: Gunter Narr Verlag.
Gutzwiller, K. and O. Çelik 2012. "New Menander Mosaics from Antioch." *AJA* 116: 573–623.
Hall, E. and R. Wyles 2008. *New Directions in Ancient Pantomime*. Oxford: Oxford University Press.
Harrison, G. W. M. 2000. *Seneca in Performance*. London: Duckworth with the Classical Press of Wales.
Harrison, G. W. M. and V. Liapis (Eds) 2013. *Performance in Greek and Roman Theatre*. Leiden, The Netherlands: Brill.
Hughes, A. 2006. "The 'Perseus Dance' Vase Revisited." *OJA* 25: 413–33.
Izenour, G. 1992. *Roofed Theatres of Classical Antiquity*. New Haven, CT: Yale University Press.
Jones, L. W. and C. R. Morey 1931. *The Miniatures of the Manuscripts of Terence, Prior to the 13th Century*, 2 Vols. Princeton, NJ: Princeton University Press.
Kotlińska-Toma, A. 2015. *Hellenistic Tragedy: Texts, Translations and a Critical Survey*. London: Bloomsbury.
Ley, G. 2007. *The Theatricality of Greek Tragedy: Playing Space and Chorus*. Chicago, IL: University of Chicago Press.
Lowe, J. C. B. 1997. "Terence's Four-Speaker Scenes." *Phoenix* 51: 152–69.
Marshall, C. W. 1999. "Some Fifth-Century Masking Conventions." *G&R* 46: 188–202.
Marshall, C. W. 2006. *The Stagecraft and Performance of Roman Comedy*. Cambridge: Cambridge University Press.
Marshall, C. W. 2013. "Three Actors in Old Comedy, Again." In *Performance in Greek and Roman Theatre*, edited by G. W. M. Harrison and V. Liapis, 257–78. Leiden, The Netherlands: Brill.
Moore, T. J. 1991. "*Palliata togata*: Plautus, *Curculio* 462–86." *AJP* 112: 343–62.
Moretti, J.-Ch. 1997. "Formes et destinations du *proskènion* dans les theaters hellénistiques de Grèce." *Pallas* 47: 13–39.
Padel, R. 1990. "Making Space Speak." In *Nothing to Do with Dionysos? Athenian Drama in its Social Context*, edited by F. I. Zeitlin and J. J. Winkler, 336–65. Princeton, NJ: Princeton University Press.
Pickard-Cambridge, A. 1988. *The Dramatic Festivals of Athens*, 2nd ed., revised by J. Gould and D. M. Lewis with new supplement. Oxford: Oxford University Press.
Poe, J. P. 1989. "The Altar in the Fifth-Century Theatre." *Classical Antiquity* 8: 116–39.
Poe, J. P. 2000. "Multiplicity, Discontinuity, and Visual Meaning in Aristophanic Comedy." *RhM* 14: 256–95.
Rehm, R. 1988. "The Staging of Suppliant Plays." *GRBS* 29: 263–307.
Revermann, M. 2006. *Comic Business: Theatricality, Dramatic Technique, and Performance Contexts of Aristophanic Comedy*. Oxford: Oxford University Press.
Romer, F. E. 1983. "When is a bird not a bird?" *TAPA* 113: 135–42.
Rouveret, A. 1989. *Histoire et Imaginaire de la Peinture Ancienne*. Rome: École française de Rome.
Russo, C. F. 1994. *Aristophanes: An Author for the Stage*. London: Psychology Press.
Scully, S. 1996. "Orchestra and Stage in Euripides' *Suppliant Women*." *Arion* 4.1: 61–84.
Scully, S. 1999. "Orchestra and Stage in Sophocles: *Oedipus Tyrannus* and the Theatre of Dionysus." *Syllecta Classica* 10: 65–85.
Sear, F. 2006. *Roman Theatres: An Architectural Study*. Oxford: Oxford University Press.
Segal, C. P. 1980. "Visual Symbolism and Visual Effects in Sophocles." *CW* 74: 125–42.

Sifakis, G. M. 1967. *Studies in the History of Hellenistic Drama*. London: Athlone Press.
Sifakis, G. M. 1979. "Children in Greek Tragedy." *BICS* 26: 67–80.
Slaney, H. 2013. "Seneca's Chorus of One." In *Choruses, Ancient and Modern*, edited by J. Billings, F. Budelmann and F. Macintosh, 99–116. Oxford: Oxford University Press.
Small, J. P. 2013. "Skenographia in Brief." In *Performance in Greek and Roman Theatre* edited by G. W. M. Harrison and V. Liapis, 111–28. Leiden, The Netherlands: Brill.
Stanley-Porter, D. P. 1973. "Mute actors in the tragedies of Euripides." *BICS* 20: 68–93.
Taplin, O. 1977. *The Stagecraft of Aeschylus: The Dramatic Use of Exits and Entrances in Greek Tragedy*. Oxford: Clarendon Press.
Taplin, O. 1978. *Greek Tragedy in Action*. Berkeley, CA: University of California Press.
Telò, M. forthcoming. *The Titular Object: Pregnant Props in Plautus and Beyond*.
Thiercy, P. 1986. *Aristophane: fiction et dramaturgie*. Paris: Les Belles Lettres.
Tordoff, R. 2013. "Actors' Properties in Ancient Greek Drama: an Overview." In *Performance in Greek and Roman Theatre*, edited by G. W. M. Harrison and V. Liapis, 89–110. Leiden, The Netherlands: Brill.
Wiles, D. 1997. *Tragedy in Athens: Performance Space and Theatrical Meaning*. Cambridge: Cambridge University Press.
Wilson, P. 1999. "The *aulos* in Athens." In *Performance Culture and Athenian Democracy*, edited by S. Goldhill and R. Osborne, 58–95. Cambridge: Cambridge University Press.
Wyles, R. 2011. *Costume in Greek Tragedy*. London: Bloomsbury.
Zanobi, A. 2008. "The Influence of Pantomime on Seneca's Tragedies." In *New Directions in Ancient Pantomime*, edited by E. Hall and R. Wyles, 227–57. Oxford: Oxford University Press.
Zimmermann, B. 2008. "Seneca and Pantomime." In *New Directions in Ancient Pantomime*, edited by E. Hall and R. Wyles, 218–26. Oxford: Oxford University Press.

14
IMAGINING THE SANSKRIT STAGE

Amanda Culp

Over the course of the last century, Indian theatre artists and scholars have debated the role that scenography and theatre architecture could play in the country's emerging modern theatre culture. Precipitated by the ubiquity of representational proscenium theatre, which took root through the scenery-laden stages that had been built and furnished in colonial Bombay and Calcutta, these debates sought a contemporary stage that incorporated the minimalist aesthetic of various Indian folk theatres, as well as the pre-modern Sanskrit tradition.[1] Nobel Laureate, poet, and playwright Rabindranath Tagore encapsulated this attitude as early as 1913 in his brief but powerful essay, "The Stage," in which he rebukes European stage practice for the limitations it places on the playwright's unbounded imagination. He queries,

> Why should the great be required to curb itself, for the sake of the petty? The stage that is in the Poet's mind has no lack of space or appurtenances. There scenes follow one another at the touch of his magic wand. The play is written for such stage and such scenes; the artificial platform with its hanging canvas is not worthy of a poet . . . is it too much to expect the audience to realize the simple truth that though the stage has its limits, the Poem has not?
>
> *(Tagore 2009: 433)*

For Tagore, the ideal stage was that which enabled the imagination – of the playwright, performers, and audience – to dominate unencumbered by restrictions of representation. In his assessment, no stage was better designed for this challenge than that expounded by Sage Bharatamuni in the comprehensive treatise on stagecraft, the *Nāṭyaśāstra* (Bharatamuni 1967).

Unfortunately, very little empirical evidence of this "stage of the imagination" survives beyond the text itself. Following in the style common to *śāstric*, or prescriptive texts,[2] the *Nāṭyaśāstra* contains dense and often esoteric instructions on every aspect of theatre production, from the aesthetic theories of *rasa* (sentiment) to genres of dramatic literature to musical techniques. Chapter 2, which describes the *nāṭyamaṇḍapa*, or theatre hall, moves formulaically through the rites and rituals required for construction, before proceeding to the particulars of the hall itself. The chapter details three different shapes that a theatre hall might take (rectangular, square, and triangular) and three corresponding sizes in which each might be built (small, medium, and large), resulting in nine possible permutations. The stage itself is described as being similar to a cave (presumably to provide for good acoustics), and is described as having two floors, though it is unclear from the text if this refers to the stage itself being of two levels, or of the theatre hall being at a different level from the stage. While the details that can be gleaned from this chapter pertaining to the organization, ornamentation, and size of Bharata's suggested stage have been well-documented by scholars,[3] without any surviving *nāṭyamaṇḍapas* from the pre-modern period it is difficult to flesh out the bare-bones instructions that Bharata's treatise provides. How, for instance, might such a stage have been used? Also, what would have been its relationship to the plays for which it was erected?[4] Luckily, a number of these plays are still extant and their dramaturgy provides a sense of the kinds of worlds the stage was required to support and some of the techniques by which those worlds were created in performance. Reading the plays with this performance in mind suggests that the architecture of the pre-modern Sanskrit stage provided a fixed frame against which the limitless scope of the stage of the playwright's mind could be played.

The structure and organization of the theatre space seem to have been designed precisely to facilitate the kind of idealized transitions and scene progressions that Tagore envisioned. According to the *Nāṭyaśāstra*, the *nāṭyamaṇḍapa* was to be divided into three sections: the *prekṣagṛha*, or place of spectatorship, from which the audience watches;[5] the *nepathya*, or backstage area; and the *raṅga*, or stage proper, itself divided into spaces similar to Euro-American concepts of upstage and downstage. Additionally, the *Nāṭyaśāstra* calls for two secondary spaces, called *mattavāraṇīs*,[6] to be built on either side of the *raṅga* in accordance with its proportion, the express purpose for which is not given by the text. The architecture of the space is therefore organized into discrete compartments, all or some of which may have been used to provide an array of possible configurations when establishing place (or, as the case may sometimes be, places) during any given performance. For clues as to how this might have worked, it helps to turn to the plays themselves.

Consider the tenth and final act of Śudraka's *Mṛcchakaṭika* (The Little Clay Cart). The central event of this act is a procession toward a burying ground where the *nāyaka* (hero), Chārudatta, is to be executed for the purported murder of his beloved, the courtesan Vasantasenā. It begins with only Chārudatta and his executioners onstage and, throughout the duration of the act, various additional characters enter and join the procession, splintering the action into multiple competing scenes in different locations. The servant Sthāvaraka, for example, enters the act "bound in a palace tower," from which vantage point he hears the executioner's proclamation but is "so far away that nobody can hear him" (Śudraka 1900: 265–6. All translations from Sanskrit are mine unless otherwise noted.) Over the course of his monologue, he hears the procession, jumps out of a window, breaks his bonds, and travels to meet up with Chārudatta and company, ultimately resolving what began as two separate scenes into one. Sansthānaka, the play's villain (and Vasantasenā's true attacker), likewise hears voices from a distance and remarks, "now I will scale the highest tower of my palace, to observe my heroic deeds," after which he regards the main scene "from afar" (Śudraka 1900: 267–8). He, too, eventually travels across the city of Ujjainī (and possibly the stage) to join the procession. Finally, Vasantasenā enters, with the Buddhist Monk who rescued her. She is unaware that Chārudatta is to be executed; he is unaware that she is alive; and yet both scenes take place within the very intimate proximity of the playhouse. The tension of the scene, therefore, relies upon keeping the two of them apart until the last possible moment, and the suggestion of the journey that she makes to come to his rescue in time.

The way this act is written suggests a theatre culture wherein the stage was flexible enough to encompass many locations simultaneously – a dramaturgical clue to the ways in which the *mattavāraṇīs*, *nepathya*, and *raṅga* may have been used to create multidimensional stage space. Perhaps the procession would have been blocked on the *raṅga*, with side-scenes taking place in either of the flaking *mattavāraṇīs*. Or, perhaps the central action itself took place in one of these secondary spaces, to create the illusion of distance as characters journeyed to join the procession. The stage directions of the play do not indicate any such specificities of staging aside from use of the *nepathya* for offstage voices and characters about to enter. (The stage direction "*nepathye*" is common in Sanskrit drama and means quite literally "in the wings." Voices are heard from offstage when there is divine intervention, when something exciting has just happened, or to announce the imminent arrival of a new character onstage.) However, the *Nāṭyaśāstra* does stipulate that certain zonal distributions of space, or *kakṣāvibhāga* (literally the apportionment of discrete spaces), be established by the actors in performance through a set of recognizable actions. "The division of stage zones is to be demonstrated by walking around the stage," Bharatamuni instructs us. "By this action, one discrete space is shown to become another entirely" (Bharatamuni 1967: Chapter 14, verse 3). The word Bharata uses to describe this scene shifting, *parikrama*, is echoed across the dramatic canon in stage directions denoting a shift of location, linking the prescribed stage of the *śāstra* to stage practice as indexed by the play text. Thus, by moving around the stage in a certain way, performers could signal to one another and to audience members that a character had moved from inside to outside, from a park to a temple, from a celestial realm to earth,[7] rendering the entire expanse of the universe accessible onstage without ever needing to signal locations scenographically.

To say that this stage was a bare platform would be misleading – even in the strictures of the *Nāṭyaśāstra* instructions are given for ornamental carving and decorative painting on the walls of the *nāṭyamaṇḍapa*. What is important, however, is that unlike the "hanging canvas" disparagingly referred to by Tagore, these paintings didn't change and had no bearing on the content of the play being staged. The *Nāṭyaśāstra* describes this ornamentation in broad strokes: "the plinth of the stage having been completed, woodwork according to a cohesive scheme should be undertaken, which may include adornment by a variety of beasts of prey" (Bharatamuni 1967: Chapter 2, verses 75–6). Or, "the walls, having been completed, should be plastered and whitewashed . . . and painted to represent men, women, vines and pleasurable activities" (Bharatamuni 1967: Chapter 2, verses 83–5). The vagueness of these directives suggests that the content of the ornamentation is less important than the fact of its being there – the static representations on the pillars and the walls will stand in stark contrast to the living stories to be presented before and among them. It is precisely this contrast that allows the imaginative worlds of the stage to emerge. The pre-modern Sanskrit dramatic tradition was notoriously self-referential: each play-text begins with a prologue, wherein a director-character (the *sūtradhāra*) and an actor-character (a *naṭī* or *naṭa*) introduce the evening's play to the audience, foregrounding the artifice of the endeavor and bridging the space between the fixed world of the auditorium and the worlds to be enacted within its bounds. Architecturally, such ornamentation preserved this distinction throughout the action of the play.

One of the most compelling suggestions of this dynamic comes from the third act of Harśa's *Priyadarśikā*. The Queen, Vāsavadattā, and her companion Saṅgkṛtyāyanī have just entered a *prekṣagṛha* as audience members to a play-within-the-play, and Saṅgkṛtyāyanī comments on the ornamentation of the stage in anticipation of the evening's performance:

> The room is resplendent with garlands of thick pearls, strung from golden, jewel-encrusted pillars. The seats are filled with young women whose beauty puts Apsarases to shame. This theatre appears equal to the palace of the gods themselves.
>
> *(Harsa 1977: Act 3, Verse 2 – Apsarases are divine beings, often described as demi-gods or nymphs)*

This is one of the only verses in the Sanskrit dramatic canon to describe a theatre hall and, whether or not it accurately represents the ways in which a stage would have been decorated, the metatheatrical juxtaposition the verse initiates speaks volumes. In describing the playhouse to the Queen, Saṅgkṛtyāyanī describes it for the audience as well, who now compare the stage before which they sit to the one invoked by Harśa. The verse thereby invites the audience to reflect and actively assess the efficacy of the performance at hand, by collapsing the manifold scenes that they have witnessed thus far into the singular frame from which they originate. Likewise, the paintings and carvings that are commissioned to adorn the actual stage space juxtapose the infinite imagination with finite representation, and assert the superiority of performance for engaging the former.

Thus, the ever-changing landscape of the pre-modern Sanskrit drama is enacted bodily, with the assistance of a theatrical architecture primed to allow for the imagination to predominate. Sanskrit theatre is, after all, a theatre of emotions, where performers labor not to convey plot, as in the Greek theatre, but *rasa*, the recognition of an essential human experience shared between performer, character and audience.[8] According to the *Nāṭyaśāstra* there are eight *rasas*,[9] each governed by a variety of supporting and transitory emotive states, and it is in orchestrating these constituent parts into an affective whole where the real work of this dramatic tradition resides. As Tagore articulates it:

> The complex of the emotions appropriate to the characters of Dushyanta and Shakuntala, Anasuya and Priyamvada[10] are doubtless . . . difficult to conjure up and retain in their exactitude, so we are grateful for the assistance [the artists] give to the corresponding play of our sympathetic emotions; but what is the difficulty about imagining a few trees, a cottage, or a bit of river? To attempt to assist us even in regard to these with painted canvas hangings is only to betray a woeful mistrust in our capacity.
>
> *(Tagore 2009: 434)*

The world and its diversity of settings, in other words, could be recognized by means other than performance, and could be conjured easily from one's personal experience; we possess the capacity to envision a tree or a cottage or even a palace to a degree of accuracy. But the richness of the lives lived within those settings, and how they influence our emotions – these were the questions of interest to the Sanskrit poets, and ones that had no straightforward answers. The stage of the *Nāṭyaśāstra*, and of pre-modern Sanskrit theatre, was therefore first and foremost a space of imagination where the poet could lead, and the audience follow, anywhere necessary in order to produce that elusive *rasa*. How exactly this stage worked, however, and what it might have looked like, requires a certain imagination all its own.

Notes

1 I categorize as pre-modern the culture of theatrical performance that spans roughly the first ten centuries of the Common Era.

2 A common genre of Sanskrit literature from this period, *Śāstras* are detailed treatises pertaining to rules of behavior, organization, and artistry that governed various fields. Other significant *Śāstras* of the period include the *Arthaśāstra* treatise on law and government; the *Kāmaśāstras* on love and lifestyle (to which the *Kāmasūtra* belongs); the *Śilpaśāstras* of various artistic guilds.

3 For more information on the details provided by the *Nāṭyaśāstra* on the Sanskrit stage, David Gitomer's chapter "The Theatre in Kalidasa's Art" from *Theatre of Memory* and G. K. Bhat's *Theatrical Aspects of Sanskrit Theatre* are excellent resources.

4 The relationship between the redacted knowledge contained in the *Nāṭyaśāstra* and the plays of the pre-modern Sanskrit canon is not entirely clear. References to a body of knowledge known as *Nāṭyaśāstra* is evinced by Kālidāsa's play *Malāvikāgnimitra* (Malāvika and Agnimitra), in which the work is cited in the adjudication of a dance contest, but our understanding of how closely playwrights and theatrical companies adhered to its guidelines in composition and performance can be speculative at best.

5 Like the English "theatre," *prekṣagṛha* also privileges the ocular experience of performance, meaning literally the place for perception or, as we often render it in the western context, "seeing place."

6 Unlike so many of the technical terms of this chapter, the etymology of *mattavāraṇī* is unclear, though it seems related to the term *mattavaraṇa*, a turret, pinnacle, or pavilion. For more on the linguistic analysis of this term, see Ghosh's translation of the *Nāṭyaśāstra*, Chapter 2 verses 63–5, footnote.

7 Verses 4–10 of *Nāṭyaśāstra* Chapter 14 enumerate the following possible locations: houses, cities, pleasure gardens, rivers, ashrams, forests, the earth, the ocean, the three worlds, the universe, continents, *Sapta Dvīpa* (an ancient name for India meaning seven islands), mountains, heaven and hell, the dwellings of gods and demigods. Not all of these spaces were necessarily present in a given play, nor is the list meant to be comprehensive. These verses simply demonstrate the great diversity that the minimalist *Nāṭyaśāstra* stage was expected to support.

8 *Rasa* means juice or essence, and is meant to connote a pure and concentrated human experience. Scholarly debates on *rasa*, particularly pertaining to where it is found (in the text? the character? the performer?) and how it is made manifest, span the centuries, and are far too complex to expand upon here. For more on *rasa*, see Barbara Stoller Miller's essay "Kalidasa's World and his Plays," and Sheldon Pollock's *A Rasa Reader*.

9 According to Chapter 6 of the *Nāṭyaśāstra*, the eight rasas are: *sṛṅgāra* (love); *hāsya* (comedy); *raudra* (rage); *karuṇa* (pity); *bhībhatsa* (disgust); *bhayānaka* (fear); *vīra* (heroism); and *adbhuta* (wonderment). Later theorists and commentators posited a ninth rasa, *śānta* (peace), but this rasa is not contemporary with the *Nāṭyaśāstra* or the plays of the pre-modern tradition.

10 These are all central characters from Kālidāsa's masterpiece, *Abhijñānaśakuntala* or the Recognition of Shakuntala, arguably the most famous work of the Sanskrit dramatic canon.

References

Bharatamuni 1967. *The Nāṭyaśāstra: A Treatise on Ancient Indian Dramaturgy and Histrionics Ascribed to Bharata Muni*, translated by Manomohan Ghosh, 2 Vols. Calcutta: Manisha Granthalaya.

Harśa 1977. *Priyadarśikā*. Delhi: Motilal Banarsidass.

Śudraka 1900. *Mṛcchakaṭika*. Bombay: Nirnayasagar Press.

Tagore, Rabindranath 2009. "The Stage." In *Modern Indian Theatre: A Reader*, edited by Nandi Bhatia. New Delhi: Oxford University Press.

15

TUDOR AND STUART SCENOGRAPHY

Andrew Gurr

The concept of the "bare stage" for the Shakespearean period is a cliché that needs cautious handling. If, in Shakespeare's own time, the repertoire of plays had to be changed every day, as Henslowe's *Diary* shows was the case at least from 1592–1597, there could never have been enough time to make radical changes to the background setting for each scene. With that in mind, we have become used to thinking of the Shakespearean stage

Figure 15.1 The two-door Swan stage, drawn by Johannes de Witt, copied by Arendt van Buchell. (Used by permission of the Folger Shakespeare Library.)

as essentially bare wood, colored only by the bright costumes of the players, and perhaps some paint on the timbers. The few references to either stage properties or "scenes" are assumed to have appeared on an otherwise vacant stage, like that on which the friend of Johannes De Witt portrayed his image of a play at the Swan in 1595.

Plays not only changed daily, but could be transferred from one venue to another very quickly. The King's Men could take plays they had staged for the public at the Globe on any afternoon for re-staging at Court the same evening. For them to be so portable, the players could not afford to augment their costumes and scripts with major scenic properties. So, besides the drastic rate of turnover that made them stage a different play every afternoon for the regular playgoers, the company must have made portability their chief priority. Any team, whether based in London or routinely travelling with just a few plays, would have carried eight or so sharers on horseback, accompanying a cart burdened with, besides a dozen or so boys and hired hands, a few carefully chosen play-books and some changes of stage apparel. Not until the leading companies became settled in London from 1594 on, and got the habit of playing constantly at the same venue, could they have begun to think of backing their shows with more than the painted wood of whatever stage frame was made available for their use.

So, did they perform, either at the Globe or at Court, without any scenic back-up at all? The assumed opposite of the "bare stage" is scenic staging. As the evidence from Henslowe's *Diary* indicates, we know that the early stages used no scenery, not least because, according to him, they always staged a different play each day. That would have reduced the time available for setting up pictorial backgrounds daily, even if the cost of mounting special props for any single performance was not a sufficient deterrent. The initial years the companies spent playing at the Rose from 1592 onwards were also the first time that we know any company had a durable tenure of one venue. Touring the country, which had been the standard practice until then, meant that scenic properties had to be portable, while the venues where they performed would change from day to day. Under such conditions elaborate sets were impossible.

Understandably, therefore, few items of evidence about any use of scenery or scenic effects appear in the texts and stage directions of the plays from this period. In extant play-texts the stage directions suggest that, only in the later years, when company income increased and the practice of companies holding their places at the one London venue gradually became standard, did the idea of imitating on the public stages the lavishly beautiful and costly sets designed by Inigo Jones for performances at Court enhance its attractions. Some of the later plays used occasional spectacles, as they were called – shows of static sets with players posing, usually uncovered (or "discovered") by drawing back the hangings that were ready set up across the central opening.

The chief question about the early stages was how many entry-ways there were from the *frons scenae*. The only drawing of a *frons* that we have is of the Swan playhouse. It shows two double doors, which is presumably what the Swan's stage offered its actors for their entrances. The bulk of the evidence about such entrances for all the other stages, however, makes a powerful case for a pair of doors, one at each side of the *frons*, with a much broader opening in the center, usually covered by a set of hangings, or a curtain drawn across the whole opening. One of the most common of stage directions demands that a spectacle be "discovered," by someone drawing the hangings back. Nerissa, for instance, does that to reveal the three caskets in *The Merchant of Venice*. Such uncoverings cannot be done at either of the flanking doors. They need hangings

(a)

(b)

Figure 15.2 Pictures showing indoor stages with cloth backdrops: (a) the title page of *Roxana* (1632) and (b) *Messalina* (1640). (*Roxana* used by permission of the Folger Shakespeare Library.)

in front of a recess or inner stage in the middle of the *frons scenae*. It is now routine to assume that the early stages had such a central recess.

Neither of the only two images we have of the later, indoor, stages offer much helpful detail, nor much reliability. The *Roxana* and *Messalina* vignettes, printed in 1632 and 1640, show players acting in front of painted cloths, which are pinned across intermittently below the stage balcony, one trailing edge dragged back to show where entrances could be made through them. The frontispiece of Nathanael Richards' *Messalina* (1640) shows two painted cloths behind the players, facing the audience. Each has a figure sketched on it, plus clouds or trees, with a single opening between the two hangings. This appears on the title page for a play staged at the third indoor playhouse, Salisbury Court, whereas the earlier *Roxana* is an academic's play, probably not meant for a London stage, although the engraver of the title page might have thought such a venue apt for his subject. Both stages are flanked by low rails. To conceive of just how the plays were enacted on such stages requires a high level of inspired guesswork.

Some scholars think the *Messalina* vignette is so similar to the *Roxana* that it might be a copy of its predecessor. If so, it must certainly have been drawn as a stock image of a typical scene. We can confirm that at least some indoor stages did have painted cloths on the *frons scenae*. The Citizen Wife in *The Knight of the Burning Pestle* (Blackfriars Boys, 1607) gossips about them at a performance by the boy company. Sitting on the stage herself, in the second Interact, she asks her grocer husband sitting by her, "What story is that painted upon the cloth? The confutation of Saint Paul?" His answer, overtly referring to standard if parodied Shakespeare, is "No lambe, that's *Raph* and *Lucrece*." They have both had to clamber effortfully onto the stage from the pit. Sadly, their exchanges tell us nothing about how and where the boys entered and exited the stage.

The hangings of painted cloth across the stage must have made the players' entrances immediately striking. They would also have provided perfect concealment for eavesdropping or other reasons to hide while on stage. Besides the painted cloths, however, other evidence about what might have clad the stages is minimal. All we have for conjecture are the stage directions specifying the massive properties that might sometimes have been taken from London to accompany the major companies on their travels.[1] A number of the many plays circuiting the country needed major set pieces, most notably *Tamburlaine*, the most famous of all the travelling plays. In *Tamburlaine* Part 2, at the beginning of 4.3, the hero enters in his chariot, pulled by four kings, whom he is scourging with his whip. The stage direction describes two of the on-foot kings hauling a chariot onstage, accompanied by seven other kings as his prisoners, plus Tamburlaine and his soldiers, in exceptional detail:

> Tamburlaine, drawen in his chariot by Trebison and Soria with bittes in their mouthes, reines in his left hand, in his right a whip, with which he scourgeth them, Techelles, Theridamas, Usumcasane, Amyras, Celebinus, Natolia, and Jerusalem, led by with five or six common souldiers.[2]

For this famous scene, whose opening line about the pampered jades of Asia is echoed by Parolles in Shakespeare's *2 Henry IV* (2.4), the company must have used a two-wheeled cart, gilded and adorned like a Roman chariot. On tour, they might have expected to acquire some such cart locally, simply adding the paint and decorations that travelled with the play.

A major precedent for spectacular entrances, Marlowe's own visual spectacle was soon imitated by Lodge in *The Wounds of Civil War* (1588–90). It has a very similar entry for Sulla "in triumph in his chare triumphant of gold, drawen by foure Moores, before the chariot: his colours, his crest, his captaines, his prisoners: Arcathius, Mithridates son, Aristion, Archelaus, bearing crownes of gold, and manacled." The printed edition of this play appears in the Stationers' Register for 24 May 1594, where it was ascribed to the Admiral's men. Not appearing in Henslowe's *Diary*, it must have had a London staging some years before the *Diary*'s first entries in March 1592, either at the Theatre, the Curtain, or the Rose. A chariot being pulled onstage by so many people, with all their accompanying kings, demanded the use of a broad central opening, rather than either of the much narrower flanking doors. Such surprising displays were usual features of the central opening, otherwise used only for royal or imperial entrances and the more startling spectacles. Most scenes involving conflict of some sort required entrance from either of the flanking doors, in opposition. Use of the central opening displayed a singular dominance, not opponents in conflict. In *The Honest Man's Fortune*, a Rose play, the heroine Lamyra makes her entrance "from the Aras," the centrally-positioned painted cloth resembling the sort of weave from Arras that normally covered the central opening. Her arrival in the center emphasized her function as the play's heroine. Cloth of Arras was a costly weave. Painted cloths were the most usual imitations, like the *Messalina* and *Roxana* cloths.

Individual locations were usually altered between scenes without much, if any, visual indicators. In his *Catiline*, another Chamberlain's play, Ben Jonson specified as a simile for high-speed actions, "a veil put off, a visor changed, / Or the scene shifted in our theatres" (1.1.184–5). Such shifts must have been almost instantaneous, changes only identifiable from references by word of mouth. The word "scene," that which is in view, came to stand equally for a location, and for the action of the moment on stage. When a character such as Dr Faustus, or Catiline in Jonson's play, was "discovered" behind the stage hangings, sitting at a table with books and sometimes a candle on it, the revelation was normal. Such directions said that only the man, often the titular character, was to be revealed on his own, in private. Almost always when he had anything to say he stepped forward onto the main stage, speaking either to himself or directly to the audience.

Particularly localized scenes do seem sometimes to need more than a casual mention in words. The stage direction that begins Act 2 scene 1 of *Julius Caesar*, "Enter Brutus in his Orchard," is suggestive, but utterly enigmatic. It gives a location for the scene, but nothing is said in the dialogue. So did it need scenery such as a symbolic tree on stage to represent the orchard?[3] Mariko Ichikawa notes that Shakespeare, in all, sets 19 scenes in a garden. In Shakespeare's time, such gardens, usually enclosed by brick walls, with mature fruit trees planted inside or espaliered against the brickwork, were private and exclusive open spaces for individuals walking and sometimes talking to a partner. Ichikawa notes that Henslowe's stage properties included "1 bay tree," "1 tree of gowlden apelles" for Dekker's *1 Fortunatus* (1596), and a "Tantelous tre[e]." Plays such as *1 Henry VI* and *Two Noble Kinsmen* required flowering rose trees, with visible roses for ready plucking. Ichikawa makes the point (Ichikawa 2013: 118) that none of the scenes other than *1 Henry VI* that needed trees on stage was said to be set in a garden.

Other early plays had scenes making more awkward demands for their staging. *The Spanish Tragedy* had its famous arbor, a bower on which Hieronymus's son is hanged, followed by his killer Pedringano, and which Bel-imperia later cuts down before killing herself. Apart from such special features, the essential bareness of the stage and its locales normally were merely announced by the speakers. That is emphasized by, for instance, *Romeo and Juliet*, where the same stage transits from being Capulet's orchard to Juliet's chamber window and then to her chamber interior, all by verbal statements (Ichikawa 2013: 119). Ichikawa even suggests that a garden might have been suggested by characters who enter carrying flowers (Ichikawa 2013: 122). For *Julius Caesar* 2.1, she considers that Brutus' reference to looking at the stars early in the scene would tell us he was outdoors, and therefore probably in his garden. Its privacy would be signified by Brutus closing the door by which he entered to start the scene.

Some of the earlier plays do seem to have demanded special London-only devices to be available. *Alphonsus of Aragon* opens with this directive: "After you have sounded thrise, let Venus be let downe from the top of the Stage, and when she is downe, say: Poets are scarce when Goddesses themselves / Are forst to leave their high and stately seates / Placed on the top of high *Olympus* Mount, / To seeke them out, to pen their Champions praise." At the end of the play, the direction is "Exit Venus. Or if you can conveniently, let a chaire come downe from the top of the stage, and draw her up." This play also had the same "brazen Head" that featured in *Friar Bacon and Friar Bungay*. The anonymous author was clearly concerned to utilize current staging possibilities. Its 1599 title page specifies that "it hath bene sundrie times acted," and it was clearly written with that in mind.

It was routine to have discoveries elaborated or explained by a viewer commenting on them. A Red Bull play of 1619, surviving in the Egerton 1994 manuscript, usually known as *The Two Noble Ladies*, has a stage direction that says (TLN 1752), "Justina is discovered in a chaire asleep, in her hands a prayer book, divells about her." At the sight, Cyprian exclaims, "O how heavenly sweet she looks in midst of hells enchantments, and charms the fierce feinds at once with rage and wonder." He tries the effect of music and song, but when he offers to kiss her, the still-sleeping Justina "looks in her booke, and the Spirits fly from her." The devilish Cantharides declares, "Her faith beats downe our incantations."

Many plays open with an announcement of the locality. Peele's *Old Wives Tale* (*c*. 1590) begins with three characters entering, one of whom, Antic, says to the others "What though wee have lost our way in the woodes, yet never hang the head, as though thou had no hope to live till to morrow." The body language accompanying such an assertion is simple to imagine, even if none of the trees specified by Henslowe were on stage. A later direction in the same play simply states "Enter Sacrepant in his studie." Further on is "He draweth a curten, and there Delia sitteth a sleepe." This is quite soon followed by the arrival of another common and portable property, "Enter Jack with a head in his hand." Few directions insist on much more than things that could be carried in the hand, such as the logs of wood that Ferdinand in *The Tempest* is required to bring onstage.

One incidental feature of early staging that may have a bearing on scenery was the use of intervals. The evidence in playbooks of written-in pauses between the acts is fairly minimal, though many later plays do mark them, and most of them show that their authors were well aware of the normal five-act structure. Scenes started and ended when groups of players entered and exited, the bare stage being the only marker of such stoppages. Frequently at scene ends, and occasionally during a scene, the stage hands must have been used, invisibly (stage directions rarely make any reference to them), but necessarily to carry off the tables and benches used when the scene demanded them.

What is now known as "continuous staging" seems to have been standard, and we cannot be sure when pauses were introduced between the acts. The usual story is that they had to be used at the indoor venues to give time for the hands to change the candles. This is rather dubious, because wax candles burn steadily for two or more hours before they begin to gutter, and even the cheaper tallows burned for more than one and a half hours. So four intervals seems excessive for such forms of control. Outdoors, of course, no mechanical pauses were ever needed, even for toilet breaks. I have always believed that the rear walls of the galleries, particularly the uppermost galleries where the viewers had to sit closest to the main railings to see the show, gave ample space behind for needy playgoers to relieve themselves against the outer walls or floor. At the more closely packed indoor venues the two hours' traffic of the stage might have run somewhat longer, and there was much less free space for folk who needed to relieve themselves. How they coped we do not know. Perhaps the intervals there, however brief, were sufficient for the menfolk to hasten out of doors for relief. Otherwise, we ought to look into the fragmentary evidence of the large number of pots found at the Rose and Globe remains, to see whether they provided relief before or after their users' bladders came to need them.

Almost all of Shakespeare's plays in the versions that have come to us in print make no provision for pauses between the acts. Only *The Tempest* has an obvious, built-in, pause, when the same characters, Prospero and Ariel, who leave at the end of Act 4 re-enter to begin the final act. Of other plays, *The Dutch Courtesan*, a Marston play written for the boys at the Blackfriars, has a similar act break involving the one character exiting and then re-entering for the next Act, when Freeville exits with Malheureux to complete Act 1, and re-enters with a group of musicians and pages to commence Act 2. We know too little about such possible breaks in the action. Beaumont, author of *The Knight of the Burning Pestle*, which marks each act-break with talk between the citizen Grocer and his wife, seems to have expected act breaks to last for less than two minutes, since he fills the last of his four written-in pauses with a speech by Rafe, the comic hero, comprising 30 lines of comic verse. Such a length of time would have been ample for Ariel and Prospero to recover from playing the dogs that hound Caliban and the other villains offstage. Two minutes is markedly less time than is now allowed for intervals, when the playgoers are expected to stretch their legs, attend the toilets, and pay for their refreshments.

However well attested, and however colorful, this narrow range of onstage activities might easily tempt us to underrate the scale of income and consequent resources that Shakespeare's company, if no other, might have used in its work. Even the most tangible evidence, stage directions, can too easily leave it unclear what might be missing. By some way the most substantial stage property we have evidence for was needed in *The Spanish Tragedy* (1588), as noted earlier, where old Hieronymo finds his son Horatio hanging dead onstage. This follows a stage direction for his murder, "They hang him in the arbour," before stabbing him. Pedringano later suffers the same fate in the same arbor. Marston appears to have recalled this famous device for his boy company play, *Antonio and Mellida*, in 1599, though he did so by exploiting the central opening commonly used for spectacles, where we are told "The Curtain's drawne, and the bodie of Feliche, stabd thick with wounds, appeares hung up."

Probably the most colorful feature of all stagings was of course the clothing people wore. Whatever the cost of laundry might have been between shows, blood was a frequent and colorful stage device that must have appeared on clothing as well as skin. In the middle of *A Warning for Fair Women*, a Chamberlain's play from 1599 or so, based on a well-known local murder story, a stage direction (sig. C4v) has "Tragedie" enter, with "a bowle of bloud in her hand." She stands holding it while she declares "in these sable Curtains shut we up / The Comicke entrance to our direful play." Shortly after, speaking "againe turning to the people" (a direction that tells us she speaks directly facing the audience), she announces, "Here enters Murther into al their harts." They sleep, and Tragedie, now given the speech heading "Murther," "settes downe her blood, and rubbes their hands."

Clothing signified much more than it does now. Blue was the servant's color, red the mark of nobility. Even the fabrics worn signified distinct social status, from royal velvet or taffeta to citizen calico or wool. The so-called "sumptuary" laws from earlier in the sixteenth century survived under Elizabeth to warn non-gentry not to use specified clothing such as velvet. The color of gowns marked their wearers. Doctors wore scarlet, friars grey, servants blue, while soldiers wore leather – that was easy. Women's gowns were more complex, though no less colorful and ornamented with frills than a gentleman's. Worn clothing could easily be patched up with furbelows of some sort. The money paid by players for a woman's costume, often over £20 each, exceeded the price of a new playbook.

Disguise, that most obviously theatrical device, was one of the most common tricks in early drama, simply as a change of costume. In Chapman's *The Blind Beggar of Alexandria* (1596, at the Rose), Edward Alleyn wore three disguises, besides that of the blind beggar himself, manifestly a disguise. A false beard was only a minimal disguise, when the clothing you wore could tell so much more about you. Robert Greene wrote enviously about a player who walked the street in

> a murrey cloth gowne, faced down before with gray conny [rabbit fur], and laide thick on the sleeve with lace, which he quaintly bare up to shew his white Taffata hose, and black silk stockings. A huge ruffe about his necke wrapt in his great head like a wicker cage, a little Hat with brims like the wings of a doublet, wherein he wore a Jewel of Glasse, as broad as a chancery sale.

For all the evidence of such finery, it is extremely unlikely that a player, after wearing the conspicuous dress of an earl or duke on stage, would even think of continuing to wear it outside the playhouse.

So much for the decorated features that might have stood on the Tudor stage. For the stage itself, we can only say that, like the costumes, its verges would have been distinctly eye-catching. Bare timbers, other than perhaps the stage floor itself, were never a feature of Tudor design. A painted and decorated *frons scenae* out of which the player emerged to perform in front of it is a given for the Globe. That assumption stands in spite of the most expensive seats being positioned at what we think of as the "back" of the stage. Knowing that the highest paying audience sat "behind" the players on the stage balcony in the *frons*, where some can be seen in the Swan drawing, we still find ourselves using the two-dimensional modern terminology for their locations as "front" and "rear" or "behind." This hardly fits well with a stage with an audience surrounding it on all sides. Cinema has profoundly influenced theatre into acting to the "front," aiming at the majority of audience in the stalls and galleries facing the stage. That means, in effect, two-dimensional acting. Shakespearean acting was in the round, truly three-dimensional. We lose a lot by treating our theatres as if they were cinemas.

Notes

1 The Admiral's travelled extensively, both before and after 1592. See Gurr (2009), Chapter 2, especially pp. 72–81; in Ludlow, two babies were given Tamburlaine's name when baptized in 1622, which suggests that a performance of the play had occurred there recently.
2 I quote from the original text.
3 Chapter 5 of Ichikawa (2013) deals with this scene and the implications of its opening stage direction.

References

Gurr, Andrew 2009. *Shakespeare's Opposites: The Admiral's Company, 1594–1625*. Cambridge: Cambridge University Press.
Ichikawa, Mariko 2013. *The Shakespearean Stage Space*. Cambridge: Cambridge University Press.

16
PLAYING WITH MATERIALS
Performing effect on the indoor Jacobean stage

Jane Collins

The opening of the Sam Wanamaker Playhouse in London in January 2014, designed to "invoke a version of the indoor playhouse Shakespeare's company occupied from 1609 to 1642" (Gurr and Karim-Cooper 2014: 1), has inspired Early Modern theatre scholars and historians to not only revisit the plays performed indoors during the winter months but also reconsider the social, economic, and *material* conditions of their production. Until recently, studies of Early Modern drama have primarily focused on these plays from a literary perspective or, when considering them in performance, discussions of acting styles, costume, and architecture have in the main concentrated on the larger outdoor amphitheatres such as The Globe. This renewed interest in the staging of Jacobean and Caroline plays in the more intimate environment of the indoor playhouses has shifted the focus away from what had been generally accepted as "an actor's and playwright's theatre" (Sturgess 1987: 37) towards a more nuanced understanding of the actor as just one component in a complex matrix of elements that constitute the performance event, as well as re-thinking the notion of a single authorial vision. Thus the emphasis of scholarly attention expands from actor presence and authorial intent to embrace wider considerations of the spatial, visual, acoustic and olfactory conditions that pertained in the indoor playhouses, as well as the social status and expectations of the audiences who attended performances there; in effect a "turn" towards scenography.

In the editorial of the inaugural issue of the journal *Theatre and Performance Design* Arnold Aronson and I argue that scenography "is reframing debates and changing perceptions and, as such, emerging as a significant challenge to established epistemologies in theatre and performance discourse" (Aronson and Collins 2015: 1). This position is supported by Farah Karim-Cooper and Will Tosh in the program for the Winter Season 2015–16 at The Sam Wanamaker Playhouse who ask us to consider: "How did the specific conditions of the indoor theatres affect the plays that dramatists produced for them?"[1] In other words, what new ways of expressing the social, political, and philosophical preoccupations of the times were afforded to the playwrights and actors by the visual, spatial and acoustic conditions of the indoor venues?

One of the most profound philosophical debates of the early modern period, sparked by renewed interest in the ideas of Plato, concerned the relative merits of words and images as the purveyors of *truth*. A contemporary disquiet about the reliability of the senses, particularly sight, is one of the themes common to many of Shakespeare's later plays, what Karim-Cooper describes as "a continuous interrogation of the idea that what you see is what you get"[2] (Karim-Cooper 2014: 198). The "turn" towards scenography in early modern scholarship extends our understanding of how these themes, identified in the surviving folios, might have been worked through in performance.

> Theatre enacts the dialectic of showing and concealing that underpins the tension between epistemology (that which is shown is true) and metaphysics (that which is concealed is true). And it questions the testimony of eye and ear through deception and illusion: theatrical narratives often turn upon whether we can trust the evidence of our senses – what we see what we hear, what we are told.
>
> *(Till 2015: 111)*

John Webster's *The Duchess of Malfi*, produced by the King's Men in the early years of the winter move into their indoor home in the Blackfriars Playhouse, has become something of a touchstone for early modern scholars analyzing the changes instituted by the move indoors. Most scholars agree that Webster probably wrote *The Duchess of Malfi* with the indoor playhouse in mind and it is significant because, among its many themes, it explores this "contemporary disquiet" by playing on theatre's capacity to destabilize the relationship between seeing, hearing and knowing.

The spatial conditions of the smaller intimate indoor playhouses, combined with the potential to control light and sound, made these venues ideally suited for playwrights and actors to explore these ideas through practical experiment with materials and through play. This chapter will discuss some of the ways the special effects made possible by the move indoors may have contributed to the realization of the thematic preoccupations of Webster's *Duchess of Malfi*.

There is no clear evidence of what the Blackfriars[3] indoor playhouse may have looked like. It was, as the name suggests, an adaptation of the upper floors of an old monastery situated "inside the city and close to St Paul's Cathedral" (Gurr and Karim-Cooper 2014: 3). A set of architectural drawings discovered in Worcester College, Oxford, in the 1960s and thought to be designs by stage designer and architect Inigo Jones for an early playhouse, were revealed in the 1990s to have been made much later, probably in the Restoration, by Jones' ex-student John Webb. The drawings however displayed a number of architectural features associated with the earlier Jacobean period and they therefore became the basis for the design of the Sam Wanamaker Playhouse, a simulacrum of The Blackfriars, adjacent to London's Globe.[4] One of these features, noted as significant by Gurr and Karim-Cooper, is "the priority it may give to hearing over seeing the plays (though this positioning does allow for privileged viewing), since nearly a third of the seats are positioned at the sides or rear of the stage in order to give the best proximity for hearing" (Gurr and Karim-Cooper 2014: 2). It is generally accepted "that the Blackfriars stage was about half the size of the Globe stage" (Ichikawa 2014: 80) and the playing space was further reduced by the presence of "gallants" seated on stage on either side of the acting area. Many of the actual and symbolic features – the heavens above and hell below – of the outdoor spaces were replicated on a smaller scale indoors, not surprising given that a company's repertoire often moved between the two spaces in the different seasons. As Ichikawa elaborates, "the requirements of plays performed at the Blackfriars suggest that its stage had two doors in the facade, a discovery space between them, a balcony above, a trapdoor to the space below and a descent machine" (ibid.). It would seem then, initially at least, that many of the staging practices of the outdoor theatres were transferred to the indoor venues with some modifications. There is evidence, for instance, that entrance and exit speeches were trimmed, possibly to accommodate the reduction in distance from the doors in the upstage facade to the downstage playing area (see Ichikawa 2014: 79–94). However, as I discuss below, this assumes that the spatial conventions of the outside theatres were replicated indoors and this may not have been the case.

Scenographic innovations and experiments adapted from painting by Italian theatre designers like the architect Baldessare Peruzzi in the sixteenth century had been widely disseminated in the writings of Sebastiano Serlio as early as 1545. In England, these ideas were celebrated by Inigo Jones in the court masques, but in the Jacobean mind, according to Keith Sturgess, there was a clear delineation between a play and a masque and "'[s]hows' were for masques and masques were not plays" (Sturgess 1987: 38). Sturgess attributes this lack of scenic display to a "deep conservatism" (ibid.) as well as the expense involved and the demands of turning round a huge repertoire. Sturgess equates "design" with costly decoration and although this was clearly "not a scene-painter's theatre" (Sturgess 1987: 37), examined through a scenographic lens early modern plays like the *Duchess of Malfi* demonstrate a complex stage-craft as visual as it is aural that attests to a highly sophisticated understanding of space and materials.

The discussion around the relative merits of words (hearing) and images (seeing) a play, identified as a characteristic of the Jacobeans, erupted in the Caroline era in 1631 into the famously public argument between the playwright Ben Jonson and stage architect Inigo Jones. They had maintained a long and successful partnership dating back to 1605 staging highly elaborate court masques. The argument centered around who should be credited as the "primary 'inventor'" of their collaborations. Jonson habitually assumed this designation for himself and finally Jones challenged him. As Nicholas Till explains:

> Jonson hit back with a series of vicious ripostes . . . mock[ing] the pretentions of Jones's increasingly grandiose settings for their court masques, complaining that 'design' has now become 'omnipotent' and intends to make poetry redundant.
>
> *(Till 2010: 154)*[5]

Jonson came down emphatically on the side of words, vehemently asserting that "the spectator must seek beyond the spectacle which is being presented for the meaning that lies within" (ibid.: 156). Paul Menzer warns against the oversimplification that the King's Men, under the pernicious influence of Jones and his foreign ideas, eventually shifted the balance "to fantastic visual scenery that appealed to the eye over verbal scenery that spoke to the mind's eye" (Menzer 2014: 180) when the company moved indoors. He argues that "the bareness of the 'bare' platform of the early modern amphitheatre is greatly overstated" and that "[we] know the outdoor theatres to have been, themselves, invested in wonder" (ibid.). He also points out that this "fabled" shift is often associated with a kind of "loss" in the way it is presented by many theatre historians, as if they too support the iconophobia of Jonson. However, underlying the egotistical rivalry between Jonson and Jones we can discern the philosophical argument about artifice and truth being played out across Europe.

> Plato's philosophy is based upon an innate distrust of the outer body of material reality as being no more than an ephemeral simulacrum of the real metaphysical truth beyond. During the Renaissance there was a fierce debate among neo-Platonists as to whether images or words offered a more immediate way of representing the essential Platonic form. Were images lesser because they were sensory, or were they superior because they more directly represented the pure form of the thing existing prior to the mediated sign system of language.
>
> *(Till 2010: 156)*

John Webster also privileged language when he complained about the lack of appreciation of the first performance of his tragedy *The White Devil*.[6] Staged at the Red Bull, an outside playhouse, it was performed on a dull afternoon – most likely in February or March 1612 – so people couldn't properly see it but, more importantly, they couldn't hear it, or they weren't listening attentively and therefore did not understand it.

> [S]ince it was acted, in so dull a time of winter, presented in so open and black a theatre, that it wanted (that which is the only grace and setting out of a tragedy) a full and understanding auditory
>
> *(Webster 1996: 5)*

Two years after the very unsatisfactory reception of *The White Devil*, *The Duchess of Malfi* was staged at the Blackfriars in the autumn of 1614. Martin White identifies that "many features of staging implied by the text . . . are clearly designed for indoor performance" (White 2014: 132). These features include not only the potential for more focused light and sound but also exploitation of new technologies in the form of wax figures, as well as the spatial opportunities offered to performers to *play* in more intimate and colluding ways with the audience. I have argued elsewhere that "[t]he explicit theatricality of Jacobean stage convention with its sensationalist effects, tricks, and fakery appears to demand an exuberant performance style" (Collins 2012: 57). Bridget Escolme makes the point that "in performance, these dramatic texts are dependent for their effects of subjectivity upon the potential for direct encounter between performer and spectator" (Escolme 2005: 8).

> They want the audience to listen to them, notice them, approve their performance, ignore others on stage for their sake. The objectives of these figures are bound up with the fact that they know you're there.
>
> *(Ibid.: 16)*

The indoor venues were ideal for this kind of direct address but also enabled more intimate asides that could draw the audience into the orbit of the protagonists. In the early stages of the play Bosola, who is paid to spy on the Duchess by her brother, is able to make jokes with the audience at her expense in the public environment of the court, with no less than four asides in a very short exchange as he tries to find out whether she is pregnant (II. ii). As the plot progresses this form of "playing" has the potential to further embroil the audience in the reprehensible actions of the characters and the moral ambiguities of Webster's world.

Scenographic thinking argues that a separation of sound and space is impossible, positing instead "that sound and space must be understood dialectically" (Till 2015: 111) and certainly the changed acoustic environment of the smaller more intimate indoor spaces opened up the possibilities for a more nuanced and subtle style of playing. "The whispering that characterizes court intrigue, and of which the Duchess complains in IV. ii. 218–19, well suited the ambiance of the Blackfriars" (Elizabeth M. Brennan in Webster [1963] 1993: xxxiii). This also begs the question how did actors actually use the space? Did they seek out the best positions from which to address the audience? Did they speak behind them or take advantage of the architectural features of the building, the pillars, for instance, to make sudden appearances. Did they enter from downstage through the audience, breaking the convention of the upstage facade? The stage entrances of important personages, Maria Ichikawa tells us, were announced with fanfares using "quieter musical instruments such as cornets and recorders" as "trumpets would have been too loud in the smaller, roofed theatre" (Ichikawa 2014: 88). She evidences this by a close reading of the stage directions of plays written specifically for these indoor spaces that call for "'*still*', '*soft*', '*sad*' or '*solemn*' music" (ibid., author's italics).

The *Duchess of Malfi* is a play that undermines our perceptual confidence by suggesting that if we can't trust what we hear, we can't trust what we see either. Did the performers experiment with the effect of a single candle suddenly appearing in total darkness? Certainly thematically and in material terms lightness and darkness are played on throughout. Scott Palmer suggests that for lighting effects indoors, "[b]ranched chandeliers with candles . . . [and] the closing of shutters on windows was on occasion part of the action, creating a cross fade from daylight to night" (Palmer 2013: 47). Particularly associated with tragedies, this technique was in use in the private playhouses before the King's Men moved into the Blackfriars. Palmer cites Thomas Dekker, a contemporary of Webster, who makes the comparison with "the city of London as shuttered . . . 'like a private playhouse, when the windows are clapt down, as if some Nocturnal or dismal tragedy were presently acted'" (Dekker, in ibid.).

It seems inconceivable that the playwrights would not have structured their texts with these effects in mind or that, experimenting in the space, they would not have adapted their ideas in response to the available technology. Martin White discusses this in relation to *The Duchess of Malfi* and his analysis of Act IV scene 1 is worth quoting at length as he illustrates just how integral lighting "effects" were to the actual plot of the play.

> With the fourth act beginning at roughly 3.45 p.m. on a winter afternoon, the daylight outside would already be fading. The act opens with the servant, Bosola, reporting to the Duchess's mad brother, Ferdinand, who has come to visit her. He has, however, vowed never to *see* her and he exits as the Duchess enters. The servant, Bosola, informs her that her brother has ordered that 'neither torch nor taper/ Shine in your chamber' (25–6), and removes what lighting there is: his own torch and her taper, and probably extinguishes the candles in the sconces either side of the stage. The stage will now not only appear, but actually *be*, darker than at any point in the play so far, and her exchange with her brother – 'FERDINAND: Where are you? DUCHESS: Here sir. / FERDINAND: This darkness suits you well' (29–30) – will be played . . . with the audience able to see as little as the characters.
>
> *(White 2014: 134)*

What follows is a macabre sequence where Webster exploits this "natural" darkness to maximum affect.

> FERDINAND:
> I come to seal my peace with you: here's a hand,
> *Gives her a dead man's hand.* (43)

The Duchess, recoiling from the coldness of the hand, calls for lights. Ferdinand exits ordering Bosola "Let her have lights enough" (53). As the servants enter with lights the Duchess and the audience see the severed hand she is holding. Almost immediately Bosola draws back the curtain at the rear of the stage to reveal the bodies of her husband and child.

> *–Here is discover'd, behind a traverse, the artificial figures of* ANTONIO *and his child; appearing as if they were dead.*
>
> BOSOLA:
> Look you: here's the piece from which 'twas tane. (56)

As I have shown elsewhere,[7] David M. Bergeron suggests that the lifelike quality of the figures would have been the result of advances in wax molding techniques and this convinces the Duchess that they are "true substantial bodies" (114). Sturgess argues that the company would not have gone to the trouble and expense of providing waxwork dummies "when the actors themselves might act them at no cost and very well" (Bergeron 1978: 112). This assumes that the companies were penny-pinching in terms of what they would spend on special effects but there is no evidence to suggest this. We know that higher admission prices for the indoor venues changed the status of the audience from the socially diverse mix of the larger outdoor venues to a wealthier elite patronage indoors who perhaps demanded more sophisticated production standards. Penelope Woods traces "a performance practice of stillness," perhaps instigated by more focused lighting in which "dead bodies, sleeping bodies or wax figures interact with the space and social dynamics in deliberate and precise ways" (Woods 2014: 157). Bergeron further "speculates that the Jacobean audience would have recognised the figures with which the Duchess is tormented as wax funereal effigies popular with high ranking people at the time. In this sense, the stage illusion or special effect would have had a symbolic as well as a dramatic impact" (Collins 2012: 63). However the effect was achieved, the illusion was easier to sustain in a dimly lit theatre and Webster takes full advantage of this "to raise the stakes of horror and the grotesque" (ibid.: 63) as Ferdinand informs the audience that the bodies are "fakes" but allows the Duchess to continue in her belief that her husband and child are in fact dead.

> Excellent; as I would wish: She's plagued in art.
> These presentations are but framed in wax . . . (110–111)
>
> *(IV. i)*

Art and artifice play tricks on the eye of the beholder. At an earlier point when Ferdinand, looking at the Duchess, asks, "Virtue where art thou hid?" (III. ii) he is voicing another neo-platonic idea that "a woman's virtue would create a luminescence that would naturally be visible on the cheeks" (Karim-Cooper 2014: 187). On stage this "naturalness" was of course artificially constructed using all the latest technologies:

> [C]osmetic spectacle was crucial to theatrical performance in this period; indeed, it was an essential technology of theatre production as it enabled boys to play women, actors to play ghosts and witches and could be deployed in a variety of ways to achieve the illusions upon which early modern theatre traded.
>
> *(Karim-Cooper 2014: 189)*

"Self-fashioning,"[8] the process of constructing one's identity and public persona, was characteristic of the moneyed classes at this time and audiences went to the new indoor playhouses to see and be seen. "Sartorial display was an indicator of social and economic status in the 17th century. Male and female clothing was rich and elaborate – the padding, starch and drapes of varying textures from velvet through to lace obscured the body" (Entwistle 2000: 94). Costume and make-up constituted a major proportion of the materials budget of the Early Modern companies. In the indoor playhouses bejeweled and sumptuously dressed audiences surrounded performers clothed in equally extravagant costumes, the whole atmosphere enhanced by candlelight. Karim-Cooper suggests that "some plays performed at the Blackfriars highlight at times not only the luxurious materiality of costume, jewels and candle light but cosmetic ingredients as well" (Karim-Cooper 2014: 194). In plays like *Duchess of Malfi* "the thematic preoccupation with female chastity and beauty is registered through this material referencing visually and textually" (ibid.), coalescing with themes of "seeing and believing" that so troubled the Jacobean mind.

In their introduction to *Shakespeare's Theatres and the Effects of Performance* the editors state:

> for Shakespeare and his contemporary playwrights, there was no binary between the materiality of the theatre and the emotional, metaphorical and poetic registers of the plays themselves . . . the written word is a kind of technology: perhaps as much a technology as stage architecture or the actor's voice.
>
> *(Karim-Cooper and Stern 2013: 3)*

Consideration of the material aspects of production is shedding new light on the processes through which plays were realized in performance in the Early Modern period. The imaginative ways contemporary writers, performers, makers and technicians exploited the opportunities offered by the indoor spaces and worked together to enhance theatrical effect has broadened the discussion of dramaturgy and aesthetics to include recognition of the way materials make meaning. The move by the King's Men into the Blackfriars, according to Menzer, "struck the death knell . . . for a theatrical norm of outside theatre that was nearly two thousand years old" (Menzer 2014: 171). The physical proximity of performer and audience in the indoor theatres heralded the beginning of "a transition in the sensory norm of theatrical presentation and attendance" (ibid.: 174). Scenography is crucial to understanding how these changes were wrought; theoretically this places scenographic research at the center of this new scholarly enquiry and in practical terms for those currently working in the field it will inform their practice and open up new possibilities for playing with sound, light, space, and materials. As scenographer Pamela Howard succinctly puts it, "[t]o imagine what can be done, we have to know what has been done" (Howard 2010: xxiii).

Notes

1 *The Indoor Performance Project*, Farah Karim-Cooper and Will Tosh, Sam Wanamaker Playhouse, Winter Season, October 2015–April 2016.
2 See *The Winter's Tale* and *The Tempest* as examples of Shakespeare's later works that play with these themes.
3 Also referred to as the Second Blackfriars as "there had been a playhouse in the precinct, a first Blackfriars playhouse constructed in 1576, which was also an indoors conversion of an existing building" (Sturgess 1987: 2).
4 There is also a Blackfriars Playhouse in Staunton, Virginia, USA.
5 For a full account of this argument see Nicholas Till, "Oh, To Make Boardes Speak!" in Collins and Nisbet 2010: 154–61.
6 See his preface to the printed edition.
7 See Collins 2012.
8 A term introduced by Stephen Greenblatt in *Renaissance Self-Fashioning* (Chicago, IL: University of Chicago Press, 1980).

References

Aronson, Arnold and Jane Collins 2015. "Editors' Introduction." *Theatre and Performance Design*, 1 (1–2): 1–6.

Bergeron, D. M. 1978. "The Wax Figures in *The Duchess of Malfi*." *Studies in English Literature, 1500–1900*, 18 (2): 331–9.

Collins, Jane 2012. "Embodied Presence and Dislocated Spaces: Playing the Audience in *Ten Thousand Several Doors* in a Promenade, Site-Specific Performance of John Webster's *The Duchess of Malfi*." In *Performing Site-specific Theatre, Politics, Place, Practice*, edited by Anna Birch and Joanne Tompkins, 54–68. Hampshire, UK: Palgrave Macmillan.

Collins, Jane and Andrew Nisbet (Eds) 2010. *Theatre and Performance Design: A Reader in Scenography*. London and New York: Routledge.

Entwistle, Joanne 2000. *The Fashioned Body*. Cambridge, UK: Polity Press.

Escolme, Bridget 2005. *Talking to the Audience: Shakespeare, Performance, Self*. London: Routledge.

Gurr, Andrew and Farah Karim-Cooper 2014. "Introduction." In *Moving Shakespeare Indoors, Performance and Repertoire in the Jacobean Playhouse*, edited by Andrew Gurr and Farah Karim-Cooper, 1–11. Cambridge, UK: Cambridge University Press.

Howard, Pamela 2010. "Foreword." In *Theatre and Performance Design, A Reader in Scenography*, edited by Jane Collins and Andrew Nisbet, xxiii–xxiv. London: Routledge.

Ichikawa, Mariko 2014. "Continuities and Innovations in Staging." In *Moving Shakespeare Indoors, Performance and Repertoire in the Jacobean Playhouse*, edited by Andrew Gurr and Farah Karim-Cooper, 79–94. Cambridge, UK: Cambridge University Press.

Karim-Cooper, Farah 2014. "To Glisten in a Playhouse: Cosmetic Beauty Indoors." In *Moving Shakespeare Indoors, Performance and Repertoire in the Jacobean Playhouse*, edited by Andrew Gurr and Farah Karim-Cooper, 184–200. Cambridge, UK: Cambridge University Press.

Karim-Cooper, Farah and Stern, Tiffany 2013. "Introduction." In *Shakespeare's Theatres And The Effects of Performance*, edited by Farah Karim-Cooper and Tiffany Stern, 1–8. London: Bloomsbury.

Menzer, Paul 2014. "In The Event of Fire." In *Moving Shakespeare Indoors, Performance and Repertoire in the Jacobean Playhouse*, edited by Andrew Gurr and Farah Karim-Cooper, 168–83. Cambridge, UK: Cambridge University Press.

Palmer, Scott 2013. *Light: Readings in Theatre Practice*. London: Palgrave Macmillan.

Sturgess, Keith 1987. *Jacobean Private Theatres*. London: Routledge & Kegan Paul.
Till, Nicholas 2010. "'Oh, To Make Boardes To Speak!'" In *Theatre and Performance Design, A Reader in Scenography*, edited by Jane Collins and Andrew Nisbet, 154–61. London: Routledge.
Till, Nicholas 2015. "Theses for a Sceno-sonic Turn." In "Sounding Out 'The Scenographic Turn': Eight Position Statements," edited by Adrian Curtain and David Roesner. In *Theatre and Performance Design*, 1 (1–2): 110–11.
Webster, John [1963] 1993. *The Duchess of Malfi*, 3rd ed., edited by Elizabeth M. Brennan. London: A & C Black.
Webster, John [1966] 1996. *The White Devil*, 2nd ed., edited by Christina Luckyj. London: A & C Black.
White, Martin 2014. "'When Torchlight Made an Artificial Noon': Light and Darkness in the Indoor Jacobean Theatre." In *Moving Shakespeare Indoors, Performance and Repertoire in the Jacobean Playhouse*, edited by Andrew Gurr and Farah Karim-Cooper, 115–36. Cambridge, UK: Cambridge University Press.
Woods, Penelope 2014. "The Audience of the Indoor Theatre." In *Moving Shakespeare Indoors: Performance and Repertoire in the Jacobean Playhouse*, edited by Andrew Gurr and Farah Karim-Cooper, 152–67. Cambridge: Cambridge University Press.

17

ARCHITECTURE AS DESIGN

Early Modern theatres of France and Spain, 1486–1789

Franklin J. Hildy

The Early Modern period in Western history begins in the late fifteenth-century, where the periods traditionally called the Late Middle Ages and Renaissance overlapped. This is significant in theatre history as it is the time when medieval dramatic traditions were in many ways reaching their zenith, while the new Renaissance theatre was working out what it could and should be. It was at this juncture that professional theatre was reintroduced to Europe after a long absence dating back to a century or so following the fall of the Western Roman Empire. It was also at this juncture that the first purpose-built theatre buildings to be erected in Europe since Roman times were constructed in the Italian States, England, France, and Spain. In all of these countries theatre professionals had to blend old traditions with new ideas, coming up with approaches to theatre art that laid the foundation for the theatre we know today. Those who designed theatre buildings for these new professionals had to accommodate the new hybrid approaches to staging that were being created. The theatre architecture they developed not only defined the relationship an audience could have with the performance on stage, it also defined the relationship an audience could have with itself. Theatre architects had to negotiate the ways in which the organization of audiences within a theatre space was to reflect the social order in the society these spaces served. The accommodation of class distinctions is often discussed as a manifestation of cultural hegemony in which the powerful used the products of culture, in this case architecture, to impose acceptance of the status-quo on the less powerful. But the organization of space in the house of an Early Modern theatre can just as readily be seen as a manifestation of a universal desire for what I would call social comfort; the right to enjoy an entertainment among those for whom one feels the greatest *esprit de corps*. This would suggest that it was not imposed from the top but insisted upon by all. Only part of the spectacle of Early Modern theatre occurred on the stage; a great deal of the appeal of attending the theatre came from watching other parts of the audience and the design of these building fully accommodated that desire. In this chapter I will examine the distinctive development of professional theatre in France and Spain as they are representative of the trends throughout Europe.

Medieval theatre: neutral, simultaneous, and sequential settings

By the end of the Late Middle Ages drama came in many forms, both secular and religious. The staging traditions of medieval drama acknowledged that a stage (variously called by such terms as platea, plateau, playne, or place) provides a space for performance but does not suggest a location for the scenes being performed. The audience must provide the setting with their imagination and the nature of the drama being performed dictated how much stimulus their imaginations might benefit from. For a great many scenes in both secular and religious drama, the imagined location is of no great importance and no two audience members need to agree on where such scenes occurred for the play to succeed. When it was important to the clarity of a performance that all members of an audience imagine a scene in the same location, a character could announce the location within the dialogue. This is often referred to as spoken decor. The judicious use of a few symbolic props can also achieve the same level of identification. These dramas did not require scenery, just a neutral background such as a curtain, through which entrances could be made and behind which props could be stored and costumes changes. Such stages might best be described as having neutral settings, and they became, for the audience, whatever location the actors told them it was, either by word or action. As plots became more complicated, dramaturgical techniques were sometimes tried before scenic solutions were sought. The Spanish *Égloga de Plácida y Vicoriano* (1513), by Juan Encina, for example, used a prologue – for the first time in Spain – to help the audience navigate through the play's 13 scenes on a neutral settings stage (McKendrick 1989: 14). By the end of the century the Spanish corral theatres would be developing techniques for using a neutral settings stage in combination with other medieval techniques to create a hybrid approach to staging that had remarkable versatility and great success.

The notion that all actors need to produce great theatre are "three boards and a passion" has been attributed to a great many theatre artists in history. Regardless of its true origin, it describes the neutral settings stage almost perfectly; almost because from the beginning of its history, theatre has never settled for quite so little as that, at least not for long. Spectacle in the form of costumes, props, and movement are part of even the most neutral of stages and special effects are rarely left out. Scenic backgrounds are the logical next step. Medieval mystery plays, for example, told stories from the Bible for which the settings were generally well known and most likely well illustrated in the local churches. The location for the action in a play like *The Magi Kings*, versions of which were performed all over Europe but especially in Spain, was never in doubt. The same was true for most Miracle or Saint's plays as well. The setting might be less clear for a mystery play like *The Wise and Foolish Virgins* but a simple neutral stage would still suffice for any of these dramas. Not surprisingly, it rarely did. By the late Middle Ages small scenic structures (variously called *loci*, *domi*, *edifice*, *mansions*, or *pageants*) were being used for most mystery and miracle plays. These were structures that symbolized locations like Heaven, the Garden of Eden, Noah's Ark, Bethlehem, Jerusalem, the entrance to Hell, etc., rather than illustrating them. They helped to minimize confusion. They also added to the visual appeal of a production and served as masking for special effects machinery that added considerably to the spectacle. This stage and location identifier (*platea* and *locus*) approach to staging lent itself to almost limitless variations. For cycles, all the location identifiers (*loci*) to be used in a day's performance were on stage from start to finish.

If a production lasted several days, as many cycles did, new location identifiers might be brought in each day. This was staging using *décor simultané* or simultaneous settings.

The *loci* for simultaneous settings could be arranged: in a circle; in a line along the back of a rectangular stage as they were for the Valenciennes Passion Play (France) in 1547; in a U shape around a market square as they were for the Passion Play at Lucerne (Switzerland) in 1583; or in a seemingly random order around a city's central square as they were for the Passion Play at Villingen (Germany) *c.* 1585. All of these spaces were outdoors, but the system was used indoors as well, especially in Italy and France. No matter what the configuration for a performance, the audience was accommodated in whatever space remained. Many audience members stood, either on the ground or on viewing stands. Others sat on bench seating arranged in tiers that might face a stage or might be worked in between the *loci*. The divisions within the audience that underscored the cultural and class distinction in the society at large were achieved through a combination of the prices charged and the natural inclination towards social comfort. These round, square, and rectangular areas were the theatres of the Middle Ages. They were intended to provide the audience with the most desirable conditions that could practically be achieved for experiencing the performances, while giving the performers the support they needed to do the best performance possible. They were an integral part of sixteenth-century festival culture.

Neutral settings stages could change location with a spoken word or with a stage convention like an exit and re-entrance. Simultaneous stages required that a scenic unit (*locus*) be activated by being used. This was done in a variety of ways, most often by having actors enter the stage through the unit or by opening a curtain that revealed a tableau within it. By convention, once a unit was activated all stage space was part of the location symbolized by that unit and all other units were ignored. To change location the active unit had to be closed and another unit had to be activated, although the two processes could overlap. These units could be fantastically complex with multiple levels, flying machinery, trap doors, water features and facilities for fireworks displays. They could also be quite simple.

An important variation on the simultaneous settings approach can be seen in the *autos sacrimentales* in Spain. There the *loci* to be used were paraded on wagons (*carros*) to the outdoor performance space before being put into their predetermined locations around a fixed stage where the actual performance took place. In Florence, for the *sacre rappresentazioni*, *loci* were paraded to a church where they joined other *loci* already in place. Such use of *loci* on wagons inspired another important development in staging in the Middle Ages, sequential settings, in which *loci* were revealed to the audience one at a time. This was most famously done in the city of York in England. Here up to 48 separate plays were staged on individual pageant wagons, each with its own *locus*, at between nine and twelve locations throughout the city. At each location the first wagon would enter, perform its play, and move on to the next location as the next wagon began its performance, each wagon following in sequence until all the mysteries in the cycle were performed at each location. Although this system was far rarer than is generally assumed, sequential settings set the precedent for changeable scenery, the offshoot of the particularly Italian obsession, perspective painting.

Renaissance theatre: neutral/simultaneous hybrids and perspective in sequential settings, 1486–1547

The Renaissance fascination with all things classical became focused on theatre in 1486. In that year *de Architectura*, by the late first-century BCE Roman military engineer and architect Vitruvius, was published in Italy. This work contains the only ancient account of how both Hellenistic and Roman theatres were designed, and indicates their use of three different kinds of scenery and mentions scene-changing equipment. Vitruvius' work changed scholarly attention from the study of drama to the investigation of performance and provided the basis for debates on theatre architecture and scenography for the next 200 years and more. Indirectly it also promoted new thinking concerning neutral settings. To celebrate its publication the Accademia Romana produced Seneca's *Phaedra*, under the title *Ippolitus*, on a Roman-style stage erected on the palace grounds of the 25-year-old Cardinal Raffaele Riario. The Accademia Romana was led by the great Italian humanist and "Professor of Eloquence," Julius Pomponius Laetus. Laetus is said to have been asked to stage all the plays of Plautus from the "Codex Ursinianus," a complete works that increased the known number of Plautus' plays by 12. It was found in Germany in 1428 and was eventually deposited in the Vatican Library. It was published in 1472 and Laetus had certainly staged Plautus' *Aulularia* by 1484, but it was the plays staged after 1486 that had the most influence. Scholars from across Europe, especially from France and Spain, came to study in Rome during this period and their presence ensured that these early experiments in staging would become widely known and copied. But it was the Duke of Ferrara, Ercole I d' Este, who made the greater contribution to theatre in 1486. He had the *Menaechmi*, by Plautus, staged at the Plazzo del Corte in Ferrara. But, unlike the Roman experiments, which were done in Latin for an aristocratic audience, the Ferrara play was done in Italian for the general public and 10,000 are said to have seen it (Touhy 1996: 257). This was the first of 14 Roman comedies Ercole I produced in translation before 1505 and he made Ferrara the leading center in the development for early Renaissance theatre.

A young Flemish scholar Jodocus Badius [Ascensius] (1462–1535) was studying in Ferrara at the time of these productions. He went on to become the foremost humanist publisher of the age, but, while he was learning his trade in Lyon, the press he worked for put out an edition of the plays of Terence (1493) with illustrations almost certainly based on the stages used both indoors and outdoors in Ferrara (Figure 17.1). The illustrations show an interesting blending of the neutral stage with its simple curtain backgrounds and the simultaneous stage with its five curtained openings, labeled with

Figure 17.1 The Terence stage from an edition of Terence (1493).

character names above, giving them the function of *loci*. This arrangement would find its way into the staging practices of early professional companies all over Europe.

As the 1493 Terrence was being published, a 19-year-old scholar, Ludovico Ariosto, participated in a de'Este production and toured with it to Pavia. Later he went into service with the de'Este family. Aristo is known primarily for his great poetic masterpiece, *Orlando Furioso*, but he also wrote five plays in Italian inspired by Roman models. Such classically inspired plays became known as *commedia erudita* (learned drama), and such plays had an enormous influence on the development of theatre in the sixteenth century. *Commedia erudita* were generally performed by gentleman amateurs, or students, in the palaces of the secular or religious aristocracy, at academies or in universities. Many of these amateurs went on to join the early professional theatre companies. With Ferrara's position as the most active center for the classical revival, it is not surprising that one of the first recorded professional theatre companies in Europe was formed there in 1529 by Angelo Beolco who performed under the name il Ruzzante. It is also not surprising that one of the Italian companies that was most influential to the development of theatre in France and Spain was formed there in the late 1560s by Alberto Naselli (fl. 1568–1584) known as Zan Ganassa.

Ariosto's first *commedia erudite* play, *The Casket* (*La Cassaria*, 1508), was staged in Ferrara with a perspective backdrop by the court painter Pellegrino da San Daniele (Pallen 1999: 22). This may be the first use of perspective painting in theatre (although a painting done by Sigismondo Cantelino for a production at Mantua in 1501 could ultimately claim that credit). These early graftings of the modern techniques of perspective painting onto the productions of plays intended to be done in the classical manner became the defining characteristic of Renaissance theatre (Figure 17.2).

But the challenge was to give the pictures more depth, and then to make them change. The first issue began to be addressed in 1513 when Girolamo Genga added a set of

Figure 17.2 From an edition of Plautus, 1518. Note that the curtains in the previous image have now been replaced with a landscape vista painted behind the facade.

angled wings (*telai*) to a perspective backdrop for *La Calandria* by Cardinal Bernardo Bibbiena, staged at Urbino. The following year (1514) Baldassare Peruzzi created three sets of angled wings and a perspective backdrop for a production of a play by Plautus in Rome. A remarkable garden theatre was built in the Plazzo Medici in Florence in 1539 featuring what many scholars consider the prototype of the proscenium arch (Pallen 1999: 32). It was also at Florence that Bastiano da Sangallo addressed the issue of changing scenery when he used periaktoi on stage. Thus all the major elements of the Renaissance scenography were in place by the 1540s – the remainder of the Early Modern period would be spent perfecting them.

Having pioneered the staging of Roman plays for the public, Ercole I d'Este began experimenting with the kinds of spaces in which Renaissance scenography was to be displayed. In 1499 he converted the Sale Grande of his palace into a theatre with the stage on one of the long walls rather than on one of the narrow ends. This was unusual and may reflect an early attempt to apply an understanding of the work of Vitruvius in which the audience space is described as being as wide as it is deep. Five years later (1504) he began construction of the first purpose-built theatre to be constructed since Roman times, the Sala dale Comedie. Sadly he died before it could be completed and his family abandoned the project. We do not know if this was intended to be a court theatre or a public one but his son, Alfonso d'Este, does seem to have helped Aristo convert a room above an apothecary shop in Ferrara into a theatre space in 1531, the first public theatre space in the Italian states. We do not know if this public theatre in Ferrara put its stage on one of the long walls, as was done in 1499, or if it followed the design seen in the temporary purpose-built theatre, the Teatro del Campidoglio, which had been erected in Rome in 1513. This was the normal *teatro da sala* arrangement that had been used occasionally for a hundred years, with its stage on one of the short walls of

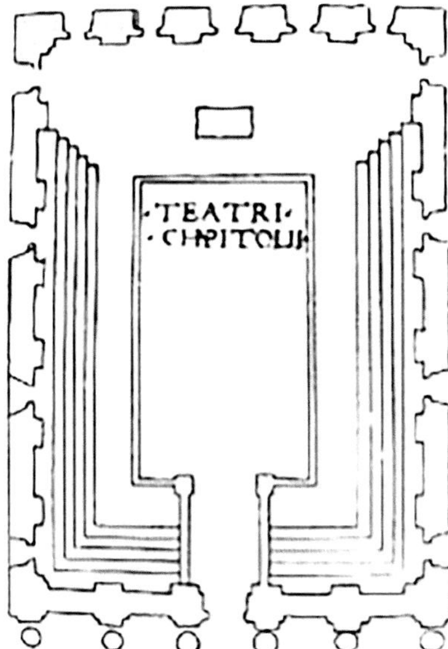

Figure 17.3 Plan of the Teatro del Campidoglio, Rome 1513. Although this was an independent structure it followed the pattern of what was known as a theatre-in-a-room (*teatro da sala*) conversion.

the hall, accommodation for audience along three walls, and an open area in the center in which people could stand or, for the honored, could sit in chairs on a raised dais. Essentially, this form of theatre architecture was used throughout Europe for the next hundred years. As with most court theatres, there was limited need for addressing the issues of class divisions in the Teatro del Campidoglio because only a very narrow range of social classes were allowed to attend. With the addition of a balcony or two along the walls above the audience, however, the Teatro del Campidoglio would have the same plan as the indoor theatres of France and the open-air theatres of Spain (Figure 17.3). It was certainly used for the first successful purpose-built public theatre when it was erected in Paris in 1548. By that time the Italians had converted spaces into theatres in Urbino (1513), Florence, at the Plazzo Medici in Via Larga (1518), Naples (1536), Vicenza (1539, designed by Serlio), Venice (1542), Rome (1546) and Bologna (1547). Many others would follow.

While the 1486 edition of Vitruvius' *de Architectura* marks the real beginning of the Renaissance focus on theatre, the full implications of the work were not realized until Sebastiano Serlio began to publish his own *Architectura* in 1534, nearly half a century later. When the first volume of this magisterial study was published in Venice, it was fittingly dedicated to the new Duke of Ferarra, Ercole II d'Este, and it credited Baldassare Peruzzi, the architect of a great many innovations in the use of perspective scenery, with many of its most important insights. By the time Serlio published Book II of his seven-book study, the one that dealt with theatre and included a ground plan and section drawings of what was probably the theatre he built in Vicenza in 1539, he had moved to France.

Theatre architecture as design in France

Despite the Italian Wars that dominated the first half of the sixteenth century, the French court recruited large numbers of Italian artists and humanists to its service. When Henry II ascended the throne in 1547, his Queen, Catherine de Medici, began a policy of inviting Italian theatre artists to France. France had a long tradition of establishing organizations to perform farces. It also had the most extensive history of medieval religious drama in Europe and many of its most spectacular productions were done in the sixteenth century, in spite of the growing tensions between the Catholics and the French Calvinists, the Huguenots, that would lead to the Wars of Religion in the century's second half.

Records of payments to small companies of professional actors date to the early sixteenth century in Italy and France. The year 1545 marks the first contract to form what appears to be a *commedia dell'arte* troupe in Italy, although the first clear reference to a *commedia dell'arte* production does not occur until 1568 (Duerr 1962: 93) An Italian company *(comédiens et comedientes d'Italie)* came to a court festival at Lyon in 1547, but they performed a *commedia erudite* play (Wiley 1960: 20). Zan Ganassa, mentioned above, led a company to France in 1571 – one of at least three Italian companies to perform there that year (Henke 2008: 27). Ganassa's was the first Italian company to attempt to perform outside the court and for the general public in Paris. Although he had a patent from King Charles IX and the support of the expatriate Italian business community, he had not secured a license from the Confrérie de la Passion, which held a monopoly on all producing of drama in Paris. As Ganassa learned to his cost, they enforced it. He was ordered to cease public performances or face arrest (Duchartre 1966: 82). The Ganassa Company was back in Paris for a performance at court on

18 August 1572, however, just six days before the infamous St Bartholomew's Day massacre in which thousands of Huguenots were brutally murdered. Understandably the company left France, never to return, and went on to influence the development of theatre in Spain. In later years, probably starting with the *I Gelosi* company that came to Paris in 1577, many Italian *commedia dell'arte* companies would come to France and do public performances. Several would reside in Paris for long periods. By the time Carlo Goldoni came to Paris to manage the *Comédie-Italienne* in 1761, near the end of the Early Modern period, France was a major center for that declining art form. *Commedia dell'arte* companies energized the theatre all over southern Europe in the Early Modern period. They carried their own props, costumes, and backdrops; rented theatres whenever possible and rented the materials to build an outdoor platform (neutral) stage when it was not; and they taught others about professional organization and tour management. They were a source of inspiration in many lands, but they were rarely copied and the French certainly came up with a theatre quite different from theirs.

Religious controversies slowed the development of French theatre and probably changed its direction, at least architecturally. The nascent professional theatre in France was being heavily influenced by the classical revival, and Serlio's work was not just published in France, it was quickly made available in a French translation. After 1553, French students were learning how to stage classical revival dramas in the newly formed Jesuit colleges. But for professional theatre to prosper, it needed to have access to the audience in Paris, and this is where the Confrérie de la Passion becomes significant. The Brotherhood lost its theatre in the Hôpital de la Trinité in 1539 and was forced to rent other spaces. In 1540 they petitioned the king for a new theatre in the "Roman style" but nothing came of it. They seem to have built such a theatre temporarily at the Hôtel de Flanders, which was described as being in-the-round with 20 tiers of seats, but it is not clear if it was indoors as their previous theatre had been or outdoors which is where they often performed both in Paris and while on tour to other cities (Arnott 1977: 7). This space too was lost to them so in 1548 the Brotherhood built a new theatre on land formerly occupied by the palace of the Dukes of Burgundy, the Hôtel de Bourgogne (Figure 17.4). This was the first purpose-built public theatre in Europe since Roman times. But the Brotherhood seems to have lost interest in the classical revival that had been behind their theatre in the Hôtel de Flanders and ignored all the experimentation with theatre design that was occurring in Italy. Even though this was a purpose-built space, they seem to have settled for a *teatro da sala* design like the one they had used at the Hôpital de la Trinité from 1402 to 1539.

The Hôtel de Bourgogne was long and narrow with two levels of galleries along three sides and a stage at the remaining short end. The resulting open floor area, the *parterre*, was where the bulk of the audience stood for performances, although some benches and chairs could be found there. Many scholars think the *parterre* extended wall to wall, under the galleries, rather than ending at the gallery fronts but there is insufficient evidence to prove that. The upper galleries on the long sides were for standing, the *paradise*, but this may indicate a third level on those sides. That was the case in later renovations. In later renovations too, the upper gallery on the short end, opposite the stage, was occupied by steeply tiered rows of benches referred to, for some odd reason, as the *amphithéâtre*, a term only used for gladiatorial arenas in classical times. It is not clear that this was part of the original structure; in 1548 the rear upper gallery may have just been a continuation of the *paradise*. (No matter when it first appeared, the *amphithéâtre* was moved to the rear of the *parterre* in the early eighteenth century.) Some parts of the

(a)

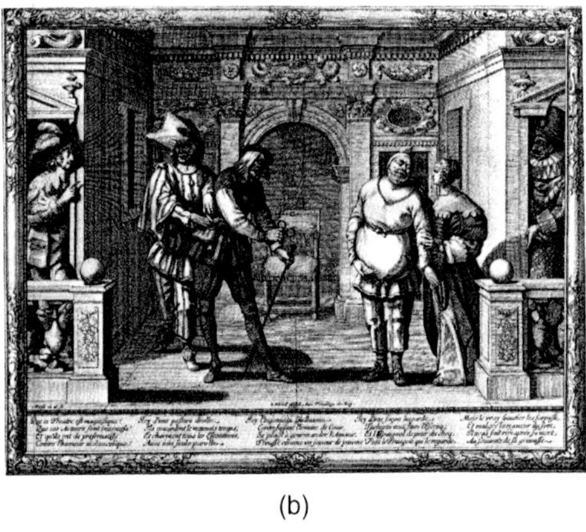

(b)

Figure 17.4 Actors of the Hôtel de Bourgogne showing two versions of *décor simultané*, *c.* 1630. The top illustration (a) is set up like the neutral stage version of the classical revival stages and the lower illustration (b) shows the use of medieval loci-like scenic units. (Illustration (b): Metropolitan Museum of Art.)

galleries were certainly divided into boxes (loges) but how many and where they were is unclear. The galleries did not extend above the sides of the stage so all audience members viewed the performances from the front. The stage was 5 or 6 feet high and perhaps as little as 17 feet deep in its original configuration although it would eventually have a depth of 40 feet. It extended wall to wall across the width of the building but both sides were occupied by those medieval style scenic units (*loci*) used for simultaneous settings. The visible stage between the gallery ends has been variously estimated to have been 25 feet, perhaps less, and certainly no more than 30 feet. A "U"-shaped second stage level, the *théâtre supérieur*, was used for special effects machinery. We do not know its height at the Bourgogne but in other theatres is was about 13 feet above the main stage floor. We do not know if there were windows into the space to supplement the candles that illuminated it nor do we know its interior decoration scheme. We also know little of the extent to which the audience who attended this theatre represented the full range of Parisian society.

Henry II came to the throne in March 1547 and on 17 November 1548 parliament banned the performance of religious dramas in Paris, the dramas the Hôtel de Bourgogne had been built for. Had the parliament stopped with this ban, the new theatre based on such an old design would have undoubtedly been quickly superseded by more modern designs created by the professional acting companies who were replacing such Brotherhoods across Europe. But it was not to be. In compensation for the loss, parliament gave the Brotherhood permission to stage non-religious plays and declared that all such plays done in Paris and its suburbs had to be done for the benefit of the Brotherhood – in effect giving them the monopoly on all theatrical activities in the capital. The Brotherhood made full use of this monopoly, insisting that all performance in Paris pay a licensing fee and eventually began renting out its theatre – until its monopoly was revoked in 1629. The monopoly, therefore, had the dual effect of preventing anyone else from building another theatre that might improve on its design, while at the same time not generating enough money to pay for significant renovations to the Hôtel de Bourgogne, thus stifling any architectural innovations in French theatre for nearly a century. It was, in fact, 1647 before the Hôtel de Bourgogne was modified to accommodate perspective scenery, and 20 years later the Confrérie relinquished its control. The theatre was modernized again in 1717 and finally closed in 1783.

The first theatre built in Paris to compete with the Hôtel de Bourgogne was the Théâtre du Marais built in 1634. However it was a converted tennis court, what became known as a *jeu de paume* theatre, and it made no real advances in design as it was about the same size as the Bourgogne. Because tennis courts had been built all over France, they became the easy, cost-effective, choice for provincial theatres despite the deficiencies of their long narrow layout. This was a problem that plagued French theatre until at least the 1750s. The real importance of the Marais, however, was that it produced Corneille's *Le Cid* in 1636. The multiple incidents crammed into the plot challenged and stretched the limits of simultaneous settings on France's narrow stages. More importantly, this was the production that caused the French Academy to insist on a strict adherence to Neoclassicism as the standard for French drama. Neoclassicism was part of the classical revival movement in Italy and its precise logic and attention to rules had great appeal for those coming out of the chaos of the Wars of Religion. It is important here because its semiofficial adoption by the French Academy also led the French to embrace the Italian Renaissance approach to theatre architecture. (It is also important as it marks the beginning of selling space on the sides of the stage to affluent audience members, an innovation that quickly spread to other theatres is France and continued into the 1750s.)

The Italian approach to theatre architecture that was embraced by the French initially appeared in Venice in 1637 with the first opera house open to the public, the San Cassiano, soon followed by three others. With these theatres, the pit, box, and gallery design had arrived in Italy, along with its prerequisite proscenium arch; behind which was a raked stage designed for sequential settings and the equipment needed for rapid scene changes. This was the Baroque theatre and soon it would be brought from Venice to Paris.

There was an inherent contradiction to the Baroque theatre. It grew out of the classical revival along with Neoclassicism. Neoclassical dramaturgy proposed that the ideal play should take place in a single location but the Baroque theatre reveled in scene changes in full view of the audience. Such was the power of perspective painting, along with the influence of aristocratic entertainments like intermezzi and *ballet de cour*, and the sixteenth-century desire for moving pictures. The first step towards bringing this new development to France was the building of the theatres at the Palais-Cardinal by the architect Le Mercier in 1641. He gave it the largest stage in the city and the first permanent proscenium arch in France. He also equipped the stage with the groove system for the rapid changing of wing-and-border used in the creation of perspective scenery. The auditorium was innovative as it was significantly wider than those of the *jeu de paume* theatres and there was no lower gallery across from the stage; instead, the *amphithéâtre* was allowed to come all the way down from the upper level to the floor, well into the *parterre*, making the space look less deep. The galleries were also not divided into boxes. The stage technology from this theatre was copied by the Théâtre du Marais when it was rebuilt after a fire in 1644. The success of the new scene-changing equipment induced the Marais company to specialize in "machine plays," high-tech dramas that depended on spectacular set changes. Sadly, the costs soon drove then into bankruptcy. The Palais-Cardinal became the Palais-Royal upon Richelieu's death in 1642. It was eventually opened to the public, but only after a complete redesign of its auditorium and stage.

The next and most definitive step was taken in 1645 when the great Italian designer, Giacomo Torelli, was summoned to Paris. He converted the Grande Salle of the Petit-Bourbon palace into a fully Italianate theatre. This large hall next to the Louvre had been the sight of the first *ballet de cour*, in 1572, played host to the *I Gelosi commedia dell'arte* troupe when it first came to Paris in 1577 and was the site for the *Ballet Comique de la Reyne* in 1581, the production that became the definitive example of simultaneous settings carried over from the Middle Ages into the court entertainments. It was now fully converted into a theatre with a stage that could accommodate Torelli's invention of the chariot-and-pole system for scene changing (also known as the carriage-and-frame system.) With this system, wing- and-border sets, painted in perspective, could be changed smoothly from one to another in full view of the audience, much like a modern cinematic dissolve, and it could be done in ten seconds or less. The court put on plays here, often including the king as a performer, until 1658 when the theatre was temporarily handed over to Molière's company. In 1660 it was torn down to make room for new construction that included the Salle des Machines, (also called the Théâtre des Tuileries), designed by another Italian, Gaspare Vigarani. When the Salle des Machines opened in 1662 it was the largest theatre in Europe with an audience capacity of over 6,000. This was a theatre for pure spectacle in which the special effects were more important than the drama being staged. That turned out to be fortunate because the acoustical properties of the structure were not sufficient to allow much of the audience to hear well in this cavernous space. A theatre of this size was appropriate for only a very limited range of productions and the technology needed for them was so expensive that the theatre was all but abandoned before the end of the decade. Several attempts were made to reduce its size and repurpose it but it was used only sporadically before being destroyed by fire in 1871.

Before leaving Paris, Torelli had converted the theatre in the former Palais-Cardinal into the Théâtre du Palais-Royal, a fully Italianate theatre with a more class-conscious audience arrangement and a stage fitted with the chariot-and-pole system. This theatre was used by Moliere's company from 1660 to 1673 and remained in service until 1763. With Torelli's conversion of the Théâtre du Palais-Royal, Paris had fully absorbed the results of the theatre history project that had been started by the Renaissance Italians and had now manifest itself in what we know as Baroque theatre architecture. Outside Paris performances were given in spaces temporarily converted for use as theatres; everything from tennis courts to old warehouses, to halls in public buildings, to market squares. By 1700 theatres had been built by entrepreneurs in Toulouse (1671), Marseille (1685), Lyon (1688), Montpellier (1692), and Lille (1699). By 1750 perhaps as many as 15 more cities had their own theatres. These were primarily, if not exclusively, of the *jeu de paume* design (long and narrow), and were likely to be unassuming on the outside, drab on the inside, and dirty (Clay 2013: 17, 24, 44). The real building boom for theatres in French cities came after 1760 and culminated with the Grand Theatre at Bordeaux in 1780. The theatre at Lyon built in 1756 is credited with inspiring the change. Designed by the city architect Jacques-Germaine Soufflot, this building brought the Italianate theatre to the provinces. It was a free-standing structure not hemmed in by other buildings, located on the central square and facing the City Hall. It had a Palladian facade and the elegance of that exterior carried into the decorations of the interior making the experience of entering the building satisfying it itself. With this building, theatres began to be thought of as works of architecture in which a community could take pride and the Lyon model began to be followed in major cities throughout France. It was not just communities that wanted a theatre to be proud of, the king had the Opéra royal de Versailles built in his palace in 1770.

Theatre architecture and design in Spain

With the completion of their conquest of the Iberian Peninsula in 1492, the Spanish had turned to the conquest of the New World. Spain, unlike France, only become a unified nation in 1516. Prior to that the Iberian Peninsula was much like the Italian peninsula with a number of independent states and kingdoms each vying for power but occasionally joining forces against their common enemy, the Moors. The election of a second Spanish Pope, Alexander VI, in 1492, was followed by the election of unified Spain's first king, Carlos I, to the position of Holy Roman Emperor, Charles V, in 1519. This and the wealth being brought back from the Americas in the second half of the century was making the newly unified nation the most envied super power in Europe. It also put it in almost constant conflict with both the Italian states and France while it sought to suppress Protestantism and defend the West against territorial expansion by the Ottoman Empire.

Religious drama had developed in the states of the Iberian Peninsula much as it had elsewhere in Europe, but it was not as well documented as it was in England or France. Its most distinctive form, the *autos sacramentales* (acts of the sacrament), was a mystery-morality-intermezzi hybrid in which biblical, allegorical, and classical stories could be intermixed in performances that were poetically intricate and visually complex. It was associated exclusively with the Corpus Christi festival. The performance of *autos* was entrusted to professional acting companies from the mid sixteenth century until *autos* were finally banned in 1765 so they had enormous influence on the development of theatre in Spain. One to three *autos* were offered at each festival and each *auto* required two highly ornate two-storied wagons (*carros*) pulled by spectacularly costumed attendants or by steers with gilded horns. The wagons were part of a large parade that also included oversized carnival figures of giants and dragons, traditional dances, and farce performances. At selected sites or at a central location, depending on the size of the city sponsoring them, the two wagons would pull up to a fixed stage and the *autos* would be performed following the simultaneous settings tradition. As wagons for the first *autos* pulled away those for the next would be moved into place so the scene shifting between *autos* was sequential. *Carros* supported scenic units made of wooden frames covered with painted canvas and equipped according to the requirements of the play. Additional scenic devices might rise out of the lower story or pivot out onto the stage. The facade of the upper story was often hinged so that it might open to reveal something within and many of the wagons included machinery for flying actors or objects. After performance in a city the *autos* sometimes toured local villages. As theatres were constructed, *autos* could be given additional performances in them. Farces known as *pasos* were part of the festival activity but could also be performed on their own on the simplest of neutral stages.

Spanish universities, like those elsewhere, taught the plays of Plautus and Terrence and by the 1530s were mandating that these plays be performed. Jesuit schools, which spread rapidly throughout Spain in the 1540s, used theatre even more extensively in their educational system. Their students were therefore knowledgeable of developments elsewhere in Europe and, in spite of Jesuit opposition to professional theatre, that knowledge found its way to the public stage. As a result, by the beginning of the sixteenth century, many Spaniards would have seen numerous examples of both neutral and simultaneous settings and, with the changing of the wagons for the *autos*, would have a clear idea of the potential of the sequential kind. They were also well aware of the classical revival and its implications for modern staging.

Italian influence in Spain

The Spanish, like the French, got much of their early experience with professional theatre from the Italians. Sicily, the Kingdom of Naples, and Milan were part of the Spanish Empire and large numbers of Spanish intellectuals studied in Rome. The first mention of a professional theatre company in Spain involved a group of Spanish actors performing in Toledo in 1538, but in that same year an Italian company of touring actors performed in Seville. Lope de Rueda (*c.* 1510–*c.* 1565), the actor-manager-dramatist, who is considered by many to be the founder of professional theatre in Spain, is thought to have worked with them (Rennert 1963: 29, f.n. 2; McKendrick 1989: 43). In 1548 an Italian company appeared in the capital city of Valladolid (Madrid did not become the capital until 1561) performing Ariosto's *commedia erudite, I Suppositi* (McKendrick 1989: 46). Soon after Rueda was contracted to produce the Corpus Christi festival there, which he did from 1552–1558. In his final year at that post he petitioned to build a theatre in Valladolid, intended to be Spain's first, but the project seems not to have been completed, at least not as a fully developed theatre space. Plays do appear to have been performed at a corral in Santisteban del Puerto from about that date, however, and this may reflect a compromise with Rueda's original plan (Allen 1990: 233, note 22).

After leaving Paris, the Zan Ganassa Company traveled to Madrid in 1574, just as the Spanish theatre was experiencing its most rapid period of expansion. Four years earlier the Cofradía de la Pasión y Sangre de Jesucristo had been granted the privilege of operating a theatre in Madrid as a means of raising money to feed and clothe the poor and support a hospital. It began by using a leased courtyard in the Calle de Sol for performances and soon added two others. Courtyards (corrales) are a distinctive feature of Spanish urban architecture. City blocks are organized around a series of such courtyards. In Madrid, three charitable "confraternities," like those that had presented religious plays throughout Europe during the Middle Ages, leased corrales, converted them to theatres, and then rented them to professional theatre companies. Most such spaces were communally owned by those whose properties surrounding the courtyard while other were entirely owned by individuals.

To convert a corral to a theatre, a stage (*scenario*) with a tiring house (*vestuario*) behind it, was placed at the end of the courtyard opposite the closest street access. In early corrales the stages were probably only slight improvements on the neutral stage which the great playwright and novelist Cervantes remembered nostalgically from his childhood; simple platforms of four to six boards placed across some benches with an old blanket as a background (Thacker 2012: 36). In the Madrid corrales, that old blanket was more likely a richly decorated curtain. When Ganassa arrived in 1574, he rented one of the early corral theatres, the Corral de la Pacheca, leased by the Cofradía de la Pasión from its owner, Isabel de Pacheco, and paid 600 reales plus the profits of two performances to have a much more substantial permanent covered stage erected in it. We know little of the design of that stage, but in 1583 he made a similar investment in the Corral de la Principe, a theatre we do know a great deal about.

The stage at the Corral del Príncipe was about 28 feet wide by 14½ feet deep (a semicircular extension about 5 feet deep was added to the front in the eighteenth century). All corral stages for which we have dimensions roughly share these measurements, although the smallest is 20 feet by 11½ feet. The stage was raised about 5 to 6 feet above the courtyard. It was equipped with several trapdoors but their number and location seem to have varied over time. The roof over the stage could support temporarily attached machinery for flying actors or objects and for other special effects when necessary.

The stage was backed by a facade of two or three levels. At stage level were three openings, a larger central opening 8½ feet deep often used for discoveries, with doorways on each side serving as entrances and exits. The central opening could be covered by a curtain. The upper facade levels could be used for everything from windows in the upper floors of houses, to city walls, towers, or even hills. When needed, visible stairways were erected to allow the audience to see a character move from the stage to the balcony above (Vidler 2014: 11). This was the neutral stage from medieval tradition on a grand scale. The arrangement of the three openings at the back, however, comes from Vitruvius and is reminiscent of the classical revival stages developed in Ferrara and Rome in the 1490s, making this a hybrid of medieval and early modern design. In spite of Ganassa's experience with the court theatres of Italy, France, and Spain, it is interesting that there was so little accommodation for perspective scenery on the Príncipe stage or indeed on any public theatre stage in Spain prior to the late seventeenth century. Unlike the French, but like the English, the theatre professionals in Spain did not embrace perspective scenery or Neoclassicism.

What the Príncipe stages did have were moveable lateral platforms 5 feet wide running the full depth on each side of the stage (Allen 1990: 214). They served as additional seating and occasionally as space for medieval-like scenic units representing castles, fountains, gardens, mountains, rocks, or trees. These side stages were both practical for adding high-priced seating and, when used for scenery, a logical carry over from the simultaneous settings traditions of the *autos sacramentales*. They were half the size of the standard *carros* used in Madrid and it is interesting that Ganassa had won a prize for his 1575 *autos sacramentales* that were staged using two "half carts" (Shergold 1967: 102). Not all corrales had such side stages but it gave those that did the opportunity to employ simultaneous settings when desired.

When in its neutral stage configuration, the facade at the back of the stage served as the sole background for the action – an exit followed by a reentry was sufficient to mark a change of place. If the new location was important, it could be indicated in the dialogue but curtains could also be drawn aside to reveal properties or scenic pieces set up in the central space when further localization was required, thereby creating the earliest manifestation of sequential settings that would come to dominate European theatres in the eighteenth century. When the lateral platforms were used for scenic units, the stage must have resembled that of the Hôtel de Bourgogne. As happened in Paris, the demand for scenic spectacle on stage increased after 1651, so painted flats and practicable windows and doors began to be set into the facade in lieu of curtains.

To complete the adaptation of a corral to a theatre, a refreshment booth (*alojeria*) was created near the entrance facing the stage. Above that, two or three galleries were constructed. It is not known how these galleries were used in the early corrales but in the later ones the lower gallery was dedicated to the exclusive use of unaccompanied women (the *cazuela*). The documents make it clear that the theatres were instructed to create such spaces but it is less clear whether this was an attempt by government to ensure public morality or a response to a demand by women that such spaces be created for their social comfort in a culture that was generally segregated by gender. Women did eventually insist on separate entrances to this gallery so the motivation may well have come from them. The gallery above the woman's gallery was divided into boxes (two of which were assigned to the City of Madrid and the Council of Castile), and the one above that was used as a seating area for clergymen and intellectuals (*tertulia*) or sometimes as an upper *cazuela*. Initially there was only standing room in the open courtyard or patio, but after 1579 stadium-style seating (*gradas*) was added along each side and by the mid-seventeenth century a row or two of benches were set up in the space nearest the stage. *Gradas* were separated from the patio by a railing and protected from the weather by an overhanging roof. Gannasa is credited with introducing adjustable awnings over the patio, which shaded the audience standing there and could also be used to dim the light in the space for a special effect (McKendrick 1989: 48). These awnings were not designed to protect against rain, however. The *gradas* extended up to the second-story level of the four-story houses that surrounded the patio at the Príncipe. Windows in the houses above the level of the *gradas* served as a theatre boxes (*aposentos*), and those on the second floor were fitted with grilles to prevent anyone from climbing from a house into the theatre. Some homeowners collected entrance fees for their boxes on certain days and the theatre lessee collected the fees on other days; some owners had sole rights to their boxes in return for allowing passageways through their property to other boxes; and some owners paid the theatre an annual fee for the right to watch the plays. Many corrales in other cities avoided this difficulty by building walls some distance in front of the houses on each side of the courtyard and attaching galleries to them, parts of which could be divided into boxes. When this was done *gradas* were not used and the patio extended under the first gallery just as it is thought to have done in the parterre of the Hôtel de Bourgogne. This is the solution found at the 1628 Corral de Comedias in Almagro, the only corral theatre still in existence, and it was briefly adopted by the corrales in Madrid in 1736 (Allen 1996: 36).

At first the corrales theatres were temporary, at least five different ones being used in Madrid, three in Seville, and one in Vallodolid during the 1570s. Lope de Rueda attempted to build a permanent theatre in Valladolid in 1558, and the Italian architect Juan (Giovanni) Marin Modeñin Bellini was contracted to build a theatre in Seville in

1574, but neither project seems to have been completed (Donoso 2015). In 1579 the Corral de la Cruz became the first permanent theatre in Madrid and probably in Spain. It was followed by the Corral del Príncipe in 1583. After 1585 these were to be the only public theatres for drama in Madrid until the Coliseo, a court theatre, but one open to the public, built in the Buen Retiro Palace in 1640.

Theatrical performances were not given regularly at the Spanish court until the reign of Philip III (*r.* 1598–1621). Court entertainments reached their peak under Philip IV (*r.* 1621–1665), who had roughly 300 different plays presented at court between 1623 and 1644. Although Italianate scenery had been used occasionally in court performances of the sixteenth century, it did not become common until Cosme Lotti (*c.* 1570/80–1643), a student of the great Italian designer Bernardo Buontalenti (*c.* 1531–1608) and an associate of Giulio Parigi (1571–1635), was brought to Madrid from Florence in 1626. Lotti quickly introduced the Spanish court to *teatro da sala* performances in rooms adapted as theatres in several palaces and to garden spectacles of all kinds. In 1638 Lotti consulted on the building of a permanent theatre in the new Buen Retiro Palace. The theatre was built into a space 95 feet wide by 110 feet long and was modeled on the corral theatres with a patio, three levels of four boxes on either side, and a cazuela at the back, across from the stage. Above the cazuela and set slightly further back was the royal box (*luneta*) and above that an additional box for guardsmen. The King, and especially the Queen consort, Elisabeth of France (1602–1644), sought an authentic experience of attending a public corral theatre so, for the first production in 1640, not only the actors but also the audience performed. Fake fights were staged in the *cazuela* and audience members "whistled derisively," rattled key rings and shouted at the actors in a manner that was most likely an exaggeration of actual behavior in the corrales (Shergold 1967: 299). The theatre was frequently open to the public, who paid the same entrance fees as at the corrales. The plays were performed by troupes that normally appeared in the public playhouses and the scenic demands for most of the plays were similar to those used in the public theatres. The audience's response to these performances was therefore at least marginally more authentic than it had been at the opening. But the theatre also did machine plays; spectacular pieces that required Italianate scenery and special effects that Madrid's corrales could only partially recreate.

The Buen Retiro theatre differed from most corrales in that it was roofed. It quickly became known as the Coliseo and after its construction roofed theatres were commonly referred to as coliseos to distinguish them from the open-air corrales. The Coliseo's most distinguishing characteristic, however, was its proscenium arch, the first in Spain. It was roughly 31 feet wide with an average stage depth behind it of 27 feet. There was just under 25 feet of wing space on each side of the stage (Dowling 1996: 127). Lotti probably installed five sets of wings in this theatre with the perspective setting they created being terminated by a set of back shutters. It is difficult to tell whether an Italian chariot-and-pole system was introduced at this early time or if the theatre used the simpler groove system, but either would have allowed for perspective sets to be dissolved from one to another in ten seconds or less. An extensive set of stage traps and flying machinery allowed for the simultaneous use of multiple special effects. This theatre was also far more sumptuously decorated than any corral could have afforded to be. Sadly, Lotti had only a few opportunities to show what this theatre stage could really do. The Catalan revolt began just four months after the theatre opened and, six months after that, the Portuguese rebelled. Lotti died in 1643, the Queen in 1644, and the King's only son in 1646. The period of mourning

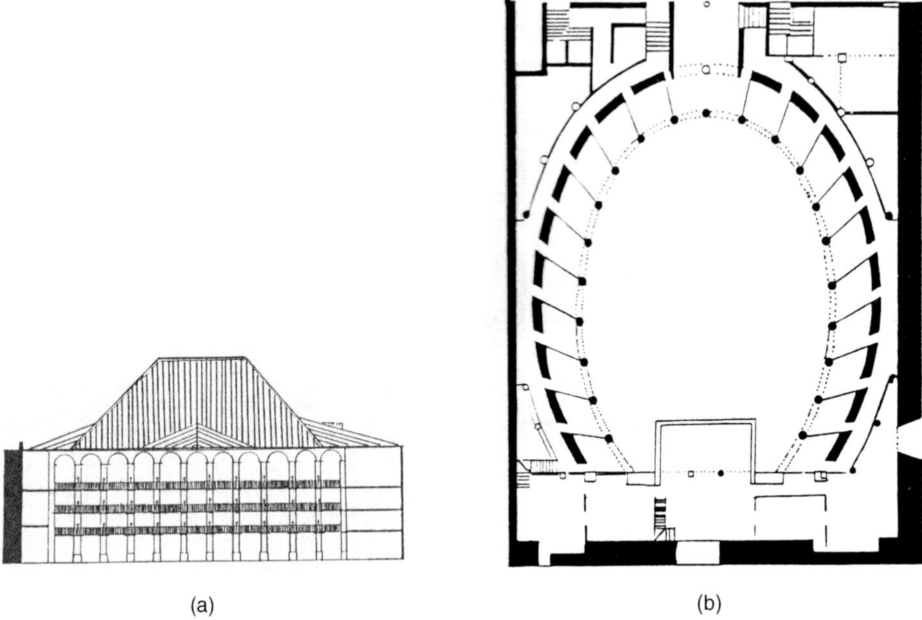

Figure 17.5 Section (a) and plan (b) of Corral de Monteria in Seville (1626), redrawn from the original drawings of 1691.

for the Queen and Prince left all theatres closed for nearly six years. Following the reopening of the theatres the King invited another Italian designer, Baccio del Bianco (1604–1657), to replace Lotti, which he did in 1651. He appears to have extended the depth of the Coliseo's stage by an additional 25 feet, added six more sets of wings to the perspective and terminated it all with a much smaller set of shutters at the rear. If the chariot-and-pole system did not already exist, he must have installed it. The Coliseo shared the fortunes of the Spanish court through the turbulent times.

Prior to the building of the Coliseo, the Corral de Comedias in Córboda (1601) and the rebuilt Corral de la Olivera in Valencia had used the "U"-shaped auditorium. The Corral de Monteria in Seville, built in 1626, had also already established the precedent for roofed public theatres (Figure 17.5). The design of its auditorium was far more groundbreaking than that of the Coliseo. The Monteria auditorium was oval, the only one in Golden Age Spain, with two levels of galleries containing 22 boxes each. All of these boxes were angled towards the stage, an arrangement only occasionally seen before the eighteenth century. There was a standing gallery above the boxes much like the *paradise* of the Hôtel de Bourgogne. The Monteria stage, however, was remarkably small, only 24 feet wide by 11 feet deep. It had a discovery space that added an additional 16 feet of depth but it also had a traditional three-level *vestuario* that prevented them from fully utilizing it (Allen 1990: 220; Peña 2015). The potential for perspective scenery existed at this theatre but there is no evidence of its ever having been realized. So it was not until 1708 that the Caños del Peral Coliseo in Madrid became the first truly public theatre in Spain to have an Italian stage equipped to change perspective scenery (Rico 2012: 124). The Corral de la Cruz was pulled down and rebuilt to an Italianate design in 1736 and the same thing occurred to the Corral del Príncipe in 1745 (Allen 1996: 36).

Other theatres in the country quickly followed or simply closed and sequential settings rapidly replaced the last vestiges of the neutral stage and simultaneous settings in Spain just as it had done in France.

Conclusion

For theatre, the start of the Early Modern Period was an applied theatre history project and can be said to have begun in Ferrara, Italy, in 1486. The classical revival experiments with staging Roman dramas began to take hold just as the long dominance of religious drama from the Middle Ages was waning in the face of the advent of Protestantism. Out of this came the reintroduction of professional theatre. Those early professionals combined the medieval traditions with which they had grown up with the new thinking overlaid of the classical revival, and had theatre buildings constructed to accommodate the new approaches they were developing. Gradually these new approaches were over-played with perspective scenery and the Italian Baroque stage was the result. This form came to dominate theatre by the end of the Early Modern period and was not really superseded until near the end of the nineteenth century.

References

Allen, John J. 1990. "The Spanish Corrales de Comedias and the London Playhouses and Stages." In *New Issues in the Reconstruction of Shakespeare's Theatre*, edited by Franklin J. Hildy, 207–235. New York, Peter Lang.

Allen, John J. 1996. "The Reemergence of the Playhouse in the Renaissance: Spain 1550–1750." *Theatre Symposium* 4: 27–38.

Andrews, Richard 2006. "Erudite Comedy." In *A History of Italian Theatre*, edited by Joseph Farrell and Paolo Puppa, 39–43. Cambridge: Cambridge University Press.

Arnott, Peter D. 1977. *An Introduction to the French Theatre*. Lanham, MD: Rowan and Littlefield.

Brand, Peter 2006. "Ariosto and Ferrara." In *A History of Italian Theatre*, edited by Joseph Farrell and Paolo Puppa, 44–57. Cambridge: Cambridge University Press.

Clay, Lauren R. 2013. *Stagestruck: The Business of Theatre in Eighteenth-Century France and Its Colonies*. Ithaca, NY: Cornell.

Donoso, Piedad Bolaños 2015. "Corral de las Atarazanas." Rutas del Teatro en Andalucía. Junta de Andalucía. Available online at: www.juntadeandalucia.es/cultura/rutasteatro/es/02_022.html.

Dowling, John 1996. "The Spanish Buen Retiro Theatre 1638– circa 1812." *Theatre Symposium* 4: 124–131.

Duchartre, Pierre Louis 1966. *The Italian Comedy*. New York: Dover.

Duerr, Edwin 1962. *The Length and Depth of Acting*. New York: Holt, Rinehart & Winston

Henke, Robert 2008. "Border Crossing in the *Commedia dell'Arte*." In *Transnational Exchange in Early Modern Theater*, edited by Robert Henke and Eric Nicholson, 19–34. Aldershot, UK: Ashgate.

Lawner, Lynne 1998. *Harlequin on the Moon* (2nd ed.). New York: Harry N. Abrams.

Lawrenson, T. E. 1986. *The French Stage & Playhouse in the XVIIth Century: A Study in the Advent of the Italian Order*. New York: AMS Press.

Lea, K. M. 1962. *Italian Popular Comedy*, 2 Vols. New York: Russell & Russell.

McKendrick, Melveena 1989. *Theatre in Spain, 1490–1700*. Cambridge: Cambridge University Press.

Newbigin, Nerida 2006. "Secular and Religious Drama in the Middle Ages." In *A History of Italian Theatre*, edited by Joseph Farrell and Paolo Puppa, 9–28. Cambridge: Cambridge University Press.

Nicole, Allardyce 1957. *The Development of the Theatre* (4th ed.). New York: Harcourt, Brace & Co.

Pallen, Thomas A. 1999. *Vasari on Theatre*. Carbondale, IL: Southern Illinois University Press.
Peña, Mercedes de los Reyes 2015. "Corral de la Monteria." Rutas del Teatro en Andalucía. Junta de Andalucía. Available online at: www.juntadeandalucia.es/cultura/rutasteatro/es/02_022.html.
Ravel, Jeffery S. 1999. *The Contested Parterre: Public Theater and French Political Culture, 1680–1791*. Ithaca, NY: Cornell University Press.
Rennert, Hugo Albert 1963. *The Spanish Stage in the Time of Lope de Vega*. New York: Dover.
Rico, Fernando Doménech 2012. "Theatrical Infrastructures, Dramatic Production and Performance, 1700–1759." In *A History of Theatre in Spain*, edited by Maria M. Delgado and David T. Gies, 120–133. Cambridge: Cambridge University Press.
Scott, Virginia 1989. "*Junon descend du Ciel sur un Poulet d'Inde*: Spectacle in the Commedia dell'Arte in Paris in the Seventeenth Century." In *The Commedia dell'Arte from the Renaissance to Dario Fo*, edited by Christopher Cairns, 178–208. Lewiston, NY: Edwin Mellen Press.
Scott, Virginia 1996. "'My Lord, the Parterre': Space, Society, and Symbol in the Seventeenth Century French Theatre." *Theatre Symposium* 4: 62–75.
Scott, Virginia 2009. *Women on the Stage in Early Modern France, 1540–1750*. Cambridge: Cambridge University Press.
Shergold, N. D. 1956. "Ganassa and the 'Commedia dell'arte' in Sixteenth-Century Spain." *The Modern Language Review*, 51 (3): 359–368.
Shergold, N. D. 1967. *A History of the Spanish Stage*. Oxford: Oxford University Press.
Thacker, Jonathan 2012. "Lope de Vega, Calderón de la Barca and Tirso de Molina." In *A History of Theatre in Spain*, edited by Maria M. Delgado and David T. Gies, 36–56. Cambridge: Cambridge University Press.
Touhy, Thomas 1996. *Herculean Ferrara: Ercole d'Este (1471–1505) and the Invention of Ducal Capital*. Cambridge: Cambridge University Press.
Vidler, Laura L. 2014. *Performance Reconstruction and Spanish Golden Age Drama: Reviving and Revising the Comedia*. New York: Palgrave Macmillan.
Wiley, W. L. 1960. *The Early Public Theatre in France*. Westport, CT: Greenwood.

18
THE OPEN-STAGE MOVEMENT

Dennis Kennedy

Of the many innovations of theatrical modernism, one of the most lasting was a movement to reconfigure the physical stage. Convinced that the proscenium theatres of the nineteenth century in Europe and the Americas hindered the relationship of the audience to the action, a number of influential practitioners sought to create a playing space that was more open, both metaphorically and actually, than the proscenium stage that implied a "fourth-wall" barrier between spectators and actors. The logic went like this: the over-decorated box settings of the period increased audience passivity by virtue of making actors and scene into an illusion of a self-contained world, rather than an unguarded place that stimulated the imagination. Further, realist three-dimensional scenography usually required numerous set changes, with a closed curtain and entr'acte music, which slowed the progress of the drama. To English and German reformers this seemed especially inappropriate for Shakespeare, whose plays had been written for a non-illusionist stage. Shakespeare's flow of scenes, moving briskly from one fictional locale to another, demanded, they thought, a swifter sequence.

The movement for architectural renovation had been preceded in part by Richard Wagner, whose Festival Theatre at Bayreuth (1876), built for the performance of his music dramas, used a fan-shaped auditorium intended to promote a sense of community among the spectators. Though indoors, the arrangement was (and is) suggestive of the ancient theatre at Epidaurus, especially as Bayreuth lacked the galleries and encircling boxes essential to most playhouses of Wagner's era. But his innovations were limited to the seating; the stage was not very different from those found elsewhere. In fact, its double proscenium, and Wagner's demand for a recessed orchestra pit hidden from view, placed the action even further away from the audience, who were deliberately separated from the singers by what he called "the mystic gulf."

It was that gulf that the promoters of the open stage wished to eliminate. Not for them Wagner's total theatre, enrapturing spectators by singing, music, drama, movement, and the visual into a dreamlike recollection of Teutonic myth. They sought a more direct, untrammelled, cleaner experience. Though a number of English commentators had railed since early in the nineteenth century against the pictorial approach to Shakespeare, the first extended experiment with an Elizabethanist open stage occurred in Germany, when in 1889 Jocza Savits created a playing space similar to Shakespeare's.

Designed by Karl Lautenschläger, the result was a conscious compromise with the proscenium architecture of the Munich Residenztheater and contemporary notions of an Elizabethan prototype. The orchestra pit was covered over by a semi-circular forestage, creating an open platform that jutted beyond the proscenium boxes. Considerably upstage of this sat a decorated false proscenium, with a second playing space three steps higher that could be closed by a curtain. At the rear was a painted backdrop, used on occasion to represent locale. An etching of the period shows a scene from *King Lear*, with Lear and an attendant far downstage on the open platform and a perspective painting of the heath scene behind the upper stage.

One of the spectators at that production was William Poel, an Englishman who had been battling against pictorial Shakespeare since 1881, when he directed an amateur performance of the first quarto of *Hamlet* in London. Though not satisfied with Savits' setting, Poel was impressed with the result. But Poel disdained compromises. He wanted to return Elizabethan plays to their original methods of performance, "so as to represent them as nearly as possible under the conditions existing at the time of their first production" (Kennedy 2001: 38).

Poel's mission was complicated by the discovery of the commonplace book of the Dutch humanist Aernout van Buchel (1565–1641) in the library of the University of Utrecht. Van Buchel had copied a sketch of the Swan Theatre made by a fellow student on a visit to London about 1596. The originator, one Johannes de Witt, accidentally provided the only visual record of the interior of a playhouse from Shakespeare's lifetime. Published for the first time in 1888, it shows a playing space that is more open and less decorated than most scholars had thought, and suggests that the stage was thrust deeply into the unroofed "yard," the area for "groundlings" or standing spectators around the stage. As a document it is difficult to analyze, since there is nothing to compare it with: we cannot know how accurately it renders details, how correct its scale, or (crucially) if the bare stage of the Swan was representative of other London playhouses.

Poel took note of the drawing but was more interested in the building contract for the Fortune Theatre, another rare document that indicates dimensions and construction materials for a theatre built for Philip Henslowe in 1600. For a production of *Measure for Measure* in 1893 Poel converted the interior of the Royalty Theatre in Soho into (in his words) "as near a resemblance of the Old Fortune Playhouse as was possible in a roofed theatre" (Kennedy 2001: 38). Its accuracy was questionable, as Poel was as much influenced by Victorian ideas about Shakespeare's stage as he was by new scholarship. He extended the playing space beyond the proscenium and built a high and narrow canopied stage behind it, ridiculed as "Poel's four-poster." He masked the proscenium arch with simulated oak panelling and decorated the existing boxes of the Royalty in Elizabethan fashion, as if the performance were a costume ball. In a sense it was, because he went to the extent of populating the stage with extras as gentlemen spectators, also dressed in Elizabethan fashion.

Needless to say, the actual audience had not become Elizabethan, were not wearing period costume, and were sitting in a nineteenth-century auditorium unaffected by the sixteenth-century pretence on stage. What Poel had actually presented was a quasi-open stage as a metonym of the lost age of Shakespeare. Since his actors were chiefly amateurs, and his notions of vocal delivery aggravatingly idiosyncratic, the result of this and later productions tended to confirm Poel as a crank in the public mind. Ultimately he was an antiquarian with limited effect on theatrical practice, but two matters make his contribution significant. First, he insisted that the original conditions of Elizabethan performance, even when reconstructed in a partial and adulterated manner, held clues to a better understanding of the theatricality of Shakespeare's plays. Second, by experimenting with stage spaces that tried to break down the physical barrier between action and audience, however unsuccessfully, he offered an example of what renovated theatrical architecture might accomplish.

In 1899 Poel directed *Richard II* in a lecture theatre at London University. Though the production was not well received, the professional actor playing the lead was considered impressive: Harley Granville Barker, then aged 22. Barker soon established himself as England's most important director in the modernist mode. All his life he acknowledged his debt to Poel, but Barker succeeded where his mentor did not because he avoided the antiquarian trap. At the time of his own *Twelfth Night* in 1912 Barker said, "I don't go as far as Mr. Poel; I think his method is somewhat archaeological; there is somewhat too much of the Elizabethan letter, as opposed to the Elizabethan spirit" (Kennedy 1985: 151). Barker was convinced that the key to a renovated Shakespeare was speed of delivery and rapid scene sequence, coupled with symbolic scenography, and all were stimulated by the open stage.

The first years of the twentieth century saw a notable change in scenographic approaches for classical plays, particularly in Germany and central Europe. Designers who exemplified the new attitude included Edward Gordon Craig, Emil Orlik, and Carl Czeschka, often working with Max Reinhardt in Berlin. Despite their differences, their general approach was based on simplicity of line, vibrant colour, and symbolic rather than figurative representation. Barker saw and admired some of Reinhardt's Shakespeare productions and took away a lesson that, when combined with Poel's principles, offered a new model. For three major productions of Shakespeare in London just before the First World War, Barker used the same basic layout, though each had substantially different scenography. Working inside the proscenium stage of the Savoy Theatre, he divided the playing space into three tiers. Like Savits and Poel, he pushed the forestage out beyond the arch. Barker's extension covered the first rows of seats, creating a curved open space 3.5 meters in depth. Footlights were of necessity abandoned and the actors lit by new electric "torpedo lamps" hanging from the first balcony. A middle tier began in front of the proscenium, rising by two steps from the forestage and incorporating most of the floor upstage of the proscenium. A final tier rose four steps above that and could be curtained off into an Elizabethan-style discovery space.

The London critics, overwhelmed by what they considered outlandish scenography of the first of these productions (*The Winter's Tale*, 1912, sets by Norman Wilkinson, costumes by Albert Rothenstein), tended not to notice the innovations to the stage structure. But they did notice the speed of delivery and the rapid flow of scenes, uninterrupted by set changes or act curtains, made possible by the architectural modifications. The next two productions, *Twelfth Night* (1912) and *A Midsummer Night's Dream* (1914), both with sets and costumes by Wilkinson, consolidated the new method and won over audiences as well as critics. Barker's renovated approach was clearly modernist in visual style and approach to acting. The label that stuck at the time was "post-impressionist."

No one, then or now, knows with any precision what performance in Shakespeare's age was actually like. Ignorance of Elizabethan methods has not stopped scholars speculating and directors experimenting, though as long as open-stage productions were squeezed into a proscenium theatre the testing could only be partial and the results indecisive. This was the case with two productions by Jacques Copeau in 1914, which openly followed Barker's example, even to the extent of using *The Winter's Tale* and *Twelfth Night* as the texts. At the Vieux-Colombier Theatre in Paris, Copeau reduced the setting to a few essential items, masked the gilded proscenium, and emphasized rapid acting. The effect of his simplicity was powerful and, despite certain reservations, even pleased Barker. But though the *Twelfth Night* was seen in New York in 1917 and revived in Paris each year in the early 1920s, after the war Copeau, like Barker himself, retired from active theatre work without major disciples.

In fact, between the wars the open stage movement caught Poel's disease: it became interested in the antiquarian rather than the performative. A number of replicas of the Fortune or the Globe were built in academic settings, chiefly in the USA, based on uncertain scholarship, and full-scale outdoor models arose in 1935 in Ashland, Oregon, and San Diego. Their tiring-house facades spoke loudly of the past.

It was not until after the Second World War that any practical open-stage theatre was built. Tyrone Guthrie, an English director in the Barker mold, had made some interesting productions at the Old Vic in the 1930s, but was dissatisfied by the limitations of the proscenium. In 1948 he was invited to direct David Lyndsay's *Aine Satire of the Thrie Estaites* for the second Edinburgh Festival. With the designer Tanya Moiseiwitsch, Guthrie set a thrust stage in the middle of the Assembly Hall of the Church of Scotland, to create a narrow acting space with an upper level and curtained recesses below. The result convinced the collaborators that a proper venue for early modern drama required breaking up the proscenium entirely.

When Guthrie was asked to start a Shakespeare festival in Canada, in a small town in Ontario that happened to be called Stratford, he and Moiseiwitsch found a simple solution: begin with the stage rather than the playhouse. Since there was no suitable building available, the organizers decided to perform under a large circus tent for the opening in 1953. Moiseiwitsch designed a permanent architectural stage on the Elizabethan model that was not limited by "a pseudo-Elizabethan appearance," as Guthrie put it. "We were determined to avoid *Ye Olde*" (Kennedy 2001: 158). A set of plain wooden back panels with doors, windows and stairs, an open playing space on two levels with steps, a stage balcony supported by six columns – that was all. Under the tent the seats were arranged in a 220-degree arc around the playing space, which meant that some spectators were behind the horizontal centreline of the stage. To keep actors' faces in view, Guthrie developed what would become a characteristic of Stratford Festival directing: frequent choreographed moves. Actors had to learn to "open out" to the entire audience, even those members at their backs. The open stage forced players to perform more directly to the audience, or at least keep the audience in mind at all times. By its shape alone the stage denied full illusion. Scenography was limited to small moveable pieces and to costumes, which, in the absence of three-dimensional and changeable scenery, assumed much greater visual significance.

After three summers in the tent, a permanent theatre was completed in 1956. It included a new curved balcony, increasing audience capacity to 2,258. Despite being a very large number for spoken theatre, no seat was further than 20 meters from the stage. Crucially, spectators were always aware of one another, in many cases looking across the stage to other spectators sitting opposite. What the new arrangement demonstrated most of all was that an open-stage without scenic distraction makes the audience more connected to the actors and more focused on the words of the play. Guthrie had proved that a renovated Shakespeare could be achieved by architectural intervention, and the Guthrie plan became, for a while, the major alternative to proscenium playhouses. His success prompted the building of a number of open-stages in 1960s in North America and England that have been regularly used for classic as well as modern plays. The trend also gave new emphasis to the studio theatre movement, which had been around since the start of the twentieth century. "Black boxes," or small interior spaces without architectural definition and with flexible seating arrangements, became another way of connecting more directly with audiences.

Though the open-stage movement was never restricted to the performance of Shakespeare, it never would have succeeded without Shakespeare as its mascot. Shakespeare's status, which in the twentieth century grew greater than ever before, allowed reformers to appeal to an internationally admired epitome. Regardless of productions that contemporize his plays, Shakespeare's heritage status is the primary reason his work remains saleable on stage, film and television. Of course that status has been achieved because the work is wonderful, and continues to play very well. But even a producer with an uncommercial heart must recognize that Shakespeare holds a unique post in the business end of theatre making.

Which brings us to the latest major development in the history of the open stage. The Globe Theatre in London is a replica version of the playhouse of that name built by the Lord Chamberlain's Men in 1599, or its larger reconstruction of 1614, after a fire. The present theatre was the creation of the transplanted American actor Sam Wanamaker, who wished to re-establish the building as a monument and as a practical space for experimenting with Elizabethan theatre techniques. The site in Bankside is a few hundred meters away from the original Globe foundations, which are partly under Southwark Bridge Road. A great deal of effort and money was expended to make the edifice conform to the best archaeological and historical scholarship. Oaks were felled, boards were manufactured, Tudor methods applied (no nails, hair-and-lime plaster). Though some elements were of necessity conjectural, and though modifications were required by safety regulations, the general architectural effect is impressive and the enterprise has been enormously successful as a tourist destination and a performance venue since opening in 1997.

The most radical aspect of Poel's theory was that the nature or style of original performance is inscribed in the texts. Given how often they were played in other venues in Shakespeare's time – in private indoor theatres, at court, probably in great dining halls – we should be suspicious of the view that they were written for the public stage and somehow confined by it. Yet it was Poel's idea that fed Wanamaker's obsession with archaeological exactitude: that rebuilding Shakespeare's theatre would provide a laboratory for uncovering clues to his proper performance. The playing space of the new Globe is controversial among scholars for its accuracy and among directors for the large pillars supporting the stage roof which obscure sightlines. Its great success is to place the action in the middle of the audience standing in the yard and sitting in the encircling galleries. The open stage of the Globe works for non-illusionist performance to a remarkable degree, especially for comedy. Spectators join the play in a collaborative way, shout at the actors, move about in the yard, and generally break down the staid traditions of English Shakespeare.

Most of the performances there tell us very little about Elizabethan acting or production methods, other than what derives from the spatial arrangement. The Globe, like any theatre dependent on box office receipts, houses productions that appeal to present-day audiences, contemporary in speech patterns and body language and similar to those seen elsewhere. No doubt the building's reconstructive manifestation contributes to the playful, willing adventure that spectators engage in, but the open stage might well do this without pseudo-Tudor trappings. If the performances follow Barker's modernist inclination to adapt the open stage to contemporary uses, the building follows Poel's antiquarian urge to imagine an earlier era nostalgically. Together they make an impure gesture toward Elizabethan methods – one that seems fitting for classical theatre under the complicated economic conditions of postmodernity.

References

Kennedy, Dennis 1985. *Granville Barker and the Dream of Theatre*. Cambridge, UK: Cambridge University Press.

Kennedy, Dennis 2001. *Looking at Shakespeare*. Cambridge, UK: Cambridge University Press.

Spatial and environmental design

The chapters in this section address, for the most part, performances that occur outside the bounds of traditional or purpose-built stages. Theatre in many societies and cultures originated in festivals, rituals, market squares, and streets. The permanent theatres, where and when they did emerge, tended to grow out of the circumstances of evolving production practices. Dengaku, a forerunner of Noh, for instance, grew out of agricultural festivals and is usually translated as "field performance." Since a great deal of theatre around the world was performed outdoors for thousands of years, or in semi-open structures, the spectators were aware, on some level, of the surrounding environment, whether rural or urban, as informing the production. One of the oldest forms of performance is procession, and the costumed movement of individuals through streets, often accompanied by music and song, transformed streetscapes into performance spaces, with urban facades becoming scenic backgrounds. While some processions, as well as some rituals, clearly delineate spectators and performers, others merge the two so that everyone is a performer and spectator simultaneously. In such instances, the performer/spectators may actually comprise the most significant aspect of scenography.

Richard Schechner coined the term "environmental theatre" to describe a type of performance that eliminates the dichotomy of stage and auditorium, that abolishes the separation of performer and spectator, in order to incorporate the spectators and the entirety of the space in which the performance occurs. Though used to describe a particular kind of experimental theatre of the 1960s and 1970s, best exemplified by the work of Jerzy Grotowski and Tadeusz Kantor in Poland, and the Living Theatre and Schechner's own Performance Group in the US, it had roots in a variety in Asian and African performance traditions (explored here by Kathy Foley and Jesse Weaver Shipley),[1] in the medieval European theatre (examined by Gordon Kipling), in the monarchical pageantry and processions of the Renaissance – and for that matter in totalitarian regimes throughout history. It flourished in the spectacles of the French and Russian revolutions as well as the Soviet theatre of Nikolai Okhlopkov in the 1920s and 1930s.

While a superficial level of audience involvement emerged as a gimmick in the latter twentieth century, with traditional seating ripped out and actors invading audience space on the slightest pretext, environmental theatre also gave rise to a much more rigorous exploration of the relationship of the performer and spectator to a given space.

Site-specific work became a major genre – the creation of a devised performance for a specific locale, one often suffused with a particular social or political history. Teatro da Vertigem in Brazil, Rimini Protokoll in Germany, Brith Gof (presented by Mike Pearson in his chapter), Punchdrunk and dreamthinkspeak in the UK, En Garde Arts and Woodshed Collective in the US, Krétakör from Hungary, and SIGNA based in Copenhagen, are or have been among the most innovative practitioners of site-specific work, devising productions in shopping centers, abandoned military bases, an abandoned hospital, etc.[2] Similar to this is found-space performance in which non-performance spaces are used for their esthetic or atmospheric qualities but may not have any specific social or political connotation.

The most recent permutation of environmental theatre is "immersive theatre," which is addressed in the chapter by W. B. Worthen. At least stylistically, immersive theatre seems to share a great deal with its environmental predecessors. Scholar Josephine Machon, whom Worthen cites, argues that its underlying principles are different as is the experience.[3] She sees its origins in installation art, gaming, and technology and she sees the total immersion of the spectator within the event as vital to the experience. The immersive performance, according to Machon, "colludes in a continuing immediate, and interactive exchange of energy and experience between the work and the audience."

I would argue that all the work discussed in this section, and other analogous work, falls somewhere on the environmental continuum, at least from a scenographic standpoint. The spectators of the late medieval theatre, moving from mansion to mansion along a cathedral nave, were as much immersed in the performance of the mystery plays as any spectator at *Sleep No More*.

Notes

1 The Ghanaian theatre described by Shipley in his chapter often occurs on the proscenium stages that are a legacy of colonial rule, but the performances have roots in non-frontal traditions, and even in their contemporary form tend to ignore the fourth wall and engage the audience.

2 See essays by Marvin Carlson and Christopher Baugh in *The Disappearing Stage: Reflections on the 2011 Prague Quadrennial*, edited by Arnold Aronson (Prague: Arts and Theatre Institute, 2012).

3 See Josephine Machon 2013. *Immersive Theatres: Intimacy and Immediacy in Contemporary Performance*, 44. Basingstoke: Palgrave Macmillan.

19
MEDIEVAL SCENOGRAPHY
Places, scaffolds, and iconography

Gordon Kipling

What we know – or think we know – of theatrical scenography in the Middle Ages has been largely shaped by two fifteenth-century images: a scene plan (c. 1425) for an English morality play, *The Castle of Perseverance* (Figure 19.1) and Jean Fouquet's miniature, *The Martyrdom of St Apollonia* (*c.* 1452–60), depicted as a scene being performed in a French *mystère* (Figure 19.2). Since the turn of the twentieth century, several generations

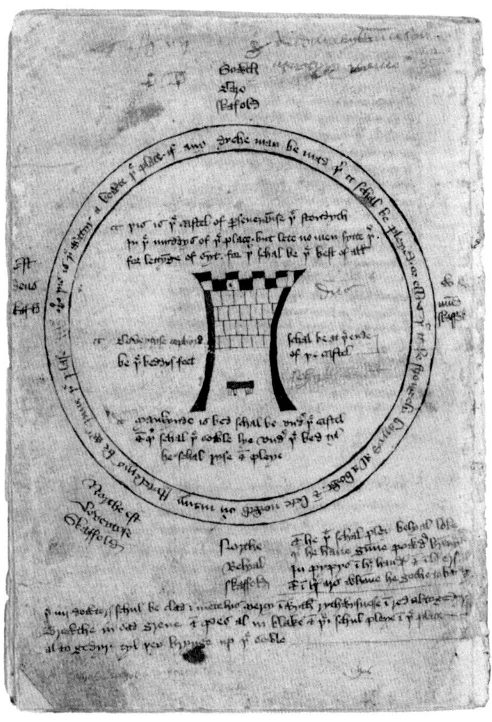

Figure 19.1 Stage plan for the Castle of Perseverance. Folger MS V. a. 354, fol. 191v. (Used by permission of the Folger Shakespeare Library.)

of historians have studied these images primarily for what they might tell us about medieval theatre architecture.[1] Plays, we are told, were predominantly performed in circular theatres; actors and audience members shared the available performance space; and theatrical spaces were defined by multiple, fixed locations. Only the last is true, but the first two propositions have badly skewed our ideas about medieval scenography.

The *Castle of Perseverance* stage plan (*c.* 1425) led to an assumption that it provided a model of a typical theatrical shape, one confirmed by the Fouquet miniature (*c.* 1460). In his influential *Medieval Theatre in the Round* (Southern 1957), Richard Southern envisions the structure as a huge theatre surrounded by a deep ditch full of water to keep non-payers out, a large circular rampart within the ditch, tiered on the inside for seating. The audience, he thought, could either sit upon the tiers or simply take places on the performance area, and he places the "scaffolds" atop the rampart rather than outside the ditch as shown in the plan. By the 1970s, other influential scholars had built upon Southern's work and argued vigorously that medieval theatres were characteristically round structures, and if, for instance, Hubert Cailleau's illustration of the Vallenciennes *Passion* (Figure 19.3) depicts the stage as a long, linear structure, then the illustration must be wrong.[2]

There are many reasons to think this architectural view is mistaken. For one thing, the massive earthwork situates the "scaffolds" inside the ditch instead of outside where

Figure 19.2 Jean Fouquet, *The Martyrdom of St Apollonia*, from *The Hours of Etienne Chevalier* (*c.* 1452–60). Engraving by F. Courboin. (©RMN-Grand Palais/Art Resource, NY.)

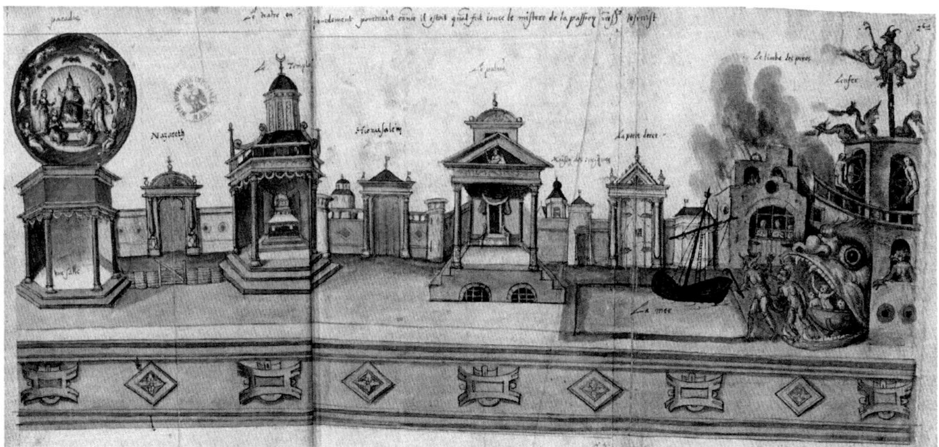

Figure 19.3 Hubert Cailleau's illustration of *The Passion and Resurrection of the Savior* as performed at Valenciennes in 1547. BNF, MS fr. 12536.

the plan places them. P. M. Ryan calculates that such a structure would require excavating 20,000 cubic feet of earth and transporting 50,000 gallons of water to fill the ditch. (See P. M. Ryan's calculations reported in Schmitt 1972: 296.) Since Southern imagines that the play was "toured and played at various places," all this labor would have to be repeated over and over (Southern 1957: 20–1). The plan makes no suggestion that audience members shared the "place" with the actors.[3]

If the *Castle* sketch does not work very well as an architectural blueprint, it makes excellent sense as a scenographical plan. Arguably the earliest medieval stage plan we possess, it introduces an authentic vocabulary for a study of the medieval scenography: its inscriptions (and the text of the play itself) repeatedly refer to the performance area as the "place," and the structures built around the stage as "skaffolds," so that modern scholars now refer routinely to large-scale outdoor plays as "place and scaffold" productions.[4]

Unlike all other medieval stage plans, it speaks to all the visual, spatial, and even aural components of what we now refer to as the play's scenography. The two circles represent a circular ditch filled with "water about the place," although if such a ditch cannot be made, then the place could instead be "strongly barred [fenced] about."[5] Scaffolds occupy compass points (N, NE, E, S, W) located just outside the circle while the castle stands at the center of the "place." Because of the castle's unusual design, the plan provides a sketch to guide the carpenters in building this essential stage structure. The plan also prescribes essential costuming, for example the Four Daughters of God must wear mantles of different colors: Mercy, white; Righteousness, red; Truth, green; and Peace, black. The plan also takes interest in essential stage furniture as well: a large compartment underneath the castle must be furnished with a bed and a cupboard. It also prescribes essential stage action. An actor portraying Mankind's soul must lie hidden "under the bed until he shall rise and play." When Belial, the Devil, "goes to battle," he must have "gunpowder burning in pipes in his hands and in his ears and in his arse." Above all, the design sets the stage for the two climactic moments of the play, the attack by the vices on the Castle and Mankind's descent into the lower chamber and his death. To this end, the plan worries about keeping spectators' sight lines clear: "This is the Castle of Perseverance that stands in the midst of the place, but let no men sit there, for letting [blocking] of sight, for there shall be the best of all."[6] The outer scaffolds look toward the central castle and prepare for these climactic moments. The plan arranges stage movement so that actors initially move between the peripheral stations and then all move vigorously into the center.

The plan thus requires six structures and a circular ditch (or fence) arranged on a reasonably flat surface, a village "green" as the text explicitly tells us.[7] If arranged in this way, the "skaffolds" can be placed just outside the ditch (where the plan says they are), and actors could descend directly into the *platea*, over the water-filled ditch, by means of ladders. The ditch, moreover, need not be anything like a "moat."[8] A relatively modest excavation, it distinguishes spectator space from performers' space. The plan mentions that *stytelerys* [wardens] will be present to ensure that spectators do not cross that ditch and infringe upon the acting area. Because they move around the inside of the circular ditch in front of seated and standing spectators, the plan observes that there ought not be too many of them, presumably to prevent interference with the actors. The *stytelerys*' duties would then resemble those of the "whifflers" who confined spectators to designated areas along the sides of the street during royal and civic processions. (For *stytelerys*, see Southern 1957: 81–8; for whifflers, *OED*, *s.v.* "whiffler," n. 1.) If we understand the ditch in this way, Pamela King observes, "the audience is excluded from the moated area 'for lettynge of syt,' but could, presumably, dispose themselves anywhere else they liked . . . The castle and the space within the moat . . . are preserved for stage action only" (King 2008: 241–2).

What the *Castle* diagram tells us about medieval scenography

As a maker of visual art, the *Castle* stage designer creates the stage and its multiple locations in the same way that other artists design panel paintings, book of hours, sculpture, and stained glass. An anonymous fifteenth-century writer observes that plays were commonly thought of as paintings-come-to-life. Why, he asks, may men not

> better read the will of God and his marvelous works in the performance of them than in painting? And they are better retained in mens' minds and more often reviewed by the playing of them than by the painting, for the one is a dead book, the other a living one.
>
> *(Davidson 1993: 98)*

Plays were written, staged, and performed in the language of iconography derived from paintings and other forms of medieval art. Playwrights, actors, stage designers, and costume makers all employed iconography as a visual language that spectators might read as if they were the "naked letters by which a clerk reads the truth."[9] Scenes are staged in order to imitate the iconography of, say, the Annunciation; when an actor representing the Angel Gabriel descends from heaven to greet the Virgin, he "makes a little pause and Mary beholds him." Briefly, the staged scene becomes a still life devotional painting, so that the spectators might fix the scene in their memories.[10] In the Mons *Mystère de la Passion* such moments of iconographical stillness are signaled by organ music that invites the spectators to read and discern the "dead book" – the painting – that is being made live through performance (Cohen 1924: 56).

The *Castle*'s circular design specifically appropriates the familiar iconography of a medieval *mappa mundi* (Figure 19.4).[11] Placing one of these medieval world maps – the

Figure 19.4 *Mappa mundi*, The *Psalter Map*, c. 1265. (British Library, Add. MS 28681 fol. 9r.)

Psalter Map is a good example – beside the *Castle* diagram demonstrates the relationship between iconographical source and its theatrical appropriation, dead book and quick book. The *mappa mundi* places Jerusalem at the center of the world. A circular ribbon of water represents the outermost margin of the world, and The Four Winds, located on the outer margin of that boundary, mark the cardinal compass points (N, E, S, W). In the stage plan, the *Castle* occupies the central position of Jerusalem while a ditch replicates the *Psalter Map*'s watery border. The "skaffolds" of God, the Devil, and the vices, occupy compass points just outside the circumference.

This *mappa mundi* design distinguishes the *Castle* plan from the five surviving diagrams for the Cornish plays (Figure 19.5). These are also round, but not because an iconographical design requires them to be so. The structures they illustrate, called *pleins-an-gwary*, were constructed to host a variety of outdoor entertainments: wrestling, hurling, sporting matches, and martial contests of various kinds. The eighteenth-century antiquarian William Borlase calls these "athleticly exercises" (Borlase [1754] 1999: 195–6). Performance of plays may well have been much less frequent than these other entertainments. These Cornish plans mark only the positions of the various scaffolds to be placed around these multi-use amphitheatres. Each of the three parts of the *Ordinalia* fit eight scaffolds around the perimeter, while the two parts of *Beunans Meriasek* required 14 each. Even though the individual structures were impressive and iconographically informed, overall scenographical design must have been, in part, exercises in custom fitting.

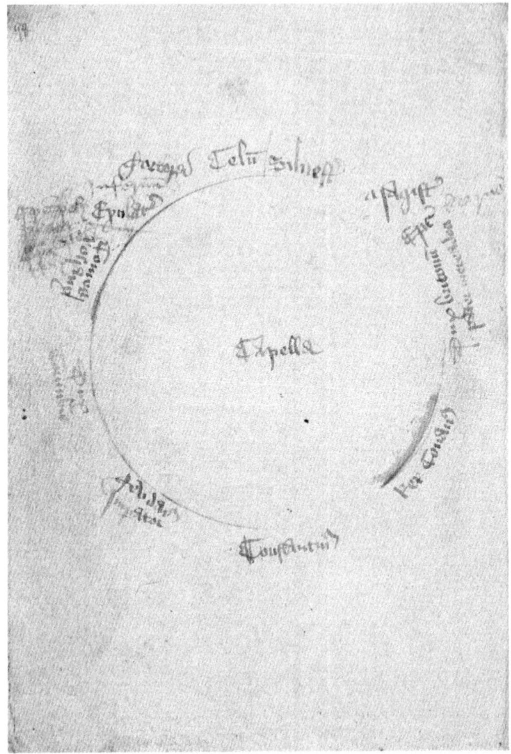

Figure 19.5 Stage plan for *Beunans Meriasek* (1504). National Library of Wales, MS Peniarth 105B, fol.51v. (Courtesy of the National Library of Wales.)

Because the *Castle* takes place in a spiritual world rather than a geographical one, the stage plan describes a spiritual *mappa mundi*. It situates the Castle of Perseverance at the Jerusalem position. Here Mankind resides under the protection of the Seven Heavenly Virtues. Just as the Four Winds occupy the cardinal compass points around the outer rim of the world's watery boundary in the geographical model, so too do the "skaffolds" representing the "houses" of the spiritual forces that contend for the soul of Mankind from these same places: God (East), the World (West), the Flesh (South), and the Devil (North). The stage designer takes one important liberty in adapting his iconographical source: eccentrically, he provides a fifth "house" at one of the four ordinal compass points, Northeast.[12] Here dwells that most redoubtable of medieval sins, Coveytyse (Avarice). Because it conceives of human spiritual life as constantly beset by sin and evil, the design surrounds the *Castle* with Mankind's spiritual enemies, who occupy "skaffolds" at the North, South, and West. Although symmetry would suggest that Avarice ought to belong in the East, not the Northeast, God logically and symbolically belongs in the East, just as the Devil belongs in the North. The plan therefore situates Avarice in the North East between God and Belial, thus completing the encirclement of the *Castle* while still placing God in his traditional location.[13]

A castle at the center of a *mappa mundi* necessarily represents Jerusalem, but the plan takes less interest in the literal city of that name than in its spiritual meanings. "Jerusalem" was commonly used in the Middle Ages to illustrate the four senses of

Figure 19.6 Siege of the Castle of Ladies, Peterborough Psalter. Brussels, KBR MS 9 61-62, fol 92r. (After the facsimile edition by Quaternio Verlag Luzern, www.quaternio.ch)

scriptural interpretation: the literal (the historical city), the tropological (the Christian soul), the allegorical (the Church Militant on earth), and the anagogical (the Heavenly Jerusalem).[14] In representing the spiritual geography of Mankind's soul, the plan takes primary interest in the tropological sense of "Jerusalem." The Seven Heavenly Virtues thus inhabit the ramparts of Mankind's Castle, from which vantage they repel the attacks of the Vices. So long as he remains faithful to the seven virtues, Mankind can repulse the inevitable attacks of the World, the Flesh, and the Devil.

In addition to all this tropological material, the *Castle* also models itself upon a popular *amour courtois* allegory, the Siege of the Castle of Ladies (Figure 19.6). Knights armed with swords and spears attempt to capture a castle defended by ladies, who hurl flowers down upon them. Despite their improbable weapons, the ladies often defeat the knights, but then they graciously capitulate and descend from the ramparts to join them. Once the male has been properly refined, female capitulation usually represents erotic surrender or matrimonial union. Ivory carvings, tapestries, murals, and manuscript paintings popularized this allegory, and courtly *entremets* featuring knights besieging a pageant castle garrisoned by ladies became widely popular (Loomis 1919; Greene 1995).

The designer necessarily transforms this romantic castle into a tropological one, as had Grosseteste and other medieval writers.[15] He replaces the courtly ladies with the Seven Heavenly Virtues who protect Mankind from their spiritual opposites, and transforms the knights into the Seven Deadly Sins led by the World, the Flesh, and the Devil. Like most of the romantic versions of the Siege, the seven virtuous ladies successfully repulse the assault by hurling roses down upon their attackers (for example, ll. 2145–6, 2217–25).

The designer divides the castle into two levels that are mirror opposites in size and shape. The top half of the structure, the Castle proper, represents an exterior view of the tower, all stone blocks and crenellation. The lower half, however, represents interior, domestic space, a chamber open to view from all sides containing a bed and a chest. If this were a conventional *amour courtois* castle, the bottom half would feature a portcullis where courtly ladies fight to prevent their lovers from entering. We might well imagine that an erotically-charged struggle might lead to a bedchamber where lovers might couple.[16] The lower chamber, however, contains Mankind's deathbed and a chest of valued possessions, symbols of death and sin. Avarice traps Mankind in this lower chamber that he calls "my castel cage" (2703) where the Virtues cannot save him.

Mankind can choose either to stay with the Virtues in a constant battle with the Vices or to accept the comfort and fellowship that Covetyse offers him. "Come and speak with thy best friend," Avarice asks, and Mankind willingly descends from the Castle battlements into Avarice's "castel cage." Because he freely chooses Avarice, the Virtues have no power to protect him. In one respect, moreover, the nature of his leave-taking draws upon the *amour courtois* castle: he deserts the Virtues as a false lover betrays his troth. As his will to Virtue decreases, his covetousness increases, and he reenacts the Fall. The Castle's mirror-image compartments illustrate Mankind's upside-down spiritual condition. From grace to sin, from salvation to damnation, from the "Castle of Goodness" he falls into the "castel cage."

How multi-locational scenography works

Technical terminology does not exist in contemporary descriptions of the medieval stage. Depending upon the play we are examining, actors' stations – the Castle calls them "Skaffolds" – might be called *lieus*, *stations*, *eschaffaulx*, *sedes*, *domus*, *stage*, *tentum*, or *pulpitum*. In France such scaffolds might be subdivided into *loges*. The performance space may be called *place*, *platea*, *plain*, or *parc*. Onstage structures may be called *eschaffaulx*, *scaffolds*, *mansions*, *maisons*, *stages*, or *places*. (See Twycross 2008: 49; Butterworth 2014: 40; Murdoch 1994: 215; Bakere 1980: 155–6.) Confusingly, *place* can be used for all three stage parts. Graham Runnalls wisely concludes, "there were no technical terms as such, but just ordinary, everyday words used in an inconsistent way to refer to parts of the stage" (Runnalls 1998: 475; *Mystère d'Adam* in Bevington 1975: 78–121). To reduce confusion among this welter of terms, we will, insofar as possible, imitate the Castle plan's use of these terms: "place" (or alternatively "platea") will identify the performance area; "scaffolds" will refer to actors' stations usually located at the edges of the "place"; and onstage structures, wherever possible, will simply be named (i.e., The Castle of Perseverance, Paradise, a chapel, Jerusalem, the Temple and so on).

Scaffolds are designed to define characters, sometimes a single individual but more commonly a group of related individuals. Meg Twycross remarks that they are "often not so much locations as the 'home ground' of the characters who preside over them. These are their spheres of influence, where their power is greatest." A character who "goes up" into a scaffold subjects himself to an overlord (Twycross 2008: 50). Both French and English plays may begin with processions of actors who enter the place and go to their designated scaffolds. The first stage direction in the N-Town *Passion Play II* explicitly refers to this convention: "When that procession enters the place, King Herod takes his scaffold and Pilate, Annas, and Caiphas take their scaffolds also" (Meredith 1990: 89). Andre de la Vigne describes a similar procession of the actors who began the performance of the *Mystère de St Martin* with a procession into the *parc*, whereupon "they circled round as was proper, and then each went to his *loge*" (Meredith and Tailby 1983: 261). These scaffolds usually sit at the edges of the *platea* as in the *Castle* stage plan. Runnalls notes that the *Mystère de Saint Martin* follows this convention: "'escaffaulx' [actors' stations] are not part of the 'parc' . . . Characters come from their 'eschaffault' onto the 'parc'; when their role is over, they return to their scaffold" (ibid.; Runnalls 1998: 360–1). French *mystères* can also situate actors' stations among the audience accommodations as Fouquet's painting (Figure 19.2) may illustrate. The emperor has left his throne in the scaffold, descended a ladder, and takes up his role on the place; it remains empty until he returns after his performance.[17]

The twelfth-century *Mystère d'Adam* (*Ordo Repraesentationis Adae*) provides us with our first circumstantial descriptions of place-and-scaffold stage structures.[18] A church standing at the east side of the *platea* serves as God's scaffold; the "gates of hell" (*portas inferni*), the Devil's scaffold, probably occupies the north side. God makes entries and exits from the church (see line 112 sd), while the Devil and his attendant demons emerge from Hell to enter Paradise, to drag characters off to Hell, or to "make a foray among the people" (line 204 sd). Three specific locations are constructed either on or raised above the *platea*: Paradise (The Garden of Eden), the earthly garden in which Adam and Eve labor, and the altars where Abel and Cain make their sacrifices. For Paradise, the playwright specifies an ideal garden full of flowers, foliage, and fruit-bearing trees; raised above the *platea*, it is surrounded by silken curtains so that, when they are closed, Adam and Eve can only be seen from the shoulders upward. Adam and Eve's worldly garden, located on the *platea* below Paradise, must contrast with the flowers and fruit trees that grow effortlessly above.[19] Adam and Eve rake, till, and plant wheat in the garden until they are so worn out that they bend over to their ankles. The Devil sneaks into the garden to plant thorns and thistles, and a special effect makes these weeds, instead of wheat, "spring up." Two "great stones" serve as altars for Abel and Cain's sacrifices. Finally, prophets emerge one by one from an offstage *locus secretus* (concealed place).

Medieval scene builders generally make both peripheral actors' stations and on-stage *loca* as visually impressive as possible.[20] The *Castle* stage plan may give the impression that the five actors' stations placed around the *platea* of the *Castle of Peservance* were unremarkable structures because it illustrates the Castle but not the "scaffolds." The text, however, describes the latter as "these towers" (lines 235, 239), and each is large enough to house an impressive retinue of attendant Vices. Much of the action takes place in and around these five towers perched on the edge of the *mappa mundi*. Only the middle third of the play involves the storming of the Castle, Mankind's betrayal, and his death in bed underneath the structure. The first third takes place upon or before the "towers" of the World, Flesh, and Devil, while the final third takes place at the heavenly throne. God's "skaffold" is grand enough to stage a debate between the Four Daughters of God, and his judgment throne is roomy enough for Mankind to sit beside him (l. 3600). Given the play's interest in pyrotechnics, Hell may have been a gaping, smoking, canine maw like those constructed on the Continent (see Figures 19.2 and 19.3). The *Castle* plan's lack of interest in describing these impressive structures suggests that they were probably iconographically conventional, so that they did not need to be illustrated. The *mappa mundi* stage and its central castle, by contrast, were unconventional stage structures and so required careful description.

A glance at the Valenciennes *Passion* image (Figure 19.3) demonstrates that on-stage structures were designed to impress: ships in full sail, apparently in a body of water; heaven with orders of angels circling around God; the Temple of Jerusalem; a great hell-mouth leading into a flaming Hell; Limbo; and a Palace among them. Some of the scenic structures in medieval plays, however, must have been small, even portable. Consider the Cross in the *Resureccion*; the "two great stones" in the *Mystère d'Adam*; the two pillars – one brick, one marble – that Seth sets up in the *platea* to preserve sacred books from fire and water in the *Creacion*; the cauldron and oven in the *Play of the Sacrament*; and the pillar and stool where Christ is scourged and mocked in the N-Town *Passion II*. The Fouquet painting provides a good example of a minimalist design. Only the Hell scaffold, its gaping maw ready to devour sinners as they make their exits, looks at all impressive. Otherwise, God, albeit seated in a golden throne and surrounded by angels, sits in a *loge* indistinguishable from those that spectators occupy, as does the Emperor's empty throne. As for the single on-stage *locus*, an *eculeus* (torture table) represents the place of the saint's martyrdom. Designed to be portable, it can be placed on the stage and then carried off again.

Plays typically start with the actors in their places on the scaffolds while the *platea* and the on-stage *loca* stand empty. Sometimes players will begin by entering the *platea* from offstage. God leads Adam and Eve into the place to begin the *Mystère d'Adam*; the first N-Town *Passion* starts when a fashionable demon and a hair-shirted John the Baptist make separate entrances from offstage. Performances usually begin in the peripheral scaffolds. God creates the world from his heavenly scaffold in the *Origo Mundi*, or even more spectacularly in the *Creacion of the World*, he does so from a "clowde" atop his scaffold; "and when he speaks of Heaven, let the leaves open" (Neuss 1983: 3).[21] Most of these place-and-scaffold plays, however, begin at the scaffolds of arrogant, worldly characters, each of whom competes to "make his boast," a convention sometimes evoked in stage directions (Bevington 1975: 761, line 148 sd).[22] These ritual boasts introduce the inhabitants of the scaffolds to the spectators and sometimes initiate preliminary interactions between scaffolds as conspiracies are formed. Having begun in the stations at the edges of the *platea*, actors then move onto the *platea*, either moving to other actors' stations or to on-stage structures.

The "perfectly logical premise" that explains "multi-locational" scenography, Meg Twycross observes, is "that if you want to represent two locations, they should be in two separate places" (Twycross 2008: 51). O. B. Hardison finds that this premise had already become conventional in vernacular plays of the twelfth century. As a rule, he observes, significant places and character groups each require a station. This representational "technique is a dramatic analogue to the brute fact that a place or human being occupies physical space in the natural world. The rule of identity – that two points cannot occupy the same place – is symbolized by having a different place for each group." The choice and organization of these places upon and around the *platea*, Hardison thinks, was more a matter of geometry than geography. The Anglo-Norman *Seinte Resureccion*, for instance, makes no attempt "to reproduce the geography of Jerusalem in the deployment of stations" (Hardison 1965: 271–2). Rather, the play deploys its stations with reference to the central position of the cross; some are located "on this side" of the cross while others are "on the other side."[23] This convention continues to dominate medieval scenography for at least three hundred years, and it still thrives well into the sixteenth century, as the Cornish and Digby plays demonstrate.[24]

Medieval scenography not only accommodates but enables the movement of characters from place to place throughout the performance. *Mary Magdalene*, according to

Meg Twycross, "is organised on a series of encounters which involve the heroine moving from location to location." She similarly admires "the web of comings and goings" in the N-Town *Passion I* that "works up the mounting atmosphere of conspiracy and the net closing on the protagonist" (Twycross 2008: 52). Peter Meredith describes these "comings and goings" at the beginning of the play: a messenger travels from scaffold to scaffold to arrange a meeting between two "bishops of the old law," Annas and Caiphas. As he travels from one station to another, he encounters the two judges of the same law, Rewfyn and Leyon, who have been moving across the *platea*; the messenger sends them to the Council House in "myd place." Then he returns to Annas and Caiphas, who descend from their scaffolds to travel together to the same Council House (Meredith 1990: 25–6, 29–30). There they will consider together what to do about Jesus' challenge to their authority and the Law they uphold.

Playwrights often invest movement between and among scaffolds with considerable symbolic significance. Dux Morad's journeys from sacred to secular *loci* across the *platea*, Scherb observes, invite "the spectators to evaluate the relative merits of worldly and spiritual glory, illegitimate and legitimate sexuality . . . The moral complexities of the *Dux Morad* are to some extent inherent in the dynamics of its stagecraft" (Scherb 2001: 60). Those same dynamics similarly explain the representation of Judas' betrayal of Christ in the N-Town *Passion I* as a series of journeys from *locus* to *locus*. Leaving Jesus and the other disciples during the Last Supper, he leaves the house of Simon Leprows and "comes into the place." Having conceived of a "prevy [secret] treason," he travels to the Council House in "the mid place" where the Jews are considering what to do about Jesus. His apostasy allows the bishops and judges to make a decision. The play does not explain his defection;[25] rather the journey from the one place to the other dramatizes a decision he has already made by showing him "go over to the other side." Once he makes his deal at the Council House, he then returns to Simon's house where he "goes in craftily where he came from." After the Last Supper, Judas again goes subtly to the Council House; along the way, he meets a Devil who addresses him as "darling mine" to make clear that this third journey completes Judas' decline from disciple to damned. Then in a fourth journey, Judas will lead the Jews from the Council House to Gethsemane, where he identifies Jesus with a kiss. These four journeys across neutral space follow a single line of continuity from Judas' secret defection from Jesus to its ultimate fruition in a kiss of betrayal.

The *Slaughter of the Innocents*[26] requires two, or perhaps three, stations: Herod's court, where he prays to false idols, is clearly counterposed across the *platea* from the Temple, where true religion is practiced. "Israelle," positioned somewhere between these two *loca*, may simply be an area marked out on the *platea*. At the opening of the play, Herod sits enthroned at his court among his "gods" (idols) and soldiers; Mary and Joseph lie asleep in Israelle; and Simeon worships in the Temple. A pattern of individual journeys now defines a continuous action in which Herod and his gods are defeated and the Holy Family saved by divine providence. First Herod orders his soldiers to "slay all the children that come into your sight" (line 111), and they "walk about the place" (line 232 sd) towards Israelle. Having been warned by an angel, Joseph and Mary flee from Israelle and "go out of the place." In response, Herod's idols fall off their pedestals. Then the women of Israel, with young children in their arms, enter the *platea* and replace the Holy Family in Israelle (line 280 sd). The soldiers then arrive, murder the children, and then return to Herod's scaffold. Upon hearing their report, Herod goes mad, his heart "bursts asunder," and he dies. All these journeys trace the consequences leading from Herod's command to its ultimate effect in Herod's madness and death.

Medieval scenographers often find oppositional arrangements of stage structures especially effective in enabling simultaneous staging. In the N-Town *Mary Play* (Meredith 1997), Joachim leaves Anna in his scaffold and travels to the Temple where he means to present his sacrifice. When the High Priest rejects his offering because he and his wife are barren, Joachim despairingly flees to join his shepherds (line 130). This bucolic *locus* must be located on the opposite side of the Temple from his scaffold to permit the contrapuntal laments of the lovers who have been separated by the Temple. "Joachim, lamenting in the desert, full of anxiety about his wife Anna," Meg Twycross remarks, "is echoed at another part of the stage by Anna herself, left at home, and worrying about Joachim" (Twycross 2008: 52).

Cornish plays often delight in staging simultaneous action, even from diametrically opposed points on a large, circular *plain-an-gwary*. In the *Passio Domini*, the action requires rapid shifts between Gethsemane at the center of the circular *place*, and two scaffolds located 90 degrees from one another on the periphery. Jesus alternately prays and admonishes his disciples on the Mount of Olives while God in heaven dispatches Gabriel to reassure him. Simultaneously Caiphas dispatches Judas and other Conspirators from his scaffold to arrest Jesus in Gethsemane. As they walk across the *place*, we hear their conversations intermingled with Jesus' praying and admonishing. An even more impressive feat of Cornish simultaneous staging occurs in the "Mother's Son" episode in *Beunans Meriasek*. The action shifts rapidly between four characters' scaffolds upon the periphery – two of them diametrically opposed to one another – and two locations on the *platea*. The virtuous King Massen and the Tyrant simultaneously decide to hunt in the same forest while the Mother's Son sets out for King Massen's court. As the Son leaves his scaffold, the Mother goes to the Chapel at the center of the *place*. The two kings meet and fight a battle in the forest, Massen is defeated, and the Mother's Son is captured and thrown into prison. The Mother's prayers in the Chapel intermingle with the Tyrant's orders for the son's execution. The Mother despairs, snatches a Jesus figure from the arms of a statuary Virgin, and returns to her scaffold with her substitute "son." The Virgin descends from heaven, frees the Mother's Son, and asks him to have his mother return little Jesus to the *Capella*, which she does to close the episode. These quick shifts in focus occurring across the *platea* at many points, either in quick succession or simultaneously, create carefully wrought dramatic ironies: the two kings deciding to go to the same place at the same time, the Mother and the Virgin exchanging "sons."

Place and scaffold staging is often remarkably flexible. The text of *The Conversion of St Paul* (Baker *et al.* 1982: 1–23) contains evidence of a long performance history in which the stage design has been adapted to suit various production circumstances. In its current form, the play requires three different *places*, one for each of the play's episodes or "stacyons," as the text calls them. The first episode requires two onstage structures, the Temple of Jerusalem, where Saul receives his commission from Anna and Caypha, and a stable, from which Saul acquires a horse. Saul rides the horse "about the place" and then "out of the place" (line 140 sd). At the second episode, God speaks to Saul and Ananias from heaven, and from this vantage he sends a "fervent" [firework] to knock Saul off his horse; later the Spiritus Sanctus descends upon Saul from the same structure (lines 182 sd, 291 sd). Other areas of the *platea* serve both as the Road to Damascus where Saul is struck down off his horse and a separate place where Saul kneels "upon this ground" to be baptized (line 318). The third episode requires no peripheral scaffolds or on-stage structures at all – a point to which we shall return.

To negotiate these different configurations, a Poeta introduces the play, and then conducts the audience from one stage setting to the next. Scherb thinks that the audience's progress from *stacyon* to *stacyon* is a devotional strategy based upon such peripatetic devotions as the Stations of the Cross; these transitions encourage "the audience to participate physically in Paul's journey from Jerusalem to Damascus." The three *stacyons*, he further observes, represent the stages of Paul's conversion: the first "Paul's worldliness, the second his encounter with the divine, and the third the spiritual nature of his conversion," and these three stages may also "provide a model of spiritual development for the audience" (Scherb 2001: 95–7). The spectators trace the continuity of Paul's conversion as he and they travel from place to place.

The text offers three different staging options. In making a transition between the first and second *stacyon*, a stage direction suggests that the Poeta's services might be dispensed with: "*Poeta – si placet*" [the Poet, if desired]. A marginal annotation – "*Daunce*" – also suggests that a dance might conclude one station and prepare for the next, but whether a dance is meant to replace the Poeta's speech or accompany it is unclear. The third "*stacyon*" originally requires only a brief conversation between Anna and Caiphas and, after their exit, a sermon from Paul. A reviser, however, inserts a new scene into the text. Echoing the "fervent" that struck Paul down in the second *stacyon*, the devils Belyall and Mercury enter with "thunder and fire" and they also vanish "with a fiery flame and a tempest" (lines 411 sd and 502 sd).

All of these options suggest that the text was constantly adapted for various performance conditions. Originally the play may have been written for a conventional production in which all the *loca* are disposed about a single *platea* (Baker 1989). Since all evidence of the audience moving from *stacyon* to *stacyon* appears in the Poeta's optional speeches, a producer could choose to eliminate them. A dance might perhaps mark the break between episodes – or not.

Most scholars have noticed that the austerity of the third *stacyon*'s scenography contrasts sharply with the presence of impressive stage structures in the first two. In a conventional single- *platea* play, Anna and Caypha would naturally reappear in the same Temple scaffold we saw at the beginning of the play. The three-*stacyon* version, however, requires no structures of any kind. Anna and Caypha walk on to the *platea* to begin their performance and, after they are done, they simply walk off.[27] The interpolated devil scene also seems to have been composed with scenographical spareness in mind. The two devils, Belyall and Mercury, make their entrances with "thunder and fire," but otherwise the scene dispenses with such spectacular special effects. Where a hellmouth would normally be expected in a place-and-scaffold production, the interpolated scene mentions only a chair for Belyall to sit in (line 411 sd). Instead of a *place* large enough to accommodate a horse and rider, the Poeta introduces the spectators to "this little stacion" (line 363). In its current form, the third *stacyon* could easily be staged in a church. Without having to accommodate a horse and spectacular effects, Saul's sermon might simply be declaimed from a pulpit. If used, the devil scene option could easily take place in the nave, perhaps using fireworks to clear the spectators aside for the entry of Belyall and Mercury. If so, then the conclusion to the play takes the form of a brief stage play, not unlike the interludes that are becoming increasingly popular at the beginning of the sixteenth century. In its three-*stacyon* format, the play experiments with highly unusual production techniques, not only by leading the spectators in a three-*stacyon* progress, but also in mixing place-and-scaffold with interlude production modes. However, the options of deleting the poet-expositor, the dances, and the interpolated scene also invite a full-scale place-and-scaffold production.

Figure 19.7 The Ommeganck in Brussels on 31 May 1615: *The Triumph of Archduchess Isabella* [detail: Nativity wagon] Denys van Asloot, Belgium, 1616. (Museum no. 5928–1859 © Victoria and Albert Museum, London.)

The play demonstrates a remarkable scenographical flexibility, one easily adaptable to religious, courtly, and popular venues.

Multi-locational scenography: beyond the place-and-scaffold stage

Guilds, Confraternities, and a variety of religious and social organizations designed and built pageant wagons to perform great biblical sequences in the streets of York, Chester, Norwich, Coventry, Lille, Leuven, Antwerp, and Brussels, among other places (see Twycross 2008: 35–42; Twycross 1980a and b). The wagon plays functioned as mobile *loca* that moved from one group of spectators to the next, each performing an episode (sometimes two or three) of biblical history. Unlike the fixed scaffolds constructed for place-and-scaffold productions, the pageant stations were built, altered, and improved, year by year, performance by performance, so that they became, in Twycross' apt phrase, "custom-built theatrical machines" that seemed both sumptuous (*ludum sumptuosum*) and costly ("great costage") (Twycross 2008: 35–6). Sophistication and splendor were important because these mobile stages manifested the prestige of the guilds that created them and of the honor of the city that sponsored them.

The creators of these pageant wagons, like the designers of other forms of multi-locational plays, worked within the tradition of medieval iconographical representation. When Joseph complains, in the York Tille-Thekers' Nativity play, that the walls of the Bethlehem stable "are down on every side, / The roof is torn open above our heads"

(Beadle 2009: 17–18), he describes the standard iconographical vocabulary for representing the structure: a ruin with few or no walls and a hole in the roof through which the star will shine upon the Christ child. As a symbol of the old, tired fallen world that is passing away at the Incarnation, the ruined stable became the dominant setting for representing the Nativity and Epiphany in medieval art,[28] and we have illustrations of enough Nativity pageant wagons from Louvain, Antwerp, and Brussels (Figure 19.7) to demonstrate that pageant devisers routinely appropriated the "dead book" of painted images to make them "quick" by live performance (Twycross 1980a: 23–7).

Pageant wagons moved through the streets, stopping at predetermined stations to perform their episodes. Given the tightness of the stage space on a pageant wagon (about 8 feet wide and 10 to 14 feet long), there simply is not much room for multiple locations (Twycross 2008: 36–7). Actors can, of course, use the street for additional performance space, lifting mechanisms can raise the Virgin from earth to heaven as in the York *Assumption* play, and trapdoors can provide entrances and exits from below. As in some place-and-scaffold plays, a single *locus* can sometimes represent multiple places; Moses can climb Sinai at the beginning of the Chester Cappers' play, then Balaam can climb the same structure, which has now become a different mountain, at the end of the same play.[29]

It is fair enough to think of the pageant wagons as mobile onstage locations and the street (or at least the performance area at each station) as a *place*, but the dynamics of pageant wagon sequences differ considerably from those of place-and-scaffold performances. The most significant journeys are those made by pageant wagons traveling from one station to another station, not by characters moving between scaffolds, although a few pageant wagons do accommodate multiple locations. Spectators experience the arrival of each new play as part of a historical sequence that comes to them, includes them, and defines the communal faith that connects all spectators at all stations.

The two surviving Coventry plays may have attempted a compromise between pageant wagon and place-and-scaffold scenography. King and Davidson doubt that either of them could be performed on a single wagon. The Shearmen and Tailors' pageant, they point out, requires no less than three separate locations: the Bethlehem stable, the shepherds' hillside, and Herod's court. At least some of the Coventry guilds may have deployed multiple wagons. Stage directions often invoke language made familiar in place-and-scaffold productions: "The shepherds . . . *go forth out of the place*" (King and Davidson 2000: 92). The "absolute distinction between place-and-scaffold staging and processional performance is misleading, and what was set up at each station was a moveable place-and-scaffold arrangement" (ibid.: 12–13). A very similar mixture of these two scenographical approaches, as we have seen, also distinguishes *The Conversion of St Paul*, except that in the one a procession of wagons brings the play to a stationary audience, while in the other spectators process from stage to stage.

Much the same development occurs indoors at great hall venues. Mummings and disguisings, essentially dance performances, did not require any further theatrical embellishment than the masks and costumes worn by the dancers. To achieve a heightened level of theatrical display, however, dancers sometimes made their entrances aboard pageant cars. At a Christmas revel in 1394, mummers arrived in Westminster Hall in a ship with a cargo of spices and other gifts to be presented to Richard II and Queen Anne (Hector and Harvey 1982: 516). Lydgate wrote texts for several mummings in the mid-fifteenth century, and these may have also involved actors making entrances on pageant cars. One of these, an Epiphany mumming for Mayor William Eastfield, probably featured the entry of several "estates" [nobles] aboard a pageant ship and perhaps other such vehicles as well (Twycross and Dutton 2014). Because the purpose of these pageants was to introduce the dancers, disguising pageants remained "fundamentally a framework for the *costumed* dances," even when "the pageant vehicles came to be involved in allegorical scenarios" (Twycross and Carpenter 2002: 136).

By the end of the century, however, these allegorical scenarios deployed pageant cars as theatrical locations. The wedding revels for Prince Arthur and Katharine of Aragon (1501) may mark the moment when these pageant prologues have become indoor place-and-scaffold performances. William Cornish, Gentleman of the King's Chapel, poet, musician, and performer, designed a disguising that was based upon the same Castle of Ladies allegory that we found in the *Castle of Perseverance.* Three remarkable wheeled pageants entered Westminster Hall during a banquet: the castle of ladies, a ship bearing ambassadors named Hope and Desire, and a mountain bearing the Knights of the Mount of Love.[30] First the castle made its entrance at the "nether part of the Hall," moved through the hall and stopped at the "upper part" before the high table. The ship next followed, mooring at one side of the castle. Hope and Desire climbed down a ladder, proceeded to the castle, and entreated the ladies on behalf of the knights "as wooers and breakers of the matter of love between the knights and ladies." When the ladies "utterly refused," Hope and Desire threatened that the knights would make such "battle and assault" that "it should be grievous to abide their power and malice." On this cue, the Mount of Love entered and fetched up on the other side of the ship. The ambassadors reported the failure of their embassy to the Knights, who immediately besieged the Castle. "The ladies, yielding themselves, descended from the said castle and submitted themselves to the power, grace, and will of those noble knights" (Kipling 1990: 55–8). A dance between the former combatants at last resolved rough wooing into matrimonial harmony.

This transformation of the "upper part" of the Hall into a place-and-scaffold theatre even displaced Henry VII, who "conveyed and set himself somewhat out of the way," to become one of the spectators, albeit a privileged one. The Castle, Mount, and Ship pageants form a linear theatre, like the scaffolds depicted in the Fouquet and Valenciennes paintings (Figures 19.2 and 19.3). Characters moving across the *platea* define theatrical continuity: the ambassadors move from the ship to castle, then from castle to Mount, then from the Mount back to the Castle, ending with a dance of ladies and knights in the *platea*. With the dance, however, the theatrical structures move out of the hall leaving the floor to the costumed dancers.[31]

The royal entry shares many scenographical conventions with the civic biblical sequences we examined briefly above. The same guilds take responsibility for designing and organizing performances at fixed stations throughout the city, and the pageants draw heavily from biblical and religious iconography. Where civic biblical sequences travel from one station to another and thus perform several times, royal entry pageants, fixed to their stations, only perform once as the king or queen pauses briefly before each pageant. From 1377, the first recorded English royal entry with pageantry, until the mid-fifteenth century, actors performed static *tableaux vivants*, but they did not speak. From 1456 (the London entry of Margaret of Anjou) onward, however, pageant characters declaimed speeches. Although complex theatrical spectacles, they were sometimes produced in as little as 10 days.

From the point of view of a spectator, the king or queen who progresses from pageant to pageant is as much protagonist of this civic pageant as merely a traveling audience of one. These pageant sequences, often called "advents," almost always take place on the first *formal* entries of kings or queens after their accession. As a general rule (to which there are exceptions) kings perform their advents by entering the city imitating Christ's entry into the celestial Jerusalem. Queens encounter similar pageants during their entries, but they do so imitating the Virgin Mary rising to her apotheosis to take her seat upon a throne next to Christ. Both frequently encounter "jasper-green castles" representing the Celestial Jerusalem as they journey through the streets and metaphorically ascend into heaven. Fountains miraculously spring with wine as they pass by. Genealogical trees declare the earthly lineage of these royal visitors as a reflection of the genealogy of Christ leading from Jesse at the root to Christ and the Virgin at the top.

Henry VI's London entry (1432), as described by Lydgate (but not, as some have thought, devised by him), stages many of these topics (Kipling 1998: 143–69). The "virgins celestiall," Nature, Grace, and Fortune, bestow their gifts upon the child king; Enoch and Elijah await the advent of the messiah from their heavenly paradise; the angelic maidens, Mercy, Grace, and Pity, draw Eucharistic wine (*aquas architriclinas*) from the Fountains of the Savior and distribute it to all; two Jesse trees place both Henry's royal genealogy and Christ's genealogy side by side. A jasper-green castle suggests that London is a type of the heavenly Jerusalem; at the last station, armies of angels, surrounding the Throne of the Indivisible Trinity, welcome Henry as a messianic king.

The devisers sometimes structure these sequences of pageants into a well-defined narrative. The royal entry pageantry for Henry V's London entry (1415) visualizes the soul's entry into paradise as described in a series of liturgical prayers in the Office of the Dead (ibid.: 201–9). At the Bridge Gate, Henry enters the *Civitas Regis Iustitiae*, "the City of the King of Justice." Saints, angels, prophets, apostles, martyrs, and confessors welcome him into heavenly communion as the Office of the Dead envisions. Many of the pageants shine "like a precious stone, as to the jasper stone, even as crystal" as the Apocalypse describes the heavenly Jerusalem. At the final pageant, Henry encounters the Sun of Justice as described in the Apocalypse: "a figure of majesty in the form of a sun . . . emitting dazzling rays" which "shone more brightly than all else." Around the heavenly throne, "archangels moved rhythmically together, psalming sweetly and accompanied by every kind of musical instrument." Represented as pure celestial glory in the form of a sun, the Lord's glory outshines that of the mortal king. To his credit, Henry understood and played the role the pageants designed for him. The king rode through the city with "a quiet demeanour, gentle pace, and sober progress . . . silently pondering the matter in his heart" and "rendering thanks and glory to God alone, not to man."[32]

A queenly ascent forms the London entry of Katharine of Aragon (1501) (Kipling 1998: 209–21). Its six pageants imagine Katharine's entry into London as her apotheosis, rising from earth, through the cosmos, to the Throne of Honor above the firmament. Saints Katharine and Ursula descend from "the court celestial" to greet her on London Bridge where they announce that she is to be conveyed "to Honor" in the heavens among the "stars bright." Thereafter she ascends from the earthly Castle of Policy to Honor (pageant two), to the sphere of the moon (pageant three), to the sphere of the sun (pageant four), to the throne of God the Father (pageant five). Finally she is invited to sit with Prince Arthur upon the Throne of Honor, a seat fixed upon the eternal foundation of the seven virtues and set above the cosmos (pageant six). Although taking the form of a courtly dream vision, the journey to heaven ending at the celestial throne where she sits beside her *sponsus* on a heavenly throne also reflects the Virgin's apotheosis.

Most of these careful narrative structures, however, would be lost on the spectators who stand at the various stations for their chance to glimpse the royal visitors interacting with the pageantry. Given the press of the crowds, even a determined spectator would find it hard to move from station to station to see more than a single pageant. The poet

Lydgate, whose poem describes Henry VI's royal entry in considerable detail, seems to have witnessed only one of the pageants himself, but he made use of a preliminary plan approved by the city to describe the others.[33] Lydgate's description would help some visualize the entire show, but it is unlikely that such descriptions circulated widely until the sixteenth century.

For spectators, viewing only one pageant would be sufficient for the most important purpose of the entry. As the king or queen passed from station to station through the city, the performances at the various stations create manifestations for the people of the "king of God among us" or the *Virga Mediatrix*. In response, the people respond by acclaiming these manifestations. Shouts of "noel, noel" and *benedictus qui venit in nomine domini* are reported, although a simple "hurrah" suffices.[34] A spectator who has participated in one such royal manifestation has little need to chase down others.

Kings and queens are not only spectators of these shows, but they are the protagonists of the drama. Their journey through the city connects pageant to pageant, *locus* to *locus*, as do characters moving across the *platea* in more conventional multi-locational plays. Despite the apparently miscellaneous selection of pageant topics in some royal entries, the king's journey defines narrative continuity. Entry pageants start at the borders of the city and move into the center – once again a pattern noticed in place-and-scaffold theatres. Most medieval London entries end up at St Paul's where a heavenly throne or celestial Jerusalem castle often closes the show. Along the way, the individual manifestations can indeed seem various, just as the biblical lessons read in church through Advent and Epiphany can seem miscellaneous. The royal entry's journey from margins to center, however, completes a public manifestation of the king as a *Christus Rex* or of the queen as a *Virga mediatrix*.

Other forms of scenography were performed in the Middle Ages. Conventional stage plays (for example, *Interludium de Clerico et Puella*), often performed in households' halls or inns, set the scene with little more than stage properties. Liturgical plays and academic plays could often be quite splendidly decorated, although most often these were "in house" productions adapted to the particular locations they were designed for. Multi-locational scenography, however, was by far the most versatile and popular form of medieval theatre scenography, and it could be adapted in various ways, as place-and-scaffold productions of moral and biblical plays, civic biblical sequences on wheeled wagons, court disguisings, and royal entry pageantry. These are often thought of as quite different forms of scenography, but once we see them as variations on the same scenographical conventions, we are better positioned to understand the most important form of theatrical production from the twelfth through the mid-sixteenth centuries.

Notes

1 See, for example, Cohen 1926; Southern 1957; Konigson 1969; and Rey-Flaud 1973.
2 Stage plans for two other late-sixteenth-century plays, the Lucerne *Passion* (1583) and the Villingen *Passion* (1585) also show long, rectangular stages. For these, see Nagler 1976: 29–32, 36–47.
3 The plan does mention that "no men" should sit near the Castle·"for blocking of sight[-lines]." Southern (1957) thinks this inscription refers to spectators who are allowed into the "place" among the actors, but it may rather refer to a small group of privileged spectators, like those who were permitted to sit on stage in Early Modern theatres, to the actors, or even to the wardens who prevent spectators from crossing the ditch onto the place (for which see p. 253–5).
4 French *mystères* also refer to *eschaffaults* in the same theatrical sense. See p. 257.
5 All textual quotations in this essay are modernized. Original texts can be found in sources cited.

6 "The best of all" probably means the most important scenes that tend to take place around the castle.
7 The "Vexillators" (flag bearers who proclaim the forthcoming performance) describe the venue in this way. The play also refers to a "hill" upon which spectators sit, but there is no warrant for thinking that this refers to a circular earthwork. On this point, see Schmitt 1972: 302–3.
8 Two excellent studies have made good progress in attacking Southern's massive rampart with its outer ditch and questioning the placement of the spectators on the *platea* (Schmitt 1972: 292–315 and King 1987: 45–58.) Both argue that the topography of the theatre is relatively flat and that the ditch represents the Castle's moat.
9 The anonymous Lollard writer, however, thinks plays were dangerous precisely because they were "quick." In viewing these living paintings, spectators accept what they see as true, even lies and idolatry, because plays are designed "more to delight men bodily than to be books for unlearned men." Paintings were safer because they could be soberly read without "too much feeding mens' wits." (Davidson 1993: 104).
10 This passage draws upon Scherb 2001: 48–9.
11 Some studies have briefly discussed the *Castle*'s appropriation of the *mappa mundi*. See Cawley 1983: 7; Stevens 1995: 38–9; and Twycross 2008: 50.
12 The artist of the *Psalter Map* follows a tradition first defined by Timosthenes of Rhodes who distinguishes four principal Winds and eight lesser ones. The *Castle* plan, however, depicts a simpler, eight-point system, where four ordinal directions (NE, SE, SW, NW) mark the medial positions between the four cardinal ones. Except for NE, however, the plan ignores the other ordinal points.
13 David Bevington characterizes the stage plan as "a theater representative of the divine universe, with little Man at its center and with vast contending forces facing their opposite numbers on every side" (Bevington 1985: 170).
14 For the commonplace "Jerusalem" trope, see Caplan 1970.
15 Grosseteste's allegory figures the Virgin's body as a Castle within which Christ is incarnated. A sinner, pursued by his three enemies, the World, the Devil, and his own Flesh, flees to the Virgin and asks for succor. No siege takes place. Loomis (1919: 264–9) points out that the *Castle* is part of a "moralistic development" of the Castle of Ladies which he details in his article. Schmitt (1972: 299–302) defends Gosseteste's influence on the *Castle*.
16 See, for example, Greene's readings of Tudor disguisings that make use of Castle of Ladies pageants (Greene 1995: 21–6).
17 In Fouquet's painting, only the Emperor's *loge* has a curtain. Perhaps it was pulled open to disclose the Emperor's first entry and pulled shut to mark his final exit.
18 Textual citations from Bevington 1975: 78–121.
19 An iconographical analogue for the two gardens – Eden above and the Fallen garden beneath – appears in the contemporaneous York Psalter; see T. S. R. Boase, *The York Psalter in the Library of the Hunterian Museum, Glasgow* (London, 1962), pp. 16–17.
20 Some "stations" may well have been relatively non-descript compartments, such as the "loges" in the *Mystère de Saint Martin* reserved for actors among the audience accommodations (Runnalls 1998: 359–61; see also Hamblin 2012: 145–56).
21 The cloud is constructed with "leaves" that open and close to permit God to appear.
22 See Butterworth 2014: 40–1 for boasting as a stage convention.
23 *Seinte Resureccion* textual citations from Bevington 1975, *Medieval Drama*, 123–36.
24 The Cornish plays, *Beunans Meriasek* and *Bewnans Ke*, are preserved in sixteenth-century manuscripts, while the manuscript of the *Creacion of the World* was copied in 1611. The plays themselves were probably composed a good deal earlier, but the manuscripts suggest a continued performance history. The Digby MS plays include *Mary Magdalene*, *The Conversion of St Paul*, and the *Killing of the Children*. See Baker *et al.* 1982. The MS seems to have been copied about 1520, but some of these plays were still being performed in the 1560s. See Coldewey 1975.
25 A later compiler apparently wanted to provide Judas with a motive, so he interpolated a scene from a different play in which Judas quarrels with Jesus. When Jesus tells Judas, "thou spekest wrong," he provides the motive for Judas' "secret treason" (Meredith 1990: 233–41).
26 Quotations cited from *Digby Plays* in Baker *et al.* 1982.
27 An editorial stage direction inserted into the text (*Digby Plays*, p. 13) muddles this point by having Caypha and Anna appear in "the temple" in Jerusalem, but there is no warrant for this in the text.

28 For the ruined stable, see Schiller 1972, Vol. I: 80–8, 111–14 and plates 202–3, 205–6, 219, 288, 292, 297–8.
29 The York Hosiers Play requires four locations: Pharaoh's court, Sinai, Goshen, and the Red Sea. Journeys between these places may be as significant as any made between locations on a place-and-scaffold stage, but they are necessarily brief.
30 William Cornish, Gentleman of the Chapel Royal, produced three of these disguisings and John English, Master of the King's Players, produced the fourth. See Kipling 1990, xix–xxiii. Quotations cited from this text. See also Loomis 1919: 256; Welsford 1962: 120–3; and Greene 1995: 4–5, 2–24.
31 Castle of Ladies performances continued throughout the sixteenth century: Loomis 1919: 256–8; Welsford 1962: 116–48; Greene 1995: 27–34.
32 For Henry's self-effacing behavior during his royal entry, see Wylie 1919, Vol. II: 178.
33 Kipling 2010: 32–6.
34 Kipling 1998: 28.

References

Baker, Donald C. 1989. "When is a Text a Play?" In *Contexts for Early English Drama*, edited by Maryanne G. Briscoe and John C. Coldewey, 20–41. Bloomington: Indiana University Press.

Baker, Donald C., John L. Murphy and Louis B. Hall Jr. (Eds) 1982. *The Late Medieval Religious Plays of Bodleian Library*, MSS. Digby 133 and E Museo 160, EETS O.S. 283. Oxford: Oxford University Press.

Bakere, Jane A. 1980. *The Cornish Ordinalia: A Critical Study*. Cardiff: University of Wales Press.

Beadle, Richard (Ed.) 2009. *The York Plays*, EETS SS 23. Oxford: Oxford University Press.

Bevington, David (Ed.) 1975. *Medieval Drama*. Boston, MA: Houghton Mifflin.

Bevington, David 1985. "'Man thinke on thine endinge day': stage pictures of Just Judgment in *The Castle of Perseverance*." In *Homo, Memento Finis: The Iconography of Just Judgment in Medieval Art and Drama*, edited by David Bevington, 147–177. Kalamazoo: Medieval Institute Publications.

Borlase, William [1754] 1999. *Observations on the Antiquities, Historical and Monumental, of the County of Cornwall*. Oxford: W. Jackson.

Butterworth, Philip 2014. *Staging Conventions in Medieval English Theatre*. Cambridge: Cambridge University Press.

Caplan, Harry 1970. "The Four Senses of Scriptural Interpretation and The Mediaeval Theory of Preaching." In *Of Eloquence: Studies in Ancient and Mediaeval Rhetoric*, edited by Anne King and Helen North, 93–104. Ithaca, NY: Cornell University Press.

Cawley, A. C. 1983. "The Staging of Medieval Drama." In *The Revels History of Drama in English*, edited by Lois Potter, 54–55. London: Routledge Kegan & Paul.

Cohen, Gustave 1924. *Le Livre de Conduite du Régisseur et le Compte des Dépenses pour le Mystère de la Passion Joué à Mons en 1501*. Strasbourg: Imprimerie Alsacienne.

Cohen, Gustave 1926. *Histoire de la Mise en Scène dans le Théâtre Religieux du Moyen Age*. Paris: Champion.

Coldewey, John 1975. "The Digby Plays and the Chelmsford Records." *Research Opportunities in Renaissance Drama* 18: 103–121.

Davidson, Clifford (Ed.) 1993. *A Tretise of Miraclis Pleyinge*. Kalamazoo: Western Michigan University Press.

Greene, Thomas M. 1995. *Besieging the Castle of Ladies*. Binghamton, NY: SUNY Press.

Hamblin, Vicki L. 2012. *Saints at Play*. Kalamazoo: Western Michigan University Press.

Hardison, O. B. 1965. *Christian Rite and Christian Drama in the Middle Ages*. Baltimore, MD: Johns Hopkins Press.

Hector, L. C. and Barbara F. Harvey (Ed. and Trans.) 1982. *The Westminster Chronicle 1391–1394*. Oxford: Clarendon Press.

Joyce, Sally L. and Evelyn S. Newlyn (Eds) 1999. *Records of Early English Drama, Cornwall*. Toronto: University of Toronto Press.

King, Pamela 1987. "Spatial Semantics and the Medieval Theatre." In *The Theatrical Space*, edited by James Redmond, 45–58. Cambridge: Cambridge University Press.

King, Pamela 2008. "Morality Plays." In *The Cambridge Companion to Medieval English Theatre*, 2nd ed., edited by Richard Beadle and Alan J. Fletcher, 235–262. Cambridge: Cambridge University Press.

King, Pamela and Clifford Davidson (Eds) 2000. *The Coventry Corpus Christi Plays*. Kalamazoo: Western Michigan University Press.

Kipling, Gordon (Ed.) 1990. *The Receyt of the Ladie Kateryne*, EETS os 296. Oxford: Oxford University Press.

Kipling, Gordon 1998. *Enter the King: Theatre, Liturgy, and Ritual in the Medieval Civic Triumph*. Oxford: Oxford University Press.

Kipling, Gordon 2010. "The Design and Construction of Royal Entries in the Late Middle Ages." *Medieval English Theatre* 32: 26–61.

Konigson, Elie 1969. *La Representation d'un Mystère de la Passion à Valenciennes en 1547*. Paris: CNRS.

Loomis, R. S. 1919. "The Allegorical Siege in the Art of the Middle Ages." *American Journal of Archaeology* 23: 255–269.

Meredith, Peter (Ed.) 1990. *The Passion Play from the N. Town Manuscript*. London: Longman.

Meredith, Peter 1997. *The Mary Play: from the N. Town Manuscript*. Exeter: University of Exeter Press.

Meredith, Peter and John Tailby 1983. *The Staging of Religious Drama in Europe in the Later Middle Ages*. Kalamazoo: Western Michigan University Press.

Murdoch, Brian O. 1994. "The Cornish Medieval Drama." In *The Cambridge Companion to Medieval English Theatre*, edited by Richard Beadle, 211–239. Cambridge: Cambridge University Press.

Nagler, A. M. 1976. *The Medieval Religious Stage*. New Haven, CT: Yale University Press.

Neuss, Paula 1983. *The Creacion of the World: A Critical Edition and Translation*. New York: Garland Publishing.

Rey-Flaud, Henri 1973. *Le cercle magique*. Paris: Éditions Gallimard.

Runnalls, Graham A. 1998. *Études sur les Mystères*. Paris: Champion.

Scherb, Victor I. 2001. *Staging Faith: East Anglian Drama in the Later Middle Ages*. Madison, NJ: Fairleigh Dickinson University Press.

Schiller, Gertrud 1972. *Iconography of Christian Art*, 2 Vols. Translated by Janet Seligman. London: Lund Humphries.

Schmitt, Natalie Crohn 1972. "Was There a Medieval Theatre in the Round? A Re-Examination of the Evidence." In *Medieval English Drama: Essays Critical and Contextual*, edited by Jerome Taylor and Alan H. Nelson, 292–315. Chicago, IL, and London: University of Chicago Press.

Southern, Richard 1957. *The Medieval Theatre in the Round*. London: Faber & Faber.

Stevens, Martin 1995. "From *Mappa Mundi* to *Teatrum Mundi*: The World as Stage in Early English Drama." In *From Page to Performance: Essays in Early English Drama*, edited by John A. Alford, 25–50. East Lansing: Michigan State University Press.

Twycross, Meg 1980a. "The Flemish *Ommegang* and Its Pageant Cars." *Medieval English Theatre* 2 (1): 15–41.

Twycross, Meg 1980b. "The Flemish *Ommegang* and Its Pageant Cars: 2." *Medieval English Theatre* 2 (2): 80–98.

Twycross, Meg 2008. "The Theatricality of Medieval English Plays." In *The Cambridge Companion to Medieval English Theatre*, 2nd ed., edited by Richard Beadle and Alan J. Fletcher, 26–74. Cambridge: Cambridge University Press.

Twycross, Meg and Sarah Carpenter 2002. *Masks and Masking in Medieval and Early Tudor England*. Burlington, VT: Ashgate.

Twycross, Meg and Elisabeth Dutton 2014. "Lydgate's Mumming for the Mercers of London." In *The Medieval Merchant*, edited by Caroline M. Barron and Anne F. Sutton, 310–349. Donington, UK: Harlaxton Symposium.

Welsford, Enid 1962. *The Court Masque: A Study in the Relationship Between Poetry & the Revels*. New York: Russell & Russell.

The Westminster Chronicle 1381–1394 1982. Edited and translated by L. C. Hector and Barbara F. Harvey. Oxford: Clarendon Press.

Wylie, James Hamilton 1919. *The Reign of Henry the Fifth*, 2 Vols. Cambridge: Cambridge University Press.

20

STORYTELLER AS TIME-TRAVELER IN MOHAMMED BEN ABDALLAH'S *SONG OF THE PHARAOH*

Multimedia avant-garde theatre in Ghana

Jesse Weaver Shipley

This chapter explores the scenography of contemporary Ghanaian theatre by examining the spatial and narrative aspects of Mohammed ben Abdallah's *Song of the Pharaoh*, which premiered at the National Theatre of Ghana in 2013. The theatrical design of this play reveals some of the multiple influences that come together in making contemporary West African theatre. More specifically, it shows how modern Ghanaian drama codifies the improvisational aspects of storytelling and popular theatre traditions through spatial ordering, narration techniques, and embedding multiple genres in a performance. In this style of staging, theatrical time-space shaped around a storytelling idiom reflects debates about historical time. *Song of the Pharaoh* is emblematic of modern Ghanaian drama and broader contemporary African theatre in transforming formal elements of older performance genres and playing with time-space through design techniques. Specifically, the play codifies older techniques of improvisation and storytelling in its script and staging. By embedding and juxtaposing purportedly traditional styles within a modernist narrative, this play provides a critical lens on the notion of tradition and how it is made and deployed and erased as a mode of power.

Abdallah directed his play. It took over a year to produce through its complex rehearsal, rewriting, workshopping, collaborating, and finding funding from state and private sources at Ghana's National Theatre in downtown Accra. It involved numerous collaborations: The National Theatre Players and the National Dance Company, both resident companies at the National Theatre, led the production but it also involved The National Symphony Orchestra, the private Noyam Dance Company, and a number of young and established guest artists.

Ghanaian modern drama is not a staging of "traditional" performance forms. Rather it emerges as avant-garde artists experiment with media and popular theatre in ways common across the continent. Particularly around political independence movements, artists experiment with recombining various popular, religious, colonial, and political forms to aesthetically imagine political transformation. Indeed, contemporary drama contests and challenges what counts as traditional ritual popular entertainment and modernist performance by showing that all theatre is a comment on historical transformation. Theatre, whether understood as traditional or modern, is performative rather than referential. That is to say, it produces the worlds it claims to portray rather than reflecting a ready-made world. African theatre shows how the present is made by telling stories about the past that use bricolage – blended pastiches of images, styles of movement and dance, multiple languages, humor, fantastical costumes, and music. In the process, new futures are called into being.

While Ghanaian drama played a role in creating national consciousness around the independence movement, I would not characterize it as resistance or protest theatre as in South Africa (Kruger 1999) or direct political commentary as in Nigeria (Banham *et al.* 2001). Rather, its primary interpretive frame is a proverbial mode of indirection. Its narration and staging encourage multilevel interpretations. In this sense, Ghanaian theatre is built on established storytelling and musical genres that use metaphor and poetic innuendo to take on grand questions of historical legacy and political legitimacy.

Abdallah's play is a blend of the minimalist and the exaggerated. This duality reflects a long history of traveling theatre groups and improvised staging. Creative designs emphasize exaggerated costuming and props that build on both the majestic and the humorous for emphasis. Ghanaian modern theatre favors simple set designs with static backdrops in contrast to exaggerated costuming that visually reflect characters' key attributes. Actors are given room to move, dance, and play with space. Design elements tend to encourage movement between stage and audience, between the imagined realm of the proscenium stage, the realm of the actors and musicians, and the audience. In this

Figure 20.1 Mohammed ben Abdallah's *Song of the Pharaoh*. (Photo: Rodney Quarcoo.)

sense, dramatic form reminds audiences of the fantastical possibilities of magical storytelling and the multiple worlds that coexist.

Song of the Pharaoh is a musical-dance drama that tells a story of love, incest, and betrayal, and of political and religious transformation in ancient Egypt. The story focuses on the rise and fall of the enlightened Pharaoh Akhenaten who ruled Egypt during a time of growth and artistic flourishing. It also tells the tale of his love for his beautiful wife Nefertiti and the dynastic struggles among the family. As Akhenaten gains power he must navigate family betrayals that will shape his rule and eventually change the history of Egypt. Abdallah the playwright portrays Akhenaten as a leader who encouraged new ways of thinking and creativity in the land of Kemet. He attempts to reform the religious beliefs of his kingdom by promoting the worship of Aten, the sun, the new merciful god. In the process he incurs the wrath of his uncle, the high priest of the ancient god Amon. This sparks a family power struggle that reshapes the religious and political world. Abdallah challenges audiences to reflect on how and why Akhenaten has been portrayed as the first proponent of a monotheistic religion and linked to myths of both Moses and Oedipus (Osman 2002). Akenaten encourages education and builds a new capital called the "City of Light," which he designed himself. During his reign, artisans, craftsmen, and common people were encouraged to think creatively. This dramatic tale is set in ancient times but uses these tales of the Pharaoh to engage existential questions of love and familial conflict, death and memory, and indirectly comment on contemporary political and religious conflict. The play's full subtitle – "Abibigoro: On the life and times of Pharaoh Akhenaten (Who was Moses and also Oedipus)" – points to some of the influences on the production, including Freud's late work *Moses and Monotheism* (1955).

History of Ghanaian avant-garde theatre: from storytelling to National Theatre[1]

Abdallah's work builds on Ghana's National Theatre Movement in the 1950s and 1960s. Ghana became independent from British colonial rule in 1957. Independence hero and first Prime Minister Kwame Nkrumah encouraged the development of new artistic forms as part of the development of both Pan-African and Ghanaian nationalist consciousness. The National Theatre Movement emerged as a state-based project to inspire and develop creative theatre through studying and developing various performance styles rooted in the experience of African peoples. It intertwined various competing views on the significance of theatre in contemporary urban Africa into an emerging performance logic that linked storytelling to European theatrical traditions. National theatre aimed to unite disparate linguistic and "cultural traditions" separated under colonialism within the modern frame of a Pan-African state (Arhin 1993). Theatre practitioners reframed styles of narration, forms of reference and indirection, and modes of address typical of rural performance genres into an overarching style suitable for urban institutional contexts. Juxtaposing music, dance, and costume from Akan, Ewe, Ga, and other Ghanaian peoples was meant to show national and Pan-African unity. In training artists, writing plays, and designing performance spaces, intellectuals, dramatists, choreographers, and actors condensed and combined various genres into a shared aesthetic to be performed for rural and urban workers and citizens.

Efua Sutherland was the architect of the National Theatre Movement. She argued that a modern Ghanaian drama should draw on Anansesem and its eclectic, irreverent offspring, concert party popular theatre (Anyidoho 1996). She wanted "to root a modern theatre programme in the dramatic traditions of this country" (Sutherland, quoted in July 2007: 163). In experimenting with theatrical forms with various drama groups and projects, she aimed to identify the crucial structural elements of storytelling to "condense and heighten [storytelling's] potency and add stagecraft and modern theatrical effects."[2] For Sutherland, Anansesem was "the body of stories and the storytelling performance itself" (Sutherland, quoted in Donkor 2008). Ananse tales are built on a proverb-like structure that provides indirect messages usually through morality tales (Cole 2001: 109; Yankah 1995).

Ananse tales were seen by ethnographers and folklorists as traditional and timeless, removed from history and politics. Rattray's collections of Hausa and Asante folktales were published as simple collections of stories in contrast to his complex ethnographic treatments of Asante religion, art, and politics. His volume *Akan-Ashanti Folk-Tales* (Rattray 1930) completed his comprehensive multivolume survey of Akan people. But rather than address storytelling through its complex staging and eclectic theatrical stylings, Rattray imagined it as a stereotypic token of traditional life that purportedly revealed some truth about Akan people "at their worst no less than at their best" (Rattray 1930). The tales give to "Western peoples a vision" of "the soul of an African people" (Rattray 1930: xii–xiv). In the colonial logic of culture, trickster tales were unlikely to stir up political upheaval or nationalist conflict. Rattray argued that Anansesem were complex allegories meant to be interpreted on multiple levels simultaneously. In contrast, many of his contemporaries subscribed to the idea that characters in folktales are hybrids of animals and humans because the "savage" mind of a "primitive" human cannot "grasp the difference in kind 'between animals and himself'" (Rattray 1930: xii–xiii). Ananse stories relied on *akutia*, or innuendo, to talk metaphorically about someone or use other forms of indirection to address the sacred and the powerful (McCaskie 2002: 81; Yankah 1995). In this way, storytelling provides "a period of licence [sic]" such that they could humorously depict Nyame (God), fetishes, ancestors, sickness, and sex, and even ridicule chiefs (Rattray 1930: x). "The names of animals, and even that of the Sky-god himself, were substituted for the names of real individuals whom it would have been very impolitic to mention" (Rattray 1930: xii). Rattray noted Anansesem's multimedia theatrical elements: "During some story-telling evenings, between the various tales, and often indeed, in the very middle of a story, actors will sometimes enter the circle and give impersonations of various characters in the stories" (Rattray 1930: x).

Colonial educators from the 1930s onwards saw the potential of Ananse stories as a basis for the development of local drama that expressed a national character because it was deemed apolitical. They tried to "make a selection of native themes, so that a large amount of African folk-tales shall be ready for dramatic use" (Anonymous 1934). African teachers were "encouraged to make plays with their pupils and the adults of the village, and the highly educated African should wherever possible see these plays and note the methods and growth" (Anonymous 1934). Interest in Ananse as a potential national icon continued as a British observer in 1954 argued that a National Theatre should be based on Ananse storytelling, drumming, and local festival traditions (Lawrenson 1954). In contrast, African dramatists and intellectuals saw Ananse stories as potential frameworks for national theatre because of the formalist flexibility that would allow for multiple inclusions. Haitian poet Félix Morisseau-Leroy, who became a key figure after independence in working with concert party and other theatre groups in Ghana, also thought "traditional" performances of Ananse stories could be adapted into a modern National Theatre (Morisseau-Leroy 1965).

For Sutherland, Akan storytelling traditions built on Ananse the spider as the main character establish narrative action as always dual: a trickster who is always scheming, and a storyteller who continually breaks the spatio-temporal frame to make metanarrative comments to the audience on his own action and that of others.[3] Storytelling sessions in rural settings are collaborative performances in which drumming, dancing, and acting are woven into the framework of the main story.[4] Performances take place in social spaces like the center of a compound house or under a communal tree. The tale's action is regularly interrupted and taken on playful detours by *mboguo* songs and musical interludes and comic interjections from storytellers and audience members (Rubin 1997: 140). Anansesem embodies a multimedia sensibility. For Sutherland, storytelling predisposes people to pay attention on two levels at once as "people come to storytelling sessions prepared to be hoaxed" (Sutherland 1975: 5). Storytelling events often begin with the storyteller claiming the role of speaker/animator by invoking trickery: "Anansesem ye sisi!" (Ananse storytelling, we are here to trick you!). Others respond, "Sisi me! Sisi me!" (Trick me! Trick me!).[5] Rattray records a variation of this exchange framing many of the tales he collected with "Ye' nse se, 'nse se o," which he translates as "We do not really mean, we do not really mean [that what we are going to say is true]." This performance frame demarcates participation roles and a space of performance at the beginning of a storytelling performance as one of complex double voicing, exaggeration, and hidden intents. By engaging audiences through trickery, Anansesem directs audiences to pay attention and to think reflexively (Yankah 1998: 27).

Ghana's concert party theatre originated in the late nineteenth century with roots in many disparate performance styles, both African and European, including storytelling, Empire Day celebrations, silent films, church Cantata plays, vaudeville, and popular music. The earliest amateur concert groups performed in the coastal cities of Cape Coast, Sekondi, and Accra (Cole 2001: 56). In the late nineteenth and early twentieth century British colonials staged plays and variety shows both for their own entertainment and in schools for Gold Coast youth (Cole 2001). For the British, theatre and pageantry was a crucial part of educating Africans in the manner of European civilization and a technique of rule that created loyalty, as well as a way for them to nostalgically recall England. Annual Empire Day celebrations also featured performances by schoolchildren that introduced them to Western theatrical genres. The films of Al Jolson, Charlie Chaplin, and minstrel and vaudeville shows by white and African American performers were extremely influential in the development of concert party in the early twentieth century in the Gold Coast (Cole 2001; Collins 1994). The plight of Chaplin's tramp character resonated well with the trickster figure Ananse from the Akan storytelling tradition as well as with the political and economic plight of colonial Gold Coasters. African teachers, students, and community members began performing comedic and musical sketches in schools and at social clubs (Cole 2001: 71). These shows began to move out into surrounding communities. Performances took place in churches, schools, social centers, and parade grounds. They recalled European and American variety shows in form using a demarcated stage, a set performance program and consisted of musical comedy and dramatic variety shows. They were initially in English but as they performed for audiences who did not speak English they performed in local languages, particularly Fante and Asante Twi. As the genre evolved it took on more characteristics of African performance genres, most notably Akan Anansesem storytelling. The use of English decreased as they identified more with the uneducated non-English speaking masses in both rural villages and growing urban centers. As Cole states (2001: 55), "concerts served as forums through which Africans expressed an active and irreverent engagement with Western performance conventions – both theatrical convention . . . and the performative conventions of daily life."

Professional concert groups in the 1930s and 1940s developed into performing trios such as The Two Bobs and Their Carolina Girl, the Axim Trio, and Fante Trio. They performed for diverse audiences of both elites and working-class people. The groups no longer solely performed in the coastal cities. Traveling all over the Gold Coast (Cole 2001: 94–5) and into surrounding countries they played in isolated villages as well as major towns. In rural areas theatre troupes would take over a compound house or community building and put out benches and improvised gate and painted backdrops or simple props. Concert party actors used minstrel-show-style costumes and black face, and the physical comedic style of vaudeville drawing on the complex racial imagery of American popular theatre (Cole 2001). Their portrayals of gender reflected the fact that theatre was seen as disreputable and unsuitable for women. In this period one actor would be a lady impersonator and the other two would be the gentlemen. Performances developed a stock formula involving two comedic actors or 'bobs' and a lady impersonator. From the 1950s a transition occurred from trios to larger groups accompanied by a change in the focus of the performances. Early variety-show formats evolved into more full-length dramatic works; musical performances and standup comedy would typically introduce the play and be integrated throughout in order to punctuate the narrative.

By the 1950s guitar-band highlife music became the focus of concert party groups though other types of African and foreign music, including rumba, jazz, and funk especially James Brown, were played. Indeed, most concert groups (with the most notable exception of the Jaguar Jokers – see Collins 1994), such as E. K. Nyame, Nana Ampedu, and Kakaiku, were built around a popular highlife band and their dramas revolved around the group's original songs and the morals that it espoused. In these concert-party morality plays the stories revolved around simple messages about regular people struggling to be successful, find love, escape difficult family situations, etc. As in the tradition of proverbial speaking and trickster storytelling, these moral messages provided a frame for the drama to explore indirectly multiple themes (Yankah 1995). Rural and poor urban audiences also saw concert-party theatre as a way for them to gain access to new music, styles, political debates, and cosmopolitan issues as performers embedded the latest references to the latest issues and trends in their performances (Bame 1985). These traveling troupes continued to improvise and make the most of various spaces by tweaking stagings each night as they moved from neighborhood to village; they worked hard to develop innovative techniques to outdo rival groups and used the latest styles to impress rural and urban poor audiences with a sort of spectacle of modern flashiness (Collins 1994). In towns and cities, groups and bands performed at social centers, nightclubs, and bars. They carried simple painted backdrops that they would drape over the wall of a house or a community center. They used oil lamps or, if there was electricity, simple bulbs (Collins 1994). Costuming often took on comedic elements with actors stuffing their clothes to exaggerate stomachs and backsides. Actors and audiences interacted directly at times and the line demarcating the stage was at times unclear. Later, with more consistent electricity, a standard form of staging evolved in which three microphones were placed in a horizontal row center stage several feet apart from each other, such that all of the dialogue was presented into the microphones by actors facing the audience, which would then be punctuated by action. This further emphasized the storytelling framework of the form.

Concert party and highlife music became forms that were seen to reflect the concerns of local people. It was an alternate public sphere; a space for articulating local concerns. Concert party was seen as rough, disreputable, and slightly dangerous and the purview of marginal groups, the poor and illiterate masses. However, in the post-war period, as anti-colonial agitation and the independence movement grew, concert party traveling theatre groups were crucial to the formation of a national aesthetic (Plageman 2013). They provided a medium for the formation of a national collective imaginary (Barber 1997; Cole 2001). After independence, concert party was central to Ghanaian cultural nationalism and state propaganda; it was appropriated by nationalist projects as a way of accessing and incorporating mass audiences into a new national public.

Efua Sutherland coined the term Anansegro ("Ananse theatre") to refer to how she used the formalist framework of trickster storytelling and its articulation through concert-party theatre to create a modern Ghanaian theatrical style. The Twi word "agro," as in "me di agro" ("I am playing"), has a double meaning, referring both to "joke" and "play." The doubleness of playfulness and playing reflects the sensibility of this theatre. For Sutherland, a modern Ghanaian theatre combines music, dance, drama, and storytelling, bringing "traditional" idioms to the formal stage to inspire new creative works. She worked with rural concert-party actors and storytellers, bringing a select few to Accra to experiment with how to adapt and refine popular techniques to suit the temporal and spatial constraints of a proscenium stage (Donkor 2016).

Anansegro has defined modern Ghanaian drama. Plays often are set in traditional contexts or involve mythic elements. They interweave narrative and scripted dialogue with music and movement. The trickster/storyteller form provides the crucial structure around which the emergent genre of Ghanaian National Theatre revolved. It has set the poetic sensibilities through which subsequent forms of popular music, film, and theatre have been presented. Sutherland abstracted what she saw as the significant elements of these rural performance forms and trained a generation of theatre and media artists in this idiom. The trickster/storyteller provided Sutherland and her students with a form of critical agency. Sometimes the trickster is consciously invoked in formal and informal speech contexts; at other times he is unspoken, embedded in the ways that stage and social actors produce authority and public performance is made meaningful. Stories rely on an oblique style to communicate moral messages, akin to the indirectness of proverbial speech and the broader values placed on metaphor, circuitousness, and indirect references in public rhetoric (Yankah 1995; Obeng 1997; Anyidoho 1983).

Pan-African Total Theatre

Abdallah, as a student of Sutherland, has been the most innovative playwright of his generation in building upon the work of first-generation National Theatre artists. Since the 1970s, Abdallah's work has pushed the boundaries of theatre through formal experimentation, linking Western and African dramatic traditions by developing a theatrical style he has termed *Abibigro*. His plays have been developed through collaborative workshops involving musicians, actors, and dancers that encourage the inclusion of various eclectic styles into the changing script. He coined the term *Abibigro* (African Play) to mean Total African Theatre. He has been critical of making an amoral trickster into a national or pan-African icon. Building on Sutherland's Anansegro he aimed to expand the logic of how to blend and combine multiple African and diasporic styles – music, dance, storytelling, comedy, dramatic narrative, experimental – and also to complicate the role of the storyteller as a figure of the avant-garde rather than one relegated to tradition.

Song of the Pharaoh is the apotheosis of the *Abibigro* style of drama that blends music, dance, and theatre from a variety of African styles around the continent into a proscenium-staged format. The play creates an overarching frame for multiple genres of performance to be embedded, displayed, and contemplated (Bame 1985: 77). Funerals, preaching, fetish worship, and rites of passage are embedded in storytelling, concert party, and avant-garde plays by inserting dances and music, such that audiences can react in appropriate ways, adopting roles they would in relation to these life events. Aside from blending various genres into a stage-play, this also builds on a key principle of the National Theatre Movement that aimed to juxtapose various linguistic-cultural styles such that people from various parts of the country and from around Africa could see "their" familiar dances and music alongside unfamiliar ones and, according to this theory of performance, feel part of a multi-cultural collective in the process.

This play has a large cast of over 60 performers, including, as I mention, collaborations between the National Theatre Players and the National Dance Company, and an opening theme song performed by the National Symphony Orchestra. The artists have a variety of expertise from various traditions of dance, music, and acting. The dance and music draw together new composition and choreography with Yoruba, Akan, and Ga music and dance through a story set in ancient Egypt. A young Accra fashion designer, Patrick, created costumes combining contemporary Afro-chic style and exaggerated ideas of ancient Egyptian imagery with sheer gold lame and well-tailored kente cloth. The script calls for minimal set. Though in the production the director and designers created painted backdrops of an Egyptian phoenix for the opening scenes, and backdrops to designate palace decorations for most of the play. Monumental columns flanked the risers placed upstage to provide three levels for action. Downstage remained bare for dance sequences. On stage left and right during the entire production were three drumming musical groups as musical accompaniment also interacted directly with the storyteller characters.

The staging expands on the trickster storytelling idiom with three main storytellers who move on and off stage as they chat with each other, the musicians, and the audience; as they move levels they travel in time and space. Indeed, key to the script and its staging are the multiple storytellers and the way they fracture the certainties of place. The opening scene is framed by the three main storytellers taken from the Ananse storytelling tradition into the modern city as time travelers who narrate the tale and mediate between the contemporary audiences and characters who populate various worlds. They each represent a different cultural-linguistic tradition indicated by their costume and dance and modes.

After the opening scene of the play in which Pharaoh waits for news about the birth of his child, the three storytellers interrupt the action by chastising everyone for beginning without official sanctioning. This quickly indicates to audiences that the formal terms of performance and speaking are under consideration. They then invoke another observer, Kumo-ji, a wiseman and fetish priest, to come and sanction the event, and call forth yet another outsider, Amenhotep the ancient Egyptian scribe, to take note of the action. Amenhotep plays the role of another storyteller but one who is an ancient Egyptian scribe and historian present in the time of the play's action who is reincarnated back in time from Kumo-ji, the modern fetish priest. This dual character played by one actor is tasked with recording the play for future generations. He moves between realms, talking and joking with various characters and audience members while being unable to communicate with others. The three main storytellers remain present in the time of the audience tasked with the ritual mediation of the space of narration and the movement between the two temporalities.

The dialogue focuses on procedural politics and struggles for power among the family and the melodramatic rise and fall of Akhenaten framed by an eclectic set of generic references. Most significantly, the play's narrative is punctuated by majestic dance sequences, choreographed by Nii Yartey, the National Dance Company's long-time director, that give a temporal frame of stages of life; musical numbers drawn from theatre and music styles from around Africa and Ghana including Yoruba, Akan, and Dagomba dances. The opening of the play marks the birth of the Pharaoh and the wedding of Akhenaten and Nefertiti. In the final scene, Akhenaten leads a procession of followers – made up of the National Dance Company moving in slow-motion, Akan funeral-march choreography – across the desert, downstage right, into exile, through the audience, as his newly built "City of Light" is destroyed upstage. Forty dancers dressed as Akan mourners lead Akhenaten off stage into the desert to the slow dirge played by the musicians perched stage left.

Conclusion

Song of the Pharaoh's production and staging design show key principles of how modern Ghanaian theatre emerges through a complex blend of literary art, oral tradition, ritual and festival forms, political protest, popular music, and community theatre. Over the course of the twentieth century artists blended a set of styles into a Ghanaian modern-theatre style of staging, scenery, directing, and performing. The emergence of a national theatre movement in Ghana, and the debates about the aesthetics and politics of staging modern African theatre that it entailed, demonstrate that African theatre is highly reflexive and entails a blending of various genres, styles, and fluencies. Crucial to the process of blending multiple influences into a modern avant-garde is resignifying what counts as tradition. Indeed, this play displays exaggerated images of the past and cultural scenes, through storytelling figures, dance, and costuming in particular. Images of hyper-tradition are framed to question the naturalization of cultural difference that was at the root of colonial rule as well as independence movements that attempted to invert and revalue colonial projects that denigrated and depoliticized "culture."

This process resonates with other styles around Africa, such as those found in Soyinka, Osofisan, and Ngugi (Banham, Martin, Gibbs, and Osofisan 2014; Kruger 1999). There are of course multiple traditions of theatre in Africa. Many sub-Saharan performance traditions tie together what in European traditions have become separate between music, poetry and eloquent speaking, masking and dance traditions, and storytelling. Perhaps the most striking continuity among various modern African theatres is a tendency towards reflexive recognition of the principles of staging and how performances and contexts are mutually constituted. That is to say, Africa theatre practitioners and audiences tend to have a complex awareness of the process by which the staged is separated from daily life. There is often the sense that artistic practices – that is public activities reflexively understood by participants and audiences to entail an attempt to achieve some sort of affective reaction through sonic, visual, somatic means – are more tied to daily activities in many African contexts when compared with Western European traditions.

African performance forms of all sorts continue to be understood as unchanging timeless aspects of exotic culture. Modern African theatre styles challenge this stereotype in how they reflect on the historicity of performance itself, forcing artists and audiences alike to rethink what counts as culture. As Fanon says, culture emerges in violent struggle over the future of political collectivity and not as a pristine type of dance or music as colonial powers defined it. In this way, popular, modern, and tradition become genres defined in political struggle; transformed, deployed, and framed within experimental performance styles by artists and audiences.

Notes

1 This section is drawn from my book, *Trickster Theatre: The Poetics of Freedom in Urban Africa* (Shipley 2015).
2 Private interview with Mohammed ben Abdallah, October 1999.
3 Private interview with Yaw Asare, February 2000.
4 Interviews and research with Samuel Dawson in Atwia and Accra, February–March 1999.
5 Private correspondence with David Donkor, November 2002. There are different variations on this call-and-response formula. Another is "Ye sisi aara" (We are tricking still, we haven't stopped). *Sisi* can be translated as "hoax," "bully," or "lie."

References

Abdallah, Mohammed ben 1987. *The Trial of Mallam Ilya and Other Plays*. Accra, Ghana: Woeli.

Abdallah, Mohammed ben 1989. *The Fall of Kumbi and Other Plays*. Accra, Ghana: Woeli.

Anonymous 1934. "African Drama and the British Drama League." *Overseas Education* 5 April: 125–28.

Anyidoho, Kofi 1983. "Oral Poetics and Traditions of Verbal Art in Africa." PhD diss., University of Texas, Austin.

Anyidoho, Kofi 1996. "Dr. Efua Sutherland: A Biographical Sketch." *African Literature Association Bulletin* 22 (3): 9–12.

Arhin, Kwame (Ed.) 1993. *The Life and Work of Kwame Nkrumah*. Trenton, NJ: Africa, World Press.

Bame, Kwame N. 1985. *Come To Laugh: African Traditional Theatre in Ghana*. New York: Lilian Barber Press.

Banham, Martin (Ed.) 2004. *A History of Theatre in Africa*. Cambridge: Cambridge University Press.

Banham, Martin, James Gibbs and Femi Osofisan (Eds) 2001. *African Theatre: Playwrights and Politics*. Oxford: James Currey.

Banham, Martin, James Gibbs and Femi Osofisan 2014. *African Theatre 13: Ngugi wa Thiong'o and Wole Soyinka*. Oxford: James Currey.

Barber, Karin 1987. "Popular Arts in Africa." *African Studies Review* 30 (3): 1–78.

Barber, Karin 1997. "Preliminary Notes on Audiences in Africa." *Africa* 67 (3): 347–62.

Barber, Karin 2000. *The Generation of Plays: Yoruba Popular Life in Theatre*. Bloomington: Indiana University Press.

Barber, Karin, John Collins and Alain Ricard 1997. *West African Popular Theatre*. Bloomington: Indiana University Press.

Cole, Catherine M. 2001. *Ghana's Concert Party Theatre*. Bloomington: Indiana University Press.

Collins, John 1994. *Highlife Time*. Accra, Ghana: Anansesem.

Collins, John 2007. "Popular Performance and Culture in Ghana the Past 50 Years." *Ghana Studies* 10: 9–64.

Donkor, David 2008. "Spiders in the City: Trickster and the Politics/Economics of Performance in Ghana's Popular Theatre Revival." PhD diss., Northwestern University, Evanston, IL.

Donkor, David 2016. *Spiders of the Market*. Bloomington: Indiana University Press.

Fanon, Frantz 1963. *The Wretched of the Earth*. New York: Grove Press.

Freud, Sigmund 1955. *Moses and Monotheism*. London: Vintage.

Gibbs, James 2006. *Ghanaian Theatre: A Bibliography of Primary and Secondary Sources – A Work in Progress*. Llangynidr, UK: Nolisment.

Gibbs, James 2009. *Nkyin-Kyin: Essays on the Ghanaian Theatre.* Amsterdam: Rodopi.
Harding, Frances (Ed.) 2002. *The Performance Arts in Africa.* London: Routledge.
Jeyifo, Biodun 2007. "When Anansegoro Begins to Grow: Reading Efua Sutherland Three Decades On." In *The Legacy of Efua Sutherland: Pan-African Cultural Activism*, edited by Anne V. Adams and Esi Sutherland-Addy, 24–37. Banbury, UK: Ayebia Clarke.
July, Robert 2007. "'Here, Then, Is Efua': Sutherland and the Drama Studio." In *The Legacy of Efua Sutherland: Pan-African Cultural Activism*, edited by Anne V. Adams and Esi Sutherland-Addy, 160–64. Banbury, UK: Ayebia Clarke.
Kennedy, Scott 1973. *In Search of African Theatre.* New York: Charles Scribner's Sons.
Kerr, David 1995. *African Popular Theatre.* London: James Currey.
Kruger, Loren 1999. *South African Theatre.* Chicago, IL: University of Chicago Press.
Lawrenson, T. E. 1954. "The Idea of a National Theatre." *Universitas* 1 (3): 6–10.
McCaskie, T. C. 2002. *State and Society in Pre-colonial Asante.* Cambridge: Cambridge University Press.
Morisseau-Leroy, Félix 1965. "The Ghana Theatre Movement." *Ghana Cultural Review* 1(1): 10, 14.
Nketia, J. H. K. 1962. "The Problem of Meaning in African Music." *Ethnomusicology* 6: 1–7.
Nketia, J. H. K. 1982. "Developing Contemporary Idioms Out of Traditional Music." *Studia Musicologica Academiae Scientiarum Hungarica* 24: 81–97.
Obeng, Samuel Gyasi 1997. "Language and Politics: Indirectness in Political Discourse." *Discourse and Society* 8 (1): 49–83.
Odom, Glenn 2015. *Yoruba Performance, Theatre and Politics.* London: Palgrave Macmillan
Osman, Ahmed 2002. *Moses and Akhenaten: The Secret History of Egypt at the Time of the Exodus.* Rochester, VT: Bear & Company.
Osofisan, Femi 2007. "'There's a Lot of Strength in Our People': Efua Sutherland's Last Interview." In *The Legacy of Efua Sutherland: Pan-African Cultural Activism*, edited by Anne V. Adams and Esi Sutherland-Addy, 201–8. Banbury, UK: Ayebia Clarke.
Plageman, Nate 2013. *Highlife Saturday Night: Popular Music and Social Change in Urban Ghana.* Bloomington: Indiana University Press.
Rattray, R. S. 1927. *Religion and Art in Ashanti.* Oxford: Oxford University Press.
Rattray, R. S. 1930. *Akan-Ashanti Folk-Tales.* Oxford: Clarendon.
Rubin, Don (Ed.) 1997. *World Encyclopedia of Contemporary Theatre*, Vol. 3: Africa. London: Routledge.
Shipley, Jesse Weaver 2015. *Trickster Theatre: The Poetics of Freedom in Urban Africa.* Bloomington: Indiana University Press.
Sutherland, Efua 1970. *The Original Bob: The Story of Bob Johnson – Ghana's Ace Comedian.* Accra, Ghana: Anowuo.
Sutherland, Efua 1971. *Foriwa.* Accra-Tema: Ghana Publishing.
Sutherland, Efua 1975. *The Marriage of Anansewa.* London: Longman.
Yankah, Kwesi 1995. *Speaking for the Chief: Okyeame and the Politics of Akan Royal Oratory.* Bloomington: Indiana University Press.
Yankah, Kwesi 1998. *Free Speech in Traditional Society: The Cultural Foundations of Communication in Contemporary Ghana.* Accra: Ghana Universities Press.

21
ENVIRONMENTAL THEATRE
Selected Asian models

Kathy Foley

The advent of purpose-built theatres (especially indoor theatres) in many areas of Asia was relatively rare prior to the eighteenth century, but we do find early open-stage models discussed in India's *Nāṭyaśāstra* (Book of Dance/Drama, 200 BCE–200 CE). Often open-air stages existed in temples for *dasiattam* (ritual temple female dance) in India, in shrines or palaces for *bugaku/gagaku* in Japan from the seventh century or for *nō* from the fourteenth century, or for various forms of Chinese regional *xiqu* (traditional opera) especially during the Ching Dynasty (1644–1911). Outdoor markets, a square in front of a palace, temple grounds, dry riverbeds, and other sites were multi-use spaces where performers presented on the ground or a raised platform. In some cases a whole village/city might, during a festival period, be repurposed to highlight religio-, political-, historical-dramas. In most areas processional performances were popular.

This chapter will only give a few examples, discussing categories of: 1) festival where important geographical sites are transformed, sometimes using multiple venues and lasting many days; 2) localized performances where an ordinary home, aristocratic abode, market square, or temple site may become a temporary performance venue, and/or parades meant to lead audiences to a pre-determined temporary performance space; and 3) processional performances where either the procession itself is the full performance or it leads viewers who join toward sites of stationary performances.

Traditionally, costumes, mask, or makeup might be more central than stage, scenery, or set pieces. However, beginning with the colonial introduction of melodrama and modern drama in the nineteenth to early twentieth centuries, proscenium stages and realistic scenography entered the mix available to local artists. I will deal primarily with traditional genres, but modern global trends using digital arts, lighting, media, and other technologies are now found in urban areas worldwide.

Festivals old and new

Traditional festivals rooted in religion and/or rituals of state continue. An extreme example is the *Ramlila* (Play of Rama) of Ramnagar, India, where at least since 1833 the Maharajas of Benares (Varnasi) have supported a performance for the autumn festival based on the sixteenth-century Tulsidas version of the epic story of King Rama and his kidnapped spouse Sita (see Kapur 2006; Schechner 2010; Swann 1990). Ramnagar's *Ramlia* extends over 30 days with scenes at multiple sites – in fields, on streets, in front of buildings – bringing the landscape to life for this sacred story. Thousands of spectators join behind the actors playing Prince Rama, incarnation of Vishnu, and his monkey army as they stream across the field to conquer the demonic forces of King Ravana. Religion, ritual, and participatory theatre unite spectators and performers who may process a mile together from one scene to the next. Spectators are embedded – physically, emotionally, and spiritually – in this annual ritual spectacle.

Another festival is the Indra Jatra in Nepal, comprised of multiple performances using masks and puppets, processions of figures, ornate carts, and presenting ritual events that take place across Kathmandu and probably originally intended to identify the kings with the Vedic god Indra (Toffin 2011). The Nepali display, believed to originate from the tenth-century King Gunakamadeva, continues, although the monarchy ended in 2008. Ritual and political impulses link with entertaining local viewers and tourists via events where masks of deities dance and the girl incarnation of the goddess Kumari processes on a cart.

Mahayana Buddhist practices encouraged performance festivals in many sites: for example, the mask dances (*cham*) of Tibetan monks has dancers create moving mandalas in Bhutan, Nepal, Sikkim, Tibet, Dharmsala (India), etc. In Bhutan spectators watch *tshechu* (festival in open-air spaces – often temple/fortress courtyards). Elaborately dressed masked monks, representing tantric forces, present scenes while teacher-director monks play clowns (*atsara*) moving among audiences in the carnival atmosphere (see Tashi 2011; Perlman 2002; Nebesky-Wojkowitz 1976; Schrempf 1997). Giant figures and/or 20 m × 30 m paintings (Tibetan *tangka*, Bhutanese *thongdrel*) are displayed including representations of Padmasambhava, the thirteenth-century saint. Viewers participating are prodded toward enlightenment.

Festival performances in North Asia included the Joseon era (1392–1910) *kwalhee* (moot court play) of students at Seoul's Sungkyungkwan, staged outside throughout the educational compound built for this Confucian school. *Kwalhee*, mentioned by 1525, was generally performed after the *ilmu*, a dance done by military and civil officers for Confucian ceremonies. Humor, participatory performance, dancing, and flexible circulation of characters around sites in the all-male school were the *kwalhee* norm.

Current festival events with celebratory energy include the birthday of the Thai monarch which takes place in the royal parade grounds in front of the Thai palace in Bangkok each December. Multiple shows running simultaneously on different open-air stages are presented through the night. Genres range from the traditional *khon* (mask dance) or *likay* (popular theatre), to modern pop bands. A shadow show (*nang yai*) in which dancer-puppeteers manipulate large (1.2 m × 1.5 m) figures in front of a stretched white screen (12 m long × 2 m high) allows them to create shadows when behind and accentuates the dancer *cum* figure when in front. These events are held out of doors at night. Today the remaining troupes perform the story of Rama (*Ramkien*). Such local groups can also present the *hun* (rod puppets) using a puppet booth. Food stalls, souvenirs, and crowds watching for longer or shorter intervals characterize these events, which, like Elizabethan Renaissance fairs, offer diverse attractions.

Festivals often support ideology. Consider mammoth performances in contemporary North Korea where up to 100,000 performers become participant-spectators in nationalist spectacles rehearsed for a year glorifying Kim Il Sung's dynasty (Kim 2010).

Boundaries between performance space and spectator space dissolve and the viewers/citizens/performers are united in *communitas* as political thought fuses with religio-emotionality via precision group acrobatics, dances, and other displays in vast stadiums (see North Korea documentary *Wide Angle – A State of Mind* [Daniel Gordon, dir.], www.youtube.com/watch?v=iR638THdoYk [accessed 9 May 2015]).

Since World War II, performance festivals use world heritage sites as backdrops for large productions that emphasize national heritage or transnational links. For example, the pan-ASEAN (Association of Southeast Asian Nations) Ramayana Festival in the 1960s at Prambanan, Central Java, used an open-air stage at the ninth-century Hindu-Buddhist compound and initiated a neo-traditional style dance drama (*sendratari*) with up to 150 dancers. It continues in a rather mechanical mode catering to Indonesian and international tourists. Angkor Wat temples are also sites for ASEAN arts festivals. The Bali Arts Festival founded in 1978 with hopes of luring tourists has been more successful in attracting local fervor: performances, parades, contests swirl around the Taman Wedhi Budaya Arts Center in Denpasar with whole villages accompanying the teams of dancers, musicians, and actors hoping to win art contests supported by the provincial governments.

Modern festivals such as the Singapore Arts Festival become secular rituals of that global city-state: performances along the Esplanade, in parks or theatres, display Singapore as a cosmopolis attracting world-class artists and generating local displays of modern and traditional arts. The Malay Cultural Center in Singapore may seek to recreate healing rituals like the Kelantanese *main peteri* in which physical or psychological traumas are cured by a patient playing the dance drama role of the wounded hero, Dewa Muda, guided by professional actors from the dance drama *mak yong*. Traditional healing, education, ethnic pride, and museum ethnography meld in such displays.

Intangible cultural heritage in times of political stress may also take to the streets. *Madang nori* (field/open air plays) and traditional farmer's band music grew popular in 1980s South Korea as part of the student pro-democracy movement, especially in Seoul, questioning the military government (Park 2011). Protests such as the 1989 Tiananmen Square Assembly in Beijing or the 2014 78-day Occupy Central Hong Kong with Love and Peace movement included happenings-like performance art. Yellow umbrellas became a sign of the Hong Kong movement. People on the street could make the choice of blindfolding themselves and sitting unmoving to represent the repression (see Kowk's *Stay or Leave?* – Participatory Theatre in Occupy Central of Hong Kong, https://vimeo.com/123375897 [accessed 9 May 2015]). Events as in the cases above are often staged in large city squares, at nationally significant heritage sites or temples, or in capitals.

Localized performances

Another type of performance is in a relatively small local site that may be an out-of-the-way home temple – making it a "center" for the event duration. For example, in Indonesia temporary stages are assembled for a *slametan* (ritual meal) for a wedding or circumcision in front of the host's house for *wayang golek* rod puppetry in Sunda (West Java) or other theatre forms. Some viewers lounge in the house, others watch from chairs set up in front of a temporary stage. General viewers stand on all sides and children may clamber up on the stage platform to sit among the musicians and female singers behind the performers. Selected viewers join onstage to joke with the puppet master and singer during the clown scene, or spontaneously dance in a song sequence. The village is for the night full of vendors and food carts as audiences watch, eat, chat, or gamble. The *pendopo* of a Javanese aristocrat's house is a multipurpose open-air pavilion that can be similarly used for elite performance gatherings of dance or drama events, with invited guests watching under the roofed area and uninvited viewers perhaps getting a glimpse from outside.

Korean local village festivals, traditionally, mixed ritual and comedy. In Korea's Hahoe village (Cho 1988), men presented a ritual comic mask drama believed to date from the twelfth century. Performers go to the shrine of the tutelary deity, then Kakshi (Bride), played by a man, would be carried on the shoulders of another male as "she" solicited donations from villagers, lions (*chuji*) would dance, a comic butcher would sell spectators "ox testicle soup" to boost sexual potency. The "loose" widow tempted the pedantic scholar and clever servants trick their *yangban* (aristocrat) master. Finally, an audience volunteer "married" the Bride in this rough open-air theatrical. Sex, class criticism, and ritual intermix in lively scenes accompanied by percussion, dance, and laughter in outdoor arena staging. Now the Andong International Mask Dance Festival in the Hahoe area allows this old performance to be played side by side with modern and traditional mask traditions from across the globe, educating viewers about national heritage, creating an annual event, and attracting tourist dollars (Saeji 2012).

Likewise, places that might usually be relatively empty village spaces for a night become a bustling performance site. A *kathakali* troupe lit by a coconut oil lamp performs on the ground outside a local temple. In a culminating battle Bhima (a heroic Pandava brother) and Dursasana (his villainous Kurava cousin) carry their fight into the audience, as viewers scurry to avoid the actors' voluminous costumes and ferocious dance-like leaps.

A Balinese temple that is normally empty will spring to life in times of festival. In the *calonarang* dance drama an inner temple court may be used for dressing. Characters may enter through the audience, playing in a rectangle surrounded by viewers as clowns and demons run regularly into the spectator space. The character playing the corpse may be carried in from the adjacent graveyard. The lion-like *barong* figure representing Wisnu (Vishnu) appears from the temple. The widow witch Rangda descends from a small raised house above the audiences' heads and, later, retreats into the graveyard to take off this mask representing the goddess's demonic manifestation. Trance behaviors sometimes allow some audience members to join the *kris* (dagger) performers who enter an altered state as the priest sprinkles holy water, insuring that no one gets hurt as they stab themselves. Staging by the cemetery/death temple adds cognitive impact in this representation of the eternal struggle of salvific preservation against the demonic forces, counter and complementary to one another.

Local events like the Balinese temple celebrations are multi-centric. A puppeteer does a shadow show without a screen, while a *topeng* mask dancer performs across the field, while a singing group chants archaic poetry on a platform, and a priest conducts a ritual using bell, mantra, and mudra (hand gestures). The busy (*ramai*) atmosphere enchants humans who wander between and confounds demons; it delivers enjoyment for ancestors, the living, place spirits, and gods. The demonic, comic, and iconic share time and space with viewers allowing them to ascend toward the extra-daily – the refined divine. In each of the above instances, the arts come to an out-of-the-way locale making it a "center" for a time. By means of performance the extramundane enters the here and now.

Processions

Processional performances are part of many Asian cultures. Parades were sometimes used as a strategy of gathering audience for a culminating show as, for example, with the Korean *namsadang nori* (male vagabond theatre), where farmer's band (*pungmul*) music and actors' costumes could draw a local audience toward an open field in which tight-rope walking, plate spinning, puppetry, acrobatics, and mask dance materials waited. In the Philippines, Good Friday brings recreations of Jesus carrying his cross as viewers follow to the knoll where Christ and the two thieves are crucified (Peterson 2007).

In other instances the parade was the entire event and showed figures throughout the wider landscape; for example, a young man who gained top marks in a Confucian imperial exam (*jinshi*), prior to its abolition in China in 1905, moved through the district accompanied by musicians and flag bearers to be applauded everywhere. In Pakistan as a riderless horse and/or other images, representing the martyred Iman Hussein and members of his party killed at Karbala plain in 680 CE/61 AH, might process through the city during the Muharram commemoration accompanied by flag-ellants from the Shia community mourning the defeat of this grandson of the Prophet. Japanese festival floats bearing manipulated or mechanical puppets, dancers, and musicians appear for the Gion Festival in Kyoto each 17 July – with carts weighing up to 10 tons and standing 20 meters high.

In some areas the performances can take place in water with the viewers watching from the shore. For example, the dance of Thai royal ladies might be seen by lower classes only as they performed on royal barges parading along the river. Traditional Vietnamese water puppets could be viewed from the perimeter of pools and the show often contained a procession that ran from the staging house, around a track hidden beneath the surface, and looped back into the house: a miniature replication of top scholar parades.

Dancing lions, dragons, and demons are widely-seen parade figures. Martial arts groups dance lions through business districts in China and Sinified areas of Southeast Asia, performing in front of shops where "greens" have been hung – the dancers balance on a partner's shoulders or use other means to get the reward in this fortune-bringing dance. Performances are traditionally associated with New Year exorcisms. The lion may process with other characters. For example, the Buddhist *gigaku* procession, a now extinct Japanese mask genre as documented in the thirteenth century, included a lion, attendant, a Chinese woman (Gojo), Baroman (Brahman), Karora (Garuda bird), and so on. The genre declined but lion dances or processions still abound in Japan, Okinawa, Korea, China, Indonesia, Laos, Singapore, Malaysia, and Vietnam.

Other parade genres may move the spectators as a group from one site to the next where entertainments are presented (rather like an Elizabethan royal progression). An example was the parade of the Chinese envoys sent to the Seoul court during the Joseon Dynasty: the Chinese would be entertained by a civil servant who borrowed from the *namsadang nori* repertoire, dances of courtesans, etc. The parade of impressive Chinese officials would formally arrive at a stopping point such as Bongsan in the north and then local entertainers presented as these officials rested. Next the impressive diplomatic parade moved down the road to the following site.

Processional performances in Indonesia include forms like *barongan* in which newly circumcised boys ride throughout the village atop dragons and other animal figures.

Figure 21.1 Processions in Bali may include the leonine Barong who brings blessings, and his witch-like opponents Rangda and her followers who flank the lion in this photo taken at the Bali Arts Festival. (Photo: Kathy Foley.)

In *singa-singaan* (lion) in Subang, West Java, the boys ride a lion figure carried/danced by four men using moves from martial arts dance. In *reog ponorogo* in Central Java a strong man wears a mask of a *singa-barong* (lion-beast) – said to be part peacock, part lion, part tiger. A boy in times past would mount a seat atop the striking 50 kg mask. Other masked characters drawn from the Panji (prince of East Java) story present simple scenes and dance as the group moves through the village or performs at a set site. There are also Indonesian parades of giant figures (*ogoh-ogoh* in Bali, *ondel-ondel* in Jakarta), which are paraded to music and dance often to celebrate the New Year or harvest.

Most parade forms include music and dance. Audience members in many genres are encouraged to join; consider, for example, the Ati-Atihan Festival of Kalibo, the Philippines, where only the costumes seem to distinguish the paraders from the myriads who join in an event that seems to get most of the city dancing.

Conclusion

Even where Asians perform on permanent stages, the space and audience seating were not traditionally divided in the proscenium arrangement. Chinese opera, *xiqu*, usually was performed in teahouses rather than theatres where seats all faced the stage. Japanese *kabuki* had the convention of the *hanamichi* (flower path) that extended though the audience. In the eighteenth century, *kabuki* theatres sometimes had two parallel *hanamichi*s with a crossover between them running behind the viewers. Chases or dances could go around the spectators, providing a 360-degree viewing experience. Eating while viewing was normal in most forms. While modern theatres for spoken drama have largely adopted proscenium arrangement, lighting effects, painted or projected scenery, set pieces, curtains, silent audiences, and other conventions of European theatre, most traditional forms had and have a porous stage – where audience and performers can co-penetrate. In these forms stage and world are not separate, but one.

References

Cho, Oh-Kon 1988. *Traditional Korean Theatre*. Fremont, CA: Asian Humanities Press.

Kapur, Anuradha 2006. *Actors, Pilgrims, Kings and Gods: The Ramlila of Ramnagar*. New Delhi: Seagull.

Kim, Suk-Young 2010. *Ilusive Utopia: Theater, Film, and Everyday Performance in North Korea*. Ann Arbor: University of Michigan.

Kwok, Freya 2015. "'Stay or Leave?' – Participatory Theatre in Occupy Central of Hong Kong." Available online at: https://vimeo.com/123375897 (accessed 9 May 2015).

Masks of Korea 1981. Introduction by Du-Hyun Lee. Seoul: Pioneer Press.

Nebesky-Wojkowitz, Rene de 1976. *Tibetan Ritual Dances*. The Hague: Mouton.

Park, Jungman 2011. "Remapping the Korean Theatre Tradition: A Case Study of *Kwalhee*, a Theatricality of the Confucian Students in the Chosun Dynasty." *Asian Theatre Journal* 28, No 2: 549–68.

Perlman, Ellen 2002. *Tibetan Sacred Dance: A Journey into the Religious and Folk Traditions*. Rochester, VT: Inner Traditions.

Peterson, William 2007. "Holy Week in the 'Heart of the Philippines': Spirituality, Theatre, and Community in Marinduque's Moriones Festival." *Asian Theatre Journal* 24 (2): 309–37.

Peterson, William 2011. "The Ati-atihan Festival: Dancing with the Santo Niño at the 'Filipino Mardi Gras.'" *Asian Theatre Journal* 28 (2): 505–28.

Saeji, CedarBough 2012. *Transmission and Performance Memory, Heritage, and Authenticity in Korean Mask Dance Dramas*, PhD dissertation, UCLA. Available online at: https://escholarship.org/uc/item/3zw204qf#page-1 (accessed 10 May 2015).

Schechner, Richard 2010. "Ramlila of Ramnagar." In *Between Theatre and Anthropology*, 151–212. Philadelphia: University of Pennsylvania.

Schrempf, Mona 1997. "From 'Devil Dance' to 'World Healing': Some Representations, Perceptions, and Innovations of Contemporary Tibetan Ritual Dances." In *Tibetan Culture in the Diaspora*, edited by F. J. Korom, 91–102. Vienna: Österrichishen Akademie der Wissenschaften.

Swann, Darius 1990. "Ramlila." In *Indian Theatre: Traditions of Performance*, edited by Farley Richmond, Darius L. Swan and Phillip B. Zarrilli, 215–336. Honolulu: Hawaii University Press.

Toffin, Gérard 2011. *La Fête Spectacle: Théâtre et Rite au Népal*. Paris: Édition de la Mason de Sciences de l'Homme.

Tashi, Khenpo Phuntsok 2011. *Invoking Happiness: Guide to the Sacred Festivals of Bhutan and Gross National Happiness*. Thimphu, Bhutan.

22
THE CITY AS THEATRE[1]

Marvin Carlson

When we begin to consider the use of the city as theatre we soon find that, around the world and throughout recorded history, a major part of human performance, even of a distinctly theatrical nature, has taken place not in theatre buildings but in the streets and hubs of cities. Some of our earliest records of cultural performance, from ancient Egypt and Babylon, involve processional movements of celebrants along urban paths to and from a central place of worship, a religious hub. In the early Christian era Jerusalem served as the model city for the Christian world, and Jerusalem, with its many sites associated with the life of Christ and especially with the passion week, served as a major urban configuration that inspired a theatricalization of its spaces. Egeria's diary of her pilgrimage as early as 381 speaks of ceremonies held "on the same day in the very place" as the Upper Room or the Mount of Olives (Egeria 1970: 127). Some ceremonies came very close to dramatic representation, such as the bishop reading the news of the resurrection to the congregation assembled before the very tomb where, legend reported, these words were spoken by the angel to the three Marys, or the Jerusalem Palm Sunday procession, where pilgrims and townspeople welcomed the bishop into the city with songs and the waving of palm fronds.

Pilgrims to the Holy Land in the twelfth and thirteenth centuries speak of a "Via Sacra," a pathway of shrines along which pilgrims were conducted. By the fourteenth or fifteenth century, this pathway had become the modern "Via Dolorosa," tying together the specific performative sites, called the stations of the cross, each marking a moment in Christ's journey from his sentencing by Pilate in the city center to his crucifixion and burial on the city's edge. By following these stations, pilgrims could follow a performative map of this final journey, not only in Jerusalem itself but in countless replicas of Jerusalem recreated in cities and churches throughout the Christian world.

Although the following of the Via Dolorosa and the stations of the cross are among the most familiar urban processional performance traditions in the Western world, the medieval and early renaissance periods saw a flowering of many types of processional performance, both religious and secular, during a period when formal theatrical structures, in the classic or modern sense, were not really a part of the urban configuration. The great religious festivals made the entire medieval city a conscious performative space. Familiar public spaces were theatricalized into scenic backgrounds, as when the fifteenth-century Viennese passion play began in the town marketplace, suggesting the secular and social connotations of that area, and then followed the actor playing Christ as he bore the cross from that center through the winding streets to the distant cemetery where the crucifixion was represented. Clearly Vienna served for this performance as a theatricalized representative of Jerusalem (Konigson 1974: 95).

Although the Vienna play moved from the center of the city to its edge, more common were religious processions that moved from city gates to the center, to either the cathedral with its facing square or the city marketplace. These large spaces, the hubs of the medieval city, were often the only significant open spaces within the city, and so, not surprisingly, were favored locations for both festival performances and religious dramas. Stage plans from the 1583 passion play in Lucerne show how the major market space was converted into a religious landscape, with the ornate town hall, the most impressive building on the square, being designated as heaven (see Liebing 1869).

A similar theatricalization of urban spaces during the middle ages and early renaissance was offered by the royal entries, a major display of princely power at a time when the monarchy was much occupied with the symbolic display of this power over the hitherto often essentially independent cities. Although these secular entries, like the religious festivals, utilized urban hubs for their most lavish displays, and sometimes for the culmination of elaborate processions, it was the processions that were favored. There is a fascinating interaction between the development of the late renaissance and the baroque theatre, the changing concept of the city during this time, and the royal displays performed in the evolving urban spaces. Almost from the beginning, royal entries imposed a theatrical and performative consciousness on the cities where they occurred. Particularly striking was the entry of Henri II into Lyons in 1548, when huge screens were set up covering the entrance to medieval streets painted with trompe d'oeil perspective in the manner of contemporary stage settings so as to make them appear to be grand open boulevards (see Guigué 1927). Such displays in fact anticipated the development of the baroque city, in which these grand boulevards and striking perspectives became the defining feature.

Although performative activity of this sort never disappeared, a much more conscious and self-conscious use of the city itself as a performance space began to gain new popularity about a century ago, and has constantly developed and expanded since that time to become one of the most significant contemporary performance phenomena. A key year in the development of this modern use of the theatricalized city was 1920, which saw two of the most famous and influential urban spectacles of the century, both providing inspiration for countless subsequent experiments. On 22 August the German director Max Reinhardt, inspired by the medieval practice of presenting religious plays on the steps and in the square before a cathedral, utilized the Salzburg cathedral square for this purpose. However, he extended the imaginary world represented by his production to the entire city in the famous "summoning of Everyman" sequence that opened the production. A cry went up from one of the cathedral towers of "Everyman!" and it was repeated and was taken up by actors stationed in various locations near the square. Then the cathedral bells began to toll, and were echoed by bells across the city, so that, aurally if not spatially, the entire city of Salzburg was utilized (Styan 1982: 89).

In November of this same year, Nikolai Evreinov created an even more ambitious production in *The Storming of the Winter Palace*, in St. Petersburg, then called Petrograd. The production re-created, in highly romanticized form, that key event in the Russian Revolution just three years before. The spectacle was staged in the huge square before the palace, involved some 2,500 performers with an audience of over 100,000 spectators. Among the sequences was an armed battle within and outside the palace, a car chase through the spectators, maneuvers of tanks, and even a cannon fired from the nearby battleship *Aurora*, also involved in the original action (Leach 1994: 46–7).

Both of these famous modern urban spectacles, while located in large public spaces outside theatres and implying an involvement with much of the surrounding city, treated their audiences as if still in a theatre, seated in rows facing the main performance area. This arrangement was also used by Reinhardt in 1934, for one of his most famous productions, Shakespeare's *The Merchant of Venice*, for which he utilized an actual public square in Venice, allowing him to bring in such elements as real gondolas in real canals (Carlson 1989: 28). Performances directly related to the city like these of Reinhardt and Evreinov remained rare and fairly isolated until later in the century when theatre performed in spaces outside traditional theatre structures became a truly significant part of the art. Peter Brook shared and even surpassed Reinhardt's interest in non-theatrical spaces. His 1968 book and manifesto, *The Empty Space*, begins with the often quoted sentence: "I can take any empty space and call it a bare stage" (Brook 1968: 1). Brook proposes calling a theatre into existence not by the construction of a particular kind of building, but simply by claiming the space for that use. Among Brook's most famous productions was a monumental open-air spectacle, *Orghast*, set among the ruins of the Persian city of Persepolis in 1971. In Moscow, Russia's leading experimental director Yury Lyubimov began during the 1960s to "theatricalize" the real world contiguous to his theatre, the Taganka. As early as his second production, *Ten Days that Shook the World*, in 1965, he began the performance in the streets outside the theatre, with loudspeakers playing revolutionary songs and ushers dressed as Red Guards who guided spectators to the theatre and punched their tickets with their bayonets (Beumers 1997: 21).

Probably the most widely used term today in English for such work is site-specific, inspired by the growing use of this term in the art world to indicate works of art inseparable from their physical surroundings. During the 1970s the Netherlands became a major European center for work of this sort, and Dutch companies like Dogtroep and Tender provided models for similar work throughout Europe and America. Such companies were specifically dedicated to presenting performance in spaces not designed for theatre – in the street, in corridors, stairwells, squares, on walls, and in windows. Today this work is perhaps most spectacularly carried on in the work of Royal de Luxe, which has displayed its signature gigantic puppets in the streets of a number of major European cities. By the 1980s, so-called site-specific performance had become an important part of the experimental theatre scene in Britain and America. Most theatre scholars now consider the peak of this movement in the United States came from the mid-1980s to the mid-1990s when America's leading site-specific company, En Garde Arts, directed by Anne Hamburger, was operating in New York.

Although the greater part of this work has taken place in urban environments, as did all of the En Garde Arts projects, the majority of such work, especially before 2000, did not engage the city as such, but more often took place within particular buildings of historical, architectural, or spatial interest. Occasionally, however, such productions would expand to theatricalize larger sections of the city, through which the audience was encouraged to move, either guided or more improvisationally. An early and influential such production in New York was one of the last and most ambitious creations of

En Garde arts, created by the innovative Iranian-American experimental director, Reza Abdoh, in 1990. This production, *Father Was a Peculiar Man*, based on Dostoevsky's *Brothers Karamazov*, was staged in a several-square-block area of the New York meatpacking district, a rather grim and forbidding area whose narrow cobbled streets somewhat suggested a nineteenth-century city. Audiences were partly guided but also partly free to wander through this area, where they witnessed some obviously staged scenes, but also many parts of the streetscape that may or may not have been part of the production. Although the area was quieter in the evening than during the day, the life of the city continued. Clearly, the dark blue limousine with American flags and John and Jacqueline Kennedy look-alikes in the rear was part of the show, but what about the line of cars and taxis following? Were they a cortege or just backed up traffic? What about people looking out of windows, or passed in the street? Were they actors, fellow spectators, or just citizens going about their own business?

The concept of utilizing the city as theatre moved from an obscure corner of Manhattan to its very heart in 2003 with *The Angel Project*, created by British director Deborah Warner. The experience started several miles from the city center in a park at the end of Roosevelt Island, a small strip of land in New York's East River. Here audience members received instructions that sent them by public transportation to the Times Square area, the central Manhattan district where most of the other eight stops were located, stops that ranged from an abandoned pornographic theatre to the elegant upper floors of the Chrysler building. The mixture of real life and staged performance, so clear in *Father Was a Peculiar Man*, was much in evidence here as well. As one reviewer observed:

> Walking around the city as part of the project opens up the possibility that anyone on the street might be an 'angel.' How about the homeless man in front of the Peep-o-rama, with his 'Tell Me Off for $2' sign? Or the well-scrubbed teens in matching red 'Bear His Name' T-shirts who swarm out of the 42 St. subway station? Warner leaves everything open, which helps you see the familiar with new eyes.'
>
> *(criticbigot.com 2010)*

Subsequent productions in Europe and the United States have similarly taken audiences to a variety of urban locations accessed by tram or subway, but rather more common has been the use of special buses, which operate much in the manner of conventional tour buses, with loudspeaker system and a performer "guide." The 2009 production, *The Provenance of Beauty*, created by the Foundry Theatre of New York, was essentially a guided bus tour of the South Bronx, a part of New York rarely visited by tourists and the symbol of urban decay in the 1970s, but since given new life by urban renewal and a strong alternative art scene, closely associated with such urban expressions as rap, hip-hop and graffiti art. As the bus toured this complex, much layered, and rapidly changing district, the "guide" pointed out places and even passing individuals as part of a poetic narrative. As with much such performance, the distinction between "real" and "staged" elements of the passing scene was deliberately left unclear. All became part of the passing show.

Walking, however, the traditional mode of urban involvement, clearly remains the dominant way of experiencing the city as theatre, as may be seen in many of the productions of Rimini Protokoll, founded in Berlin in 1999 and today one of the European groups best known for mixing theatrical material with elements of reality. Probably the most well-known of its productions was the 2005 *Call Cutta.* Here audience members reported to Hebbel-Theater, a center for experimental work in Berlin, where they were given a mobile phone and connected with an operator in a call-center tower in another major city, but one on the opposite side of the globe: Calcutta, India. The Indian operator then gave directions to the audience member, taking him or her on an individual rambling tour through a generally unfamiliar and somewhat desolate section of the nearby Kreuzberg district. The interaction was complex, since the operator had never been in Germany but relied on maps and written instructions when guiding the spectator along the path. For *50 Aktenkilometer*, in Berlin in 2011, based on the history and activities of the Stasi, the notorious secret police of East Germany, audience members created their own experience within a section of the city. Starting from the Lookout Tower in Alexanderplatz and aided by headphones, a cellphone with an electronic map to show their location, and a physical map showing the locations of a hundred "bubbles" where they could access recorded data from the Stasi files, they could wander and create their own trajectory.

Rimini Protokoll has now taken its utilization of the city as theatre around the globe. In 2015 it offered a headphone-guided theatricalization, taking audience members from Brooklyn to Manhattan in *Remote New York*, a production that had, before that time, been similarly staged in 17 other major cities around the world, in Europe, Asia, and South America. Although certain sequences may be staged, the very fact that a living city is accepted as the co-creator of such works demands an openness to indeterminacy. The experience is thus centered not upon the development of a traditional narrative, but on an open-ended experience.

Note

1 This chapter first appeared, in somewhat different form, as "Streets, Squares and Strollers: The City as Performative Space," *Parabasis*, Journal of the Department of Theatre Studies, University of Athens, 12 (1) 2014.

References

Beumers, Birgit 1997. *Yury Lyubimov at the Taganka Theatre, 1964–1994*. Amsterdam: Harwood Academic Publishers.

Brook, Peter 1968. *The Empty Space*. New York: Atheneum.

Carlson, Marvin 1989. *Places of Performance*. Ithaca, NY: Cornell University Press.

Criticbigot.com, posted 16 November 2010.

Egeria 1970. *Diary of a Pilgrimage*, translated by George E. Gingras. New York: Newman Press.

Guigué, G. (Ed.) 1927. *La Magnificence de la Superbe et Triumphante Entrée . . . .* Lyons: Société des Bibliophiles Lyonnais.

Konigson, Elie 1974. *L'espace théâtrale medieval*. Paris: CNRS.

Leach, Robert 1994. *Revolutionary Theatre*. London: Routledge.

Leibing, Franz 1869. *Die Inszenierung des zweitätigen luzernes Österspiels*. Elberfeld: Friderichs.

Styan, J. L. 1982. *Max Reinhardt*. Cambridge: Cambridge University Press.

23
SITE-SPECIFIC THEATRE

Mike Pearson

In the late 1980s and early 1990s, Welsh theatre company Brith Gof created a number of site-specific performances in disused, often semi–derelict, industrial buildings and large public spaces: car factory, ice rink, railway terminus, iron foundry and empty swimming pool (see Pearson 2010: 68–72). Designer Cliff McLucas supposed that the particular properties of such sites – their extent and height, ground-plan, layout of integral features and distribution of vernacular details – might offer unique opportunities for scenic design: to create installations at the scale of the building itself, employing materials unusual in the auditorium but commonplace at such locations, and to construct another architecture within the existing architecture (see Pearson 2010: 112–15). In *Gododdin* (1988) (see Pearson and Shanks 2001: 102–8), McLucas employed hundreds of tons of sand and dozens of trees and wrecked cars in a formal setting of circles, avenues and cones, that was gradually flooded with thousands of liters of water during the performance; in *PAX* (1990) (see Pearson 2010: 68–70), he built a section of a Gothic cathedral from metal scaffolding. This overlay and interpenetration of the found (the site) and the fabricated (the production) he eventually characterized as the co-existence of host (the extant building with its fixtures, fittings, ambiance; that which pre–exists the work; all that is at site) and the ghost (that which is temporarily brought to and emplaced at site; that which remains spectral, transparent). Significantly, host and ghost may have quite different origins or natures. Their relationship may be frictional or anachronistic – in *Gododdin* a sixth-century battle elegy was staged in a twentieth-century car factory – and they might effectively ignore each other's presence. They are not necessarily congruent – they need not inevitably fit easily together as complementary functions of a particular narrative theme – though both are always apparent and cognitively active for an audience: ancient military defeat and contemporary industrial decline resonate against one another. Site itself becomes an agency of performative meaning, rather than simply acting as a convenient, neutral space for spectacular exposition. It is not converted into a thermostatically controlled auditorium, and the prevailing environmental conditions of host and those manufactured within ghost impact upon performers and audience alike.

McLucas's preliminary drawings for these works include plan, section *and* axonometric projection (see Pearson 2010: 105): a looking down into from an oblique perspective available only to the designer. He regards performance as three-dimensional in the placement of components, including its audience, any one of which may, in any one moment, constitute a dramatic carrier; anything may come into perceptual or dramatic play including phenomena beyond either containment or the control of the work, such as the site's ambient qualities. In an unpublished company document, he writes:

> Site-specific performances that fold together place, performance and public have no natural edges or frame to hold their identity discrete, no stage backdrop against which their outlines might be thrown into crisp focus and they do not rely on containment for their identity and integrity. They have the characteristics of the field rather than the theatre 'object'.

At ground level, this is scenography as landscape: it is as large as the room, reaching the walls, though often askew, on a different orientation to host building; and performers and audience are co-present as occupants of the conjoined environment.

The non-pristine nature of such sites, their lack of seemliness and their specialist characteristics might allow the use of materials, resources and techniques unusual, undesirable or dangerous in creating scenographies and conjuring dramatic situations and events unseen in the cloistered world of the auditorium: quantities of water and electricity; objects, elements and phenomena not conventionally used – fire, smoke, machinery, animals, wind, rain, snow, excessive light; or that which is of industrial production itself, such as machinery and equipment.

Site-specific performance here might allow the suspension and transgression of the prescribed practices and bye-laws of theatre, including disturbances of the spatial partition of performance and audience. Equally, it might necessitate the employment of non-theatrical techniques to address and counter the material realities of the site – its specificities – such as its scale, the nature of its surfaces, the distribution of its in-built features. There is little attempt at scenic illusion, at the substitution of theatrical properties and devices constructed in replica forms; rather, fragments of the real world – real things – are selected, enter into and are reconfigured in unfamiliar juxtapositions of like and unlike, in assemblages unique to each production, albeit within the selective metonym of performance.

There are here two contiguous domains. Within the built scenography it may be possible to conspire live climatic effects, such as wind generated from appropriated extractor fans; but the extant conditions within or of the site will be inescapable. National Theatre Wales's *The Persians* (2010) (see Pearson 2012: 69–83) was staged in a village built by the British Army to rehearse urban warfare on the military ranges in mid-Wales, principally in an open-fronted three-story house faced by a small grandstand. To provide protection from the elements, audience members were issued with protective ponchos. On some evenings their view included distant mountains, rainbows, vivid crimson sunsets, a large moon; on others, they huddled in driving rain. Weather became an active and affective component of dramaturgy and of reception – most strikingly in scenes riven by diagonals of beating rain, or part-obscured by intervening moorland mist.

For performers, host and ghost are jointly *affective*: the materialities and climate of site-specific performance present a shifting oscillation of *ergonomic challenge* and *affordance*. We might regard site and scenography as the workplace of the performer: whatever the degree of verisimilitude of setting and objects – whether they are made of cardboard or of steel – it provides the physical milieu within which the performer goes to work. Although the dramatic theme may be fictional, the place is never so: performers do not experience it metaphorically. It may indeed be that the constructed environment of performance is active and the ecology of this special world – of surface, illumination and temperature – is much better or much worse perhaps than in everyday life, changing from moment to moment, necessitating the substitution of patterns of engagement – including real tasks – for stage illusion and theatrical gesture. Beyond questions of representation, the performer's encounter with scenography is *phenomenological.*

Here, the nature of the contracts – body to scene, body to object, body to body – and the physical and emotional experiences they conspire may be extra-ordinary. The performer's methods of coping as an expressive entity may include those *planned*, those *improvised* and those *informed* by previous experience. Environmental conditions may compromise or restrict signaling abilities and capacities – through increases in hazard, stress, demand, overload; they may cause duress through increasing durations and limiting the potential to adjust posture and reach. Performance might be a difficult place to work. In the dynamic relationship between the action and the specific circumstances of its enactment, we watch the performer's methods and organization of effort, her flexibility of response, and her use of tools, both designed and appropriated. We appreciate her endurance, and her relentless application to the task. Above all, we are aware that we are witnessing real responses, the *symptoms* of her engagement with the milieu. Performance then exists as a chain of corporeal engagements and reengagements: its substance may be comprised, at least in part, by the performer dealing with the realities of existing in this workplace, this landscape, this environment, this climate. Here between body and material environment, dramatic conflict is forged, in the clash between energetic activities and intractable materials.

But all here need not be problematic. German dramatist Bertolt Brecht describes how actress Helene Weigel selected her properties "for age, function and beauty" (Brecht 1987: 427–8); a found object may be chosen for intrinsic qualities – its dimensions, appearance, patina, texture or feel. But it may also be included for its ergonomic potential: its fit, balance, weight and potential dynamism in manipulation – or for the converse – "what we perceive when we look at objects are their affordances, not their qualities" (Gibson 1979: 134). The object in performance is always double: within the narrative, it may represent status or act as a token of exchange; but it is also one of the "tools of the trade" of the performer – it allows her to go to work. Through rehearsal, it is invested with value; it becomes a companion, part-embodying the action that is to be achieved.

Host and ghost may provide – in James Gibson's formulation – unique *affordances*: "[t]he medium, substances, surfaces, objects, places and other animals have affordances for a given animal. They offer benefit or injury, life or death" (Gibson 1979: 143); and "[t]he *affordances* of the environment are what it *offers* the animal, what it provides or furnishes, either for good or ill" (Gibson 1979: 127). Surfaces provide vertical support: they are also "climb-on-able or fall-off-able or get underneath-able relative to the animal" (Gibson 1979: 128); and "[s]urfaces afford posture, locomotion, collision, manipulation, and in general behavior" (Gibson 1979: 137). However their array may equally provide obstacles and create barriers to movement, upsetting equilibrium and influencing corporeal engagement. In performative encounters with different layouts, we witness a rich and complex set of interactions in which the fundamentals are the substances, the medium and the surfaces: in positing constraints and challenges that afford different behaviors, require adjusted practices and lead to demonstrations of unexpected or extra-daily virtuosity.

For audiences too, site and scenography may afford unique theatrical experiences, the outcome of scale, of three-dimensionality, of atmosphere, of altered viewpoint. The co-presence of performers and audience in adverse conditions may even enhance that sense of being in it together, inescapably: of art versus the elements.

Performers come to know the terrain of performance at the most intimate of scales – in close-up – as surface and slope and angle and facade, as topographic detail, as the best place to achieve this or that, as the places where danger lurks.

For the late geographer Denis Cosgrove, landscape gathers together "nature, culture and imagination within a spatial manifold" (Cosgrove 2004: 69). It has no pre-existing form that is then inscribed with human activity: both environment and its inhabitation are co-emergent, continuously brought into being, together. There is no privilege of origin: a place owes its character not only to the experiences it affords – as sights, sounds, etc. – but also to what is done there – as social and cultural practices. Landscape as "a dimension of existence, collectively produced, lived and maintained"; "to apply the term *landscape* to their surroundings seems inappropriate to those who occupy and work in a place as insiders . . . For the insider there is no clear separation of self from scene, subject from object" (Cosgrove 1984: 19).

For anthropologist Tim Ingold, landscape is the "familiar domain of our dwelling"; "the world as it is known to those who dwell there," "And through living in it, the landscape becomes part of us, just as we are part of it" (Ingold 2000: 191). The theme in both Cosgrove and Ingold is of landscape as inhabited lifeworld, an enfolding of people and environment, of natural and cultural phenomena, of features and practices. Inhabitants know their environs not as spectators but as participants. In emphasizing human activity, Ingold characterizes landscape as *taskscape*. A *task* is "a constitutive act of dwelling" – a practical operation carried out by a skilled agent in an environment, that only gets meaning from its position within an array of related activities. Moving between familiar places – what Ingold calls *wayfinding*, feeling one's way "*through* a world that is itself in motion, continually coming into being through the combined action of human and non-human agencies" (Ingold 2000: 155) – more closely resembles story-telling than map-using, as one situates one's position within the context of journeys previously made and tasks achieved by oneself and others; it is this intimate perception of a familiar landscape "that distinguishes the countryman from the stranger" (Ingold 2000: 219).

For French theorist Jean-Luc Nancy, a countryman is someone whose occupation is the country and the land. He occupies it and takes care of it, and he is occupied with it: that is, he takes it in hand and is taken up by it. He works *on*, *at*, *in the land*. It is a matter of *holding* – I hold it, it holds me, it holds together (see Nancy 2005: 53). Geographer Yi-Fu Tuan suggests that *topophilia* for those who work "on the land" is the result of "physical intimacy, of material dependence and the fact that the land is a repository of memory and sustains hope" (Tuan 1974: 97). For Tuan, the peasant's attachment to land is profound. The relationship here is as much haptic as optic: in the need to win a living, nature – landscape – enters their bodies. "We were created by the world we live in" (Gibson 1979: 130).

A proposition: to regard the scenography of site-specific performance as landscape rather than architecture, as worked ground, as co-emergent with performance – its performers as Ingold's dwellers, as knowledgeable inhabitants of performance as taskscape.

It is their activities that bring the performance landscape into being and *vice versa*: performers as Cosgrove's insiders – those who don't need a map to get around, as Nancy's countrymen, as Tuan's peasants attuned to all the topographical and climatic features, for good or ill, of this landscape. The scenography, post-performance, bearing traces in its marking of the effects of occupancy; and the bodies of performers, in their bruises and scars, showing the impacts of living in such landscapes.

Performance existing for performers as a series of places to be, as a pattern of tasks to be undertaken; rehearsal involving processes of acclimatization and habituation, of developing ways of going on, with acute attention to the business of dwelling; choreography imagined as way-finding – in a terrain of locales linked together as nodes in a matrix of movement, in the itineraries of performers. At the core of performance is not the play-script but complex sets of rules and engagements within particular circumstances: places to be, things to do. Given changing conditions, performance might be as much tactical as strategic, for although the "what" may be fixed, the "how," in terms of delivery, timing, and qualitative improvisation, may be decided in the moment.

Performance as three distinct but interlocking constituents – site, constructed scenography, and performance in all its constituents – text, action, soundtrack, and levels of rhetoric – in, after Bernard Tschumi's formulation, relationships of reciprocity, conflict and indifference, with three-way, long and short-term shifts of operative predominance (see Tschumi 2012: 184–6). A constructed world, both utopian and dystopian, in which performers and audiences occupy the same site, in which the moderating conventions of the auditorium are absent; in which the weather itself might be "changeable."

In September 2015, National Theatre Wales presented a seven-hour staging of Christopher Logue's poetic rendering of Homer's *Iliad* at the Ffwrnes Theatre in Llanelli, Wales (Figure 23.1). The eight-hour production tracked the repercussions of Achilles's quarrel with Agamemnon and his refusal to fight against the Trojans. In Mike Brookes' scenographic design – that regarded the theatre as a site equipped in a particular but non-prescriptive manner – the floor of both stage and auditorium was tiled with sheets of medium-density fibreboard (MDF) to create a single unified space; a wall of similar sheets disguised the retracted seating, filling the void between the circle balcony and the floor. Installed elements included a large screen 12 meters by 4½ meters hanging obliquely in the stage area on which were projected four slowly moving videos – 280-degree panning shots of Welsh landscape, not as background but rather to expand the space, and to create a window into the outside; 10 microphones hanging on their cables, 30 centimeters from the floor; five video monitors on which pre-recorded footage appeared from time to time – head-and-shoulders shots of the gods, played by local teenagers; and a repertoire of materials including 250 rubber tires, 400 white plastic chairs, 10 loose MDF boards, lengths of timber and rolls of adhesive tapes. The main lighting element – an array of sodium lights – bathed the space in a single glow. All components were in plain view, a scenography that upset the familiar use of the venue and confounded audience expectations. As they entered for the first of four two-hour sections, *Kings*, the tires were piled in a single sweeping curve that suggested a wrecked ship, with the chairs stacked in unassigned piles. At all times they were free to move and to take a chair to sit in any position of their choice.

Six narrators delivered the text, their voices mixed in a pre-recorded musical soundtrack issuing from 45 audio speakers, in an enveloping sonic architecture. Over the four sections, the loose materials were employed, shifted, reconfigured, manipulated and modeled by four "constructors" in a continuous series of task-based activities

Figure 23.1 National Theatre Wales production of Christopher Logue's adaptation of Homer's *Iliad* at the Ffwrnes Theatre in Llanelli, Wales, 2015. (Photo: Farrows Creative, courtesy of National Theatre Wales.)

independent of, but complementary to, the text; building and deconstructing provisional structures, contexts and set ups that were at times used and occupied by the narrators, at others, analogous to or redolent of images in the narrative, without ever directly illustrating it. Guided by outlines marked on the floor, they created platforms, daises and runways; barricades and palisades; and ship-like forms and machinic tripods. They shepherded and reorganized the audience into new configurations; rolled tires; hurled chairs to form a huge wall; pushed rows of chairs into heaps resembling a dune landscape; and hoisted bound clusters of chairs on the tripods to suggest clouds or skeletal trees. They resembled army engineers, set-builders or film extras.

Here then was a scenography in flux, ever-changing – created and reconfigured by a group of experienced performers, going about their business, using mundane materials in unexpected ways, making space for their activities. At times, they were barely perceptible in the on-rush of text; at others, they engaged in actions that brought the full implications of the words into focus, through their skillful works of construction and energetic activities. Always seeking affordance, encountering and confounding ergonomic problems, in a landscape in which, through rehearsal, they became experienced dwellers.

The critical apprehension of such site-specific performance with scenography as landscape might attend to its overall ecology, to the interaction of all its components: to the relationships between the human activity and the context in which it is set; to the impacts of the constituents and elements of site upon the conceptualization, design and presentation of the work; to how performance design itself conspires conditions, both benign and adverse; and to what any of that might mean for performers, those who have to survive, dwell and work in such climes and niches. Any full description of a site-specific production surely requires as much said about the site – its architecture, its atmospheres, its climate, its history – and the emplaced scenography – its surfaces, substances, objects, locales – as about the themes and dramaturgy, to fully account for what happened: about the specifics of a place, about performance as eco-system.

References

Brecht B. 1987. *Poems 1913–1956*, edited by J. Willett and R. Manheim. London: Methuen.
Cosgrove, D. 1984. *Social Formation and Symbolic Landscape*. Beckenham: Croom Helm.
Cosgrove, D. 2004. "Landscape and Landschaft." *German Historical Institute Bulletin* 35: 57–71.
Gibson, J. J. 1979. *The Ecological Approach to Visual Perception*. Boston, MA: Houghton Mifflin.
Ingold, T. 2000. *The Perception of the Environment*. London: Routledge.
Nancy, J. L. 2005. *The Ground of the Image*. New York: Fordham University Press.
Pearson, M. 2010. *Site-Specific Performance*. Basingstoke: Palgrave.
Pearson, M. 2012. "Haunted House: Staging *The Persians* with the British Army." In *Performing Site-Specific Theatre* edited by A. Birch and J. Tompkins, 69–83. Basingstoke: Palgrave.
Pearson, M. and M. Shanks. 2001. *Theatre/Archaeology*. Abingdon: Routledge.
Tschumi, B. 2012. *Architectural Concepts: Red Is Not A Color*. New York: Rizzoli.
Tuan, Y-F. 1974. *Topophilia: A Study of Environmental Perceptions, Attitudes, and Values*. New York: Columbia University Press.

24
FREE REIGN?
Designing the spectator in immersive theatre

W. B. Worthen

Theatre has always been "immersive": it would be hard to say that Athenian spectators, sitting among their tribe, watching its members compete for a prize in singing and dancing dithyrambs, or the courtiers in the highly-charged political and social atmosphere of a Stuart masque, or postwar European tourists crossing into East Berlin to see the Berliner Ensemble were not *immersed* in a complex social and theatrical event. At the same time, though, both the spread and conceptual grip of the aesthetic, architecture, practice, and ideology of proscenium realism from the 1880s – "an inevitable consequence of the incandescent bulb," according to Brander Matthews – and the reactive rise of a range of more participatory spectacles influenced, however eccentrically, by Artaud, has lent the patina of innovation to the rhetoric of contemporary "immersive theatre" (Matthews 1910: 64). Phrased at the intersection of theatre and digital media, exploiting cognate notions of "immersion" and "interactivity," and conceptualized in reaction to the conventions of proscenium performance, immersive theatre articulates not only a changing sense of the uses of theatre, but a complex understanding of the *technicity* of theatre as well, its implication as a technology in a projection of the human.

Theatre does considerably more than merely incorporate its ambient technologies. As a medium of constant technological renovation, theatre is itself a technology that at once creates and represents technologies of the human, staging them, so to speak, to the view. As David Wills puts it, the human is "understood to become technological as soon as it becomes human, to be always already turning that way," and the history of theatre is itself one history of that turn (Wills 2008: 4). Yet when Bernard Steigler argues that "the human invents himself in the technical by inventing the tool – by becoming exteriorized techno-logically," he quickly notes that his own phrasing is misleading, appearing to articulate an "illusion of succession," as though there were an "interior" (the human, the drama) to give rise to the exteriority of technology (theatre). For this reason, while theatre participates in the logic of the *prosthesis*, that logic is neither successive nor supplemental: although the prosthetic "is added," the technological "is not a mere extension of the human body; it is the constitution of this body *qua* 'human'" (Steigler 1998: 141, 42, 152–3).

How does immersive theatre articulate the transformational technicities of the contemporary stage? In *Immersive Theatres*, Josephine Machon defines the genre largely in terms of the function ascribed to its spectator. Anticipated by digital gaming, virtual reality, and installation art, immersive theatre as a distinctive theatre practice arises for Machon in the 1980s; the apparatus of immersive theatre – first labeled as "immersive" around 2007 – is devised to put the audience "in 'the playing area' with the performers, physically interacting with them" in a space that has been *designed* for aesthetic production (Machon 2013: 65–6, 67). Some events take on spectators one at a time: *You Me Bum Bum Train* (London 2004), devised by Kate Bond and Morgan Lloyd, takes individual spectators through a series of familiar social scenarios, requiring them to perform. Others lead small groups: Third Rail Projects' *Then She Fell* (Brooklyn 2012) guides groups of spectators down Alice's, and Lewis Carroll's, rabbit hole. Still others – several works of Punchdrunk Theatre, perhaps now most famously *Sleep No More* – occupy a huge and richly-designed space, incorporating a large number of (masked) spectators who roam the installation more or less at will, encountering performers where their journeys intersect. Unlike site-specific performance, immersive theatre generally ignores the historical, cultural, and social significance of the location, redesigning it as a fully technologized venue in which all aspects of the production can be aesthetically governed. Punchdrunk typically develops a *themed* site (the McKittrick Hotel reanimating 2.5 acres of unused warehouse and club space in New York's Chelsea neighborhood); *Natasha, Pierre, and the Great Comet of 1812* – a musical adaptation of a section of *War and Peace*, music and libretto by Dave Malloy and directed by Rachel Chavkin – originated in a New York theatrical venue, Ars Nova, in 2012 but moved the following year to "Kazino," a tent in New York's meatpacking district, where the performance transpired among the tables of a Russian-style "restaurant."

Appearing to refuse the technical, social, and aesthetic apparatus that took shape toward the turn of the twentieth century (the box set, the boundary of the fourth wall, an invisible audience silently consuming the artwork before it), immersive theatre locates its spectator by indirectly emulating the forms of performance enabled by contemporary device culture: it demands, requires, and rewards "interactivity." Rather than presenting a work *to* spectators, immersive theatre asserts a prosthetic interdependency between performer and immersant, a bivalent reciprocity between the player and the played, the machined human and, well, the machined human. Redefining theatre by refiguring its prosthetic relation to the spectator, immersive theatre urges a distinctive means of entertaining – a holding-together apart, as Victor Turner conceived it – and so of fashioning its human participants, laying claim to a specific vision of theatre as a technology of the human, a vision simultaneously avowing and disavowing the ideological structure of the technological apparatus it invokes, shapes, and deploys (Turner 1982: 41).

Sustained by a conceptual, often material, reciprocity with interactive digital media, immersive theatre is defined, produced, advertised, and performed through the means of digital culture and, whether free-roaming or not, the spectator is immersed in a virtual field that – like devices, social media, the internet itself – conceals its productive apparatus. This interplay is particularly visible in what might be called massive multiplayer immersive performances, such as Punchdrunk's *Sleep No More* (which opened in New York in 2011, after versions in Boston and London). Punchdrunk's vast, meticulously designed spaces allow audiences what director Felix Barrett calls "free reign" (perhaps a suggestive transcription error for "free rein"), framing a spectatorial activity structured within a gaming performative (Barrett and Machon 2007). The experience of the immersed spectator, or "player" as Brainy Gamer has it, not only provides "a familiar sense of open-world freedom, bound by intentional designer-imposed limits," but one "ultimately responsive to my desire to test those limits, tweak the system, and observe the results" (Brainy Gamer 2011). Brainy Gamer *plays* Punchdrunk's *Sleep No More* by engaging its designs on the player, "digging to figure how the system works; looking for the seams; seeking ways to give myself an advantage over the other audience members; developing strategies to overcome the system's rules." Like the brilliantly-designed spaces spread over six floors of the "McKittrick Hotel," the faux-hotel where *Sleep No More* takes place, the system itself is both seductive – will I get a one-on-one with a performer tonight? be asked to find Hecate's lost ring? be dragged by a frantic Lady Macbeth up five flights of stairs to the hospital bath, where she'll step into the tub, the water reddening with blood? – and frustrating, designed to enable a kind of narrative arrhythmia. Although, as Dan Dickinson notes, there's "no way to win this game," *Sleep No More* allows its *players* – used to exploring, tracking, and stealthily following other online players both anonymously and voyeuristically – to use highly-developed skills "generally not acceptable to use in real life" in the "meticulously designed playground" of the performance (Dickinson 2011).[1]

Sleep No More participates directly in the techniques framing the human as the subject and the instrument of distributed gaming: the immersant is engaged in a virtual collaboration/competition with other players "known" only as virtual presences in the game space. This reciprocity is visible in the vertiginous array of online commentary and information about playing Punchdrunk's work, especially *Sleep No More*. Some sites – *Behind a White Mask*, for example – archive a massive array of information, including links to similar sites, published news articles, and individual blogs; others like *Scorched the Snake* are more openly fan blogs, following "news, events, rumors, silliness and sexyfuntimes at *Sleep No More NYC*," or follow several Punchdrunk works, as "*Blood Will Have Blood They Say*" does.[2] Most theatre productions today, immersive or otherwise, have an online presence, and typically a social media presence as well. But for *Sleep No More*, which was and is marketed virally through social media, this dimension of mediation is not conceptually alongside or outside the performance. The performance of *Sleep No More* is multiplatform, ubiquitous, always available in online circulation. Like the internet, perhaps especially so given the deployment of a pervasive internet-of-things, immersive performance is interminable, uncircumscribed, and – despite the apparent free "reign" of its ostensibly sovereign subjects – a site of rigorous and pervasive surveillance and discipline.[3]

The social mediation of immersive performance dramatizes the complicity between theatre and media in what is now widely known as the "experience economy" (see Pine and Gilmore 2011).[4] Users post photos, "likes" online, experiences purchased as part of *Sleep No More*. But the websites, blogs, Facebook and Twitter posts don't merely provide a record of past "journeys," or useful information advising future players on how to maximize their pleasure in the event; they are also performances in themselves, positioning the "live" but evanescent experience of theatrical immersion within an always available resource for virtual (re)performance.[5] To the extent that audiences "*actively exploit* opportunities to be expressive," as Jen Harvie suggests, they are exploited by the medium that transforms them into a resource, what Keren Zaiontz calls a "resourcing of spectators" that extends to their interactive performance on the social media so often used to advertise and publicize the event (Harvie 2013: 28; Zaiontz 2014: 406). Mediated performers are resourced during the show and after, tweeting out experiences that market the show in a medium (Facebook, Twitter) in which users are readily, voluntarily resourced as content for advertisers.

In immersive theatre, the spectator performs – even dines – within a technologized aesthetic environment: a designed platform sustaining both the spectator's performance and the visible virtuosity of the event, which continuously evokes the operational work of an unseen backstage armature, a structure enforced directly by the performers, the material design of the space (doors), and often by audience minders.[6] If there is an older paradigm lurking behind the interactivity prized by immersive theatre, it's the characteristic "distribution of the sensible" of the much-scorned proscenium house, with its ostensible emphasis on a solitary, private, disciplined voyeurism (Rancière 2009: 12).

When Punchdrunk "rejects the passive obedience expected of audiences in conventional theatre," using a "cinematic level of detail" to create a "theatrical experience where the lines between space, performer and spectator are constantly shifting," it casts its spectator as the reciprocal of that old-fashioned consumer of internalized experience in the dark, that unfortunate, unsociable, merely virtualized agent of a surpassed technology, deprived even of making "*human* contact, often with another human as much as with the work itself."[7]

Yet, many immersive events provide little opportunity for the spectator to *play interactively* in this dynamic sense, however much the event transpires 360 degrees and involves the spectator's motion, mobility, and physical exploration. It is astonishing to be withdrawn by the White Queen in *Then She Fell* into a small, beautifully cluttered and curious bedroom, be placed in bed (with a companion), have the lights turned off and be told a bedtime story; or to be one of the four spectators seated at the Mad Hatter's tea party, with the Red Queen, White Queen, and Hatter performing a fast, elaborate, seated dance with one another, with us, cups and saucers flying around the table. However engaging it is to be addressed, even to be unprotected and unmasked to the performers, there's little room for volition here; perhaps revealingly, when the Mad Hatter asks one spectator to take dictation while she fits another with a hat, she dictates at a frantic pace that's impossible to capture (even if you recognize some of the Carroll lyrics she recites). When I was asked by one of the Alices to brush her hair, and then about my "first love," did she take my hand in response? Or on cue? (And don't try to depart from the group or your guide: you will be strenuously directed back on course. No "free reign" through this looking-glass.)[8] While the Punchdrunk aesthetic creates a richly detailed space and then lets the audience loose within it, the audience's activity is hardly unstructured, however much latitude is given to move through the space, to take things, read the books, have sex (which the dancers have observed frequently), and pilfer from other immersants.[9] The performance structures interactions, but they transpire within the algorithmic instructions of the performance script: the spectator is part of the machine.

Moreover, regardless of the qualities of interactive agency experienced in different genres of immersive performance, such performances generally take place in a vividly *designed* environment, one that recalls and perhaps reanimates the only apparently discarded aesthetic relations of late-nineteenth century naturalism. As Jen Harvie notes, in works like the Punchdrunk or Third Rail Projects events, realism's usual "fourth wall is not so much removed (as on a proscenium arch stage) as moved, such that the other 'three' walls of the theatrical fictional space encompass the audience along with the theatre performers" (Harvie 2013: 30). While the spectator's epistemological "objectivity" is surrendered by this device, moving the audience *into* the scenery, *into* the visual and ideological design, far from repudiating the relations of realism, stages a continuity with them. Immersion, in Punchdrunk's case, cannot escape the ideology materialized by realist theatre because it provides the company's sustaining model of commodified experience. To construct a Punchdrunk performance space is first to "black out the windows," because "it's the impact of the space" – designed, theatrical space – "on the audience that establishes the show" (Barrett and Machon 2007).[10]

For Barrett, though, Punchdrunk space is practiced in different ways than is typical of the "conventions of going to the theatre" where, "irrespective of whether you like it or not, you sit there in silence, you observe, you praise and then you have the interval and so on" (Barrett and Machon 2007). This "formulaic," "passive and mechanical" performance (as though speaking to others next to you before the show, hearing their laughter, talking in the bar during intermission were irrelevant) in the modern theatre requires both a thoroughly designed space and the imposition of rules for its proper use (Barrett 2011). Yet while the audience of the proscenium theatre remains seated more or less quietly in the relative darkness, the differential degree of its captivity in relation to the free-roaming immersant is significantly overstated. In many forms of immersive theatre the spectator is led, guided, placed, even served dinner. Even in Punchdrunk's productions, where the immersed spectator improvises his or her way around the space, the performance is hardly "interactive" in the sense of depending improvisationally on the spectator's performance. Like most immersive theatre work, Punchdrunk performances are very highly scripted, though perhaps "choreographed" – rather than dramatically plotted – would be more accurate. As Barrett often remarks of *Sleep No More*, "Nothing in the show is improvised. At five past eight we'll know where everyone in the show is . . . Every single gesture, every single action has been rehearsed" (Andersen 2011). The three cycles of each production are – as anyone immersed in the production can't fail to notice – stopwatch-timed, so that actors in one scene can flow across six floors and appear a few minutes later among a different cast in a different scene. Even the one-on-ones, in which the spectator is taken into a confined space, usually unmasked, by a performer and involved in some kind of disarmingly intimate-feeling activity, are completely scripted. Inside the clock, we're watching the clockwork, and becoming the clockwork, too.

Immersive theatre models both the actor's and the spectator's performance on environmental theatre, resembling the one advocated by Richard Schechner in the 1970s Performance Garage, but actually more fully thematized a century before by Émile Zola, that theatre in which dramatic character – like the spectator in this case – "is asking more and more compellingly to be determined by his setting, by the environment that produced him" (Zola 1978: 370; see also Schechner 1973).

This reciprocity between space, design, narrative, acting, and spectating is, of course, an animating principle of Stanislavsky's work, in which the "given circumstances" motivating the actor's approach to "building a character" arise from the dramatic narrative, from the actor's prepared backstory and "emotion memory," and from the scenographic detail of the space itself. For Barrett, the environment lets the cast "build their character and leave memories all over the space"; the set is understood both to materialize and to provoke sense memory, much as Chekhov's Gaev and the actor playing him take their cue, so to speak, from the bookcase they apostrophize (Barrett and Machon 2007). Immersive performance moves the spectator on to the naturalistic stage, and so keeps in place the conceptual structuration of naturalism itself, in which a powerful offstage or backstage ideological order – male, institutional, moral, objectified, economic, technological – determines what characters, actors, and spectators can legitimately see and do, both in the social world shown on the stage (all those confining drawing rooms) and in the theatre as well.

While the distinction between "the audience model of a passive individual in a darkened theatre" and "real interaction" is often belabored in accounts of immersive performances, its evident conceptual limitations go well beyond Jacques Rancière's sense that the passivity ascribed to the conventional spectator is a means of artificially disqualifying a mode of potential agency in the theatrical "distribution of the sensible" (Carson 2008: 184; Rancière 2009: 12).

As in neoliberal political philosophy, and in more conventional theatre as well, the individualized immersant is "free" to work within a symbolic and economic structure or to depart, but not to improvise very far within the system; in this sense, *Sleep No More* stages the "lie of the pure voluntarity of consumption" (Jain 1999: 46). Harvie notes that "immersed" spectators are directly making the performance event, and yet "in immersive theatre events where all *professional* performers are paid, audiences often contribute their labour for free by, for example, peopling crowd scenes"; like the huge casts of volunteers and unpaid student interns, audiences articulate the situation of people in "insecure contemporary economies," who are "persuaded to undersell themselves by taking underpaid and unpaid work in the hope that it will lead to future paid work" (Harvie 2013: 28).[11] In this regard, the immersive theatre is characteristic of the contemporary performance field more generally, in which an "increasing reliance on – or demands for – volunteer labour" not only articulates an "'entry criterion to the cultural labour market'" but as part of a neoliberal "propensity to extend inequality" (Harvie 2013: 81).

What is the human that the technicity of immersive theatre articulates and produces? How does it create desire, what we want, want to do, to see, to be, through theatrical performance? The realist theatre defines spectatorial desire as the desire to subject others, to see them from an institutionalized position of protected invisibility, a position that enables us to interpret, perhaps even control those we see before us by *knowing* them (all those confessions, all those secrets) in a way only fantasized in the social world. As Judge Brack puts it, "People don't do such things" in his social world, but they *do* in the theatre; the entire apparatus – architectural design, lighting, scenography, acting – of theatrical realism is complicit in this process. The proscenium house, with its fiction of an objective public of unique but associated individuals, is, we might say, also the instrument of a lost liberalism. As Bernard E. Harcourt suggests, the "liberal ideal – that there could be a protected realm of individual autonomy – no longer has traction in a world in which commerce cannot be distinguished from governing or policing or surveilling or just simply living privately" (Harcourt 2015: 26).

What does immersive theatre say about us by constituting us within its prosthetic apparatus, bringing us from an artificial position of (only) apparent epistemological advantage into its inescapably disciplinary environment of *experience*? Immersive theatre assumes a desire to be spectacularized but not to perform; it withholds the attribution of representational power to its spectatorial agents, playing at the intersection of spectacle and surveillance that is today sustained by a specific means of performance, what Harcourt calls the "*exhibition*, or *exposition*, or perhaps more simply *exposure*," required for satisfying performance in the arena of digital life (Harcourt 2015: 89). But while it may feel active to "like" a Facebook post, or to share an article with "friends," or to tweet a brief commentary to the world of one's followers, *exposure* is not agency: it is the surrender of autonomous action shaped in the figure, the mask so to speak, of individual will. It's exciting, but unnerving, to be seated at the Mad Hatter's tea party and be unable to keep up with its complex choreography of crockery, but to try to play along is, literally and figuratively, to smash the performance. As a performative structure, immersive theatre generally resembles and rewards the habits of social media networking and gaming, arenas in which one plays with "friends" who share a virtual sphere in which actions have a momentary, interconnected consequence, but where relationships remain virtual, and can be quickly unfollowed, unfriended, or simply turned off. The power to define the means, purpose, and extent of virtual interaction in immersive performance is even less in the gamer's hands than it is on much social media. Like the performance of social media, the individualized experience of immersive theatre is always already a commodity, marketed virally, already anticipating the social mediation that's driven by, and so indistinguishable from, advertising.[12] The physical environment of immersive theatre recalls that of the naturalist stage, a foreground of intensely intricate and detailed activity, in which spectators figure as present but virtualized subjects, and also as objects, furniture of the production, whose freedom is controlled by an offstage, backstage apparatus that joins the social and economic to the technological and representational in ways that offer the illusion of knowledge (fourth-wall realism) or of individual experience (immersion) while simultaneously withdrawing access to the structuring mechanism, the hardware and software running the machine. Like the stage realism that it both displaces and refigures, immersive theatre is not open-source. While the technicity of proscenium realism projects, however deceptively, the theatrical audience as the social "public," immersive theatre projects the human as part of the set, an object of work, its radical individuality merely the means of its use, its experience routinely rationalized and instrumentalized, uploaded to a media platform that – like *Sleep No More* itself – commodifies its anonymous and voyeuristic interactivity as capital.

Whether as masked wanderers or themed diners or tourists in wonderland, we enact an illusion of agency that stands in for experience, an "individual" agency, a "'flexible entrepreneurial identity'" fashioned in the total apparatus of the economy of immersion.[13] As a theatrical allegory of the human, the technicity of immersive theatre, perhaps like the device culture it emulates, engages not the individual subject construed before the vanishing point of the picture-frame stage, but a different kind of fashioning, the absorption of the subject to the immersive fiction of "free reign." If the box, staging a world of economic constraint and enforced confession to an apparently disconnected audience of onlookers, materializes an ideological image of the social figuration of late-nineteenth-century social power, immersive theatre stages a rather more desperate figuration of the contemporary social order: an audience that's neither sociable nor cognate with a larger public, but instead a collection of atomized individuals presuming a richly constructed and literally captivating experience as the sign of an evanescent freedom.

Notes

1 As Keren Zaiontz notes, *Sleep No More* emulates "level design: the process of creating navigable levels of interaction for gamers through the mise en scène," and in so doing has in fact inspired the work of game designers; see Zainotz 2014: 418.

2 See *Behind a White Mask*, behindawhitemask.tublr.com (accessed 25 October 2015); *Scorched the Snake*, scorchedthesnake.tumblr.com (accessed 25 October 2015); "Blood Will Have Blood They Say," bloodwillhavebloodtheysay.tumblr.com (accessed 25 October 2015).

3 My thanks to Danielle Drees for sharing a preliminary version of her article, "The Sleeping Spectator: A Sleep Cultures Critique of Punchdrunk's *Sleep No More*." *Performance Research* 21.1 (2016), and for pointing me toward the extensive social-media industry surrounding Punchdrunk's work.

4 For an application of Pine and Gilmore's sense of "experience" as a product genre to venues and experiences like Shakespeare's Globe in London, see Worthen 2003: 95–7, and Chapter 2 *passim*.
5 As Zaiontz notes, the retailing of experience on social media reflects "not only an expectation that you produce what you consume (prosumerism), but that you collaboratively strategize on *how* to consume and, in this case, bring those strategies with you to the playhouse." He reports feeling that he might have consulted Facebook and other blog posts "before setting foot in the warehouse" (Zainotz 2014: 414). Adam Alston, in remarking on how spectators might become "sufficiently savvy to reap the benefits of being in the right place at the right time," perhaps implies social media as the source of such savviness (Alston 2013: 133). On social media, see also Jennifer Flaherty 2014: 134–54.
6 Graham White argues that, while immersive theatre "often surrounds audience members, makes use of cleverly structured interiors and ingenious invitations for them to explore, addresses their bodily presence in the environment and its effect on sense making, and teases them with the suggestion of further depths just possibly within reach," in many respects both the design and the processual experience of theatrical immersion seem familiar, generally predicated as they are on the aesthetics of realism: immersive theatre "has no strong claim to creating either fictional or imaginative interiors in a way that is different in kind than in more conventionally structured audience arrangements" (White 2012: 233).
7 The first phrase is quoted in Nield 2008: 532; the second phrase appears on the Punchdrunk website, Punchdrunk.com (accessed 25 October 2015); and the final phrase is from Machon 2013: 25. It might be noted that the remarks Nield found in 2008 on Punchdrunk's website no longer appear there.
8 One measure of the pervasiveness of *Sleep No More* is the assumption of the work of the mask. As one blogger reported of attending *Then She Fell*, in which audiences are unmasked and interact frequently with the performers, "Really, I was more worried about being in this environment and not having a mask. The idea of being utterly emotionally naked, both to performers and to other participants, had me on edge"; see "More Limen, Please: Thoughts on *Then She Fell* (11-28-12)," *The Stomach Flip*, akajakeedwardmarks.tumblr.com (accessed 25 October 2015).
9 On the dancers' report of immersant sex, see "Fear thy Nature," *Freakonomics*, 14 September 2012, http://freakonomics.com/2014/01/16/fear-thy-nature-a-freakonomics-radio-rebroadcast/ (radio podcast, accessed 25 October 2015). D. B. Wilson reports an immersant's sense that a stolen wallet seemed potentially a part of the immersive experience in "Spotting a Thief in a Roomful of Masks at 'Sleep No More,'" *New York Times*, 1 November 2015, www.nytimes.com/2015/11/02/nyregion/spotting-a-thief-in-a-room-full-of-masks-at-sleep-no-more.html?smid=nytcore-iphone-share&smprod=nytcore-iphone (accessed 1 November 2015).
10 Barrett and Machon 2007, "Conversation." As Barrett remarked on *Freakonomics*, a "huge swath of darkness" is essential to Punchdrunk's work; when they were forced by law to leave the lights on during a performance in the Boston run of *Sleep No More*, "it didn't work at all." See "Fear thy Nature."
11 Casting the audience as, in effect, casual workers who perform work according to an invariable, and unquestionable, script – costumed in reflective vests that dramatize their subjection *as* workers – is the central gesture of Ant Hampton's engaging piece, *The Extra People*, which premiered in 2015.
12 Punchdrunk is also deeply networked into corporate advertising, not only using a sister company, Gideon Reeling, as a means to offer immersive services, as a means to launch new products, but also directly collaborating "with like-minded, imaginative organisations to bring original and extraordinary ideas to life," organizations including "Louis Vuitton, Stella Black, Sony Playstation, Bacardi, W Hotels, Alexander McQueen, Xbox and Virgin Media" (Punchdrunk). While this effort extends to the performance space itself – the McKittrick Hotel, the current Chelsea site of *Sleep No More*, now features two themed restaurants, and has headline entertainment many evenings – it also locates immersive theatre as exemplary of Pine and Gilmore's "experience economy." Adam Alston discusses Punchdrunk's launch of Stella's *Black Diamond* brand, as well as its efforts to market "exclusiveness" through its "key" series to performances: Key Holder, Valet Key, Skeleton Key, Master Key. See "Funding, product placement and drunkenness in Punchdrunk's *The Black Diamond*." *Theatre & Performance* 32.2 (2012): 193–208.
13 Harcourt cites Phillip Mirowski's comments on Facebook as the "'neoliberal technology par excellence': a 'wildly successful business that teaches its participants how to turn themselves into a flexible entrepreneurial identity'"; see Harcourt 2015: 99.

References

Alston, Adam 2013. "Audience Participation and Neoliberal Value: Risk, Agency and Responsibility in Immersive Theatre." *Performance Research* 18.2.
Andersen, Kurt 2011. "Interview with Felix Barrett." *Studio 360*, 10 June. Available online at: www.studio360.org/story/139730-sleep-no-more/ (accessed 25 October 2015).
Barrett, Felix 2011. "Director Felix Barrett on the Dark and Dangerous Interactive World of *Sleep No More*." *Broadway.com*, 1 November. Available online at: www.broadway.com/buzz/158377/director-felix-barrett-on-the-dark-and-dangerous-interactive-world-of-sleep-no-more/ (accessed 25 October 2015).
Barrett, Felix and Josephine Machon 2007. "Felix Barrett in Conversation with Josephine Machon." *Body, Space & Technology Journal* 7.1. Available online at: http://people.brunel.ac.uk/bst/vol0701/home.html (accessed 25 October 2015).
Brainy Gamer 2011. "Bloody Play." *Brainygamer.com*, 6 July 2011. Available online at: www.brainygamer.com/the_brainy_gamer/2011/07/bloody-play.html (accessed 25 October 2015).
Carson, Christie 2008. "Democratising the Audience?" In *Shakespeare's Globe: A Theatrical Experiment*, edited by Christie Carson and Farah Karim-Cooper. Cambridge, UK: Cambridge University Press.
Dickinson, Dan 2011. "Games of 2011: *Sleep No More*." *Dan Dickinson: The Primary Vivid Weblog*, 25 December. Available online at: http://vjarmy.com/archives/2011/12/games-of-2011-sleep-no-more.php (accessed 25 October 2015).
Flaherty, Jennifer 2014. "Dreamers and Insomniacs: Audiences in *Sleep No More* and *The Night Circus*." *Comparative Drama* 48.1–2.
Harcourt, Bernard E. 2015. *Exposed: Desire and Disobedience in the Digital Age*. Cambridge, MA: Harvard University Press.
Harvie, Jen 2013. *Fair Play – Art, Performance and Neoliberalism*. Houndmills, Basingstoke: Palgrave Macmillan.
Jain, Sarah S. 1999. "The Prosthetic Imagination: Enabling and Disabling the Prosthetic Trope." *Science, Technology, & Human Values* 24.1.
Machon, Josephine 2013. *Immersive Theatres: Intimacy and Immediacy in Contemporary Performance*. Basingstoke: Palgrave Macmillan.
Matthews, Brander 1910. *A Study of the Drama*. Boston, MA: Houghton Mifflin.
Nield, Sophie 2008. "The Rise of the Character named Spectator." *Contemporary Theatre Review* 18.4.
Pine, II, Joseph B. and James H. Gilmore 2011 (updated edition). *The Experience Economy*. Boston, MA: Harvard Business Review. Kindle e-book.
Rancière, Jacques 2009. *The Emancipated Spectator*, translated by Gregory Elliott. London: Verso.
Schechner, Richard 1973. *Environmental Theater*. New York: Hawthorn Books.
Steigler, Bernard 1998. *Technics and Time, 1: The Fault of Epimetheus*, translated by Richard Beardsworth and George Collins. Stanford, CA: Stanford University Press.
Turner, Victor 1982. "Liminal to Liminoid, in Play, Flow, Ritual." In *From Ritual to Theatre: The Human Seriousness of Play*. New York: PAJ Publications.
Wills, David 2008. *Dorsality: Thinking Back through Technology and Politics*. Minneapolis: University of Minnesota Press.
White, Graham 2012. "On Immersive Theatre." *Theatre Research International* 37.3.
Worthen, W. B. 2003. *Shakespeare and the Force of Modern Performance*. Cambridge, UK: Cambridge University Press.
Zaiontz, Keren 2014. "Narcissistic Spectatorship in Immersive and One-on-One Performance." *Theatre Journal* 66.3.
Zola, Émile 1978. "Naturalism in the Theatre," translated by Albert Bermel. In *Theory of the Modern Stage*, edited by Eric Bentley. Harmondsworth: Penguin.

Pictorial and illusionistic design

> The true stage-illusion . . . consists – not in the mind's judging it to be a forest, but, in its remission of the judgment that it is not a forest.
>
> *(Samuel Taylor Coleridge,* Progress of the Drama *[1818])*

The invention of mathematically precise perspective painting is generally attributed to Filippo Brunelleschi and Leon Battista Alberti. In his 1436 treatise, *Della Pittura* (On Painting), Alberti described his process. "First of all, on the surface on which I am going to paint, I draw a rectangle of whatever size I want, which I regard as an open window through which the subject painted is seen" (Alberti 1991: 54). The image of the open window, of course, has become a classic metaphor for pictorial realism in all the arts. Not only does it propose a separation of viewer on one side and subject on the other, but it establishes the notion of the frame through which the subject is seen. The development of perspective painting, and the concomitant development of the frame, was quickly adopted in the Renaissance and Baroque theatre of Europe to create pictorial illusionistic scenery.

The illusion created in the Baroque era was often for the fantastic worlds of allegorical intermezzi, so it was not "real" in the sense of recreating an experiential reality. But it employed perspective technique to create a realistic sense of distance and scale to whatever was depicted – whether phantasmagorical landscapes or urban streets. Though the specific content and style changed over the next centuries, pictorial illusionism continued to be a major scenographic strategy of much Western theatre and opera well into the twentieth century. The flickering light of candles and oil lamps aided the illusionistic project, but the increasing brightness of gas led to highly talented scene painters whose technical skill could fool the eye of spectators beyond the footlights. Particularly through the seventeenth and eighteenth centuries, the perspective vistas painted on parallel rows of flats, often set in grooves on raked stage floors, meant that actors could not enter into the scenic stage. Actors were relegated to the apron stage in front of the proscenium, with scenery trapped upstage. Although the scenic stage had physical depth, the use of forced perspective excluded the presence of the actor, and scenery thus functioned analogously to projected scenery of later eras – an image that provided semiotic information to the audience, but remained inaccessible to the performer. In other words, an illusion.

One way of understanding the history of Western theatre from the seventeenth through nineteenth centuries is to observe the changes to lighting technology coupled with the increased use of three-dimensional scenery, along with a shrinking forestage, so that ultimately the actor moved behind the proscenium and into a three-dimensional – if still illusionistic – environment. As the actor moved into the scenic space, the relationship of costume to the physical environment became ever-more significant. Actors could no longer incongruously wear the latest fashions regardless of the ostensible time and place of the play. The identification of the actor with the character, and the character with the locale, mandated historically accurate costumes as well as sets.

One aspect of pictorial illusion that is applicable to painting and stage alike is the implication that the world seen within the frame continues beyond the frame. As Rudolph Arnheim explained in relation to painting, the world inside the frame "came to be conceived of as boundless – not only in depth, but also laterally – so that the edges of the picture designated the end of the composition, but not the end of represented space" (Arnheim 1974: 239). This applies equally well to the image within the proscenium.

The naturalist movement, spearheaded by Émile Zola, believed that the theatre should address the ills of society and that in order to do so the stage needed to depict an absolutely accurate – a scientific or clinical – rendering of the external world. Thus, it became the ultimate illusionism. But the invention of photography in 1839, and film at the end of the century, created new ways of capturing reality (or at least convincing an audience that it was observing reality) that rendered the techniques of the stage seemingly quaint and inadequate. Declaring that truth lay within the soul of the individual and could not be depicted through superficial means, the Symbolists in the 1880s and 1890s called for the "detheatricalization" of the theatre, by which they meant a rejection of the detailed clutter of the naturalist stage. In the late twentieth and early twenty-first centuries, naturalist illusion, particularly in the depiction of domestic interiors, sometimes re-emerged as a scenographic trope – naturalism in quotes, as it were. Audiences often greeted the revelation of such decor with applause, taking delight in the theatricality of illusionism. It also resurfaced in the highly detailed scenographic environments of much immersive theatre. In an event such as *Sleep No More*, spectators move through fully constructed rooms which are, in essence, Baudrillard-like simulacra: every element within each room is "real," and yet the room is a carefully constructed theatrical space.

In the same essay quoted in the epigraph, Coleridge describes his young son seeing an engraving of a storm at sea. As Coleridge relates,

> He instantly started, stood silent and motionless, with the strongest expression, first of wonder and then of grief in his eyes and countenance, and at length said, 'And where is the ship? But that is sunk, and the men are all drowned!' still keeping his eyes fixed on the print.
>
> *(In Clark 1965: 412–13)*

Coleridge then concludes, "What pictures are to little children, stage illusion is to men, provided that they retain any part of the child's sensibility." Despite centuries of technological change and the welter of "isms" of the modernist movement, there is still a child-like delight and emotional appeal to what Coleridge called "the willing suspension of disbelief."

References

Alberti, Leon Battista 1991. *On Painting*, translated by Cecil Grayson. London: Penguin.

Arnheim, Rudolph 1974. *Art and Visual Perception: A Psychology of the Creative Eye*. Berkeley and Los Angeles: University of California Press.

Clark, Barrett H. 1965. *European Theories of the Drama*, newly revised by Henry Popkin. New York: Crown Publishers.

25
SCENOGRAPHY IN THE FIRST DECADES OF OPERA[1]

Evan Baker

Stage design as an independent component of operatic production began in the first decades of the seventeenth century. The festivals of the preceding era in the great towns of Florence and Rome as well as in smaller towns presented splendid opportunities for great artists – particularly Bernardo Buontalenti and the father/son team of Alfonso and Giulio Parigi – to create designs for grand spectacles of horse ballets, naval battles, celestial scenes, appearances of deities, and especially devils and demons, many set to voice and music as precursors to opera.

Even a lesser ruler of a province to the north was inspired to create his own grand theatre. In 1618 Ranuccio I Farnese of Parma was ready to present his own spectacles for the visit of the Medici prince Cosimo and commissioned Giovanni Battista Aleotti to create a new theatre. Aleotti designed a huge space, the Teatro Farnese, which is of seminal importance to opera and theatre history.[2]

Situated above the ground on the second floor of the Palazzo della Pilotta, the large theatre measures over 285 feet in length and is 105 feet in width. The auditorium, shaped in the form of an elongated U, is capable of seating over 4,000 spectators.[3] One architectural plan of the theatre reveals a clear delineation of an orchestra "pit," one of the earliest of its kind, albeit placed at the same level as the auditorium floor. The stage measures 140 feet deep with the proscenium opening 39 feet wide.[4] Pumps brought in water from nearby wells to flood the auditorium floor for sea battles. The stage space included flying machines, traps, and other complicated machinery. Unfortunately, Cosimo's illness forced the cancellation of the events, scheduled for 1619, and the theatre remained unused for 10 years.

More successful was Ranuccio's heir, Odoardo, who in 1628 celebrated his marriage to Margherita of the Medici family with splendid festivals of his own. Among the entertainments was a play with *intermedi*, performed in the smaller court theatre near the Palazzo, while the primary event, a tournament entitled *Mercurio e Marte* ("Mercury and Mars") was staged in the Teatro Farnese on 21 December 1628.[5] Its realization required five orchestras: one in the pit, one each above the two side entrances before the pit, and two hidden behind the proscenium. Heavens and hell, deities of all kinds, and exotic animals appeared throughout the huge spectacle. Cities materialized and disappeared and, on command, water flooded the auditorium floor, providing the locale for sea battles (Nagler 1964: 153–61). One witness nervously reported, "I was afraid to sit in such a large hall overloaded with thousands of spectators and many machines. Moreover, the [floor of the] same hall later had to sustain the weight of the water which rose to a height of more than [twelve inches]" (ibid.: 159).

Aleotti's achievements with his design of the stage and its machinery in the Teatro Farnese proved fundamental to the development of operatic staging and theatre technology. His innovations included permanently separating the stage space from the audience using the proscenium arch. In addition to functioning as decoration, with a dedication to the Farnese family above its family crescent, the arch also masked the elaborate machinery above the stage.[6] The notion of hiding all technical apparatus, however, did not take hold until the end of the nineteenth century.

Equally significant was Aleotti's invention for moving stage sets by means of rolling wagons or wing chariots (*carozze*), situated on tracks beneath the stage (Figure 25.1). Upon the chariots were mounted frames extending through slots in the floor. Stagehands affixed the painted flats to these frames, set on the same line in the left and right sides of the stage, and rolled the contraption in and out of view of the audience. Although the mechanism for propelling the wagons would be refined in the following decades, this cardinal method of changing scenery remained constant for over 250 years.

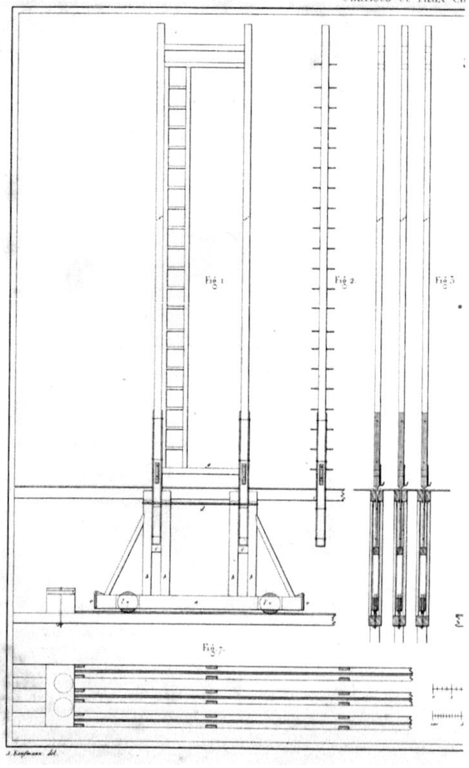

Figure 25.1 Chariot. A wood frame was inserted through a slot in the floor into a wagon beneath the stage and affixed to a single-rail rolling carriage. Detail from Giulio Ferrario, *Storia e descrizione de' principali teatri antichi e moderni corredata di tavole col saggio sull'architettura teatrale*. "Tavola B." Milan, 1830. (Collection of the author.)

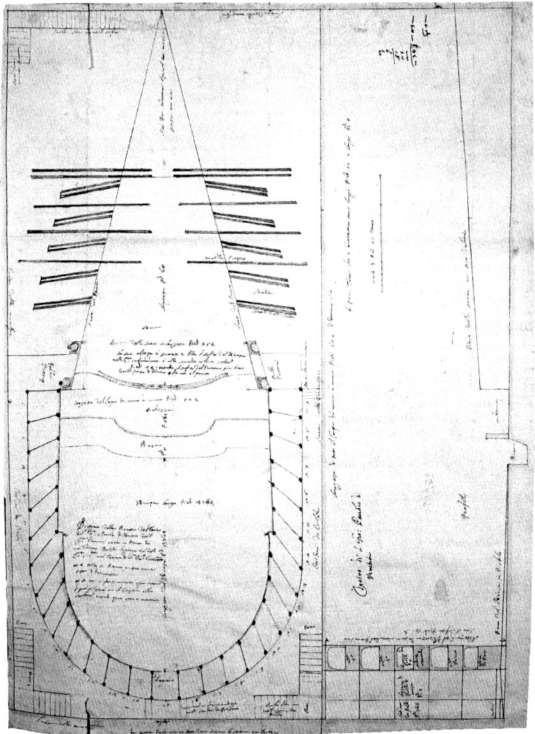

Figure 25.2 Plan (after 1692) of *Teatro SS. Giovanni e Paolo*, the earliest surviving architectural document of a Venetian public theatre. (Sir John Soane's Museum [London], SM Vol. 117/34.)

When in 1637 the curtain opened to reveal the sea scene to the spectators attending the first performance of Francesco Manelli's *Andromeda* at the Teatro San Cassiano in Venice – the first public opera house to charge an entry fee – the spectacle evoked gasps of wonder. Memoirs described "marvelous transformation scenes, the crowded stage, the ingenious mechanism, the flying figures, the scenery representing the heavens, Olympus, the ocean, royal palaces, forests, groves, and innumerable other enchanting spectacles" (Molmenti 1908: 158). The final scene of the opera paid homage to Venice with pictorial representations of the city-state.

Few documents detail the early workings of the San Cassiano theatre; the earliest eyewitness accounts date only from the 1680s. Thus the architectural layout – including the number of galleries, boxes, seating capacity, and the size of the stage – remains a mystery. Judging from earlier theatrical structures like those in Padua, Ferrara, Mantua, and Bologna, however, it is reasonable to assume that the auditorium took a U-shaped form (Figure 25.2). At least five galleries of boxes complemented the theatre with its total capacity of perhaps 900 seats. The parquet had a number of benches, with space for standing room at the rear (Mancini *et al.* 1988: 97). The only account of the theatre's first production, *Andromeda*, comes from Benedetto Ferrari's foreword to the libretto published two months after the premiere in 1637.[7] That description has been confirmed by one of the first published histories of Venetian opera, Cristoforo Ivanovich's *Memorie Teatrali di Venezia* (1687).

After the reconstruction of the San Cassiano, it is likely that the backstage areas were equipped with the newest machinery necessary to produce the marvelous changes of scenery outlined in the *Andromeda* libretto.[8] This stage spectacle attracted audiences of not only aristocrats and members of the diplomatic community, but also of wealthy bourgeoisie, including the merchants. Indeed, anyone who could afford the price of a ticket now had the opportunity to witness the scenic marvels. The influence of the paying public has governed the business of public opera ever since.

In the portion of the libretto for *Andromeda* addressed to the reader, the production's description is laced with superlatives for the settings and costumes. Management spared no expense. All five of the opera's scenes took place on an "imaginary shore of Ethiopia" (scenario in Worsthorne 1968: 25–7). The view of a seascape with stars in the heavens filled the audience with amazement. Above the stage a cloud machine revealed Aurora circling, followed by the entrance of Juno in "a golden cart drawn by two peacocks." The cart could move and turn to the right or left sides of the stage, "to the wondering delight of the spectators." At the end of the prologue, Mercury "flew" across the stage by means of a flying apparatus.

As would remain typical for many decades, the change of setting from the prologue to the first act was performed in full view of the audience (*a vista*): "In an instant, one saw the scene change from a seascape to a wood so natural that it carried our eyes to real snowy heights, real flowering countryside, a regal spreading wood and unfeigned melting of water" (ibid.). After scenes with Andromeda and nymphs, the setting changed to the seashore for the appearance of Neptune, probably from below stage. He emerged "on a great silver shell drawn by four sea horses. A sky blue cloak covered him: a large beard descended down to his breast and a long shock of hair garlanded with seaweed hung down to his shoulders. His crown was made as a pyramid tossed with pearls."[9] Prometheus appeared "from the bosom of the sea . . . Astrea appeared in the sky, and Venus in the sea; one in a silver cloud and the other in her seashell drawn by swans" (ibid.).

The second act changed into another woodland. After a highly praised dance by Andromeda and her retinue, "suddenly, from below [as if from the underworld] arose the magician Astarco as a ghost. This character was clad entirely in a long, gold coat with long hair and beard white as snow. He held in his right hand a sorcerer's scepter." Suddenly the sky opened up, and in a burst of light, "one saw sitting on a majestic throne Jove and Juno."

> At the beginning of the third act with the representation of a seashore, a magnificent machine appeared from one side of the scene with Astrea and Venus upon it. It turned to the right and left as these goddesses most pleased. Opposite them Mercury came out and, as the sky opened, sat in the middle. This little scene had a most wonderful effect for the quantity of machines and for the successive arrangements of silent characters and movement [on the stage]. In a flash, the sea scene became a superb palace. It was a beautiful sight to see a well laid out and constructed building suddenly born out of rough stone and coarse sand. This represented the royal palace of Andromeda . . . ; suddenly the palace disappeared, and we saw the scene entirely consisting of the sea with Andromeda bound to a rock. The sea monster came out. This animal was made with such beautiful cunning that, although not real, he put people in terror. Except for the act of tearing to pieces and devouring he did everything as if alive

> and breathing. From the sky Perseus arrived on Pegasus, and with three blows of a lance and five with a rapier, he overthrew the monster and killed it . . . The sky opened and one saw Jove and Juno in glory and other divinities. This great machine descended to the ground to the accompaniment of a concerto of voices and instruments truly from paradise. The two heroes, joined to each other, were raised to heaven. Here the royal and ever worthy occasion had an end.
>
> *(Worsthorne 1968: 26–7)*

Such was the spectacle of the first production of an opera for a paying public. More than nine significant theatres opened and closed up to the end of the eighteenth century, in which more than 200 operas received their premieres (see Baker 2013: 10, note 7).

Until the final decades of the seventeenth century, productions in Venetian theatres did not place importance on stage design as a genuine element of the opera, relying instead on the music for inspiration. The surviving illustrations found in many frontispieces and title pages of Venetian librettos demonstrate that most early designers trained chiefly as architects and engineers. Technical elements, such as the development of machinery to effect the changes of décors, received much of the attention: machine-driven devices of gods descending from the heavens, demons appearing from hell (that is, from below the stage through traps), and oceans transforming into woodlands. What is interesting is how simply, by today's standards, these effects were created.

At the same time as public opera made its debut in 1637, a fundamental treatise appeared: *Pratica di Fabbricar Scene e Macchine ne'Teatri*, or "The Practice of Building Scenery and Stage Machines for Theatres." Authored by Nicola Sabbattini (1574–1564), it imparted much practical information to theatre technicians and designers of the time, and it continues to be instructive today. A year later, a second volume together with a reprint of the first appeared in Ravenna, and this edition is the one best known today.[10] *Pratica* detailed the design elements from the perspective of standing "behind the scenes." Sabbattini did not invent any of the effects or machines described; in fact, many of the machines had been around for decades, and some were outdated. Nonetheless, the treatise's value lies not in theories but in Sabbattini's clear, precise descriptions of the machines and scenic effects. Because of its simplicity, this book served as a guide for theatre practitioners throughout seventeenth-century Europe.

Book I of Sabbattini's treatise describes more than 40 items, chiefly involved in theatre construction, seating arrangements for the audience, construction and painting of scenery, and lighting in the auditorium. The most striking effects are described in Book II. Fifty-seven chapters discuss theatrical machinery, including dimming stage lights, using traps, special effects such as hellfire and water fountains, and raising the front drop at the beginning of the performance – all fundamental components of many productions of the period. Many effects described by Sabbattini are similar to those used today.

Book II discusses several methods of using the traps to allow people to enter the stage. Each chapter describes moving a segment of the stage floor attached to a downward swinging hinge. One suggests placing dancers in front of the trap to cover the appearance of the performer. Another outlines a method for quick entrances by having the person stand on a lever that, at the appropriate moment, is quickly raised after which the trap is closed. Sabbattini strongly recommended using "persons experienced in this business and trustworthy, so that movements go smoothly" (Hewitt 1958: 121).

Dimming illumination cast by candles appeared simple. Merely lowering or raising cylinders of soldered tin over each candle by a system of cords operated by several stagehands will dim or illuminate the stage (ibid.: 111–12). Truly impressive lighting effects, such as hellfire, required considerable ingenuity. Sabbattini describes a trap opened at the center of the stage, and men waiting below with specially prepared pots filled with ground resin. They place a torch in a sealed pot, with the flame above the seal. The top of the pot has numerous small holes, and when the pot is shaken the resin comes out, causing a burst of flame. Performed by several persons and within the right stage decorations, the hellfire can be quite effective. The author cautions that "great care" must be taken, "since very often mishaps result, and fools and thick-witted persons should not be allowed to participate" (ibid.: 126–7).

Four chapters of *Pratica* contain instructions for displaying the sea, in either a calm or a tempestuous state, a vital element of staging, particularly if Neptune appears in the opera. Stagehands stood on each side of a wide cloth, gripped cords running under it, raised and lowered the lines at different speeds that caused the cloth to billow and thus created the illusion of a rolling sea. Another method involved several painted cylinders resembling waves across the width of the stage. A scale model of a ship rolled across the stage between the waves while stagehands cranked the cylinders at varying speeds. If the ship is to travel through a tempest, the model is set on a curved rail. When pulled by a rope, the ship bobs up and down, as if rocked about in a storm (ibid.: 130–43).

In Sabbattini's day, gods and goddesses descended from the heavens in machines commonly known as *gloires*. These devices took the shape of a sun, a moon, or, most frequently, a cloud that could expand in size. Performers could appear either standing or seated. Theatre technicians perfected several methods for making the clouds grow as the machine descended from the heavens. In Chapter 46, Sabbattini recommends constructing an "elevator post" with a winch behind the backdrop. A beam, parallel to the stage floor with a small platform on which the performer could stand or sit, could then be lowered from above as if the gods were descending from the heavens, or raised from the underworld below the stage. Another method used a counterweighted pivoting crane with its neck also protruding through the backdrop. Painted cloth attached to a series of ribs expanded at the pull of the line by an operator below, using the same principle as that of a hand fan unfolding. In every effect he described, Sabbattini emphasized concealing the machinery to prevent spoiling the theatrical illusion (ibid.: 146–70).

In 1640 stage machinery for changing settings in the wings and borders was clumsy to operate and required a large work force. Shifting scenery – then and now – is not easy. The labor is physically demanding and frequently dangerous. Large and tall flats required at least two stagehands to move and affix them to the wing chariots.[11] Borders – wide strips of canvas that traversed between the wings above the stage and hid the upper spaces from view of the public – were hoisted up into place by several rope lines pulled by stagehands through pulleys mounted on wood crossbeams. Large canvas objects, tall flats, wide borders, or large drops, are very heavy, especially with the additional weight of the wood frames.

Hence it was a great step forward in operatic production when a stage machine was invented to allow a complete change of scenery in one smooth, flowing motion in full view of the audience. The opening of Venice's Teatro Novissimo in 1641 with Giulio Strozzi's musical setting of Francesco Sacrati's *La finta pazza* ("The feigned madwoman") provided the opportunity to implement the new system.

The story of this opera revolves around the Greeks' search for Achilles before he departs for the Trojan War. Amid the tumult of the search, the gods appear and utter their support variously for the Greeks or the Trojans. Deidamia, in despair at the thought of the departure of her lover Achilles, feigns madness. After she is placed in chains, Achilles is touched and takes her hand in marriage. As the warriors (including Achilles) depart for Troy, a celestial chorus bears Deidamia's chains up to the heavens.

La finta pazza was a phenomenon. The opera held 12 performances in 17 days – an extraordinary success. To satisfy public demand, two separate printings of the libretto followed. Descriptions of the production, accompanied by elaborate illustrations, showered praise on the marvels of rapid and effortless changes of scene at a level of sophistication not found in other theatres.[12] The libretto describes five distinct scenes in a prologue and three acts. The locales mandated rapid changes between a royal courtyard, a rich garden, a seaport, and a setting in hell, with the final scene being a royal garden.

What were these scenic "marvels," and who created them? A copy of a sixteenth-century manuscript preserved in the archives of the Correr Museum in Venice offers a clue: "Giacomo Torelli of Fano invented the system of shifting scenery with winches, and was involved with the four famous theatres of Paris, Venice, Parma, and Fano."[13] Torelli (1608–1678) appears to have received his early training in the theatres of Ferrara and Pesaro where there was more theatrical activity than in his birthplace of Fano. By 1640, he was working in Venice, probably at first in the employ of the naval shipyards in the Arsenale. His talent with ropes, winches, pulleys, and rigging played a key role in his creations for the theatre.

Torelli's newly installed machinery in the understage area of the new Teatro Novissimo allowed complete changes of scenery in one easy, continuous movement. Through an ingenious construction of rope lines and pulleys, clouds for gods transformed effortlessly into royal courtyards or woodland glades, thus amazing and astonishing the public. Several published writings detail Torelli's productions, from which we can deduce the existence of the sophisticated stage machinery. Although no plans of the theatre exist, recent documents show it to have had four sets of wings. The auditorium probably had three galleries of boxes and seated about 500.[14]

Maiolino Bisaccioni's *Il cannocchiale* is a 55-page booklet – issued after *La finta pazza* finished its run at the Novissimo – describing the production, the singers, and the public reactions.[15] The title word "cannocchiale" is a pun on the Italian for "telescope" – the public looking closely at the specifics of theatrical production through a telescope from afar. This *Il cannocchiale* was both an examination of the magical elements of the production and publicity for Torelli, the technical team, and the performers, and it spread word of the marvels at the production at Teatro Novissimo.[16]

Torelli's invention enabled a rapid transformation of scene with far less manpower. Below the stage, a series of rope lines were attached to the chariots, with their frames extending through parallel slots in the floor on both sides of the stage. The rope lines ran through a series of pulleys joined at a central winch. A single person cranking the winch could regulate the speed of the transformation from one scene into the next and pull the ropes attached to one set of chariots onto the stage while simultaneously pulling the other set of chariots into the wings and out of view. After the transformation, several stagehands immediately shifted flats off and placed different sets of flats onto the chariots. The mechanism was so simple that a "young boy of just fifteen years of age" can pull it into motion. It was hard to believe "that so many flats may be moved into their locations to vary a scene, all at the same time in one moment" (Bisaccioni 1987: 1032). Torelli was not so much a scenic designer as a master mechanical engineer; his invention fundamentally changed the method of stage production for all genres of theatre everywhere. The visual aspects of operatic production became an integral part of the aesthetics of opera itself.

Il cannocchiale also showed that audiences delighted in the spectacle. Bisaccioni wrote of the "marvels" of the scenery changes, which repeatedly drew the public to the theatre. "[*La finta pazza*] closed, but the public's desire to see [the opera] again never ended" and the theatre was so crowded that many "cursed their own laziness when they arrived and could not find a place to sit" (ibid.: 1052). The foreword to the libretto noted that 12 performances were required to satisfy the demands of the public and that it was necessary to reopen the Novissimo for several additional performances.

All we know of the production's looks comes from prints of a later version in 1645, also staged by Torelli but in Paris at the behest of Cardinal Mazarin.[17] These prints can only offer tantalizing clues to Torelli's stage effects. Some of the imagery corresponds with the descriptions in the *Cannocchiale*, but for the Paris production important scenes were changed or cut. Views of Paris replaced all visual references to the Republic of Venice. The productions at the Teatro Novissimo were splendid but expensive, and the theatre lost money. Brilliant stagings continued, but after six years and only seven productions, the Novissimo closed its doors in 1646 and burned down soon after.

Still, these productions had great and lasting impact. Venetian opera had won acceptance by a public that hungered for even more vocal virtuosity and grand scenic presentations. Since Venice was the seat of a sovereign state and the site of many foreign embassies and businesses, the Venetian opera's performance and production styles became known throughout Italy and the rest of Europe. Torelli's achievements set a standard against which other operatic productions were measured, not only in Venice but elsewhere in Europe. Torelli himself became one of the first exports of Italian operatic productions. His successes in Venice and later in Paris earned him the sobriquet *Grand Sorcier* – the "Great Wizard."

Although illustrations of the stage apparatus for the Teatro Novissimo have not survived, we can reconstruct the machinery based on the writings of Fabrizio Carini Motta (1627–1699), a theatre architect and scenographer at the court of the Duke of Mantua. In 1676 he published *Trattato sopra la Struttura de' Teatri e Scene* ("Treatise on the Structures of Theatres and Scenes"), an important architectural monograph.[18] It includes observations regarding sightlines, placement of the central perspective, the proscenium arch, and the stage area necessary to accommodate the machinery, wings, and drops.

Carini Motta prepared an even more significant document in 1688, *Costruzione de Teatri e Macchine Teatrali di Fabrizio Carini Motta Ingeg.º. Architetto del Ser.mo Duca di Mantua 1688* ("Construction of Theatres and Stage Machinery by Fabrizio Carini Motta, Engineer and Architect to His Most Serene Highness, Duke of Mantua"). The manuscript, however, remained unpublished until 1987, when it appeared in an English translation accompanied by facsimiles of the original illustrations.[19] Carini Motta's manual contains a series of drawings detailing theatrical machinery and dates from the latter part of the seventeenth century. The surviving manuscript, in a copyist's hand from 1773, is based directly on Carini Motta's work 85 years earlier. In 22 chapters, Carini Motta codifies Torelli's mechanics of scene changing. He concentrates on the use of the slots traversing the width of the stage floor for freestanding objects, such as braziers, ships, or fountains. The spaces between the groups of slots were called *strade* (streets), or more commonly, wings. Carini Motta emphasizes maintaining enough space between the wings so that

> the chariots carrying the [flats] will have sufficient space to move back and forth . . . without any concern that they will foul one another, as they often leap because of the change of speed, or because of the great force generated as they accelerate, causing them to rise out of plumb. When the circumstances prohibit sufficient space [for them] to travel smoothly, they jam into the chariots ahead causing great confusion and inconvenience.
>
> *(Larson in Carini Motta 1987: 70)*

Borders, painted cloths hung above and between the wings that spanned the width of the stage, also figure in the manual. Not only did borders complete the scenic picture with skies, heavens, leafy branches, and ceilings, they also served to mask flies and machinery from public view.

The descriptions by Sabbattini and Carini Motta demonstrate that these scenic marvels were refinements of existing engineering techniques rather than innovations. Torelli previously utilized many existing pieces of theatre machinery to merge disparate scenic effects into one seamless whole. Hence, all ropes, pulleys, and wheels were incorporated into a theatrical machine that could be operated in many instances by a single person. Although theatres and their backstage spaces expanded as stage machinery evolved, the process of moving flats on and off stage, and of raising and lowering drops and borders in one single movement, remained constant for over 250 years.

One of the most dazzling theatrical productions outside of Italy took place in Vienna at the new Theater auf der Cortina on 12 and 14 July 1667 featuring Antonio Cesti's *Il pomo d'oro* ("The golden apple"). For the wedding festivities of the Hapsburg Emperor, Leopold I, and Margaretha of Spain, which *Il pomo d'oro* was to celebrate, the architect Lodovico Burnacini (1636–1707) not only designed plans for a new theatre, but also

Figure 25.3 Ludovico Burnacini, *Il Pomo d'oro*, Act I, sc. 5: "Jupiter and His Court at Banquet . . . With Discord Floating in a Cloud above the Table" (1688). (Musiksammlung der Österreichischen Nationalbibliothek, Vienna.)

23 magnificent settings for the opera (Figure 25.3). Construction of the theatre, which was made entirely of wood, began early in 1666 in a space next to the royal palace now occupied by the Austrian National Library. Ensuing difficulties in building and financing the house forced the delay of the opera's premiere, originally planned for December 1666, until July 1667.

At the Theater auf der Cortina, a raised dais in the center in the first row of the auditorium provided the place of honor for the emperor and his family. The symbol of state, a huge double-headed eagle, topped off the elaborately decorated proscenium arch. Leopold's court sat on chairs behind the emperor's party, with the other officials in the three surrounding galleries. The auditorium's design meant that the emperor's seat in the first row center of the auditorium afforded the best view of the stage. Only members of the imperial court and visiting dignitaries attended performances; the public was not admitted.

The main acting area downstage, more than seven meters deep, was equipped with at least five sets of wings on wagons. The entire stage measured over an astounding 26 meters deep (Griffin 1972: 45). Machinery beneath the stage raised scenic pieces from below. The 14 meters of space from the stage floor to the ceiling allowed flying machines for the appearances of deities.

The story of *Pomo d'oro* revolves loosely around the legend of the judgment of Paris. At a banquet of the gods, the goddess Discord appears riding a dragon. From her perch she throws a golden apple, upon which is inscribed, "to the fairest." Harmony is shattered as Juno, Minerva, and Venus squabble for the honor. After elaborate scenes of betrayals, revenge, destruction, dragons, and hell, Leopold I, in the persona of Jupiter, restores calm by awarding the golden apple to the one he judges to be the noblest person on earth, that person whose wisdom will unite the virtues of love, honor, and beauty. In Burnacini's staging, the figure of Emperor Leopold appeared frequently as a godlike character on horseback at the center of the stage or descending as a *deus ex machina* from the heavens. Margaretha, Leopold's wife, embodied the figure of Wisdom. Burnacini exploited the large stage space and theatre machinery with elaborate scenery. The settings alternated between seven scenes of interiors and courtyards, with the remaining sixteen scenes using the deeper part of the stage for the perspective views of encampments, caverns, woodlands, seascapes, heavens, and hells.

Other operas for the Viennese court followed sporadically. Burnacini designed the productions of *Il fuoco eterno custodito delle vestale* performed on 23 October 1674, and *La monarchia latina trionfale* four years later on 10 October 1678. Most of the operas received only a single performance, leaving the theatre otherwise empty. When the Turks laid siege to Vienna in 1683, Leopold ordered the theatre razed to avoid any dangers of fire spreading to the royal residences.

Burnacini's designs for *Pomo d'oro* accompanied the publication of Francesco Sbarra's libretto, serving to publicize both the staging and the power and glory of Leopold I and the Austrian Empire. Twenty-three engravings depict the auditorium and scenes from the opera. In the foreword to the libretto, Sbarra regrets that the reader could not see either the original production or the magnificent theatre.[20] Nevertheless, the results of Burnacini's achievements were important for they sowed seeds that flourished a decade later in the creations of the Galli-Bibienas for their stage designs and plans of new theatres throughout Europe (see Sommer-Mathis *et al.* 2016).

By 1700 significant emphasis in the Italian opera libretto had shifted away from the dramatic action of the plot toward the visual aspects of opera production and staging.

Production practices at the time required that all changes of scenery be played in full view of the audience seated in a fully lit auditorium. While Torelli's invention for changing the scenes – ropes attached to wings, moved through a series of pulleys and powered by several men either working separately or rotating a single winch – continued to be refined, the mechanical principles remained the same. The paraphernalia of theatrical machinery remained visible to all until 1876, when Richard Wagner began the practice of lowering the curtain to mask all scenic transformations.

At the same time, librettists of Italian opera created increasingly convoluted plots demanding greater suspension of disbelief from the public. In late sixteenth and early seventeenth-century Italian operas gods intervened in human affairs constantly, providing a pretext for elaborate scenery changes and displays of theatrical machinery. Spectacle promoting elaborate musical settings became a raison d'être for staging new operas, at the expense of quality of the drama.

Numerous polemics, treatises, and even theatrical satires protested this trend. Critics lampooned excesses in singing, acting, and theatrical production. Sparing no aspect of operatic production, Benedetto Marcello's essay *Teatro alla Moda* (Venice, 1720) was the most pointed satire.[21] Throughout the essay, pungent observations mock the mediocre librettos, the overindulgences of the singers, the dependence on scenic effects, and the fatuous behavior of all concerned. A taste of Marcello's style is apparent early on in a paragraph "advising" the librettist on how to include the maximum scenic display:

> Before the librettist begins writing he should ask the impresario for a detailed list giving the number and kind of stage sets and decorations he wishes to see employed. He will then incorporate all these into his drama. He should always be on the lookout for elaborate scenes such as sacrifices, sumptuous banquets, apparitions, or other spectacles. When those are to occur in the opera the librettist will consult with the theatre engineer [machinist] in order to find out how many dialogues, monologues, and arias will be needed to stretch each scene of that type, so that all technical problems can be worked out without hurrying. The disintegration of the drama as an entity and the intense boredom of the audience are of no importance in connection with all this . . . For the finale of his opera he should write a magnificent scene with most elaborate effects, so that the audience won't run off before the work is half over.
>
> The libretto's subject matter need not be historically true . . . the modern librettist is faced with the task of inventing a fable and adding to it all kinds of oracles, realistic shipwrecks scenes, ominous prophecies gathered by examining the flesh of a roasted animal, etc. All that is needed is to have an historical name or two . . . the rest can then by freely invented and the only further thing that matters is that the number of verses must not exceed twelve hundred, arias included.
>
> *(Pauly 1948,* MQ *24: 375,* passim*)*

To sustain the demand for opera, private business groups, municipalities, and royal courts of Europe constructed, extensively renovated, or expanded more than 35 theatres during the first half of the eighteenth century. While some theatres remained solely for the royal courts, others began admitting a paying public. Interior decorations in court theatres, along with financial standards for theatrical production, became an integral part of the opera aesthetic. Most of the larger theatres were similar, each stage being elaborately equipped with up-to-date machinery.

The most prominent German and Austrian theatres were the Kärntnertortheater in Vienna (1709), the Opernhaus in the royal palace of Dresden (1719), and the court theatre in Mannheim and the Berlin Opernhaus opened in 1742. Smaller important court theatres included the Ludwigsburg Schlosstheater (1730) and the Margrave's Theater in Bayreuth (1748). France, with its monopoly of opera controlled by Lully's descendants in Paris, lagged behind in numbers with only three new, significant opera houses: Marseilles (1733), Bordeaux (1735), and Toulouse (1737).

Architectural exteriors and interiors of theatres reflected their local demographics. Italian theatres placed emphasis on the interior decorations but, with the exception of the court theatres in Turin and Naples, less on the exterior facades. The Regio Ducal Teatro, Milan (1717), despite its smaller and cramped stage, became the most important in northern Italy.[22] Fire destroyed the edifice in February 1776 and two and a half years later it was replaced by the magnificent Teatro alla Scala. In Turin, the grand and elegant Teatro Regio opened its doors in 1740. Two years later Naples inaugurated the splendid Teatro San Carlo with its well-equipped enormous backstage.

While staged spectacles dominated the first two decades of the eighteenth century, conformity in scenic design became the rule. There was little experimentation with colors or architectural forms in the settings depicted on the stage. Generalized settings with military encampments, groves of trees, or rooms in royal apartments became common. This practice at times proved financially advantageous since the impresario recycled sets from one opera to another. If a performer needed to hide behind a tree at the center of the scene, a painted flat of a tree of the necessary width was positioned either on a wagon that traversed the stage through a track, or placed as a freestanding unit at the specified spot. Built units (called *praticabili* in Italian – literally, "practicals"), such as actual stairs, balconies, doors, or windows, generally were not yet part of a production.

Many productions, however, paid no heed to the continuity of settings as required by the plot of the libretto and drama. Before the Metastasian reforms transformed Italian opera, stagings often neglected the balance between the drama and the production. Marcello's *Teatro alla Moda* sheds light on the absurdity of the theatre, when productions, settings, lighting, and acting ran amok.

> *Instructions for Stage Machinists and Painters of Scenery*
>
> The modern stage designer or painter must avoid any familiarity with perspective, architecture, decorating, or lighting. For that reason he should see to it that all architectural sets are designed as if viewed from four or six different points at the same time, and that the horizon is assumed at a different level for each. This kind of variety will greatly please the eye of the spectator.
>
> For the first two scenes he should provide rich cloth draperies which then can be used for all other scenes not requiring an outdoor setting. In fact, they are very nice to have around in a garden or forest scene, too, since they will protect the singers from the danger of catching cold in the open air . . .
>
> Halls, prisons, small rooms, etc., need not have any doors or windows; the singers will climb on the stage directly out of [the proscenium] boxes anyway . . .
>
> In scenes representing the seashore, the open country, sheer precipices or caves, the stage must be kept free from cliffs, rocks, grass, or tree stumps as those might restrict the virtuoso in his acting . . .

> The modern stage technician or painter must take care to employ stronger colors on props or decorations towards the rear of the stage, the farther they are removed from the spectators' eyes. This is necessary since he must distinguish himself from the old school of stage painting which sought to use softer shades the larger the distance from the audience, thus creating the illusion of spaciousness. But the modern theatrical engineer or painter must strive to achieve the opposite effect . . .
>
> The modern stage technicians and painters must outdo themselves when it comes to the set for the opera's finale. That scene will receive the greatest amount of applause since it will be judged by the crowds from the street who by this time have been let into the theatre without having to pay admission. Therefore this last scene should represent a summary of all previous scenes. Seashores, groves, dungeons, halls, smaller rooms, fountains, and fleets of ships should all be there, along with a bear hunt, large and beautiful tents, banquets, thunderstorms, and bolts of lightning.
>
> *(Pauly 1948/49: 89* passim*)*

Through the first decades of the eighteenth century, scenic designers continued to place the vanishing point of perspective at the center of the stage, with the staging and blocking of the singers concentrated at downstage center. Objects toward the rear of the stage were painted smaller than those downstage to maintain the central perspective upstage and center. At first, this scheme was intended to create settings primarily for the viewing pleasure of the ruling potentate seated both front and center in the auditorium or in his box centrally located in the first tier of boxes at the rear of the auditorium. An unobstructed view for the remainder of the audience was secondary. The concept of clear sightlines had yet to take hold and the location of this central perspective remained unchanged.

This approach to scenic perspective tended to limit entrances and exits for singers to the downstage areas. When performers remained downstage, their physical relationships to the perspective of the settings appeared normal. However, the upstage entrances of the soloists or chorus sometimes inadvertently destroyed the illusion. Francesco Algarotti, a noted critic and aesthete, acidly observed:

> Another most important article, not so much attended to as it should, is in the not leaving convenient openings in the scenes, particularly of architecture, that the actors may come on, and go off the stage, in such a manner, as that their figures may appear, to an observer's eye, to be in a just proportion with the columns. We often see them obliged to advance from the bottom [rear] of the stage, because it is there that the only entrance is contrived for them, which makes their persons shew very incongruous and offensive to a discerning spectator. The apparent magnitude of an object depends on a judicious comparison made of the exhibited figure, with its distance from us. So . . . the performers, presenting themselves from the bottom of the stage, appear like so many towering giants, by the artificial magic of the scene, through the illusive power of perspective, inducing us to fancy them at a prodigious distance. Yet these imaginary giants dwindle by degrees, as they come forward, and are dwarfed down to their native size, as they approach nearer to us.
>
> *(Algarotti 1768: 75)*

Figure 25.4 Ferdinando Galli-Bibiena, "Operation 68: Designing another scene viewed at an angle." Pen and ink drawing from *L'Architettura civile*, published in Parma 1711. (©Staatliche Graphische Sammlung, Munich.)

In 1711 the publication of Ferdinando Galli-Bibiena's *Architettura civile* presented unique methods that enabled designers to break from the strictures of the central perspective. These ideas profoundly influenced the evolution of the scenic arts in opera, spoken theatre, and dance, and remain tangible today (Figure 25.4).

A family dynasty led by the brothers Ferdinando (1657–1743) and Francesco (1659–1739) Galli added the name Bibiena to honor their father, Giovanni Maria Galli, who was a painter and the mayor of that Tuscan town. During the last two decades of the seventeenth century, the brothers worked as stage designers, scenic painters, and theatre architects in Parma, Piacenza, Reggio, Rome, Milan, Bologna, and Vienna.

In 1704 the Austrian imperial court summoned Francesco to Vienna, where he created magnificent designs for a new court theatre in the Hofburg. Francesco designed other theatres in France and Italy as well: Nancy (1709), Teatro Alibert (Rome, 1719–22), and the Teatro Filarmonico (Verona, 1728). In 1714, Francesco returned to Italy and established his workshop in Bologna. With his students, he continued to create vast numbers of architectural plans and theatrical designs.[23] Ferdinando, following his brother's path, moved to Vienna in 1712 and became the chief court architect five years later. Three of his sons became illustrious designers and architects in their own right: Alessandro, Giuseppe, and Antonio.

Ferdinando Galli-Bibiena's *magnum opus* was his treatise *L'Architettura civile*, which consists of five parts: geometry, perspective, civic architecture, painting of perspective, and equipment for transporting heavy machinery.[24] Part Four, notwithstanding its lengthy title, revolutionized theatrical production: "A Short Discourse on Painting and the Perspective for Painters of Figure: With a new Perspective of Viewing Theatrical Scenes at an Angle, along with Practical Applications for Others." Ferdinando's key formulas gave designers the capability to create scenes viewed at angles, using the technique commonly known as *scena per angolo*.

Bibiena offered a method for skewing perspective at 45° angles left and right. The vanishing point in this case was no longer restricted to an area upstage and center; it could be placed anywhere within the stage. No longer were viewers forced to endure the effect of two lines seemingly retreating into the distance and joining together at a point of perspective fixed centrally at the rear of the stage like a railroad track. Portions of corridors, grand rooms, chambers, prisons, encampments, and gardens offered different opportunities to "peer around the corners" of doorways, arches, gates, and stairs, thereby engaging the viewer's imagination. This sophisticated use of optical illusion delighted audiences and aided immensely in creating the appearance of stage depth through painted wings and backdrops.

The most important theories for the *scena per angolo* are in the sections "How to locate on wings and borders lines that converge toward the vanishing point" and "How to design scenes viewed at an angle" (Operations 62 and 67, respectively; Ogden 1978: 53, 60). The latter is accompanied by an illustrated example of a courtyard drawn both in perspective and with a detailed ground plan. Bibiena provided another illustrated example showing how to design another "scene viewed at an angle" in a large hall.[25] The floor should ramp upwards from the front edge of the stage to the rear, which aids greatly in creating the illusion of perspective. No longer was the axis for the vanishing point to be determined from the center of the first row of seats in the auditorium. Instead, the new viewpoint is pinpointed to the central box in the first gallery. This change acknowledges the new social hierarchy and its growing influence on the development of theatre architecture. Consequently, stage designs began emphasizing the importance of clear sightlines for the general audience instead of the ruler alone.

Before creating the settings, the scene designer must know the precise location of the wings. Bibiena provided instructions on "how to put theatrical scenes in perspective – first, how to find the positions of the wings and how to find scaled dimensions determined by their positions" (Ogden 1978: 49). This operation calculated the amount of space required between each set of wings for proper lighting and ease of access to the stage. The latter was especially important because of the practical difficulties encountered by singers of both sexes wearing the era's wide costumes. Theatre architects and stage machinists strove to include more space between the individual wings, in the construction of new theatres and in the renovations of existing stages.

Bibiena's theories of perspective were not new. Earlier artists and architects such as Sabbattini had used similar ideas; however, Bibiena's methods of *applying* the ideas of *scena per angolo* were previously untried. However, his treatise elucidated applications for creating diverse perspectives clearly and simply. Illustrations in the *Architettura civile* enabled most scenic artists and designers to grasp these theories immediately and to apply them with relative ease. Bibiena's techniques freed the designer's eye and imagination and gave the audience a multitude of vistas within one stage picture.

The scenic and staging possibilities thereby offered were staggering. Performers were no longer restricted to a single area downstage center and parallel to the proscenium. Now they could move back as far as the first set of wings and in a diagonal pattern. Clever designers could create an illusion of seemingly limitless stage depth for larger and, even more critically, for smaller stages.

Algarotti called Bibiena the "Paul Veronese of the Theatre" and effusively praised his invention:

> The introduction, especially, of accidental points, or rather the invention of viewing scenes by the angle, produces the finest effects imaginable; but that requires the nicest judgment to bring properly into practice. FERDINANDO BIBIENA was the inventor of those scenes, which, by the novelty of the manner, drew the eyes of all the curious upon him. They soon began to look upon, as unpleasing objects for a stage, these streets, and narrow passages, those galleries that were always made to tend to its center, there at once to limit the spectators imagination and sight.
>
> *(Algarotti 1768: 77–8)*

Figure 25.5 Fabrizio Galliari, design for Antonio Salieri's *Europa riconosciuta*, Act II, sc. 7: "A majestic hall for the meeting of the supreme council." This was one of 28 settings Galliari created for the opera for the opening of the Teatro alla Scala in Milan, 1778. (Courtesy of Civico Gabinetto dei Disegni–Castello Sforzesco – Milano, ©Commune di Milano, all rights reserved.)

Bibiena's theories took years to make their impact. When they did, however, the results fundamentally changed the direction of scenic design for all of the theatrical arts.

A boom in construction of opera houses throughout the second half of the eighteenth century resulted in more than 140 new theatres, large and small, opening throughout Europe. The Bibiena family and their students were prolific; they designed more than 20 theatres.[26] Antonio alone designed eight, the most famous being the Teatro Comunale in Bologna (1763); Giuseppe Galli-Bibiena designed the Margrave's Theater in Bayreuth (1748). The latter theatres are prime examples of contemporary tastes and baroque styles running delightfully amok.

Italian designers and architects continued to dominate the stage and extended their influence throughout Europe. Ferdinando Bibiena's theories took root, and many smaller theatres were able to create grand settings previously seen only on larger stages. The three brothers Galliari (Bernardino, Fabrizio, and Ferdinando) were chief designers at the Teatro Regio in their hometown of Turin and the Regio Ducal Teatro and, later, the Teatro alla Scala in Milan (Figure 25.5). Production values in their work and that of others changed through constant evolution in scenic design and stage painting so that it began to incorporate simple "practicals," that is, three-dimensional elements such as steps, stairs, and platforms within the settings. Designers gradually relied less on only painted wings and borders to create an optical illusion.

Spectacle, however, was still an important part of production. Then, as now, new productions were very expensive in material costs and also manpower. Even though most opera productions were far simpler than earlier in the century, impresarios and theatre directors could still concoct elaborate effects. Designs became more realistic but often generic: a room within a palace, a tented city, a garden, a grand gallery, or a mausoleum. The use of flying machines and traps continued, but more selectively.

Generic scenery and drops became standard because they saved money and needed only minor repainting or retouching to lull the public into believing they were seeing new settings. Stage designers and scenery painters were (and still are) exceedingly clever; they knew how to draw out the best effects in order to make the greatest impact on the public.

Effective stage lighting is vital to achieve optimum scenic effect. Given the relatively subdued illumination possible in the seventeenth and eighteenth centuries, various techniques improved its effect. For example, reflective material in both scenery and costumes made them more visible. Open flames from small pots of oil provided most of the lighting, supplemented by tallow candles placed primarily at two locations on the stage.[27] The most common placement was at the edge of the forestage, hence this area was known as the footlights. In many theatres raising the ramp of candles above or lowering it below the stage floor regulated the intensity of the illumination. More lamps were mounted behind each chariot, which slid on or off the stage as necessary. Another method placed a series of lamps affixed on a pole in each of the wings. To dim the illumination, the poles revolved away from the stage. Controlling the intensity of the light for illuminating the actors and settings was no easy task. The larger the stage, the more flames were required, and the greater the costs. Light sources could not be recycled as could scenery, backdrops, and costumes; consequently, illumination frequently was the largest expenditure for any production.

Candles needed daily replenishment and tending during a performance. Lamps frequently emitted clouds of smoke along with occasional foul odors. Tapers for each candle required constant trimming during the course of the opera to maintain a consistent flame. Often a worker had to enter the stage during the change of scenery or between the acts to adjust the candles in the footlights, and avoid interrupting the scenic action. (In France, these *moucheurs* ("snuffers") were much loved by the public.) Despite these drawbacks, economics dictated that management of many theatres favor tallow candles over the more expensive, though brighter, wax candles.

Pre-twentieth-century stage lighting did not reach the same artistic level as scene design. Up to the end of the eighteenth century oil and candlepower continued to light the stages, providing sufficient illumination to make the settings and costumes visible. Attempts to control the intensity and color of the light remained crude. At the same time, lighting continued to be costly. Surviving eighteenth-century documents show that oil and candles for illumination were among the most expensive items of any production budget.

Three positions in the stage area provided sites for lighting: at the front edge of the forestage (footlights), behind both sides of the proscenium, and on the rear of the frames of the rolling wing chariots. Each lamp, backed by a reflective metal sheet, cast its light towards the stage and decors. Light spread only several feet from the wings, and gloom enveloped the large backdrops. The purity of the wax or tallow, together with the quality of the candlewicks, determined the brightness of the light. Consequently, controlled dimming of the light was difficult. Once a candle was lit, the only change easily effected was a greater degree of darkness, obtained either by covering the flame in varying degrees – as suggested by Sabbattini one hundred years earlier – or by extinguishing it altogether. To dim the lights at the Drottningholm court theatre, where eighteenth-century techniques are still used (along with electricity), stagehands gradually turn groups of candles mounted on poles away from the stage and toward the wings. Other attempts, such as lowering the footlights below the stage floor, remained clumsy and rudimentary.

Footlights created unique problems. If the singers came too far downstage, the extreme angle of the light distorted their facial features with shadows and exaggerated the hand gestures and body movements. Fire was an ever-present danger, especially if the performers came too close to the open flames of the footlights. Drafts of air passing over the flame caused unwanted variations of intensity and sometimes unexpected flickering. Smoke frequently rose from the flames, obscured the stage, and created health hazards. If the candle or the oil was of poor quality, a terrible stench assaulted the performers and the public. Stagehands continued to enter the stage to trim the footlight wicks, thus distracting from the performance.

Stage design and scenic painting compensated in some degree for the dimness of the stage. Artists prepared formulas that enabled colors to stand out in the shadows. New techniques in painting scenery increased optical illusions of perspectives, shadows, and highlights. Reflective material might be added or stronger colors painted on the canvas to emphasize scenic contrasts. For special effects, such as twinkling starlight or fireworks, small holes were punctured through the drop with large batches of candles lit behind a second upstage drop to hide the glowing flames. At the specified moment in the performance stagehands quickly raised the masking drop, which resulted in a marvelous display of starlight shining through the holes of the backdrop.

Candelabras and chandeliers, complete with their copious wax drippings, were the norm for illuminating the auditoriums. The main chandelier, which remained lit throughout the entire performance, required large quantities of candles. Sconces or candelabras affixed to the fronts of the boxes provided additional light. For gala or festive events every available candelabra and sconce brilliantly lit the auditorium. Additional candelabras hung in front of the boxes, all of which required even greater expenditure for more candles and oil lamps. Lighting was an expensive commodity. When hundreds of lamps were required for both stage and auditorium, theatre administrations frequently requested the local government or court to underwrite the extra costs.[28]

Despite all the difficulties, lighting technology continued to improve, gradually resulting in greater illumination with less expense. Wax candles that gave somewhat more light and less smoke began to replace tallow candles. In oil lamps flat, twisted, ribbon-like wicks generated twice the amount of illumination in contrast to older single-string wicks.

A great advance in theatre illumination occurred in 1783 when Emile Argand (1755–1803) received a patent for a lamp that emitted ten times greater light. It was soon dubbed the "Argand burner." A separate reservoir housed the oil for the flame. Attached by a feeding tube from the oil reservoir, two short concentric metal tubes housed a cylindrical wick that soaked up the oil, providing fuel for the flame located in the inside tube. A glass chimney-like tube increased the intake of air through the inside tube, thus burning the oil more efficiently and producing a cleaner, clearer flame with far less smoke. A metal reflector attached to the same mount as the glass cylinder bounced the light of the flame off the shiny surfaces towards the stage (see Pougin 1885: 318; Baker 2013: 91 and Plate 46).

The artistic advantages of the new invention quickly became evident. No longer would audiences view thick smoke emanating from the tallow lamps. Stacking the lamps on the scenery frames in the wings closest to the stage, as well as in the footlights, radiated bright light and produced dramatic improvements in illuminating the stage, the performers, and the stage decors. The primary drawback of Argand lamps was economic; the burner consumed more oil and tubes frequently shattered, particularly if the quality of the glass was poor, which required replacement.

Breakage costs notwithstanding, the Argand lamps proved extremely beneficial and quickly came to be widely used. Scenic artists resourcefully adapted to the new medium, which required changes in applications of color and shading during the painting of scenery and backdrops. New techniques included the application of sparkling material on canvases to create glittering effects. Controlling the flames for achieving a consistent light became more precise.

Notes

1 This essay is a condensed and edited extract from the first three chapters of Evan Baker (2013), *From the Score to the Stage: An Illustrated History of Continental Opera Production and Staging* (Chicago, IL: University of Chicago Press).

2 "Teatro Farnese" is a contemporary name; originally, it was known simply as *Teatro nel Salone*, a large room for theatrical events (Nagler 1964: 152).

3 Nagler's description of the Teatro Farnese is derived from Marcello Buttigli's report, *Descrittione dell'apparato fatto per honorare la prima e solenne entrata in Parma della serenissima principessa Margherita di Toscana, duchessa di Parma, Piacenza* (Parma, 1629). Buttigli claimed the theatre could seat 10,000, which Nagler rightfully called an "exaggeration" (Nagler 1964: 153 f.n. 63). Although this number is high, it must be remembered that in past centuries the human physiognomy was much smaller, thus allowing considerably more people into the space.

4 Marzio dall'Acqua provides a concise general overview with excellent illustrations, "Farnese Illusion" for the Italian periodical, *FMR* (English edition) 1 (June 1984): 77–98. A fuller account may be found in Luca Ronconi, Marzio dall'Acqua, *et al.*, *Lo Spettacolo e la Meraviglia: Il Teatro Farnese di Parma e la Festa Barocca* (Turin, 1992).

5 Claudio Monteverdi composed the tournament music set to the libretto by Claudio Achillini.
6 The translation from Latin reads, "Ranuccio Farnese, fourth duke of Parma and Piacenza, fifth duke of Castro, opened this theatre to Bellona [goddess of war] and the Muses with august liberality in the year 1619." Dall'Acqua (Ronconi, Luca, Marzio Dall'Acqua *et al.* 1992: 81) also noted that the front curtain behind the proscenium arch was lowered during the preparations for the performance to hide the effects from the craftsmen in the auditorium so they would not be distracted by the wondrous scenic effects unfolding on the stage.
7 *Andromeda*'s plot centers on the myth of Perseus and Andromeda. The goddess Juno, angered that Cassiopeia boasted that her beauty was greater than her own, orders Neptune to have a sea-monster devour Andromeda, the braggart's daughter. Perseus laments Andromeda's decision to accept her fate. After much fussing by the gods, Perseus arrives and slays the monster. Perseus asks for Andromeda's hand, and Juno's heart softens. Jupiter raises the two lovers to heaven.
8 Much of the production had its seeds in Felice Sanches and Pio Enea degli Obizzi's *Ermiona*, staged in Padua one year earlier with similar appearances of deities and monsters, such as a dragon and the sea monster. Cf. Pierluigi Petrobelli, "Francesco Manelli: Documentazione e Osservazioni" in *Chigiana*, 24 (1967): 43–66.
9 It is worth noting that Manelli, the composer of the opera, performed Neptune himself.
10 Nicola Sabbattini, "Pratica di Fabricar Scene e Machine ne' Teatri" (Ravenna, 1638). An English translation is provided by John H. McDowell as "Manual for Constructing Theatrical Scenes and Machines" in *The Renaissance Stage: Documents of Serlio, Sabbattini and Furttenbach* (Miami, 1958). All Sabbattini citations refer to this English translation. Several facsimiles of the original Italian editions have been published, the latest being Alberto Perrini (Ed.), *Nicola Sabbattini. Scene e Macchine Teatrali: Della Commedia dell'arte e Della Scenotecnica Barocca con i Disegni Originali* (Rome, 1989). An online edition is available at: https://archive.org/details/praticadifabrica00sabb.
11 No one standard terminology exists for this mechanism. "Wing wagon" is one description, whereas the French use "chariot," which is the same in English. Italian is *carretto* or *carrozza*, a carriage. German is *Kulissen*, also "Wing wagon." For consistency, the term "chariot" will be used throughout.
12 This is not a new phenomenon; earlier opera librettos such as Pio Enea degli Obizzi's *Ermiona* (Padua, 1636) also were published with illustrations.
13 "Giacomo Torelli da Fano inventò il moversi delle scene coll'argano, e fece quattro famosi teatri in Parigi, Parma, Venezia e Fano." Museo Correr Venice, Cod. Cicogna 2991, fasc. II, fol. 30. Cited by Molmenti, 3: 158. The standard works on Torelli are Per Bjurström's *Giacomo Torelli and Baroque Stage Design* (Stockholm, 1961) and the exhibition catalogue, *Giacomo Torelli: L'Invenzione Scenica nell'Europa Barocca* (Fano, 2005).
14 The size of the Teatro Novissimo and its spaces was recently extrapolated from several surviving documents. The complete area measured 14.70 meters wide and 29.50 meters long with the width of the proscenium opening measuring 9.00 meters and a height of 6.70 meters. When the first season at the Novissimo began in 1641, the depth of the stage from the proscenium to the furthest upstage wings measured 12.00 meters with another 4.10 meters added for the 1642 season (Mancini *et al.* 1985–95, Vol. 1: 323).
15 Only one copy survives at the Biblioteca Marciana, Venice. A complete transcription is printed in the program book of the Teatro la Fenice for the first modern production of *La finta pazza*, July 1987, pp. 1020–52. All references, unless otherwise noted, are to this edition. Extracts in English may be found in Bjurström 1961 and Rosand 1991, available online at: http://ark.cdlib.org/ark:/13030/ft3199n7sm/.
16 Torelli himself wrote two pamphlets with scenic descriptions that included engravings of stage designs for the subsequent operas: *Bellerofonte* (1642), and the *Apparati scenici per lo Teatro Novissimo di Venetia* (1644), the latter discussing the productions of *Venere gelosa* (1643) and *Deidamia* (1644). Both pamphlets are extremely rare, since they were separate, ephemeral publications with detailed descriptions of the production. They foreshadowed the staging manual, known as the *disposizione scenica*, or *Regiebuch*, or *livret de mise en scène*, common in nineteenth-century Italy, Germany, and France.
17 A low resolution digital reproduction of the designs is available on Gallica, beginning with page 62: http://gallica.bnf.fr/ark:/12148/bpt6k111118c.

18 Fabrizio Carini Motta, *Trattato sopra la struttura de' teatri e scene* (Guastalla, 1676). A facsimile of the original in the Bavarian State Library can be viewed at http://reader.digitale-sammlungen.de/de/fs1/object/display/bsb10862738_00003.html

19 The manuscript is located at the Biblioteca Estense in Modena. Orville K. Larson (Ed. and Trans.), *The Theatrical Writings of Fabrizio Carini Motta: Translations of "Trattato sopra la struttura de' Theatri e scene, 1676" and "Costruzione de teatri e machine teatrali, 1688"* (Carbondale, 1987).

20 Twenty-four prints reproducing each scene were published in 1668. A folio-sized and gloriously handcolored set of the prints are available in the music collections of the Austrian National Library and for online viewing at: http://data.onb.ac.at/rec/AL00161749. A facsimile of the libretto with the 24 designs in a German edition appeared in 1965 for the members of the Wiener Bibliophilen-Gesellschaft with an afterword by Margret Dietrich.

21 Benedetto Marcello, *Il Teatro alla Moda* (Venice, 1720). Without a doubt, Marcello exaggerated to make good stories. Nonetheless, there is much truth in what he wrote. All references here are to the English translation by Reinhard G. Pauly, "Benedetto Marcello's *Il Teatro alla Moda*." *Musical Quarterly*, 24 (1948): 222–33, 371–403; and 25 (1949): 85–105. Hereafter cited as Pauly.

22 A contemporary description of the Milanese theatre, with two plates, is in Serviliano Latuada, *Descrizione di Milano, ornata con molti disegni in rame delle fabbriche più cospicue, che si trovano in questa metropoli*, 5 Vols. (Milan, 1737–38) 2: 136–9.

23 The original designs of the Bibiena family and their workshops are scattered throughout the world. The largest number is in the Staatliche Graphische Sammlung in Munich, which holds over 600 designs. Other significant repositories include the Austrian Theater Museum, Graphische Sammlung Albertina, and Akademie der bildende Künste, all of Vienna, and the Metropolitan Museum of Art, New York. See the exhibition catalogue by Deana Lenzi and Jadranka Bentini, *I Bibiena: Una Famiglia in Scena Da Bologna all'Europa* (Venice, 2000).

24 Ferdinando Galli-Bibiena, *L'Architettura civile* (Parma, 1711). All references are to the English translation in Dunbar Ogden, *The Italian Baroque Stage: Documents by Giulio Troili, Andrea Pozzo, Ferdinando Galli-Bibiena, and Baldassare Orsini* (Berkeley, 1978). The original Italian edition can be viewed at: http://dx.doi.org/10.3931/e-rara-9304.

25 The published print for this "operation" (1711 edition, opposite p. 139 and reproduced in Odgen 1978, *Baroque Stage*: 63) does not do justice to the theories of Bibiena. The original drawing for Operation 68 survives in the Staatliche Graphische Sammlung in Munich. See Baker 2013, *From the Score to the Stage*, plate 24 for a reproduction of the original drawing.

26 This number does not include projects that did not come to fruition.

27 Tallow candles were manufactured from animal fats, with a cotton wick for the flame.

28 Occupants of boxes provided their own lighting. Many people brought a candle for extra light to read their personal copies of the libretto. Librettos from the period housed in the Museo Teatrale alla Scala in Milan still show wax droppings on numerous pages.

References

Adami, Giuseppe 2003. *Scenografia e scenotechnica barocca tra Ferrara e Parma (1625–1631)*. Rome: L'Erma di Bretschneider.

Algarotti, Francesco 1768. *An Essay on the Opera. Written in Italian*. London: R. Urie.

Allevy, Marie Antoinette 1938. *La Mise en scène en France dans la première moitié du dix-neuvième siècle*. Paris: E. Droz.

Aronson, Arnold 2005. *Looking into the Abyss: Essays on Scenography*. Ann Arbor: University of Michigan Press.

Austin, Paul Britten and Inger Mattsson 1991. *Gustavian Opera: An Interdisciplinary Reader in Swedish Opera, Dance, and Theatre, 1771-1809*. Stockholm: Royal Swedish Academy.

Badenhausen, Rolf and Harald Zielske (Eds) 1974. *Bühnenformen, Bühnenräume, Bühnendekorationen: Beiträge zur Entwicklung des Spielorts: Herbert A. Frenzel zum 65. Geburtstag von Freunden und wissenschaftlichen Mitstreitern*. Berlin: E. Schmidt.

Baker, Evan 2013. *From the Score to the Stage. An Illustrated History of Continental Opera Production and Staging*. Chicago, IL: University of Chicago Press.

Bapst, Germain 1893. *Essai sur l'histoire de théâtre: La mise en scène, le décor, le costume, l'architecture, l'éclairage, l'hygiène*. Paris: Hachette.

Bastistelli, Franco 2005. *Giacomo Torelli: L'Invenzione scenica nell'Europa barocca*. Fano: Fondazione Cassa di Risparmio.

Baumann, Carl Friedrich 1988. *Licht im Theater: Von der Argand-Lampe bis zum Glühlampen-Scheinwerfer*. Stuttgart: F. Steiner Verlag.

Beijer, Agne 1933. *Slottsteatrarna pä Drottningholm och Gripsholm*. Malmo: John Kroon.

Biach-Schiffmann, Flora 1931. *Giovanni und Ludovico Burnacini: Theater und Feste am Wiener Hofe*. Vienna: Krystall-Verlag.

Bianconi, Lorenzo and Giorgio Pestelli 1988. *Storia Dell'Opera Italiana*, Vol. 5, *La spettacolarità*. Torino: EDT/Musica.

Bisaccioni, Maiolino 1987. "Il cannocchiale per *La finta pazza*." In *La finta pazza*, edited by Cristiano Chiarot, 1020–63. Program book. Gran Teatro la Fenice, Venice.

Bjurström, Per 1961. *Giacomo Torelli and Baroque Stage Design*. Stockholm: Almqvist & Wiksell.

Bjurström, Per 1966. "Unveröffentlichtes von Nicodemus Tessin d. J.: Reisenotizen über Barock-Theater in Venedig und Piazzola." *Kleine Schriften der Gesellschaft für Theatergeschichte* 21: 14–41.

Blumenthal, Arthur 1980. *Theater Art of the Medici*. Hanover, NH: Dartmouth College Museum and Galleries.

Brockett, Oscar, Margaret Mitchell and Linda Hardberger (Eds) 2010. *Making the Scene: A History of Stage Design and Technology in Europe and the United States*. San Antonio: Tobin Theatre Arts Fund.

Carini Motta, Fabrizio 1676. *Trattato sopra la struttura de' theatri e scene*. Guastalla: Alessandro Giavazzi.

Carini Motta, Fabrizio and Orville K. Larson 1987. *The Theatrical Writings of Fabrizio Carini Motta: translations of* Trattato sopra la struttura de' theatri e scene, *1676 and* Costruzione de teatri e machine teatrali, *1688*. Carbondale, IL: Southern Illinois University Press.

Cavicchi, Adriano 1976. "Scenotecnica e Macchinistica Teatrale in un Trattato Inedito di Fabrizio Carini Motta (Mantova, 1688)." In *Venezia e il Melodramma nel Seicento*, edited by Maria Teresa Muraro, 359–77. Florence: L.S. Olschki.

Fabbri, Paolo and Angelo Pompilio (Eds) 1983 [1989]. *Il corago, o vero Alcune osservazione per metter bene in scena le composizioni drammatiche*. Studi e testi per la storia della musica, no. 4. Florence. English translation (partial) by Roger Savage and Matteo Sansone, "*Il Corago* and the Staging of Early Opera: Four Chapters from an Anonymous Treatise circa 1630." *Early Music* 17(4): 495–511.

Ferrario, Giulio (Ed.), Pierre Patte and Paolo Landriani 1830. *Storia e descrizione de' principali teatri antichi e moderni corredata di tavole : col saggio sull'archtettura teatrale*. Milan: G. Ferrario.

Galli-Bibiena, Ferdinando 1711. *L'Architettura civile sú la geometria*. Parma: Paola Monti.

Gamba, Enrico and Vico Montebelli 1995. *Macchine da Teatro e Teatri di Macchine: Branca, Sabbattini, Torelli; Scenotecnici e Meccanici del Seicento*. Urbino: Quattroventi.

Glixon, Beth L. and Jonathan E. Glixon 1992. "Marco Faustini and Venetian Opera Production in the 1650s." *Journal of Musicology* 10: 48–73.

Glixon, Beth L. and Jonathan E. Glixon 2006. *Inventing the Business of Opera: The Impresario and His World in Seventeenth-Century Venice*. Oxford: Oxford University Press.

Griffin, Robert Arthur 1972. *High Baroque Culture and Theatre in Vienna*. New York: Humanities Press.

Hadamowsky, Franz 1962. *Die Familie Galli-Bibiena in Wien: Leben und Werk für das Theater*. Vienna: G Prachner.

Hansell, Kathleen Kuzmick 1979. *Opera and Ballet at the Regio Ducal Teatro of Milan 1771–1776: A Musical and Social History*, 3 Vols. PhD diss., University of California, Berkeley.

Hewitt, Barnard (Ed.) 1958. *The Renaissance Stage: Documents of Serlio, Sabbattini and Furttenbach*, translated by Allardyce Nicoll, John H. McDowell and George R. Kernodle. Coral Gables, FL: University of Miami Press.

La Gorce, Jérôme de 1997. *Féeries d'Opéra: Décors, Machines et Costumes en France, 1645–1765*. Paris: Patrimoine.

La Gorce, Jérôme de 2010. *Dans l'Atelier des Menu Plaisirs du Roi: Spectacles, Fêtes et Cérémonies aux XVIIe et XVIIIe Siècles.* Paris: Archives Nationales-Versailles, Artlys.

Landriani, Paolo [1815] 1996. "*Osservazioni sui difetti prodotti nei teatri dalla cattiva costruzione del palcoscenico e su alcune inavvertenze nel dipingere le decorazioni*," Milan, translated by Briant Hamor Lee in *European Post-Baroque Neoclassical Theatre Architecture.* Lewiston, PA: Edwin Mellen Press.

Lenzi, Deanna and Jadranka Bentini 2000. *I Bibiena: Una Famiglia Europea.* Bologna: Marsilio.

Mancini, Franco, Elena Povoledo and Maria Teresa Muraro (Eds) 1985–95. *I Teatri del Veneto*, 6 Vols. Venice: Corbo e Fiore.

Molmenti, Pompeo 1908. *Venice: Its Individual Growth from the Earliest Beginnings to the Fall of the Republic.* London: John Murray.

Nagler, A. M. 1964. *Theatre Festivals of the Medici, 1539–1637.* New Haven, CT: Yale University Press.

Ogden, Dunbar (Ed. and Trans.) 1978. *The Italian Baroque Stage: Documents by Giulio Troili, Andrea Pozzo, Ferdinando Galli-Bibiena, and Baldassare Orsini.* Berkeley: University of California Press.

Patte, Pierre 1782. *Essai sur l'Architecture Théâtrale, ou De l'Ordonnance la plus Avantageuse à une Salle de Spectacles, Relativement aux Principes de l'Optique et de l'Acoustique.* Paris.

Pauly, Reinhard G. 1948 and 1949. "Benedetto Marcello's *Il Teatro alla Moda.*" *Musical Quarterly*, 24: 222–33, 371–403, and 25: 85–105.

Pougin, Arthur 1885. *Dictionnaire Historique et Pittoresque du Théâtre et des Arts qui s'y Rattachent* [etc.]. Paris: Firmin-Didot.

Rapp, Franz 1930. "Ein Theater-Bauplan des Giovanni Battista Aleotti." *Neues Archiv für Theatergeschichte* 41: 79–125.

Ronconi, Luca, Marzio Dall'Acqua, *et al.* 1992. *Lo Spettacolo e la Meraviglia: Il Teatro Farnese di Parma e la Festa Barocca.* Turin: Nuova ERI.

Rosand, Ellen 1991. *Opera in Seventeenth-Century Venice: The Creation of a Genre.* Berkeley: University of California Press.

Solf, Sabine 1975. *Festdekoration und Groteske: Der Wiener Bühnenbildner Lodovico Ottavio Burnacini; Inszenierung barocker Kunstvorstellung.* Baden-Baden: V. Koerner.

Sommer-Mathis, Andrea, Daniela Franke and Rudi Risatti 2016. *Spettacolo Barocco! Triumph des Theaters.* Vienna: Michael Imhof Verlag.

Wolfe, John J. 1999. *Brandy, Balloons, & Lamps: Ami Argand, 1750–1803.* Carbondale: Southern Illinois University Press.

Wolff, Hellmut Christian 1968. *Oper: Szene und Darstellung von 1600 bis 1900.* Leipzig: Deutscher Verlag für Musik.

Wolff, Hellmut Christian 1969. "Bühnenbild und Inszenierung der italienischen Oper 1600–1700." In *Congresso Internazionale sul tema Claudio Monteverdi e il suo tempo: Relazioni e Comunicazioni*, edited by Raffaele Monterosso, 105–15. Verona: Valdonega.

Worsthorne, Simon Towneley 1968. *Venetian Opera in the Seventeenth Century.* Oxford: Oxford University Press.

26

RESTORATION AND EIGHTEENTH-CENTURY ENGLAND

David Kornhaber

"It is an Argument of the worth of the Plays and Actors, of the last Age . . . to consider that they cou'd support themselves meerly from their own Merit; the weight of the Matter, and goodness of the Action, without Scenes and Machines," observes James Wright in his *Historia Histrionica* from 1699 (Wright 1699: 6). Unlike the public playhouses of England's early modern period, the theatres of Wright's day – those that opened in London after the restoration of the monarchy in 1660 and the lifting of the Interregnum ban on theatrical performance in that same year – could boast no such similar achievement. Modeled largely on the European (and especially French) theatres that England's exiled aristocrats and theatre practitioners had come to know intimately during their years on the Continent, the playhouses of Restoration-era London all prominently featured the "Scenes and Machines" of which Wright seemed so skeptical and that were relatively new to the English theatrical tradition. There were a few prominent English models, to be sure: the Blackfriars Theatre was probably the closest in-country correlate from the era before the Civil War, and Italianate perspective scenery had been used before by Inigo Jones in his legendary Jacobean court masques. But as Wright's undisguised nostalgia attests, a new era in English scenographic design had begun.

It was, at first, a moment of some hybridity. Despite Wright's wistful remembrances, aspects of the Elizabethan and Jacobean public playhouses did in fact persist into Restoration-era theatre design through the element of the forestage, with significant implications for the era's scenographic practices. Often seen as a holdover from the thrust stages of the early modern era, the forestage was an area of undecorated stage space in front of the proscenium arch that allowed for a degree of intimacy between the actor and the audience in the pit. On the other side of the proscenium arch, painted canvas wings of decreasing size lined the edges of the raked stage, with horizontal borders masking the top of the stage and painted flats called shutters masking the back. (The shutters would be replaced by painted drops toward the turn of the eighteenth century.) Standing in grooves on the floor with matching grooves above, the wings and shutters could be easily slid onstage and off by stagehands, often revealing a second set positioned directly behind the first, while the borders could be pulled up or down from the flies.

The effects of this construction were twofold. On the one hand, the grooved system allowed for rapid changes of scenery to become a normal feature of Restoration play production, and the at times peripatetic written drama of the era reflects this newfound capacity. At the same time, the division between the upstage portions of the stage space devoted to the mechanics of wing-shutter-border shifting and the downstage space of the forestage on the other side of the proscenium arch created a visual disjunction between the space of the actors and the space of the scenery. More than likely, the majority of a play's action was performed in the forestage area while the scenery remained behind the proscenium, although the boundary point was far from solid and the arrangement of the actors may have varied depending on the play. Regardless, the natural divide between scene and performer created by the placement of the proscenium kept at bay any notion of an enveloping illusionism. The effect was closer to that of an idealized pictorialism, with the scenery serving more of an indicatory function than an illustrative one – pointing toward the locale to be imagined rather than specifically representing it within a shared space with the performers.

For early Restoration audiences, the scenographic effect of these wing-shutter-border arrangements was no less vivid for their indicative rather than illustrative qualities. "The scenery is very light, capable of a great many changes, and embellished with beautiful landscapes," wrote one Italian visitor during a trip to Drury Lane in 1669 (Magalotti 1960: 159). Audiences were likewise won over by the stage effects that were newly enabled within the design of the Restoration theatres. With their system of masked wings and flies at the sides and top of the stage, Restoration theatres were able to create the illusion of flight using a series of cranes and rolling platforms, appearances from below using trap doors and elevators, the image of rolling ocean waves using movable flats, as well as rapid reveals and changes of locales using the wings, shutters, and borders. Hence the more spectacular features of an opera like John Dryden's *Albion and Albanius*, which calls for, among many other attractions, a moment when "the clouds divide, and Juno appears in a Machine drawn by Peacocks; while a Symphony is playing, it moves gently forward, and as it descends, it opens and discovers the Tail of the Peacock" (Dryden 1976: 26).

Such costly moments of visual extravagance were far from the norm in Restoration productions, however, and most plays of the era called for only a few relatively simple and standard interior or exterior set pieces. In fact, the general scenographic trend of the Restoration and early eighteenth-century stage was one of complacent visual repetition rather than innovative spectacle. The majority of set pieces were generic and recyclable, and the major London theatres each maintained a storehouse of reusable wings, shutters, and borders – an expanded scene room was added to the rebuilt Drury Lane in 1674 specifically for this purpose. These familiar set pieces would even become well-known to a theatre's more regular patrons: "I never see those wings slide on but I feel as if seeing my very old acquaintance unexpectedly," as one theatre-goer of the age sardonically observed of a certain palace scene (Wilkinson 1790: 92).

By the 1730s, barely 60 years after the reopening of the playhouses, accounts were already beginning to appear depicting the London stage as a moribund institution – "a sight of so much shabbiness and majesty" in the words of one dramatist and theatrical pamphleteer (Hill 1735). It was a narrative of decline premised to a significant degree on the sorry state of the era's perpetually recycled scene paintings. "It cannot but be acknowledg'd it wou'd be much more reasonable that the scenery should always represent at least the place where the action represented is said to be perform'd, than that it should be left at random in this point," wrote another account (Hill 1750: 222). Such complaints stemmed at least in part from a growing intolerance with the double-vision that lay at the heart of the Restoration-era stage. As London's population grew, the managers of the city's major theatres engaged in a series of architectural re-designs over the course of the early eighteenth century that first shortened and then eventually eliminated the forestage of the Restoration playhouses, replacing it with more paying seats in the pit. The two sequestered worlds of the Restoration stage, the scenographic and the actorly, were thus slowly brought together, with no corresponding change in the nature of English scenographic practice. It is one thing to watch a performance where a shifting array of generic flats transition behind the actors to broadly gesture toward the locations of the play, quite another to see those same actors playing directly against those same generic backdrops. The problems of visual discordance were only exacerbated by the lingering tradition of placing audience members on the stage – relatively discreetly in boxes on the sides of the stages for regular performances and then quite obtrusively throughout the main playing space during special benefit nights, when patrons paid for the privilege of watching their favored actors up close. The calls for greater illusionism that start to be seen around the middle of the eighteenth century were also calls for a resolution to the contradictions between the relative positions of actor, audience, and scenery that were becoming increasingly intractable.

The figure who did the most to rescue the eighteenth-century English stage from its position of visual incoherence was not a scene designer but an actor: the famed David Garrick. In his capacity as manager of Drury Lane from 1747 to 1776, Garrick introduced a number of innovations that fundamentally transitioned the English stage away from the visual model of the Restoration era and toward the illusionistic conditions that would become dominant during the nineteenth century. The most notable and most celebrated of these was the elimination of spectators from the stage, which Garrick put into force in 1763. (Ever the conscientious manager, he first found a means of expanding the auditorium so as to offset the lost revenue from those pricey stage seats.) Less noted but of no lesser consequence was the introduction of candle lighting along the sides of the stage to supplement the chandelier lighting that emanated from the center of the stage space. The effects of this change on the possibilities for English scenographic design were substantial: for the first time, the upstage portions of the stage reserved for scenery might be seen with as much clarity and detail as the downstage portions dominated by the chandelier lighting. A new visual equivalency between the different portions of the stage had been established, and with that space newly cleared of intruding spectators the conditions were set for a new approach to scenographic illusionism.

Garrick found that new approach in the work of a French landscape artist newly relocated to London named Philippe-Jacques de Loutherbourg. Starting in 1772, De Loutherbourg served as Drury Lane's primary scenic designer for nine years, and "in that wink of time," as Ralph Allen observes, "a century seemed to pass" (Allen 1981: 97). During De Loutherbourg's reign, the London stage transitioned from a realm of bifurcated pictorial and actorly spaces that still maintained vestiges of early modern stage practice to a place of unified illusionism in which the actor was enveloped in and supported by a realistic set design. First and foremost among De Loutherbourg's innovations was the modification of the wing-shutter-border apparatus that had defined

Figure 26.1 Set design, *c.* 1772, by Philippe Jacques de Loutherbourg for a production of *Richard III* (most likely at the Theatre Royal, Drury Lane, on 30 May 1772), showing an asymmetrical arrangement of foreground tents, built pieces of scenery in the middle distance, and a painted backdrop beyond. (© Victoria and Albert Museum, London.)

English scenographic practice for the better part of the last century. In its place, he substituted a so-called "broken scene" – overlapping flats of various rather than uniform dimensions, placed at irregular intervals on the stage so as to create an impression of depth and distance.

The change created a degree of dimensionality that had not yet been seen on the English stage; rather than perform in front of the perspective scenery, the actor could now perform alongside and move through the scenographic elements. In some cases, De Loutherbourg coupled this to an articulation of the stage space itself that meant to adjust the playable area to the contours demanded by the design. The 1772 stage plans for *A Christmas Tale*, for instance, indicate the use of a series of ramps masked by painted raking pieces so as to allow the actors to move up and down the rocky landscape. In such a realm of carefully articulated stage space, specificity in the painted imagery became for once the rule rather than the exception. Gone were the days of dusty flats featuring generic palace chambers dragged out from the theatre's scene room time and again. De Loutherbourg exalted in a studied and widely celebrated exactitude in his depictions, traveling to the English Midlands to draft the scenery for *The Wonders of Derbyshire* or creating a carefully observed replica of a particular naval review that took place in

Portsmouth in 1773, crafting scale models of each ship featured in that review and placing them against a painted backdrop of the city's harbor.

During De Loutherbourg's heyday, the scene designer became a star attraction. By the 1780s, De Loutherbourg was being paid as much for his work as were the city's best dramatists – £100 for a new scene design – and the designer, once an ancillary figure who only occasionally painted new flats for an upcoming production, became a prime creative collaborator. De Loutherbourg's status reached such heights, in fact, that it was not uncommon for plays to be written so as to highlight his pre-designed scenes, as in the much-revived *Christmas Tale*, written "in a hurry & on purpose to shew some fine Scenes where were designed by Mons De Loutherberg" (Hopkins [1773] 1960). De Loutherbourg's designs, one account raved, depicted "the most beautiful scenes next to those in the opera at Paradise" (Walpole 1906: 37).

As great as De Loutherbourg's influence was on the English stage, his time as an active participant in London theatre was ultimately short-lived. If his innovations helped in large part to answer calls for greater verisimilitude on the London stage, he eventually fell victim to renewed public calls for theatrical change. In a way, De Loutherbourg represented an overcorrection in the ongoing balancing act between scenographic spectacle and dramatic interest, and his career was dogged by complaints that Drury Lane was privileging scenery over substance. Of De Loutherbourg's *Wonders of Derbyshire*, one critic wrote, "This subject was judiciously chosen for the display of Mr. Loutherbrough's abilities; but he should have been accompanied into Derbyshire by a man of some dramatick genius; or at least of talents for the invention of a pantomime" (*The London Magazine* 1779: 31). Fewer than 10 years after he first started at Drury Lane, De Loutherbourg was off the theatre's payroll; the company's new manager, Richard Sheridan, no longer felt that the designer's waning appeal warranted his high salary. Beginning in 1781, the better part of De Loutherbourg's energies became focused on a quixotic design project of his own devising – a miniature theatre called the Eidophusikon wherein he displayed spectacular scenographic effects at a reduced scale as a form of entertainment and attraction in itself, charging entry for spectators to behold the tiny theatre in his home and at commissioned events. Here, at last, scenography was the true star of the show.

Within London's life-sized theatres, the world of dimensional stage design, specific scenographic locales, and spectacular effects that De Loutherbourg helped inaugurate remained, but it became more frequently paired to the major play texts of the era. The designer who was arguably De Loutherbourg's most prominent successor, William Capon, was well known for his exacting architectural depictions, but those depictions were rarely the substance of a theatrical attraction unto themselves and were typically paired to substantial dramas. By one account, Capon "really seemed expressly fashioned, as a scene-painter, to carry into effect the true and perfect decorations which he meditated for the plays of Shakespeare" (Boaden 1825: 316). This was the theatrical world that would carry forward into the nineteenth century with its integration of performer and scenographic space and its somewhat more equitable marriage between dramatic text and scenic spectacle. In location and in name, the Theatre Royal at Drury Lane where both De Loutherbourg and Capon plied their trade was the same as the theatre first opened in 1663 under a commission from the newly restored Charles II. But the scenographic worlds depicted inside those theatre doors were worlds away from their Restoration origin.

References

Allen, Ralph G. 1981. "Irrational Entertainment in the Age of Reason." In *The Stage and the Page: London's "Whole Show" in the Eighteenth-Century Theatre*, edited by George Winchester Stone, Jr. Berkeley: University of California Press.

Boaden, James 1825. *Memoirs of the Life of John Philip Kemble, Esq*. New York.

Dryden, John 1976. *Albion and Albanius*. In *The Works of John Dryden, Volume XV*, edited by Early Miner and George R. Guffey. Berkeley: University of California Press.

Hill, Aaron 1735. "Letter" (signed Jeff'ry Cat-Call). *Prompter*, 24 January.

Hill, John 1750. *The Actor*. London.

Hopkins, William [1773] 1960. "*Diary*, December 27, 1773." In *The London Stage, 1660–1800*, Part 4, edited by William Van Lennep. Carbondale: Southern Illinois University Press.

The London Magazine, Or, Gentlemen's Monthly Intelligencer 1779. "The British Theatre," Vol. 48 (January).

Magalotti, Count Lorenzo 1960. "Travels of Cosomo III, in England, AD 1669." In *The London Stage, 1660–1800*, edited by William Van Lennep. Carbondale: Southern Illinois University Press.

Walpole, Horace 1906. "Letter to the Countess of Ossory, Arlington Street, Dec. 30, 1773." In *The Letters of Horace Walpole: Fourth Earl of Orford, Volume* 6, edited by Peter Cunningham. Edinburgh: John Grant.

Wilkinson, Tate 1790. *Memoirs of His Own Life, Volume* 4. London.

Wright, James 1699. *Historia Histrionica: An Historical Account of the English Stage*. London.

27
EIGHTEENTH-CENTURY FRANCE

Pannill Camp

Scenography in France underwent profound transformations during the reigns of the last three monarchs of the *ancien régime*. In some ways, these changes were conspicuous. The attention to supposed historical and cultural accuracy that marked the revival of Voltaire's *Brutus* in 1790, in which custom replicas of Roman furniture appeared on stage, marked a sharp departure from the generic painted sets mounted for tragedies at the Hôtel de Bourgogne during the time of Louis XIV. But the most meaningful changes that transpired had to do with the way that stage space was theorized and constructed on paper. The decades of high Enlightenment saw the overhaul of the conception of theatre space taken for granted by architects and designers in the neo-classical era. In the second half of the seventeenth century, unified perspective compositions became the state-of-the-art in court and major public theatre sets. By the 1780s, new thinking informed by the physical science of optics challenged linear perspective in theoretical and practical ways.

Louis XIV's direct rule began when his Chief Minister Mazarin died in 1661, the same year in which Carlo Vigarani completed the enormous Salle des Machines in the Tuileries Palace in Paris. This building stood as a testament to the prestige attached to a certain model of scenic spectacle that had been imported from Italy. Patrons asked architects including Vigarani for stages dressed with perspective compositions painted on flat sliding wings arranged in mostly symmetrical patterns along the sides of the stage. The grander theatres also supported a range of machinery that could manipulate these flats, and fly objects and people in from above the stage. The pictorial style that ruled here, heavily influenced by the Italian scenic impresario Giacomo Torelli, produced grandiose rhythmically arranged fantasy architecture: endless rows of columns, lavishly decorated arches, and fanciful combinations of statuary, fountains and other architectural curiosities that seemed to repeat into the distance beyond where the eye could see.

The work of Jean Bérain, who the Vigarani family employed as head scenic designer of the Paris Opera in the 1680s, perpetuated a style that was in many ways a stage picture of monarchical hegemony. The illusory central depth of field, like the architectural fantasies that surrounded it, externalized an image of concentrated power and political dominion that appealed to seventeenth-century potentates. Unified and lavish views of architecture, manicured landscapes, and other such constructions produced a kind of soft power like that generated by real buildings, military parades, and much of the visually-overpowering art typically associated with the Baroque era in European art (see Jarrard 2003).

These displays of visual power proliferated in court and other playhouses financed, directly and indirectly, by royal coffers. Meanwhile, at the popular Hôtel de Bourgogne, crude if versatile scenic decorations were made to serve the needs of the repertoires heavy with Racine and Corneille. The *Mémoire de Mahelot*, a scene-dresser's notebook that records decades of stage sets, shows that settings for many far-flung locales were depicted with little concern for lavish detail, pictorial unity, or historical specificity (see Herzel 1993). Such approaches to scenery can certainly be faulted for lacking artistic sophistication, but they served a theatrical culture far more concerned with quality of language than with resources expended on *mise-en-scène*. As the dazzle of unified and moveable perspective sets became known and associated with halls of power, however, private theatres and public houses including the Bourgogne attempted to imitate the extravagances of the Opera and the Salle des Machines.

The eighteenth century saw two major shifts in scenographic paradigms that bore lasting consequences for theatre in France and beyond. The first of these was an aesthetic development with legible ramifications concerning political ideas: the decentering of vanishing points. This particular shift owed its theoretical genesis to Andrea Pozzo and its popularity in practice to the Galli-Bibiena family of scenic designers. Ferdinando Galli-Bibiena, who was trained by the Bolognese painter Carlo Cignani and theatrical engineer Ercole Rivani, worked with his brother and sons to build awe-inspiring perspective sets that broke the monotony of central vanishing-point perspective. Whereas Torelli, Bérain, and others had arranged architectural figures on stage as if they were retreating parallel to the central axis of the building, the Galli-Bibiena placed vanishing points off-center, often using one to the right and one to the left of the stage, simulating a view from an oblique angle. In ways that would define eighteenth-century architectural fantasies painted by Piranesi, these sets also depicted truncated views of enormous buildings that towered over actors and seemed to rise above and beyond the proscenium arch. Portions of ceiling complemented the effect of scenery that towered over the human figure. The so called *scena per angolo* unlocked new powers of scale and visual complexity.

The work of the Galli-Bibiena family was best known in Vienna and in the Hapsburg network of patronage, but the hallmarks of *scena per angolo* made their way to France in the eighteenth century. Jean-Nicolas Servandoni, who took charge of decorations at the Paris Opera in 1724, refined and pushed linear perspective to dizzying new extremes. His work nearly bankrupted the Opera and wiped out his own fortunes on multiple occasions, but Servandoni developed a reputation for producing stunning spectacles, including series of mute scenes in the *Salle des Machines*, including one depicting the interior of St Peter's Basilica in Rome. Servandoni's sets refined and exploited perspective visual effects. He set his wing flats at irregular intervals, placed taller flats in the upstage recesses, and decorated flats with new materials, including precious jewels (see Olivier 2005 and La Gorce 2009). Such productions were uniquely extravagant and, while they clearly impressed the public, by all accounts they did not transform the sets likely to be seen at the Comédie-Française. These and most public theatre sets remained largely determined by seventeenth-century conventions and suggested only in a general way the settings of the plays for which they were mounted.

But Servandoni's importance shouldn't be assessed solely on the basis of its immediate influence on other decorators. The rotation of vanishing points off the central axis of the stage may be read as an implicit challenge to a scenic model that overtly propped up a vision of monarchical power. Perspective sets cohere around a central spectatorial point of view; from here the picture is unified and the visual sensation of false depth most compelling. Central vanishing points externalized the concentricity of good sightlines, laying bare the scene's political and ideological scaffolding. Obliquely pivoted scenic architecture did not in fact disrupt the way that linear perspective conferred optimal views on a single point in the theatre, but it masked this defect and drew the eye to one and another side instead of down an orderly alley of limitless reach.

The decentralizing pull on the eye that Servandoni helped popularize in Enlightenment-era scenery had an analogue in mid-century political thought. Montesquieu, in the 1748 *The Spirit of Laws*, compared absolute monarchical power with other systems and praised the separation of powers. Rousseau wrote bitingly about the starkly unequal status of human beings in modern Europe. Comparable impulses to counterbalance extreme concentrations of privilege exerted themselves in other areas of French theatre space as well. Beginning in the middle of the century, there was a concerted movement to improve the state of France's theatre buildings. The initial objective was to replace the converted tennis courts and other modified structures that constituted most French public playhouses. But as this movement gained momentum in the 1760s and 1770s, radical new designs sought to more fairly distribute the sensory pleasures of spectatorship around the audience.

Many of the playhouse designs that circulated at this time – both those meant to demonstrate theoretical principles and some intended for specific locations – proposed to divide the stage into three parts, so that even spectators on the sides of the house could see a perspective scene aimed roughly in their direction. While it is tempting to see this reformist approach to theatre design as evidence of a democratization of sightlines, architects and others ensconced in Louis XV's administration found ways to re-affirm the supremacy of the central point of view. Charles-Nicolas Cochin proposed a three-part stage, with a "petite scène" on either side of a central "grand scène," which partially curved around the audience. Cochin, however, intended for these side stages to merge with the picture of the center stage, and for all three together to offer an impressive view to the luxuriously sized and decorated King's box in the center of the first ring of *loges*. Cochin, who served as an engraver to Louis XV, did not let his distribution of scenic pleasures prevent him from making sure that the King's seat was "the most advantageous spot" (Cochin 1765: 17).

The practice of centralizing the ideal spectatorial position was not just a matter of stubborn political habits resisting architectural reform. It was tied to the deeply entrenched conventions of perspective stage design. For all the ingenuity of Servandoni, the rotation of vanishing points on stage did not undermine the formal attributes of perspective scenery. The very mechanism that allowed a scenic composition painted across many flats set on different planes to be unified also forced it to be drawn in reference to a single viewing spot. While separate elements of a stage picture could be made to alleviate this limitation – a distant hillside or cloudscape could be rendered in an indistinct scale, for instance – the fact remained that the further one sat from the set decorator's point-of-view, the more distorted the set would tend to look.

This underlying static feature of eighteenth-century scenography is vividly evident in the work of Pierre-Adrien Pâris, an architect, painter, and set designer whose service to

Louis XVI as *Dessinateur du Cabinet du Roi* and architect of the *Menus Plaisirs du Roi* allowed him design abundantly for the most prominent stages in France. Pâris' style was highly creative and novel, but he did not meaningfully deviate from the repertoire of linear perspective design that had reigned in France since the 1660s. His sketches preserved at the Municipal Library of Besançon divulge a conception of stage space and a method of drafting still bound to Alberti's manual of perspective staging. In one sketch from the 1780s for an unknown play, Pâris created a detailed ground plan for a fictional scenic environment, located a point-of-view in the center of the audience, and traced lines between that point and individual pieces of scenic architecture. This process assigned pieces of his composition to optimal places on the grid of wing chassis, and would have given the centrally seated audience a remarkably verisimilar view of a capacious arcade rotated about ten degrees to the house right side of the theatre's central axis.

Pâris shows that linear perspective scene design continued, and continued to see new refinements, through to the end of the eighteenth century, and it was commonly used deep into the modern era. But the conceptual reformulation of theatre space that took place in the last decades of the *ancien régime* foretold its eventual demise. In an effort to design a uniquely French and optimally functional model for public theatre space, reform-minded architects looked to experimental physics and absorbed the latest philosophical ideas about sensation. Experiments showing optical principles and the physical traits of the atmosphere, as well as sensationist psychology – which understood the mind to be wholly dependent upon the senses – renovated the way architects thought of theatre space. In a series of French treatises on theatre design between 1760 and 1782, the term perspective diminishes, while "optics" and "acoustics" take an increasingly central place.

The communication between Enlightenment philosophy and theatre architecture theory in this era presaged the major tenets of modern "rational" theatre design, which takes great account of engineering principles. Already in the eighteenth century, however, there were signals that theatre space and the space of experimental science were merging, conceptually and practically. Experimental physics, during the middle decades of the century, expanded and began to separate itself from the older catch-all tradition of natural philosophy. This way of investigating the natural world bore numerous theatrical trappings, involving rehearsed, audience-oriented, spectacular effects and short, but discernibly neo-classical, dramaturgical arcs: sequences of events were consciously trimmed and simplified, suspense ably cultivated, and titanic forces suddenly overcome in crowd-pleasing reversals. Some of the more famous experimentalists overtly wove sentimental and romantic themes into their performances. Jean Antoine Nollet's "electric kiss" experiment contrived to make a visible spark jump between the lips of two young volunteers, one of whom was suspended from non-conductive materials.

While physicists borrowed from the dramatic arts, architects drew increasingly from optics. In their efforts to discover what playhouse shapes would most advantageously serve the senses, some particularly visionary architects bet that mimicking the shape of ocular anatomy would provide evenly distributed views. Charles de Wailly and Claude-Nicolas Ledoux, who received prestigious theatre design jobs in Paris and Besançon, designed capacious, three-part stages joined to auditoria built partly on circular plans. These designs seen in plan view replicate the forms of diagrams of the eye that circulated widely in optical treatises. In other ways too, spaces of physical optics and theatre merged, as, for example, when the chemist Antoine Laurent de Lavoisier blocked out all the daylight in the Salon Carré in the Louvre, creating what he called a "simulacrum of a playhouse" in which he experimented with early versions of focused lighting instruments (Lavoisier 1862–1893: 100).

The mutual approximation, in theory and practice, of spaces understood to be theatrical and those conceived as spaces of physical optics, was a defining turn in the way theatre space was understood in the modern era. This way of thinking became the bedrock of holistic critiques of perspective scenery in the early nineteenth century, such as that deployed by Joseph-François-Louis Grobert in 1809. For Grobert and others, perspective not only created absurdities of scale when actors wandered upstage, it committed the scenic designer to "inseparable errors" linked to the arbitrary placement of the single unifying point-of-view (Grobert 1809: 122). Once detached from this single point, scenographers explored new techniques, including scenery in relief, which we now associate with the nineteenth century. The theoretical and conceptual shift that made such innovations possible, however, was firmly rooted in the restive intellectual milieu of eighteenth-century France.

References

Cochin, Charles-Nicholas 1765. *Projet d'une Salle de Spectacle pour un Théâtre de Comédie*. Paris: Chez Jombert.

Grobert, Joseph-François-Louis 1809. *De l'Exécution Dramatique, Considérée dans ses Rapports avec le Matériel de la Salle et de la Scène*. Paris: Schoell.

Herzel, Roger W. 1993. "Racine, Laurent, and the Palais à Volonté." *PMLA* 108 (5): 1064–82.

Jarrard, Alice 2003. *Architecture as Performance in Seventeenth-Century Europe: Court Ritual in Modena, Rome, and Paris*. Cambridge: Cambridge University Press.

La Gorce, Jérôme de 2009. "Une Scénographie de Servandoni Conservée pour les Spectacles de l'Opéra à Paris: le Décor de la Ville de Thèbes du Triomphe de l'Harmonie (1737)." *Journal for Eighteenth-Century Studies* 32 (4): 577–90.

Lavoisier, Antoine Laurent de 1862–93. *Oeuvres de Lavoisier*. Paris: Imprimerie Impériale, III.

Olivier, Marc 2005. "Jean-Nicolas Servandoni's Spectacles of Nature and Technology." *French Forum* 30 (2): 31–47.

28

BOXED ILLUSIONS

From melodrama to naturalism

Amy Holzapfel

In 1888 Swedish dramatist August Strindberg proposed an idea for a new theatre: instead of "a Bible in pictures for those who can't read" (Strindberg 1983: 63), theatre would become a venue for social and literary debate or, as he described it, a "place of entertainment for educated people" (ibid.: 75). Such a monumental transformation would demand the construction of a new dramatic repertoire, as well as radical shifts in scenography and theatre design, including: making the orchestra invisible, raising the auditorium floor "so that eye level for the spectator was higher than the hollow of the actor's knee," removing the stage boxes along with their "grinning late arrivals from dinners," and darkening the house during performances (ibid.: 75). Above all, Strindberg desired "a small stage and a small auditorium" (ibid.).

In the decades that followed the publication of his "Author's Preface" to *Miss Julie*, Strindberg's vision would materialize in such new spaces as: André Antoine's Théâtre Libre, Otto Brahm's Freie Bühne, Lady Gregory and W. B. Yeats' Abbey Theatre, J. T. Grein's Independent Theatre, and August Falck and Strindberg's own aptly named Intimate Theatre. The century that began with perspectival scenery, painted flats, raked stages, and footlights ended with box sets, gas and electric lighting, and real furniture and props on flat stages. How did a changing view of the world impact the shift in theatre scenography from an emphasis on grandiose moving spectacles to a focus on intimate and authentic stagings of everyday life?

This chapter argues that while it may be tempting to view the developments of theatrical styles like melodrama and naturalism as opposing paradigms, such movements may more accurately be positioned on the same historical continuum: the rise of modern visual culture. From the invention of photography and the handheld *carte-de-visite*, to the popularization of the stereoscope and storefront glass display window, the nineteenth century witnessed a massive increase in new technologies and media that sought to capitalize on rising middle-class consumer culture's unquenchable thirst for all things visual. Over the course of the century, new crowds would flock to the theatre as well, seeking illusions of fantasy, history, mythology, and reality – all packaged, bound, and sealed within the confines of a life-size black box.

Boxes of fantasies: melodrama

By all accounts, the nineteenth century was the "century of the visual." In his major comparative study of nineteenth-century art, literature, and theatre, *Realizations*, Martin Meisel, for example, writes of the veritable "explosion of print and picture" (Meisel 1983: 4) occurring widely throughout the period. Meisel's study tracks the growth of a fully realized pictorial theatre, in which dramaturgy and scenography sought to merge into a continuous visual form, one that could rival painting and photography (and eventually film) in the manufacturing of its illusions. Art historian Jonathan Crary also approaches the importance of the visual alongside the science of vision during the nineteenth century, documenting the rise of the historical construction of a "new observer," a physiological subject who encounters and takes in the seen world through an unstable, autonomous, and fluctuating body. Crary examines particularly how, over the course of the century, "vision, rather than a privileged form of knowing, becomes itself an object of knowledge, of observation" (Crary 1992: 70), interrogated by scientists and artists alike. As a central component within an emergent and, at the same time, destabilizing culture of the visual, theatre both participated in and aided in the construction of a "new observer" through its own scenographic developments, including those of stage melodrama.

As the English critic Percy Fitzgerald wrote in 1870, referring to the melodramas of Irish dramatist Dion Boucicault: "We go not so much to hear as to *look*. It is like a giant peep-show, and we pay the showman, and put our eyes to the glass and stare" (Meisel 1983: 49). Fitzgerald's criticism of the melodramatic spectacle echoes the French poet Charles Baudelaire's earlier disgust towards the fad of the stereoscope, which drew, as he saw it, "thousands of pairs of greedy eyes" to its peepholes as if they were "skylights towards the infinite" (Baudelaire 1980: 87). Both Fitzgerald and Baudelaire were criticizing what they, and many others, viewed as popular obsession with new forms of visual media and their variety of enthralling, titillating and sensational effects. The early French melodramas of René-Charles Guilbert de Pixérécourt, for example, produced between 1800–1840 and designed largely by the scenic artist Julien Michel Gué, were filled with elaborate visual special effects, including volcanic eruptions, rushing floods, and earthquakes. As the century wore on, melodramatic and operatic spectacles flourished in major cities and theatres across the globe, such as the Bowery Theatre in New York, Garnier's Opera House in Paris, and Samuel Phelps' Sadler's Wells Theatre in London.

Within the theatre of melodramatic spectacle, two figures became indispensable: the machinist and the scene painter, who collaborated to produce elaborate stage pictures by means of hydraulics, flying apparatus, traps, pulley systems, and sliders in stage floors. Aided by new technologies, artists and craftspeople sought to create the illusion of nearly seamless scene-shifts. Referring to this very effect, the English critic Henry Morley wrote of Phelps' 1853 production of *A Midsummer Night's Dream* at Sadler's Wells as "dreamlike" for the ways the scenes were made "to glide insensibly into another" (Nagler 1952: 479). Morley was also impressed by the scenic innovation of a curtain of green gauze positioned between the actors and the audience during the "fairy portion" of the play, which further heightened the impression of the stage world as a dream (ibid.). Writing of Phelps' *Pericles*, produced a year later, Morley praises the scene painter and machinist most of all, describing how, "When he sails at last to the temple of Diana of the Ephesians, rowers take their places on their banks, the vessel seems to glide along the coast, and . . . the whole theatre seems to be in the course of actual transportation to the temple at Ephesus, which is the crowning scenic glory of the play" (ibid.: 480). As Morley's criticism suggests, melodramatic spectacles appealed to audiences seeking sensations and effects conjured by adept scenographers working alongside highly skilled technicians.

To further enhance the depth of its illusions, scenography began to move away from features that brought attention to theatre's artifice and presentationality – the apron, the raked stage, proscenium boxes, and wing and groove mechanisms – towards those that allowed for greater impressions of actuality and representationality. In 1869, for example, Edwin Booth introduced the first theatre possessing a level (rather than raked) stage, allowing for the innovation of the "free plantation" of scenery, which no longer needed to be nailed into the floor or set into pre-existing grooves but could instead be supported by stage braces in order to maintain its position in the space. During the 1870s at Henry Irving's Lyceum Theatre as well, leading designer Hawes Craven used a backlit upstage scrim to reveal precisely detailed and authentically rendered tableaux. As the English critic Sir Edward Russell wrote of Irving's pictorial-driven production of *Macbeth* in 1888, "By the cooperation of costumiers and scene painters, each scene is a very noble picture" (Nagler 1952: 502). Going even further, the playwright Thomas William Robertson lavished praise on the scene painter as one who "copies Nature on a large scale," and, for this, stands out as a "far more important person in a theatre than the Tragedian" (ibid.: 495).

Almost from their earliest debut, melodramatic spectacles were rivaled and, in some cases, aided by other popular, new visual technologies, such as the panorama, diorama, and cyclorama. During the 1820s, theatre designer and would-be photographic innovator Louis-Jacques-Mandé Daguerre introduced the panorama along with a new invention, the diorama, in Paris. Originating in Scotland in 1788, the panorama surrounded its audience by a circular wall, on the inside of which rotated a single, continuous, painted scene. In contrast, Daguerre's later innovation of the diorama, striving to produce an even more exacting scenic illusionism, positioned the audience on a platform that rotated to face different picture-frame stages, upon which appeared realistic images traced from *camera obscura* photographs. Like stage melodramas, which utilized advanced technology to produce even greater scenic effects, both the panorama and diorama claimed to provide their spectators with the illusion of being transported to new and foreign times and places. The authenticity of a scene, desired above all else, was further accomplished by the incorporation of real props and other three-dimensional scenic elements positioned against the flat, painted drops, along with masterful and nuanced lighting, to induce in audiences the feeling of greater absorption into the depths and contours of a different reality. Seen in this way, the manufactured illusions of melodrama, panorama, and diorama, were, as Fitzgerald and Baudelaire bemoaned, not all that different from those boxed and sold to the public via other visual technologies, such as the stereoscope or peep-show, which varied only in the scale, price, and content of their offerings.

Boxes of history and mythology: from Kean to Wagner

What melodrama packaged for audiences was, in essence, fantasy. What realism packaged for nineteenth-century audiences was at least touted as the very opposite: truth. Nevertheless, fantasy and truth intermingle in melodrama and realism, making it, in some cases, difficult to tell the styles apart from one another. While realism in theatre is often defined as the quest to produce an exact copy of reality objectively on stage, a more accurate definition of realism might be the struggle to make visible the act of seeing reality (Holzapfel 2014: 8). Given that we interpret the world through our subjective physiological bodies, as many nineteenth-century scientists and visual artists were beginning to understand, how can we ever hope to interpret the world objectively? Realist theatre artists, too, while driven by a quest for truth, remained uncertain about the best ways to represent the unstable act of seeing or perceiving such truth. Should one depict reality as it might allegedly be perceived in an abstract universe, in which pure objectivity is possible, or should one instead cop to the fact that the *way* one subjectively perceives reality may be the only real truth worth telling? Such a debate may be seen to have manifested not only textually, in the dramatic literature of the nineteenth century, but also scenographically, on its vast variety of realist stages.

Among the countless "truths" sought after in nineteenth-century realist theatre was that which was believed to have belonged to a particular historical or cultural period. We have our own version of this trend, of course: today, archival restoration and refurbishment has become the foundation of a massive consumer-based cultural enterprise, which, in the US alone, includes everything from stores like Restoration Hardware, to television shows like *This Old House*, to living history museums such as Massachusetts' Sturbridge Village. Yet, antiquarianism – the relentless and often futile search for the reenactment of authentic historical culture and forms – was extremely popular in the nineteenth century as well, driving shifts in theatre scenography towards innovations that provided what appeared to be more accurate and precise renderings of what were, at best, enticing and easily digestible historical fictions.

Believing in theatre's capacity to reconstruct lost truths, the English actor and manager Charles Kean, influenced by his predecessor Charles Kemble, strove for precise historical accuracy in his productions, particularly of Shakespeare's works. Kean, whose name became synonymous with the relentless quest for historical authenticity, based his dramaturgy and designs on information acquired from historians and scholars. Kean's lavish, elaborate, period renderings of Shakespeare's plays or classical works by poets established his theatre as one of the most innovative and popular forms throughout the 1850s. "Why should I present to you what I know to be wrong," Kean wrote in defense of his theatre, "when it is in my power to give what I know to be right?" (Nagler 1952: 490). Asserting that in no "single instance" had he ever "permitted historical truth to be sacrificed to theatrical effect" (ibid.), Kean heralded a new orthodoxy in design, one in which the authenticity – the fiction of being "right" – began to trump theatricality – the truth of being "wrong."

Following in the steps of Kean, many theatre artists increasingly began to insist upon the substitution of actualized scenic environments for more conventionally fake, painted backdrops, although, more often than not, a combination of two- and three-dimensional elements prevailed. One of Kean's greatest admirers was George II, Duke of Saxe-Meiningen, who established a theatre company at the Court Theatre in Saxe-Meiningen in 1866. Saxe-Meiningen, who presided over all aspects of design, insisted that even the tiniest element, a button on a coat or a wooden stool, must be historically correct in order to preserve the illusion of an authentic past reconjured on the stage of the present. Noted for its dynamic stage designs involving large ensemble casts, the Saxe-Meiningen Company made an enormous impact in London, where, in the spring of 1881, they performed works by Shakespeare and Schiller at Drury Lane. Praising the troupe for their outstanding vitality, and "*vraisemblance*" in their production of Schiller's *The Robbers*, a critic from the *Athenaeum* objected only to one casting detail: "The robbers look too old" (Nagler 1952: 502).

Desire for historical accuracy flourished as well in the theatre of the English impresario Herbert Beerbohm Tree, who in 1878 became the manager for the Haymarket Theatre and, a little more than two decades later, founded his own theatre, Her Majesty. Like Kean, Irving, and Saxe-Meiningen before him, Tree was yet another stickler for historical truth on stage. Spectacle and realism combined in Tree's designs for a production of *A Midsummer Night's Dream* in 1900, which famously debuted live rabbits. Following suit, the American director and designer David Belasco also strove for extreme accuracy and authenticity in his attempt to recreate the "feeling of a scene" (Nagler 1952: 570), using elements like historic wallpaper and real plants and food on stage. "Everything must be real," wrote Belasco, "I have seen plays in which thrones creaked on which monarchs sat, and palace walls flapped when persons touched them. Nothing so destructive to illusion or so ludicrous can happen on my stage (Nagler 1952: 575). Alongside Tree, Belasco is often credited with transforming theatre into a compelling, affective and pictorial spectacle, capable of competing with the rising industry and technology of cinema. Deeply methodical in his approach, Belasco came to rely particularly on new lighting innovations, even going so far as to suggest that "lights are to drama what music is to the lyrics of a song . . . as essential to every work of dramatic art as blood is to life" (Nagler 1952: 571). Recalling his production of *The Girl of the Golden West*, Belasco notes how he struggled with the lighting for three months to create the perfect illusion of "the soft, changing colors of a California sunset over the Sierra Nevadas" until, in exasperation, he was forced to turn to a different method entirely, admitting that "it was a good sunset, but it wasn't Californian" (ibid.).

While history would remain an enticing subject for theatre long into the twentieth century, mythology became another kind of truth sought after by artists working within the industry of manufacturing illusions. Strindberg's own late-century vision for an "intimate theatre" was, of course, indebted to the innovations of one of his chief influences, composer and director Richard Wagner, whose Festspielhaus at Bayreuth, opening in 1876, revolutionized scenography and theatre architecture. Among the many modernizations pioneered by Wagner and designer Otto Brückwald at Bayreuth was that of the "mystic gulf," or sunken orchestra pit, hidden below the proscenium so that the business of the musicians would not pose a distraction from the stage. Bayreuth signals one of the first shifts in theatre architecture to accommodate the interests of a broader class of spectators, who, as Wagner saw it, desired a theatre of total illusions, a theatre that would combine all arts into a single total work of art (*Gesamtkunstwerk*). With its fan-shaped auditorium set on a single slope, containing gangway seating that reached the full length of the auditorium, and its double proscenium, which, when unlit, "separated the real world of the auditorium from the illusionistic stage world" (Leacroft and Leacroft 1984: 114–15), Bayreuth claimed to offer direct sightlines of its stage to every single audience member in attendance.

Wagner's Bayreuth shared with Kean's antiquarianism, as well as Boucicault's melodramatic spectacles, a desire to reach a broader and rapidly growing leisure class of theatregoers. With public outbursts – beginning as early as 1809 with the Old Price Riots at London's Covent Garden, incited by audience members objecting to privatizing third-tier boxes as well as increased prices for most seating areas – on the rise, the call for theatre to embrace more democratic configurations began to be reflected in both the theatre architecture and scenography by the later nineteenth century. Dedicated to meeting the demands of a more egalitarian viewing space, the People's Theatre at Worms, for example, constructed from 1887–9, eradicated all individual auditorium boxes, striving instead to "promote the spirit of community by assisting the spectator to see his neighbor near him" and to assure him that there would be no experience of "exclusion or privilege with regard to view or position" (ibid.: 115). The People's Theatre exemplifies a broader scenographic movement that, increasingly, saw the private boxes of the auditorium absorbed by the all-consuming box of the picture-frame stage, upon which were produced spectacular visual effects. In the case of the People's Theatre, at least more of the public could now purchase them.

Boxes of reality: from the box set to the *Doll House*

Among its many upheavals – social, political, artistic – the nineteenth century witnessed a massive rise in the variety of transportable goods and products suited to the economically average household. Such goods were made readily available through the introduction of arcades and shopping districts into urban spaces, such as those discussed by cultural critic Walter Benjamin in his legendary *Arcades Project*. Benjamin's cryptic musings on the rise of the middle-class shopper is linked to his inquiry on the advent of the "private individual," one for whom the "interior" of the home becomes a protected sanctuary that not only contains the self but, in fact, *defines* the self. For the "private individual," writes Benjamin, "the living room is a box in the theatre of the world" (Benjamin 1999: 9). So too, however, by the latter part of the nineteenth century, theatre had become a box in the living room of the world.

Enter the box set. In today's music industry, a "box set" refers to a group of albums packaged in a box and sold as a single unit; in a related way, in theatre, the term "box set" connotes a type of scenography that uses three walls on stage and the proscenium arch as a fourth to package and sell the illusion of a single unit interior. No one quite knows exactly when the first box set appeared; some sources credit the Italian designer Fabrizio Carini Motta with its earliest designs, which appear in a manual for constructing theatrical scenery published in 1668 (Brockett and Mitchell 2010: 175). In London, the box set is widely believed to have debuted in 1832, constructed for a production of W. B. Bernard's *The Conquering Game* by the illustrious English theatre manager Madame Vestris (Eliza Lucy Bartolozzi), whose Olympic Theatre, by one critic's estimation, "served as a life boat to the respectability of the stage, which was fast sinking in the general wreck" (Nagler 1952: 462). Despite these and other early cameos (such as Heinrich Laube's Burgtheatre in Vienna in the 1840s), however, it would take several more decades for the innovation of the box set to catch on; once it did, however, there was no going back to the wing and groove systems of the past.

By the 1860s, in theatres across Europe, the UK, and the US, three-dimensionality began to outmode two-dimensionality as box sets increasingly challenged the illusionism of outdated mechanisms for scenography, which began to look highly theatrical and, more to the point, fake. In Paris, the Comédie-Française increasingly produced new bourgeois dramas by Victorien Sardou, Alexandre Dumas *fils*, and Émile Augier that challenged conventional perspectival scenography by demanding the recreation of

Figure 28.1 Photograph of a rehearsal of Act IV of Émile Zola's *Thérèse Raquin* at the Odéon. (Courtesy of the Bibliothèque nationale de France.)

elaborately detailed domestic interiors on its gilded-framed proscenium stage. Sardou, like Kean, requested the use of real props, bric-a-brac, and furniture for his *mise-en-scène*, as did the English author Thomas W. Robertson, whose penchant for real porcelain earned his dramas of the 1860s the diminutive title of "cup and saucer plays." French author and critic Émile Zola's interest in physiology, psychology, and the hidden depths of the mind and body, similarly inspired an emphasis on scenographic interiority, as in his 1873 production of his dramatic adaptation *Thérèse Raquin*, set in a single room with one window and an upstage alcove containing only a curtained bed. It was Zola, of course, who first envisioned a new genius of the theatre "scorning the tricks of the clever hack, smashing the imposed patters, remaking the stage until it is continuous with the auditorium, giving a shiver of life to the painted trees, letting in through the backcloth the great, free air of reality" (Innes 2000: 47).

Taking cues from Zola, Norwegian playwright Henrik Ibsen also pioneered a new form of realistic drama largely set within the confines of four interior walls, seen in works such as *A Doll House* (1879), *Ghosts* (1888), and *The Wild Duck* (1890). Theatre critics fond of musing over Ibsen's inclusion of the infamous "bag of macaroons" in the first act of *A Doll House* may overlook the "armload of packages" that Nora also carries with her into the house (Ibsen 1978: 125). Nora's array of parcels and bags signify her middle-class consumerism and also, in a more meta-theatrical sense, gesture to the bourgeois theatre itself as an illusion that is boxed-up, presented and distributed for leisurely consumption. It's a delightfully ironic coincidence that *A Doll House* premiered in 1879, the same year that the Scottish-born American entrepreneur Robert Gair introduced the first die-cut and scored cardboard box, which could be stored flat and refolded for future use. Gair's cardboard box revolutionized the global, commercial industry much in the way that Ibsen's *A Doll House* transformed modern drama and scenography, a point perhaps not lost on contemporary director Lee Breuer, who set his production of the play within the confines of a three-walled, foldable, life-size doll house, in other words, a giant fold-out cardboard box.

When Ibsen's dramas occasionally break from their suffocatingly intimate confines they do so with resounding theatricality, as in Nora's own door-slam departure – a gesture made possible precisely because of the box set – or John Gabriel Borkman's wolf-like ascent to the mountains. Such scenographically attuned dramaturgy suggests Ibsen's tacit awareness of the link between the construction of Benjamin's "private individual" and the bourgeois domestic interior itself. In order to break free from social, economic, and moral constraints, the individual must necessarily depart from her elaborately constructed box set. Ibsen's realism, in this sense, offers not so much a transcript of reality as a series of boxes set inside other boxes. Like his earlier picaresque figure of Peer Gynt, who peels back the layers of his onion-self, so too do the audiences of Ibsen's dramas peel back the layers of the playwright's realist scenography, revealing, with each layer, a deeper appreciation for the empty space that lies within its center.

Boxes in boxes: naturalism's photographic interiors

Realism's double orientation of boxes within boxes is also suggestive of the black boxes of nineteenth-century photography, an art form that initially grew out of theatrical forms like the diorama, as Daguerre's legacy confirms. Photography was, in turn, hugely influential to many pioneers of the new art-oriented, independent movement in theatre occurring towards the end of the century, among them the French director André Antoine. Beginning with the staging of "*tranches de vie*" ("slices of life"), a term that nods to photography, and later producing full-length dramas, such as Ibsen's *Wild Duck*, a play concerning the tragic downfall of a family of photographers, Antoine's Théâtre Libre in Paris debuted a rigid form of naturalism that demanded freshly designed sets and actualized environments for each new production.

It was Denis Diderot, the eighteenth-century French philosopher and critic, who first introduced what, in theatre vernacular, became familiarly referred to as the "fourth wall." As early as 1758, in his essay "On Dramatic Poetry," Diderot championed a theatre of illusions, offering practical advice to theatre makers such as: "Whether you write plays or whether you play them, do not think any more about the spectator than you would if he didn't exist. Imagine on the edge of the stage a large wall that separates you from the audience; write or act the play as if the curtain had not risen" (Diderot 1974: 292). Strictly adhering to Diderot, André Antoine designed his staged interiors with all walls intact and without "worrying about the fourth wall, which," he instructed his actors, "will later disappear so as to enable the audience to see what is going on" (Innes 2000: 53). Although Antoine was also greatly influenced by the Saxe-Meiningen Company, which he saw perform on several occasions in Brussels in 1888, he was at the same time highly critical of many aspects of their work. Obsessed with details, Antoine particularly objected to small problems that, in his mind, sacrificed the illusion of reality produced on the Meiningen's stage, such as, for Schiller's *Wilhelm Tell*, their use of the "same stage carpet" for every act, the "squeaking floorboards among the mountains," and the "white hands and spotless knees" of the mountaineers, who looked as clean as actors from "the Opéra-Comique" (Nagler 1952: 582). For his own productions, Antoine advocated for an "abundance of little objects" to fill his interiors; such properties he viewed as "imponderables that give a sense of intimacy and lend authentic character to the environment the director seeks to recreate" (Innes 2000: 53).

Antoine's critiques of theatre's conventions and tendency towards artificiality echo those cited at the top of this chapter by one of those whose work he produced:

Strindberg, who was himself a noted painter and photographer. Like Antoine, Strindberg abhorred theatrical scenic conventions, preferring to borrow from the art of the impressionist painters the "device of making a setting appear cut off and asymmetrical, thus strengthening the illusion" (Strindberg 1983: 73). These visions prompted him to make significant changes, such as getting rid of "tiresome exits through doors because scenery doors, made of canvas, wobble at the slightest touch" (ibid.). Also much like Antoine, who preferred to illuminate a mere "slice" of life, Strindberg too was drawn to showing less rather than more on stage: "[w]hen we see only part of a room and a portion of the furniture" he wrote of his idea for the staging of *Miss Julie*, "we are left to conjecture, that is to say, our imagination goes to work and complements what is seen" (ibid.). As rigid as Antoine in his articulation of a staged illusion that would not require audiences to overly suspend their disbelief, Strindberg called for the end of painted scenery, seeking to spare his spectators the strain of "trying to believe in painted pots and pans" (ibid.: 74). Despite calls for an end to overt theatricality in scenography, however, illusions continued to be created on the basis of a fraught and imperfect tension between reality and artifice, such as in the 1906 production of *Miss Julie* at The People's Theatre in Stockholm, during which the actress Sacha Sjöström, playing Kristin, fried real kidneys on a working stove (Ekman 2000: 84) within an interior whose side walls were nevertheless cheated out at an almost 70-degree angle to allow for better sightlines.

Both Antoine's Théâtre Libre and Strindberg's Intimate Theatre inspired the formation of many other smaller theatres throughout Europe and the UK, such as J. T. Grein's Independent Theatre in London and Otto Brahm's Freie Bühne in Berlin, which also evoked intimacy, authenticity, and everydayness as a mantra for their own modern stages. Topping all of these in its legacy within theatre and scenography, however, was the Moscow Art Theatre. Founded in 1898 by Konstantin Stanislavsky and Vladimir Ivanovich Nemirovich-Danchenko, the Moscow Art Theatre offered the first playhouse in Russia to cater to new drama, particularly works of naturalism. Yet another admirer of the work of the Saxe-Meiningen Company, Stanislavsky sought to establish a new theatrical paradigm, one that would unite the literary and the artistic rather than viewing them in isolation. Emphasizing a play as something that should not only be "clear, comprehensive, and true," but, more importantly, must "live," Stanislavsky focused all of his collaborators on the task of finding the "inner line" of the drama (Nagler: 587). Discovering the emotional arc of the play was a primary goal within Stanislavsky's sensitive approach to new drama, particularly works by the Russian dramatist Anton Chekhov.

At the Moscow Art Theatre, dramas like *The Seagull*, *Uncle Vanya*, *Three Sisters*, and *The Cherry Orchard*, set a new standard for nuance and subtlety in theatre, pushing the style of naturalism into more symbolic terrain. As Arnold Aronson observes, "Chekhov's scenography aims at an emotional sensibility, not a documentary recording of domestic décor" (Aronson 2005: 118). Despite such innovation within the drama, Aronson suggests, Stanislavsky's scenography remained tied to the "illusionistic practices of fourth-walled naturalism" (Aronson 2005: 119), causing Chekhov himself to famously propose adding a speech to *The Cherry Orchard* in which one of the characters asserts, "How wonderful! We hear no birds, no dogs, no cuckoos, no owls, no clocks, no sleighbells, no crickets!" (Innes 2000: 139). Yet, while both Stanislavsky and designer Victor Simov were criticized for "encasing [Chekhov's] plays in a highly detailed, representational, physical world" (Aronson 2005: 118), their designs signal as well a collaborative desire to achieve a *mise-en-scène* that was much more psychologically based than those of either Kean or the Saxe-Meiningens, or even Antoine. In his memoirs, Stanislavsky recalls that Simov aided him particularly in the "creation of the mood" for Chekhov's plays (Innes 2000: 159). Simov's famous design for *The Cherry Orchard*, for example, with its real objects and furniture pieces, patterned wallpaper, and other materials chosen to produce psychic energy for the actors, arguably borders as much on an ontological as naturalist theatre.

Despite such preferences for authenticity, there remained in the scenography of the Moscow Art Theatre a surprising degree of theatrical conventionality, testifying to the difficulty of producing illusions in a way that did not ultimately appear artificially contrived to audiences. Between the genius of an idea and its material realization on stage resides, of course, a gulf of mediocrity and compromise, a point suggested by Stanislavsky's paradoxical description to Chekhov of the scenography for Act Four of *The Cherry Orchard*: "Down front there is something like a shrubbery. Further upstage are the stairs and billiard room. The windows are painted on the walls" (Innes 2000: 171). All in all, what Stanislavsky desired with his call for trains puffing with smoke, frogs and corncrakes croaking, and mounds of real hay, alongside the almost completely antithetical aesthetic of fake windows painted on walls was the creation of a psychological context deep enough to get the actors "into the spirit of their parts" (Innes 2000: 171). In this manner, the initial signs of a shift towards a new and more modernist type of theatre practice and scenography, one that paradoxically combined both theatrical and anti-theatrical tendencies, may be unearthed in the Moscow Art Theatre's designs for Chekhov's plays, even if it would take another decade for Edward Gordon Craig's *Hamlet* to appear on its wooden boards.

Damaged goods: illusionism as imperfection

When viewed within the context of the rise of modern visual culture, the nineteenth-century theatre of boxed illusions almost appears as an evolutionary given. Panoramas, photographs, dioramas, peep shows, stereoscopes, cardboard boxes, postcards, cartes-de-visite, storefront glass window displays, zoetropes, and the first motion pictures, arose alongside the development of a new scenography oriented around framing stage pictures, delivering authenticity, and optimizing sightlines. Yet, what connects the dots between the spectacles of Phelps, the archives of Kean, and the intimate theatres of Strindberg, is more than simply a common historical context: it is a shared desire to achieve a perfect illusionism by means of a totally imperfect art.

No one recognized the imperfections of the theatre of illusions more than Belasco, who describes, for example, a "most troublesome problem" that arose during rehearsals for the scene of the River of Souls in his 1902 production of *The Darling of the Gods*:

> I had built the translucent scene of the river at a cost of $6,500 and have devised a sort of harness in which fifteen girls were suspended to represent a passage of the souls. When I tested the scene with manikins in my miniature theatre, it invariably worked perfectly; but when I tried it on the regular stage something was sure to go wrong. Some of the girls swam well, while others swam badly, and almost always one or two got tangled in their harnesses.
>
> *(Nagler 1952: 573)*

Keenly attuned to the commercial aspects of the art form, Belasco knew that "such accidents in a performance before an audience would have caused laughter, which would have been fatal to a production that had cost $80,000" (Nagler 1952: 573–4). Belasco promptly instructed the carpenters to remove the costly, opaque setting, built especially for the production, leaving only a thin gauze curtain hanging at the front of the stage. "Just at this moment," Belasco recalls, "one of the workmen happened to pass between the curtain and a light at the back" such that, when viewed through the fabric's delicate folds, his movements were "almost ghostly" (Nagler 1952: 574). For Belasco, the illusion he'd been seeking all along had suddenly, by complete accident, come to him "ready-made" (Nagler 1952: 574). That very same afternoon, Belasco restaged the scene with the fifteen girls swimming in front of the gauze, building the scene "in a day for $90" (Nagler 1952: 574). As more than an amusing anecdote, Belasco's incident offers a healthy reminder of the degree to which contingency and chance factor into both the manufacturing and delivering of modernity's neatly packaged productions of fantasy, history, myth, and reality. As Belasco understood, inside the box of every theatrical illusion may be discovered a charming array of cheap tricks.

References

Aronson, Arnold 2005. *Looking into the Abyss: Essays on Scenography*. Ann Arbor: University of Michigan.

Baudelaire, Charles 1980. "The Modern Public and Photography." In *Classic Essays on Photography*, edited by Alan Trachtenberg, 83–9. New Haven, CT: Leetes Island Books.

Benjamin, Walter 1999. *The Arcades Project*, translated by Howard Eiland and Kevin McLaughlin. Cambridge, MA: Belknap Press of Harvard University Press.

Brockett, Oscar G. and Margaret Mitchell 2010. *Making the Scene: A History of Stage Design and Technology in Europe and the United States*. San Antonio, Texas: Tobin Theatre Arts Fund.

Crary, Jonathan 1992. *Techniques of the Observer: On Vision and Modernity in the Nineteenth Century*. Cambridge: MIT Press.

Diderot, Denis 1974. "On Dramatic Poetry." In *Dramatic Theory and Criticism: Greeks to Grotowski*, edited by Bernard G. Dukore, 292–3. Fort Worth, TX: Harcourt Brace Jovanovich College Publishers.

Ekman, Hans-Göran 2000. *Strindberg and the Five Senses*. London: Athlone Press.

Holzapfel, Amy 2014. *Art, Vision and Nineteenth-Century Realist Drama: Acts of Seeing*. London: Routledge.

Ibsen, Henrik 1978. "*A Doll House*." In *Ibsen: The Complete Major Prose Plays*, translated by Rolf Fjelde, 119–96. New York: Plume.

Innes, Christopher (Ed.) 2000. *A Sourcebook On Naturalist Theatre*. London: Routledge.

Leacroft, Richard and Helen Leacroft 1984. *Theatre and Playhouse: An Illustrated Survey of Theatre Building From Ancient Greece to the Present Day*. London: Methuen.

Meisel, Martin 1983. *Realizations: Narrative, Pictorial, and Theatrical Arts in Nineteenth-Century England*. New Jersey: Princeton University Press.

Nagler, A. M. 1952. *A Source Book in Theatrical History*. New York: Dover.

Strindberg, August 1983. "*Miss Julie*: Author's Preface." In *Strindberg: Five Plays*, translated by Harry G. Carlson, 63–75. Berkeley: University of California Press.

Symbolic and emblematic design

In contrast to illusionistic design, symbolic and emblematic scenography emphasizes and acknowledges its theatricality. It seeks to convey its meanings through the vocabulary of the stage rather than a replication of the external world. Nineteenth-century critic Teodor de Wyzeva, a contributor to *La Revue Wagnérienne*, wrote of art that it "must consciously re-create, by means of *signs*, the total life of the universe, that is to say the soul, in which the varied drama we call universe is played" (Wyzeva [1886] 1995: 149). He goes on to suggest that "the whole life of our soul" is constituted by "sensation, thought, and emotion" and that the role of art is the "aesthetic reconstitution of these three vital modes" (ibid.). Emblematic scenography, through the use of its particular vocabulary of light, sound, costume, and visual-spatial imagery – signs – creates emotion, thought, and sensation just as art does.

There is no single style, and certainly no prescribed technique, for this approach to scenography. It may range from the blatantly symbolic in which one thing serves directly as a sign for something else – think of the wild duck in Ibsen's play, or Williams' glass menagerie. Or it may consist of more ambiguous and evocative symbols such as the water or sheep in Materlinck's *Pelléas et Mélisande* and the sound of a breaking string in Chekhov's *The Cherry Orchard*. It manifests in Alexandra Exter's cubo-futurist designs at Tairov's Kamerny Theatre in Moscow or Lyubov Popova's Constructivist assembly for Meyerhold's *The Magnanimous Cuckold*. It literally looms over the stage in Robert Edmond Jones' representation of *Macbeth*'s witches as giant masks.

Its origins are as old as theatre itself – the masks of ancient Greek tragedy are a form of emblematic design. It is found in the medieval European theatre, the pine tree of the Noh stage, the throne that would appear on the Elizabethan stage to represent a kingdom, and the allegorical costumes and settings of court masques. But in modern times it essentially begins with the Symbolists with their curtains and pre-Raphaelite imagery, and notably in the pastiche that made up the scenery and costumes of Alfred Jarry's infamous masterpiece of 1896, *Ubu Roi*.

In more recent times, it is found in Ming Cho Lee's set for *Electra* (1964), inspired by the work of Boris Aronson and various German theatre designs, that consisted of what appeared to be massive fragments of stone walls that floated on scaffolding above the stage floor. As Lee noted, realism gave way to something else: "[s]uddenly they become sculptural pieces. Suddenly they become icons rather than walls" (quoted in Aronson 2014: 85). George Tsypin's *Ring Cycle* with the Mariinsky Theatre in 2003 with its giant gods towering on and over the stage or his 2016 *Guillaume Tell* with deer suspended upside down above the stage is yet another example.

But it need not be so blatant or spectacular. Any time the theatrical, the formal, the visual, the structural, etc., takes precedence over the realistic and illusionistic, we are in the realm of the symbolic and emblematic. One could probably make the case that, from the end of the nineteenth century onward, Western theatre was dominated by symbolic and emblematic design. In some ways, much theatre throughout history employed the vocabulary and strategies of the emblematic and symbolic.

References

Aronson, Arnold 2014. *Ming Cho Lee: A Life in Design*. New York: Theatre Communications Group.

Wyzeva, Teodor de [1886] 1995. "Notes sur la Peinture Wagnérienne et le Salon de 1886." In *Symbolist Art Theories*, edited by Henri Dorra, 147–9. Berkeley: University of California Press.

29

RICHARD WAGNER, GEORG FUCHS, ADOLPHE APPIA, AND EDWARD GORDON CRAIG

Christopher Baugh

No aspect of theatre history is more likely to be constructed within a narrative of evolution than that of scenography. It is hard, for example, to resist describing Renaissance scenic perspective as the beginning of a coherent trajectory leading towards late nineteenth-century stage realism. It is similarly tempting to portray artists such as Wagner, Fuchs, Appia, and Craig as knights in shining armor, blazing onto the theatrical battlefield and mercilessly slaughtering existing practices with their visionary insights. Instinctively we warm to the rhetoric of Craig who taunted "this false-witnessing Realism – this traitor to the Imagination – this idolatry of ugliness" (Craig 1913: 90). Rejection of "false-witnessing Realism" and appreciation of the material reality of the stage, serve as benchmarks of theatrical modernism, but we should not oversimplify the nature of this artistic revolution. Jonathan Crary warns against creating a "conceptual division" leading to the belief that "something called realism dominated popular representational practices, while experiments occurred in a distinct . . . arena of modernist art making" (Crary 1992: 4). He argues for a shift in perceptual sensibilities "signaled by the passage from the geometrical optics of the seventeenth and eighteenth centuries to physiological optics, which dominated both scientific and philosophical discussion of vision in the nineteenth century" (ibid.: 16). We might characterize this as a shift from a theatre where actors played before the perspectival formality of a painted scene witnessed by an objective audience, to a theatre that unified actors within a scenic environment, and which sought subjective involvement and absorption within a darkened audience. Modernization of vision progressed throughout the nineteenth century as more was discovered about the subjectivity of perception. It is perhaps useful, therefore, to think of stage realism and modernist theatre as complementary components functioning within the shared social context. Amy Holzapfel's important and decisive re-evaluation of the scenographies of Ibsen, Strindberg, and even Zola and Hauptmann, has shown that, when viewed within the context of contemporary science, their scenic realism was "nuanced, metatheatrical, and self-conscious" (Holzapfel 2014: 7). She rightly cautions that, when viewed within contemporary conceptions of vision, "the realist stage ceases to be a fixed stylistic category" (ibid.: 20). Similarly, arguments about empathy and abstraction that concerned modernist artists early in the twentieth century may be traced back to the early nineteenth century when absorption and involvement began to condition scenographic thinking. It is an oversimplification, therefore, to present the arguments of modernist theatre artists as a straightforward consignment of realism to the past. But, of course, these cautions cannot undermine the crucial importance of attitudes and acts of renaissance proposed by Wagner, Fuchs, Appia, and Craig: ideas that are made more potent by their longevity and enduring energy.

Richard Wagner (1813–1883)

> The highest conjoint work of art is the *Drama*: it can only be at hand in all its possible fullness, when in it each *separate branch of art* is at hand in *its own utmost fullness.*
>
> *(Wagner 2008: 101)*

In 1849 Richard Wagner's great achievements lay in the future: the music-dramas *Tristan und Isolde*, *Die Meistersinger*, the *Ring* cycle, and *Parsifal*, and the 1876 Bayreuth Festspielhaus theatre. Nevertheless *The Artwork of the Future* (*Das Kunstwerk der Zukunft*), which he wrote in that year, undoubtedly lies right at the heart of twentieth-century scenographic theory and practice.

During the 1830s Wagner scraped a living as musical director in a number of theatres and had composed several operas; but *Die Feen* (*The Fairies*) written in 1833 was not performed until after his death, and *Das Liebesverbot* (*The Ban on Love*) a version of Shakespeare's *Measure for Measure* closed after just one performance in 1834. From 1839, he spent a miserable period in Paris, pitching his talents against what he considered to be a decadent cartel of musical and theatrical management that ignored his work. However, with the help of Giacomo Meyerbeer, his opera *Rienzi* was successfully produced in Dresden (20 October 1842) where Wagner moved to live in 1842, and where he staged *Der fliegende Holländer* (2 January 1843) and *Tannhäuser* (19 October 1845). But the politics of socialist German nationalism increasingly occupied his attention. Among dissident and anarchist friends he met the architect Gottfried Semper who would provide the model for Otto Brückwald's Festspielhaus in Bayreuth. After the abortive uprising of May 1849 warrants were issued for the arrest of the leaders, including Wagner, and he fled to Zurich to live in exile for the next 12 years. Wagner did not gain any significant recognition as an artist until the 1860s when *Tristan und Isolde* was performed in Munich in 1865. This opera had an enormous influence upon the development of modernist music towards the end of the century and upon symbolist writers and artists.

Unfortunately the tortuous philosophical prose of *The Artwork of the Future* is not helped by the continuing dominance of the severely dated English translation by William Ashton Ellis published in 1892. Nevertheless its significance in expressing core values of scenography is very clear. For example, in the twenty-first century, most articulations of scenography describe the collaborative artistic inter-relationships of different theatrical arts: arts of space, scene, costume, light, and sound. Scenography is frequently glossed as the act of drawing with the stage wherein the combined arts respond to dramatic action – whether that action is enshrined in dramatic literature, or within an act of performance created by a collaboration of artists. Wagner said:

> [E]ach separate art can only bare its utmost secret to their common public through a mutual parlaying with the other arts; for the purpose of each separate branch of art can only be fully attained by the reciprocal agreement and corporation of all the branches in their common message.
>
> *(Wagner 2008: 101)*

Wagner used the word *Gesamtkunstwerk* (variously expressed as a combined, united, or a "coming together" art work) to express this dominant idea of an artwork that, through combination, becomes greater than the sum of its individual parts. This became an idea that would run like a leitmotif through modernist theatrical manifestos. Rejection of the formal Italianate *opera seria* and the repetitions of *da capo aria* opera dramaturgy had been central to the ambitions of German romantic "reforming" opera early in the nineteenth century, and it was in discussion of opera that the word *Gesamtkunstwerk* was probably first used by Friedrich Trahndorff (1782–1863) in his 1827 essay "Aesthetics, or Theory of Philosophy of Art" (*Ästhetik oder Lehre von Weltanschauung und Kunst*). Wagner's concept of *Gesamtkunstwerk* found its unifying force in the dramatic action, which must be the core driving force of the drama:

> The Art-work of the Future is an associate work, and only an associate demand can call it forth . . . But the thing that makes this sharing possible to all – nay that renders it necessary, and which without their cooperation can never come to manifestment [*sic.*] – is the very kernel of the Drama, the dramatic Action.
>
> *(Ibid.: 112)*

This "manifestment" represented an artistic *process* both in its creation (a process of collaboration in rehearsal) and also in its unfolding, presentation and reception by an audience. At the time of writing *The Artwork of the Future*, Wagner was a keen follower of the philosopher George Hegel (1770–1831) whose ideas of historical growth, change and development influenced the understanding of his own presence in history and, importantly, discussed relationships between societies and cultural forms. Bryan Magee in his analysis of philosophical thought upon Wagner's work explains: "Hegel's fundamental insight . . . was that reality is not a state of affairs but a process: *it is something going on* . . . Even a material object is a process: it comes into existence and passes away, and is never the same for two consecutive moments" (Magee 2000: 43).

Wagner was undoubtedly the first to articulate the phenomenology of time-based creation *and* the unfolding process of audience reception. He had produced a theory of performance that suggested the amalgamation of art forms, uniting to create an artwork, as he says, of the future. Each would respond to the dramatic will, and to that extent Wagner's *Gesamtkunstwerk* proposed egalitarianism within the arts, which could, through the processes of creation and reception, become "the maximally expressive artwork" (ibid.: 238). But Wagner also acknowledged the possibility of what might today be called a transient scenographic focus; that the *Gesamtkunstwerk* should not suggest a process of performance where all the individual elements of theatre would work *simultaneously*. He clarified:

> Thus supplementing one another in their changeful dance, the united sister-arts will show themselves and make good their claim; now altogether, now in pairs, and again in solitary splendour, according to the momentary need of the only rule- and purpose-giver, the Dramatic Action.
>
> *(Wagner 2008: 107)*

Although we may question Wagner's understanding of cultural relativism and his belief in the power and efficacy of the art of the "Folk," his idealistic vision of antiquity initiated an atavistic strand of thought that would be extended by Appia, Fuchs, and Craig, and continue throughout the twentieth century: "let us look far hence to glorious Grecian Art, and gather from its inner understanding the outlines for the Art-work of the Future!" (ibid.: 19). The argument of such atavism is that present-day theatre and its conventions have become artistically corrupt; that materialism has connived with decadence to produce meaningless and trivial art manufactured to meet consumer demand. Healthier forms and attitudes might be discovered in the past – in the theatres of antiquity, in theatre forms of the Renaissance and in theatres of non-Western cultures where the cultural *necessity* of performance has not been morally degraded and corrupted by social custom and mercantile appropriation.

> Tragedy flourished just so long as it was inspired by the spirit of the Folk, and this spirit was a veritably popular, i.e. *a communal* one. When the national brotherhood of the Folk was shivered into fragments, when the common bond of its Religion and primeval Customs was pierced and severed by the sophist needles of the egoistic spirit of Athenian self-dissection, – then the Folk's artwork also ceased . . . [and] threw Art upon one side for two millennia.
>
> *(Ibid.: 59)*

The exception for Wagner, as it was to be for Craig and a great many twentieth-century theatre artists, was the Renaissance when, in *Commedia dell'arte* and in Shakespeare's theatre:

> the boorish figure of the homely Folk's-comedian takes on the bearing of a hero, the raucous clang of daily speech becomes the sounding music of the soul, the rude scaffolding of carpet-hung boards becomes a world-stage with all its wealth of scene.
>
> *(Ibid.: 63)*

In 1854 Wagner discovered the writings of Arthur Schopenhauer (1788–1860) and in particular *The World as Will and Representation* originally published in 1818, but expanded and re-published in 1844. For two decades, this work became Wagner's guiding testament and freed him to create the major operas. There were two aspects of Schopenhauer's ideas that are relevant: first, the idea that all the arts, with the exception of music, are representational. However, what they represent is not just the physical object itself – not the plot, or the stage scene or characters – but they talk *about* something, which is represented by these means. In other words, the work of art leads towards the universal through the representation of the particular. This understanding became central to the symbolic and emblematic functioning of art, and underpinned early twentieth-century movements that rejected artistic mimesis. Second, and especially important for Wagner, music, being non-representational, became more than "first among equals" within the artistic pantheon of the *Gesamtkunstwerk*, it became the *will* of art: the bearer of the over-riding dramatic action. This, of course, became central for Adolphe Appia when he developed Wagner's ideas into an explicitly practical theory of scenography.

Schopenhauer also enhanced Wagner's understanding of the cultural significance of the arts as he suggested that through forms of empathy, art has the capacity to take us out of ourselves, to offer absorption into a world of the artist's making. This was an ambition of Loutherbourg in the late eighteenth century as he sought artistic control over all visual elements within performance and, by implication, to remove the fore-stage and harmonize the actor within the designed scenic environment. It is important to locate this philosophy within Wagner's thinking since it achieved an architectural culmination within his expression of the proscenium arch at Bayreuth. The design of the Festspielhaus (Figure 29.1) presented music as something transcending empirical reality – so fulfilling his understanding of Schopenhauer. Wagner expressed this within the speech that he made at the opening of the theatre in 1876:

> In the proportions and arrangement of the room and its seats, however, you will find expressed a thought which, once you have grasped it, will place you in a new relation to the play you are about to witness, a relation quite distinct from that in which you had always been involved when visiting our theatres. Should this first impression have proved correct, the mysterious entry of the music will next prepare you for the unveiling and distinct portrayal of scenic pictures that seem to rise from out an ideal world of dreams.
>
> *(Wagner 1977: 358)*

The Artwork of the Future advocated new forms of relationships between individual artistic practices and presented them within a framework of history and cultural understanding. For theatrical reform late in the century these ideas were "modern," advanced, and revolutionary: "to many it seemed the voice of the future" (Magee 2000: 99).

Figure 29.1 Wagner's *Festspielhaus* at Bayreuth. (Photo: akg-images.)

Georg Fuchs (1869–1949)

The harmony of the arts is the beautiful symbol of a stronger *Volk*.
(Peter Behrens, Feste des Lebens und der Kunst *1900)*[1]

Georg Fuchs rarely figures in the histories of theatre and scenography. He has earned a paragraph or two in the general histories that reference the Munich Artists' Theatre (Künstlertheater) that opened in May 1908. These histories acknowledge its auditorium as a reflection of Wagner's Festspielhaus, and refer to Fuchs' attachment to the "relief" stage – a shallow stage with a proscenium area that placed the actors on a deep forestage. He wrote several plays that have not survived their historical moment; he was not himself a practicing visual artist, using artists such as Fritz Erler (1868–1940) to design his productions; and he was not an especially significant director, being over-shadowed by the emerging talents of his contemporary Max Reinhardt. Nevertheless, he has a significant place within the development of scenographic theory and practice and shares important contemporary links with Appia and Craig.

There is no published study on Fuchs, although he does feature significantly in Peter Jalevich's *Munich and Theatrical Modernism* (1985). But Jalevich pays little attention to the architectural and scenographic achievements of the Artists' Theatre, and is more concerned to locate Fuchs within the contemporary campaigns for the cultural (re)formation of the German *Volk*. The elitist, nationalist, and implicitly racist attempts by artists and thinkers to create a truly German culture, following the unification of the German state in 1871, has tarnished the reputation of many artists. The only serious and properly balanced study of Fuchs is the important PhD thesis by Juliet Koss, *Empathy Abstracted: Georg Fuchs and the Munich Artists' Theater* (Koss 2000).

However, Fuchs published two books, whose titles should command our attention: *The Stage of the Future* (*Die Schaubühner Zukunft*) was a 1905 manifesto for the Artists' Theatre, and the 1909 *Revolution in the Theatre: Conclusions Concerning the Munich Artists' Theatre (Die Revolution des Theaters)*. While these writings are by no means as racist or as anti-Semitic as those of Wagner, they can, out of context, be easily mined for progenitive material and ideas that point towards the future barbarism of German National Socialist cultural policy. Nevertheless, the articulation and descriptions of theatre architecture, actor-audience relationships, scenic approaches and especially the awakening of the value of stage lighting cannot be ignored, and must be rightfully located within the narrative alongside ideas by Appia and Craig.

Fuchs studied literature at the University of Giessen and then art history in Leipzig, moving to Munich in 1890. Fundamentally he was a critic whose art journalism supported the Munich Secession – an alternative exhibition framework for young artists – and the *Jugendtsil* movement that emerged in the mid-1890s. He was involved in the project of Ernst Ludwig, the grand Duke of Hesse, to create the Artists' Colony in Darmstadt, and he wrote a play that formed part of the opening ceremony in May 1901. *Jugendstil* advocated forms of low relief and surface decoration in the applied arts, and Fuchs's relief stage developed from these values. With the architect and decorative artist, Peter Behrens (1868–1940), whom he met in Darmstadt, Fuchs began to develop a theory of *Jugendtsil* theatre.

Fuchs shared Wagner's belief in the pivotal role of culture within national consciousness and developed a similar appreciation of historical cultures. For example, Fuchs admired the theatre of antiquity and endorsed the views of Friedrich Nietzsche (1844–1900) expressed in *Birth of Tragedy* (1872), that forms of spiritual intoxication were essential elements of the theatrical experience. This served to underpin his concept of theatre architecture and the actor-audience relationship: "[i]n the theatre, art can fulfill its purpose – become an independent and specifically theatrical art – only when it engenders something of this primitive excitement and throws it back again into the audience" (Fuchs [1909] 1972: 7). He shared with Wagner, and indeed Craig, a deep admiration for Renaissance theatre, and through the mythologizing of Hans Sachs in *Die Meistersinger* idealized them into his practice: "[j]ust as our forefathers created their cultural life out of the stylized elements of their simple handicrafts, so shall we to create a culture peculiarly our own through a similar domination of our more complicated machine" (ibid.: 9). Like Craig he rejected ideas of reform, demanding out and out revolution: "we are not required to reform what exists. Our obligation is toward new creation, the creation of a theatre for those who do not yet have one worthy of them" (ibid.: 10). He questioned the artistic subjection implicit within the *Gesamtkunstwerk* and demanded the autonomy of theatrical art: "[i]t does not attain perfection solely as a synthesis of all the other arts, but as an art in itself" (ibid.: 47).

In 1904, after Fuchs concluded a lecture on the topic of theatre reform, the architect Max Littman (1862–1931), who had designed the Munich Schauspielhaus (1901) and the Prinzregententheater (1901), introduced himself in order to discuss shared ideas. Littman sketched designs, which appeared in Fuchs' *The Stage of the Future* the following year, and which, four years later in 1908, were realized as the Artists' Theatre, forming part of the *Ausstellung München* exhibition. Littman's plans were closely modeled upon those of Gottfried Semper for the unrealized Munich Festspielhaus. Littman and Fuchs' auditorium rose in a single amphitheatre with no central aisle, and with audience access through side doors. The orchestra, as at Bayreuth, was located beneath the stage but was frequently covered thereby creating a deeper forestage. The precise relationship of the audience with the act of performance was vital to Fuchs:

> For it is in the audience that the dramatic work of art is actually born – born at that time it is experienced – and it is differently experienced by every individual member of the audience. The beginning of a dramatic work of art is not upon the stage or even in a book. It is created at that moment when it is experienced as movement of form in time and space.
>
> *(Fuchs [1909] 1972: 43)*

Fuchs vehemently opposed literary and naturalistic theatre, which he exemplified by Ibsen and the Meiningen Company. He claimed that the literary school of dramatists took for its "heroes" neurasthenics, hysterical persons, patients of "certain doctors" and turned the art of the theatre into a psychological laboratory investigating nervous diseases, and in which the art of acting was being ground into dust by the tyranny of literature. He said that it would be difficult to find a person so naive as to really

Figure 29.2 Georg Fuchs' production of *Twelfth Night* at the Munich Künstlertheater, 1908. (From *Dekorative Kunst*, December 1910.)

believe in a naturalistic art of scene design, or one who would consider it possible to build a setting that was actually true to nature: "[f]or the actuality is a stage set and one must let it go at that" (ibid.: 99). He asserted that:

> Odious ostentation, scholastic pedantry, and the bombastic acting of an earlier age were byproducts of the Meiningen stage. Plays and performers sank beneath the burden of this egregious rubbish. They grimaced and cavorted; with ranting and roaring they overacted. Things came to such a pass that, although this was an era in which taste was universally debased, the stage stood upon the very lowest level of degradation.
>
> *(Ibid.: 156–7)*

Fuchs believed that actors must perform within the same architectural volume as the audience; the forestage was therefore the principal acting area, and the actors would appear in a form of bas-relief. The aim was to keep the performer close to the audience so as to establish a sense of community and to emphasize plasticity by using light to frame actors against a simplified background. Placing the actors in this relationship with their audience encouraged empathy (*einfühlung*), and he considered the spectator's experience as "a form of embodied vision, an emotional absorption that helped to create the work of art" (Koss 2000: 14). Absorption and involvement were in direct contrast with the sense of calm objectivity that was traditionally supposed to govern the appreciation of art. In this state of empathy, Koss argues, "all sense of the spectator's carefully delineated identity disappeared as the individual melted into a sensation of ecstasy. Reconfigured as the god of a spectatorship that is active, passionate, and communal, Dionysus – and the notion of spectatorial ecstasy more specifically – would haunt European aesthetics for decades (Kos 2000: 33).

The key feature of the scenography was the design and functioning of its extensive proscenium. The "special correspondent" of *Le Figaro* (Paris) provided a clear description of this in reviewing the opening production of Goethe's *Faust*:

> The rising of the curtain revealed an inner proscenium, a middle stage, and an inner stage, sometimes on one level, and sometimes on different levels. At the sides and continually visible are two square towers of wood, each with a door and a window, plain and without colored glass. A movable bridge unites them above, a bridge which carries a complete outfit of lights and which may be raised and lowered at will. Lowered at its farthest point upstage until it almost approaches the curtains, it diminishes considerably the dimensions of the scene and suffices to create of itself the frame of an extremely intimate interior. The second scene is bounded on the right and left sometimes by a movable frame supporting curtains when an interior scene is to be played on the second level, sometimes by two walls when a more open space is desired. These two walls are both movable. They may be completely withdrawn on wagons into the wings, or, on the other hand, they may be brought together so as to shut off the horizon.
>
> *(*Le Figaro*, No. 233, 18 August 1908; quoted in Fuchs [1909] 1972: 185)*

This three-dimensional mobile proscenium structure, complete with entrances and upper level "windows," similar in some ways to the permanent proscenium of early baroque theatre, defined Fuchs' concept of stage practice. The movable nature of both the lateral towers and the overhead bridges served to both model space and to provide an extremely flexible rig for the lights. Gorelik is more precise in his description when he says that the bridges "masked a battery of light-projectors" and that "[i]n the rear . . . four differently colored cycloramas rolled across when needed, at the touch of an electric button" (Gorelik 1957: 177). Fuchs claimed that the reason for the depth of the stage was to enable light to transform and "dematerialize" the physicality of back scenes. He stresses the fundamental place of light in scenography:

> Light is, and will continue to be, the most important factor in the development of stage design. Modern electrical technique offers possibilities, which it would be folly to disregard. To use them correctly, to distribute and regulate these immense and manifold masses of lights with artistic effect, requires the creative spirit of a sculptor . . . Engineers and electricians who have so much to contribute may no longer be ignored. Workers in the plastic arts must recognize and welcome them.
>
> *(Fuchs [1909] 1972: 85)*

Along with Appia and Craig, Fuchs believed that rhythm fused all the elements of production into a single coherent art. Unlike them, however, he placed the actor in front of the setting rather than within it, thereby reducing the three-dimensionality they so avidly sought. Notwithstanding, the work of the Munich Artists' Theatre and the theories of Georg Fuchs reinforced those of Appia and Craig and furthered the modernist trend toward stylization in the theatre.

Adolphe Appia (1862–1928)

Appia was born in Geneva within a strict environment of humanitarian endeavor; his father, Louis Appia, was one of the co-founders of the International Red Cross. He studied music at the Leipzig Conservatoire from 1882 to 1883 and then, following an intermission in Paris, at Dresden from 1886 to 1890. He enrolled in the Conservatoire, but, as Palmer's research[2] has shown, he developed a relationship with the Dresden Hopftheater as audience member from 1886 and, more significantly, as a formal technical apprentice for the year 1889–1890. Between 1886 and this apprenticeship, however, he seems to have assisted backstage as perhaps what we would call an intern. During this period the Meiningen company visited Dresden on several occasions and through them Appia met Germany's leading lighting artist, Hugo Bähr, who lived in Dresden and who created lighting and special effects for the Company. Appia moved to Vienna in 1890 and immediately entered into a period of internship at the Vienna opera. Palmer convincingly demonstrates that this intense period of theatrical experience and technical education, between his arrival in Dresden in 1886 and his time in Vienna, "provided an ideal grounding as well as the inspiration for Appia's radical scenographic vision" (Palmer 2015: 43).

Appia therefore possessed invaluable practical experience, which he applied to the fundamental problem that had not been addressed by Wagner in either his writings or in practice at Bayreuth: that was the function of lighting in the theatre. For most of the nineteenth century, stage lighting, dominated by gas burners, was placed at the service of painted scenery, and the lighting "designer" was usually the painter who arranged the borders and battens of burners to produce the best effect on the scenes. However, the use of electric battens, and the increasing use of electric arc lights such as the Duboscq units that Appia had experienced working with Hugo Bähr, could provide more intense and focused light. The resulting shadows and variations in light intensities all rendered the scenery ineffective at best or, at worst, ludicrous. Appia summarized the problem in 1899:

> The arrangement of painted canvas to represent the setting demands that the lighting be exclusively at its service in order to make the painting visible, a relationship having nothing to do with the active role played by lighting and quite distinctly in conflict with it . . . If we introduce the actor onto the stage, the importance of the painting is suddenly completely subordinated to the lighting and the spatial arrangement, because the living form of the actor can have no contact and consequently no direct rapport with what is represented on the canvas.
>
> *(Appia [1898] 1962: 22)*

While in Leipzig, he had discovered the music dramas of Wagner, whose international popularity accelerated following his death in 1883, and was enhanced by the advocacy and publications of Houston Stewart Chamberlain with whom Appia had formed a friendship in 1883. Since Wagner was the first director of the music-dramas at Bayreuth, their scenography quickly acquired canonical status. This was encouraged by Wagner's wife Cosima, who became artistic director following his death and whose son Siegfried maintained Wagner's production approach throughout the repertoire until the 1930s.

In *La Mise en Scène du Drame Wagnérien* (Paris, 1894), Appia's aim was to make an interpretation of the *Gesamtkunstwerk* of *The Artwork of the Future* by providing what he thought was the correct approach to *mise en scène*. He proposed a formal arrangement of simple, abstract, non-representational geometrical structures. Stage settings, he suggested, should serve to evoke "place" where the focus would be upon the moving bodies of actors; and their illumination would be undertaken by what he called "living light." One of Appia's early memories concerned the nature of stage "place." In 1921, in "Theatrical Experiences and Personal Investigations," he recalled:

> One of my friends at boarding school had seen *Tannhäuser* in Germany and gave me a report of it. I tried to pin him down and inquired whether the characters were really "in a place" and what this "place" was like. He didn't understand me. I remember having been rather insistent and having finally asked almost in despair, "Where were their feet?"
>
> *(Quoted in Beacham 1994: 7)*

In the theatre of Appia's youth, the actors' feet existed on a formal stage floor marked with the lines of traps and grooves, while their upper bodies were framed against painted scenic illusion. *Die Musik und die Inszenierung* (Music and the Art of the Theatre) was published in Munich in 1899 and contained a detailed analysis of current stage practice and a development of his ideas on the use of light. Although extended in later publications and influenced by his work with Émile Jaques-Dalcroze (1865–1950) at Hellerau from 1910 to 1914, this book represents the primary account of Appia's theory of the stage and its lighting. The work contained 18 illustrations of scenographies for Wagner's music-dramas which, as Lee Simonson says in his foreword to the first English translation in 1962, "embodied Appia's aesthetic principles with such finality that they became a revelation of a totally new kind of stage setting and stage lighting" (Appia 1962: xi). Fuerst and Hume, in *Twentieth-Century Stage Decoration* (New York, 1929), the first comprehensive survey of new approaches to scenography, quite simply accept the publication of Appia's work in 1899 as the beginning of the modern period in the theatre.

The starting point for all Appia's theory was a response to Wagner's unification of music with poetry – in his judgment, an achievement of the utmost artistic and human significance. However, productions at Bayreuth utterly failed to realize this artistic potential. Appia said that Wagner was clearly aware of the value of the visual in the theatre because of the Festspielhaus design: "but strangely enough this otherwise purely idealistic genius did not have an idealistic visual sense" (Appia 1962: 22). In order to find a suitable model for the temple of the Holy Grail for *Parsifal* (1882), Wagner sent scenic artists on an extensive research trip to Italy. The Baptistry of the *Duomo* in Sienna was chosen and carefully re-created on the stage. Appia described the effect:

> In *Parsifal* at Bayreuth, when the curtain went up on the scene of the interior of the Grail Temple, the painted scenery had to be sacrificed to the darkness necessitated by the scene change – imparting a marvelous life to the setting. As the lights started to come up, the illusion was continuously dispelled until finally, in the full glare of the border lights and the footlights, the knights made their entrance into a pasteboard temple.
>
> *(Ibid.: 23)*

The historicism of costumes and scenic detail attracted a similar judgment:

> Characters in scrupulously historic costumes proudly descend a wooden staircase. In their luxurious and authentic footgear they tread boards cluttered with set pieces, and appear outlined against walls and balustrades, which the well-lighted painting indicates to be of marvelously sculptured marble. The costume, in contact with the set pieces and the drops, lighted by light not designed for it, is completely devoid of meaning – a museum piece, nothing more.
>
> *(Ibid.: 62)*

Appia's theory of scenography is built upon his ability to move from observation and description to reflection and rigorous analysis, which together make his conclusions so compellingly inevitable:

> Because living light was not used, the audience became accustomed to using its imagination to interpret the flat painted perspectives of the vertical canvas . . . And so the real life which only lighting and a three-dimensional setting can give is sacrificed to the desire to behold in *indication* many fascinating and spectacular things.
>
> *(Ibid.: 24)*

Unlike Craig, who consistently rejected the primacy of dramatic literature within production practice, Appia did not. He believed that the *mise en scène* should exist in order to create a realization of core dramatic action, which would emerge from the inspiration of the musician-poet. The musician-poet would control all aspects of production, and the *mise en scène* should be a synthesis of all elements. He did not consider an especially collaborative process of theatre making and therefore, like Craig, proposed the individual artist/director as being responsible for making the production in the theatre of the future. The logic is clear:

> It is the word-tone poet, then, who possesses the guiding principle which, springing as it does from the original intention, inexorably and of necessity dictates the *mise en scène* . . . this principle is an integral part of his drama and shares its organic life.
>
> *(Ibid.: 17)*

In this way there would be an absolute integration between dramatic intention and its realization as *mise en scène*. This is more fundamental than simply seeking a closer relationship between content and form; Appia's assertion was that the actual forms and means, including light, of theatrical presentation should *become* the content. In this way production would *embody* the dramatic idea, and not simply *interpret* the idea. Music lay at the heart of this synthesis of sound, movement, space and light:

> The word-tone drama is the one dramatic form which dictates most accurately the actor's role in all its proportions. It is therefore the only drama which empowers the actor through his use of the setting to determine the relation of the spatial arrangement to the lighting and to the painting, and thus to control, through his role, the entire visual expression.
>
> *(Ibid.: 26)*

The actors' reality is that of their stage presence – not that of fictional, rounded characters. The actor should be an expressive medium who responds in sympathy with the living force that emanates from the will of the musician-poet. Appia would have agreed with Fuchs when he said, "For it is in the audience that the dramatic work of art is actually born – born at that time it is experienced" (Fuchs [1909] 1972: 43).

Appia made these arguments precisely at the time when Stanislavski was suggesting quite the reverse. Six years later Craig wrote his provocative essay "The Actor and the Über-Marionette" (1905), in which he said that he wanted the fire and passion of the actor on stage, without the personality of the actor, who currently served merely as an instrument for literature and impersonation. He proposed a way forward for the actor, along a route that Appia would advocate: "[b]ut I see a loophole by which in time the actors can escape from the bondage they are in. They must create for themselves a new form of acting, consisting for the main part of symbolic gesture" (Craig [1911] 1962: 61). However, such a form of "living" acting must be located within an equally "living" scene. In 1904, in the essay "How to Reform our Staging Practices," Appia argued:

> [T]he human body does not seek to create the illusion of reality *since it is itself reality!* What it demands of the scenery is simply that it bring out that reality; which has the natural consequence of completely changing the whole object of the scenery: in one case the desire is to achieve the real appearance of objects; in the other, to give the highest degree of reality to the human body.
>
> *(Appia [1904] 1995: 237)*

For the preface to the 1918 edition of *Die Musik und die Inszenierung*, Appia refined this concept of a synthesis between music, human action, and light, first articulated in 1899:

> Eleven years later, I became acquainted with the Eurhythmics of Jaques-Dalcroze . . . and there I found the answer to my passionate desire for synthesis! By closely following this musical discipline of the body, I discovered the living germ of the dramatic art, in which music is no longer separated from the human body in a splendour which is after all illusory, at least during performance, nor subjugated to it, a dramatic art which will direct the body towards an externalization in space, and thus make it the primary and supreme means of scenic expression, to which all other elements of production will be subordinated.
>
> *(Appia [1898] 1962: 3–4)*

Musical terminology consistently provided Appia with metaphors for his analysis of light. "Light is to production what music is to the score" (ibid.: 72). He conceived of an organization of stage lighting – the lighting plot – that would begin with the first chords of an overture and continuously change, blend and harmonize throughout the entire production. Such a conception of lighting would operate beyond illumination, beyond visibility, or even beyond an accompaniment. Appia considered stage lighting to be capable of the deepest and most profound human expression; like music it would be capable of expressing "the inner essence of all vision" (ibid.). In *La Vie Musicale* (1908) he wrote, "Where the other arts say, 'that means', music says, 'that is'. When forms and colours seek to express something, light says, 'I am'; forms and colours will come into being only through me." Appia described practical ways by which *mise en scène* could embody Wagner's understanding of Schopenhauer's presentation of music as the expression of dramatic will.

Notwithstanding the infancy of electric light, Appia identified the essential qualities of light in the theatre and, by implication, the nature of the necessary equipment and installation. He described the principal functioning of light as a "[d]aylight [that] floods the whole atmosphere, but nevertheless we are always aware of the direction from which it comes" (ibid.: 74). But he also realized that the direction of light could only be sensed by means of shadow, and therefore it was the quality of shadows, which would express the quality of light. He logically deduced that, in the real world, "[s]hadows are formed by the same light which illuminates the atmosphere." However, he also appreciated that this could not be achieved artificially: "On stage this task must therefore be divided, so that part of the lighting equipment will be used for general illumination, while the rest will cast shadows by means of exactly focused beams. We shall call them 'diffused light' and 'living light'" (ibid.: 74). To these he added the idea of projecting images using what today would be called gobos – cut-out shapes placed between a light source and the focusing lens that would produce broken or textured light when projected onto a cloth or the stage. Appia had experience of the Duboscq electric arc light that could provide a powerful source of light for such projection. He illustrated the value of gobos where

> coloured illumination, filtered and brought into play in various ways, throws onto the stage light characteristic of the forest, the quality of which leaves to the imagination of the audience the existence of obstacles they have no need to see . . . and thus the characters as well as the three-dimensional portions of the setting are immersed in the *atmosphere* suited to them.
>
> *(Ibid.: 67)*

In identifying these three kinds of stage light, Appia's conclusions have not been significantly changed to the present day. The catalogues of equipment manufacturers in the twenty-first century display luminaires for producing a soft, diffused light – generally the wide-focusing halogen or LED lamp with a diffusing fresnel lens; luminaires with lenses that will create hard-edged pools of "living light" – spotlights and beam lights; and luminaires that have condensing and lens capabilities to project sharply focused images. Inevitably the technology of the intervening period has made improvements to safety, flexibility and light output, but the essential functions and purposes of theatre light as identified by Appia in 1899 have changed little.

In 1910 Appia worked with architect Heinrich Tessenow (1876–1950) and with the painter Alexander von Saltzmann (1874–1934) to design Europe's first studio theatre at Hellerau, a "garden suburb" community of Dresden. The rectangular hall had no proscenium arch and there was no demarcation between audience space and performance space. An orchestra pit traversed the space but, when covered, the hall was in daily use for Dalcroze's eurhythmic classes and exercises. Dalcroze insisted that eurhythmics was not an art form in itself, but an educational path towards art: performance was a by-product of eurhythmics, not the planned end-product. The installation created by

Appia and Saltzmann was invisible and reflected light provided a calm, neutral space. In "Eurhythmics and the Theatre" (1911) Appia said:

> Up to now . . . comfortable seats have been provided in semi-darkness, to encourage a state of total passivity – *Eurhythmics will overturn this passivity!* . . . Light, no longer forced to illuminate the painted flats, can radiate, carrying form into space, filling it with living color and the limitless variations of an ever-changing atmosphere.
>
> *(In Beacham 1994: 93)*

The walls of the hall were hung with cedar-oil-impregnated linen, which provided a warm translucency, and must have provided a wonderful perfume to the hall. Battens of lights (reported to consist of 7,000 individual bulbs) were placed behind the linen and were reflected back from the white painted walls of the building onto the surface of the fabric. This "diffused light" created an environment for performance that was illuminated by the glowing "walls." No distinction was made between the linen hangings surrounding the performance space and those surrounding the audience. Saltzmann said: "instead of a lighted space, we have a light-producing space. Light is conveyed through the space itself, and the linking of visible light sources is done away with" (ibid.: 94).

In order to achieve the "living light," spotlights were placed in the ceiling of the hall, and the whole installation, both diffusing battens and spotlights, was centrally controlled. The entire place of performance at Hellerau could respond to the dramatic action, the emotion, the music, the atmosphere, and indeed to the totality of the living performance. Music achieved a physical embodiment through both its placement within the sunken space at the center of the hall and through the eurhythmic movement of the performers, while the light could represent the music throughout the entire space. There are enthusiastic comments from audience members about the unearthly and ethereal qualities of the light. George Bernard Shaw, who visited Hellerau in 1913, described the lighting installation: "acres of white linen and the multitude of light behind and above it. It needs only a transparent floor with light beneath it to make it capable of anything heavenly" (quoted in Dent 1952: 137).

In the festivals taking place at the Dalcroze Institute during the summers of 1912 and 1913, the community-living ideas of Hellerau, eurhythmics, and Appia's ideas for scenography were seen by most of the leading theatre artists of Europe whose reactions were consistently enthusiastic. Hellerau created an alternative model for theatre architecture in parallel with the mainstream architectural model of Littman in Munich and of Wagner's Festspielhaus (Figure 29.3). In his "Theatrical Experiences and Personal Investigations" (1921), Appia theorized the concept of the "study site":

> The designs I first produced for Dalcroze were still in essence oriented towards a spectacle presented to the eyes of others; they therefore only partly encompassed the auditorium. Today I have reached extreme conclusions with regard to the hierarchic principle of stage production. Reaching beyond theatre, it will serve all living art. I imagine a rectangular, empty and unadorned hall equipped with complete lighting installations. On either side are large annexes for storing sections of three-dimensional units. These would be built with lines and

> proportions appropriate to the human body and broken up into segments that could be joined together to form every possible arrangement of levels, whether horizontal, vertical or sloping. They would be combined with curtains, folding screens, etc., and everything would be covered with canvas of a uniform type . . . This would be called the 'study site'.
>
> *(In Beacham 1994: 272–3)*

Revolutionary in 1921, Appia's "study site" describes the ubiquitous studio space and scenic equipment of the theatre complex, arts center or educational campus of the twenty-first century.

But Appia went further in locating the "study site" within his belief in the living nature of art. His ambition was that performance space should no longer reflect the binary distinction between the act of performance and its reception by a spatially located audience: "[a] moment of living art with no one viewing it except the performers themselves exists fully, and with more dignity than when reflected in the eyes of passive onlookers" (quoted in ibid.: 272). To clarify, he invited a comparison between the experience of participating in singing the first great chorus of Bach's *St Matthew Passion*, and being an audience listening to a choir sing it. In other words Appia's ultimate living work of art reflected the engagement of direct participation. The "study site" represents an inter-active, environmental scenography – a place – that enables, welcomes and locates performance. He concluded:

> The obstacle to living art is the audience. We are in it, and it in us! Therefore the very concept of an audience, the expression of passivity, must be neutralized through an effort to overcome this passivity.
>
> *(Ibid.: 274)*

Figure 29.3 Appia's design at Hellerau for Gluck's *Orfeo*, Act 2.

Edward Gordon Craig (1872–1966)

Gordon Craig the actor left Henry Irving's Lyceum Theatre in 1896. In 1910, he was 38 years old and seemed to be close to achieving the recognition and theatrical opportunities for carrying into practice his radical ideas for performance and scenography. The volume of essays, *On the Art of the Theatre*, published in 1911, consolidated his writings, bringing together essays written in the period 1905–1909, and including the "Art of the Theatre" dialogues. The book also contained the provocative "The Actor and the Über-Marionette," which many critics and most of the theatrical profession understood as a manifesto to banish the actor and create a theatre of purely scenographic action animated by marionettes. During the period 1910–1913 his vision of theatre and scenography was being recognized internationally, and in the preface to *On the Art of the Theatre* he identified international artists with whom he confidently associated himself: a grouping that included Stanislavski, Meyerhold, Fuchs, Antoine, Yeats and Appia. He concluded the preface:

> It is a great honour for me to feel that among my friends are the names of the first artists in Europe. And I think we can all feel happy on the progress, which our movement has made, a movement, which is destined ultimately to restore the Art of the Theatre into its ancient position among the Fine arts.
>
> *(Craig [1911] 1962: viii)*

Two of the most important "art" theatres of Europe, the Moscow Art Theatre and the Abbey Theatre in Dublin, were actively seeking his collaboration; through exhibitions, his name was linked alongside that of Appia as co-founder of scenographic modernism. Two years later, in 1912, plans that he had begun to develop in London in 1904 for establishing a theatre school would be achieved at the Arena Goldoni in Florence. It is important, therefore, to set aside interpretations of rejection and failure that we may have of Craig's later life and consider the period 1910–14 as an extremely positive and optimistic one. At the age of 85 in *Index to the Story of My Days* he summarized his situation in 1907: "[f]rom now to the middle of 1913 is a very productive period of my life. All came along this year – 1907: Screens, and SCENE, the 'Übermarionette,' Black Figures, *The Mask*" (Craig 1957: 297).

On 24 January 1910, Craig submitted to the King's Patent Agency[3] in London a draft specification for what he modestly called "Improvements in Stage Scenery." On 15 April he submitted the complete specification describing his scenic proposals in detail and accompanying them with four sheets of technical drawings. Under the terms of the Patents and Designs Act (1907), a search would then have been made through the last 50 years of patent submissions to ensure originality. His submission was completed and published on 1 September 1910. The patent that Craig now owned was for the design for a stage scene, created by "screens."[4] He described the screens in his book *Scene*:

> They stand on the stage just as they are; they do not imitate nature, nor are they painted with realistic or decorative designs. They are monotone – 'A nice place', said a dear old friend to me on looking at the model of the scene [probably W. B. Yeats] – and I have always thought this was the best word to use – far better than scene – it is a place if it seem real – it is a scene if it seem false.
>
> *(Craig 1923: 1)*

Craig stressed the physical reality of the constructions and clearly described their relationship with the performer, arguing that their primary characteristic was to create a solid, three-dimensional structure that would, through light, adapt itself to the actors' movement. Like a musical instrument, the setting could be brought to life through performance:

> The relation of light to this scene is akin to that of the bow to the violin, or of the pen to the paper. For the light *travels* over the scene – it does not ever stay in one fixed place, – travelling it produces the music. During the whole course of the Drama the light either caresses or cuts, – it floods or it trickles down, – it is never quite still.
>
> *(Ibid.: 25)*

The scenography of Craig's screens, with its *continuo* accompaniment of defining light, established the idea of scenery as performer. The formally structured screens covered in unbleached canvas represented nothing; they neither imitated nor represented any actual relationship with the real world. This modernist concern with the physical reality of the stage closely links these screens with the scenic units used by Fuchs in Munich, alongside the scenes of geometrical levels sketched by Appia. Craig's patent proposal exemplified what might be considered an agenda for the future of theatrical art that he had proposed in 1907: "Today they *impersonate* and interpret; tomorrow they must *represent* and interpret; and the third day they must create" (Craig [1911] 1962: 61).

Craig's screens, therefore, did not try to reproduce a pre-existent place – a room, a street, or a palace, although they *might* serve as a device or construction to *represent* such places should the act of performance require them. The screens simply created a *place* for performance that might represent any *scene* while responding to the movements of the actor. Their essential realism was that of their material presence before an audience – hence Craig's description of them as a "place" rather than as a "scene." "Place" de-localized scenographic effort and removed all sense of topography: "[y]et the aim of the Theatre is to restore its art, and it should commence by banishing from the Theatre this idea of impersonation, this idea of reproducing Nature; for, while impersonation is in the Theatre, the Theatre can never become free" (Craig 1909: 77). The purpose and the aesthetic of a scene by Craig may be defined by its performative function rather than by representational purpose. In a very practical way, the screen scenes tried to achieve the relationship between architecture and scenic design that underpinned so much of Craig's thinking, whether expressed in models, words, or designs. As a statement of scenographic intent he wrote: "I wish to remove the *Pictorial Scene* but to leave in its place the *Architectonic Scene*" (ibid.: 75).

Craig's belief in the screens underpinned his scenography for the production of *Hamlet* that he made at the Moscow Art Theatre in 1912 (Figure 29.4). In spite of the technical complexities of realizing such scenography upon a raked stage, Stanislavski clearly understood and appreciated this ambition:

> It seemed that nothing simpler than the screens could be imagined. There could be no better background for the actors. It was natural, it did not hurt the eyes, it had three dimensions, just like the body of the actor, it was picturesque, due to the endless possibilities of lighting its architectural convexities which gave

> freedom of play to light, half-tone and shadow . . . The public was to come to the theatre and see no stage whatsoever. The screens were to serve as the architectural continuation of the auditorium and were to harmonize with it.
>
> *(Stanislavski [1924] 1948: 511)*

But he regretted the inability of contemporary technology to achieve the functionality that he and Craig wanted:

> What a tremendous distance there is between the scenic dream of an artist or a stage director and its realization upon the stage. How coarse are all the existing scenic means of incarnation. How primitive, naive and impotent is scenic technique . . . Why is it that the same mechanics are so coarse and primitive where man strives to satisfy not his personal bodily needs but his best spiritual longings which arise from the clearest aesthetic depths of the artistic soul? In this region there seems to be no inventiveness. The radio, electricity, light rays, create wonders everywhere but not in the theatre, where they could find a completely exceptional use in the sense of beauty and forever banish from the stage disgusting glue-paint, papier-mâché and properties. May a time come when newly discovered rays will paint in the air the shadows of colour tones and the combinations of lines.
>
> *(Ibid.: 519)*

Figure 29.4 Craig, preliminary design (1910) for court scene (1.2) of *Hamlet* at the Moscow Art Theatre, produced in 1912.

In spite of the technical challenges, Stanislavski concluded:

> The production of *Hamlet* met with great success. Some people were enthusiastic, others criticized, but everybody was excited, and debated, read reports, wrote articles, while the other theatres in the country quietly appropriated the ideas of Craig, publishing them as their own.
>
> *(Ibid.: 523–4)*

Hamlet remained in the Moscow Art Theatre repertory for three seasons, with a total of 47 performances in all.[5] Sadly for serious critical attention and his reputation, Craig's achievement was overshadowed by Stanislavski's frequently referenced irritation and loss of patience. But it is evident that the director's anger concerned the technical problems and not Craig's scenographic vision. The screens were in process of being re-positioned following a late rehearsal, ready for the first performance, when they collapsed. The angry irritation of the director is understandable. However, the problems were resolved very shortly before the audience entered the auditorium, and there is no evidence that similar technical problems were to affect future performances in Moscow or when the production toured to St. Petersburg.

Craig's concern for the architectonic qualities of "place," rather than the imitative qualities of "scene," stemmed from his response to theatre architectures of the past:

> Once upon a time, stage scenery was architecture. A little later it became imitation architecture; still later it became imitation artificial architecture. Then it lost its head, went quite mad, and has been in a lunatic asylum ever since.
>
> *(Craig 1913: 6)*

The theatres of antiquity, the bare *commedia* trestle stage, the architectural theatres of Palladio and Scamozzi at Vicenza and Sabbioneta in northern Italy, the large forestage of the eighteenth-century English playhouse, all of these seemed to structure within their architectonic frame a liminal place, a place that might "become" anywhere that the act of performance might wish. Importantly for Craig it was not the building and painting of scenes that would achieve this, but the act of performance as it encountered the imagination of the audience. Like Fuchs, Craig suggested that the act of theatre should take place within this liminal place of meeting and that, accordingly, the arts of scenography and architecture must combine to create these places that have the potential for performance. As liminal places they are not, of course, impositions by architect or scenographer. Their acceptance as places of performance, possibility, and imagination, whether on the orchestra of the theatre of antiquity under the bright sun, or upon the forestage within the dimly lit playhouse of the eighteenth century, was an expression of the complex social contract that performance involves. Craig's struggle to articulate this distinction between "scene" and "place" initiated this most critical of debates for contemporary scenography.

The scenographer is constantly faced with issues of presentation. Both Appia and Craig were always anxious to point out the difference between a two-dimensional design on paper and its realization in living time in performance. Contemporary theatre photography (albeit quite primitive), the account of the eye-witness, the evidence provided by designs and sketches, all carry a heavy burden in enabling the scenic historian to assess the ambitions and ideas that lie beneath the pencil, ink, and chalk.

Craig created beautiful, haunting graphic images of possible stages. They resonate with qualities of space, contour and mood; they also suggest possibilities of stage lighting that only became technically achievable towards the end of the twentieth century. But they are not images *of* the stage; they are representations of the *qualities* that the stage might create. Craig was very clear about this:

> When I make the same scene on the stage it is sure to be quite different in form and colour, but it will create the same impression on you as this design . . . a design for a scene on paper is one thing; a scene on the stage is another. The two have no connection with each other. Each depends on a hundred different ways and means of creating the same impression. Try to adapt the one to the other, and you get at best only a good translation.
>
> (Craig 1921: 93–4)

There were many phases in his long working life. In Florence, for a short period in 1912–1914, he achieved his ambition to run a school of theatre, but at the onset of World War One it closed down, as did Fuchs' Munich Artists' Theatre, and also the experiments of Dalcroze and Appia at Hellerau. Craig produced some magnificent books of designs and, under countless *nom de plume*, he wrote and published the journals *The Mask* and *Marionette*. He also constructed a two-meter-high model of a proposed scenography for a staging of Bach's *St Matthew Passion* based upon the tiny Romanesque church of San Nicolao in the town of Giornico in the Swiss canton of Ticino.

All Craig's projects share ambitions with those of Wagner, Fuchs, and Appia: the combination of artistic practices; the inseparability of architecture and scene; the understanding that the scene should be an active performer creating and sharing significance; but that the vital touchstone for all this would be the living interaction with an audience.

Notes

1 Fuchs' artistic collaborator at the Darmstadt Artists' Colony, Peter Behrens, wrote a manifesto, "A Celebration of Art and Life: a consideration of the theatre as the highest symbol of culture" (*Feste des Lebens und der Kunst: eine betrachtung des theaters als höchsten kultursymbols*), Leipzig, 1900.

2 Palmer describes Appia's connections with the Hopftheatre, his acquaintance with Hugo Bähr and the Dubosc electric arc lamp and rightly corrects historians who have asserted that Appia had no practical experience of stage technologies before he began to propose his theories. See Palmer 2015.

3 King's Patent Agency served as an approved interface between inventors and the Patent Office, providing legal and technical advice on the nature of submissions.

4 For a detailed account of Craig's Patent and the computer reconstructions of the plans, see Christopher Baugh, Cat Fergusson and Gavin Carver, "Gordon Craig and Improvements in Stage Scenery, 1910" in *Scenography International*, 1 (1999). Available online at: www.iar.unicamp.br/lab/luz/ld/C%EAnica/Artigos/Gordon%20Craig.pdf

5 See the very full and detailed account in Laurence Senelick (1982) *Gordon Craig's* Hamlet *– a Reconstruction*, (Westport, CT, and London: Greenwood Press).

References

Appia, Adolphe [1898] 1962. *Music and the Art of the Theatre* (*La Musique at la Mise en Scène*). Translated by Robert W. Corrigan and Mary Douglas Dirks. Coral Gable, FL: University of Miami Press.

Appia, Adolphe [1904] 1995. "How to Reform our Staging Practices," in *La Revue des Revues*, Vol. 1 (9). In *Twentieth-Century Theatre*, edited by Richard Drain. London: Routledge.

Beacham, Richard C. 1994. *Adolphe Appia: Artist and Visionary of the Modern Theatre*. London: Harwood Academic Press.
Craig, Edward Gordon 1909. *Daybook 1*, 3 February 1909. Archive in the Humanities Research Center, University of Texas at Austin.
Craig, Edward Gordon 1913. *Towards a New Theatre*. London: J. M. Dent.
Craig, Edward Gordon 1921. "Proposals Old and New." In *The Theatre Advancing*. London: Constable.
Craig, Edward Gordon 1923. *Scene*. London: Humphrey Milford and Oxford University Press.
Craig, Edward Gordon 1957. *Index to the Story of My Days*. London: Hulton Press.
Craig, Edward Gordon [1911] 1962. *On the Art of the Theatre*. London: Heinemann (reprint, Mercury Books).
Crary, Jonathan 1992. *Techniques of the Observer: On Vision and Modernity in the Nineteenth Century*. Cambridge, MA: October Books MIT Press.
Dent, Alan 1952. *Bernard Shaw and Mrs. Patrick Campbell: Their Correspondence*. New York: Alfred A. Knopf.
Fuchs, Georg [1909] 1972. *Revolution in the Theatre: Conclusions Concerning the Munich Artists' Theatre*, translated by Constance Connor Kuhn. Port Washington, NY: Kennikat Press.
Gorelik, Mordecai 1957. *New Theatres for Old*. New York: Samuel French.
Holzapfel, Amy 2014. *Art, Vision, and Nineteenth-Century Realist Drama: Acts of Seeing*. New York and London: Routledge.
Koss, Juliet 2000. *Empathy Abstracted: Georg Fuchs and the Munich Artists' Theater*. PhD Thesis, Massachusetts Institute of Technology.
Magee, Bryan 2000. *Wagner and Philosophy*. London: Penguin Press.
Palmer, Scott 2015. "A 'choréographie' of light and space: Adolphe Appia and the first scenographic turn." *Theatre and Performance Design* 1 (1–2): 31–47.
Stanislavski, Konstantin [1924] 1948. *My Life in Art* (5th ed.). London: Geoffrey Bles.
Wagner, Richard 1977. *Wagner on Music and Drama*, edited by Albert Goldman and Evert Sprinchorn, translated by H. Ashton Ellis. London: Victor Gollancz.
Wagner, Richard 2008. *The Artwork of the Future* (*Das Kunstwerk der Zukunft*), translated by William Ashton Ellis. Gloucester: Dodo Press.

30

RUSSIAN STAGE DESIGN AND THEATRICAL AVANT-GARDE

Julia Listengarten

Intense experimentation in early twentieth-century Russian stage design was inspired by the modernist vision of a unified and expressive theatrical space that would integrate design elements with the actor's performance. As Russian theatre experienced a period of incredible innovation and extraordinary artistic growth between the two Russian revolutions of 1905 and 1917 and during the early years of the Soviet regime, the concept of theatre design evolved from a purely decorative function. The theatre designer was no longer a stage decorator but an artist, working closely with a visionary director to create a unified scenic composition that would poetically express the playwright's intentions or reimagine the play's themes.

Associated with the early twentieth-century avant-garde, designers Nikolai Sapunov, Alexandra Exter, Lyubov Popova, and Alexander Vesnin, among others, applied the aesthetics of Symbolism, Cubo-Futurism, and Constructivism to theatrical forms. Their search for a unique visual language in theatre was often fueled by their collaborations with avant-garde directors such as Alexander Tairov and Vsevolod Meyerhold, who rejected the idea of theatrical representation and a realistic box set, and who sought new ways to express poetic symbols on stage or capture the revolutionary spirit of the time. These artistic partnerships between directors and stage designers began to reflect a new approach to theatre-making as a creative process that celebrated the importance of visual storytelling and which ultimately resulted in a variety of collaborative models. Collaboration between stage designers and directors (or choreographers), however, expanded beyond avant-garde theatres and their focus on entirely experimental work, including dialogues between Russian studio artists – Alexandre Benois, Léon Bakst, Natalia Goncharova, and Alexander Golovin, to name a few – and the Ballets Russes, Sergei Diaghilev's famed Parisian enterprise. Konstantin Stanislavski's scenic explorations with his creative teams at the Moscow Art Theatre also contributed to the birth of the modern scenographer.

By examining diverse scenographic practices in early twentieth-century Russia, this chapter traces the emergence of the modern scenographic tradition.[1] The development of this tradition – closely connected to the relationship of art and politics in Russia, especially in the early Soviet period – prompts challenging questions about the ways in which theatrical designs reflected cultural and political changes, and whether they helped reshape social assumptions or bowed to the ideological pressures of the time.

The Ballets Russes, the Moscow Art Theatre, and the emergence of the modern scenographer

The beginning of modern scenographic tradition in Russia is often associated with set and costume designs for the Ballets Russes and theatrical experiments with Symbolism by stage directors and studio artists in Moscow and St. Petersburg. Influenced by Richard Wagner's concept of *Gesamtkunstwerk* and the modernist ideas of Adolphe Appia and Edward Gordon Craig, Diaghilev founded the Ballets Russes based on the principles of the art group Mir Iskusstva (World of Art), whose members included Diaghilev himself, Benois, and Bakst. Their artistic approach to the performing arts was rooted in the concept of artistic synthesis and the spirit of experimentation. Their productions delighted audiences from 1909 to 1929, encompassing a variety of artistic styles from Russian folk tradition and Oriental exoticism, frequently identified with Russian culture, to the sumptuous revisions of classical antiquity. Their technique at first relied on a decorative approach to designing scenery, then shifted to embody the dimensionality of theatrical space. Whereas the primary goal of the Ballets Russes, at least at its inception, was to "showcase 'Russianness' for Western consumption" (Bowlt *et al.* 1988: 76), the company became a laboratory for most of the modernist movements of the early twentieth century, including Neo-Primitivism, Cubism, Futurism, Simultanism, and Constructivism. Art historian John E. Bowlt writes that "in some cases the Ballets Russes served as an extension of theoretical ideas that the radical artists of the 1910s (Larionov, Kazimir Malevich, Vladimir Tatlin, *et al.*) entertained in their studios" (1989: 44).

Uniquely positioned between the two cultures, the company developed its aesthetics at the intersections of multiculturalism and successfully promoted its native culture through flamboyant images of Russia's Oriental sensibility in Bakst's costume designs for Igor Stravinsky's *Firebird* (1910) and captivating pictures of pagan Russia in Nikolai Roerich's sets and costumes for *The Rite of Spring* (1913), another celebrated Stravinsky work. For Stravinsky's *Petrushka*, Benois evoked the spirit of St. Petersburg's fairgrounds from his childhood memories of visiting Russian bazaars and fairs and watching Punch and Judy puppet shows. Russian folk motifs also emerged in the neo-primitivist and cubo-futurist designs of Goncharova (*Le Coq d'Or*, 1914) and Mikhail Larionov (*Kikimora*, 1916), which established a close artistic link between the Ballets Russes and the Russian avant-garde.

The Ballets Russes attracted a remarkable number of visual artists, Russian as well as European, and soon became a fertile ground for performances that demonstrated consistency of style and artistic unity. Bowlt argues that these designers' "initial training as studio artists contributed to their stylistic vitality and facilitated their automatic suspension of disbelief each time they were confronted with a new design commission. Undoubtedly, this spontaneity and freshness added much to the distinctive collective psychology of the Ballets Russes" (ibid.: 49). The artists' commitment to collaboration – two or more designers frequently worked on the sets or costumes for a production – guided their approach to stage design and informed their keen understanding of the connection between the stage composition or costume elements and the dancer's movement. Regarding "the body as a kinetic force," Bakst – through his costume designs – worked to amplify the expressiveness of the dancers' physical language. To extend or accentuate the body's movement, he created "intricate abstract patterns of dress" and attached "appendages such as veils, feathers, and jewelry" (ibid.: 51). He also collaborated with the company's leading choreographer, Michel Fokine, suggesting ideas for choreography and integrating design, dance, and music. Dancer and choreographer Bronislava Nijinska recalls that "Léon Bakst worked with Fokine and inspired us during the rehearsals; from time to time he would correct us, showing us proper position of a hand or the movement of an arm, sometimes even demonstrating an oriental pose for us and extending the way we should move our bodies during the dance" (quoted in Van Norman Baer 1989: 64). This methodology in which the body's movement is integrated into stage and costume design would later develop in cubo-futurist and constructivist sets of Exter, Popova, and Varvara Stepanova.

As the Ballets Russes explored non-representational aesthetics in its designs in Paris, Russian theatres, too, began to incorporate non-realistic principles in their productions. The development of Russian symbolist scenography is often attributed to the bold experimentation of modernist directors such as Meyerhold and Nikolai Evreinov in partnership with visual artists during the first decade of the twentieth century. Paradoxically, Stanislavski, a self-proclaimed realist, was among the first theatre practitioners of the Silver Age to explore non-realistic, innovative forms.[2] Encouraged by prominent writers Anton Chekhov and Valery Bryusov, he turned to staging symbolist plays. Although his experimentation with this aesthetic at the Moscow Art Theatre was fraught with tension, it revealed his search to strike a delicate balance between the explicit and the abstract, the material and the spiritual, and to imbue realistic expression with visual poetry. Stanislavski's early experiments with symbolist drama began in 1904, when he introduced Maurice Maeterlinck's three one-act plays, *The Blind*, *The Intruder*, and *The Interior*, to the predominantly realistic repertoire of the Moscow Art Theatre, preceding Meyerhold's symbolist period at the Vera Komissarzhevskaya Theatre in St. Petersburg (1906–1907). Other experimental projects followed: the failed partnership with Meyerhold at the Theatre-Studio on Povarskaya in Moscow in 1905; the staging of several symbolist works (Knut Hamsun's *The Drama of Life,* 1907; Leonid Andreyev's *The Life of Man,* 1907; and Maeterlinck's *The Blue Bird,* 1908); and the both challenging and rewarding collaboration with Craig on the Moscow Art Theatre's production of William Shakespeare's *Hamlet* from 1908 to 1911.

Stanislavski's work on Maeterlinck's symbolist miniatures in 1904 led to a series of discoveries in stage design that – although timid and inconsistent at first – resulted in scenographic breakthroughs, advancing the use of theatrical space and challenging the principles of realistic acting. To transport Maeterlinck's mood-driven poetic images to the stage, he invited St. Petersburg-based Armenian studio painter Vardkes Surenyants, a new artistic voice at the Moscow Art Theatre, to replace Victor Simov, Stanislavski's longtime collaborator whose realistic sets had become the staple of the Moscow Art Theatre during its initial phase. The production's painted sets (for instance, in *The Blind*), which offered images of tree branches cutting the stage diagonally and disappearing in the sky, seemed to tap into a new kind of theatricality or theatrical stylization – a shift from Simov's realistic box sets – but were still rooted in realistic representation. Diaghilev, in particular, was disappointed with the failure of the set design to express the unspoken and capture the intangible, the essential qualities of Maeterlinck's poetic drama. He wrote, "an arid wooden set [in *The Intruder*] immediately made impossible any kind of mysterious contemplation whatever; then a series of crude symbols – the scrape of the scythe, the net curtains blowing in the air – profoundly contradicted Maeterlinck's very subtle symbology which strays eternally between reality and fraud" (quoted in Schumacher 1996: 222).

Stanislavski's encounters with symbolist scenography reflected his often-unsuccessful attempts to reconcile realistic staging with symbolist dramaturgy that offers little or no action, explores extreme emotional conditions, and conjures images of impending catastrophe. Equally important, these encounters trace various developments in early twentieth-century Russian scenography, particularly in response to the aesthetic requirements of symbolist drama. Moreover, they point to visual artists' struggle to embody the grotesque, the imaginary, and the poetic in a three-dimensional theatrical space.

After his fiasco with Maeterlinck's drama, Stanislavski partnered with Meyerhold at the Theatre-Studio to continue experimentation with non-realistic forms. At a dress rehearsal, however, he disapproved of the two-dimensional scenery in Meyerhold's staging of Maeterlinck's *The Death of Tintagiles* and Meyerhold's attempts to create a stylized form of acting that manifested in barely visible, lifeless figures whose movements and voices were intentionally synchronized. In the words of Nikolai Ulyanov, one of the Theatre-Studio visual artists, "on stage semi-darkness, only the silhouettes of the actors visible, two dimensional scenery, no wings, the back-drop hung almost level with the setting line" (quoted in Braun 1995: 42). The actors' lack of experience with stylized acting and the production's stylistic inconsistencies – the unintended mixture of realistic and non-realistic visual effects – likely compounded the problem. Indeed, as Edward Braun writes, "Sapunov and Sudeikin (who designed *The Death of Tintagiles*) had been incapable of translating their brilliant atmospheric sketches into three-dimensional scenic terms. Not only did they introduce crude naturalistic details which marred the overall impression of stylisation, but they had failed to allow for the effects of stage lighting, and it altered their original designs beyond recognition" (ibid.: 41).

Despite his disagreement with Meyerhold's staging choices and scenic effects at the Theatre-Studio, a year later, in 1906, Stanislavski invited Ulyanov, Meyerhold's collaborator, to work with Vladimir Egorov in designing the Moscow Art Theatre's production of *The Drama of Life*. Pointing to the nightmarish environment created on stage, Stanislavski described "the dark moving shadows of the merchants [that could] be seen against the white stalls, as on screen . . . The stalls are set up on rising levels to the mountains, from downstage almost to the flies upstage, where mountainside is filled with shadows. The same shadows turn and turn furiously in the air on a roundabout, up and down, up and down" (Stanislavski 2008: 263). The combination of the rectangular, tall, white stalls on the black background with the feverishly moving shadows created a grotesque, phantasmagoric effect, which distinguished this staging from Stanislavski's earlier works. This production also was a milestone for Stanislavski's discovery of the "black velvet" technique, which redefined the architectural possibilities of stage space, as well as the relationship between performers and scenery.

Working on the productions of *The Blue Bird* and *The Life of Man*, Stanislavski and his design team addressed the necessity of creating a scenic background that would highlight the three-dimensionality of the stage and facilitate the interplay between the visible and invisible in performance. Somewhat fortuitously, they stumbled upon the idea of using light-absorbing black velvet that would unify the floor with the stage wings and the borders of the proscenium arch. Stanislavski explained, "With the stage draped in black, I could reveal the actors' faces, or their whole bodies, or entire groups as on a black sheet of paper, at the top, the sides, the bottom, or, finally whole sets could appear and disappear in full view of the audience, hidden by large pieces of black velvet" (ibid.: 273). The "magic" space created in the production of *The Life of Man* accentuated fragments of the interior in relation or juxtaposition to characters' silhouettes emerging out of the black infinity and disappearing into the abyss. "Picture a huge, black sheet of paper," Stanislavski elucidated, "with white lines in perspective to indicate the shape of the room and its contents. Beyond these lines, on all sides, a terrifying, measureless void can be felt" (ibid.: 275). Asymmetrical shapes, fragmented contours, and syncopated rhythms of the set suggested the influence of Aubrey Beardsley's grotesque drawings (see Stroeva 1973: 220) or pointed toward Art Nouveau, a prevalent movement in art and architecture in the early twentieth century. Still, the construction of negative theatrical space signaled a major shift toward uniform visual composition on stage. Furthermore, the "black velvet" technique foregrounded avant-garde experiments in scenography involving an intricate relationship between positive and negative space.

Stanislavski's other significant contributions to scenographic practice in early twentieth-century Russian theatre included his collaborations with Benois, whose international fame for designing extravagant costumes and sets for the Ballets Russes had reached his native country, and Craig, whose vision of three-dimensional architectural units on stage meshed with Stanislavski's interest in creating architecturally and stylistically unified sets. In 1913, Benois was appointed principal stage designer of the Moscow Art Theatre, responsible for artistic advising of all productions and co-directing one production a year. This appointment signified Stanislavski's recognition of the importance of visual language in theatre and challenged the artistic and administrative hierarchy, which championed the subordination of stage design to the directorial concept.

A few years before Benois joined the Moscow Art Theatre, Stanislavski's often-tense partnership with Craig (1908–1911) disrupted the traditional roles of stage designer and director and led to a series of unresolved disagreements between these two artists. By introducing movable screens and platforms in the staging of *Hamlet*, Craig offered a bold, architectonic stage composition[3] that required stylized stage movement and, therefore, a rather non-realistic interaction between actors and scenic elements. His spatial metaphors clashed with Stanislavski's psychological theatre. Commenting on Stanislavski's unwillingness to embrace the design's spatial possibilities and minimize the focus on characters' motivations, Bryusov wrote:

> a conventionalized staging requires conventionalized acting: The Art Theatre failed to understand this . . . A house without windows, doors and ceiling, the monochromatic denuded walls, even the stone graveyard itself with its square pillars would not have seemed strange and inappropriate if we had seen them filled with substantially 'conventionalized' creatures, with conventionalized gesture and vocal intonations.
>
> *(Quoted in Schumacher 1996: 243)*

Stylization, grotesque, and symbolist scenography in Meyerhold's theatrical experiments

It was Meyerhold who, in his subsequent productions in the late 1900s and early 1910s, seemed to fully explore a marriage of stylized design elements with "conventionalized" acting. He was the driving force in pushing against realistic representation in stage design and exploring the potential of applying symbolist and other non-realistic principles to theatrical forms, thus questioning representational practices in theatre.

A visionary director with a strong artistic purpose to innovate and reimagine in order to capture the complexity of life and create new ways to communicate with the audience, he surrounded himself with visual artists who shared his artistic goals. In many instances, he was the instigator of artistic reforms in both directing and stage design, inspiring visual artists to experiment with new scenographic ideas.

For Meyerhold, "the concept of 'stylisation' is indivisibly tied up with the idea of convention, generalization and symbol." He believed that "to 'stylise' a given period or phenomenon, means to employ every possible means of expression to reveal the inner synthesis of the period or phenomenon, to bring out those hidden features that are deeply rooted in the style of any work of art" (quoted in Braun 1995: 35). Working exclusively with studio artists, rather than scenic painters and craftsmen, and considering stage and costume designs the key aspects in the production synthesis, Meyerhold experimented with a variety of artistic styles and theatrical forms, such as the Ancient Greek and the Japanese. Rather than authentically recapture a style or period, however, he distilled a mood or synthesized the essence of a character by painstakingly coordinating architectural, scenic, and costume designs and integrating them with stylized gestures and vocalizations in acting. In *Hedda Gabler* (1906) at the Vera Komissarzhevskaya Theatre, Meyerhold and set designer Sapunov synthesized the production's visual elements to articulate their vision of the main character. The drama unfolded on the narrow strip of stage where the characters appeared to be trapped between the footlights and a single decorative backdrop offering a glimpse of the blue sky. Peter Yartzev, the theatre's literary manager, described how the production employed "unfamiliar means of scenic presentation to create an impression (but only an impression) of a vast, cold blue, receding expanse." He wrote,

> Hedda is visualized in cold blue tones against a golden autumnal background... [Autumn] is suggested by the pale golden tints in the tapestry, the upholstery and the curtains. The theatre is attempting to give primitive, purified expressions to what it senses behind [Henrik] Ibsen's play: a cold, regal, autumnal Hedda.
>
> *(Quoted in Braun 1995: 53–4)*

Despite overwhelmingly negative critical reception pointing to the production's excessively stylized qualities, which conflicted with Ibsen's realistic style, Meyerhold continued his "polemic against stage naturalism and the whole materialist philosophy from which it sprang" (ibid.: 56). Inspired by the symbolists' appeal to selectivity and suggestion in dramatic form, and their quest to evoke ideal beauty and communal spirit through performance, he collaborated with visual artists to alter the traditional confines of the stage. His permanent artistic collaborators in the early twentieth century included Sapunov and Sergei Sudeikin,[4] the studio artists he befriended during the short Theatre-Studio period, and later Golovin, his primary designer during his work at the Imperial Theatres, but it was often Meyerhold who was at the forefront of advancing or disrupting prevailing scenographic practices.

As Meyerhold led the experiments with innovative approaches to stage lighting and architectural composition, he and his creative team worked to embrace a three-dimensional quality and plasticity of stage space. He was driven to create a visual synthesis and organic harmony in theatre expressed in a unified image of the set and the performer – the concept that Appia and Craig espoused. In his staging of Andreyev's

The Life of Man, Meyerhold explored the sculptural power of lighting to unify design elements and grotesquely exaggerate the actors' bodies and fragments of interior furniture. He explained that, "[b]y enveloping the stage in grey shadow, using a single light source to illuminate one area (the lamp behind the divan and the lamp over the round table in Scene One, the chandelier in the ball scene, the lamps above the table in the drunk scene), we managed to create the impression of actual walls which were invisible because the light did not reach them" (quoted in Braun 1995: 70). To challenge the architectural principle of the proscenium arch that separates performers from the audience, in his production of Feydor Sologub's *Death's Victory* (1907), Meyerhold contemplated extending "a broad flight of steps" from the stage into the auditorium, "thereby enabling the action of the tragedy to culminate amongst the audience" (ibid.: 76).[5] This reimagining of the relationship between the stage and the audience was most likely informed by Meyerhold's interest in forging a spiritual communion between actors and audience members, turning both performers and spectators into participants in a sacred ceremony – a recurring vision in symbolist thought.

Meyerhold outgrew his fascination with Symbolism, but his engagement with symbolist ideas contributed to the theatrical aesthetic that integrated the tragic sensibility of disillusioned Russia at the time of the first revolution (1905–1907) with *commedia dell'arte*, masquerade, puppetry, and play-within-a play. His production of Alexander Blok's *Fairground Booth* in 1906 signaled the beginning of a phase in his approach to staging that heightened the ambivalent, incongruent, and tragi-farcical in theatre and reflected the tragic carnival of everyday life. As I have argued elsewhere, in Blok's play "Meyerhold saw the tragic-grotesque in the incongruities between visual and verbal means, between the appearance of 'the injured clown with his convulsed body hanging across the footlights' and the clown's announcement that he is bleeding cranberry juice" (Listengarten 2000: 74). The tragic phantasmagoria was created on stage through ironically juxtaposed images: joyous Harlequin confused a painted landscape for paradise and leaped through the window, tearing a hole in the cardboard set and vanishing into the void; beautiful Colombine transformed into the terrifying figure of Death with a scythe; the Mystics, a satirical reincarnation of symbolist characters, turned into grotesque marionettes – life-sized puppets devoid of humanity – when their heads disappeared in their cardboard torsos. This production therefore both embraced and ridiculed the symbolist aesthetic. As Bowlt noted, Sapunov designed "a stage within a stage, the outer one hung with blue canvases, the inner one denuded to reveal the ropes, footlights, boards, prompter's box, etc. – as if to affirm that the ulterior reality that the Symbolists aspired to disclose was just as mundane as the everyday world of appearances" (Bowlt *et al.* 1988: 142, 144).

The fusion of unabashed, carnivalesque theatricality with irony and tragi-grotesque motifs reemerged in Meyerhold's productions of *Don Juan* (1910) and *Masquerade* (1917), this time in Golovin's lavishly designed sets. *Masquerade* culminated Meyer hold's experiments with stylization, ornamentation, and architectural unity of the proscenium and auditorium. It also signified the end of the entire artistic epoch, symbolically premiering at the Alexandrinsky Imperial Theatre in St. Petersburg on the eve of the February Revolution of 1917. Critic Konstantin Rudnitsky wrote of the production's emotional leitmotif of "impending catastrophe," juxtaposed with the exquisite ornamentation and decorative artistry of Golovin's set: "the spell-binding succession of noiselessly moving curtains," "the semi-circular forestage . . . extended to the first row of the stalls over the orchestra pit and . . . framed on the left and right by two staircases with handrails descending to the orchestra," the "tall frosted mirrors facing the illuminated auditorium and reflecting a sea of lights," and "white ornamentation against gold" (Rudnitsky 1988: 23). Meyerhold's earlier explorations into the architectural possibilities of theatrical space and the sculptural power of lighting were fully realized in this production, which celebrated theatricality and tragi-farcical ambivalence – a "tragedy within the frame of a carnival" (ibid.: 22) – as revolutionary momentum was growing on the streets outside the theatre.

Modernist scenographic practices at the Kamerny Theatre

Inspired by early twentieth-century avant-garde art, pre-revolutionary and early Soviet theatre applied cubo-futurist geometric forms and asymmetrical, colorful compositions to stage and costume designs and transformed static sets into moving constructions. The development of modernist scenography in Russian theatre around the time of the 1917 Revolution is closely connected to the history of the Kamerny (Chamber) Theatre in Moscow under Tairov's artistic direction. Founded in 1914 by Tairov and closed in 1949 by the Soviet authorities, the Kamerny Theatre, perhaps the longest-surviving avant-garde theatre during the Soviet regime, experimented with Cubo-Futurism and Constructivism. In the 1930s, the early period of state-imposed socialist realism, it cautiously navigated the official aesthetic doctrine by investigating so-called structural realism in scenographic application.

The production of *Famira Kifared* (1916), a result of the collaboration between Tairov and visual artist Exter, who designed both costumes and scenery for this occasion, marked the beginning of the cubo-futurist phase at the Kamerny Theatre. In his artistic approach to staging Innokenty Annensky's stylized antique tragedy, which in a symbolist fashion reaffirms the absolute power of fate, Tairov rejected stylization and juxtaposed cubo-futurist style with the play's implied symbolist tendencies. Russian critic Nikolai Efros admired the monolithic quality of the set and its flawless rhythmic organization: "[c]ubes and cones, large, densely colored, blue and black masses, rose and fell along the steps of the stage," where "harmony of blocks dominated" and "the forms and rhythmic arrangement of steps were finely regulated" (quoted in Rudnitsky 1988: 18). Efros recognized in this production "the birth of a new theatricality"; Rudnitsky contended that the staging of *Famira Kifared* "was the first theatrical victory for Cubism, preceding Massine and Picasso's Parisian *Parade* (1917) by one year" (ibid.). A dazzling fusion of angled lines, geometric shapes, and multi-level platforms signified the Kamerny Theatre's shift toward an abstract theatrical composition, which "transcend[ed] the confines of the pictorial surface and . . . organize[d] forms in their interaction with space" (Bowlt 1991: 64). Exter's innovative set design offered a variety of spatial arrangements for the performers and undoubtedly informed Tariov's carefully choreographed *mise-en-scènes* interacting with the "rhythmically organized space" (ibid.).[6]

The staging of *Famira Kifared*, however, was hardly the first effort to apply the concept of abstraction to a theatrical design. From 1909 to 1914, Vassily Kandinsky experimented with abstract, non-representational scenery in his stage compositions, such as *The Yellow Sound* (1912). As noted, Goncharova and Larionov explored, perhaps still with some caution, Cubism and Futurism in their designs for the Ballets Russes. Even more important, Malevich, a celebrated avant-garde artist, contributed his geometric and angular sets and costumes to the production of *Victory Over Sun*

(1913), "a pivotal work in the early avant-garde's attempt to forge a new theatrical aesthetic" (van Norman Baer, 1991: 38). This production coincided with Malevich's conceptualization of the suprematist style in visual art and signified perhaps the first truly non-representational accomplishment in the history of modern theatre. In *Victory Over Sun*, "a three-dimensional, volumetric design [was realized] through the distribution of freestanding geometric forms onstage and the use of mobile lighting" (ibid.).

What distinguished the work of Tairov and Exter from some of these earlier artistic efforts, though, was the collaborative nature of their discoveries. Sharing a strong vision of abstract theatrical compositions, they transcended the static quality of scenery and heightened the rhythmic complexity and musicality of theatrical space, which they envisioned as a character in constant interplay, harmonious or discordant, with the performers. For Tairov, colorful, dynamic, and abstractly designed stage compositions provided a scenic environment conducive to his directing principles rooted in the actors' physical plasticity and expressiveness of gesture. For Exter, this period foregrounded her future constructivist works,[7] in which she would completely abandon the idea of decorating the stage and build sets that were kinetic, economical in form, and utilitarian. If the set in *Famira Kifared*, in Rudnitsky's opinion, could still suggest a representational landscape in which "the cubes were stacked like rocks [and] the cones resembled cypresses" (Rudnitsky 1988: 18),[8] the next Tairov-Exter collaborations further disrupted the realistic conventions of stage design and approached stage space sculpturally and architecturally, an idea that Meyerhold explored during his symbolist period but could not fully realize because of technical and artistic limitations.

In Tairov's production of Oscar Wilde's *Salome* (1917), Exter refashioned the dimensions of the proscenium stage "by lowering the proscenium arch, extending . . . steps along the line of footlights and erecting very wide columns" (ibid.). Rudnitsky describes the production's tightly enclosed space in which "the columns projected forward, and the steps dictated the actors' movement downward, toward the proscenium. The silvery-black and silvery-blue costumes sparkled against the background of drapery which billowed out intermittently . . . The movement of the coloured canvases imparted a sensation of fluidity to the scene, illuminated by crimson-red beams of light" (ibid.). To heighten the fluidity and dynamism of the stage, Exter in *Romeo and Juliet* (1921) designed an "intricate system of curtains, which fell from above and moved apart diagonally, parallel to the footlights, dividing or reducing or expanding the space of the stage" (Georgii Kovalenko, "Alexandra Exter," in Bowlt and Drutt 2000: 137). The spatial limitations resulting from Exter's vertical sets dictated laconism, graphic clarity, and choreographic precision in the actors' movements and sculptural group compositions.

Tairov's post-revolutionary productions avoided propaganda[9] and embraced the euphoria and romantic idealism that Russian artists experienced in the wake of the revolution. "The revolution was destroying the old forms of life and we were destroying the old forms of art," he reflected in 1936, at the height of the Stalinist purges. "It followed that we were in step with the revolution. This was, of course, an illusion but, at the same time, we sincerely believed ourselves to be revolutionaries" (quoted in Worrall 1989: 16). Drawn to the portrayal of strong, individualistic, and passionate figures in defiance of society, Tairov in 1922 turned to Racine's *Phèdre*, this time underscoring the structural simplicity and austerity of both sets and costumes designed by Vesnin. This collaboration also signaled his aesthetic shift from the colorful extravagances and unrestrained geometric fantasies of Cubo-Futurism to purely functional, kinetic structures inspired by the constructivist style. For *Phèdre*, Vesnin constructed the stage floor, which in Nick Worrall's description was "broken up into three planes patterned on a sloping, diagonal structure." Phèdre's first entrance was striking, "made along this broken diagonal, very slowly . . . trailing a heavy purple cape which streamed out behind her" (ibid.: 38). The stage built as a series of diagonal panels anticipated constructivist sets on the stage of the Kamerny Theatre, which would celebrate the power of machinery and fully engage in dialogue with other constructivist experiments in Soviet theatres in the early 1920s.

Originating in Russia in the 1913, Constructivism was an artistic movement and philosophy that advanced futurist principles in industrial and textile design and architecture and posited the primacy of social and political function in artistic practice.[10] The program of the movement's First Working Group formed in 1921, which included Stepanova, Alexander Rodchenko, and the Stenberg brothers (Vladimir and Georgii), among others, declared that constructivist artists needed to contribute to "the practice of Soviet construction" and to "determine the place [for] . . . constructivist constructions [to] occupy in communist life" (quoted in Lodder 1983: 94). As Lodder asserts, "It was . . . in the theatre, at the very beginning of the 1920s, that constructivist ideas of the interrelation of the environment with life – albeit hypothetical, but active and real – became first demonstrated and tested" (ibid.: 173). Despite the constructivists' denial of artistic activity for aesthetic purposes, it was the theatre that "acted as a micro-environment in which it was possible to explore spatial and material structures which could act as prototype components of a new, completely constructivist environment" (ibid.: 174). Constructivist theatrical designs, which often resembled Tatlin's sculptural works or Kurt Schwitters' dadaist assemblages, rejected the decorative principles of painted sets, used a variety of materials and objects to build constructions, and embraced the futurist vision of integrating motion in otherwise-static structures.

Georgii Yakulov's constructivist design for Tairov's production of Charles Lecocq's operetta *Giroflé-Girofla* (1922) offered a playful combination of "folding ladders, screens, revolving mirrors, [and] trap doors" (Worrall 1989: 39), an approach similar to the intricate constructivist sets that Popova and Stepanova built for Meyerhold's productions in the early 1920s. Although the application of constructivist theory to this light-hearted operetta seemed random and lacked political purpose, Tairov's next experiment with constructivist scenery, the production of *The Man Who Was Thursday* (1923), a stage version of G. K. Chesterton's novel, embodied Soviet ideology through its explicit critique of mechanized capitalistic society. Regarded as an extraordinary accomplishment in constructivist scenography, Vesnin's multi-level set occupied most of the proscenium stage vertically and horizontally, with several segments – working elevators or rotating billboards – set in intermittent motion (see Mel Gordon, "Russian Eccentric Theatre: The Rhythm of America on the Early Soviet Stage," in van Norman Baer 1991: 122).

The production's central image, "a constructivist skeleton, the elements of which combined to suggest a modern urban landscape consisting of skyscrapers, oil derricks, pitheads, moving walkways, ironwork bridges and lift shafts" (Worrall 1989: 39), heightened the sense of entrapment and claustrophobia. But it also prompted a reassessment of powerful machinery and its function in society, in this case exploiting people and turning them into mannequins. The ideological principles of Constructivism clashed with the production's expressionistic motif, exposing the dehumanizing power of society as a relentless, crushing machine.

The evolution of the Kamerny Theatre's visual aesthetics in the late 1920s and 1930s shows the theatre's artistic negotiations under increasing ideological pressure. Perhaps in response to the mounting accusations of formalism, but also as a reflection of the director's own disillusionment with the revolution, the space in Tairov's productions lost the playfulness of earlier constructivist sets, becoming austere and monumental. In the Stenbergs' design for Eugene O'Neill's *The Hairy Ape* (1926), simple geometric outlines – a visual expression of an industrial or urban environment that suggested a ship's deck, a stokehole, and Manhattan skyscrapers – replaced Vesnin's complex and clever construction of the modern city landscape for *The Man Who Was Thursday* just three years earlier. Working toward simplicity and purity in form, the Stenbergs designed most of Tairov's productions in the mid- to late 1920s, including Lecocq's operetta *Day and Night* (1926) and O'Neill's naturalistic tragedy *Desire Under the Elms* (1929).[11] To articulate this monumental design, lacking detail and stripped of the witty and eccentric quality of previous scenographic practices, Tairov coined the phrase "structural realism" (see Rudnitsky 1988: 195). The Stenbergs, in Rudnitsky's assessment,

> bridled and tamed the Constructivist set. In their hands it lost the importunate mechanistic and fragmented quality, ceased flashing and flickering. The construction calmed down, quietened down and turned into a rigid framework that dictated an economical and clear sculptural form. This framework retained the ability to change, although metamorphoses were rarely executed and, as a rule, only during intervals and not in front of the audience. The place of action was designated honestly but sparingly. The space remained fundamentally unlived-in although its functions were not concealed: a house was a house, a street was a street, and the deck of a ship – the deck of a ship.
>
> *(ibid.)*

The starkness and asceticism of the Stenbergs' theatrical style – at times excessively schematic and emotionally detached – laid the foundation for the Kamerny Theatre's socialist realist aesthetic. The production of Vsevolod Vishnevsky's *Optimistic Tragedy*, a retelling of the crushed revolt of Russian sailors in the Baltic fleet, directed by Tairov and designed by Vadim Ryndin in 1934, won critical recognition as a model of socialist realism in theatre.

Meyerhold and post-revolutionary theatrical designs

Early Soviet avant-garde theatre embraced the exaltation and euphoria that followed the Bolshevik Revolution; theatre artists rejected traditionalism in art, perceived as a reflection of bourgeois life, and celebrated the innovation that reverberated with the Soviet platform to build a utopian society. Meyerhold was at the forefront of this cultural revolt, his theatrical experimentation with circus forms and constructivist designs in the 1920s reflecting his artistic and political agenda. Along with the other avant-garde theatre directors Nikolai Foregger, Yuri Annenkov, and Sergei Radlov, he infused circus elements into theatre productions to invigorate performance, disrupt continuity in storytelling and visual presentation, and create a theatricality to appeal to a new type of audience – mostly uneducated peasants and workers who began to fill theatres after the revolution. Describing Annenkov's production of *The First Distiller* (1919), Robert Leach writes "Trapezes swung, ropes dangled, odd-shaped platforms were suspended from the flies, tubes and steps gave actors height but led nowhere. There were no stage curtains and the performance consisted of a series of circus-like turns" (Leach 1994: 53–4).

It was during this period of adapting circus forms to his own theatre practice that Meyerhold began to develop principles of Constructivism, biomechanics, and a montage of attractions. His 1921 production of *Mystery-Bouffe*, Vladimir Mayakovsky's futurist allegory-farce, completely abandoned the conventions of the box set and painted backdrops and entirely eliminated the imaginary fourth wall that separated performers from the audience. The set design, "a system of staircases and gangways" (Rudnitsky 1988: 62) devised by sculptor Anton Lavinsky in collaboration with painter Vladimir Khrakovsky, anticipated constructivist sets – soon to become a distinct feature of early Soviet scenographic practice. The wings were eliminated to clear the space for "a series of platforms of different levels, interconnected by steps and vaguely suggestive of various locations" (Braun 1995: 167) signifying "Earth," "Hell," and "Paradise." A few rows in the auditorium were removed to accommodate the action that spilled beyond the stage into the orchestra: "a broad ramp extended deep into the auditorium, bearing a huge hemisphere over which the cast clambered and which revolved to expose a 'hell-mouth'" (ibid.). The actors performed on various levels of the set, highlighting its multidimensional character and expanding the action vertically to the ceiling; renowned circus performer Vitaly Lazarenko, dressed as a devil, made a dramatic entrance descending from the flies on a wire.

The work on the constructivist set for *Mystery-Bouffe*, albeit still in "embryonic and underdeveloped form" (ibid.: 168), inspired Meyerhold's fruitful collaborations with constructivist designers Popova and Stepanova during his next phase at Moscow's newly founded Theatre of the Revolution, where he staged his most famous productions in the 1920s, including *The Magnanimous Cuckold* and *The Death of Tarelkin.* Popova, the designer of *The Magnanimous Cuckold*, came to Constructivism through her artistic engagements with Cubism and Suprematism. The "architectonic" and "spatial-force compositions" in her abstract paintings prepared her for energy, force, and multi-direction in theatrical designs. As art critic Dmitrii Sarabianov posits, "The radical accomplishments that we associate with Popova's stage, fashion, and book designs of the early 1920s, while public, utilitarian, and often ideologically inspired, are organic extensions of her studio painting of several years earlier" (Sarabionov, "Liubov Popova and Artistic Synthesis," in Bowlt and Drutt 2000: 195).

Popova's design for *The Magnanimous Cuckold* consisted of a single construction resembling a windmill or a flying machine with rotating wheels, but it was also suggestive of a child's playground that could be "walked round, entered, bumped into, [and] climbed on" (Leach 1989: 97). In this design, she realized the performance potential of the set itself. "[A] concrete object of wood and metal with its own shape [and] its own contribution to the action" (ibid.: 96–7), the set performed in interaction with the actors. The actors' numerous somersaults, jumps, and falls – a result of Meyerhold's application of biomechanics in acting – seemed to exist in accord with the movements of the wheels and wings of Popova's construction. The entire stage transformed into a performative environment in which the kinetic quality of the set highlighted the well-trained physical apparatus of the actors, underscored the characters' traits, and informed the production's meaning, extending or somewhat reimagining the play's themes. In addition to infusing urbanism into Fernand Crommelynck's farce about a husband's psychopathic suspicion of his wife's marital infidelity, the movements of the set – "the wheels and propeller whirled round with increasing speed" (ibid.: 96) – accented emotional peaks in the story and exaggerated characters' aggression or frustration. Meyerhold acknowledged that Popova's kinetic sculptural set influenced his direction, resulting in the constructivist synthesis of form and content (see Lodder 1983: 172). Blue coveralls, prozodezda, that the actors wore throughout the play, in combination with the biomechanics in acting and Constructivism in stage design, contributed to the production's uniform visual language and, perhaps, a cohesive narrative.[12]

Similarly to Vesnin's designs for Tairov's productions, Popova's set transcended its purely utilitarian purpose. Her construction defined the space, functioned to evoke an emotional response, and added an effective layer in visual storytelling, which intentionally worked with or against the text of the play. Its ability to perform and invite the actors to perform with it was, however, unique, highlighting the performative potential of theatrical space. Stepanova's design for Meyerhold's next constructivist production, *The Death of Tarelkin* (1922),[13] a reimagining of the nineteenth-century comedy by Russian playwright Mikhail Saltykov-Shchedrin, likewise possessed the performative quality. Rather than a unified multi-level structure, it offered a combination of smaller constructions conceived as circus devices that were strewn along the proscenium and performed multiple functions. As Stepanova explains, "The task had been to provide apparatus-objects as instruments for playing on the stage" (quoted in Lodder 1983: 173). Performing objects propelled the action of the play and could be shifted or transformed as needed. "Each one concealed a trap: the table's legs gave way, the seat deposited its occupant onto the floor, the stool detonated a blank cartridge. Most spectacular of all was the cage used to simulate a prison cell into which the prisoner was propelled head-first through something resembling a meat-mincer" (Braun 1995: 185). Although Stepanova's circus objects functioned individually and differed in approach from Popova's unified construction – "an all-embracing apparatus for acting" (Lodder 1983: 173) – devised the same year, both designs pointed to the set's transformative, fluid nature that would characterize later scenographic practices.

If Meyerhold's post-revolutionary productions intended to provide an image or visual narrative that strengthened the playwright's message or underscored the play's themes (in *Mystery-Bouffe* and productions in his constructivist period), in his later work – particularly his expressionistic staging of Nikolai Gogol's tragi-farce *The Inspector General* – the set increasingly assumed a central role in re-envisioning the script or refashioning the playwright's vision. This approach to stage design coincided with Meyerhold's experimentation with the montage of attractions; it also reflected the tendency of modern design to consider the set, as Arnold Aronson observes, "the dominant element of a production, establishing the whole tone and shaping the interpretation of the script as well as determining the rhythm and movement of the performers" (Aronson, "Postmodern Design" in Collins and Nisbet 2010: 149).

By the mid-1920s, Meyerhold's fascination with objectified reality, realized on stage by constructivist designs, gave way to his interest in subjectivism and expressionist aesthetics that revealed the individual's agonized, distorted perception of this reality.[14] The kinetic abilities of the set, which Constructivism advanced considerably,[15] continued to guide his vision of stage design, however. Braun writes that in *The Inspector General*, Meyerhold "devised a principle of kinetic staging" (Braun 1995: 231) executed through a complex stage composition. The set design, mostly conceived by Meyerhold himself,[16] foregrounded the idea of transformative or transformable theatrical space that informs, if not determines, rhythmically punctuated and musically coordinated *mise-en-scènes*. The set in *The Inspector General* transformed with each new episode or attraction, enhancing the psychological effect of montage. It also visually communicated the characters' anxieties and accentuated the production's nervous dynamism and tragic-grotesque sensibility. In Braun's description,

> The stage was enclosed by a semicircular, imitation polished mahogany screen containing a series of eleven double-doors . . . The centre section of the screen opened to admit a tiny truck-stage . . . which rolled silently forward on runners to face the audience with actors and setting ready assembled. At the end of the scene the screen reopened and the truck retreated, to be replaced by another similarly prepared. All but four scenes were played on these trucks, with Episode Three . . . alone lowered from the flies. The remainder occupied the full stage area, with the final 'grand rond' overflowing into the auditorium.
>
> *(Braun 1995: 231)*

The provincial town in Gogol's satire about Imperial Russia's political corruption turned, through Meyerhold's staging, into a carefully orchestrated, nightmarish microcosm of society characterized by the catastrophic loss of humanity and individual identity. Criticized for distorting Gogol's humor and abandoning his laughter,[17] this production activated the concept of single authorship, in which the responsibilities of scenographer and director are fused to reshape the play's themes and structure and articulate a singular artistic vision.

Then and now

Pamela Howard, a designer and director, defines the role and responsibilities of the contemporary scenographer accordingly: "The scenographer visually liberates the text and the story behind it, by creating a world in which the eyes see what the ears do not hear. Resonances of the text are visualized through fragments and memories that reverberate in the spectator's subconscious, suggesting rather than illustrating words" (Howard 2002: 33). This understanding perhaps reflects a postmodern perspective on visuality in theatre that points toward separating visual language from spoken text rather than producing a unified effect on the audience. Nevertheless, Howard's attention to the suggestive rather than illustrative quality of stage design resonates with the modernist scenographic practices discussed in this chapter.

Challenging and later abandoning the practice of the set designer as a decorator of the stage, visual artists of Russia's Silver Age and early Soviet period experimented with styles and materials to advance stage design from decorated backdrops to complex kinetic compositions, positioning it as a key element in shaping or reshaping the playwright's vision. Embracing the performative potential of set and costume elements, they foreshadowed the current discourse in scenographic studies that conceptualizes stage design as performance design, which not only "actively extend[s] the performing body, but also perform[s] without and in spite of the human body" (Hannah and Harsløf 2008). The idea that theatre environments and objects perform on their own has emerged recently and does not necessarily reflect a modernist vision, yet the concept of kinetic sets as a dynamic force inspiring the audience's creative participation guided the evolution of modern scenography in Russia in the early twentieth century. A pivotal period in the history of scenography, Russian modernism paved the way for further exploration with the embodiment or disembodiment of space, movement, and light in traditional and non-traditional theatre environments.

Notes

1 Evgeny Vakhtangov, Michael Chekhov, Nikolai Evreinov, and Fyodor Komissarzhevsky were also among key Russian directors who, through their collaborations with visual artists, contributed to the shaping of the scenographic tradition.
2 For a more extended discussion about Stanislavski and the Avant-Garde, see my article "Stanislavski and the Avant-Garde" in the *Routledge Companion to Stanislavski*, edited by Andrew White, Abingdon and New York: Routledge, 2013.
3 See the analysis of Craig's architectonic scenic compositions in McKinney and Butterworth 2009: 20.
4 Ulyanov, who collaborated with Meyerhold at the Theatre-Studio and then worked with Stanislavski at the Moscow Art Theatre, later designed costumes for Meyerhold's production of Griboedov's *Woe from Wit* in 1928.
5 This idea did not materialize owing to a number of concerns expressed by theatre management.
6 Bowlt quotes Soviet critic Konstantin Derzhavin, *Kniga o Kamernom teatre*, Leningrad: Khudezhestvennaia literatura, 1934: 70.
7 During her later constructivist period, Exter collaborated with choreographer Nijinska and dancer and acrobatic gymnast Kasian Goleizovsky, and designed costumes for the science-fiction film *Aelita* in 1924. After she left Russia in 1924 she remained at the forefront of the European avant-garde, and her works were exhibited internationally, in Paris, Berlin, London, and New York. In later years, she experimented with a mix of materials and the power of light to produce immaterial décor.
8 Rudnitsky acknowledged Exter's innovative stage design for *Famira Kifared*, but also noted that "the three dimensional set was stationary [and] its outlines were dominated by horizontals, recalling the Wagnerian sketches of Adolph [sic] Appia" (*Russian and Soviet Theatre*, 18).
9 I discussed the fraught relationship between Tairov's aesthetic and the state ideology in "Problematics of Theatrical Negotiations: Directing, Scenography, and State Ideology," in *Directors & Designers*, edited by Christine White, Bristol, UK and Chicago: Intellect, 2009.
10 The beginning of Constructivism is traditionally attributed to Tatlin's first non-utilitarian constructions created in 1913. Art historian Christina Lodder argues that the experiences of the Russian Revolution of 1917 and the Civil War prompted Constructivism's radical reassessment of "a new relationship between the artist, his work and society" elevating constructivist artists to the level of "active participants in the process of social and political transformation" (Lodder 1983: 1).
11 Other productions included Ostrovsky's *The Thunderstorm* (1924), Shaw's *St Joan* (1924), O'Neill's *All God's Chillum Got Wings* (1929), and a new Soviet play, *Natalya Tarpova* (1929), among others.
12 In Popova's subsequent collaboration with Meyerhold on the production of *The Earth in Turmoil* in 1923, props – field phones and machine guns – also played a significant role in articulating the production's connection with modern technology.
13 Stepanova also designed costumes for the production that resembled various geometric shapes.
14 Meyerhold's productions of the mid- to late 1920s, such as *The Mandate* and *The Inspector General*, dwelled on the theme of dehumanization expressed in staging through nervous rhythms, mannequin-like character movements, and overall tragi-grotesque images. Most important, their focus on revealing the frightening opposition between the individual and mechanized society seemed to be out of tune with the Soviet ideology.
15 It is noteworthy that, four decades later, renowned Czech scenographer Josef Svoboda articulated the importance of "a transformable, kinetic, dramatic space and movement," stating that "[d]ramatic space is psycho-plastic space [meaning] that it is elastic in its scope and alterable in its quality" (quoted in Burian 1974: 30). Constructivist designs, therefore, anticipated later scenographic experiments with plasticity and kinetic possibilities of theatrical space.
16 This was not the first instance when Meyerhold functioned as both designer and director articulating the single vision for his theatre. As in his earlier symbolist period, Meyerhold, conceiving the production score for *The Inspector General*, collaborated with a series of

designers including Golovin, but his visionary perspective always guided their discussions. The set design was eventually attributed to Victor Kiselyov.

17 The production's critical reception was mixed. Among its vehement critics was Russian poet Demyan Bedny, who exclaimed in an epigram addressed to Meyerhold, "Laughter, you have murdered Gogol's laughter outright" (quoted in Rudnitsky 1988: 192).

References

Bachelis, T. I. 1983. *Shekspir i Kreg*. Moskva: Nauka.

Behr, Shulamith 2013. "Kandinsky and Theater: The Monumental Artwork of the Future." In *Vasily Kandinsky: From Blaue Reiter to the Bauhaus, 1910–1925*, edited by J. Lloyd, 65–85. New York: Neue Galerie Catalogue.

Benedetti, Jean 1988. *Stanislavski*. London: Methuen Drama.

Bowlt, John E. 1989. "From Studio to Stage: The Painters of the Ballets Russes." In *The Art of Enchantment: Diaghilev's Ballets Russes, 1909–1929*, edited by Nancy Van Norman Baer, 44–59. San Francisco: Universe Books.

Bowlt, John E. 1991. "The Construction of Caprice: The Russian Avant-Garde Onstage." In *Theatre in Revolution: Russian Avant-Garde Stage Design, 1913–1935*, edited by Nancy Van Norman Baer, 61–83. New York: Thames and Hudson.

Bowlt, John E. 2008. *Moscow & St. Petersburg, 1900–1920: Art, Life & Culture of the Russian Silver Age*. New York: The Vendome Press.

Bowlt, John E. and Matthew Drutt (Eds) 2000. *Amazons of the Avant-Garde: Exter, Goncharova, Popova, Rozanova, Stepnaova, Udaltsova*. New York: The Solomon R. Guggenheim Foundation.

Bowlt, John E., *et al.* 1988. *Masterpieces of Russian Stage Design, 1880–1930*. Woodbridge, Suffolk, UK: Antique Collectors' Club.Braun, Edward (Ed.) 1969. *Meyerhold on Theatre*. New York: Hill and Wang.

Braun, Edward 1995. *Meyerhold: A Revolution in Theatre*. Iowa City: University of Iowa Press.

Burian, Jarka 1974. *The Scenography of Josef Svoboda*. Middletown, CT: Wesleyan University Press.

Collins, Jane and Andrew Nisbet 2010. *Theatre and Performance Design: A Reader in Scenography*. London and New York: Routledge.

Davis, Mary E. 2010. *Ballets Russes Style: Diaghilev's Dancers and Paris Fashion*. London: Reaktion Books.

Garafola, Lynn and Nancy Van Norman Baer (Eds) 1999. *The Ballets Russes and Its World*. New Haven, CT, and London: Yale University Press.

Gladkov, Aleksandr 1997. *Meyerhold Speaks; Meyerhold Rehearses*, translated, edited, and introduction by Alma Law. London and New York: Routledge.

Hannah, Dorita and Olav Harsløf 2008. *Performance Design*. Copenhagen: Museum Tusculanum Press.

Howard, Pamela 2002. *What is Scenography?* Abingdon and New York: Routledge.

Ioffe, Dennis G. and Frederick H. White 2012. *The Russian Avant-Garde and Radical Modernism*. Brighton, MA: Academic Studies Press.

Khan-Magomedov, Selim Omarovich 1986. *Alexandr Vesnin and Russian Constructivism*. New York: Rizzoli.

Leach, Robert 1989. *Vsevolod Meyerhold*. Cambridge: Cambridge University Press.

Leach, Robert 1994. *Revolutionary Theatre*. London: Routledge.

Listengarten, Julia 2000. *Russian Tragifarce: Its Cultural and Political Roots*. Selinsgrove, PA: Susquehanna University Press.

Lodder, Christina 1983. *Russian Constructivism*. New Haven, CT: Yale University Press.

McKinney, Joslin and Philip Butterworth 2009. *The Cambridge Introduction to Scenography*. Cambridge: Cambridge University Press.

Meyerhold, Vsevolod 1968. *Stat'i, pis'ma, rechi, besedy*, edited by A. V. Fevral'sky, 2 Vols. Moskva: Iskusstvo.

Milner, John 1983. *Vladimir Tatlin and the Russian Avant-Garde*. New Haven, CT, and London: Yale University Press.

Rudnitsky, Konstantin 1988. *Russian and Soviet Theatre: 1905–1932*, translated by Roxane Permar. New York: Harry N. Abrams.

Sarabianov, Dmitri V. and Natalia L. Adaskina 1989. *Popova*, translated by Marian Schwartz. New York: Harry N. Abrams.
Schumacher, Claude (Ed.) 1996. *Naturalism and Symbolism in European Theatre; 1850–1918*. Cambridge: Cambridge University Press.
Stanislavski, Konstantin 2008. *My Life in Art*, translated by J. Benedetti. London: Routledge.
Stroeva, M. N. 1973. *Reshisserskie iskaniia Stanislavskogo (1898–1917)*. Moskva: Nauka.
Tairov, Alexander 1969. *Notes of a Director*, translated and introduction by William Kuhlke. Coral Gables, FL: University of Miami Press.
Van Norman Baer, Nancy (Ed.) 1989. *The Art of Enchantment: Diaghilev's Ballets Russes, 1909–1929*. San Francisco, CA: Universe Books.
Van Norman Baer, Nancy (Ed.) 1991. *Theatre in Revolution: Russian Avant-Garde Stage Design, 1913–1935*. New York: Thames and Hudson.
Vinogradskaya, Irina 1987. *Stanislavskii repetiruet: zapisi i stenogrammyi repetizii*. Moskva: STD.
Worrall, Nick 1989. *Modernism to Realism on the Soviet Stage: Tairov, Vakhtangov, Okhlopkov*. Cambridge: Cambridge University Press.

31

EXPRESSIONISM AND THE EPIC THEATER IN EARLY TWENTIETH-CENTURY GERMAN STAGE DESIGN

The Expressionist ethos

Mel Gordon

When German critics employed the word *Expressionismus* during the years 1910–1911, it had already acquired an elusive – and often contrary – set of definitions and characteristics. For the most part, it denoted a kind of primitive anti-rational, post-Romantic, non-Realistic creation. Various graphic artists, writers, philosophers, playwrights, and dancers from Central Europe began to label their work "Expressionist." Without a center or an adjudicating leader, without any authoritative pronouncements or clearly stated manifestos, now a trend, rather than a movement, was growing up around the term.

In one Berlin art gallery, Sturm, founded by Herwarth Walden in 1910 and promoted in its influential periodical, *Der Sturm*, art from nearly every contemporary European avant-garde school – French Cubism, Italian Futurism, and Russian abstractionism – were gathered together under the single rubric of Expressionism. Some journalists, on the other hand, linked this current anti-materialist craze to the spiritual zealotry and artistry of medieval German or Eastern mystics.

One aspect of Expressionism was commonly acknowledged: its psychological roots sprang from the most extreme human sensations – mainly anguish, revolt, and ecstasy. From its beginnings to its demise as an aesthetic in Germany some 15 years later, literary and dramatic Expressionism promulgated the existence of a higher order of humanity, of a certain kind of individual who was neither merchant nor "blond beast," of an intellectual who could act, of the New Man. But the Expressionists' conception of this idyllic type underwent numerous and extreme transformations. At first he was described as a Nietzschean Nay-Sayer, the slayer of fathers and teachers, the destroyer of all bourgeois traditions (i.e., the students in Gottfried Benn's *Ithaka* [1914]). Later, during the war, the New Man appeared as an apostle of peace; he became an activist Christian, one who was capable of great feats of leadership and self-sacrifice, a lover of Mankind (i.e., Antigone in Walter Hasenclever's *Antigone* [1917]). In the last phase of Expressionism, or its "Black Period," the New Man was revealed as a Übermensch/Gandhian manqué, the individual with all the conventional attributes of the enlightened hero except the powers of social or political potency (i.e., Jimmy Cobbett in Ernst Toller's *The Machine-Wreckers* [1922]).

The followers of Expressionism propagated the philosophy of the worth of Man – of all men. Essentially, they thought, Man was good, born good. Only a restrictive society and a denatured consciousness were preventing Man from searching and feeling the true, inner ecstatic reality of life. Instead, society's institutions – the family, the government, the military, the business and land-owning classes – were pushing Mankind into cycles of materialism and misery. There was only one solution, the Expressionists felt: revolution – not necessarily the substitution of one government for another, but rather a revolution of the spirit. If Man could learn to trust his emotions, then he would love all men, would experience "new love," and therefore would be in touch with the laws of the universe.

What united all of these conceits was the New Man's unique awareness of Mankind's – as well as his own – place in the universe and his ability to act upon it. No books of philosophy or psychology could instruct the New Man in this cosmic understanding; instead, he would have to seek it directly. Sometimes this could be accomplished through the exploration of his unconscious in dream, hypnotic trance, or drug-induced states. Occasionally in physical states of pure action where the brain's censor would not function adequately, the New Man could discover that ineffable condition of "absolute Rapture." The Expressionists believed that only the possessed individual was capable of transcending his daily existence to make contact with the *Seele*, or soul. (In such a primordial state, one's entire being is expressed outside space and time; the possessed's muscles and joints may be twisted and contorted, sounds akin to animal barks or single syllables may be produced in his throat. According to the Expressionists, a man in that condition was experiencing the Cosmos.)

Expressionist art changed the rules by which performances could be visualized and staged. For the first time, the author and directors' primary fantasies and thoughts, or ego, leaped over the pages and promptbooks directly onto the minds of the spectator. The play structures and the objective filters of the past were swept away; the Expressionist theatre revealed twisted but purer realities beyond the bourgeois facades of social piety and the rationally bound conscious life. Because it dealt unswervingly and forcefully with the artist's own wounded psyche and his antagonist relation to a corrupt society, Expressionist drama – although it had a seductive appeal to writers internationally – only found its real audience in the morally shattered young generation of post-World War I Germany.

Theories of Expressionist stage design

Expressionist scenic designers, like Emil Pirchan, Ludwig Sievert, and Ernst Stern, drew scores of identifiable and highly praised stage pictures. Illustrations and photographs of their productions were reprinted in dozens of international art monthlies. Unfortunately, they published surprisingly few theoretical statements about them. Even the prominent Expressionist playwrights and directors rarely discussed the underpinning of their visionary innovations, except in the most vague terms of fabricating spectral nightmares; indeterminate, spooky environments; or psychotic dreamscapes. Yet a small number of writers did theorize about the specific and unique features of Expressionist scenography.

In 1909, the Russian painter Vassily Kandinsky composed the scenario *The Yellow Sound*, later published with an introduction in the *Blaue Reiter Almanac* (Munich, 1912). Kandinsky's theatrical premise was based on the formation of "delicate vibrations" that affect the "strings" of the audience's souls. In part, Kandinsky's program was a further development of Symbolist operatic tendencies in Germany, France, and Russia. But, unlike Richard Wagner's idea of the *Gesamtkunstwerk*, Kandinsky's theory called for a production style that abstracted and separated the various theatrical elements, rather than allowing them to overlap and reinforce one another. Each expressive feature of the performance – like the music, "the physical-psychical sound and its movement," or color-tone – while existing independently of the others, functioned only as a means to the artist's ultimate goal. In the text of the second picture of *The Yellow Sound*, for example, actors, dressed in assorted primary colors, were instructed to speak ecstatically in unison, and then repeat themselves individually in various tones, keys, and tempos. Sometimes they were to shout as if overcome, then hoarsely, before their voices and costumes faded into the sounds of orchestra and stage-lights. Although *The Yellow Sound* was not staged, Hugo Ball, the future Dada, then a theatrical producer in Munich in 1914, asserted that Kandinsky's abstract performance theories would be the basis of "The Expressionist Theatre."

Possibly the most coherent and detailed analysis of the philosophical/technical aspects of theatrical Expressionism was published in a book that appeared during its decline, Felix Emmel's *Das Ekstatische Theater* (1924). In his chapter on Expressionist, or ecstatic, stage pictures, Emmel described the atmospherics behind the anti-Naturalism impulse. The new scenic designer had to depict the inner world of the proscenium, where the furniture, backdrops, costumes, makeup, and lighting all existed as individual and menacing realities. The lines and forms could not be merely stylistic or even painterly; they had to be part and parcel of the drama's overriding phantasmagoric message. For the spectator, the visual decor had to be "experienced, felt, breathed, internalized." After parsing the most successful of Expressionist productions and their specific application of set design, Emmel declared, "The rhythmic space, the dynamic images, the dramatic color – these are the three major necessities of the ecstatic theatre" (Emmel 1924: 50).

Modes of Expressionist stage design

Borrowing some of the terminology from Bernhard Diebold's influential study, *Anarchie im Drama*, that was used to describe models of pre-Expressionist and Expressionist dramas, German Expressionist performances can be subdivided into three general styles based on their expressive relationship to the audience – the creation of ecstasy through induction, association, or identification. These three categories are: 1) the *Geist* (purely spiritual or abstract) performance, which could be viewed as an ultimate vision of pure expression without the conventional intervention of dramatic characters or intricate plot – a sort of absolute communication between the playwright/director's *Seele*-mind and his audience; 2) the *Schrei* (scream or ecstatic) performance, which could be likened to an actual, if hazy, intense dream-state where movement, exteriors, language, motivation, and inner logic were uniformly and bizarrely warped; and 3) the *Ich* (I or ego) performance, which resembled the second type in certain ways, but focused upon a central performer who acted less – or more – grotesquely than the other, often stereotypical, characters and who was the subject of the playwright's and audience's identification – a kind of dream told to another person, or a dream remembered.

I. The Geist *performance*

In the July 1916 issue of *Der Sturm*, the Berlin dramaturg Lothar Schreyer published his first statements on the yet unseen Expressionist theatre. Following Kandinsky's abstract-mystical stage theories, he maintained that the new theatre must be pure, absolute – in the way that nonrepresentational painting and sculpture were absolute, without any lifelike referents. For Schreyer the perfect performance consisted of pure sound, pure movement, pure color, and pure form. Schreyer was most concerned with structuring theatrical elements in spiritual and dynamic compositions of synesthesia, where each of the performance's audio and visional components became linked up with another, adhering to a mystical pattern. Although Schreyer's scenic theories and otherworldly language show strong resemblances to the French Symbolists, his acknowledged influences came from certain Christian mystics and Goethe. For instance, Schreyer's theories on stage color exhibit both medieval and early scientific interests:

> **Color meaning**
>
> *Silver lighting expresses natural illumination.*
> *Gold expresses the supernatural.*
> *Blue expresses the binding principles of belief.*
> *Green expresses development or aging.*
> *Yellow expresses strength or contamination.*
>
> **Color shape**
>
> *White presses to an egg-shape.*
> *Blue stretches out forms into spheres.*
> *Violet divides form.*
> *Orange reproduces form.*
>
> *(Schreyer 1948: 85–6)*

While Expressionist directors outside Berlin attempted to impart the deranged awareness of their protagonists via their actors' mimicry and otherworldly stage sets, Schreyer wished to use the mechanical gestures and rote sounds of his performers as lightning rods to directly induce visions in the spectator. Only an absolute, "actorless," theatre could accomplish that, Schreyer claimed.

Advertised in *Der Sturm* and Schreyer's own new periodical, *Sturmbühne*, as "Expressionist theatre," his production of August Stramm's *Sancta Susanna* opened on 15 October 1918. This was to be Schreyer's first realization of his scenic alchemy. Despite an audience limited to subscribers of *Der Sturm* and newspaper critics, Schreyer requested police protection – perhaps more a manifestation of his unfashionable apolitical beliefs than any aesthetic fear. Instead of highly-made up, emotionally inflamed performers, gigantic, almost nonhuman, figures appeared making strange unintelligible singsong noises. Against a brightly colored backdrop of black, yellow, green and red, an arm appeared, then an oversized mask, then the chant of a bizarre litany. Expecting something quite different, the opening-night audience quickly responded in restlessness and irritation. The next day's newspaper reporters ridiculed the *Sturmbühne*'s "megaphone art," their "secret speech and limb-exercises." Many wondered how this could be called Expressionism and suggested that Schreyer was only attracted to the titular commercial aspect of the word. Schreyer was devastated by these morning-after critiques. *Sancta Susanna* went just as he had planned. Each performer was instructed to first find his "base note" and his "internal sound"; Schreyer rehearsed each actor until a spiritual dimension was experienced. When that occurred, the *Sturmbühne*'s "sound speakers" could reproduce any "vibration of the soul" vocally. Granted the simple megaphones and the thick cardboard costumes distorted certain low-pitched sounds; the performance was enacted as well as it might have been.

Although some later reviews proved much kinder, Schreyer made the decision to return to his native Hamburg. There, in 1919, he founded the *Kampfbühne*, a sister theatre to the *Sturmbühne*. With the assistance of a local organization of a few hundred, called the "Friends of Expressionism," Schreyer was able to stage premiere productions of Expressionist plays as well as original adaptations. Using students from the local academies, Schreyer and his *Kampfbühne* mounted eight productions in Hamburg. After some encouragement from Herwarth Walden, Schreyer returned to Berlin in the spring of 1920 to reactivate his old Sturm-troupe. He presented *Man* at Max Reinhardt's Deutsches Theater. But Reinhardt himself found the production too esoteric, too cultish, and declined to further any other *Sturmbühne* projects.

Although Schreyer was appointed to direct the stage-workshop of the Weimar Bauhaus in 1921 and obviously influenced the more purely abstract director, Oskar Schlemmer, he always considered himself an Expressionist. In fact for this reason, besides being thought something of a mystic among functionalists, Schreyer resigned from his post in 1923 and maintained that only the *Sturmbühne* exemplified Expressionism in the theatre; everything else was pseudo-Expressionism. The *Geist*-performance's position is best summarized in Schreyer's statement in the final number of the *Sturmbühne* periodical.

"Art is the artistically logical formulation of optical and acoustic relations. Art comes from the senses and appeals to the senses. It has nothing to do with understanding. The theatre is the formulation of focal color forms" (Schreyer 1919: 1).

II. The Schrei *performance*

Most critics associate the *Schrei*-performance with the bulk of Expressionist productions. Certainly, the irregular and ghoulish set designs were directed toward this style. As in the 1919 German film, *The Cabinet of Dr Caligari*, the performers and their environment constantly shifted from a kind of cataleptic stasis to a powerful, if epileptic, dynamism. The buildings and alleyways as well as stationary objects were marked with jagged, nonparallel lines and were often concealed by lopsided shadows. Photographs of *Schrei*-performances, even posed ones, show the distraught states of the actors as they performed before a milieu of asymmetrical and indistinct gloomy backdrops. Nearly every *Schrei* interior set resembled a claustrophobic parlor with skewed doors and cell-like window frames. The external scenes were often dimly lighted from above and reduced into elongated, compressed landscapes without any heavenly prospects or divine concern.

Two of the foremost *Schrei*-directors, Karl-Heinz Martin and Richard Weichert, utilized a new technological apparatus known as "telegraphic lighting." Intense shafts of illumination from overhead projectors created isolated pockets of scenic activity that emphasized the seclusion and lack of communication between characters and their surroundings. Their productions were perceived as primitive woodcuts that moved and spoke. The entire stage picture now cast a blanket of despair across both the vertical and horizontal planes.

III. The Ich *performance*

In the winter of 1919 still another variety of theatrical Expressionism came to be seen in Berlin. It differed from the intimate *Geist* and *Schrei* productions in scope and audience focus. These performances were massive in scale and more commercially targeted toward the traditional arrangement of prominent leads interacting with rigidly drilled secondary performers and walk-ons.

The marriage of Max Reinhardt's star system and mass choruses formed the basis of the *Ich*-performance. Characteristically, an *Ich*-performance focused upon the single ecstatic actor surrounded by or confronted with dozens of choral-performers who moved in unison, creating grotesque, if picturesque, poses. Frequently, the central actor, like Fritz Kortner or Alexander Granach, received his earliest training in both *Schrei* and Reinhardt productions. For the most part, *Ich*-directors absorbed much of Reinhardt's use of *mise-en-scène*, whether they worked in competition with him or under his auspices. The best known of these were Leopold Jessner and Jürgen Fehling.

Jessner mounted a version of Friedrich Schiller's *William Tell* at the State Theatre in December 1919. Heavily influenced by the scenic experiments of Adolphe Appia and Émile Jaques-Dalcroze, Jessner's designer, Emil Pirchan, reduced and abstracted all the dramatic elements that could be used to spotlight the soul-state of Schiller's revolutionary character. Pirchan's sparse platforms, labeled *Jessnertreppen* or Jessner steps, represented the icy mountaintops and embankments of the Swiss Alps. It was there that Kortner's conflicted gesticulations could be underscored from multiple perspectives. Newspaper columnists and foreign reviewers were thrilled.

The historical becomes the abstract, the human focuses itself into the symbolic, external fades into an adumbration, space and the scene are reduced to the simplest common denominator, costumes are resolved into masses of color. The poetry, the characters, and

Figure 31.1 Design by Emil Pirchan for *William Tell*, directed by Leopold Jessner at Staatliches Schauspielhaus, Berlin, 1919. (KHM-Museumsverband, Theatermuseum Vienna.)

passions remain dominant, but with a treble, a tenfold force and meaning. It is indeed an expressionistic summary, but also a compressionistic one (Scheffauer 1924: 209).

Pirchan's *Jessnertreppen* abetted the Expressionist endeavor. They magnified the link between characters and their individual psychic states; they increased the actor's plastic possibilities, allowing him to be more easily perceived in depth; they rhythmically sharpened the impact of slow, fast, or disjointed movements; and they created a novel aesthetic unity that was thought to be lacking in other Expressionist productions.

Jessner accomplished many of his mathematically calculated effects through an unwavering reliance on enormous set pieces, startling transformations, and stark symbolism. In his celebrated production of *Richard III* (5 November 1920), colored bars over the proscenium arch and carpeted-platforms of unadulterated black, gold, red, and white signified the protagonist's mood and destiny while eerie shadows foretold the ultimate doom of Shakespeare's other combatants. It was this last Neo-Romantic feature that most caught the critics' attention. The American architect and set designer Lee Simonson enthusiastically described their use:

> How immensely the movement of the second part was enhanced by the staircase when Richard appeared at the summit, when his men in red and Richmond's in white moved up and down it with all the symbolism of opposing forces, groups mounting toward its apex in imminent struggle. And what a contrast to all heightened movement as Richard descends slowly at the end in utter lassitude, to dream his last dream at its base.
>
> *(Simonson 1922: 126–7)*

The stage settings in Jessner's *Othello* (11 November 1921) instantaneously merged from one huge emblematic object into another. For instance, in Act One, the walls of a Venetian side street rotated as it transformed into the Council-Chamber pillars; and in the final act, a mammoth Cypriot tree magically rematerialized as Desdemona's lethal Bedchamber. Yet, an otherwise comic anecdote points up the peril of Jessner's multi-leveled scenery: at the premiere of *Macbeth* (10 November 1922), Kortner, in a "possessed" state of mind, lost his footing on the stairs and went sliding down the length of the platforms. While mass actors could be precisely choreographed in the negotiation of the complex staging, an ecstatic actor could not.

Another Berlin director, Fehling, also used a rhythmic mass-chorus and Appia-like platforms for his *Ich*-production of Ernst Toller's *Mass-Mensch* (29 September 1921). Here the actors were set off against a background of black curtains and concentrated beams of cross-fading lights. As in the Jessner productions, the abstract *mise-en-scène* and highly choreographed groups of actors compelled the audience to concentrate on the histrionics of a single performer (Mary Dietrich). Between each harsh and dismal political scene, which unfolded across the stairway incline, a dream sequence was enacted on the forestage. Despite Fehling's public success with *Mass-Mensch* and the international attention it received, Expressionist productions began to recede from the German stage by 1923.

Epic Theater in Germany

Like its Expressionist predecessor, Epic Theater was a distinctive avant-garde theatre genre that came of age in Weimar Germany during the 1920s. Both heralded left-wing communal doctrines and utilized modern technical means for their productions, but the Epic Theater defined itself as a correlative to Expressionism, in fact a Counter-Expressionist rebuke. Erwin Piscator and Bertolt Brecht, respectively the founder and main theoretician of Epic Theater, eschewed raw sentiment, emotionalism, and cathartic denouements, the basic elements of Expressionism. Stirred by the radical beliefs and aesthetic models of Karl Marx and the French Naturalist Émile Zola, Piscator and Brecht proselytized that effective political art had to be objective and "scientific." Like a trial courtroom, the Epic stage would be an open forum for competing societal narratives, a public venue that would dramatize class warfare.

Piscator and the political stage

The Bolshevik Revolution in 1918 not only upended the feudal order in Czarist Russia, it inspired civic and national unrest throughout Europe. Marxism as interrupted by the Soviet intellectuals provided a momentous impetus for the creation of novel popular art forms at home and abroad. "Agitation and propaganda" to secure and broaden the Communist insurgency, or agitprop, materialized overnight into street parades and Mass Spectacles, itinerant amateur theatricals, and musical concerts and comic sketches presented in factories and workers' clubhouses.

After the surrender of the German armed forces in World War I, Piscator joined the Berlin Dadas as a militant propagandist and freelance director. His *Red Revue*, a German-language imitation of Russian agitprops, played before local proletarian audiences. But one evening, when his stage designer and collaborator John Heartfield belatedly dragged his just-painted flat to a performance that had already begun, Piscator discovered that this backstage mishap, or "anti-illusionary interruption," actually increased the spectators' interest in the production and its "behind the scenes" reality. This "showing the seams" moment would inaugurate the first element of Piscator's Epic Theater: the calculated display of the stage's artifice.

Beginning in 1924, Piscator added slide projections, sound recordings, and film clips to his experimental productions. (The Soviet directors, Vsevolod Meyerhold, Sergei Eisenstein, and Les Kurbas had already pioneered the use of these audio-visual techniques some months and years before.) Like the inter-titles in silent movies, word captions that highlighted the injustice of American Capitalism appeared on stage screens (*Flags*, 1924). For *In Spite of Everything* (1925), a documentary investigation of the German Socialist Party support for the Kaiser's war, Piscator fashioned a peep-show montage of live action, newspaper clippings, photographs, taped speeches, and newsreel segments in 23 scenes. It was a *succés de scandale* and elevated Piscator's Epic ideas in the eyes of Berlin's Communist elite.

More technological stage novelties followed. In *The Drunken Boat* (1926), cartoon triptychs by George Grosz were cast on the backdrops to indicate the play's exotic settings. In *Storm Over Gotland* (1927), a medieval costume drama about Baltic fishermen, their Hanseatic League overlords, and the pirate chieftains who led a peasant revolt in 1398, Piscator accompanied the antiquated dialogue spoken by the heroic figures with filmic images of the Russian Revolution projected on the theatre's cyclorama. The historic parallels could not be made more scenically.

Later that year, Piscator established his own independent theatre and studio collective, the *Piscator-Bühne* in Nollendorfplatz. Designed by Walter Gropius, the head of the Dessau Bauhaus, this "Total Theater" was to be an architectural phenomenon. His blueprints featured flexible revolving stages, concentric thrusts, and steeply racked auditorium arenas. Colossal in size, it would accommodate 1,100 spectators. The still incomplete *Piscator-Bühne* opened with Toller's *Hoppla, We Live!* (1927). This was a tendentious melodrama about the workers' deprivation, government corruption, and left-wing betrayal during the last decade in Berlin. A 25-foot-high scaffolding portrayed a prison block, a dilapidated apartment building, a police station, a polling booth, and a grand hotel. Backlighted images and cinematic location shots introduced each act. Meanwhile simultaneous bits of action were created on the nine-box set through synchronized lighting and sound effects.

The second production at the theatre, *Rasputin, the Romanovs, the War, and the People Who Opposed Them* (1927), was generally considered to be a superior example of Epic dramaturgy. Screens of unfolding documents and newsreel fragments provided ironic contrasts to the follies of the Czar and his wartime court who were sequestered inside a double-storied hemispheric interior. For instance, in an early scene, the audience witnessed Nikolai II writing to the Czarina. On the side of the stage, the words of his letter unfolded, "Today the front was quiet" and other solipsistic inanities. Above, a motion-picture clip of the Battle of Tannenberg, one of the bloodiest clashes in modern history, divulged a different reality.

The final major *Piscator-Bühne* production was *The Good Soldier Schweik* (1928), a comedy about a hapless Czech recruit in the Great War. Here, Piscator reengaged Grosz to construct cartoon characters as backstage animations and life-size cardboard cutouts. These were placed on a conveyor belt that pulled set pieces and caricatured authority figures across the elongated central stage.

Brecht's contribution to Epic Theater

In 1927, Bertolt Brecht was accepted into Piscator's collective as a collaborative writer and helped adapt *Rasputin* and *Schweik* for the stage. He extolled Piscator's mechanical wonder succinctly as "the theatrical style of our time."

The essential point of the Epic Theater is perhaps that it appeals less to the feelings than to the spectator's reason. Instead of sharing an experience the spectator must come to grips with things. At the same time it would be quite wrong to try and deny emotion to this kind of theatre (Brecht 1964: 23). The economic downfall of Germany beginning in 1929, however, soured the climate for experimental and politically motivated theatre. In the Depression period that followed, Piscator and Brecht reverted to simpler varieties of propaganda, the extended agitprop. Both of them escaped the Nazi coup in 1933, eventually landing in America, where their Epic Theater techniques found adherents in the 1930s workers' theatre and Federal Theatre movements.

(For Brecht and scenography see Chapter 32 by Christopher Baugh, "Bertolt Brecht and Scenographic Dialogue.")

References

Brecht, Bertolt 1964. "The Epic Theater and Its Difficulties." In *Brecht On Theatre*, translated and edited by John Willett. New York: Hill and Wang.

Diebold, Bernhard 1921. *Anarchie im Drama*. Frankfurt: Frankfurter Verlags-Anstalt.

Emmel, Félix 1924. *Das Ekstatische Theater*. Prien: Kampmann & Schnabel Verlag.

Scheffauer, Herman George 1924. *The New Vision in the German Arts*. New York: B.W. Huebsch, Inc.

Schreyer, Lothar 1919. *Sturm-bühne*, May No. 6.

Schreyer, Lothar 1948. *Expressionistisches Theater*. J. P. Hamburg: Toth Verlag.

Simonson, Lee 1922. "Down to the Cellar." *Theatre Arts Monthly* 6 (2): 119–39.

32

BERTOLT BRECHT AND SCENOGRAPHIC DIALOGUE

Christopher Baugh

Bertolt Brecht (1898–1956) possessed an intense visual sensibility; in his writing for and about the stage his poems and stories are filled with admiration for lightness and material elegance, and for stage settings that display an "aesthetic of selective precision and implied human presence" (Willett 1986: 15). The scenographic played a fundamental role as Brecht and his collaborators grappled with innovative narrative methods and rehearsal practice. He found joy in working alongside scenographers and his writing is filled with reference to the theory and practices of scenography. Dialogue within the process of making performance, and dialogue whereby the spectator constructs meaning in performance, continue to be significant issues of interest within contemporary theory and practice.

Brecht worked with three scenographers: Caspar Neher, Teo Otto, and Karl von Appen. Von Appen was the successor to Neher at the Berliner Ensemble, and Otto worked with Brecht on the 1941 production of *Mother Courage* when Neher was unavailable. The collaboration with Neher was the most durable and significant for Brecht in the development of scenographic practice. They had been classmates, and their friendship was based on the free and pleasurable (*lustig*) dialogue involved in devising theatre. Neher was as stimulated by dramatic literature as Brecht was by stage space, theatrical imagery and properties; neither could consider a stage aesthetic that was separate from the political rationale for theatre.

During the period 1919–1922 Brecht wrote *Baal*, *Drums in the Night*, *Galgei* (an early version of *Man is Man*), worked on film scripts, and sang in cabaret. Neher prepared visual propositions that illustrated theatrical ideas and in turn led to revision and development. Notwithstanding this creative dialogue, the Munich Kammerspiele rejected Neher's drawings, preferring the pictorial coherence of their resident expressionist designer Otto Reigbert. However, Brecht won the Kleist prize and received good reviews, while Neher acquired credibility by designing Kleist's *Kätchen von Heilbronn* for the Berlin Staatstheater. In May 1923, therefore, their professional collaboration began with *In the Jungle of the Cities* at the Munich Residenz-Theater. Neher worked with Brecht on the adaptation of *Edward II* at the Kammerspiele and moved as designer, with Brecht as junior director, to the Deutsches Theater in Berlin, where *Jungle* opened in October and work began on the adaptation of *Coriolanus*.

Brecht and Neher rejected the pictorial coherence of contemporary expressionist art: distorted lines and tightly focused steeply angled light creating dramatic shadows. They wanted a theatre equivalent of the sketch: looking for ways of endowing wood, canvas and paint with the softness of definition similar to those achieved by drawing with ink upon damp watercolor washes – Neher's favored medium. The dialogue involved Neher sketching in rehearsals and providing material for debate between the team of collaborators. Drawings of actors and their groupings created outlines of dramatic action: von Appen insisted on the importance of this method:

> Arrangements (*Arrangementskizzen*) fix the movement on the stage. They determine the position of groups and decide on how they are changed. It is their task to elucidate the plot. Finding arrangements should be the starting point of any rehearsal work.[1]

These sketches became a vital methodology of rehearsal, drawing strength from the actors, feeding back to them and serving as models for blocking and textual development. Egon Monk[2] described rehearsals for *The Tutor* in 1950:

> They [Neher's sketches] always lay ready to hand on the director's table . . . Nearly all the blocking of the Berliner Ensemble derived directly from Neher's sketches. If there was a particular scene, or a particular moment within a scene – a 'nodal point' as Brecht and Neher would call it – that had no sketch, or if Neher for once was not there . . . then that rehearsal might well be broken off. As for instance when the last scene but one of *The Tutor* was being rehearsed . . . On stage, a large number of actors, glasses in their hands, drinking a toast (yes, but how?). Projected behind them, falling snow. Brecht rehearsed somewhat indecisively, asked first one then another of his aides to try blocking the scene, looking helplessly at the actors on stage, who looked equally helplessly down on him, then finally said: 'It's no use, we'll have to wait till Cas gets here.'
>
> *(Quoted in Willett 1986: 109)*

As the theatre text emerged, energies of meaning were created by confrontations between actors and scenic material. Monk continues:

> Wenzeslaus the Schoolmaster . . . One Hand holding Neher's sketch, the other holding the long quill pen with which the sketch shows him driving Count Vermuth and the Major's armed domestics from the room. A most impressive moment, clarifying the scene as no subsequent performance could do.
>
> *(Ibid.: 111)*

This is scenography inextricably integrated within the construction of dramaturgy. *The Threepenny Opera* at the Theater am Schiffbauerdamm in 1928 was the first production in which a *mise en scène* achieved the status of a "model," in the sense that the scenography existed as a layer of meaning within the text of performance – a layer as inseparable as the dialogue and Kurt Weill's musical score.

Brecht's *Lehrstücke* (learning plays) of the period 1928–1932 were experiments in audience/performer redefinition that extended the collaborative dialogue of theatre-making to one that engaged the spectator within the process of making performance. The theoretical basis of the *Lehrstücke* expressed the relationship between Brecht's view of theatre and his expectation of scenography. Traditionally, practitioners and theoreticians have suggested that theatre operates by means of a series of strategies developed during rehearsal aimed at achieving an interpretation that is communicated in performance. *Lehrstücktheater* redefined the nature of an audience, treating the act of theatre as dialectic: a process in which the audience take upon themselves the role of interpretation. Brecht describes *Lehrtheater* in terms of Marxist political philosophy:

> Marxism posits certain methods of looking, certain criteria. These lead it to make certain judgments of phenomena, certain predictions and suggestions for practical action. It teaches a combination of thinking and active intervention as a means of dealing with reality in so far as social intervention is able to deal with it. It is a doctrine that criticizes human action and expects in turn to be criticized by it. A true *Weltanschauung*, however, is a picture of the world, a hypothetical knowledge of the way in which things happen, mostly molded in accordance with some ideal of harmony.
>
> *(Brecht 1978: 36)*

But this posed the problem of names: designer or scenographer, *bühnenbildner* or *bühnenbauer*?[3] This distinction lay at the heart of Brecht and Neher's understanding of scenography. The *bühnenbildner* (stage picture maker) proposes a harmoniously composed knowledge of the world, and offers an interpretation of a play's topic and themes. Whereas the *bühnenbauer* (stage builder) creates and builds a scene as a component *within the dramaturgy* and which should be considered as an act of performance: Brecht's "combination of thinking and active intervention." The *bühnenbauer* will be co-responsible for the building of "gests" involving the combination of performance elements. This differs fundamentally from traditional practice where a *bühnenbildner* designs, in advance, a complete setting. We easily recognize Brecht's account:

> Normally the sets are determined before the actors' rehearsals have begun, 'so that they can start,' and the main thing is that they evoke an atmosphere, give some kind of expression, [and] illustrate a location . . . it is considered with regard to creating a space with some good possibilities for performance . . . It seems very strange that set designers (*bühnenbildner*), who feel and claim that they are artists with a "vision" which they must realize, seldom reckon with the actors.
>
> *(Brecht 1967: 442–3)*

The practical alternative is spelt out:

> The good scene designer (*bühnenbauer*) proceeds slowly and experimentally. A working hypothesis is based on a precise reading of the text, and substantial conversations with other members of the theatre, especially on the social aims of the play and the concerns of the performance, are useful to him. However, his basic performance ideas must still be general and flexible. He will test them constantly and revise them on the basis of results in rehearsals with the actors . . . This is how a good stage designer (*bühnenbauer*) works: now ahead of the actor, now behind him, always together with him. Step by step he builds up the performance area, just as experimentally as the actor.
>
> *(Ibid.: 443–4)*

This concern for taxonomy clarifies Brecht's aversion to expressionist theatre and the revolutionary theatres of Piscator[4] and Meyerhold, and designers such as Georg Grosz whose stage "pictures" firmly proposed a *Weltanschauung*. Brecht considered such theatre to be anti-revolutionary because it was passive and relied on reproduction of existing views and judgments. For Brecht, paradoxically, it represented "the ultimate form of bourgeois naturalistic theatre" (Völker 1979: 116). Concern for reality in theatre remained with Neher; he thought of the title *bühnenbildner* as a "Nazi" term since it pretended to offer a coherent view of the world as being "real." But Neher argued that the stage is *always* realistic, "[t]hat's why I maintain that the realistic stage picture is a nonsense."[5]

The *Lehrstücke* should not be understood, therefore, as short-lived attempts to create didactic Marxist theatre. In terms of Brecht's scenography, they articulated the very basis of his theory, and their performances offered radical scenographic exploration: the rejection of traditional architecture and its proscenium arch; the presence of large choirs who, in *The Flight over the Ocean* and *Baden-Baden Cantata of Acquiescence* (1929), defined and maintained the narrative process; and the use of a boxing ring in the *Songspiel, Mahagonny* (1927). There were projections by Neher and exhortations to the audience ("follow the words in your programs and sing along loudly!"), which must have created, even within the context of a new music festival in Baden-Baden, a disturbing and provocative atmosphere. Teo Otto[6] designed *The Measures Taken* (1930) at the Berlin Grosses Schauspielhaus with a workers' choir beneath the projection screen and with actors lit by low-hanging industrial lamps. For the *Baden-Baden Cantata* a 3-metre high grotesque figure was constructed. Two "clowns," theatricalizing man's inhumanity, sawed off the figure's limbs, all of which took place in front of and among the choir.[7]

Dialogue between writer, director, musician, and scenographer was fundamental, not only for making a stage aesthetic but also for the development of dramaturgy. This was inseparable from Brecht's political and social philosophy that sought the "refunctioning" (*umfunktioniert*) of theatre. The multiplicity of creative contribution within the rehearsal process was essential in creating a theatre that relished diversity and encouraged conscious separation of elements within the *mise en scène*. Brecht and Neher had served no apprenticeship, so neither acquired "professional" practices and skills that tempered their passion and joy in the dialogic work of shared creativity. Egon Monk describes them rehearsing *The Tutor*:

> Brecht and Neher sitting next each other at rehearsal. Both of them leaning back, their knees pressed against the seats in front. Brecht appreciatively studying his cigar; Neher, his eyebrows exaggeratedly raised or exaggeratedly frowning over his glasses, more severe . . . They are rehearsing 'by interjections.' Each interjection is prefaced by Neher or Brecht naming its originator. 'Neher thinks . . .,' 'Brecht thinks . . .,' 'Monk thinks . . . .' The interjection is listened to, then tested. If a detail works, then Brecht giggles with pleasure and Neher gives him a look of amusement . . . This lasts a long time.
>
> *(Quoted in Willett 1986: 111)*

The progression from *Lehrtheater* that united political and theatrical ideology, to practical grappling with rehearsal was inevitable. Building the imagery of the stage was as much a process as that of building the performances of actors. In this way Brecht and Neher enfranchised scenography, empowering it with opportunities for

Figure 32.1 Design by Caspar Neher for the village school in Act 4 of *The Tutor* (*Der Hofmeister*), 1950. (KHM-Museumsverband, Theatermuseum Vienna.)

comment, criticism, humor and disruption. But the collaborative dialogue of rehearsal must not produce the Wagnerian *Gesamtkunstwerk*. While working on the *Mahagonny Songspiel* (1927) Brecht wrote:

> [S]o long as the arts are supposed to be 'fused' together, the various elements will all be equally degraded, and each will act as a mere feed to the rest . . . Showing independent works of art as part of a theatrical performance is a new departure. Neher's projections adopt an attitude towards the events on stage, as when the real glutton sits in front of the glutton whom Neher has drawn. These projections of Neher's are quite as much an independent component of the opera as are Weill's music and the text.
>
> *(Brecht,* Versuche 2 *[1930] quoted in Willett 1964: 37–8)*

Scenography happens in time, working in dialogue with the actors; the scenographic is an act of performance working in dialogue with the audience. The plain wooden poles and simple door (*The Caucasian Chalk Circle*, scenography by von Appen, 1954) have minimal architectural and theatrical significance until they are crowded with wedding guests. The final result, originating from the placement of actors who articulated and defined the spaces, created a beauty of haunting significance.

> [T]he *Neher principle* of building the set according to the requirements established at the actors' rehearsals allowed the designer to profit by the actors' performance and influence it in turn. The playwright could work out his experiments

> in uninterrupted collaboration with actor and stage-designer; he could influence and be influenced. At the same time the painter and the composer regained their independence, and were able to express their view of the theme by their own artistic means.[8]

Brecht was no dour utilitarian when it came to the appearance of properties and stage furnishings. Much is made about his love of objects, which recounted the history of their use – the sociology of prop-making. But from his earliest statements on theory to the last examples of practice, there was a demand for the beauty that was the product of artistry. The beauty of a well-used kettle, certainly, but also that of stage architecture joyfully chosen and designed so that it might take its individual place, and not merely "service" the action. The joy and the self-referential beauty of Brecht and Neher's theatre, with its constant reminders of illusion and mutability, invited its audience to engage with the theatrical in their own lives. This was central to Brecht's concern to "refunction" the stage, and is not well served by the bleak utilitarian aesthetic of many revivals.

It is unclear whether the "break" that occurred between Brecht and Neher over the winter of 1952–1953 was intended to be final. However, Neher seems to have made his position clear when he became a regular designer at the Volksbühne in West Berlin and in 1954 became head of design at the Munich Kammerspiele. Significantly, in December of that year, Brecht received the Stalin Peace Prize and Neher was appointed to the Board of the Salzburg Festival.

Karl von Appen had a considerable theatre career behind him when Brecht invited him to the Ensemble in 1953, and he became principal designer when the company moved into the renovated Theater am Schiffbauerdamm in 1954. Von Appen collaborated on the first production of *The Caucasian Chalk Circle* later that year. Ironically, it is the scenography of von Appen and Teo Otto that travelled the world and established the image of the "Brechtian" stage. *Mother Courage*, arguably the most scenographically influential, toured in what was essentially the original scenography created by Otto for its première at the Zurich Schauspielhaus in 1941.[9] Indeed, Neher's work was not represented at all when the company visited London shortly after Brecht's death in August 1956.[10]

Although indebted to Neher, there was a distinct change of attitude apparent in von Appen's work. If teeth were still bared, then they were shown with a pictorial skill, which frequently prevented the eye going beneath the surface to engage in dialectic. Scenography now offered visual unity: the coherence of a "world-view" with pre-interpreted ideology.[11] Battles with definitions of stage reality, which had taxed Neher and Brecht, could not be engaged in Stalinist East Germany other than by offering completed solutions – "realism within a utopian horizon."[12]

> [W]e have developed a realistic style in the theatrical work of our Republic. In this theatrical work socialist realism is a method aimed at selecting the socially fruitful means out of the whole wealth of means at the stage designer's disposal.
>
> *(Von Appen 1971: 1)*

Nevertheless, von Appen was the agent whereby Brecht and Neher's dialogue of collaborative creativity became enshrined into the practice of the Berliner Ensemble. Through the heavily funded training schools of Eastern Europe, the Ensemble's influence spread. Throughout most Western theatre, aesthetic preference tended towards the more accessible von Appen scenographies, reflected in reverential approaches to staging "authentic Brecht." Reception outside Germany has suffered considerably from fetishization of the Berliner Ensemble's solutions and their aesthetic. "Solutions" have a disarming way of disassociating themselves from their theoretical context and becoming *the* object of study and imitation. Unfamiliarity with the language and ignorance of the plays' context has resulted in a thorough distortion of Brecht's theatre.[13] This was an objectification of practice that Brecht recognized:

> When studying the following remarks, consisting of a number of thoughts and ideas conceived while rehearsing a play, one should – when faced with certain solutions to problems – recognize primarily the problems.
>
> *(Brecht 1958 in* Encore *1965: 6)*

Nonetheless, it is still tempting to try to create a production that is "true" to Brecht, since he is the rare dramatist who has written copiously and clearly about the scenography of his plays. Performance iconography attained the power of dramatic utterance: harsh white lighting from exposed instruments, bare stripped stages, "earth" colors, hessian and canvas costumes, half stage-height curtains running on horizontal wires across the stage and terse, combative captions projected onto screens straddling the stage. But these were solutions to problems generated by the historical collision of a play with its production team within a theatrical and political context. There can be nothing truly Brechtian in reconstructing the performance conditions of the original productions, beyond the nostalgic or the historicist. But to stage *Mother Courage* and ignore the sparse screens, the bleached revolving stage and the images of Courage's wagon seems tantamount to ignoring or re-writing the spoken text. If the scenography is as central as the written text, then surely the original scenography *should* be endowed with a similar "textual" status. In the *Courage-Modell 1949* Brecht offered a resolution resisting permanence:

> Provisional structures must be erected, and there is the danger that they may become permanent . . . As far as the theatre is concerned, we throw our Models into the gap . . . And the Models will be misused by those who accept them and have not learnt how to handle them. Intended to make things easier, they are not easy to handle. Moreover, they are not made to exclude thought, but to inspire thought; they are not made to replace artistic creativity, but to compel it.
>
> *(Ibid.: 5)*

We should remember that the original scenographies gained power by virtue of their contrast with prevailing audience expectations. So many "Brechtian" practices have been assimilated that any sense of disturbance or shock is unlikely. Contemporary audiences are prepared for the separation and dislocation of dramatic and scenic elements; for a narrative borne along by differing media, and for a variety of "effects" designed to jolt us out of any tendency to believe that what we see is any other than the product of art. West End and Broadway theatre can usually offer its audience a whole catalogue of "Brechtian" techniques.

The refunctioning of stage practice proposed by Brecht and Neher signified a major shift in theatrical philosophy – from a Romantic aesthetic founded upon the principle of the "absorption" of the spectator in the product of art, towards a theatre of rhetorical gesture and process. Aristotelian catharsis is frequently cited as the arch villain of Brechtian theatre, but the scenic "world" of topographical verisimilitude advocated by Romantic theory presents an equally significant opponent. Contemporary practices have extended Brecht's concept of scenography as active performance: developments that are undoubtedly more truly "Brechtian" than the reverential revival of his plays. For example, in performance where interpretation is resisted and the audience become participants in a dialogue to create meaning and significance. Heiner Müller said about Robert Wilson's work:

> There's a text and it's delivered, but it is not evaluated and not colored and not interpreted either, it's just there. Then there's noise, and that's there too and is also not interpreted . . . Interpretation is the work of the spectator and is not to take place on the stage. The spectator must not be absolved from this work. That's consumerism . . . capitalist theatre.[14]

Wilson suggests that absorption creates fascist theatre: "I want the spectator to have sufficient space to have his own thoughts and ideas, inner impressions that are analogous to the outer ones on the stage" (quoted in Wright 1989: 129). Strategies of contemporary performance may well serve as the most appropriate model for practical Brechtian research today.

Brecht and Neher's scenographic dialogues offered political and aesthetic "space" for both the artists and the audience whose integration can establish the dialectic nature of performance. Brecht's accounts of collaborative practice are extensive and offer coherent and lucid ideas: but they are ideas that demand the continuous re-assessment of personal practices and responsibility. They are predicated upon a ceaseless continuum of "refunctioning" theatre.

Notes

1 Karl von Appen, "On Arrangement Sketches (*Über Arrangementskizzen*)" in "Introduction to the GDR Contribution to the Prague Quadrennial, 1971" (possibly written by von Appen himself) in *Stage Design in the German Democratic Republic* (in an anonymous translation prepared for the International Quadrennial of Scenography, Prague, 1971) Berlin: Sektion DDR der Internationalen Organisation der Bühnenbildner und Theatertechniker (OISTT), 1971, p. 1.

2 Egon Monk (1927–2007) was an acting stage manager/assistant director in the Ensemble during the period *c*. 1950–1954.

3 *Bühnenbildner* is someone concerned with creating stage pictures. "Stage" or "scene" builder is, of course, a more correct translation of *bühnenbauer*. However, within contemporary practice in Europe and in North America, the word "scenography" is understood to represent a collaborative and integrated approach to the stage and its relevant practitioners, which is precisely the point that Brecht's and Neher's semantic distinction initiates. See a more extended discussion of this in my "Brecht and Stage Design: the *bühnenbildner* and the *bühnenbauer*" (Baugh 2006).

4 Brecht's biography usually deals with this issue in terms of theatre status, copyright on ideas and personal rivalry see, for example, John Fuegi, *Bertolt Brecht; Chaos According to Plan*, Cambridge: Cambridge University Press, 1987, p. 49.

5 Letter from Neher to Brecht, *ca* 1951, cited by Willett 1986: 75.

6 After study in Kassel and Paris, Otto had taught at the Bauhauschule in Weimar in 1926 and was an assistant at the Berlin Staatsoper in 1928. He always maintained a commitment to

painting and exhibited at the Berlin Exhibition in 1930. Shortly after *The Measures Taken*, as the Nazis seized power, Otto returned to his native Switzerland and began a 25-year residency at the Zurich Schauspielhaus.

7 John Fuegi considers this giant figure in some detail and examines contemporary audience response, which seems to have bordered upon the hysterical. The contemporary reports that he cites, however, do not indicate whether the depth of feeling was generated by a heightened awareness of man's inhumanity to man, or merely by the gruesomeness of the theatrical effect. *Bertolt Brecht: Chaos According to Plan*, Cambridge: Cambridge University Press, 1987, p. 34.

8 From "Über experimentelles Theater" a lecture given by Brecht in Helsinki in October 1940, published in *Theater der Zeit*, East Berlin: 1959, No. 4, cited in Willett 1964: 134.

9 Otto's scenography was adapted by Heinrich Kilger when Brecht directed the play at the Deutsches Theater in 1949.

10 Neher's opera designs had been seen at Glyndbourne in 1952, and Sam Wanamaker used a Neher scenography in his production of *The Threepenny Opera* at the Royal Court Theatre in February 1956.

11 Neher had already expressed qualms about some of the scenic tendencies at the Ensemble, which he had sensed in the "realistic" conventionalism of John Heartfield's designs for *Kremlin Chimes* in 1952.

12 This is the title given by Friedrich Dieckmann to his valedictory essay on von Appen in *Théâtre International*, Nos. 3–4, pp. 10–15. Significantly, von Appen is referred to as *bühnenbildner* of the Berliner Ensemble.

13 See a particularly clear survey of this theme in Maro Germanou, "Brecht and the English Theatre" in *Brecht in Perspective* edited by Graham Bartram and Anthony Waine, London: Longman, 1982, pp. 208–24. Jocelyn Herbert's scenography for the English Stage Company at the Royal Court Theatre during the 1960s and her relationship with new writing clearly benefited in positive ways from the Ensemble's example. John Bury's work at the Royal Shakespeare Company, and especially for the adaptation of Shakespeare's history plays as *The Wars of the Roses* (1964–5), was an important attempt to define an English scenographic attitude in line with Brecht and Neher's ideas.

14 Heiner Müller and Olivier Ortolani, "Die Form entsteht aus dem Maskieren," *Theater*, 1985, p. 91, quoted and translated by Elizabeth Wright, *Postmodern Brecht*, London: Routledge, 1989. Wright's is an important study that centralizes the ideology of the *Lehrstücke* and also, in locating Brecht's dialectics within more recent performance theory, offers important directions for re-interpretation and analysis.

References

Appen, Karl von 1971. "Introduction to the GDR Contribution to the Prague Quadrennial, 1971." In *Stage Design in the German Democratic Republic* (in an anonymous translation prepared for the International Quadrennial of Scenography, Prague, 1971). Berlin: Sektion DDR der Internationalen Organisation der Bühnenbildner und Theatertechniker (OISTT).

Baugh, Christopher 2006. "Brecht and Stage Design: The *bühnenbildner* and the *bühnenbauer*." In *The Cambridge Companion to Brecht*, 2nd ed., edited by Peter Thomson and Glendyr Sachs, 259–77. Cambridge: Cambridge University Press.

Brecht, Bertolt [1958] 1965. *Courage-Modell 1949* (Berlin: Henschel Verlag), translated by Eric Bentley and Hugo Schmidt, reprinted in *Encore* Vol. 12 (3), May–June.

Brecht, Bertolt 1967. *Gesammelte Werke*, Vol. 15. Frankfurt: Suhrkamp. [All translations from this volume of the *Gesammelte Werke* are by Juliette Prodhan and myself.]

Brecht, Bertolt 1978. *The Messingkauf Dialogues*, translated by John Willett. London: Methuen.

Völker, Klaus 1979. *Brecht: A Biography*, translated by John Nowell. London and Boston: Marion Boyars.

Willett, John 1964. *Brecht on Theatre: The Development of an Aesthetic*. London: Methuen.

Willett, John 1986. *Caspar Neher: Brecht's Designer*. London: Arts Council/Methuen.

Wright, Elizabeth 1989. *Postmodern Brecht: A Re-presentation*. London: Routledge.

33
THE NEW STAGECRAFT

David Bisaha

The New Stagecraft was a scenographic movement that adapted European modernist practices for the American theatre. Its adherents were stage decorators and architects, who would only later call themselves scenic designers. The New Stagecraft rejected conventionalism and the detailed realism of the previous generation, instead valuing simplification, suggestion, and unity of the stage picture (Macgowan 1914: 416). It also supported the professionalization of designing and, as a result, New Stagecraft tenets undergird much twentieth-century American scenic practice. Robert Edmond Jones, Lee Simonson, Jo Mielziner, Norman Bel Geddes, and Joseph Urban were practitioners of the New Stagecraft, and their designs have become touchstones for the movement.

The New Stagecraft is frequently traced back to Adolph Appia and Edward Gordon Craig. Craig's call for the synthesis of the stage picture under the creative authority of a single designer-director and Appia's experiments with flexible settings and the development of mood through light and "atmosphere" did inspire Americans. However, critics cited more diverse influences. Touring productions introduced European methods to New York audiences, including Max Reinhardt's *Sumurun* (1912), the Irish Players' tour in the same year, and Sergei Diaghilev's Ballets Russes (1911).[1] In these productions scenery suggested rather than represented, featured creative restraint, and employed colorful lighting. Continued experimentation with simplified scenic environments, striking use of color, and flexibility became the subject of American periodicals and publications, especially Macgowan and Jones' *Continental Stagecraft* (1922).

The first New Stagecraft artists trained in Europe as well. Austrian-born architect Joseph Urban moved to the United States after a design commission for the Boston Opera in 1911 blossomed into his artistic directorship. Urban's work introduced the Viennese architectural style, his idiosyncratic taste for theatrically arranged interiors, and "Continental methods" of scenery construction. Among these new techniques were the painting of scenic drops on the floor instead of on vertical paint-frames; "pointillage," or the spattering of paint in order to provide visual interest under colored lights; and the use of portals or successively smaller frames upstage of the main proscenium (Larson 1989: 45).[2] Though Urban's contributions were later eclipsed by others, his conception of unity predates the writings of Jones: "The new art of the theatre . . . is a fusion of the pictorial with the dramatic" (Urban quoted in Macgowan 1917: 106).

Urban's notable designs include Broadway's *The Garden of Paradise* (1915), his operas for the Metropolitan Opera (1917–1933), and his several-times-yearly designs for Florenz Ziegfeld (1915–1931). Similarly, Livingston Platt, an American who had studied in Paris and Bruges, had been hired by the Boston Toy Theatre to emulate the Irish Players' spare scenic style. Like Urban, Platt emphasized that the role of the setting should be to support the author's intention and the performers' craft: "All superfluous details should be eliminated, and the settings . . . should suggest the mood of the play at a glance" (Ranck 1915: 84, 92).

From these beginnings, several collaborations between designers and director/producers ignited interest in the New Stagecraft. Jones and George Pierce Baker's *The Man Who Married a Dumb Wife* (1915), Urban and Ziegfeld's *Follies*, and Urban, Jones, and Percy MacKaye's "community masque" *Caliban of the Yellow Sands* (1916) shared similar styles. In Macgowan's formulation, these were "simplification," "suggestion," and "synthesis" or unity (Macgowan 1915). These designs used stage space economically; rather than arranging realistic props, the New Stagecraft simplified lines, abstracted stage objects, and emphasized multi-use design. Simplicity refocused attention on the actor and ornate decorations were used sparingly. Suggestion meant that the sweep of a line or the mood of a space became a significant design consideration. Macgowan, for example, claimed that "one candlestick can carry the whole spirit of the baroque" (ibid.) While designers cited economy and effect as main reasons for suggestion, emphasizing qualia of single objects also afforded designers an advantage as it placed design (and the designer) at the center of creative discussions.

Unity was often noted in its absence and failures of New Stagecraft design were often attributed to the lack of cohesion. The Arthur Hopkins-directed *Macbeth* (1921),

Figure 33.1 Design for *Macbeth* (1921), the banquet scene. Setting by Robert Edmond Jones.

designed by Jones and starring Lionel Barrymore, was one such production, poorly received by audiences despite its striking design. While Jones' ghostly arches and giant floating masks for the Witches suggested expressionism, Barrymore's Macbeth was "tedious and unimaginative . . . never for a moment simulating any natural emotion" (Macgowan 1921: 95). Critics "focused on Jones, lambasting him as the culprit for the evening" when the fault truly lay with the acting and direction being "out of key" with the design concept (Larson 1989: 63–4).

Simplicity and suggestion took root in the smaller art theatres where designers had few resources. New York-based outgrowths of the Little Theatre movement, such as the Provincetown Playhouse and the Washington Square Players, were an early proving ground for New Stagecraft designers. The Provincetown employed several in its first incarnation, notably Cleon Throckmorton for *The Emperor Jones* (1921), but the movement became firmly associated with the downtown theatre when the Provincetown was resurrected in 1924 under the "triumvirate" of Eugene O'Neill, Hopkins, and Jones. Jones' designs became part of its dually experimental and Broadway-oriented brand. For O'Neill's *Desire Under the Elms* (1924) and *The Fountain* (1925), he designed functional, multi-location sets that framed the costumed actor in compositions of scenery, gesture, and light (Pendleton 1977: 54–7).

Figure 33.2 Scene aboard "HMS Europa." Setting by Lee Simonson for Theatre Guild's production of *Roar China* (1930). (Photo by Vandamm Studio © Billy Rose Theatre Division, The New York Public Library for the Performing Arts.)

Meanwhile, Lee Simonson worked with the Washington Square Players, and helped found its successor company, the Theatre Guild. Simonson's realism utilized clean lines, simplified architectural interiors, and large-scale scenic statements, such as a proscenium-length viaduct (*Lilliom*, 1920), an expressionistically distorted courtroom for *The Adding Machine* (1923), and 15-foot, rear-projected shadows for the time-traveling epic *Back to Methuselah* (1922) (see Simonson 1943). Simonson differed markedly from Jones; his methods used an architectural approach and his writings praised economic reform through labor unions, while Jones fashioned himself as an independent bohemian poet-artist. Nonetheless, these disparities showed the New Stagecraft to be a field of many designers, not merely a single artist's new style.

As the New Stagecraft moved to Broadway, designers took on larger projects. Artists with name recognition and commercial associations dramatically accelerated public acceptance of designers as freelance artists. Urban's reputation for creating spacious, colorful interiors led him away from theatre toward architectural design, where businesses and wealthy individuals sought meticulous, opulent interiors (Mahnken and Mahnken 1963: 61). A similar grand scale animated the work of Norman Bel Geddes, whose unrealized plan for *The Divine Comedy* envisioned a five-story amphitheatre for hundreds of performers and thousands of spectators. Showings of these drawings and scale model photographs, especially at the International Exhibition of Theatre Art (toured 1922–1926), and the publication of the project in 1924 raised Bel Geddes' reputation to rival Urban and Jones. Later, Bel Geddes transformed the Century Theatre on Broadway into a European cathedral for Max Reinhardt's American premiere of *The Miracle* (1924) (see Larson 1989: 68, 76 and Essin 2012: 30–4, 150–3). Many of Bel Geddes' subsequent projects, particularly his 1932 memoir *Horizons* and his General Motors-sponsored *Futurama* exhibit at the 1939 World's Fair, persuasively demonstrated the potential commercial benefit of simplified design. Throughout the interwar period, both Urban and Bel Geddes became self-fashioned design celebrities; not solely artists of the theatre, these renaissance men applied the techniques of theatre art to problems of industry and modern living.

The Depression transformed the visionary dreams of many designers to the professionalism of a few. While production slowed somewhat after the 1929 crash, theatre production rebounded quickly. Several famous designers, including Jones, Simonson, and Throckmorton, maintained or increased their productivity during the thirties. The main reason for this was the consolidation of design work among a small number of professionals with name recognition and reputations for quality work (Simonson 1943: 65–73). Simultaneously, the contributions of design to successful runs were becoming well-known among producers, and designers conceived larger-budget productions. For example, Lee Simonson's designs for *Dynamo* (1929) and *Roar China* (1930) realistically rendered the dangers of industrialization and the history of colonial intervention in Asia. In these and other productions, the spare, suggestive aesthetic of the previous decade gave way to more elaborate spectacle, though still maintained the idea that the visual world should support a play's individual needs.

Two versions of a new spectacle-driven New Stagecraft emerged in the late thirties. On one hand, it was used to spread ideology. A younger generation of designers applied the principles of simplification and suggestion to political projects, notably in Mordecai Gorelik's work with the Group Theatre and Elia Kazan (*Golden Boy*, 1937; *Casey Jones*, 1938; *Thunder Rock*, 1939; *All My Sons*, 1947), and also in Howard Bay's designs for the Federal Theatre Project, epitomized in his cutaway apartment building for *One-Third of a Nation* (1938). By crafting designs that evoked the feel of a boxing ring, charging locomotive, tall lighthouse or backyard-as-graveyard, Gorelik placed actors inside a space that visually echoed his metaphorical interpretation of the play (Fletcher 2009: 1–12, 159–71). Bay's Federal Theatre Project work applied New Stagecraft aesthetics through restricted realism, ultimately emphasizing the role of the individual and the laborer (Essin 2012: 73–8, 125–8). On the other hand, the desire for large-scale spectacle prompted Jo Mielziner's signature "concentrated" or "poetic realism." *Winterset* (1935) was an early success; later he became known for work with postwar dramatists Arthur Miller (*Death of a Salesman*, 1949) and Tennessee Williams (*Cat on a Hot Tin Roof*, 1955). Mielziner felt that his main goal was an "essentialization of stage settings" accomplished by "accenting the most telling object in each scene" (Mielziner 1939).[3] He enveloped the playing space in the mood of a particular geography, such as the dock underneath the Brooklyn Bridge in *Winterset*, or the penned-in Loman house of *Salesman*. His use of shadows, scrims, and projected patterned lighting pioneered filmic transitions between scenes.

After World War II, the New Stagecraft lost its defining characteristics. Designers no longer strictly adhered to simplification and suggestion, and the concept of stage unity was widely practiced. The New Stagecraft's legacy is most strongly felt in the organizational changes it encouraged. Jones' protégé Donald Oenslager joined the faculty of the Yale School of Drama in 1925, where he constructed a design curriculum based on New Stagecraft ideas. Through his teaching the idea of the designer as an accomplished technician, creative artist, and interpreter of the playscript became standard. Similarly, scenic designers' affiliation with the scene painters' union, United Scenic Artists Local 829, delineated working processes and legal frameworks for the new profession. Simonson, Bay, and other union leaders protected designs as intellectual property, assured members fair contract wages, and provided a venue for designers to see themselves as freelancers within a larger profession. These developments shaped contemporary notions of theatrical design labor; many designers began to enjoy relative freedom and economic independence because the New Stagecraft had affirmed the design idea as inherently valuable.

The New Stagecraft was a uniquely American movement; it adapted European style for a commercially-oriented theatrical ecosystem that emphasized individual artistic contributions, reliance on the market, and heightened realism. It was also the first time that a group of designers attained celebrity status. It lives on through the words of artists, still cited in American design classrooms; Simonson explains that a set is a "plan for action" (1943: 48), and Jones sees the designer as an "artist of occasions," whose sets must "enhance the natural powers of the actor" (1941: 37, 69). So long as Craig, Appia, Jones, and Simonson inspire designers, the New Stagecraft will remain influential in American scenography. As a movement it introduced and institutionalized the designing workman-artist, an idea that has remained as powerful, if not more so, than any single sketch or photograph.

Notes

1 For discussion see Beard 2010 and Larson 1989: 45.

2 See also Mahnken and Mahnken 1963; Aronson 2000; and Anon 1915, "Viennese Art Wrought on the Shore of Boston Bay."

3 For discussion of "poetic realism" see Arnold Aronson 2000, "American Theatre in Context: 1945–Present," *The Cambridge History of American Theatre, Vol. 3: Post-World War II to the 1990s*, edited by Don B. Wilmeth and Christopher Bigsby, New York: Cambridge University Press, 95–6.

References

Anon 1915. "Viennese Art Wrought on the Shore of Boston Bay." *New York Times*, 7 November, X9.

Aronson, Arnold 2000. *Architect of Dreams: The Theatrical Vision of Joseph Urban*. New York: Miriam and Ira D. Wallach Art Gallery, Columbia University.

Beard, DeAnna Toten 2010. *Sheldon Cheney's Theatre Arts Magazine: Promoting a Modern American Theatre, 1916–1921*. Lanham, MD: Scarecrow.

Essin, Christin 2012. *Stage Designers in Early Twentieth-Century America: Artists, Activists, Cultural Critics*. New York: Palgrave Macmillan.

Fletcher, Anne 2009. *Rediscovering Mordecai Gorelik: Scene Design and the American Theatre*. Carbondale: Southern Illinois University Press.

Jones, Robert Edmond 1941. *The Dramatic Imagination: Reflections and Speculations on the Art of the Theatre*. New York: Duell, Sloan and Pierce.

Larson, Orville 1989. *Scene Design in the American Theatre from 1915–1960*. Fayetteville: University of Arkansas Press.

Macgowan, Kenneth 1914. "The New Stagecraft in America." *Century Magazine* 87 (January): 416–21.

Macgowan, Kenneth 1915. "The New Path of the Theatre." In *American Stage Designs: An Illustrated Catalogue*. New York: Bourgeois Galleries.

Macgowan, Kenneth 1917. "The Myth of Urban." *Theatre Arts Magazine* 1.3 (May): 99–109.

Macgowan, Kenneth 1921. "The Centre of the Stage." *Theatre Arts Magazine* V.2 (April): 91–112.

Mahnken, Harry and Janine Mahnken 1963. "Joseph Urban: An Appreciation." *Educational Theatre Journal* 15.1 (March): 55–61.

Mielziner, Jo 1939. "Is There Scenery in this Play?" *New York Times*, 22 October.

Pendleton, Ralph 1977. *The Theatre of Robert Edmond Jones*. Middletown, CT: Wesleyan University Press.

Ranck, Edwin Carty 1915. "An American Stage Wizard." *Theatre Magazine* XXII: 83, 92–3.

Simonson, Lee 1943. *Part of a Lifetime: Drawings and Designs, 1919–1940*. New York: Duell, Sloan, and Pierce.

34
BAUHAUS SCENOGRAPHY

Melissa Trimingham

"Since there was the urge to perform, a stage was available from the first day of the existence of the Bauhaus" (Neumann 1993: 155).[1] Are we still as surprised, I wonder, to hear this, as Tut Schlemmer's 1950s audiences were, when she lectured on the work of her late husband and Bauhaus stage director Oskar Schlemmer? Today the existence of the stage work is at least better known. Yet there still seems confusion about its importance in theatre history with some extravagant claims on the one hand: "Schlemmer's influence from this period has had such an enormous impact on the theatre of Western Europe and North America that it continues to be experienced in the theatre of today" (McKinney and Butterworth 2009: 25), and near total neglect on the other. Schlemmer and the Bauhaus stage receive scant attention, for example, in Collins and Nesbitt's reader in scenography (2010: 236). Why was there an active stage at the best-known experimental art school of the early twentieth century in Germany?

Scenography is identified by Sodja Lotker as "a discipline between visual arts and theatre" (Lotker 2011: 51), which is a good starting point to consider the Bauhaus.[2] Bauhaus scenography was an "all-encompassing visual-spatial construct" (Aronson 2005: 7), which potentially encompasses a range of creative activity that took place within the institution – not only the specifically theatrical and costumed "dance" work of Oskar Schlemmer, and the "mechanical" machine-driven stages made by students and staff, but also architecture that was the site for performances on and off the stage, the pervasive experimentation with light (Trimingham 2012), even the sounds that enlivened the reverberating spaces of the buildings, and the music propelling the parties that rocked until the small hours.

The Bauhaus theatre work reveals a huge variety of activities: early plays in Weimar full of mystical yearning and poetry by the Expressionist Lothar Schreyer;[3] the disrespectful Dadaesque sketches and humorous debunking by students, especially in the Weimar days, some of it no doubt directed at Schreyer's earnestness;[4] the intricately engineered (and sometimes rather unstable)[5] mechanical stages of Joost Schmidt, Kurt Schmidt, and others, work which continued throughout the Dessau period (see Trimingham 2011: 24); puppet performances and inventive puppet stages (see Michaud 1978: 95);[6] the extravagant architectural plans for immersive "Total Theatre" by Walter Gropius and others (Gropius and Wensinger [1925] [1961] 1996: 11–14 and 73–7); and "multi-sensory" theatre events planned (but not executed) by

László Moholy-Nagy[7] and Wassily Kandinsky.[8] Finally, Oskar Schlemmer's work on and off the Dessau Bauhaus stage (*The Triadic Ballet*[9] from 1922 onwards and *The Bauhaus Dances* 1929) as Master of the Stage Workshop was the most sustained and considered scenographic practice that took place in the Bauhaus. One or two Bauhaus artists might be described as stage designers at some point in their careers, but their Modernist stage design work[10] outside the Bauhaus walls is mainstream[11] compared with the radical activities – and, admittedly, aspirational dreamings – within it.

In this short chapter there is not the space to expand upon every aspect of stage work at the Bauhaus. Instead I shall concentrate on what I consider to be its central and most important idea for the twentieth and twenty-first century, that is, Bauhaus visions of affective, transformative space, and its realization both through actual theatre performance, and also through its social practices, shared spaces and communal celebrations. Performance in the Bauhaus was part of their larger social vision of art as life. This is the Bauhaus belief in (to risk an anachronism in the terminology) scenography and scenographers "not as a service to directors, but as equal artistic *co-creators* of the totality of the performance as well as being artists in their own right and *authors* of scenographic, installation and performance projects" (Lotker 2011: 51). Beginning with the large scale, frequent and all-encompassing parties and festivals at the Bauhaus at Weimar and then Dessau, and extending on a grand scale into the new Bauhaus Dessau building designed by Walter Gropius, Bauhauslers as "co-creators" and "authors" "lived" their space as something experienced, provisional and open to change, and not something merely looked at or looked into.

Space is articulated by the material form within it. Johannes Itten, as leader of the first arts foundation course ever, refused to confine designing artifacts to paper, and throughout the Bauhaus there was sheer determination to handle and work with real materials, extending to pulverizing and transforming junk and discarded objects (driven by poverty, they made virtue of necessity). These were the concerns of the Bauhaus community: a quasi-scientific desire to discover the "nuts and bolts" of both their art and their product design. Schlemmer translated this experienced materiality into stage work. His theatre did not pretend to be anything other than what it showed – objects in the handling, for example, bodies walking, materials exposed, light and dark experienced, shapes worn, surfaces and angles pitted against the human body. The theatre was not the same as the "theatricalist" (Aronson 2013: 91) approach of the Constructivists that exposed the stage as stage but nevertheless remained representative of another space (for example, Vsevolod Meyerhold's *Magnanimous Cuckold* 1922 using a bare stage). Instead Schlemmer stripped down, isolated and analyzed the physical elements of both the theatrical and illusionist (naturalistic) stage and turned these elements into the staged content itself: for example, short pieces that showed the dynamics of the stage curtain opening and shutting (*Curtain Play*, 1927); or the play, even wondrous discovery, involved in hesitantly climbing three stair treads (*Staircase Joke*, 1925); or the "hide and reveal" of the human figure in relation to screen flats (*Flats Dance*, 1929); or the affective presence of light and dark; and the drama of motion and stillness. He discovered the embodied meaning of form, stripped of mimetic function. In *The Bauhaus Dances* (1929) he dressed his performers in heavily padded body suits and full-head "neutral" masks, and engaged them in simple movements, sitting and standing, handling objects such as poles and hoops and cubes (importantly, seminal Bauhaus basic forms for artifact designs were the triangle, the circle and the square), developing into simple slapstick comic sketches (for example, *Gesture Dance*) so that mimetic and social function emerged by tiny degrees from a shared very basic vocabulary of the stage.

Much of Schlemmer's theatre attempted "non-dramatic events," to adopt Sodja Lotker's words (Lotker 2011: 52), in real time, where "all elements, verbal, visual, spatial, and gesticular, are equal narrators" (ibid.: 53). Lotker identifies theatre with the temporary and the fragile; but the stage's temporality and fragility, of which Schlemmer was well aware, were subsumed or at least de-emphasized at the Bauhaus because of the Modernist desire for unity, permanence and gestalt forms.[12] Schlemmer also explored the experience of the performer which few others did in or out of the Bauhaus. Schlemmer's use of costume, such as the padded suits but also the more extreme geometrical and beautiful costumes of *The Triadic Ballet* (1922), deliberately heightened the performer's experience of the space. In this way his work is an important transition point between stage scenography and performance art (see Trimingham 2011). Another transition point is the famous Bauhaus parties.

Parties at the Weimar Bauhaus were held on weekends, often out of town in village halls, and the student and staff community festivals (adapting a German tradition) further drew the Bauhaus together, centering on winter lanterns, autumn kites, and, later in Dessau, Christmas, and (an annual highpoint) Gropius' birthday. Like the practice of close handling and analysis of scarce materials that poverty nurtured, and that plenty might have swamped, the social spaces and special events grew from necessity. As an isolated community in conservative Weimar, the Bauhaus stuck together doing what they liked most – having fun making, adapting, gluing, sticking, sawing, sewing, and inventing. Marvelous costumes, kites and lanterns emerged from very little, and extraordinary music was made by Xanti Schawinsky, Werner Jackson, and others, forming the Bauhaus Band that later became a permanent fixture. In Dessau, Oskar Schlemmer took charge of the parties, the most memorable of which were the White Party (1926), where everyone had to wear something spotted, checkered or striped, the humorous Slogan Party (1927) where guests wore slogans to satirize – humorously – their institution, its staff and ideals (Schlemmer had a great sense of the comic), and, as a grand finale before he left the Bauhaus, the Metal Party in 1929 that filled the spaces with gleaming silver that reflected out through the windowed walls. An immersive and socially situated scenographic practice grew up around these events, direct precedents for affective *experience* displacing the art object, that became a feature of experimental performance later in the century in America. This transformative aspiration underpinned Allan Kaprow's 1950s installations that developed into Happenings (Kaprow 1965) and Schechner's 1960s environmental theatre (Schechner 1994). More recently it is evidenced in the changing curation of the Prague Quadrennial (Lotker 2011; 2015).[13]

Finally, "total theatre" was perhaps the most intoxicating vision of transformative space and the least materially realized. A smaller version of the "total theatre" aspirations was the mechanized technical theatre that Joost Schmidt pushed for at the new Dessau Bauhaus ("no chance!" said Schlemmer, "as I had anticipated" as there were no resources for such a stage [Schlemmer [1958] 1977: 83]); and besides, he had his own plans working within the practical resources and limits actually available, on a simple, small, framed stage space, with card and cloth and the human body.

Moholy-Nagy envisaged a total theatre that was way ahead of itself in terms of available technology, but surely inspired some aspects of the Bauhaus parties such as the long metal slide depositing guests into the Metal Party in 1926.[14] Transformation, as Lehmann reminds us, is at the heart of theatre (Lehmann 2006: 77, cited in Lotker 2011: 52). Moholy-Nagy was a truly creative spirit and we should not be put off by his uniform boiler suit. He loved technology, but he also loved technology as a tool for the imagination. He explored the aesthetics of "Produktion" rather than "Reproduktion," a difference that exactly parallels Currie and Ravenscroft's distinction between the creative and the recreative imagination (Currie and Ravenscroft 2002). Photography, one of Moholy-Nagy's favorite media, can either reproduce images as close as possible to what we are used to (and this of course parallels the mimetic stage rejected by the Bauhaus) or it can (like the Bauhaus stage) produce the wholly unexpected and new, fresh "Gestalten" (a coming together of forms) to stimulate and surprise. Moholy-Nagy believed "the man of a given period is most perfect when the functional mechanism of which he is composed . . . is being used to the limits of its biological capacity" (Moholy-Nagy [1925] 1969: 30). He experimented along the lines of challenging and expanding perception with the stage. He produced designs in the 1920s for a *Lichtrequisit* (*Light Prop* – "requisit" is the name for a theatrical stage "prop"), a machine designed to sit alone on stage and produce wondrous shadows and shapes transforming the audience's perception of the space (see Trimingham 2012: 201). We are reminded of Schlemmer's plea in his public lecture of 1927: "Let us open our eyes and expose our minds to the pure power of color and light" (Gropius and Wensinger [1925] [1961] 1996: 96). Moholy-Nagy's essay "Theater, Circus, Variety" (Moholy-Nagy [1925] 1969: 49–70) expands upon his immersive scenography with an extravagant vision of a theatre to assault the senses where the figure of man is "on an equal footing" with all other media, such as light and sound, and uses moveable platforms, drawbridges, elevators and even airplanes. The spectator in this total theatre was placed inside the action in a theatre with stages thrusting out "far into the auditorium" – a long way from Schlemmer's modest and entirely practical tiny framed stage at the Dessau Bauhaus. In the same book he employs innovative printing techniques to give a reader a physical experience that moves beyond the ocular, conveying his vision of the "Mechanized Eccentric" theatre. The pull-out section in full color is so long that the reader is forced to adjust physically in order to read it, especially if we wish to see it as a whole rather than in sections.[15] The Bauhaus visions of "total theatre" manifested in the architectural plans of Gropius, and Farkas Molnár, and Andreas Weininger's "Spherical Theatre" (Gropius and Wensinger [1925] [1961] 1996: 10–14, 73–7, 89). In 1926 Gropius collaborated with Piscator, hoping to create an infinity of stage space with his "Total Theatre,"[16] using back-wall projections among other devices. In the end however plans came to nothing.

Bauhaus influence on scenographies and performance spaces of the twentieth and twenty-first century are pervasive, mainly, I would argue, through the work of Bauhaus exiles, many scattered across the United States, who had experienced firsthand the affective power of space harnessed within the social and cultural context that was the Bauhaus. In a more profound sense Bauhaus opened up extraordinary possibilities we are still pursuing today: simply because they had the courage to dream them.

Notes

1 The Bauhaus was founded in Weimar Germany 1919 by architect Walter Gropius, who had a vision of a better world led by developing art and an art education more relevant to modern life. The Bauhaus ('building house') put architecture at the center of its aesthetic and cultural ideals and later, in 1925, it moved to a purpose-built building, designed in the high Modernist style by Gropius himself, in Dessau to the North. Thanks to hard "PR" and promotion work by its founder Gropius after his exile in the 1930s from Nazi Germany to the United States, and the seminal influence of Bauhaus thinking in American art schools by émigrés (such as László Moholy-Nagy at the New Bauhaus in Chicago), the Bauhaus established a reputation in the course of the twentieth century as the cradle of Modernist design and the "face of twentieth century" (Whitford 1994).

2 See Collins and Nisbet (2010: 140–3) for summary of ideas clustering around the "scenographic."
3 The stage work of Schreyer within the Weimar Bauhaus had has a bad press through the years, evaluation of it being dominated by the outright and universal rejection of his final performance at the Bauhaus of *Mondspiel* in 1923. Yet Schreyer's work was an integral part of the prevailing Expressionist and neo-Romantic ethos that dominated the Weimar Bauhaus and which intimately connected with Kandinsky's Expressionist "Bible," *On the Spiritual in Art*. It also needs to be evaluated within the wider context of the German Expressionist stage where Schreyer was a well-respected stage director at the Kampfbühne in Hamburg. His talents, integrity, personality and generosity of spirit in the face of Bauhaus rejection are formidable and, for him, the Bauhaus was only an episode in a long career.
4 See Schawinsky 1971 for a lively insight into students making and enjoying such work.
5 See the performance of Kurt Schmidt's *Mechanical Ballet* in 1923 that formed part of the Bauhaus Week, an international showcase of work where the stage mechanisms ran less than smoothly on the Jena Theatre stage (Trimingham 2011: 16).
6 Little has been written on the puppetry work at the Bauhaus and it crosses over into the so-called "mechanical" theatre work. See Trimingham 2011: 14–15.
7 See principally Moholy-Nagy's essay "Theater, Circus, Variety" in Gropius and Wensinger ([1925, 1961] 1996): 49–70.
8 Kandinsky wrote a number of Expressionist stage scripts, the most famous of which is *Yellow Sound* 1912, none of which were performed at the Bauhaus. Mystical, highly visual, without story or characters, they conform to his stage vision as laid out in "On Stage Composition" in *The Blue Rider Almanac* (Kandinsky 1912: 257–64). He continued to theorize: see "Abstract Synthesis on the Stage" 1923 in Lindsay and Vergo [1982] 1994, 504–5.
9 *The Triadic Ballet* was not in fact a Bauhaus production but funded by Schlemmer himself, causing him much personal hardship; but the Bauhaus, particularly Gropius, liked to claim it as its own. It formed the centerpiece of the performances in the 1923 Bauhaus Week in Weimar.
10 Kandinsky designed Modest Mussorgsky's *Pictures at an Exhibition* for a performance at the Friedrichtheater, Dessau, 1929. Schlemmer himself worked frequently as a stage and costume designer in major theatres in Germany (see Scheper 1988: 391–2), but he always felt these designs were a compromise with mainstream theatre, describing the work as "cooperation with the stage in its present form – productions in which he [the stage designer] places himself at the service of writers and actors in order to give to their work the appropriate optical form. It is a rare case when his intentions coincide with those of the author" (Gropius and Wensinger [1925, 1961] 1996: 31). The trend in stage design even for mainstream productions was commonly less naturalistic than we perhaps imagine: see Trimingham 2011: 67.
11 Schlemmer's stage designs for example, like those of the Constructivists in Russia and however abstract in appearance, essentially conform to the fragmentary stage of illusion (Aronson 2011: 26–7), that is, to the "symbolic and emblematic" design that is the title of this section.
12 See Dorita Hannah on the architectural and especially Modernist architectural quest for permanence, unity and stability (2011: 59). She later quotes Nietzsche, which is apposite in connection with Oskar Schlemmer, who was well aware of the differing pulls of the disruptive "Dionysian" dancing body on stage and the supposed static "Apollonian" certainties of art and architecture: "The ecstatic sensorium of the performing body displaces the more static ocularcentricism of architecture" (Hannah 2011: 60).
13 Especially in *The Heart of the PQ* (2003) and the installation *Intersection: Intimacy and Spectacle* (2011) (Lotker 2011: 48–9, 55).
14 I am indebted to Torsten Blume, Director of the Bauhaus Stage Workshop, for this insight into Moholy-Nagy's influence.
15 The difficulties of printing his "pullout" section no doubt led to its omission in the 1961 English language version of the book *The Theatre of the Bauhaus*. The plan for simultaneous action is laid out in four columns: Form and Movement in columns one and two, spectacular contrasting light effects in column three and music/sound in column four. This "score" downgrades the human performer to a filmed brief appearance towards the end. Moholy-Nagy is here attempting to find an alternative to then current innovative but human-centered (and verbally dominated) "eccentric" (illogical) performances of Dada and the Futurists.
16 See Christopher Baugh 2005: 159–61, who contextualizes Bauhaus architectural plans for theatres within widespread early twentieth century aspirations to affect the audience through the total built space and the use of technology.

References

Aronson, Arnold 2005. *Looking into the Abyss: Essays on Scenography*. Ann Arbor: University of Michigan Press.

Aronson, Arnold 2011. "Desire and Décor." In *Space and Desire: Scenographic Strategies in Theatre, Art and Media*, edited by Thea Brejzek, Wolfgang Greisenegger and Lawrence Wallen, 20–9. Zurich: University of the Arts.

Aronson, Arnold 2013. "Time and Space on the Stage." In *Performance Research* 18.3: 84–94.

Baugh, Christopher 2005. *Theatre, Performance and Technology: The Development of Scenography in the Twentieth Century*. Basingstoke: Palgrave.

Collins, Jane and Andrew Nesbitt (Eds) 2010. *Theatre and Performance Design: A Reader in Scenography*. London and New York: Routledge.

Currie, Gregory and Ian Ravenscroft 2002. *Recreative Minds*. Oxford: Oxford University Press.

Gropius, Walter and Arthur Wensinger (Eds) [1925, 1961] 1996. *The Theatre of the Bauhaus*. Baltimore, MD, and London: John Hopkins University Press.

Hannah, Dorita 2011. "Building Babel." In *Space and Desire, Scenographic Strategies in Theatre, Art and Media*, edited by Thea Brejzek, Wolfgang Greisenegger and Lawrence Wallen, 58–67. Zurich: University of the Arts.

Kandinsky, Wassily [1912, 1982] 1994. "The Blue Rider Almanac." In *Kandinsky, Complete Writings in Art*, edited by K. C. Lindsay and P. Vergo, 229–85. Cambridge, MA: Da Capo Press.

Kaprow, Allan 1965. *Assemblages, Environments and Happenings*. New York: Abrams.

Lindsay K. C. and P. Vergo (Eds) [1982] 1994. *Kandinsky, Complete Writings in Art*. Cambridge, MA: Da Capo Press.

Lehmann, Hans-Thies 2006. *Postdramatic Theatre*, translated by Karen Jürs-Munby. London and New York: Routledge.

Lotker, Sodja Zupanc 2011. *The Prague Quadrennial at the Intersection: Nostalgia for Desire or: Perverted by Theatre as Well as Some Gaps*, edited by Thea Brejzek, Wolfgang Greisenegger and Lawrence Wallen, 46–55. Zurich: University of the Arts.

Lotker, Sodja Zupanc 2015. "Expanding Scenography: Notes on the Curatorial Developments of the Prague Quadrennial." *Theatre and Performance Design* 1.1/2: 7–16.

Maholy-Nagy, László [1925] 1969. *Painting, Photography, Film*, translated by Janet Seligman. London: Lund Humphries.

McKinney, Joslin and Philip Butterworth 2009. *The Cambridge Introduction to Scenography*. Cambridge: Cambridge University Press.

Michaud, Eric 1978. *Théâtre au Bauhaus (1919–1929)*. Lausanne: L'Age d'Homme.

Neumann, Ekhard 1993. *Bauhaus and Bauhaus People: Personal Opinions and Recollections of Former Bauhaus Members and their Contemporaries*, translated by Eva Richter and Alsa Lorman. New York: Van Nostrand Reinhold.

Schawinsky, Xanti 1971. "From Bauhaus to Black Mountain." *The Drama Review* (*TDR*), 15.3: 30–44.

Schechner, Richard 1994. *Environmental Theater*. New York: Applause.

Scheper, Dirk 1988. *Oskar Schlemmer, Das Triadische Ballett und die Bauhausbühne*. Berlin: Akademie de Kunste.

Schlemmer, Oskar [1958] 1977. *Letters and Diaries of Oskar Schlemmer*, edited by Tut Schlemmer, translated by Krishna Winston. Evanston, IL: Northwestern University Press.

Trimingham, Melissa 2011. *The Theatre of the Bauhaus: the Modern and Postmodern Stage of Oskar Schlemmer*. Routledge, New York and London.

Trimingham, Melissa 2012. "bauhaus lighthouse: der bau als bühne das bühne als bau." In *Bauhaus: Art as Life* [Barbican Art Gallery exhibition catalogue], 200–4. Köln: Koenig Books.

Whitford, Frank 1994. *The Face of the Twentieth Century* (DVD). BBC/RM Arts.

Modern and contemporary design

Is it possible to provide an overview of scenography today? In the mid-twentieth century there were a series of books edited by René Hainaux, beginning with *Stage Design Throughout the World Since 1935* (1956), and continuing with volumes covering 1950–60, 1960–70, and 1970–75. In 2012 Peter McKinnon and Eric Fielding picked up the ball with *World Scenography 1975–1990*, a second volume covering 1990–2005, and another on the way. There are other publications from around the world focusing on individual countries. These invaluable resources consist mostly of production photos with some sketches and renderings and identifications of relevant creative personnel and some contextualizing essays. But, inevitably, for every production or designer that is included, there are many more that are absent. The Prague Quadrennial, that now has representation from over 60 countries, still has gaps since economics, politics, or simple lack of organization has prevented some countries from participating. Among those that do exhibit, there are a host of decisions that result in, at best, a selective view of what is happening scenographically. So the answer, of course, is that one can provide a window onto the international scenographic landscape, but it is, to borrow the parlance of the box office, a partial or obstructed view.

And so it is with this final section. It essentially looks at some major sites of scenographic practice in the post-World War Two era. To quote Andrew Marvell (though for obviously different ends), "Had we but world enough, and time" – and in this case, pages – this could be more inclusive. But, despite the omissions, I believe that a reader of the following section will come away with a reasonable sense of what has been happening in modern scenographic practice in the past 75 years or so in many different parts of the world, particularly in places or genres where some of the most innovative work has been occurring.

35

METAPHOR, MYTHOLOGY, AND METONYMY

Russian scenography in the Yeltsin era

Amy Skinner

> To the casual observer the exhibit of the Soviet Union seemed creative and playful, if a bit puzzling. But more than any other, it was a reflection of internal politics and economics. The Soviet Union used to dominate the PQ . . . Past exhibits displayed the works of Kochergin, Levental, Barkhin, Borovski, Lider and Vasiliev – some of the best-known designers in the world. This year the Soviet exhibit consisted of a room carved out of cardboard by Irina Akimova, a young scenographer who works for the M. N. Yermolova Theatre in Moscow . . . It was cheap, easy to transport, and when the PQ was over the exhibit could be thrown away.
>
> *(Aronson 1993: 67–8)*

The Soviet Union's contribution to the 1991 Prague Quadrennial of Stage Design (PQ) was, as Arnold Aronson notes, a clear reflection of the tumultuous political changes the country experienced in the late 1980s and early 1990s.[1] The Gorbachev reforms (notably the principles of glasnost and perestroika, "openness" and "restructuring," respectively) provided the context for stage design during the Yeltsin presidency (1991–1999).[2] Akimova's design for the PQ reflects the social and political flux of this historical moment, and, in its conscious use of cardboard as a material placed in situ, fundamentally embodies the notion of construction, or even "re-structuring," within its visual idiom. In its departure from previous Russian PQ exhibits, Akimova's disposable room seems to embody a culture searching for a new, functioning aesthetic in a changing political climate, an apt metaphor for Russian design during the shift from the Soviet to post-Soviet eras.

From Soviet to post-Soviet: practitioner contexts

The relationship between Soviet and post-Soviet Russian design is a complex one. The scenographers of the 1970s and 1980s that Aronson sees as dominating the PQ prior to 1991 continued to practice during the Yeltsin era. Sergei Barkhin and David Borovsky, whose work forms the mainstay of analysis in this chapter, began their careers during the 1960s and rose to prominence in the 1970s, during what Birgit Beumers identifies as a period of theatrical "stagnation," paralleling the extended political *zastoi* under Leonid Brezhnev, a result of reactionary cultural policies following the Thaws of the previous two decades (Beumers 1999: 372). Alma Law's survey of the developments in Russian theatre during the early 1980s highlights the on-going control of theatre by political forces during the late Soviet period:

> Theatre was the first of the arts to be targeted for criticism following Leonid Brezhnev's death in November 1982, and it continues to be the focus of a great deal of attention as first the Andropov, and now the Chernenko government strive to bolster the role of the Communist Party in controlling the arts. As Konstantin Chernenko stated in a recent speech, 'Artistic creation outside of politics does not exist.'
>
> *(Law 1984: 1)*

The complex, metaphorical scenographies that are seen in the work of Russian designers during the 1970s and 1980s are a clear legacy of the Soviet period, where the necessities of censorship led to the emergence of specific modes of expression. Designs that sit in tension with the performance text, or provide additional levels of meaning to the production, exploit the power of scenography as a tool of visual communication under the Soviet government. These aesthetic metaphors can be traced back to the early Soviet period, for example, in the use of a revolving stage to pull the world out from beneath the characters' feet in Meyerhold's production of *The Mandate* (1924).

The metaphorical scenographies of the late Soviet period are characterized by a clarity in visual idiom, an interest in the material qualities of the space or costumes (for example, in Kochergin's felt settings for *The Inspector Recounting*) and a striking use of atmospheric color (in Alexander Vassiliev's designs for the ballet). The artists' concerns are perhaps summarized in this description of Daniil Lider's work:

> Active and metaphoric imagery and deep philosophical interpretation of the subject are characteristic of [Lider's] work, as well as the polyphonies of textures and volumes and the functioning of space.
>
> *(Meyer-Dinkgräfe 2000: 178)*

In 1985, Gorbachev introduced perestroika. Although his intentions were reformist, perestroika was, ultimately, to bring down the CPSU and subsequently the Soviet Union from within. The uncertainty, and in some senses disillusionment, of this period was felt keenly in the theatres, as Anatoly Smeliansky observes:

> The period of delight and euphoria which began with Gorbachev's 'thaw' very quickly became one of decay, disintegration and disappointment . . . The new state took shape amidst chaos . . . The police state collapsed, but from the ruins a very strange social phenomenon arose, unparalleled in history (just as the very process of moving from socialism to capitalism itself has no precedents).
>
> *(Smeliansky 1999: 383)*

However, as Smeliansky goes on to note, the post-Soviet period in Russian theatre – and particularly in Russian stage design – is not without innovation or merit. Much of this innovative practice, it can be argued, related exactly to the problem that Smeliansky articulates, that is, to the negotiation of process without precedents, where the relationship between citizen and state, and between performance and society, has undergone a fundamental shift. Smeliansky discusses the "transcendent" potential of the Russian theatre in the Soviet era, which in "circumstances of relative freedom . . . lost its special significance" (Smeliansky 1999: 384), and concludes that: "[w]ith the disappearance of Soviet transcendent theatre came the difficult birth of another language, another method of relating to the public, another type of theatre as yet unnamed" (386).

Smeliansky associates this process with directors (Fomenko, Ginkas, Dodin, and Vasiliev), but the resistance implied by transcendence also parallels the resistant or transcendent potential of scenographic space in eras of strict textual censorship. As the 1980s and 1990s in Russia are characterized by political and social flux, the question of scenographic idiom is a vital one: to borrow Smeliansky's phrase, the Russian designers of the 1990s were operating within a "scenography as yet unnamed."

"A scenography as yet unnamed"

In the context of social or political flux, shifts can also occur in the key idiomatic devices used in design practice (that is, the devices that link modes of scenographic representation to individual cultural frames). The utility of metaphor as a device is that it functions in relative freedom, and the stage can use metaphor to construct ideological relationships that are particularly bound to the context of the production itself, speaking indirectly to the world outside the theatre. More problematic are other sorts of visual relationships, for example, structures using mythology or metonymy, where there is a reliance on stable and shared cultural codes. The undermining of these codes, for example in a culture in flux, allows the designer the unique opportunity to engage not only with the scenographic deployment of these structures, but with their re-negotiation or debate within the theatrical frame.

What follows is the analysis of two productions, exploring the operation of mythological and metonymic structures in the context of 1990s Russian scenography. The first is David Borovsky's design for Nikolai Erdman's satire *The Suicide*, directed by Yury Lyubimov at the Taganka Theatre (1990). A production of the perestroika era, Lyubimov and Borovsky use the flux of the historical moment and the abolition of theatre control (1987) to explore a text whose performance history was, until the 1980s, virtually non-existent. The Taganka staging uses Erdman's text to engage in an extended reflection not only on the Soviet era, but on the life of the playwright, who had a close personal association with the theatre, and on the fate of Meyerhold, who staged the ill-fated original production. The staging is suffused with political and theatrical mythologies, enhanced and debunked in equal measure.

The second analysis deals with a later, post-Soviet, production: Sergei Barkhin's work on Ostrovsky's *The Storm* at the Moscow Theatre of the Young Spectator, directed by Genrietta Yanovskaya (1997). Ostrovsky's text is part of the Russian classical canon, with an extensive performance history, particularly under the Soviet regime (see, for example, Gunn 2014). Reading Barkhin's work from the perspective of metonymic structures reveals how the scenographer creates a network of internal metonymic relationships in the design that have their own idiomatic function. The scenographic choices in both productions explore the implications of a society in flux, and the results of imposing what Smeliansky calls "freedom . . . from above" (Smeliansky 1999: 383).

Unmaking mythologies: David Borovsky and *The Suicide*

David Borovsky's career includes association with the best-known theatres in Moscow and St. Petersburg, from the Bolshoi Dramatic Theatre to the Maly, the Moscow Art Theatre, and, particularly, the Taganka.[3] His collaboration with the Taganka's artistic director Yury Lyubimov formed what, for Beumers, was "a perfect symbiosis between director and designer" (Beumers 1999: 374), as:

> Borovsky only works with natural materials and authentic objects, an approach which ideally matched Lyubimov's concept that there should be nothing "false" on stage . . . Lyubimov and Borovsky created a central metaphor, which concentrated the contents of the literary material in a formal image . . . Borovsky condensed the central idea in Lyubimov's often overflowing theatricality into a straightforward image, without which the production would not work.
>
> *(Beumers 1999: 374)*

Borovsky's designs for *The Suicide* demonstrate this use of the "straightforward image" to elucidate a complex dramaturgy, which combined Erdman's play with episodes from his life. The central visual motif not only directs the spectator's attention towards specific parts of the stage, shaping their phenomenological engagement with the production, but also points their intellectual attention towards the key themes: questions of mythologies, lineages, and their provocative ability to connect past and present. Beumers describes the main element of Borovsky's design which "comprised a curtain with Karl Marx's face printed on it . . . the curtain was never fully raised, but only by a third so that both the actors and Marx's eyes remained visible" (Beumers 1997: 65).

The prominent placement of Marx's face has the effect of turning the scenography into an additional character in the production, reminiscent of Meyerhold's spinning wheels in *The Magnanimous Cuckold* (1922):[4]

> Marx's eyes could be lit up at the mention of revolution, socialism, leadership, state, or government. Goloshchapov pointed to Marx, expecting his name to be Podsekalnikov's answer to his question 'Who do you blame?'; Podsekalnikov blamed Theodor Hugo Schultz, the author of the wretched manual 'Teach yourself to Play the Horn.'
>
> *(Beumers 1997: 65)*[5]

Marx's light-up eyes provide a commentary on the action: he appears to be watching, engaged with what is taking place. He is a pseudo-spectator, facing the auditorium, meeting the stares of the audience. His position, however, is highly ambivalent and he is not simply a mirror for response: the design seems to ask the question, in the throes of the collapse of the Soviet system, should the audience's eyes light up along with those of Marx? The interaction of the performers with Marx further establishes the complexity of his role: the playful, almost mocking, exchange between Goloshchapov, an intellectual whose desire is to see the political system blamed for (what he presumes will be) the suicide of Podsekalnikov, and Podsekalnikov himself, a man who simply wants to erase his troubles by learning to play the horn, uses the physical presence of Marx on stage to embed Erdman's carefully crafted satire into a concrete image. Marx's other contribution to the production, as noted by Smeliansky, is that the actors remove suicide notes from his beard (Smeliansky 1999: 391): Marx's role in Podsekalnikov's dilemma is both made explicit and simultaneously undermined by a sense of playful irreverence. Borovsky embeds the political flux of the moment into the stage space through the omnipresent face of Marx and his liminal status as character and spectator.

The debunking of Marx is a very obvious exposure of the mechanics of mythology, what Barthes calls the "falsely obvious" (Barthes 2000: 11). One device that Beumers identifies – the only partial raising of the curtain leading to Marx's omnipresence on stage – inflects this mythological approach further, suggesting an alternative mythology to that of Marxist politics. When the curtain is half raised, the scene played beneath it appears to replace Marx's mouth. The scenes appear to issue from Marx, being spoken – or perhaps spat-out – by Marxism's founding father. The image is a powerful collaged moment, in which the play text is simultaneously "spoken" by Erdman (who is present on stage as a character in the production) and Marx, providing a counterpoint visual answer to Goloshchapov's question of blame. The power of words is a key theme in Lyubimov's production, which includes voice-over readings of Meyerhold's correspondence with Molotov, and of Stalin's letter to Stanislavsky banning the performance of Erdman's play; in this context, the scenography frames Marx as provocatively both a silent, painted figure and a visual mouthpiece.

Set against the use of Marxist myth, there is an alternative mythology in operation in Borovsky's scenography, that of the theatrical past. Beumers describes the opening of the second act:

> The second part began in the foyer, where Meyerhold's portrait (displayed alongside those of Stanislavsky, Brecht and Vakhtangov) was taken off the wall and carried onto the stage. Erdman appeared, this time in exile and remembering his work at the Meyerhold Theatre.
>
> *(Beumers 1997: 64)*

The removal of Meyerhold's portrait from the foyer and its placement on stage is a clearly symbolic placement of Meyerhold, and Meyerholdian theatre, at the center of the production. A new face, and a new mythology, are placed on stage: that of Meyerhold and the early Revolutionary theatre. Borovsky's design begins to mediate between these mythologies: of the (nearly collapsed) Soviet state, the ideals of Marxism, the exiled playwright, and finally, the avant-garde innovator who attempted, for much of his career, to appear himself as the mediator between Marx and the theatre.

This visual reference to Meyerhold suggests a complex relationship between late Soviet design and the giants of the early-twentieth-century avant-garde. For Smeliansky, it is this tension between the context of Erdman's writing and the strictures of the Soviet period that problematize the Taganka production, whose playing style was reminiscent of the old theatre, but in a new, more liberal, setting:

> If we are to believe the journalist from *Soviet Culture* who reported on rehearsals of *The Suicide*, the director was begging actors to play it so that 'they would be closed down.' But there was no-one around to close them down.
>
> *(Smeliansky 1999: 391)*

The identification of mythologies in Borovsky's design highlights a similar pattern: by 1990, the aesthetic devices that were necessary under the Soviet regime were beginning to feel out of step with current theatrical and political developments. Although the power of the early Soviet theatre was undeniable, it did not function as a replacement for the mythologies of Leninist-Marxism. The theatre needed new representational systems to respond to the moment of perestroika, which was soon to give way to closure of the CPSU and the collapse of the Soviet Union.

Making metonymies: Sergei Barkhin and *The Storm*

Like Borovsky, Barkhin has collaborated with significant Russian theatres including the Taganka, Moscow Art Theatre and Bolshoi, and, since the 1980s, has worked regularly with Kama Ginkas and Genrietta Yanovskaya at the Moscow Theatre of the Young Spectator. Barkhin's designs for *The Storm* demonstrate a sense of narrative and light in his white-on-black drawings that embed the sketches with theatricality. In contrast with other sketches for productions at the Theatre of the Young Spectator, however, drawings for *The Storm* indicate a different and more diffuse sense of focus in the performance space.[6] Figure 35.1, a "sketch-illustration" for *The Storm*, indicates a highly detailed setting in which it is difficult to identify a single focal point. Barkhin's design contrasts with the strong visual focus created by Borovsky for *The Suicide*: in this design, the viewer's eye is scattered across and through the stage space, reflecting the placement of the audience on stage during the performance. John Freedman describes the design:

> Sergei Barkhin's eclectic, suggestive and highly theatrical set surrounds and towers above us with a rain-making machine situated high up in the flies, thunder sheets hanging on the walls and entire communities of traditional Russian clay dolls scattered everywhere. The Volga, with a birch tree bearing painted eggs standing nearby, is depicted as a tin trough set into a strip of real dirt. It all suggests a play you've never heard of.
>
> *(Freedman 1998: 45–6)*

Figure 35.1 Sergei Barkhin: sketch for *The Storm* (1997); Moscow Theatre of the Young Spectator (MTYUZ). Director G. Yanovskaya. (Courtesy of Sergei Barkhin.)

Photographs of the production, alongside Freedman's description and Barkhin's sketch, indicate that the design comprises three referential spheres. Barkhin triangulates these in order to create a stage space in which associations can be made between the different spheres, their performance function, and the worlds outside the production to which they refer. The first sphere is that of the theatre itself. Barkhin's design emphasizes the functional features of the performance space: the sketch shows clearly stage lights and flies; the photographs of the production indicate the visibility of these features in performance. Barkhin adds features of the design that collapse into the theatre architecture through their formal similarity: in Figure 35.2, the spiral staircase, raised platform and two sewing machines blend with the black, metallic structures of the theatre flies, and it is difficult to tell which elements are permanent features of the theatre building.

The second referential sphere is that of folk Russia – seen clearly in Freedman's reference to the traditional clay dolls, but also in the eggs hung on the birch tree and in the costumes of the characters in Barkhin's sketch. What makes these elements stand out, and unites them across the performance space, is Barkhin's choice of colors and materials: unlike the structural elements, the folk references are vividly colored and make use of textured and natural materials (clay, dirt, wood). The final referential sphere is the storm, a self-evidently metaphorical feature of Ostrovsky's writing hanging over the characters throughout the play, which Barkhin makes manifest in the two

Figure 35.2 Photograph of *The Storm*. (Courtesy Sergei Barkhin.)

shapes suspended over the performance space. These resemble lightning bolts, whose multiple planes give a sense of crushed perspective, and whose distorted windows also recall a house spinning in a tornado.

The points at which the separate referential spheres connect demonstrate the potential of Barkhin's design from a metonymic perspective. There are some straightforward metonymic devices in operation – for example, in the clay dolls representative of Russian folk culture. However, beyond this simple use of metonymy, Barkhin appears to embody an additional, self-referential, metonymic network. Metonymy functions in two stages: firstly, establishing an association between different ideas; secondly, enacting the substitution of one element of the association for the other. The creation of a scenographic idiom with a diverse focus across three referential spheres allows for associations to emerge within the performance space: the overlaps between the theatre, folk Russia, and the storm creates space for associations to emerge that perhaps would not emerge outside of the theatrical context.

The enactment of substitution occurs, for example, in the use of a rain-making machine and thunder sheets. These are, in effect, already operating as synecdoche (arguably a form of metonym) in that they use a small element of a thunderstorm to represent the idea of a storm as a whole. However, their simultaneous participation in the referential sphere of theatricality allows for them to also function as a metonym for theatrical illusionism. The combination of the clay dolls and the sewing machines, where the contrast between the colored dolls and the dark machines creates a false shadow effect (the machines can be read as the distorted shadows of the dolls) is also an interesting example of the association–substitution relationship, where cause and effect is undermined by a form of visual illusion. This makes explicit the relationship between the colorful folk elements and the darker structural features, emphasizing the locatedness of Ostrovsky's folk culture in the current theatrical moment. The alienation effect of the complex visual schema in Barkhin's design, what Freedman refers to as "suggesting a play you've never heard of," is partly achieved through this association and substitution relationship between the three referential spheres of the design.

From unnamed scenography to Golden Triga

Perhaps what emerges most clearly from Borovsky and Barkhin's work on these productions is the communicative and aesthetic potential of a "scenography as yet unnamed." In the negotiation of the transition from a Soviet to post-Soviet context, the social, political and economic flux opens Russian design to its own process of restructuring, in which "freedom . . . from above" becomes freedom from within and the relationship between representational modes and reality is up for debate. The mythological paradigm of the "falsely obvious" becomes a battleground in *The Suicide*, and, in *The Storm*, the possible function of metonymic devices emerges as a self-referential system that can create, as well as reflect, relationships between ideas in reality. At the 1995 PQ, Russia exhibited four artists, including Barkhin; in 1999, at the end of the Yeltsin era, nine artists were included. Eight years later, the Russian exhibition entitled "Our Chekhov: Twenty Years On" was dedicated to the memory of David Borovsky, who died in 2006. The exhibition won the Golden Triga: Russia's scenographies, it seems, did not remain unnamed for long, but perhaps the opportunity to become nameless allowed Russian design to encounter, survive, and enhance an unprecedented moment of political and representational flux.

Notes

1 More information on the Prague Quadrennial and archives of national exhibits can be found on the PQ website: www.pq.cz/en/ (accessed 29 January 2016).

2 Mikhail Gorbachev became General Secretary of the Communist Party of the Soviet Union (CPSU) in 1985, and served as the final head of state for the USSR from 1988 to 1991. His policies of glasnost and perestroika were intended to reform the Soviet system from within, tackling corruption and stagnation through instigating political and economic reform. Richard Sakwa outlines the progression of perestroika towards the eventual collapse of the CPSU and Soviet Union: "in the space of six years [perestroika] moved from hesitant attempts to rationalise the system, through a phase of liberalisation to a democratisation phase that began to transform the society and polity but which culminated in a final stage of disintegration" (Sakwa 1993, 1996: 3).

3 Borovsky was Chief Artist at the Taganka from 1973 to 1984, and continued to collaborate with the theatre into the 1990s.

4 The wheels used in Lyubov Popova's designs for *The Magnanimous Cuckold* responded to the action, providing an additional layer of commentary on the mood of the protagonist, Bruno. As Bruno became more frustrated with his personal situation, the wheels turned faster (see Braun 1998: 178).

5 *The Suicide* concerns the fate of Semyon Podsekalnikov, an ordinary man who makes an idle suicide threat to his wife. As news of Podsekalnikov's threat spreads, various parties begin to petition him to buy space in his suicide note (working on the premise that, in Stalin's Russia, the only ones who can safely speak their minds are the dead). Podsekalnikov, who has no intention of committing suicide (much preferring the idea of learning the horn and making his fortune), is nonetheless caught up in the enthusiasm of others, and ends up having to hide in his coffin, staging his own death. When Podsekalnikov's deception is revealed, and just as those who have paid for his suicide note surround him demanding their satisfaction, news arrives that another man, Petunin, has killed himself – because "Podsekalnikov is right. Why live?" (Erdman 1979: 90).

6 Compare, for example, the black and white sketches for *The Storm* with those for *Hedda Gabler* (1987) or *A Taste of Honey* (2003), in which chiaroscuro is used to create clear points of visual focus (see barkhin.ru for images from these productions).

References

Aronson, A. 1993. "The 1991 Prague Quadrennial." *The Drama Review*, 37 (1): 61–73.

Barthes, R. 2000. *Camera Lucida*, translated by R. Howard. London: Vintage Classics.

Beumers, B. 1997. *Yury Lyubimov at the Taganka Theatre (1964–1994)*. Amsterdam: Harwood Academic Press.

Beumers, B. 1999. "The Thaw and After." In *A History of Russian Theatre*, edited by R. Leach and V. Borovsky, 358–81. Cambridge: Cambridge University Press.

Braun, E. 1998. *Meyerhold: A Revolution in Theatre*. London: Methuen.

Erdman, N. 1979. *The Suicide*, translated by P. Tegel. New York: Samuel French Inc.

Freedman, J. 1998. *Moscow Performances II: The 1996–1997 Season*. Amsterdam: Harwood Academic Publishers.

Gunn, W. D. 2014. "'Back to Ostrovsky!' and 'Forward to Socialist Realism': Stanislavsky's *Ardent Heart* and the Staging of Ideology at the Moscow Art Theatre." In *The Routledge Companion to Stanislavsky*, edited by R. A. White, 52–66. Abingdon and New York: Routledge.

Law, A. 1984. *Soviet Theatre in Transition: The Politics of Theatre in the 1980s*. Washington, DC: Woodrow Wilson International Center for Scholars; Kennan Institute Occasional Paper Series #195, 1985, PDF 31 pages. Available online at:. www.wilsoncenter.org/publication/soviet-theatre-transition-1985 (accessed 29 January 2016).

Meyer-Dinkgräfe, D. 2000. *Who's Who in Contemporary World Theatre*. London and New York: Routledge.

Sakwa, R. 1993, 1996. *Russian Politics and Society*. London and New York: Routledge.

Smeliansky, A. 1999. "Russian Theatre in the Post-Communist Era." In *A History of Russian Theatre*, edited by R. Leach and V. Borovsky, translated by S. Holland, 382–406. Cambridge: Cambridge University Press.

36
TRANSFORMATION OF FORMS
Polish scenography after 1945

Dominika Łarionow

TRANSLATED BY KATARZYNA GUCIO

If Polish aesthetics of the latter half of the twentieth century has left its mark on the history of theatre, it is mainly owing to two important artists, Jerzy Grotowski (1933–1999) and Tadeusz Kantor (1915–1990). Grotowski founded *Teatr 13 rzędów* (Theatre of 13 Rows; renamed *Teatr-Laboratorium 13 Rzędów* – Laboratory Theatre of 13 Rows in 1962), lauded for productions such as *Apocalypsis cum figuris* (1969–1973) and *Książę Niezłomny* (*The Constant Prince*, 1965). Kantor started his own experimental theatre, Cricot 2, in 1955, best known for *Umarła klasa* (*The Dead Class*, 1975) and *Wielopole, Wielopole* (1980). The two artists significantly altered traditional approaches to stage space, particularly the relationship of the spectator and performer, as well as transforming the dramaturgical structure of a performance. They both redefined the function of the actor in a spectacle, although they did so through opposing theories. Grotowski saw the individual ("the total actor") as the principal agent in his concept of poor theatre. For Kantor, the focal point of art was the personality of the director, whom he regarded as the main creator. In Cricot 2, actors were often placed alongside mannequins and, while they were crucial to the performance, of course, they remained subordinate to the overall concept of the work. The theatres founded by Kantor and Grotowski operated outside the formal mainstream of Polish art, in a niche created by the political system.

Between 1945 and the beginning of the new millennium, Polish scenography underwent significant changes. In simple terms, it evolved from filling the stage with decorative scenery to annexing the entire building for performance, to creating productions in post-industrial spaces. The scope of all these transformations cannot be covered in a single chapter and therefore I will focus on three issues: the exploration of stage space; the metaphoric function of props or objects; and the increasing use of multimedia.

Polish scenography in the era of socialist realism

In 1945, Polish theatre was still dominated by the aesthetics formed in the interwar period. However, a new generation of artists was beginning to emerge. Kantor, for example, had already been active in the years 1940–1944. This intergenerational conflict produced a creative tension that might have taken Polish theatre in interesting directions. But the political situation after the liberation from Nazi occupation had a direct impact on the development of art. Under Soviet domination a totalitarian regime took power. In 1949 the doctrine of socialist realism was proclaimed and then promptly enforced in the arts. According to this doctrine, artists were expected to create only in the spirit of a proper ideology glorifying the working classes and based on a new interpretation of realism. It had nothing to do with experienced reality; rather, it was meant to present an idealized image that conformed to official ideology. The new approach had a significant impact on the field of scenography. The most famous performance of that era was *Brygada szlifierza Karhana* (*Grinder Kurhan's Brigade*), based on a play by Czech journalist Vašek Kania (pen-name Stanislav Rada), which premiered in Poland in 1949 at the Nowy Theatre in Łódź. The main storyline revolved around a conflict between two generations of grinders: the old master and his son. Actors involved in staging the play visited factories in Łódź, observing actual workers. Scenographer Ewa Soboltowa-Rachwalska (1914–1974) designed highly naturalistic settings such as factory halls. Props, which were essential for the performance and its underlying message, had to be genuine. Therefore, a real grinding machine was brought from one of the factories to the theatre. Costumes were also authentic and consisted of coveralls supplied by a factory warehouse; they were stained with grease, as if ravaged by hard labor. This was not a particularly innovative approach as it echoed similar attempts a half century earlier by naturalists such as André Antoine and Konstantin Stanislavsky. This time, however, the objectives were different. The stage design was not meant to represent the world as it was, but as it should be. It served to idealize reality, even at the cost of appearing ridiculous. Realism was treated as a synonym for the word *truth*. For maximum credibility, in a return to the nineteenth-century-style box set, the designer even incorporated ceilings, which had largely been abandoned on the stage by the 1920s and 1930s. Socialist realism placed great emphasis on attention to detail. The stage was filled with things needed to authenticate the ideological message; they were not meant as metaphors but were intended to be taken literally. The structure of the piece had to be unambiguous so that its reception would match the exact intentions of the propaganda.

Socialist realism in Polish theatre is important for understanding the great departure from reality evident among scenographers from the 1960s through 1980s. In 1956 the Polish People's Republic (known under its Polish acronym as "PRL") lifted the rigid rules they had imposed earlier, and the avant-garde was granted a place in the discourse. While this was a crucial moment in the development of Polish scenography, within the popular culture of film and television design it was still expected to create an idealized vision. The world of a TV series, for instance, had to be beautiful, clean, and filled with luxury goods. Thus, stage design served propaganda purposes in some capacity for the entire duration of the totalitarian regime in Poland.

Spaces of Polish theatre of the twentieth century

One of the turning points in the history of Polish theatre and scenography came when Jerzy Grotowski met the architect Jerzy Gurawski (b. 1935) who designed environments for six plays staged by the Laboratory Theatre of 13 Rows. In his works, Gurawski broke from the traditional division of stage and auditorium that separated the spectator from the actors, situating them at a seemingly safe distance. Instead, Gurawski developed a new spatial layout, in which the viewer was closer to the narrative unfolding on stage. The resulting proximity to the intense and powerful actors of Grotowski's theatre was meant to induce in the audience a sense of isolation from reality and to encourage a contemplative environment. For Grotowski, theatre was not a social institution. From the outset, it was seen as a ritual arena and later a laboratory. The director always sought the appropriate space that would allow participation of both actors and spectators as two equal elements.

Grotowski and Gurawski's first collaboration was *Shakuntala*, based on the classical Sanskrit text by Kalidasa, in Opole in 1960. It was then that Gurawski broke the traditional stage frame for the first time. He placed the stage in the center while the audience was seated on platforms on either side of the stage. Placed behind the spectators were the thrones of two Yogis – heroes commenting on the story. For certain scenes, the audience platforms were illuminated, thus integrating the spectators into the area of the performance. At one point, for example, the audience represented a group of courtiers. The original text was expanded with excerpts from the Kama Sutra, which was one of the reasons critics described the performance as somewhat controversial. Furthermore, the sculpture Gurawski placed on the stage was clearly phallic in shape. The events of the story were played out around and against it. Since the audience had never encountered such an innovative arrangement, Grotowski issued instructions for the spectators in which he informed them how to behave when an actor suddenly appeared from behind. For example, he asked audience members not to turn their heads and to refrain from reacting in any way.

This ritual interdependence of audience and actors was again evident in Gurawski's design for Adam Mickiewicz's romantic drama, *Forefathers' Eve*, in 1961. This time, he decided to forego the division between stage and audience altogether. Instead, Gurawski created a multi-level space where seats for spectators were installed at different heights and at different angles. The audience was in the center of the action, but often had a limited field of view, while actors performed among the spectators. Thus, the area of the stage mixed with the sphere of the audience, and the proximity between the characters and the viewers produced an interaction that significantly altered the character of the spectacle.

Gurawski went a step further in Grotowski's subsequent project, *Kordian* (1962), by Juliusz Słowacki, Mickiewicz's contemporary and fellow poet and playwright, one of the key figures of the Romantic era. Their version of the drama was set in a space reminiscent of a psychiatric hospital, with the character of Doctor (added by Grotowski) overseeing the unfolding events. The performance space contained rows of hospital beds on which the audience sat. Around them various events played out with spectators observing them from different points of view. Additionally, in the first sequence Grotowski informed the audience that all those present in the theatre would be treated as patients. Thus, the viewer became an active element within the performance, no longer voyeurs as they had previously been. The reception of the production was informed by the knowledge, shared by spectators and performers alike, that psychiatric hospitals in the totalitarian system were often used as places of forced isolation for politically inconvenient individuals.

This was followed by *The Tragical History of Doctor Faustus* (1963), based on Marlowe's play. Gurawski filled the entire room with a T-shaped construction consisting of two parallel platforms abutting a single platform running horizontally at one end. These functioned as banquet tables at which the audience sat. Thus, the events in the life of Faustus unfolded in front of the audience invited to a "feast." In *The Constant Prince*, based on the play by Pedro Calderon de la Barca in Słowacki's translation (1965),

Gurawski once again used a bridge or platform, only this time placed in the center of an otherwise empty stage. It marked the space of the protagonist, Don Ferdinand, played by Ryszard Cieślak, while all the other characters of the play moved around him. Calderon's play tells the tragic story of a Portuguese prince captured by the Moors, who sacrifices himself for the sake of higher ideals. Gurawski's design was essential to Grotowski's approach, which concentrated mainly on the actor – Cieślak's performance was later dubbed "a total act" by the director. The space arranged by Gurawski emphasized his central position in relation to the entire production.

Although Grotowski's theatre developed alongside the official mainstream theatre of that era, Gurawski's disruption of the traditional arrangements of stage space soon emerged in other areas of Polish theatre. Leszek Mądzik (b. 1945) offers an interesting take on Grotowski's approach. At Scena Plastyczna (the Visual Stage), which he founded at the Catholic University of Lublin in 1970, Mądzik used visual elements somewhat as Grotowski used actors. This is an almost purely scenographic theatre consisting largely of a constantly transforming visual field in which the actor's role was marginal. Most Scena Plastyczna productions began with the audience entering the auditorium lit by a single spotlight. It is then turned off plunging the room into darkness; spectators cannot even see the person next to them. In doing so, Mądzik isolates the viewer from the reality of everyday life and forces them to focus on the emerging image. For 40–50 minutes the audience watches blurred images looming against a black background, only occasionally lit sufficiently for their shapes to be accurately identified. Sequences of images are arranged in an iconic narrative. They are composed of people, dummies, sometimes stuffed birds, dried vegetation, feathers, water. The color scheme is dominated by black, gray, and white, with occasional splashes of color: red, blue, or deep green. The images are accompanied by a music score composed to correspond to the movement of the images appearing on the stage. What matters is not only the quality of music, but also the intensity of the sound. In fact, it has a technical function because it covers the noise made by the staff working backstage. Constructing his images, Mądzik does not rely on any modern techniques but achieves the desired visual effects with very simple means: wrapping paper, black foil, rope, and lights. Mądzik's productions tackle complementary themes such as old age and death on the one hand, and love, youth, vitality, and God's presence on the other.

Mądzik's theatre emphasizes spectacle primarily as an art of looking. The visual space is filled with images conveying meaning through nonverbal methods. Using scenographic means, he manages to evoke in his audience the same kind of silence and meditation that accompanied the experiments of Grotowski's Laboratory Theatre.

Gurawski's ideas of extending the performance beyond the traditional stage space were adopted by many designers within the milieu of repertory theatre. For example, in a 1973 version of *Forefathers' Eve* at the Stary Theatre in Krakow, Konrad Swinarski (1929–1975) expanded the performance space outside the theatre itself. The spectacle began for the viewers as soon as they entered the building. The first scenes played out in the main foyer. The audience subsequently entered the auditorium which had been rearranged for the production. The spectators took their seats facing what appeared to be the stage, however the performance area was not the stage as such, but a T-shaped space composed of the proscenium and a wooden platform that stretched over a section of the auditorium. For the viewers it was an extraordinary meeting with this play, which now literally surrounded and absorbed them. While Swinarski's production was initially poorly received, it has since earned an important place in Polish theatre history, both in terms of the significance of the interpretation of the Romantic drama, and the innovative use of space. It was the first time in Poland that the traditional theatre space was transgressed on such a large scale in a repertory theatre.

Artists active in Polish theatre in the 1970s were fascinated by the possibilities of expanding the existing traditional stages. This is evident in the works of scenographer Jerzy Juk-Kowarski (b. 1944) who, like Gurawski, had originally trained as an architect. In 1977 he designed the set for *Turoń* by Stefan Żeromski, directed by Izabella Cywińska (b. 1935) at the Nowy Theatre in Poznań. He built a platform in the auditorium extending out from the stage. Wooden pillars on top of the platform gave the illusion of supporting a (non-existent) ceiling, giving the audience the impression of entering a countryside manor house where the story was set. Still, the audience remained in traditional seats and everyone had a good view of the entire stage. In the mid-1970s, Juk-Kowarski started working with another director, Jerzy Jarocki (1929–2012). Together they staged more than 20 productions, mainly plays by authors such as Anton Chekhov, Sławomir Mrożek, and Witold Gombrowicz. Typically, Juk-Kowarski's designs were extremely simple. In 1988, once again in collaboration with Jarocki, Juk-Kowarski designed the stage for *Portret* (Portrait) by Mrożek at the Stary Theatre in Krakow. The play addressed the difficult issue of denunciations during the Stalinist era in Poland. The stage was arranged to resemble a cage-like room, with characters sitting as if political prisoners. A large portrait of Stalin was visible in the background at all times. It was a prop that communicated a very important dramaturgical message.

The team of Juk-Kowarski and Jarocki went on to stage Gombrowicz's play *Ślub* (Wedding) six times. In the 1991 production at the Stary Theatre in Krakow, the designer combined minimalism with the principle of functionalism. The stage was almost empty, with only a handful of basic items such as a table, a wardrobe, and later a throne. In order to achieve a metaphysical space, particularly significant in the play because the characters wander through time as if in the realm of dreams, Juk-Kowarski designed movable sidewalls. Through the moving and lighting of the walls he created the illusion of compressing space, suggestive of condensing time.

Jerzy Grzegorzewski's (1939–2005) approach, on the other hand, could not be further from minimalism and metaphysics. An accomplished scenographer and director, head of the Narodowy Theatre in Warsaw from 1997–2003, Grzegorzewski experimented with theatrical space from the beginning of his career. In 1973 he took advantage of the configuration of the Ateneum Theatre in Warsaw for his adaptation of Kafka's *Amerika*. The building contained two stages. Grzegorzewski's production was performed in the small auditorium, but he left a door wide open so that the audience leaving the larger auditorium at the end of the production in that space was visible. The departing crowd unwittingly became part of the performance of *Amerika*, symbolizing refugees disembarking on the coast of the United States – a reference to the opening scene of the novel about a country its author never visited.

Grzegorzewski went even further in appropriating theatre space in his 1974 adaptation of Episode XV of James Joyce's *Ulysses* entitled *Bloomusalem*, also staged at the Ateneum Theatre. Colorful processions passed through the entire building – from the cloakroom to the storage space to the stage, followed by the audience who thus lost their privileged seating position. In his later works, Grzegorzewski applied constructivist principles of composition to the traditionally understood theatre space. He arranged the stage using unusual elements such as, for example, propeller blades and kayak paddles which created vertical and horizontal planes. He talked about finding

Figure 36.1 Jerzy Grzegorzewski, *Halka Spinoza* at the Narodowy Theatre, 1998.

compositional balance and rhythm within the stage frame not unlike Kazimir Malevich did in his Suprematist paintings. The space created by Grzegorzewski always had a metaphorical dimension, complementing the text, props, and costumes, shaping the meaning of the entire production. Already in the 1970s he was filling his famous prop room with unusual items, such as an old wooden mangle, a pew, an agricultural harrow. Within his productions, objects could literally *embody a role*. In *Halka Spinoza* at the Narodowy Theatre in 1998 (Figure 36.1), for example, a pantograph represented a physical therapy machine used by the heroine. Grzegorzewski used props in a way that was reminiscent of Marcel Duchamp's use of objects in his art.

For Gurawski, Grotowski, and other artists experimenting with space, such changes were associated with their desire to incorporate the spectator as an important dramatic and even scenic element, essential for the spectacle. Tadeusz Kantor, on the other hand, chose a different approach. In 1973 at the Cricot 2 Theatre, as part of the so-called Impossible Theatre, he directed *Nadobnisie i koczkodany* (Dainty Shapes and Hairy Apes, also known as Lovelies and Dowdies) by Stanisław Ignacy Witkiewicz, better known under his pen-name "Witkacy" (1885–1939) (Figure 36.2). The performance was held in the Krzysztofory Gallery, located in the basement of one of the houses in Kraków. The director divided the space into three separate areas: a cage-like cloakroom, an auditorium, and a theatre stage, albeit the latter, invisible to spectators, was hidden behind a sliding door labeled: *Theatre – Entry*. Members of the audience seated on either side of the cloakroom were led to believe that the play was being performed behind that door, though all they could see were brief glimpses when the door occasionally slid open.

Figure 36.2 Cricot 2 Theatre's production of *Nadobnisie i koczkodany* (Lovelies and Dowdies) by Witkiewicz, directed by Tadeusz Kantor, at the Edinburgh International Festival, Foresthill Theatre, 1973.

The cloakroom was ruled by two attendants played by twin brothers, Wacław and Lesław Janicki, one of whom was dressed as a woman. They "brutally" pulled on the spectators' outerwear, ordered audience members to sit on the benches and prevented them from accessing the performance area. Thus, deprived of the safety of a regular auditorium and subjected to oppressive treatment at the hands of the attendants, the spectators watched helplessly as actors emerged for a moment and delivered random fragments of their lines, only to disappear behind the door again. As Kantor wrote, "behind that door there was the theatre. Nobody could go there. Actors who gathered there were thrown out because actors always strive for fiction and illusion" (Kantor 2004b: 462). Kantor described his approach as "illusion traps" (ibid.). To emphasize the effect, a kitchen trolley in the cloakroom functioned as a giant rat-trap that was operated by a character called Bestia Domestica. Paradoxically, the director's emphasis on oppression revealed its ridiculous and illusory character, which was important in the context of the political situation in Poland. Kantor's action, therefore, placed him in opposition to the ideas proposed by Gurawski and Grotowski. In Cricot 2, the claustrophobic trapping of the spectator did not serve to invoke a ritual, on the contrary, it was meant to emphasize the separation of external reality from the world of illusion which belongs to the realm of art.

The initial fascination with the space of theatre buildings in the stage design of the 1970s and 1980s was eventually replaced by a desire to escape from it altogether, a trend noticeable among the new generation of artists whose careers started after 1989, that is after the fall of communism in Eastern Europe. As a result of the political upheaval, the landscape of the country changed and the industrial sector largely collapsed, allowing artists to capitalize on these newly available post-industrial spaces. Exhibitions and performances were held in empty halls or courtyards of factories. Notable was a series of meetings of artists from the East and the West, known as *Construction in Process*,[1] one part of which – *Mój dom jest Twoim domem/My Home Is Your Home* – was held in Łódź over the years 1990–1993. More than 100 artists, critics, poets (including Allen Ginsberg) arrived in the city and took over abandoned spaces formerly occupied by the textile industry. Art installations gave new meaning to the destroyed and degraded areas, reclaiming them for avant-garde art of the late twentieth century.

Theatre also appropriated abandoned spaces. By its very nature theatre is a medium that creates complex metaphors, and this was exploited for a distinctive spectacle called *H*, based on Shakespeare's *Hamlet*. Directed by Jan Klata (b. 1973), with stage design by Justyna Łagowska (b. 1970), it was performed in the legendary Gdansk shipyard in 2004. Upon entering, the audience went through the famous gate where, in 1980, the Solidarity labor movement, led by Lech Wałęsa, posted their demands. The strikes at the shipyard were a critical factor in the fall of the communist regime in 1989. In Klata's take on the Elizabethan drama, Elsinore was set in spaces directly related to recent Polish history. The audience followed the characters throughout the spaces of the now-defunct shipyard. Łagowska added some rusted metal pieces in the empty halls. Using metal rods and wooden countertops, she constructed furniture, such as tables, that could also serve as a platforms for actors. Łagowska always strove to separate the performance area from the rest of the large postindustrial space, often using small architectural elements, such as stairs or colonnades, to mark the zone of movement for the actors. Costumes were mostly white or gray. The minimalism of her decorations turned Hamlet into a character lost in the web of intrigue – a figure all too familiar to the Poles, who also had problems coping with the exigencies of this period of transition.

Małgorzata Bulanda-Głomb (b. 1964) went a step further than Łagowska in the performance of *Made in Poland* by Przemysław Wojcieszek in the Modjeska Theatre in Legnica in 2004, directed by the author himself. The play, set on a housing estate among concrete blocks of flats built in the 1970s, was performed in the middle of an actual estate, both in front of the building and in its interior. The play tells the stories of people in the era of social transformation. Just as in the case of *H*, the audience was assigned places outside the theatre, in a space inextricably linked to the social history of recent decades. Bulanda did not introduce any significant changes into the existing structure; she only added a handful of essential props. Her goal was to make the story as real as possible. This designer often collaborates with director Jacek Głomb (b. 1964), head of the theatre in Legnica, who also, since the mid-1990s, has been seeking unusual spaces marked by history for his productions. One of the most famous projects by this team was the stage adaptation of *Zły* (The Evil One) based on the novel by Leopold Tyrmand, performed in a former German munitions factory in Legnica in 1996. The spacious interior enabled Bulanda to use actual cars from the 1950s, the period in which the story is set. The cars raced through the former factory hall, much to the audience's delight.

Another duo composed of scenographer Małgorzata Szcześniak (b. 1954) and director Krzysztof Warlikowski (b. 1962) have been staging their performances exclusively outside traditional theatre spaces for years. Szcześniak has developed a model of trapezoidal open space erected in defunct factory halls or large film studios, where, with the help of multimedia screens and walls made of transparent plastic, glass, or Plexiglas, she constructs a space that can be divided in various ways, allowing the director to set any scene easily, as the scenery can be changed fluidly and dynamically. Warlikowski uses the stage space created by Szcześniak to build a double narrative. Breaking down the stage by introducing multimedia screens or Plexiglas walls made it possible to isolate two performance areas for the actors. The action often plays out simultaneously as a projection on the screen and as a live performance in front of the viewers. Both areas are visible to the audience, which decides what the focus is at the moment of the performance.

Another distinctive aesthetic of the late twentieth century in Poland was the type of space introduced in theatre by director and scenographer Krystian Lupa (b. 1943). Lupa constructs fully operational, often multilevel spaces for his magnetic, hours-long adaptations of twentieth-century novels, including *The Sleepwalkers* by Hermann Broch (Teatr Stary, Cracow, 1995) and *The Dreamers* by Robert Musil (Teatr Stary, Cracow, 1988). His characters roamed through scenery turned into a metaphor by the door, bridge, stairs, and furniture that were placed on the stage. Additionally, Lupa adds realistic furniture, such as wardrobes and tables. His characters eat real meals in real time, even if it means extending the duration of the performance. The director supervises everything, often offering comments from off-stage, thus becoming a narrator who, like a guide, leads the spectators to subsequent scenes or events. Lupa often points to Tadeusz Kantor as his chief inspiration. A significant element of Lupa's performances is the aesthetic tension that arises between the illusion of theatre and the realism of objects or situations arranged on the stage, such as the smell of the food being consumed onstage by the actors.

The object, the prop, the metaphor

The metaphoric use of realistic props became a significant aspect of Polish theatre in the latter half of the twentieth century. This stemmed in part from a tendency among artists after 1956 to experiment with new materials. Also, while the communist regime continued to censor all artistic activity, it was not as thorough as in the years 1949–1956, and directors and designers discovered that scenographic elements could convey meanings that would have been forbidden if expressed verbally.

In this regard, the work of Andrzej Stopka (1904–1973) is particularly interesting, especially the productions done in collaboration with director Kazimierz Dejmek (1924–2002). Their most famous collaboration was the staging of Mickiewicz's *Forefathers' Eve* at the Narodowy Theatre in Warsaw in 1967. In this production, the dominant prop was the shackles worn by the main character, Konrad-Gustaw, as he delivered his climactic soliloquy, the so-called Great Improvisation. The actor's gesture – raising his shackled hands – along with references to Muscovite torturers in the original text of Mickiewicz's play set the tone for the whole performance. The communist regime interpreted it as a reference to the country under Russian influence and the performance was shut down after several performances. The production was one of the events that sparked the uprisings of March 1968 in Poland, and the shackles used on the stage became an iconic element, inspiring other artists to use objects in analogous ways. When officials came to the dress rehearsal they often failed to decipher the scenographic metaphors, as those only came to life with a real audience. The use of scenography as a conduit for political protest was widespread throughout the Soviet-dominated countries of eastern Europe. For those who lived under the Soviet rule, art provided the possibility to express ideas that were otherwise suppressed.

Stopka, who taught stage design at the Academy of Fine Arts in Krakow since 1950, trained such scenographers as Andrzej Kreütz-Majewski (1936–2011), Krzysztof Pankiewicz (1933–2001), Jan Polewak (b. 1945), and Kazimierz Wiśniak (b. 1931). Another artist, Józef Szajna (1922–2008), taught scenography at Warsaw's Faculty of Stage Design for over ten years. He was not only a master of creating metaphors, but he was also one of the first designers to experiment with using new materials on the stage. In his design for Shakespeare's *The Tempest*, directed by Krystyna Skuszanka in the Ludowy Theatre in Nowa Huta (1959), for example, he used thin and thick plastic panels or jute sacks. He constructed the phantasmagorical space of Prospero's island by through a combination of lighting and unusual materials.

Szajna first worked with Grotowski and Gurawski in 1962 on the production of *Akropolis* by Wyspiański at the Theatre of 13 Rows. It was a highly unusual spectacle because, while the original play was set at the historical Royal Wawel Castle in Krakow, Grotowski set the play in a Nazi concentration camp. In the middle of the theatre Szajna placed a large crate, which became the centerpiece for the unfolding story. On it and next to it he arranged rusty pipes, wheelbarrows, nails, a bathtub, hammers, and so forth as if a pile of rubbish dragged from a scrapheap. The crate, constructed by Gurawski and placed in the center, became a symbol of the crematorium, where all characters entered after the final scene. The costumes, also designed by Szajna, were canvas bags with holes worn over the actors' naked bodies; they had wooden clogs on their feet and black berets on their heads. Critics dubbed the designs "a poetic version of camp uniforms" (Flaszen in Raszewski 1993: 235). Indeed, Szajna had been a prisoner at the Nazi concentration camp Auschwitz-Birkenau. His work on Grotowski's production marked the first time he translated his own experience into the language of art.

The 1970s, 1980s, and 1990s saw Szajna lauded for his unique artistic vision of theatre as a playwright, designer, and director. In 1972, he founded an art center in Warsaw called simply, "Studio," where he staged several productions, including *Gulgutiera* (1973), *Dante* (1974, loosely based on *The Divine Comedy*), and *Cervantes* (1976). His most famous production was *Replika*, which premiered in 1971, though later heavily edited and revised by the author. As the curtain rose the audience was confronted with a pile of garbage, old shoes, human limbs, fragments of mannequins, and the like. The characteristic feature of all Szajna's realizations was his use of elements representing a degraded world, such as destroyed or discarded objects or waste left behind by civilization. In this it bore some relation to Turpism, the Polish literary movement characterized by the use of ugliness intended to shock. It could be understood as Szajna's attempt to describe the destruction of this part of Europe as a result of World War Two.

A different approach to the use of objects can be observed in the work of Tadeusz Kantor, who had experimented for 40 years with objects and sculptures in his various theatrical projects. One of his famous designs was for Goplana, the mythical Slavic heroine living in the lake Gopło in Lithuania and the protagonist of Juliusz Słowacki's Romantic drama *Balladyna*, which Kantor staged in 1943 in a private apartment in Krakow as part of the Underground Independent Theatre. In his version of the play, Goplana was the so-called phantom form. It was a large, immobile sculpture with an abstract anthropomorphic form, built of plywood, aluminum, and foil, meant to resemble a cold, dead nymph whose metallic beauty was an allusion to the ubiquitous nightmare of the war and destruction. In 1963, after Theatre Cricot 2 had been established, Kantor changed his approach to the use of fixed objects on stage, which is evident in his production of Witkacy's play *Wariat i zakonnica* (The Madman and the Nun). He built a large structure out of chairs and named it the "aneantisating machine." It was moved rhythmically by an actor sitting inside it. The sculpture, serving as a fixed prop, was supposed to make a rattling noise so that the characters could not say their lines. Thus, an object dominated the stage space, preventing actors from performing. Kantor later dubbed that period in his career *Teatr Zerowy* (Zero Theatre).

During his Theatre of Death period, beginning with his iconic spectacle *Umarła klasa* (The Dead Class, 1975), the artist once again changed his approach to objects. He fused actors with fragmentary elements of objects and mannequins: *Staruszek z rowerkiem* (An Old Man with a Bike) and *Staruszek z dziecińżstwem* (An Old Man with a Childhood). The affixed prop lent new meanings to Kantor's characters. Items featured in many Cricot 2 productions had another quite alarming quality: they were lethal objects that were destructive for the characters of Kantor's world. One famous item was a "photographic machine gun" in *Wielopole, Wielopole* – a construction whose shape was reminiscent of the equipment used by travelling photographers at the beginning of the twentieth century but with a machine gun jutting out from the lens opening. The object was operated by a demonic female character – played by a man – named Owner of the Photographic Studio, and her action of shooting a group of soldiers posing for a photograph was described by Kantor as "proper use of the invention of the Lord Daguerre" (Kantor 2004b: 219). Thus, the artist made an ironic reference to the cultural role of the photographer who, since photography was invented, has always been the one who can save us from death (Gombrich 1997: 105).

Kantor had a collection of favorite objects which, in the hands of this versatile artist, easily migrated from Cricot 2 to the realm of painting or happenings. One such item was an oblong wooden board, originally part of a garden latrine from a Krakow house. Kantor turned it into an almost sacred object of his art. It became the basis for the construction of space in his *Powrót Odysa* (The Return of Odysseus), based on Wyspiański's play and staged in 1944 in Krakow. Next, it was part of a series of paintings *Wszystko wisi na włosku* (Everything is Hanging by a Thread), and finally it became the metaphorical figure of *Dwaj Chasydzi z Deską Ostatniego Ratunku* (Two Hasidim with the Last Achorage, literally "the board of last resource/help") featured in several performances of Cricot 2.

Another important prop/object associated with Kantor was a chair, featured in his visual art projects (including the 10-meter tall wooden chair on the motorway near Oslo in 1971), as well as theatre. He treated the chair in which he sat during rehearsals and performances of Cricot 2 with an almost religious reverence. After his sudden death in December 1990, the theatre continued performing sold-out performances with his chair standing empty and silent. It became an important sign of the author's absence. In 1995, the first 10-meter concrete chair installation was erected on Kantor's private estate in Hucisko near Krakow. In 2011, an almost identical chair was erected in Wrocław. Thus, the object/prop surpassed its own context. It is now a sculpture existing in public space. One could conclude that it no longer simply shapes the layout of theatrical scenery or the visual arrangement of installation art, but that it has become part of the scenography of urban area.

The screen: multimedia in Polish theatre of the twenty-first century

In Poland, the use of projection in performance dates back to the times of Stanisław Wyspiański (1869–1907), who was the first to entertain the idea of using it in the 1899 production of his own drama *Protesilas i Laodamia* (*Protesilas and Laodamia*). His stage directions (never implemented in his lifetime) suggested projecting a portion of the action on a canvas screen stretched across the back of the stage. Despite such early experiments, it was only in the new millennium that contemporary artists began to discover the advantages and disadvantages of introducing film and projection into theatre.

Boris F. Kudlička (b. 1972) is a Slovak artist who has lived and worked in Poland since 1995. In his works he uses multimedia in a unique painterly way. He positions screens on the stage at different angles, then, through the expert use of lighting and rear projection, Kudička creates phantasmagorical spaces into which he sometimes introduces abstract elements such as square blocks or staircases. Such an approach has worked well for operas, which Kudlička has done mostly with director Mariusz Treliński (b. 1962).

Krzysztof Garbaczewski (b. 1983) offers a new approach to the use of media in contemporary theatre. In 2012, he staged *Iwona księżniczka Burgunda* (*Ivona, Princess of Burgundia*) by Witold Gombrowicz at the Jan Kochanowski Theatre in Opole. It is a story of Prince Filip and his ill-fated love for the silent, mysterious Iwona. The entire royal court in the fictional state of Burgundia tries to dissuade the heir to the throne from the troublesome marriage. There are 11 characters in the original text but Garbaczewski's production expanded the cast and also added four cameras, a mixing table, and a screen. The production bore a close resemblance to a multimedia installation and the camera served as a catalyst for action. At the opening of the performance, translucent screens separated the spectators from the performance space. As the play begins two characters are standing on the stage and facing the audience, accompanied by a cameraman who films them. They speak their lines and then one of them gestures to the cameraman, inviting him (and thus, implicitly, the audience) to follow them into the interior of the palace located behind the translucent walls. From that moment the audience watches the subsequent scenes projected on the screen, while actors performing on the stage are hidden from view by the walls. The entire performance is filmed in real time. In his production, Garbaczewski made a significant distinction: as long as all courtiers and royal family accepted Filip's actions aimed at marrying Iwona, the audience followed the story on the screen only. However, when first conflicts arise in the court, the characters slowly begin to tear the paper screens covering the proscenium opening and expose the real performance space and the actors themselves. The structure of the stage space is gradually exposed, although it is not fully revealed until the finale. By using projections, created by lighting designer Wojciech Puś (b. 1978), Garbaczewski could control the spectators' gaze. They initially has no choice but to see only the image displayed on the screen. The destruction of the screens somehow marks the return of the traditional operation of theatre. In Garbaczewski's version, the main author of the spectacle is the visual director operating the mixing table and selecting which images the audience can see on the screen.

While this chapter focuses on theatre scenography, Polish cinema has also produced outstanding designers. Allan Starski and Ewa Braun received Academy Awards in 1993 for Art Direction for Steven Spielberg's *Schindler's List* and, in 2003, the Académie des Arts et Techniques du Cinema in France awarded Starski a César for his production design for *The Pianist* by Roman Polanski.

The latter half of the twentieth century saw a significant transformation in Polish scenography as it shifted from painted décor to experiments with space. In particular, Polish scenography was at the forefront of investigations of environmental and immersive theatre as it radically transgressed age-old barriers between stage and auditorium. Polish scenography, as well as art, also took the lead in appropriating the abandoned industrial structures of the post-communist world. This, in conjunction with a focus on the metaphoric life of objects, also moved stage objects out of theatre and into the area of urban architecture. Although multimedia and projection came relatively late to Polish theatre, it is functioning as it is elsewhere in the world – calling into question the nature of theatrical space and time. But even with new media and new technologies, Polish artists are mindful of the history of Polish stage design and willing to draw on the achievements of their predecessors.

Note

1 *Construction in Process* was an international celebration of art focusing on exchanges between artists of the East and West. It grew out of an interest in the "Solidarity" movement in the early 1980s. Its main initiator was the Polish artist Ryszard Wasko. In 1981 he invited artists from abroad to Łódź who came at their own expense. After the decree of martial law in December 1981, however, such initiatives were no longer feasible. After the political changes in Poland in 1989 Wasko returned to the idea. He prepared two editions of *Construction in Process* in 1990 and 1993, both titled *My home is your home*. Subsequent editions took place outside Poland: *Coexistence* in 1995 in the Negev Desert in Israel; *Bridge* in 1998 Melbourne; and *The Creators* in 2001 in Venice.

References

Deglera, Janusza and Grzegorza Ziółkowskiego (Eds) 2006. *Misterium grozy i urzeczenia. Przedstawienia Jerzego Grotowskiego i Teatru Laboratorium*. Wrocław.

Gombrich, E. H. 1997. *O sztuce*, translated by Monika Dolińska. Warszawa: Wydawnictwo Arkady.

Jarmułowicz, Małgorzata 2003. *Sezony błędów i wypaczeń. Socrealizm w dramacie i teatrze polskim*. Gdańsk: Wydawnictwo Uniwersytetu Gdańskiego.

Kantor, Tadeusz 2004a. *Metamorfozy. Teksty o latach 1934–1974*, Pisma tom 1. Wrocław–Kraków: Ossolineum-Ośrodek Dokumentacji Sztuki Tadeusza Kantora Cricoteka.

Kantor, Tadeusz 2004b. *Teatr Śmierci. Teksty z lat 1975–1984*, Pisma tom 2. Wrocław-Kraków: Ossolineum-Ośrodek Dokumentacji Sztuki Tadeusza Kantora Cricoteka.

Kuligowska-Korzeniewska, Anna (Ed.) 2010. *Teatr Kazimierza Dejmka*. Łódź: Wydawnictwo Uniwersytetu Łódzkiego.

Kuźnicka, Danuta 2006. *Obszary zwątpień i nadziei. Inscenizacje Jerzego Grzegorzewskiego*. Warszawa: Instytut Sztuki Polskiej Akademii Nauk.

Łarionow, Dominika 2008. *Przestrzenie obrazów Leszka Mądzika*. Lublin: Towarzystwo Naukowe Katolickiego Uniwersytetu Lubelskiego.

Łarionow, Dominika 2015. *Wystarczy tylko otworzyć drzwi . . . Przedmioty w twórczości Tadeusza Kantora*. Łódź: Wydawnictwo Uniwersytetu Łódzkiego.

Łarionow, Dominika and Magdalena Raszewska 2015. "From Painted Decoration to the Screen. The Turn in Stage Illusion in the Late 20th and Early 21st Century." *Art Inquiry* XVII (XXVI): 291–308.

Raszewski, Zbigniew 1993. *Sto przedstawień w opisach polskich autorów*. Wrocław: Wiedza o Kulturze.

Strzelecki, Zenobiusz 1963. *Polska Plastyka Teatralna*. Warszawa: Państwowy Instytut Wydawniczy.

Strzelecki, Zenobiusz 1970. *Kierunki scenografii współczesnej*. Warszawa: P.W.N.

Strzelecki, Zenobiusz 1983. *Współczesna scenografia polska*. Wydawnictwo Arkady, Warszawa.

Szajna, Józef i jego świat 2000. Warszawa: Wydawnictwo Hotel Sztuki Galeria Sztuki Współczesnej "Zachęta."

Walaszek, Joanna 1991. *Konrad Swinarski*. Warszawa: Państwowy Instytut Wydawniczy.

37

MODERN AND CONTEMPORARY CZECH THEATRE DESIGN

Toward dramatic spaces of freedom[1]

Barbora Příhodová

Czech theatre design, commonly called "scénografie" (scenography) in the Czech language, experienced an unparalleled boom with the establishment of the modern state of Czechoslovakia in 1918.[2] The turbulent geopolitical developments of the twentieth century framed the emergence of several generations of designers who influenced both Czech theatre and the wider international scene.[3] These designers responded to the challenges posed by the extreme political, economic and social transformations of the Czech territory that has both benefited from its strategic intercultural positioning in the center of Europe and repeatedly suffered at the hands of Western and Eastern colonial powers. In this environment, the designers became unique participants in the staging of the dramatic text: working in partnership with directors, they became co-authors of the performance and transformed the world of the play into an autonomous, non-empirical dramatic reality. Often trained as architects, they ingeniously developed a highly imaginative, evocative use of performance space that engages audiences in a multi-faceted visual communication. Historically, the general principles of Czech theatre design have developed through the shifts from strictly mimetic to metonymic to metaphorical and loosely associative deployment of space, oscillating between the rejection and re-incorporation of flat decoration and more and more advanced technologies. Taking selected artists and their projects as examples and emphasizing the underappreciated contribution of the founding generation and the inter-war avant-gardes,[4] I focus on the multiple ways Czech theatre designers have assumed a crucial role in creating the whole of the performance, taking on the role traditionally ascribed solely to the director and/or playwright. In doing so, they claimed the creative freedom of an artist who challenges the dominant aesthetic, and at times political, orders.

"Our first stage designer"

Following a number of symbolist experiments in small improvised theatre spaces, the new, anti-realistic, modern styles striving to break down the static two-dimensional illusionism of the stage arose in the official Czech theatre as early as 1900 and

Figure 37.1 *King Oedipus* (1932). Designed by Vlastislav Hofman. (Collections of National Museum in Prague, Czech Republic, H6D-1473.)

continued throughout the 1910s with the emergence of scenic expressionism. Vlastislav Hofman (1884–1964) was the founding personality of Czech scenography, recognized by the generations to come as "our first stage designer" who "for the first time in the history of our theatre . . . does not describe but *creates* dramatic space" (Svoboda 1964: 5; my translation). Hofman was a successful Cubist architect, painter, and interior designer whose first design for theatre, *The Hussites* (Vinohrady Theatre, 1919, dir. K. H. Hilar), depicts the mythically grand period of Czech medieval history. This design reveals the artist's struggle to find a new approach to staging that would appeal to the sensibilities of the contemporary audiences in both its content and form. Even though painted as a two-dimensional backdrop, the decorations depicting differently rendered clouds aimed to capture the dark, heavy atmosphere to express the inner meaning of the play as interpreted by the director and the designer, rather than its location. Integrating the designer's vision of an architect, Hofman's sets for *Heracles* and *The Dawn* (National Theatre, 1920, dir. K. H. Hilar) brought about a modernistic shift towards the more dynamic non-mimetic performance space. In both cases the stage was dominated by a monumental staircase accompanied by expressive lighting that shaped the stage space into an autonomous spatial reality while creating opportunities for the actor's body to perform at different levels. This use of staircase as a dramatic element defining the space of performance culminated in the production of *King Oedipus* (National Theatre, 1932, dir. K. H. Hilar) (Figure 37.1) with its central monumental staircase creating the world where the king's tragic destiny is fulfilled.

The inter-war avant-gardes and František Tröster's dramatic space

The emergence of the scenographer as a fully-fledged author who substantially contributes to the signifying process of the performance was furthered by a number of versatile artists working in 1920s and 1930s, many of whom were also trained as architects. Scenographers such as Jiří Kroha (1893–1974), Bedřich Feurstein (1892–1936), František Zelenka (1904–1944), and František Tröster (1904–1968) constituted the immensely rich and varied landscape of the Czech inter-war avant-gardes. They exercised their talents across genres (opera, ballet, drama, revue) and types of theatre, and often worked for both the official theatre and cabaret-like stages, bridging the gap between "high" art and "low" entertainment. Their work marked a shift from the national project of theatre as a tool for validating "Czechness," as they sought inspiration in the Soviet and French avant-gardes, while putting scenography in the service of their own political agenda. Their approach to theatre design is marked by its transnational scope, fascination with the "modern civilization" of jazz, cinema, and technological inventions, and the defiance of the bourgeois normative conventions, an attitude that later became a means of resistance against rising Fascism.

The idea that a set works with the actor to co-create the dramatic action was central to the design that Jiří Kroha, the architect, painter, and interior designer who briefly put himself in service of theatre, developed for the Czech play *Honest Matthew* (National Theatre, 1922, dir. V. Novák). The design for this fantastical comedy satirizing corruption in the newly formed Czechoslovakia relied on unseen technical devices such as screens for projection of texts and human silhouettes for the dancing room scene, or mobile components for the scene set in the forest. Admired by both critics and the audience, the forest scene was composed of cubist-like tall cylinders carrying colorful abstract structures representing leaves that could be mechanically set in motion. The whirling tops of trees not only created the atmosphere of the forest as an environment for dramatic action but further animated the set, endowing it with performative agency.

While scenographers such as Kroha emphasized the potential of theatre design by developing movement in the set to convey dramatic action, others inserted aspects of humor into this modern, architecture-driven scenography. Drawing on *poetism*, a deliberately playful and optimistic Czech version of avant-garde movements such as dada, futurism, and constructivism, these scenographers used cultural tropes of irony and hyperbole to playfully refer to two-dimensional mimetic decoration.[5] In the context of the pre-war developments their scenographic designs became acts of bold political commentary. For instance, in his design for *The Ass and His Shadow* (Liberated Theatre, 1933, dir. J. Honzl), architect Bedřich Feurstein emphasized the comically subversive potential of the play[6] by creating a set with features that we would today call postmodern. Instead of moving away from flat decoration, the set of *The Ass and His Shadow* revisited it in an ironic citation that highlights its theatrical fakeness. Denying empirical spatial logic defined by the scale and size proportion of objects, the design points to its own absurdity, suggesting that it can extend beyond the stage as a metaphor of the pathological political climate.

František Zelenka similarly made critical political statements by creating sets and costumes that merged humorous, almost childlike, naivety with a pointed use of irony. Zelenka's scenographic career successfully developed on both official and experimental stages, and even continued after his deportation to the ghetto of Theresienstadt in 1943. In the extreme conditions of the concentration camp the humor translated into shapes, colors, and materials of theatre design, and became the ultimate act of resistance against the genocidal efforts of totalitarian power, defying fear, desperation, and death. Zelenka's quest for modern design that would efficiently speak to its audiences also involved constructivism-inspired use of authentic materials (fabric, glass, wood, or whatever was available, including plain bed sheets in Theresienstadt). The scenography of *The Last Cyclist* (Theresienstadt, 1944)[7] made good use of Zelenka's rich experience in typography by incorporating the visuality of the modern city to establish the setting of the dramatic action, using huge, graphic inscriptions of "Blázinec" [Madhouse] on a simple architectonic structure.

The work of František Tröster illustrates the peak of the scenographer's determining role in a performance. Tröster was the leading personality of the later phase of the Czech inter-war avant-garde in the 1930s, and a key collaborator of the director Jiří Frejka (1904–1952). Opened only three weeks after the propagandistic Nazi Olympics in Berlin, the design for Tröster and Frejka's *Julius Caesar* (National Theatre, 1936) (Figure 37.2) grew out of their reading of Shakespeare's character as a representative of a deceitful, manipulative power, visually marked by a "false monumentality" as exemplified by Baroque architecture and sculpture (Tröster quoted in Koubská *et al.* 2007: 23). Hailed by architect Oscar Niemeyer as "the beginning of modern stage architecture" (ibid.: 26),[8] Tröster's design sought to evoke the effect such power has on the individual, and strategically drew inspiration from cinematic devices: using the turntable, the set altered the audience's perspective and positioning by exposing them to a monumental bust of Pompey, many times taller than actors' bodies, menacingly looming over the stage, and a similarly gigantic sculpture of a horse's leg, seen as if from the frog's perspective. Tröster referred to this dynamic organization of space as "dramatic space," as one that not only co-creates the highly topical political meaning of the staged play but also manipulates the audiences' visual field by possibly evoking sensations such as awe and discomfort. This special type of space emerging in the moment of a performance is an "artificial" space that is "not identical with the stage space, it overruns it in every direction, it has an independent shape and dimension, it is . . . elastic and changeable, it reacts sensitively to changes of the action, and time is ascribed an active role" (ibid., 15).

Figure 37.2 *Julius Caesar* (1936). Designed by František Tröster. (Private archive of Tröster family.)

With this concept of dramatic space as a flexible entity that transforms with the flow of the action and in cooperation with the actors while affecting the audience's perception, Tröster, who also excelled as a teacher,[9] directly influenced several post-war generations of designers.

Post-World War Two developments: Josef Svoboda and action design

Following the Communist takeover of the country in 1948, Czech theatre design continued to be characterized by the avant-garde movements but, at the same time, scenography maintained an uneasy and complex relationship vis-à-vis totalitarian power. Despite the restrictive regime, Josef Svoboda (1920–2002) cultivated and exported his particular vision of "scenography" as a site of aesthetic and political freedom. Benefiting from the state's financial and symbolic support Svoboda played a fundamental role in establishing Czechoslovakia as a scenographic superpower in the 1960s. (Ladislav Vychodil, Jiří Trnka, and Vladimír Nývlt were other significant internationally recognized scenographers.) With their abstract use of space, Svoboda and directors such as Alfréd Radok and Václav Kašlík broke through the limits of 1950s' state-promoted Socialist Realism, cultivating scenography as an autonomous system, driven by its own logic but inextricably linked to the whole of the performance, and especially enmeshed with directorial concept. This system fully unfolded in the very moment of the performance, in front of the audience's eyes and skillfully drew upon the most advanced scientific and technological inventions of its time. The continuous quest by Kroha, Tröster, and others for the dynamic set that transformed over time, affecting the spectator's perception as the dramatic action unfolded, was reconceptualized by Svoboda as a "psychoplastic space." This space was realized through mobile sets composed of stage elements that mechanically changed their positions according to the rhythm of the performance, and creative use of light, including his innovative low-voltage stage lights that he often used to create luminous walls or curtains of light, better known as "Svoboda ramps," combined with reflective surfaces, and of different types of projections and multimedia systems. Svoboda's design for *King Oedipus* (National Theatre, 1963, dir. M. Macháček) (Figure 37.3), a monolithic, timeless, abstract macrostructure of a staircase, filling the entire width of the stage and rising from the orchestra pit to the height of 15 meters, on the other hand, reveals the scenographer's training in architecture and an artistic genealogy that can be traced back to Vlastislav Hofman's work.

Working more often abroad than in Czechoslovakia from the mid-1960s onward, Svoboda successfully transformed the rich inter-war heritage through the use of rather complex mechanical and technological devices to create ideologically suspended artistic forms resonating with the transnational contemporary sensibilities of the "West." Simultaneously, another generation of emerging designers often stood in antithesis to massive Svobodian designs and echoed the global "revolutionary" shift towards "poor theatre" of the 1960s: Libor Fára (1925–1988), Luboš Hrůza (1933–2008), Jaroslav Malina (1937–2016), and Jan Dušek (b. 1942) deliberately cherished simplicity and authenticity, choosing to define the performer as the major driving force in performance. Coming from the fields of painting and graphics and/or trained by Tröster at DAMU's Department of Scenography, they turned the disadvantage of working on small underequipped stages into an aesthetic program and a political statement against the regime. Later labeled as representatives of so-called "action design," these

Figure 37.3 *Oedipus Rex* (1963). Designed by Josef Svoboda, Smetana Theatre, National Theatre, Prague. (Photo: Jaromír Svoboda. Courtesy of National Theatre, Prague.)

Figure 37.4 *A Midsummer Night's Dream*. Designed by Jaroslav Malina. (Courtesy of Estate of Jaroslav Malina.)

designers worked with found objects and accessible materials such as textiles, looking for innovative ways to create a metaphorical dramatic space in which inanimate elements continuously shift and multiply their meanings instigated by the performer's actions. For *A Midsummer Night's Dream* (ABC Theatre of the Prague Municipal Theatres, 1984, dir. K. Kříž) (Figure 37.4), Jaroslav Malina designed a set consisting of several huge pieces of fabric hung on the ropes above the stage and extending into the auditorium space as well. The stage floor was covered with a soft foam-rubber mattress with two layers of flexible fabric, allowing the actors to dive in and reappear at different spots and actively serving as their working tool.

Contemporary Czech scenography

After the 1989 transition to democracy, contemporary scenographers strove to survive in the rough conditions of the neoliberal jungle, while furthering the authorial approach to scenography inherited from previous generations. One of the most striking shifts was the access gained by female artists to the traditionally male-dominated arena of theatre design.[10] Jana Preková (b. 1956), Kamila Polívková (b. 1975), Iva Němcová (1980–2015), and Lucia Škandíková (b. 1984), among others, collaborate with directors on the most prestigious state-supported stages and in independent, often low-budget, projects to create dramatic spaces of aesthetic and political freedom that intensely communicate with the audiences of the post-totalitarian era. Preková and director Jan Nebeský's *King Lear* (National Theatre, 2013) invoked an intricate space charged with a number of competing semantic layers by situating the play in a swimming pool and in an art gallery where Lear and Cordelia hang on the wall as living artifacts. Filled with projections, sounds, and countless visual cultural and historical references, this dense "post-dramatic" space dissected the canonical work, inviting the audiences to embark on an affective journey through chains of associations while reaching out to individual and collective memories of a traumatic past. Whether loved or hated, the fact that this bold scenographic gesture unfolded on the most distinguished stage in the country suggests that even though scenographers may feel underappreciated and their budgets are relatively limited, their distinctive voices are heard and their work is highly recognized as an important contribution to theatre culture and beyond.

Notes

1 This chapter was written under the auspices of the Jan Hus Educational Foundation Fellowship.

2 Although Czechoslovakia split in 1993 to form the separate Czech and Slovak republics, a political division reflected in the title of this chapter, the arts embody a different cultural reality: bonded by history, culture and similar languages, Czech and Slovak scenographers have commonly migrated between the two countries, forming an interconnected world of Czecho-Slovak scenography that transcends geopolitical borders. Furthermore, stemming from the national and cultural diversity of the region, the category of "Czech theatre design" becomes a slippery one in light of the fact that, until 1945, theatre culture in Czechoslovakia was shaped by the coexistence of mutually influential and competing Czech and German speaking populations. It is noteworthy that the territory falling under the Austro-Hungarian empire before WWI gave birth to designers such as Alfred Roller (b. Brno, 1864), Emil Orlik (b. Prague, 1870) and Emil Pirchan (b. Brno, 1884) who, after a ground-breaking collaboration with Leopold Jessner in Berlin, worked for the German Theatre, today's State Opera, in Prague in the 1930s.

3 In 1967, following the repeated successes of Czech and Slovak scenographers at *Bienal de São Paulo*, the international community recognized the exceptional character of Czechoslovak

theatre design by establishing the Prague Quadrennial, the largest competitive display of scenography, theatre architecture and technologies.

4 In the Czech discourse, as in the whole of Central Europe, the term avant-garde is applied to modernist artistic movements that reached their peak in the 1920s. In stylistic terms, they rejected everything that had preceded them such as realism, naturalism, symbolism and expressionism. Led by a "strong impulse to reveal new paradigms" they pursued "underlying structures or forces beyond the visible surface of the nature" (Benson and Forgács 2002: 23). In the context of Czech theatre design, these avant-gardes brought onto stages the newest developments in fine arts and architecture, most significantly cultivating the use of spatial and visual metaphor as a key principle of scenographic means of expression. Even though the period of the avant-gardes is historically limited, their legacy is still present in the Czech culture, largely constituting the aesthetic norm. In fact, the anti-realistic, playful, and deliberately theatrical principles of staging that permeate theatre design in its use of space, light, shape and color, and that were accompanied by the theoretical foundations of the Structuralist concepts of the Prague School, have become and continue to be the most critically lauded form of theatre.

5 Humor, irony and metaphor were identified as important sources of Czech theatre design in two exhibitions presenting Czech scenography of the twentieth century curated by Joe Brandesky. See Brandesky 2007.

6 The Liberated Theatre was known for its political satire. The play was written and performed by the leading artistic duo of the theatre, Jan Werich and Jiří Voskovec, in the year when Hitler seized power in Germany. It was based on Aristophanes' adaptation of Lucian's fable and unfolds around the nonsensical dispute between two citizens about which one is the owner of a shadow cast by an ass. Featuring characters clearly referring to Hitler, Mussolini and Dolfuss, it addresses the destructive mass manipulation carried out by political leaders.

7 This play, written by Karel Švenk, allegorically addresses the continuous persecution of the Jewish populations. The performance in Theresienstadt never went beyond the first dress rehearsal. The set of surviving designs by Zelenka also include costumes, ingeniously showing the artist's ability to translate the comical into visual signs in performance.

8 Niemeyer stated this on the occasion of the 2nd Biennial of Stage Design in São Paulo in 1959 where František Tröster won the Golden Medal for the Best Foreign Stage Design, while a special exhibit, designed by Tröster and curated by Vladimír Jindra, that presented the development of Czech and Slovak stage design and theatre architecture between 1914 and 1959, won the Prize for the Best Foreign Exposition.

9 He was co-founder of the Academy of Music and Performing Arts (AMU) in Prague and founded The Department of Scenography at the Theatre Faculty (DAMU) there in 1946.

10 In contrast with set design, women artists traditionally found more acceptance in costume design. See Ptáčková *et al.* 2011.

References

Benson, Timothy O. and Éva Forgács 2002. "Introduction" to *Between Worlds: A Sourcebook of Central European Avant-gardes, 1910–1930*, edited by Timothy O. Benson and Éva Forgács, 17–42. Cambridge: The MIT Press.

Brandesky, Joe (Ed.) 2007. "Czech Theatre Design in the Twentieth Century." In *Metaphor and Irony Revisited*. Iowa City: University of Iowa Press.

Koubská, Vlasta, Jiří Hilmera, Magda Wagenknechtová Svobodová and Martin Tröster 2007. *František Tröster. Artist of Light and Space*, translated by Barbara Day. Prague: Obecní dům.

Ptáčková, Věra, Barbora Příhodová and Simona Rybáková 2011. *Czech Theatre Costume*, translated by Barbara Day, Mark Newkirk and Eva Dvořáková. Prague: Arts and Theatre Institute.

Svoboda, Josef 1964. "Náš První Moderní Scénograf" [Our First Modern Scenographer]. *Literární noviny* 8 (36) (1965): 5.

38

WORLDS OF GERMAN DESIGN IN THE TWENTY-FIRST CENTURY

Matt Cornish

Much of what is seen in German theatre today feels *sui generis* or even *ex nihilo* but has precedent in the twentieth century, particularly in the work of Bertolt Brecht and his close collaborators Caspar Neher, Teo Otto, and Karl von Appen. Neher, one of Brecht's earliest and longest-serving artistic partners, saw himself as a *Bühnenbauer* rather than a *Bühnenbildner*, the latter being an "artistic creator of the stage," while the former means something like "builder of the stage." A *Bühnenbauer* is less concerned with interpreting a play and producing harmony; instead, he or she make scenes that are "integral component[s] of the play's dramaturgy," elevating scenography, as Christopher Baugh states, to "an act of performance" (Baugh 2006: 263).

Scenography only became more integral to dramaturgy after the 1960s. In "Revolutions in Scenography on the German Stage in the Twentieth Century," Wilhelm Hortmann discusses how artists – Wilfried Minks working with director Klaus Michael Grüber, Peter Pabst with Peter Zadek, Karl-Ernst Herrmann with Peter Stein – began to experiment wildly with design, moving performances out of theatre buildings and using dissonant material objects to disrupt neutral spaces (Hortmann 2008: 291–3). "[S]cenography had become established as an autonomous artform," Hortmann writes (2008: 296), pointing at Robert Wilson's dreamscapes as exemplars, including *Death, Destruction and Detroit* (Schaubühne am Halleschen Ufer, 1979). The turn of the twenty-first century witnessed ever-increasing freedom for designers, but also, Hortmann asserts, "an almost absurd pressure for originality" that was forcing "younger directors and stage designers to seek ever more particularist solutions" (2008: 301). Theatre artists, he argued, were no longer presenting the text but its interpretation.

In his examination of postdramatic theatre in the late twentieth century, Hans-Thies Lehmann connects Wilson's metamorphosing tableaux with Anna Viebrock's cavernous, post-communist waiting rooms. Writing about space (*Raum*), Lehmann opposes the "metonymic" design of drama – "not so much framed as itself a frame" – to the parataxis of postdramatic theatre, in which scenography is as important, often far *more* important, than the play text (Lehmann 2005: 289; translations by the author unless otherwise noted). Scenography serving its own ends is one of the hallmarks of the postdramatic theatre, taking the form of tableaux vivants, location-based theatre, dramaturgical space, and the heterogeneous space of the everyday (Lehmann 2005: 291–308). Lehmann's *Postdramatic Theatre* has continued to actively influence designers, critics, and pedagogy in Germany. But the category *postdrama* is not always useful for understanding twenty-first century scenographic developments.

The contemporary designers I find most remarkable and will discuss here are Bert Neumann (who died in 2015 at the age of 54), who defined the Volksbühne's aesthetic under long-tenured *Intendant* (managing artistic director) Frank Castorf; Aleksander Denić, a Serbian designer, who has worked with Castorf subsequently on the Ring Cycle in Bayreuth and at the Residenztheater Munich; Katrin Brack, who worked often with Bulgarian auteur Dimiter Gotscheff; and Jan Pappelbaum, who creates rooms in which stories are told, designing intricate homes and elemental Shakespearean sets for director Thomas Ostermeier at the Schaubühne Berlin. Moving away from director-designer pairings and into the *freie Szene*, or "free-scene" independent theatres, where artists work from show to show, without the long-term contracts of state theatres, we find collectives experimenting in space. In the final section of this chapter I touch on Rimini Protokoll's smart-phone and tablet-enabled explorations of cities and personal stories, as well as the dadaistic sculpture-park-like stages, outfitted with DJ-mixing tables, constructed by andcompany&Co.[1]

Bert Neumann's autonomous spaces

Approaching the Volksbühne Berlin on Rosa-Luxemburg Straße from 1993 until 2017, one saw, from a distance, the theatre's famous "walking wheel" logo designed by Neumann, a hulking 15-foot tall rusted steel wheel with spokes set atop two legs. Behind it is the brutal Volksbühne building itself, all concrete and colonnades, crowned by a neon sign that reads O-S-T (East) and framed by vinyl banners announcing, in blackletter scripts, the title of the evening's provocation. For Neumann, a plastic artist born in Magdeburg in 1960 and raised in East Berlin, neon, vinyl, and lettering were some of his favorite materials. From 1992 until 2015, except for a two-year interregnum during a dispute with Castorf, Neumann served as the primary designer at the Volksbühne, setting the pace for German scenography.

Neumann first collaborated with Castorf in 1988, in a small space on the third floor of the Volksbühne, and they worked together again in 1990 with an adaptation of Friedrich Schiller's *Die Räuber* (*The Robbers*) on the Volksbühne mainstage – Neumann's ratty costumes for the merry highwaymen, tights in primary colors, like the rags of criminal-minded jesters, hung for many years in shallow alcoves scattered throughout the building. It was for this production that Neumann sketched the walking wheel that became the Volksbühne logo. At the time, during the heady and unstable early days of reunification, the Volksbühne could have closed at any moment. It didn't. Instead, Castorf became *Intendant* in 1992. Their 1997 *Hauptmanns Weber* (*Hauptmann's Weavers*, an adaptation of Gerhard Hauptmann's proletarian tragedy) is a telling example from Castorf and Neumann's collaborations in the 1990s. Over the stage a sign read "HUNGER?" in block sans-serif type, stolen from a billboard off the B96 highway, and underneath it Neumann placed an actual weaving machine, a heavy steel relic of the GDR. The actors, their characters trashy and low-class and underemployed, wore t-shirts stamped with aspirational corporate logos (Chanel, Deutsche Bank, and Hugo Boss), behind them radiated what must have been hundreds of fluorescent tubes, shining irregularly. East: meet West. West: meet East.

In 1999 Neumann invented his "Container," a totally enclosed space on the stage that challenged the creativity of Castorf as well as René Pollesch, playwright and director, who was just beginning to work with Neumann. For Castorf's adaptation of Fyodor Dostoevsky's *Dämonen* (*Demons*) in 1999, the Container was an enclosed apartment: "Life takes place onstage behind four real walls," wrote Neumann in his book *Imitation of Life* (2001: 199). The walls were glass, but the actors could pull the curtains to shield themselves from outside eyes. Slowly, culminating in the dual premieres of Castorf's *Der Idiot* (*The Idiot*) and Pollesch's *24 Stunden sind kein Tag* (*24 Hours Are Not a Day*) in 2002, among other events, Neumann added spaces alongside the container to create a maze of buildings he called the *Neustadt*, or new city, including three apartment buildings or hotels, a nail salon, a barber shop, and a brothel. For *Der Idiot* (Figure 38.1), the audience sat onstage on the Volksbühne's turntable, on scaffolding, the *Neustadt* all around them, a performance playground. In the five-hour-long performance, "American capital enters the picture in the form of a loquacious Texan," wrote Elinor Fuchs. "The chorus of whores trades its cheap dresses for cowboy hats and jeans jackets. Global capital invades, rates of exchange are flashed on video screens. In the east, above the old Las Vegas joint, apartments are being renovated." In *Der Idiot* Fuchs saw "the devouring of Berlin by global capital" (Fuchs 2009: 328).

Figure 38.1 A view of the set for *The Idiot*, directed by Frank Castorf and designed by Bert Neumann (Volksbühne Berlin, 2002). Through windows in the many rooms onstage, you can see some of the performers, and above the set is a projection screen (not being used at this point in the production). This perspective is of the auditorium of the Volksbühne's mainstage space; Neumann's set wrapped around the entire theatre. Joachim Fieguth/drama-berlin.de.)

As Volksbühne scenographer, Neumann was a lead artist. He made the *Neustadt*, and it changed how Castorf and Pollesch made theatre. It was because of the Containers that Castorf and Pollesch began using live video cameras. In a speech in honor of Neumann's receiving the 2015 Hein-Heckroth-Bühnenbildpreises (stage design prize), Pollesch said of the cameras, now a near-omnipresent marker of Castorf's work especially: "we only used them so that the spectators could see anything of what was happening" (Pollesch 2005). Addressing Neumann, Pollesch continued, noting that Neumann designed rooms for directors to fill: "[i]t isn't that the scenic designer makes a set, but rather the opposite. Every room you built made clear this autonomy, dear Bert. And they allowed us in turn to build our own autonomy."

In recent years, working on the cavernous Volksbühne mainstage, Neumann designed extraordinary objects and costumes for Pollesch: an enormous chandelier made from lighting instruments for *Ich schau dir in den Augen, gesellschaftlicher Verblendungszusammenhang!* (*I'm Looking You in the Eyes, Social Context of Deception!*) (2010); a tank on wheels for *Der General* (*The General*) (2013); and a life-size hot-air balloon for *Glanz und Elend der Kurtisanen* (*The Splendors and Miseries of Courtesans*) (2013). Listed as such, the objects feel both imaginative and random, but from the list one cannot grasp their beauty nor how *useful* they were for Pollesch. As Pollesch said, Neumann's sets "were robust, they smelled good, they beguiled all the senses, and did so in concrete ways" (Pollesch 2005). You always wanted to touch Neumann's materials, Pollesch remarked. Pollesch made the objects key elements of his productions: actors hang from them, crawl on them, float away on them, and discuss their political meanings in lengthy monologues.[2]

The final design Neumann completed for Castorf was *Die Brüder Karamasow* (*The Brothers Karamazov*), which premiered in Vienna in May and in Berlin in November 2015, an epic six-and-a-half-hour evening that recalls *Der Idiot* and other extraordinary Castorf/Neumann Dostoevsky adaptations; in fact, *The Brothers Karamazov* was the final Dostoevsky novel Castorf had yet to adapt. As described by critic Kai Krösche, Neumann's design included "a multiplicity of small scenic images, from the Russian Orthodox cupola to an entire small house with living rooms, a hip artist-apartment, countless hallways, and niches with beds and props" (Krösche 2015). There was a sauna, a dark pond, and a pavilion. During the performance, the actors scampered through the entire Volksbühne building, from cellar to roof. Neumann had the seats removed from the auditorium, leaving it as row after row of bare concrete, with spectators arranged on beanbags. In one image, Castorf regulars Marc Hosemann as Dimitri in a shiny red track suit, and Kathrin Angerer as Gruschenka, wearing only a long red t-shirt and reddish cowboy boots, sit on either side of a portrait of a young Stalin, who stares off into the future; on the floor, black and white stripes shoot out from Stalin's face like sun beams. The floor is covered with US dollars. The Berlin depicted in *Hauptmanns Weber* and then *Der Idiot* has now evolved into a fully westernized, gentrified, haute bourgeois city. But, though it feels finally and completely of Western Europe, this is clearly a Berlin perched unsteadily between the European Union and Vladimir Putin's Russia: Castorf incorporated angry text by Russian arch-anarchist DJ Stalingrad. Castorf and Neumann's *Die Brüder Karamasow* violently bursts forth from the abysses in our souls that cannot be bridged, much less filled, by piles of dollars, and reminds audiences that the Cold War will never truly end in Berlin, just as the East-West struggle did not actually begin in 1945.

Announcing *Die Brüder Karamasow* to the city, banners on the Volksbühne read "Nadryw" in Cyrillic letters (надрыв), which, as critic Dirk Pilz wrote in his obituary for

Neumann, is "a barely translatable word from Dostoevsky's novel . . . *Nadryw* means the irruption of emotion into thought, words breaking out of their housing" (Pilz 2015). For Pilz, *Nadryw* captures the aesthetic of the Volksbühne and Neumann: "rejection of the belief that you are in control, giving in to the accidental. But accidents don't simply happen, they happen only in exactingly created rooms, and only for the prepared spirit. That was Neumann's art" (ibid.).

Aleksandar Denić's monumental nightmares

Since 2013 Castorf has been collaborating, especially when outside Berlin, with Aleksandar Denić, a Serbian set designer, born in 1963, who also works in film and television. It is with Denić that Castorf made his infamous 2013 "Ring" cycle in Bayreuth, described by *New Yorker* critic Alex Ross as "a sprawling act of operatic Dadaism that falls between Buñuel and 'South Park'" (Ross 2013), and which Anthony Tommasini of the *New York Times* characterized as cynical, entitled, and hostile (Tommasini 2013). Denić's monumental sets rotated the opera between, among other locations, a communist Mount Rushmore – Marx, Lenin, Stalin, and Mao – with an Airstream-like trailer at its base; a recreation of Berlin's Soviet-era Alexanderplatz transport hub (its space-age world-time-clock in the foreground); and a roadside "Golden Motel" complete with

Figure 38.2 Bibiana Beglau (right, as Ferdinand Bardamu) and Götz Argus in Frank Castorf's production of *Reise ans Ende der Nacht* (*Journey to the End of the Night*) (2013) at the Residenztheater Munich, designed by Aleksandar Denić. In this image you can see the piles of detritus on Denić's stage, as well as the "Liberte Egalite Fraternite" sign, mimicking the entrance sign to Auschwitz. The projection screen above the set shows video from inside one of several enclosed rooms onstage. (Photo: Matthias Horn, courtesy of the Residenztheater.)

swimming pool. All of these locations, intimately and richly detailed, were cast in cinematic lighting by Rainer Casper, with videography by Andreas Deinert and Jens Crull. Adriana Braga Peretzki designed the costumes. Meanwhile, Wagner's music continued as usual, mostly undisturbed by Castorf's high concept.

Denić and Castorf met in Serbia in 2012 and had an immediate rapport. They share, Denić said in an interview, a "post-socialist horizon of experience," with its "contradictions and absurd paranoia" (Denić 2015: 30). Working with Castorf at the Residenztheater in Munich, Denić created post-colonial, war-torn environments for *Reise ans Ende der Nacht* (*Journey to the End of the Night*, 2013), an adaptation of Louis-Ferdinand Céline's World War One novel interspersed with Heiner Müller's *Der Auftrag* (*The Task*) and set in the Congo; and *Baal* by Bertolt Brecht, moved to an "Apocalypse Now"-style Vietnam, which greatly offended Brecht's heirs, and thus received only two public performances.

Denić's sets for *Reise ans Ende der Nacht* (Figure 38.2) and *Baal* (Figure 38.3) sat on the Residenztheater's turntable, fully-realized and hyperreal, but also impossible nightmares. The entrance to the trash-heap village of *Reise ans Ende der Nacht* was an Auschwitz-style metal gateway reading "Liberte, Egalite, Fraternite." Fans slowly mixed the smoky air; a decrepit USAID mini-bus rested on blocks amid temporary-looking structures made of corrugated metal and bare wood. Over it all was a projection screen, which somehow gave the set the feel of an abandoned drive-in movie theatre in

Figure 38.3 Inside one of the rooms on the set of an adaptation of Bertolt Brecht's *Baal*, directed by Frank Castorf and designed by Aleksandar Denić at the Residenztheater Munich (2015). Aurel Manthei, playing Baal, stands in the background; in front are Katharina Pichler, as the older sister, and Bibiana Beglau, as Isabella, the Hell Wife. Costumes by Adriana Braga Peretzki. (Photo: Thomas Aurin, courtesy of the Residenztheater.)

the African jungle. Inside the mini-bus and scattered throughout the camp were advertising posters – for pulp movies, like "Gorilla Woman," and Cassius Clay – visible only when a camera swept over them. Chickens pecked around oil barrels and half-filled gas cans. For *Baal*, a helicopter painted in shades of military green camouflage (the Playboy logo affixed to its nose) was surrounded by army tents, and an orientalist pagoda with an advertisement for what could have been a communist Kentucky Fried Chicken. Once again posters decorated the set, especially interiors, and two projection screens towered over the madness. Live videography has enabled Denić's installation-like designs: the cameras delve and zoom and focus and linger on the minutiae he has carefully arranged. "I leave stories everywhere," he said in an interview (Denić 2015).

Katrin Brack's *mise-en-scène*

Katrin Brack does not build sets. She creates climates: designing, for example, using only living plants for *Tod eines Handlungsreisenden* (*Death of a Salesman*) in 2006, directed by Luk Perceval at the Deutsches Theater Berlin; fog for *Ivanov* (2005), directed by Dimiter Gotscheff at the Volksbühne Berlin; and rain for *Prinz Friedrich von Homburg* (2006), directed by Armin Petras at Schauspielfrankfurt. "When the curtain goes up," writes Robin Detje of Brack's designs, "everything is already there" (Detje 2010: 243). It just keeps coming, like the rain for Petras' *Homburg*, which fell for three interminable hours, leaving actors soaked and audiences damply cold. The isolated materials and empty space in her scenes has encouraged critics to call her aesthetic minimalist – there are no drawing rooms, much less samovars, in her *Ivanov*, as figures appear and disappear in fog like half-remembered dreams. But we would do just as well to call her a maximalist: how else to describe endless, brightly colored confetti streamers shot from a cannon (*Tartuffe* in 2007, with Gotscheff at the Thalia Theater Hamburg) like the most awesome party you never attended?

Born in 1958 in Hamburg and trained at the Staatliche Kunstakademie in Düsseldorf under Karl Kneidl, Brack began her career as an independent designer by working with Belgian director Luk Perceval. Her early designs were architectural, including three layers of wooden platforms, which could tilt and open, for *Schlachten!* (*Battles!*), directed by Perceval at the Spielhaus Hamburg in 1999. Gradually Brack's designs became more abstract and idea-driven, as she both opened the stage to its full volume and made that volume tangible by filling it. For *Kampf des Negers und der Hunde* (*Battle of Black and Dogs*), by Bernard-Marie Koltès, directed by Gotscheff in 2003 at the Volksbühne Berlin, confetti was slowly raining onstage as the audience entered the auditorium, as it was when they departed. "I began thinking about the land to which we as white people travel, where we have a good time, take what we want and leave our rubbish behind," Brack said of the production in an interview. "Then I wrote down a whole lot of terms about Africa as they came to me . . . From all that I tried to develop an image which encompassed all the aspects." The confetti, she said, "brings together the colours of the continent, reflects colonial arrogance and a different sense of time, one we've become estranged from" (Brack 2015: 16).

Brack works to make manifest the essential spirit of a play in a director's concept. *Prinz Friedrich von Homburg* can be seen as a celebration of Prussian values and masculinity, obsessing over violence and obedience. For Petras, *Homburg* became the story of an East German man nostalgic for a Germanic past that never existed, except maybe for a brief period in the 1930s and early 1940s. Bald, in military boots and a leather jacket,

Figure 38.4 *Kampf des Negers und der Hunde* (*Battle of Black and Dogs*) (2003), by Bernard-Marie Koltès, directed by Dimiter Gotscheff, with sets and costumes by Katrin Brack. Brack's confetti falls on the cavernous Volksbühne Berlin stage. (Holger Foullois/drama-berlin.de.)

the man dreams of Prussia. Brack set Petras' production on a dark, tarp-covered, raked stage. The rain-drenched actors hit one another and wrestled, falling and sliding on the slick tarp down towards the audience, barely in control. The only reality in this world was war: Brack and Petras created a dreadful vision of Germany's future.

These designs are often allegorical. For Perceval's *Tod eines Handlungsreisenden*, she created a living, potted forest, isolated, arranged as a rectangle on the large Schaubühne stage, lit by sodium lamps, surrounded by darkness. Willy sat on a black pleather couch in a sleeveless undershirt and khakis, facing a television and the audience, fantasizing about the great wilderness Alaska, a kind of wilderness behind him; his itinerant brother appeared and vanished through the green leaves. As Willy died, the plants grew upwards, towards their artificial suns.

Many of Brack's most productive collaborations have been with Gotscheff, who died in 2013 and was renowned for his productions of Heiner Müller's plays. In 2005 they created Chekhov's *Ivanov* at the Volksbühne. The set for *Ivanov* was sculptured fog, carefully controlled by Brack. It rolled up out of the stage floor, enveloping the actors and even, at times, the first rows of the auditorium. Amid the fog, stasis ruled. Instead of shooting himself, Ivanov walked to the back of the stage, fog disappearing around his ankles; he spray-painted a stick figure with a flaccid line between the legs, a middle finger raised and a gun in the other hand. He sprayed a dot between the gun and the figure's head. A body fell from the rafters, hitting the floor with a soft thud.

Jan Pappelbaum's simple models

Jan Pappelbaum has been working with Thomas Ostermeier since the mid-1990s, first at the Baracke, the former secondary space of the Deutsches Theater Berlin, and, since 1999, at the Schaubühne Berlin, which has become the favored theatre of the European bourgeois creative-class, as popular in Paris and New York as Berlin. Trained in architecture as well as scenic design, Pappelbaum has made chic and sexy home interiors for five productions of plays by Ibsen, all directed by Ostermeier – sometimes looking like showrooms for modern furniture with towering glass walls, rich wood trims, and long, minimalist sofas. Ostermeier reveals these dream rooms of the upper middle class to be concealing, just beneath their slick surfaces, consuming disease. At the same time, Ostermeier has directed five Shakespeare plays, all designed by Pappelbaum. With Shakespeare, Pappelbaum has gone elemental, designing with dirt, water, and clay, separating the play from our contemporary moment while also enabling actors, especially the magnetic Lars Eidinger, to speak across the divide and make Shakespeare's emotions and themes palpable for Schaubühne audiences.

"Designing sets usually consists of collecting impressions and moods, putting together objects and images, and putting them in a new and clear order," Pappelbaum said in a 2006 interview. "The world only reveals itself in simplicity, in models" (Pappelbaum 2006: 16). The models Pappelbaum created for Ostermeier's Ibsen productions radiate a glossy realism, resembling the rooms pictured in the pages of *Architectural Digest*, perfectly arranged and sterile. For *Nora* (2002), he placed the Helmer family in a modernist house, with polished woods and a glass facade. A ten-foot long, four-foot tall fish tank, with living fish, faced the audience. At the end of the play, after Nora shot Torvald, sending his bleeding body into the fish tank, the stage began to rotate. At an angle, you could see the room's fakery, the empty bookshelves and stage tricks. It was all so obviously a facade.

Pappelbaum's set for *Hedda* (2006) (Figure 38.5) functioned in a similar way, working to seduce the audience with its glossy aesthetic according to Pappelbaum (ibid.: 24). This was a luxurious space, modeled on Mies van der Rohe's Farnsworth house, with walls of glass, shiny floors, and a low, modular couch. Rain showered the glass to the harmonies of the Beach Boys' "Pet Sounds." Here again the Schaubühne's audience watched itself, or some idealized version of itself, lounge, attractive and bored, in a house that was more waiting room than home. For *Ein Volksfeind* (*Enemy of the People*, 2012), Ostermeier and Pappelbaum moved into the gentrifying city: the Stockmann family (youngish, in their early 30s) lived in a loft, playing music, smoking dope, and sitting around on Ikea furniture: old enough to live on their own, but not old enough to have purchased all the objects they will want. Leftist creatives, they drew furniture on blackboard-like walls, scrawled over and defaced the images and, in a stunning gesture, whitewashed the walls before Stockmann's confrontation scene. By the end of the play, the kids had either become fanatics or, to use David Brooks' formulation, Bobos.

Educated in Weimar – he was born in Dresden in 1966 – Pappelbaum sees himself as craftsman, "ordering and structuring function" (ibid.: 17). So even though his designs for Ostermeier's Shakespeare productions look entirely different from the contemporary bourgeois tragedies, their functionality, influenced by the Bauhaus, is the same. *Hamlet* (2008) was a ready-made gravesite, an earthen pit, but also equipped for a party, with a long white-bedecked table fit for celebrating a wedding. Rain quickly turned

Figure 38.5 From left to right: Lars Eidinger (as Tesman), Joerg Hartmann (Judge Brack), Kay Bartholomäeus Schulze (Lovborg) and Katharina Schueüttler (Hedda) in Henrik Ibsen's *Hedda Gabler*, directed by Thomas Ostermeier and designed by Jan Pappelbaum (Schaubühne am Lehniner Platz Berlin, 2005). Rain falls on the plate glass wall; a mirror reflects the action from above, while the buffed black floor reflects from below. (Joachim Fieguth/drama-berlin.de)

the dirt to mud. *Othello* (2010) played in ankle-deep water, with chairs arranged in a square, as if for a high-level cabinet meeting, but placed around a bed instead of a table. A wall of neon tubes provided lighting, giving the wavy reflective water an exotic appeal. For *Richard III* (2015), Pappelbaum transformed the interior of Saal C of the Schaubühne into a version of Shakespeare's Globe Theatre. It was more like a new auditorium inside the Schaubühne, with the rounded wall of the building as the back of the auditorium and wood panels mostly hiding the building's bare concrete. The clay half-circle stage, semi-hard and chalky, offered the public little protection from the actors. With Eidinger playing the infamous hunchback, Ostermeier utilized Pappelbaum's design to enable interaction, while balconies gave Eidinger the chance to reign over the space. In translations by Schaubühne resident playwright Marius von Mayenburg, these Shakespeares come from the mythic past but belong to our time. Pappelbaum's sets provide functional bridges between those spaces, without trying to cover up the divide between them.

Experimentation in the *freie Szene*

Since the early 2000s especially, a wave of artists have been creating (often as collectives) theatrical experiments in space, freed from the constraints of *Staatstheater* stages and rehearsal processes. (The division between the state-funded, repertory- and ensemble-based *Staatstheater* and the *freie Szene* is far from absolute – the Volksbühne in particular has engaged artists from the independent theatre scene.) Here I present a sampling of this work.

Rimini Protokoll – founded in 2000, the theatre collective of Helgard Haug, Stefan Kaegi, and Daniel Wetzel, who met at the Gießen Institute for Applied Theater Studies – makes documentary drama for the contemporary media-driven and -addled world. Their productions sometimes look like traditional theatre, with performances happening onstage and spectators watching from the auditorium. In such productions, generally by Haug and Wetzel – the most recent is *Adolph Hitler: Mein Kampf Vol. 1 & 2* (2015) – "experts of the everyday," people untrained as actors, tell their own stories, which Haug and Wetzel weave together and place in conversation with theatre history. But Rimini Protokoll has also pioneered the city tour as theatre with productions like *Remote X* by Kaegi. For *Remote X*, cityscapes provide the scenography as small groups go on customized tours of Berlin, Santiago, New York, and Moscow, directed by a computerized voice to board subway trains and dance, learning about their city as they move through it, seeing it anew as elaborate performance. *50 Aktenkilometer* (*50 Kilometers of Dossiers*, 2011), by Haug, Kaegi, and Wetzel, contrasted the East Berlin of the 1980s with the Berlin of today. With smartphone in hand, participants wandered through Alexanderplatz and surrounding areas; as they walked, stories played through their headphones, triggered by their GPS-determined location. A map guided them, with story locations marked in orange circles, listing street names that have changed to erase the communist past and accommodate a capitalist society. The city was transformed for me when I participated, layers of history added to my everyday travels through Berlin.[3]

One of their most elaborate creations combined the tour-format with installation theatre: *Situation Rooms* (2013) created by Haug, Wetzel, and Kaegi together. In the foyer of Hebbel am Ufer 2 in Berlin, I was assigned an iPad and a door, my entrance into Rimini Protokoll's world, the scenography created Dominic Huber, a Swiss German and member of the design team blendwerk. The rooms – simply appointed but indicative and interactive – were transformed by the iPad, which I held up in front of my face. In the video that played there, people affected by the international weapons trade, from a child soldier to a sport shooter to a diplomat to a salesman, told their stories in their spaces. We, the participants, did not just see the world through the experts' eyes, we became them, raising a flag when their arm reached out to do the same, putting on their clothing, inserting a thumb drive into a computer for them. With its scenography, videos (created by Chris Kondek, formerly of the Wooster Group), and stories, *Situation Rooms* created conditions that encouraged radical empathy and critical thinking.

Many *freie Szene* groups create their sets as they develop a performance. For andcompany&Co. – founded in 2003 by Alexander Karschnia, Nicola Nord, Sascha Sulimma, and a rotating cast of collaborators – scenography both shapes and is shaped by the production as both are built. The designs are functional and outlandish. For *little red play: "herstory"* (2006), Hila Flashkes (an Israeli artist and puppeteer) set word sculptures, in English, German, and Russian, amid practical lights and small tables, including a place for Sulimma to mix the sound. The actors in the non-narrative communist fairy-tale – little red is a time traveler whose parents were West German communists – ran around the set pieces, shooting each other with pop guns. The company's *Mausoleaum Buffo* (2009), a sequel to *little red* in a way, also designed by Flashkes, was constructivist, like Liubov Popova's set for the 1922 Soviet production of *The Magnanimous Cuckold*. A geometric tomb for Lenin and Lennon (the Russian communist *and* the British pop star) was also a boat; a wind-turbine-like machine dominated stage left, with the Cyrillic letter "Я" at center, covered eventually by Mickey Mouse ears that folded up from the floor. For *Black Bismarck* (2013), a debate on race in the German nation and its *Kultur*, visual artist Jan Brokof created a white elongated star that functioned as a table. Behind it, a projection screen showed videos and images. Refracting Brecht through neoliberal dada, andcompany&Co like to talk and interrupt each other: when one performer hits his or her light, the others must shut up. Their aesthetic can be reduced to a table with microphones, a sound mixer, and lightbulbs as it was for their lecture-performance *Sounds Like War: Kriegserklärung* (*Sounds Like War: Declaration of War*, 2014).

Categorizing design today

It is clear that no one scenographic movement dominates the stages of Germany today. Radicalizing the trend noted by Hortmann at the start of this chapter, Neumann and Castorf did not allow the text to dictate their work. Neumann made frames, not metonymic but concrete, in and of themselves, which have pushed Castorf and Pollesch, among other artists, to innovate. But Neumann's scenography was still rooted in theatre history. Pollesch especially is trying to make a post-Brechtian, post-communist theatre that is also anti-capitalist, in theme and means of production. Neumann's autonomous spaces pick up on the legacy of Brecht's designers, but shape action even more directly. With Rimini Protokoll and andcompany&Co., however, Hortmann's criticism of directors and designers who ignore the original playtext does not apply at all; their theatre and theatrical experiments do not begin or end with plays. Here too are the legacies of past design, reinvented for today's world: constructivism, dada, and documentary theatre. While andcompany&Co. adapts Lehmann's ideas – they studied with him in Frankfurt – much of Rimini Protokoll's work stretches the category, sometimes non-dramatic and sometimes like drama, as in the individual stories of *Situation Rooms*. Finally, in the designs of Jan Pappelbaum, it is clear that Hortmann was simply incorrect. Pappelbaum sees the same world that Neumann saw – an increasingly bourgeois Berlin – and addresses it in a completely different manner, replicating its surfaces, criticizing its lack of depth, showing its tragedies. Although influenced by the aesthetics of postdramatic scenography, Pappelbaum creates stages for the dramatic theatre.

Terms such as "postdramatic" or "postmodern" are inadequate concepts for gathering together these diverse artists; the binary *drama–postdrama* is less useful today, even as design has become more autonomous than ever. Perhaps this is most clear in Katrin Brack. Gotscheff directed *Ivanov* as if he were directing a Heiner Müller text, a concept that demanded a scenography such as that created by Brack, in which atmosphere is more important than storytelling. But in working with Perceval for *Death of a Salesman* and Petras for *Homburg*, Brack created environments that enabled specific versions of those two stories to be told. In contemporary Germany, where one style does not rule, audiences and critics delight in designers with inimitable, always evolving, and immediately recognizable styles creating imaginative spaces and places tailored to particular directors, plays, theatres, and experiments.

Notes

1 Of course there are many other designers who could be included in this survey. For a more comprehensive list see *Bild der Bühne / Setting the Scene, Volume 2*, which boasts nearly 200 pages of color photography alongside biographies and interviews – in English as well as German – of

17 contemporary designers working in Germany. Mirka Döring and Ute Müler-Tischler (Ed.) *Bild der Bühne / Setting the Stage Volume* 2, trans. Lindsay Jane-Munro and James J. Conway (Berlin: Theater der Zeit, 2015).

2 For more on Pollesch's work with Neumann see Matt Cornish, "Stop Just Going Along: The Dysfunctional Theatrics of René Pollesch," *TheatreForum* 40 (Winter/Spring 2012): 58–66.

3 For more see Matt Cornish, "Performing the Archive: History and Memory in Recent German Theater," *Theatre Journal* 67.1 (March 2015): 63–82.

References

Baugh, Christopher 2006. "Brecht and Stage Design: The *Bühnenbildner* and the *Bühnenbauer*." In *The Cambridge Companion to Brecht* (2nd ed.), edited by Peter Thomson and Glendyr Sachs, 259–77. Cambridge: Cambridge University Press.

Brack, Katrin 2015. "Space of Experience," interview by Anja Nioduschewski. In *Setting the Stage Vol. 2*, translated by Lindsay Jane-Munro and James J. Conway. Berlin: Theater der Zeit.

Denić, Aleksander 2015. "Reality of the Absurd," interview by Ute Müller-Tischler. In *Setting the Stage Vol. 2*, translated by Lindsay Jane-Munro and James J. Conway. Berlin: Theater der Zeit.

Detje, Robin 2010. "The Universe is an Atom in the Thumbnail of a Giant." in *Katrin Brack: Bühnenbild/Stages*, edited by Anja Nioduschewski, translated by Lucy Renner Jones. Berlin: Theater der Zeit.

Döring, Mirka and Ute Müler-Tischler (Eds) 2015. *Bild der Bühne / Setting the Stage, Vol. 2*, translated by Lindsay Jane-Munro and James J. Conway. Berlin: Theater der Zeit.

Fuchs, Elinor 2009. "An Idiot's Guide to Theatre in Berlin." In *Changing the Subject: Marvin Carlson and Theatre Studies 1959–2009*, edited by Joseph Roach. Ann Arbor, MI: University of Michigan Press.

Hortmann, Wilhelm 2008. "Revolutions in Scenography on the German Stage in the Twentieth Century." In *A History of German Theatre*, edited by Simon Williams and Maik Hamburger, 275–305. Cambridge: Cambridge University Press.

Krösche, Kai 2015. "Dämonen in der Sargfabrik," *Nachtkritik*, 29 May. Available online at: www.nachtkritik.de/index.php?option=com_content&view=article&id=11041%3Adie-brueder-karamasow-mit-einem-all-star-ensemble-und-in-knapp-sieben-stunden-schliesst-frank-castorf-in-wien-seine-dostojewski-auseinandersetzung-ab&catid=38&Itemid=40, archived at perma.cc/J9XW-U7X5.

Lehmann, Hans-Thies 2005. *Postdramatisches Theater* (2nd ed.). Frankfurt am Main: Verlag der Autoren.

Neumann, Bert 2001.*"Imitation of Life": Bert Neumann Bühnenbilder*, edited by Hannah Hurtzig. Berlin: Theater der Zeit.

Pappelbaum, Jan 2006. "You Should Be Able to Sit in an Ibsen Play," interview by Anja Dürrschmidt. In *Dem Einzelnen ein Ganzes / A Whole for the Parts: Bühnen / Stages*, edited by Anja Dürrschmidt, translated by Joe W. Compton. Berlin: Theater der Zeit.

Pilz, Dirk 2015. "Neumann türmte Landebahnen für das Unvorhersehbare auf." *Berliner Zeitung*, 2 August. Available online at: www.berliner-zeitung.de/kultur/volksbuehne-buehnenbildner-bert-neumann-ist-tot--neumann-tuermte-landebahnen-fuer-das-unvorhersehbare-auf,10809150,31366820.html.

Pollesch, René 2005. "Jeder Raum, den du gebaut hast, erzählt diese Autonomie, lieber Bert. Und lässt einen an der eigenen Autonomie bauen." *Nachtkritik*, April. Available online at: www.nachtkritik.de/index.php?option=com_content&view=article&id=11355:laudatio-fuer-bert-neumann-von-rene-pollesch-zur-verleihung-des-hein-heckroth-buehnenbildpreises-im-2015&catid=53:portraet-a-profil&Itemid=83>, archived at <perma.cc/M755-T23Y.

Ross, Alex 2013. "Wagner Summer: A new 'Ring' in Bayreuth; 'Die Meistersinger' in Salzburg." In *The New Yorker*, 26 August. Available online at: www.newyorker.com/magazine/2013/08/26/wagner-summer.

Tommasini, Anthony 2013. "At Bayreuth, Boos and Dropped Jaws." In *The New York Times*, 1 August. Available online at: www.nytimes.com/2013/08/02/arts/music/at-bayreuth-boos-and-dropped-jaws.html.

39

MODERN BRITISH THEATRE DESIGN

UK design for performance since 1975

Kate Burnett

> I think two designers absolutely changed the course of British Theatre design: one was Jocelyn [Herbert] and the other was John Bury. Before them most designers were encouraged to wrap up the pill in a lot of fancy paper, but John and Jocelyn affected a whole generation of designers and directors and made them insist on the question, "It may be nice, but is it necessary?"
>
> *(Sir Peter Hall in Courtney 1993: 223)*

British theatre design, like British theatre itself, was transformed in the 1950s and 1960s, in part, as Peter Hall suggests, by Jocelyn Herbert, working at the Royal Court Theatre, and John Bury at Joan Littlewood's Theatre Workshop, then by both of them at the Royal Shakespeare Company (RSC) and National Theatre. Each, in their own way, continued a pre-war trend developed by the Motley design team away from the decorative. The reverberations of these innovations would ripple through British scenography over the next decades. Regarding Herbert, Margaret "Percy" Harris, one of the founders of Motley, noted, "There are two kinds of designers; there are designers and there are decorators. The big difficulty . . . Jocelyn has solved so well is to remain simple, but to maintain enough decorative feeling to keep her sets alive and, where appropriate, beautiful . . . everything she does is absolutely pure but always beautiful too" (Courtney 1993: 211). Bury was influential as an organizational and mobilizing force, also as an innovative lighting and set designer, who, in Hall's words, "believed in the real functioning of material and . . . dealt out the reality of textile, of soil and brickwork. His sets were less 'designed', less aesthetic than Jocelyn's. She removed everything from the stage that didn't fulfill a function and made something beautiful out of that minimalism" (Courtney 1993: 223).

That this involvement in the devising, conceptualizing, and sharing of production ideas led many designers to describe their practice or development in terms of a flight from "decor," is significant. John Bury as curator of the UK exhibit at the 1975 Prague Quadrennial (PQ) declared,

> They [British designers] inherited their role from a previous generation, active as decorators, bred in a theatre that served to entertain the moneyed classes. Today's designers have benefited from changes in social attitudes and work for an audience with a less frivolous outlook . . . They believe that the best way to put an idea on stage is to put a man on stage possessed by that idea, and this puts the actor and the singer safely at the centre of their work, diminishing for them the interest in stage mechanics for their own sake, and nourishing a belief in an economy of means of expression.
>
> *(Bury 1975)*

For the 1979 exhibit at PQ Bury again wrote that there is "a tendency both in the design of settings and costume, towards a clarity of vision, a creative economy and a cutting back of inessentials. Comment is inherent rather than explicit. The actor takes the centre of our stage – his presence is necessary to complete the design" (Bury 1979).

Building on the aesthetic foundations promoted by Herbert and Bury, the "modern" era of British design for performance could be considered to start in July 1975 when the Society of British Theatre Designers (SBTD) was formally established with the aim of achieving union representation for designers. But its identity was forged in January 1976 when Britain first took part in the Prague Quadrennial (the 1975 edition, but six months late). This act of participation by four designers – John Bury,

Figure 39.1 *A Midsummer Night's Dream* by Benjamin Britten, Glyndebourne Festival Opera, 1981. Set and lighting design John Bury, costume design Elizabeth Bury. Directed by Peter Hall. (Guy Gravett/Glyndebourne Productions Ltd./ArenaPAL.)

Ralph Koltai, Timothy O'Brien, and Tazeena Firth – achieved immediate status for UK theatre design in an international event of 28 participating countries. Winning a completely unexpected Gold Medal, the four returned, inspired, and committed to the idea of the SBTD holding national exhibitions from which representative selections would be made for future PQs. The SBTD has organized UK participation in PQ ever since and their national exhibitions and catalogues have not only evidenced many designers' careers, changing styles and technologies but have also contributed to and influenced successive bodies of work and their documentation.

The 40 plus years since 1975 have seen the extraordinary development of a vast variety of performance and performance design in the UK. In the same period the number of UK full-time courses in Performance Design and related specialisms has grown from four to approximately 27 and the subject has become a recognized and growing area of academic research. It has also been both a beneficiary and an agent of social, political, aesthetic, and technological change in the shifting culture of the late twentieth century and millennial United Kingdom. Throughout, this chapter will consider the training/education of theatre designers in the UK and the creation of new performance spaces alongside professional practice as these are intertwined.

Pre- and post-WWII influences and developments

In order to set the scene for the auspicious events of 1975/6 some background is necessary. There were perhaps three principal tendencies emerging from the nineteenth and early twentieth centuries in the UK. First, the so-called naturalism of the furnished stage "room" that responded to the domestic contexts of Ibsen, Shaw, Pinero, Granville Barker, etc.; second, the monumental explorations of form and light by Appia and Craig that led to a twentieth-century "epic" style of staging and the "simplifying" modular approach developed in the UK by Motley (Jump 2015: 40); and third, the embrace of vigorous pattern, exotic architectural decoration, and stylized painted landscapes that arose from the combined impact in the UK of the Ballets Russes, the Arts and Crafts Movement, and nineteenth-century Romantic landscape painting that fed scenic art. In addition, there was the heady mix of twentieth-century Surrealism and Expressionism in Fine Art and the stylization of early cinema as influences. The interwar years saw visual artists such as John Piper, Rex Whistler, Edward Burra, and Robert Medley designing for the stage along with scenic artists Vladimir and Elizabeth Polunin, Oliver Messel, illustrator Charles Ricketts, dancer William Chappell, designers Sophie Fedorovitch and Roger Furse, and designer, photographer, and decorator Cecil Beaton (see Hainaux 1957: 26) among the most noted designers of theatre, opera, and ballet in Britain. In all these forms, costume design was considered as, if not more, important than set design, which remained primarily pictorial, or sculptural, sometimes atmospheric, abstracted and evocative, as with Piper's backdrops. Architectural designs often involved three-dimensional entrance and wing flats but "morphed" into painted drops mid- and upstage.

Roy Strong's essay in the 1989 book, *British Theatre Design – the Modern Age*, is quoted at length here for his lucid appraisal of 1960s and 1970s British styles and influences. In it he recalled that Oliver Messel preferred to be "credited as having 'decorated' a production" (Goodwin 1989: 17) and that although the above pre-war artists designing for theatre had rather disappeared, the painterly tradition continued into the 1960s in the delicate and characterful work of Peter Rice, Carl Toms, Nicholas Georgiadis, and the "verismo" style of Franco Zeffirelli and Lila de Nobili which:

> took onboard the change in perception generated in the public by both film and, by 1960, television, which made any stage experience flimsy in comparison. The new lightweight construction materials permitted a new realism on stage: sets were elaborately built and there was a huge multiplication of props.
>
> The verismo style looked back to the nineteenth century in its desire to recreate gigantic stage pictures – breathtaking in concept, but still bound by optical rules of single-point perspective. It was a style particularly suited to the great war-horses of opera and ballet, but it was not one that produced any recognisable 'school' in this country except de Nobili's protege, Henry Bardon, and . . . Julia Trevelyan Oman . . . [whose detailed evocation of nineteenth-century Paris for La Bohème at Covent Garden (1974) was in use until 2015].
>
> The main thrust in theatre design after 1960 . . . was affected by a new generation of theatre directors, above all, Peter Hall and Trevor Nunn; by new theatres such as Chichester, which are open arena stages; by the advent of stage design as an academic discipline within the colleges of art; and by huge advances in technology, above all in the emergence of lighting expertise which could literally make or break a production. The new approach was certainly not painterly, nor over concerned with historical exactitude or detail. Its focus lay in that dramatic celerity familiar to audiences used to television and film. Nothing was either to impede the action, the development of dramatic tension, nor to detract from the centrality of the text, or divide the audience and actors from a shared experience. The theatre ceased to be an escape from the dreariness of post-war Britain into a magic world; rather in the 1960s and 1970s it was a theatre which reminded its audiences – buoyant in the 'You never had it so good' era – that an unpleasant real world still existed. Black and grey predominated and whole theatres and sets became monuments to a stygian gloom.
>
> *(Goodwin 1989: 18–20)*

Strong also singled out what was arguably, for other British designers, the most influential post-war design – *Oliver!* by Sean Kenny:

> The first designer to overwhelm the public with this new dynamism and vision was Sean Kenny, whose background was in architecture and not painting and who came out of the left wing stable of Joan Littlewood. Tragically he died young, but no one who saw his designs for the musical *Oliver!* (1960) will ever forget the impact of those vast moving constructions on stage which were quite thrilling to watch. Overnight they rendered the post-war painterly vision not only obsolete, but effete.
>
> *(Ibid.: 20)*

Many directors and designers of the post-war period cite the influence of the Berliner Ensemble's visits to London in 1956 and again in 1965. They particularly noted the work of Brecht's designers Caspar Neher, Karl von Appen, and Teo Otto. Pamela Howard remembers the impact of von Appen's *Coriolanus* (1965):

> The Berliner Ensemble demonstrated a new method of using colour and composition, working from the actor outwards by using indicative but imagined locales, encouraging the audience to believe what they could see and imagine what they could not. This was the break from stage-painted naturalism, to using the stage as Brecht and Neher described – 'to make a significant statement about reality', by working on the essentials of the play, finding out what the players really needed, what was happening to and through them, and composing an eloquent response in colour and form.
>
> *(Howard 2009: 107)*

Howard also describes how Jocelyn Herbert, inspired by the collaborative and economical work of Brecht's designers, "began a lifetime of influential searching to create an equivalent form of poetic realism on stage, and in so doing influenced a generation of scenographers, . . . her gifts of drawing, common sense and practicality enabled her to make stage compositions of incomparable beauty" (ibid.: 106).

Brecht and Neher's focus on the object and its performer rather than the "setting" was an inspiration to the collaborative approaches of designers Bury and Herbert, followed by William Dudley (*The Mysteries* at the Cottesloe and Lyceum), Alison Chitty, as well as Howard. In their work the artifact is made particular by its usage and poetic by its placing and juxtapositions, hence the increasing contribution of designers and their development of sketch-storyboards made in rehearsal.

Stage and costume design training

Stage and costume design were identified as a discrete training in Britain in the early twentieth century and taught in art school contexts, of which the following, all in London, are the longest established.

The Central School of Arts and Crafts (now Central Saint Martins – CSM) was founded by William Lethaby in 1896, its Southampton Row building of 1907 influenced by William Morris. By the 1930s Costume Design was being taught by Jeanetta Cochrane and in 1937 a Set Design course was established there under Ruth Keating. Cochrane planned to have a theatre built at Southampton Row but died in 1957; it was eventually opened and named after her in 1964. Ralph Koltai, who trained at "Central" from 1948–51, returned shortly after to teach and became Head of Theatre Design from 1965–72. He invited Ballet Rambert to be resident in the Jeanetta Cochrane Theatre affirming Craig's assertion of the primacy of dance and visual communication in performance (Walton 1983: 52–3). Dance continued at the Cochrane in collaborative projects until its closure in 2012 and CSM's move to its Kings Cross site.

Wimbledon College of Art was established in 1890, with Theatre Design taught from 1932 and becoming a department, one of only three, along with Visual Arts and Foundation Studies at its current site in 1948. Royal College of Art graduate Peter Bucknell taught at Wimbledon from 1948, becoming Head of Theatre Design, then College Principal from 1964–9. He was succeeded in Theatre Design by the inspirational Richard Negri who had trained with Motley and Michel Saint-Denis at the Old Vic Theatre School (see below). Negri's career included renowned work at the Royal Court, Old Vic, and also in Oldham and Manchester where he worked with directors Michael Elliott, Caspar Wrede, Braham Murray, and James Maxwell to design, develop, and design for the spaceship-like Royal Exchange theatre in-the-round

Figure 39.2 Set drawing by Jocelyn Herbert for *A Woman Killed with Kindness* by Thomas Heywood. The National Theatre at the Old Vic, 1971. Director John Dexter, set and costume design Jocelyn Herbert, lighting design Andy Phillips. (© Jocelyn Herbert, courtesy National Theatre Archive.)

(Architects Levitt Bernstein) built inside Manchester's defunct Cotton Exchange. After its opening in 1976 he also returned to Wimbledon, becoming Head of Theatre Design until 1988. CSM, Wimbledon, and the also notable Byam Shaw Art School have all now been absorbed under the umbrella University of the Arts London (UAL).

The Slade School of Art opened its Theatre Design course in 1929 established by Vladimir Polunin, who, with his English wife Elizabeth, were designers and scenic artists with Diaghilev's Ballets Russes. Their students included Oliver Messel, Jocelyn Herbert, and Nicholas Georgiadis who came from Greece on a British Council scholarship to study Painting and Theatre Design from 1953–5. Quickly developing a life-long working relationship with the Royal Ballet choreographer Kenneth MacMillan, Georgiadis taught at the Slade for 30 years from 1958 with painter-designers Robert Medley and Peter Snow, who were each Head of Theatre Design in 1958–67 and 1967–92 respectively. Students included Philip Prowse, William Dudley, Pamela Howard, and Yolanda Sonnabend who perhaps most identifiably continued a fluid, fluent painterly style of design for dance.

The first design course in a drama school environment also started in the 1930s, with three young designers, Elizabeth Montgomery, Margaret "Percy" Harris, and her sister Sophie, who had trained together at the Chelsea Illustrators Studio and found success as the team "Motley" with their first stage and costume designs for the already-celebrated

John Gielgud for the Oxford University Drama Society. They were recruited by director Michel Saint-Denis to teach a strongly text- and director-focused collaborative design course at his experimental new London Theatre Studio, which lasted from 1936 to the outbreak of war in 1939.

After the war Margaret and Sophie Harris re-joined Saint-Denis (who had also recruited directors George Devine and Glen Byam Shaw), teaching design at his Old Vic Theatre School (1947–52). From 1966 Margaret "Percy" Harris established the Sadler's Wells Theatre Design course, initially at Sadler's Wells Theatre, only the first of many different names and homes the Motley design course would have in corners of theatres around London. Jocelyn Herbert, who had trained with Motley at the Theatre Studio after attending The Slade, went on to work with George Devine and the English Stage Company at the Royal Court Theatre in 1953. The Motley design course was remarkable in staying independent of universities; it was taught by and produced a disproportionate number of notable and fiercely loyal designers in its peripatetic history. In 1991 Alison Chitty (alumnus of CSM) became co-director with Percy Harris who continued to teach until just before her death in 2000. By 2011, with Chitty and her colleague Ashley Martin Davis' retirement, the course was finally deemed to be financially unsustainable and, at least temporarily, closed.

The London courses, above, established the dominant forms of twentieth-century theatre design training in the UK reflecting, though not exclusively, the orientation of designers trained as problem-solving artists at art school. The drama schools did not introduce design courses until the 1970s, and usually with an uneasy balancing of the needs of student performers and directors with those of student designers and makers developing their vocabularies. It was against this background of training that Peter Hall commented on the supportive role of the designer as "helpmate and critic" (Goodwin 1989: 14), but it was on the Motley course, taught by Hall's most frequent collaborators (after Bury) – Jocelyn Herbert and Alison Chitty – and at CSM under Pamela Howard that the equality and sometimes leadership of the designer within the "creative team" was understood.

Post war regeneration and theatre spaces

The 1944 Education Act for post-war Britain had brought free education to all up to age 15, then 16 years. In 1946 The Arts Council was established with a mission to make the arts available to communities across the country, "the best to the most" as Minister Jenny Lee promised (Harvie 2005: 20), to improve social and educational standards, as central to the restoration of civic confidence and cultural identity in the rebuilding of badly bombed and damaged cities. However, as Harvie argues, its initial priority was London, and by "prioritising the centrally located national arts institutions . . . [it] denigrated the regional by setting it up as the metropolis' devalued binary opposite" (ibid.: 17). During the 1940s and 1950s the number of UK theatres is reported to have dropped from approximately 1,000 to fewer than 500 (Elsom in Harvie 2005: 20). But with a government report, "Housing the Arts in Great Britain," published in 1959 and 1961, the situation was turned around and approximately 100 theatres were built in the next 25 years, mostly in the regions and with an emphasis on resident producing/repertory companies, most including design departments.

In London the Royal Festival Hall, built for the 1951 Festival of Britain, was added to and adapted in 1964 and 1967, becoming in 1998 the Southbank Centre, offering increasing opportunities for a wide range of artists, performances, exhibitions and events to the present day. In 1982 the City of London opened its multi-venue, Brutalist-style Barbican Centre (designed by Chamberlin, Powell, and Bon), built in part as a London home to the RSC. The National Theatre was inaugurated in 1963 at the Old Vic Theatre, Waterloo, moving to its new building designed by Denis Lasdun also on the South Bank in 1976 and Sadler's Wells Opera company moved into the 2,000-seat London Coliseum in 1968, becoming the English National Opera Company. The 2,200-seat Royal Opera House continued in Covent Garden behind its 1858 facade.

In *Making Space for Theatre: British Architecture and Theatre Since 1958*, Mulryne and Shewring examine the "modern era" of UK theatre building and its impact on the designing and making of theatre performance and events. The Belgrade Theatre in Coventry was the first of the post-war civic theatres outside London, opening in 1958, with Chichester (1962), Nottingham Playhouse (1963), Bolton Octagon (1967), the Crucible, Sheffield (1971), and many others following on through the 1970s. All of these new theatres sought to re-invent the audience–stage relationship in a more "democratic" way, some with wider prosceniums and seating in cinema-style "flattened rows" to achieve egalitarian sight lines; some, such as Bolton's Octagon and the University (later Contact) Theatre in Manchester were designed as "adaptable spaces" to suit different types and periods of drama; other studio spaces with completely flexible seating units were designed as black boxes to be re-arranged as the occasion demanded.

Thrust stages were of particular interest, inspired by Tyrone Guthrie's specially built thrust for *A Satire of the Three Estates* at the first Edinburgh Festival in 1947. This shape was then developed with UK stage designer Tanya Moiseiwitsch into their influential design for the Shakespeare Festival Theatre at Stratford, Ontario, Canada in 1957. Other thrust-style stages were subsequently built on both sides of the Atlantic, as discussed in Mackintosh (2011), including in the UK, Chichester Festival Theatre (1962), the Young Vic (1971), the Olivier in the National Theatre complex (1976), and the new Royal Shakespeare (2011) and Swan (1986) theatres in Stratford-upon-Avon. Moiseiwitsch later collaborated on the design of Sheffield Crucible (1971, Renton, Howard, Wood, Levin Architects), arguably "Britain's only pure thrust stage . . . in a direct line of evolution of the Guthrie Thrust Stage" (Mackintosh 2011: 15). Another visionary of this time was director Stephen Joseph who became committed to the idea of theatre-in-the-round, which he realized at the Victoria Theatre, Stoke-on-Trent (1962), and in the Library Theatre, Scarborough (1955). Both were conversions that, after his early death, resulted in permanent in-the-round auditoria: the New Vic in 1986, and the Stephen Joseph, Scarborough in 1994.

In these new non-proscenium theatres painted cloths and stock flats were redundant. Designers and production departments were employed, often as resident staff, to continually reinvent these adaptable spaces using 3D structures, artifacts and light, with concomitant budget implications for labor and time.

This "golden age" of funding for theatre was short lived, with support for the "reps" dwindling from the 1980s onwards. Even so, the strategy of using the visual and performing arts to drive regeneration continued. The new arts facilities made possible by these grants have increased the amount of cross-artform and arts education work that many performance designers engage in, perhaps mitigating the disappearance of resident posts in theatres, but creating little regular work.

The RSC in Stratford-upon-Avon and London, like the National Theatre, has consumed a substantial portion of state funding, but similarly has been a huge employer of design and production staff, host of visiting companies, and commissioner of new work. They have also played significant roles in developing huge commercial successes, due in large part to spectacular visuals, that subsidize much of their programs. Both have systems of associate designers and directors, design-room managers and assistants, production departments and apprentices, but have not always had Heads of Design as the designer-follows-director approach to employment is still common practice in the UK.

The RSC's period of development of new thrust theatre spaces from 2005–2010 was driven by the Artistic Director Michael Boyd and his Head of Design Tom Piper (with architects Bennetts Associates and Ian Ritchie Associates, and Charcoalblue theatre consultants). Piper's belief in the "inventiveness of rehearsal" stems from his youthful work with Peter Brook's company in Paris, and informed his passion to find "ways to create a focused and charged space, to enhance the actor's power of storytelling and engage with the imagination of the audience" (Piper 2016). Piper's range of collaborations, demonstrating the versatility of many theatre designers, includes exhibitions for the V&A and British Museums as well as the hugely evocative World War One memorial installation, *Poppies*, with ceramicist Paul Cummins, at the Tower of London in 2014, and touring to sites around the UK until 2018.

In recent years the preference for "pre-loved" spaces by audiences and artistic teams has seen theatre architects and consultants in the UK frequently involved in redeveloping existing theatres, adapting industrial and other found spaces for performance, while building new theatres for the education sector and multi-purpose performance venues that host rather than house companies and production teams.

Expansion and experiment

The London impresario Peter Daubeny regularly brought foreign dance and theatre companies to London from 1951–1973/4, including the Berliner Ensemble, the Moscow Art Theatre, the Comédie Française, the Piccolo Teatro of Milan, the Noh Theatre of Japan, the Negro Ensemble of New York, among many others. Many designers remember his World Theatre Seasons at the Aldwych Theatre in this period and the opportunity to encounter different aesthetics and styles of working, in particular the idea of the "ensemble" in which the visual was a part of the company's vocabulary. Particularly influential was the technologically mesmerizing work of Czech scenographer Josef Svoboda, whose opera designs for the Czech National Theatre were first seen at the 1964 Edinburgh Festival. He visited the UK many times between 1964–76, mostly designing for Covent Garden and the National Theatre where his designs for Ostrovsky's *The Storm* won the English Critics Award for best design in 1966.

A major influence on British theatre design and directors' approach to it was that of aforementioned French director Michel Saint-Denis, who had co-founded the London Theatre Studio 1935–9, the Old Vic Theatre School 1947–52, and was invited to join the RSC by directors Hall and Brook in 1962. There he founded the RSC Actors Studio "a workshop for actors, directors, writers, designers, and technical staff, to develop singly and together their own craft and imagination, and that of the [Royal Shakespeare] Company, as a company" (Chambers in Harvie 2005: 123). From his period as Director of the Strasbourg National Theatre School he brought his Algerian head of design, Abd' Elkader Farrah. Saint-Denis died in 1971, but Farrah continued with the RSC as Resident Associate Designer until 1991, working in particular with director Terry Hands.

Director Peter Brook was also experimenting, particularly with Antonin Artaud's ideas of "total" theatre in his 1964 *Theatre of Cruelty* season with Charles Marowitz. But, as Harvie comments, "many of that first season's principles – of collective creation, emphasizing the visual and pursuing profound emotional expression" (ibid.: 122) continued throughout his work. Designer Sally Jacobs worked with him on that season's *Marat/Sade*, and later on *US*, *Antony and Cleopatra*, and the "white box" *A Midsummer Night's Dream* of 1970 in which she and Brook rejected traditional "prettiness" and created a playful, circus-skills-inspired ensemble piece that toured the world. This *Dream* further inspired the development of black- and white-box studios as abstracted spaces and surfaces in or onto which the object, costume, and movement achieved significance. It was uncluttered, enabled sharp contrasts of color and form and aligned with contemporary visual and graphic art. In 1970 Peter Brook left Britain to found his Centre for Theatre Research in Paris. Jacobs designed *The Conference of the Birds* with his company, but continued her design career in opera, theatre, teaching, and her own art practice in the USA and UK.

Perhaps the most enduring influence during this "modern" period has been the work of Ralph Koltai, a Hungarian who arrived in the UK aged 14 in 1939. After war service Koltai studied Stage Design at Central School of Art and Design (later Central Saint Martins – CSM). He worked first in opera and dance, frequently with costume designer

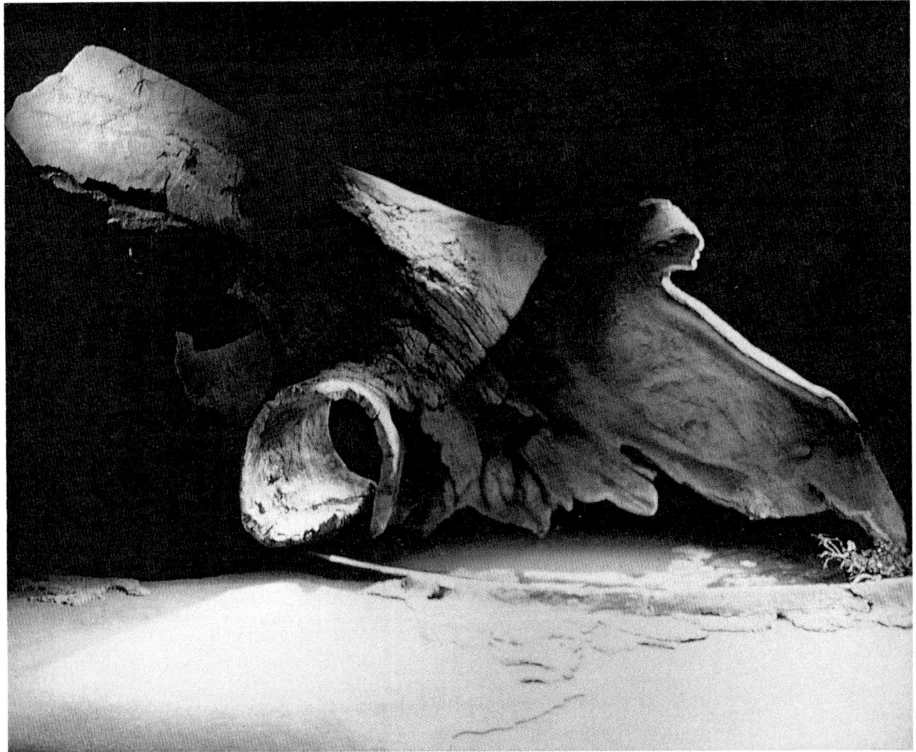

Figure 39.3 Set by Ralph Koltai for Howard Brenton's *Romans in Britain*, Crucible Theatre, Sheffield, 2006, director Samuel West, costume design Peter McIntosh, lighting design Peter Mumford, set builder Stephen Pyle. (Photo: ©Ralph Koltai.)

Annena Stubbs, before becoming an RSC Associate Designer in 1963. He has created his uncompromising poetic and sculptural abstracted forms and surfaces for a huge range of productions internationally. His acknowledged effect at CSM, as Head of Design, on designers such as John Napier, Maria Bjornson, Sue Blane, and many others has infused the UK design aesthetic, particularly through his juxtapositions of scale, use of plastics, mirror, metal effects, sculpting of light and a sensual and anarchic humor. His prize-winning work has featured in most UK selections for the PQ since 1975.

The flow of designers and companies in and out of the UK has greatly increased since the 1980s, with many designers choosing to live or regularly work here and exhibiting in the UK national exhibitions, such as Romanian Marie-Jeanne Lecca, South African Johan Engels and Hayden Griffin, Zimbabwean Richard Hudson, Greek designers Stefanos Lazaridis, Yannis Thavoris, George Souglides and Mayou Trikerioti, Iranian Rajah Shakiry, Japanese designers, Shizuka Hariu and Kimi Nakano. Companies such as the Traverse Theatre in Edinburgh, the Citizens Theatre, Glasgow, The Gate, Notting Hill, and the new National Theatre have been keen to work with "foreign" texts, enriching the diet of designers and stimulating the visual acuity of audiences. The Edinburgh Festival, but more recently the LIFT Biennial (since 1981), BITE (at the Barbican since 2002), and regular international festivals in Manchester, Liverpool, Brighton, Belfast, and elsewhere, have brought a variety of influential performances including circus, puppetry and physical and visual theatre that contribute to an increasingly "hybridised theatre culture" (Harvie 2005: 127). Timothy O'Brien's 'Introduction' to the UK's exhibition at PQ1987 summed up the growing sense of internationalism:

> Traditionally, the British Theatre has been known for its writers and actors and for designers, who obtained their results characteristically quietly and supported the performers and their text. However, repeated exposures to the international display of work at each successive Prague Quadrennial has broadened our outlook and led to developments in our design education. This and the clear need for ingenuity in the face of economic bad weather has led to a versatility of approach to our work. Nor is the British designer neglected by the theatre, opera and ballet of other countries. Thirty years ago designers from abroad came to our Royal Opera House, but few of our designers worked outside Britain. Now – in all fields – British designers travel: from Broadway musicals at one end of the spectrum to avant-garde touring theatre in undefined spaces at the other.
>
> *(In Pleskačova 1987: 373–4)*

Similarly, the growing numbers of design courses from the 1970s, and the opportunities afforded through exchange and study abroad programs, have also been important in attracting international design students and academic staff enriching the UK's "visual language" as a key component in contemporary performance narratives.

The Theatres Act 1968, and the alternative theatre design world of the 1970s and 1980s

Several major events in the 1960s enabled a wider range of theatre makers to become pro-active in an otherwise increasingly director-dominated arts scene. Dominic Shellard describes how the great changes in social policy such as the legalization of abortion, decriminalization of homosexuality (over 21 years), the abolition of the death penalty, and critically, the removal of censorship with the Theatres Act of 1968 affected the makers and making of theatre and performance (Shellard 1999: 149). Although critical aspects of the censorship battle were waged at the Royal Court over *A Patriot for Me* by John Osborne and *Saved* by Edward Bond, a wider effect of the Act beyond "the freedom to explore any subject-matter that did not corrupt or deprave, [was] the fact that writers no longer had to submit scripts for time-consuming vetting, [which] introduced a revolutionizing spontaneity to seventies drama" (ibid.: 148). Almost overnight, improvisation, experimental "arts-labs," co-operatives, community companies and venues, pub-theatres, and working men's clubs appeared and stimulated new writing. The new alternative magazine *Time Out* (first published in London in 1968) helped gain recognition for the work and develop new audiences. Designers and visual artists initiated or co-devised many of these impromptu, challenging, and politically and socially responsive performances, events, and provocations.

Unfinished Histories is a project set up in 2006 by Susan Croft and Jessica Higgs to document the history of the UK alternative theatre movement, a constantly developing rich source of interviews and archive materials for just some of the approximately 700 companies that arose between 1968–88. Croft writes:

> The art schools of the 1960s were the starting points for a wealth of experiment across art forms, channeling Dada, surrealism and happenings from New York's art scene to create companies . . . and large scale events, like the Russian Revolution staged in the streets of Bradford, inspired work by Welfare State, who created fire rituals and site-specific celebrations in spaces from rubbish tips to docks, drawing on folkloric traditions and vernacular narratives. Work and influences crossed national and disciplinary boundaries. Companies experimented with physical and visual vocabularies, creating hybrids drawing on clowning, mime, opera, drag acts, interrogating conventional performance of gender and sexuality, developing theatre laboratories to explore the theories of Artaud's Theatre of Cruelty and Grotowski's Poor Theatre.
>
> *(Croft and Higgs 2013: 18)*

Although designers and visual theatre makers, particularly women, such as Natasha Morgan, Kate Owen, Andrea Montag, and Geraldine Pilgrim, were significant contributors to this alternative theatre, there was no career path, no obvious progression, few reviews – which prior to digital media meant minimal profile. Key companies with strong visual styles or imperatives include(d): The People Show (1966–), Welfare State International (1968–2006), Lumiere & Son (1973–), Forkbeard Fantasy (1974–), Brith Gof (1981–), Bubble Theatre (1972–), Theatre Centre (1953–), Belt & Braces (1973–84), Gay Sweatshop (1974–97), Women's Theatre Group/Sphinx (1974–), Footsbarn (1971–), 7:84 (1971–2008), Impact Theatre (1979–86), Avon Touring (1983–93), Solent Peoples Theatre (1976–), and Perspectives (1972–). All of these companies have received Arts Council funding at some point and have worked or do work with designers but are now more likely to be project, rather than revenue, funded due to major cuts and the prevalence of the festival and events culture that is based on "hits" rather than developing bodies of work.

One of several projects to support emerging artists and practitioners was the Arts Council Bursary scheme, started in 1965 to fund assistant designers. As part of the centralized funding of repertory theatres, it provided a nine-month (one season) vital first step into the industry including at least one realized design and was often extended. Alison Chitty, studying at Central School of Art with Ralph Koltai, won an Arts Council bursary in 1970 to the Victoria Theatre, Stoke-on-Trent, with director Peter Cheeseman. She stayed for nine years, becoming resident designer and helping to develop the New Vic theatre-in-the-round and her own powerfully spare design and teaching philosophies (Chitty 2010: 5–6). Sadly this Arts Council scheme, which benefitted hundreds of recipients, was axed in the mid-1980s. This loss was fortunately ameliorated by the introduction of the biennial Linbury Prize for Stage Design, established in 1987 through the Linbury Trust by Lady Anya Sainsbury, who had, herself, studied at the Slade. This prize has helped to launch approximately 200 emerging designers, many of whom are now leading practitioners.

Changes in funding, arts strategy, and higher education

The 1990s were a time of rebuilding for the SBTD and for the arts and higher education in general, attempting to re-group after the destruction in the Thatcher years (1979–90) of what had been built up in the postwar era. Anthony Jackson writes of the "chorus of noisy dissent from . . . those working in community arts, political theatre and TIE [Theatre-in-Education] to the Arts Council's strategy document [of 1986], *Theatre is for All*" (Jackson 2007: 265). It had advocated substantially increased funding for "centers of excellence," but severe cuts in grant aid to "minor" or declining companies. While the document argued for support of the "wider theatre of tomorrow," Jackson insists that it failed to see that the "tomorrow" was already present in the alternative and TIE sector (ibid.: 265). The far more dynamic and positive Arts Council document, *National Policy for Theatre in England*, in 2000 announced in contrast, "We expect most forms of funded theatre to place education at the heart of their work. Involving young people is the key" (ibid.: 266).

However, the damage had been done by a mix of funding cuts and the dominance of directors' choice – or whim – in wanting a marketplace of freelance designers to choose from for each production. Only a handful of resident design departments continued, resident TIE teams and production departments were cut and a new (or revived) emphasis on touring companies was developed to create "product" for "receiving houses" and the often called "white elephant" arts centers. Co-productions between impoverished "reps" requiring the expense of only one design, designer, and production team between them, aimed for extended tours and West End runs to pay for the rest of their seasons.

The relentless marketing of high-profile, long-running musicals, such as *Cats* and *Les Miserables* (designer John Napier), *Phantom of the Opera* (designer Maria Bjornson), and *The Lion King* (designers Richard Hudson and Julie Taymor), focused on their spectacular designs and made new generations of secondary students aware of design and production crafts as training and career options. Ironically, as more designers became freelance with fewer opportunities for any career progression, more full-time HE courses in Theatre Design and Production were set up around the country focused on recruiting increasing numbers of students who, since 2012, pay hugely inflated fees.

The absorption of art colleges into polytechnics followed by their progression to universities under the 1992 Further and Higher Education Act propelled the change from training to academization in the applied arts including Theatre Design. It is arguable that Design for Performance became a "subject area" more focused on its transferable skills and potential for post-graduate research than for its application to the limited prospects of this industry. Ironically the 2017 agenda in UK Higher Education is once again on employability and skills, but in a far more complex environment of student satisfaction surveys, hugely increased fees, and funding-driven staff teaching and research ratings.

The "bodies of work"

During the 40-plus years since the UK started participating in the Prague Quadrennial, the range of resident and freelance performance design opportunities has produced distinctive companies and individuals who have built striking and influential bodies of work. The mutability of the various director-designer roles and relationships is at the heart of this period of stage design. In particular the conundrum of director as both employer/senior employee and close collaborator has led many designers to create their own work and companies. The following is an overview of some influential UK designer-directors, designer-led companies, and designer-director partnerships.

The Glasgow Citizens – Philip Prowse

The influence of the Glasgow Citizens "house style(s)" under the triumvirate of Giles Havergal, Robert David MacDonald, and designer-director Philip Prowse has been significant since director Havergal and Prowse arrived in Glasgow in 1969, joined in 1972 by writer-director MacDonald. Prowse had trained with Georgiadis, Snow, and Medley at the Slade, and worked with Kenneth MacMillan, The Group, and Watford Palace with Havergal before their 34-year collaboration at the Citizens. Ferociously imaginative but pragmatic with minute budgets, Prowse worked as both designer and designer-director. He was hugely influential for many young designers who worked with the Citizens, including Maria Bjornson, Sue Blane, Bob Ringwood, Geoff Rose, Kenny Miller, Kathy Strachan, and Stewart Laing. He became Professor of the Stage Design MFA at the Slade, which was closed when he retired in 2003. Although famous for the visual decadence and detail of his work, Prowse is quoted as insisting, "our primary duty [at the Citizens] is to the audience, not to the playwright . . . I believe in trying to make Socialism work in a practical way. We put on good shows and we balance our books. We employ a lot of good people and we entertain large numbers of even better ones" (Coveney 1990: 127).

Neil Murray

> I'm not interested in 'naturalism' in the theatre. I don't see it as a naturalistic medium . . . The theatre is an extraordinary place where extraordinary things happen . . . Theatre for me is not just about the work of playwrights. Plays are the work of playwrights. Words can only ever be one component of a performance. Thus, the ideas, words, music, visuals, *et al.* – must exist equally and work together to produce the whole.
>
> *(Murray in Northern Stage 2010: 11)*

Neil Murray's influential body of work started with training in Fine Art before an invitation to become Resident Artist in Theatre at the Arts Lab in Birmingham. After forming his own company, Performance Group, Murray joined Dundee Rep in 1980 as Head

Figure 39.4 Design drawings by Pamela Howard for *Macbeth*, Theatr Clwyd, 1994. Director Helena Kaut-Howson, set and costume design Pamela Howard. Howard states that "Actors are scenery. This production uses actors, their groupings and their costumes to create the locations on the saucer shaped slope that forms the acting space on the stage" (in Burnett and Hall, 1994: 59). (© Pamela Howard.)

of Design working with director Alan Lyddiard, moving with him to Northern Stage, Newcastle-upon-Tyne, and becoming Associate Director. As a freelancer, Murray works with Edinburgh Lyceum, Nottingham Playhouse, and many other companies including Kneehigh, on their internationally award-winning *Brief Encounter* and *Steptoe & Son* with director Emma Rice. Murray's Expressionistic work with film, collage, objects, heightened color, and quotation creates landscapes and characters full of reference points and narrative possibilities. In tandem with the Citizens designers he has helped to build a visually arresting Scottish and Northern design identity.

Pamela Howard

Pamela Howard has achieved a central role in contemporary scenography as a designer-director, educator, and curator. Her practice is strongly rooted in collaboration, deep research for all her projects and in the concept of "thinking through drawing." Having studied at the Slade, Howard taught with Ralph Koltai at Central School of Art, succeeding him as Head of Theatre Design and setting up a pioneering European Scenography MA. A committed internationalist, she re-imagined the European term "scenography" to encompass a "holistic method of visual theatre making" (Howard 2009: xx) with the scenographer as the essential contributor to, and orchestrator of, the total visual experience of performance. Her own career as designer-director, educator and curator has combined passion for the detail of observation and theatre-making with more passion and the ability to share and make her discoveries universal.

Alison Chitty

Alison Chitty is a sought-after collaborator in opera and theatre who became an inspiring teacher and champion of the Motley design course with "Percy" Harris, and director of the course after Harris' death in 2000, until 2011. She returned to

London from the Victoria Theatre, Stoke-on-Trent, in 1979, working with Royal Court director Peter Gill and moving to the National Theatre as Resident Designer. She has worked for many years with Peter Hall on theatre, opera, and on his new Globe-inspired theatre space, The Rose at Kingston-upon-Thames. Chitty has developed long working partnerships with writer-director Mike Leigh on films and theatre, poet Tony Harrison, and composer Harrison Birtwhistle. The core of Chitty's work is her drawing, and, like Herbert and Howard, it is a large part of the dialogue with all of her collaborators. As she says:

> I couldn't work without drawing, it is central to the way I clarify what I know and investigate what I don't. It is my way of ordering ideas and the way I experiment and work my way through confusion and blocks. Designing for theatre, you must be obsessive, organised, open and free: a balancing act. There are many collaborators and unlimited ingredients and through drawing I communicate what I am thinking. In a new work we start with nothing, we all need to have solidarity around a black hole and a sense of adventure. Drawing is my way out of the black hole. It is immediate and fast; for me it is the foundation of the design process.
>
> *(Chitty 2010: 23)*

Bill Mitchell

Designer Bill Mitchell trained at Wimbledon School of Art and worked across the vibrant alternative theatre and repertory scene of the 1970s and 1980s, moving to Peterborough to form a design team with Annie Smart at the touring community theatre collective, Perspectives. Their collaborative, workshopping methodology was an essential preparation for Mitchell's move to Cornwall in 1988 to work with the Kneehigh company, founded in 1980 by actor-director Mike Shepherd. Mitchell has designed and directed many shows for Kneehigh, again essentially a community company that, with director-choreographer Emma Rice, achieved national and international renown. Their particular style of visual storytelling with versatile actor-musicians is rooted in their Cornish communities but joyously shared with every audience.

Wanting to "explore the thrill of making theatre in unconventional places" (Mitchell in Burnett 2015: 128), Mitchell set up a new company, Wildworks, in 2005, also based in Cornwall, which has achieved considerable success with productions involving quarries, dockyards, palaces, forests and their local communities. In 2011 the Wildworks team under Mitchell's direction and now working with designer Myriddin Wannell won awards for their epic collaboration on *The Passion* with local actor Michael Sheen and the population of Port Talbot in Wales. This work continues the deeply community-based work of Welfare State International, Footsbarn, Ann Jellicoe, and Brith Gof, of exploring the interpretation and re-presentation of sites, people and their stories.

Designer-director teams

Opera has been the artform in which key British designer-directors Tom Cairns, Anthony MacDonald, and more recently Isabella Bywater, have had international impact, composing strong visual narratives independently, in collaboration with other designers, or sometimes with directors. Strongly visual directors are also key to the most impactful – and controversial – of opera creative teams. Writing about opera, John Higgins notes, "The style of . . . the [London] Coliseum in the eighties, principally under the influence of [director] David Pountney was one of concept. The single biggest development there was of the one-set conceptual opera, based on the director's view of the work" (in Goodwin 1989: 97). David Pountney and Graham Vick are two of the most prolific and influential visually oriented directors who challenge but stimulate design partners to create spectacular opera productions, in particular for the huge Austrian lakeside stage at Bregenz, for Glyndebourne, for Welsh and English National Opera companies. They worked together at Scottish Opera in the late 1970s where they met designers Maria Bjornson and Sue Blane (working with Philip Prowse at the Citizens). They have also worked with Ralph Koltai, Richard Hudson, Stefanos Lazaridis, Johan Engels, Marie-Jeanne Lecca, and Paul Brown on some of the most celebrated, poetic, surreal, and political designs of the last 30 years.

In particular, Paul Brown's work with Graham Vick is savagely exquisite, including: their fragmented Statue of Liberty *Aida* for Bregenz (2009); terrorist-attacked shopping center for *Nabucco* in Tokyo (2013); and a giant doll and Princess Diana funeral mound of flowers for *La Traviata* in the Verona amphitheatre (2004). They also worked together on productions for Birmingham Opera Company, of which Graham Vick has been director since 1987. Winning international awards, this is an opera project by, with, and for the diverse population of Birmingham, in a variety of disused industrial spaces. Performances are in English, with the Birmingham Philharmonic orchestra, multi-ethnic soloists and choruses of local people, and complete commitment to high quality, integrated, promenade, music experiences. Their work has included *He Had it Coming (Don Giovanni)* with 100 coffins in an old bank (2007), and Stockhausen's

Figure 39.5 *Aida*, Bregenzer Festspiele 2009. Set and costume design Paul Brown,lighting design Wolfgang Göbbel. Director Graham Vick. (Photo © Karl Forster.)

Mittwoch Aus Licht with soloists on swings over the audience, and cellists in helicopters above the warehouse (2014).

Paul Brown also works with director Jonathan Kent on both theatre and opera. Their often surreal but deeply insightful worlds and characters fill the spaces of both proscenium opera houses and adapted spaces as in their Almeida and Gainsborough Studio seasons of 2001–2.

From their Glasgow Citizens start in 1971, Maria Bjornson and Sue Blane have worked across drama, musicals, and opera. Bjornson designed many productions for Director Pountney, including the Janacek cycle of operas over several years, but she is most remembered, since her early death in 2002, for her extravagantly theatrical designs for *Phantom of the Opera* (1986). Blane's witty opulent costume designs include the original, still touring, *Rocky Horror Show* (1969), the celebrated National Theatre production of *Guys and Dolls*, costume designs for many films including *Dance of the Vampires* (1995), also ballet and opera costume designs including *Figaro Gets a Divorce* at Welsh National Opera (with Ralph Koltai's set design) in 2016.

More recent partnerships include designer Ian MacNeil with director Stephen Daldry (*An Inspector Calls*, 1992), Christopher Oram with Michael Grandage, Bunny Christie with Phyllida Lloyd. There is not enough space in this chapter to do justice to the prolific and identifiably different designers and directors who have dominated late-twentieth and early-twenty-first centuries UK performance design. Recruited through the major subsidized companies, mostly from the identified courses, there has been a pool of designers who have worked variously and intensively with the correspondingly dominant group of directors. John Gunter, Bill Dudley, John Napier, and Deirdre Clancy were Royal Court designers in the 1960s. Along with Robin Don, Alison Chitty, Tanya McCallin, Tim Goodchild, Bob Crowley, and others, they have been at the forefront of UK design for drama, musicals, and opera over the past 30–40 years, working in West End, opera houses, and regional proscenium theatres as well as the open/thrust stages of the Almeida, Donmar Warehouse, National Theatre – Olivier and Cottesloe, Young Vic, Chichester Festival Theatre, and many smaller experimental spaces. While skilled at architectural stage designs their work is essentially sculptural rather than painterly and belongs to the Brecht-inspired world of "essential" aesthetics. Robin Don's *A Midsummer Marriage* of 1982, Stefanos Lazaridis' *Rusalka* (1983), and more recently Bunny Christie (*Baby Doll*, 2000), Vicki Mortimer (*Ivanov*, 2002), and Conor Murphy (*Orphee et Eurydice*, 2015) reflect the mix of architectural, sculptural and domestic, differently scaled, planes and lines, celebrations of surreally combined materiality and intense lighting effects that are the vocabulary of much of this modern era's design.

Key touring companies with whom designers have built distinctive visual styles include Cheek by Jowl with designer Nick Ormerod working in partnership with director Declan Donnellan, creating minimal but atmospheric environments for mostly classic texts since 1981; Propellor, an all-male company focused on Shakespeare and touring internationally, started in 1997 at the Watermill Theatre Newbury, led by director Ed Hall, designer Michael Pavelka and lighting designer Ben Ormerod.

Designer Lez Brotherston has developed long partnerships with choreographer Matthew Bourne at Adventures in Motion Pictures (AMP), notably their all-male *Swan Lake*, *Edward Scissorhands*, *Dorian Gray*, and *Cinderella*; also with choreographer Christopher Gable at Northern Ballet Theatre on *Carmen*, *Hunchback of Notre Dame*, and *Dracula*. With both ballet companies he has been integral to developing their distinctive visual narrative styles, combining abstracted and often re-scaled and colored architecture with strongly characterized and usually period-inspired "real clothes."

Intensely collaborative design relationships are required within the physical and visual theatre companies (almost all touring) that have developed and influenced a wide cross section of modern UK theatre, dance, and even opera productions. The most influential of these, Complicite (founded in 1983 as Théâtre de Complicité), worked initially without designers, the visuals being developed along with the devising of the production, items of clothing, set, mask, etc. being created or found as needed. Their success required the integration of designers to deal with increased production ambitions and the more formal contexts they were being booked into. Designers Rae Smith and Tim Hatley both say that the designs arose from rehearsals, with the company responding to the materials and artifacts they supplied, and developing more requirements as they were used. Walls that could be climbed, tipped, or collapsed, pulleys and lines, moveable frames were useful for trying ideas and instincts. Designers working with Complicite and other similarly inspired companies such as DV8, Volcano, Frantic Assembly, Forkbeard Fantasy, and Kneehigh have to be confident as artists, collaborative and problem solving, not so very different from John Bury and Sean Kenny 30 years before, working with Joan Littlewood's Theatre Workshop or Jocelyn Herbert at the Royal Court.

In the contemporary companies that take an alternative approach to creating work, in which the investigative process *is* the work and the performances (just) a part of the journey, designers are integral, as founders, initiators, and contributors to creating performance material, images, and moments, and are also important in articulating, framing and witnessing the work. Such designers include Janet Vaughan of Talking Birds, David Wheeler of IOU Theatre, Bob Frith of Horse and Bamboo, and Julian Crouch of Improbable Theatre.

Designer Simon Banham joined artistic directors Richard Gregory and Renny O'Shea to set up Quarantine in 1998. Their award-winning projects are made with "real" people and their stories, working with "the people in the room" (Quarantine: qtine.com). Banham works with immense elegance and economy of style to frame complex on-going situations, distilling visual metaphors as potent as those in his designs for new operas for Music Theatre Wales, theatre, and site specific work with National Theatre of Wales.

Fine artists and fashion designers in performance

Many UK designers maintain an art practice alongside their stage design. Ralph Koltai, Robin Don, and John Napier, for example, have all created sculpture. Napier, discussing his hugely influential RSC Other Place production of *Macbeth* (1976) with Ian McKellen and Judy Dench in 1976, comments,

> I worked on so many *Macbeth* productions, and subsequently felt a passionate necessity to create artworks in parallel with the work I was doing in theatre. I had wanted to work with people, to fill the amphora – I then realised there was an inevitable 'disposability' of theatre work, as it is constantly being reinterpreted, . . . only remembered by the generations who actually saw it. I wanted to create some pieces that have a real permanence.
>
> *(Napier 2015/16: 10)*

Fine artists continue to be invited to design for performance, particularly for dance perhaps more than opera or drama, and more often for proscenium theatres in which the frame and sculptural side lighting enable the artforms to coexist and comment on each other. Napier, who started his career with Ballet Rambert, said, "my understanding of why the artists are so intrinsically drawn to them, is perhaps, the non-narrative structure and freedom to visually create in the abstract" (ibid.: 17). From the 1970s the Royal Ballet and Ballet Rambert (later Rambert Dance company) were responsible for commissioning artists such as Bridget Riley, Howard Hodgekin, Patrick Caulfield, with sculptors such as Derek Jarman, Anish Kapoor, and Bruce MacLean creating more interactive elements, and, more recently, Chris Ofili, Mark Wallinger, Conrad Shawcross, and Anthony Gormley's *Sutra* with Sidi Larbi Cherkaoui and his company of Buddhist Shaolin monks (2008).

Since 1966 when asked to design *Ubu Roi* for the Royal Court Theatre Upstairs, David Hockney has been interested in designing for theatre. He explains, "I had . . . thought of all my pictures as drama. Even the way I was painting at that time was a kind of theatrical exaggeration" (Friedman 1983: 11). He famously went on to design *The Rake's Progress* (1974) and *The Magic Flute* (1978) for Glyndebourne Festival Opera. John Cox, director of both operas, acknowledged a difference in inviting a renowned artist to design: "A stage designer, like a director, at least in so far as drama and opera are concerned, is a mere interpreter . . . With David it was a case of inviting an artist established in his own right to come in and use the operas as inspiration" (ibid.: 78). Hockney subsequently designed *Parade*, *Les Mamelles de Tiresias*, and *L'enfant et les Sortileges* for New York's Metropolitan Opera in 1982, and a Stravinsky triple bill of *Le Sacre du Printemps*, *Le Rossignol*, and *Oedipus Rex* later the same year. He also designed *Tristan und Isolde* (1986), *Turandot* (1992), and *Die Frau Ohne Schatten* (1992). For the exhibition *Hockney Paints the Stage* at the Walker Gallery in Minneapolis in 1983 he created a series of environments that were based on his previous production designs but were, in themselves, new works, "crossovers" of a narrative art in a visual art space.

Similarly, fashion designers have been invited to design costumes for performance, in particular for dance, including: Jasper Conran, Red or Dead, Versace, Christian Dior, Yves St Laurent, Alexander McQueen, Vivienne Westwood and Zandra Rhodes. However, a distinct genre of costume *as* performance has developed with particular roots in the London College of Fashion postgraduate courses (Jessica Bugg, Madeleine Trigg, Alexander Ruth, Daphne Karsten), but also internationally as exemplified in "Extreme Costume," a section of PQ2011 curated by Simona Rybakova, and the Costume in Action program of World Stage Design 2013 curated by Donatella Barbieri.

Puppetry

While puppetry in the UK has become a key part of stage design vocabulary since the fantastical creations of Jenny Carey were shown at PQ1979, and the macabre figures of *Shockheaded Peter* (Crouch and McDermott, 1998), traditional marionette companies have been in decline. Designers have embraced the mechanics and controls in the narrative potential of various types of puppetry concerned with the interaction of puppet and performer, rather than with illusion, as demonstrated in the designs of Lindy Hemming (*Good Soldier Schweyk* at the National Theatre, 1982), Jenny Carey (*Doctor Faustus*, RSC, 1975; *Animal Farm*, National, 1984), Penny Saunders (of Forkbeard Fantasy), Rae Smith (*War Horse* and *Or You Could Kiss Me* with South African puppeteers Handspring at the National Theatre, 2007, 2010), Marie-Jeanne Lecca (working with prop maker-sculptor Robert Allsopp and puppeteers Blind Summit on puppets for

The Magic Flute, Bregenz, 2014), Improbable's Julian Crouch and Phelim McDermott's giant newspaper puppets in *Satyagraha* (2007), and, perhaps most influentially, Julie Taymor's *The Lion King* animals. Kneehigh Theatre Company, working with Little Angel Marionette Company, are actively incorporating puppets into their ensemble work (*Dead Dog in a Suitcase*, 2014; *946: Adolphus Tips*, 2015) to push narratives into the surreal and create different layers of characterization.

The continuing influence of Welfare State International and the American Bread and Puppet company can be seen combining with carnival aesthetics and visible construction techniques in Clary Salandy's spectacular creations for the 2012 London Olympics, Joe Rush and Mutoid Waste's anarchic vehicles for the 2012 Paralympics Closing Ceremony, and in many street carnivals and festivals around the UK each year. Giant figures such as the *Cornish Miner* (2016) animate whole town centers influenced by Royal de Luxe's giant elephant, little girl, and spider visiting UK cities. Artist Anthony Gormley's epic *Waste Man* – an installation constructed from some 30 tons of waste material, subsequently burned as part of the Margate Exodus (2006) – wonderfully demonstrated the ancient ritual and symbolic capacity of such giant figures (Gormley 2016).

Site-specific and found space performance

Whether through the juxtapositions of surreal figures in landscape or re-staged industrial interiors, "sited" performance design has been a rapidly growing area of work for designers and visual artists driven by desire to engage outside of the designated spaces, by desperation to make work in a poorly funded sector and perhaps in order to generate and take control of one's own work.

Seven Sisters Group is a dance and performance company led by director Susanne Thomas and designer Sophie Jump. They combine site-specific performance, installation, video, and spoken word in places ranging from museums, libraries, swimming pools, forests, and railway stations. Jump's designs, as with Wilson's below, seem to be as powerful in photographic record as in the performances, actively harnessing the viewer/participant's own experience and curiosity.

Louise Ann Wilson is a Nottingham Trent theatre design graduate who formed a company to explore the stories of people and places through promenade performance in found spaces based on intensive on-site research. Her landscape performance and installation work has moved from the narratives of urban spaces in Sheffield (*Mapping the Edge*, 2001), to the Yorkshire coast and dales (*Mulgrave*, 2005), the Lancashire moors and Morecambe Bay in Cumbria (*Still Life*, 2008; *Jack Scout*, 2011) and increasingly into contemplative 'walking-experiences' (*Warnscale*, 2015), with her "performance" existing as much in exhibited photographic records as in the events themselves.

Punchdrunk (founded in 2000) and Shunt Collective (1998) are two celebrated companies that make hugely influential site-specific installation-performances. Though often text-based these are essentially visual experiences requiring large labor forces in their unlikely sites. Punchdrunk's designers Livi Vaughan (who studied theatre design at Central St Martins) and Beatrice Minns (who studied fine art) work with many volunteers to create complex multi-space journeys for their audiences to navigate. The carnivalesque qualities of Punchdrunk's often one-to-one performances are taken to new levels of engagement, isolating audience members into their own experience by making them wear Venetian carnival-style masks, as in their productions of *Faust* (2006) and *Sleep No More* (2011).

Designer Lizzie Clachan studied fine art and co-founded Shunt performance collective to explore "the live moment." The company make immersive installations and performance in various found spaces, including London railway arches, a clock tower, disused factories and a coal jetty on the Thames. Clachan also works in theatre and opera in the UK and abroad. In a 2015 interview she articulated very clearly the current situation for emerging designers with no career structures and only freelance opportunities or self-generated work:

> The economics don't work. In Shunt we used to use lots of people who'd work for free, and give them lunch, . . . I didn't intend to be a designer, I was making work with my own company, but it's really difficult for young designers to afford to do anything . . . You have to have rich parents to survive and do things like internships, and if people come and work for me, someone has to support them. I was comprehensive-educated, and if I was coming through now I wouldn't have been able to do any of this. It makes me angry, actually. On a show to show basis there's not enough time, not enough money, and you just have to pull it out the bag. But the trouble is, there comes a point where you can't continually do that.
>
> *(Clachan 2015)*

Cross-over designers

The "cross-over" or multi-context designer seems to be a feature of twenty-first century scenography, whether from lack of paid work, as above, or through a hybridization of experience in digital and live media performance. Increasingly, theatre, opera, or dance are only one aspect of a designer's portfolio. Many are working with installations, responding to 'Heritage' sites, creating film, events, and designing for the music industry. Misty Buckley studied fashion, but works as set designer for arena concerts and events such as the UK 2012 Paralympics closing ceremony and regularly for the Glastonbury Festival, collaborating with teams of other artists, designers, and engineers.

Designer Es Devlin studied Music and English before training on the Motley course and works internationally in opera and theatre, as well as designing arena concerts and events including the closing ceremony of the UK 2012 Olympics and shows for Lady Gaga, Beyoncé, Kanye West, and other music industry stars. Working with light sources and effects from early on, her spectacular designs for *Don Giovanni* at Covent Garden in 2014 incorporated complex projections mapped by designer Luke Halls onto a revolving double-story cube that filled the stage. Concept, aesthetics and technical virtuosity were completely aligned with the spiraling drama of the music as described by Devlin (in Burnett 2015: 68–70).

Developments in hand-held technology have led to the cross-over of gaming and live performance. In the work of companies such as Blast Theory, Seven Sisters, Dream, Think, Speak, and by designers Sophie Jump, Simon Daw, and Roma Patel, audiences become participants in usually urban, found-space multi-choice narratives. In large-scale community promenade performances with simultaneous filmed action – such as Streetwise Opera's *The Passion* (2016), designed by Dick Bird, combining Manchester's homeless with professional musicians, audiences, and performers appear to themselves on large and small screens, recorded-live, as in a rock concert. They/we have become actors too, recalling Howard's contention, "Actors are scenery" (Hall and Burnett 1999: 59).

Figure 39.6 *The Curious Incident of the Dog in the Night-Time* at the Lyttleton Theatre, National Theatre, 2012. Set and costume design Bunny Christie, lighting design Paule Constable, video design Finn Ross, director Marianne Elliott. (Photo © Brinkhoff/Mögenburg.)

This phrase cuts to the heart of UK design for performance in which performers are the who and what we work with in this visual medium. It also unconsciously builds on John Bury's comment quoted earlier, "the best way to put an idea on stage is to put a man on stage possessed by that idea." We are all performers now.

In this chapter there has been little mention of lighting and projection designers, nor sound designers. The enormous developments in control and operating systems for lighting, in color management, and complex projection mapping have enabled music industry lighting designers such as Patrick Woodruff, Durham Marenghi, and theatre and dance lighting designers Peter Mumford, Rick Fisher, Paule Constable, and many others to create designs of undreamed of complexity. The spectacular *The Curious Incident of the Dog in the Night-Time* combines the production design of Bunny Christie, lighting by Paule Constable and video design by Finn Ross into a dynamic and enveloping box of light and digital imagery.

The original partnership of stage and lighting designers established in the Society of British Theatre Lighting Designers (SBTLD) between 1961–75 would perhaps be even more appropriate in 2016 in our contemporary hybridized event culture.

If there were defining themes to modern UK design for performance they might be: the artifact-oriented work that can be traced to the influence of the Berliner Ensemble's visits to London, and the re-investigation of performance space as "chamber" or "clearing" rather than the perspectived contrivance organized within the frame. Found space performance is exploring and experiencing real land/cityscapes, or exploiting the claustrophobia of hotel rooms and vaults. In our newer built spaces, the emphasis seems to be on gathering the audience around some or all of the performance, still referencing Shakespeare's or Guthrie's thrust stage, while "the frame" is now the entrance to a digital "other." The spaces in front of and behind the proscenium are now seen for what they are: boxes – white, black, brick, or gilt.

> Theatre is a spectacle to see and hear, and not a text to read.
>
> *(Howard in Goodwin 1989: 198)*

References

Brotherston, L. 2013. *Interview with Lez Brotherston, costume designer – Victoria and Albert Museum*. Available online at: www.vam.ac.uk/content/articles/i/lez-brotherston-in-conversation/ (accessed 4 October 2016).

Burnett, K. (Ed.) 2015. *Make/Believe: UK Design for Performance 2011–2015*. United Kingdom: Society of British Theatre Designers.

Burnett, K. and P. R. Hall (Eds) 1998. *Make Space! Design for Theatre and Alternative Spaces*. London: Society of British Theatre Designers.

Bury, J. 1975. "Velká Británie-Grande-Bretagne-Great Britain." In *PQ 1975* Catalogue, 715. Prague: Theatre Institute. Available online at: http://services.pq.cz/res/data/256/026696.pdf (accessed 2 October 2016).

Bury, J. 1979. "Great Britain: Stage and Costume Design." In *PQ 1979* Catalogue. Available online at: http://services.pq.cz/en/pq-79.html?itemID=135&type=national (accessed 2 October 2016).

Chitty, A. 2010. *Alison Chitty Design Process 1970–2010*. London: Royal National Theatre.

Clachan, L. 2015. Available online at: http://exeuntmagazine.com/features/lizzie-clachan-im-interested-in-the-stage-as-a-place-for-images/ (accessed 4 October 2016).

Courtney, C. (Ed.) 1993. *Jocelyn Herbert: A Theatre Workbook*. London: Art Books International.

Coveney, M. 1990. *The Citz: 21 Years of the Glasgow Citizens Theatre*. United Kingdom: Nick Hern Books.

Crawley, G., P. Farley and S. Jump (Eds) 2011. *Transformation and Revelation: UK Design for Performance, 2007–2011*. United Kingdom: Society of British Theatre Designers.

Croft, S. and J. Higgs (Eds) 2013. *Re-Staging Revolutions: Alternative Theatre in Lambeth and Camden 1968–88*. London: Rose Bruford College of Theatre and Performance and Unfinished Histories.

Davis, T. 2001. *Stage Design*. Switzerland: Rotovision.

Farthing, S. (Ed.) 2011. *The Sketchbooks of Jocelyn Herbert*. London: Royal Academy of Arts in association with the Centre for Drawing at the University of the Arts London.

Fielding, E. and P. McKinnon (Eds) 2014. *World Scenography 1990–2005*. Taipei and London: OISTAT and Nick Hern Books Ltd.

Friedman, Martin 1983. *Hockney Paints the Stage*. New York: Abbeville Press.

Georgiadis, E. 2004. *Nicholas Georgiadis: Paintings, Stage Designs (1955–2001)*, edited by Robert Oresko. Greece: Olkos E. P. E., Ekdoseis.

Goodwin, J. (Ed.) 1989. *British Theatre Design: The Modern Age*. London: Weidenfeld and Nicolson.

Gormley, Anthony 2006. *Waste Man*. Available online at: www.antonygormley.com/projects/item-view/id/260#p0 (accessed 6 October 2016).

Hainaux, R. (Ed.) 1957. *Stage Design Throughout the World since 1935*. London: Harrap for International Theatre Institute.

Hainaux, R. 1964. *Stage Design Throughout the World since 1950*. London: Harrap for International Theatre Institute.

Hainaux, R. 1973. *Stage Design Throughout the World since 1960*. London: Harrap for International Theatre Institute.

Hall, P. R. and K. Burnett (Eds) 1999. *Time+Space: Design for Performance: 1995–1999* [a companion to Time+Space, an international exhibition that opened at the Royal College of Art, London, in March 1999]. London: Society of British Theatre Designers.

Harvie, J. 2005. *Staging the UK*. Manchester: Manchester University Press.
Howard, P. 2009. *What is Scenography?* (2nd ed.). London: Routledge.
Jackson, Anthony 2007. *Theatre, Education and the Making of Meanings: Art or Instrument?* Manchester: Manchester University Press.
Jump, S. 2015. "The Convergence of Influences on and Evolving Praxis of Mid-twentieth century British Theatre Design (1935–1965) Through a Close Study of Selected Works by Motley and Jocelyn Herbert." PhD diss., University of the Arts, London.
Mackintosh, I. (Ed.) 2011. *The Guthrie Thrust Stage: A Living Legacy*. London: ABTT.
McKinnon, P. and E. Fielding (Eds) 2012. *World Scenography 1975–1990*. Taipei: OISTAT.
Napier, J. 2015/16. *Stages: Beyond the Fourth Wall*. Eastbourne, Towner Art Gallery.
Northern Stage 2010. *Northern Stage Design*. Newcastle upon Tyne: Arts and Social Sciences Academic Press.
Piper, T. 2016. *Design Approach*. Available online at: www.tompiperdesign.co.uk/about-tom/design-approach/ (accessed 2 October 2016).
Pleskačova, Jana (Ed.) 1987. *PQ'87* Catalogue. Prague: Theatre Institute.
Prague Quadrennial of Performance Design and Space 2015. Available online at: www.pq.cz/en (accessed 31 July 2016).
Prior, M. 2006. *Dreams and Reconstruction: A Cultural History of British Theatre: 1945–2006*. United States: Lulu.com.
Quarantine. Available online at: http://qtine.com/ (accessed 2 October 2016).
Shank, T. (Ed.) 1996. *Contemporary British Theatre*. Basingstoke: Palgrave Macmillan.
Shellard, D. 1999. *British Theatre Since the War*. New Haven, CT: Yale University Press.
Walton, M. J. (Ed.) 1983. *Craig on Theatre*. London: Methuen Publishing.

40

LATIN AMERICAN SCENOGRAPHY

Lidia Kosovski and Luiz Henrique Sá

TRANSLATED BY ANITA PETRY

From the south of Chile to the north of Mexico, more than 20 countries and territories comprise Latin America, a mix of new republics, with neo-Latin languages, that were colonized by European powers, mainly Spain and Portugal. In the nineteenth century, Simón Bolívar had unsuccessfully attempted its political unification but, despite his failure, this portion of the American continent can be unified culturally and artistically in multiple ways – even if certain national differences remain noticeable.

The imposition of the Iberian culture on the indigenous populations and, later, on African traditions, is one of the unifying elements. Latin America's theatrical history was defined, in the same way, by the forces of colonization. Nevertheless, we do not consider the dominance of foreign models as detrimental to the development of theatre on the continent; there is no judgment, only the acknowledgement of the specific realities deriving from the historical situation.

One must acknowledge the scenography of Latin America's multifaceted cultural traditions, commonly identified as folkloric expression. These include para-theatrical festivities, which were rooted in the complex system of religious syncretism among the various countries (a result of the cultural amalgam of the migration process) and based on native-born and immigrant popular traditions, exerting significant influences on the aesthetics of our modern theatre. In the countries that managed to preserve traditional customs (or to maintain their development as part of the artistic industry), actors and spectators still converge in a process of entertainment, rite, and performance. Examples include *Mama Negra*, a festive Ecuadorian narrative presented in honor of the *Virgen de la Merced*, which resembles, in its form, a Christian procession. Its origin can be traced to the arrival of African slaves brought over by the Spanish (Escudero 1988: 18–22). Allegorical elements are a fundamental part of these festivities. In the Bolivian *Diablada de Oruro*, for example, which originated in the nineteenth century through the fusion of Hispanic and Ayamara cultures, the grotesque depiction of demons plays a central role, as does a choreographed battle between troops led by a costumed Saint Michael the Archangel against the Seven Deadly Sins (Wilde 1988: 30–2). One of the most recognized Latin American para-theatrical events is the Brazilian Carnival parade (Figure 40.1): a grand spectacle that reflects the traits of a culturally assimilating population, where references to Venetian Carnival are interlaced with African cults and

Figure 40.1 Brazilian Carnival Parade. Opening allegory Resumo da ópera for the parade *Ouvindo tudo o que vejo, vou vendo tudo que ouço* (Listening to everything I see, I see all I hear), of the Unidos da Tijuca Samba School, Rio de Janeiro, 2006. Scenographer: Paulo Barros. (Photo: Alexandre Vidal – FotoBR.)

the allegorical floats of medieval processions (Heliodora 1988: 36–41). Currently, the parade is associated with a luxurious spectacle geared to the television media.

In this sense, it would be wrong to minimize the specific socio-cultural characteristics of each nation, assuming that Latin American theatre is a homogeneous whole (Milaré 1998: 6); one must always search for individual artistic efforts that stand out within the national and international landscapes. However, from the beginning of the twentieth century onward, historical records suggest that tours throughout Latin America by musical companies coming from abroad created a range of theatrical techniques; in this way, scenographic methods were disseminated across national borders to such a degree that one can find similar aesthetic trajectories among these countries (which nonetheless retained their distinct national identities).

Colonial ties: pre-Columbian aesthetics

In order to better understand the region's contemporary scenography, we need to trace a brief history of Latin American theatre; even though, intending to maintain a focus on the modern, it was necessary to omit some older historical background, such as the catechetical theatre used as a strategy for Christian domination or the cultural relations established between the agents of power and the indigenous and African populations. We seek the modern Latin American scenography that, sustained by colonial traditions, evolved at great expense, reflecting each nation's historical path (Milaré 1998: 6–9).

The rise of independent states in Latin America in the nineteenth century did not translate into financial independence, and the newly founded countries remained subject to the interests of colonizers and other dominant powers. Even with the consolidation of the republics at the end of that century, democracy remained compromised due to the control exercised by local elites. In artistic terms, while the academic theatre inherited from Europe remained the dominant aesthetic, reactions to such classicist norms were already occurring in Europe and this new repertoire of styles would gradually make its way to the Americas (Gutiérrez and Viñuales 2000: 49).

Within the new theatre that emerged out of the European repertoire, one can detect incipient interest around pre-Hispanic aesthetic models as part of a general appreciation for distant and "exotic" cultures. One of the most significant examples was the life-size reproduction of the *Quetzalcoatl* temple at the International Exposition of 1867 in Paris, which created the impression of a Mexico whose cultural achievements were limited exclusively to its pre-Columbian past (Carranza 2010: 93). This aesthetic trend developed even further after World War One as part of the nationalist and Pan-American movements present in a continent at odds with the European model. In Cuba, the architects Evelio Govantes Fuertes and Felix Cabarrocas Ayala designed the *Lutgardita* theatre in a "modern Mayan" way.[1] In Peru, the Spanish sculptor Manuel Piqueras Cotolí developed a new style with his vision of racial synthesis, which he called *neo-Peruvian*. In Bolivia, the *Hernando Siles* stadium was adorned with replicas of decorative motifs from the *Gate of the Sun* from Tiwanaku (Gutiérrez and Viñuales 2000: 51). This alleged Pan-American cultural sentiment, made manifest through pre-Hispanic expression, goes directly towards the thinking of artistic vanguards: the search for new models based on the exotic and the distant, not unlike Gauguin's Tahitian "primitive paradise," Picasso's African-inspired cubism, or Matisse's Orientalism.

Shaping modern scenography: "colonized" by the avant-garde

The major avant-garde movements that transformed European theatrical aesthetics had little impact on early twentieth-century Spain and Portugal. The Spanish publication *Escenografía Española* (Morillejo 1923), for instance, continued to emphasize illusionist pictorial scenography based on the Renaissance tradition of scenic perspective, with *trompe l'oeil* painted backdrops. The École de Paris, however, fostered Latin American disciples who had ventured there in search of new approaches to content and artistic form. Several Argentine artists, for example, financed by the government, relocated there in order to study the new practices, manifestos, and directions being explored by the avant-garde.[2] From the 1910s on, many of those artists would frequent the Parisian studio of Catalan painter Hermenegildo Anglada Camarasa (whose work had strong Eastern and Arabic influences), where they were introduced to avant-garde trends, with special attention to the traditional artistic styles of different cultures. Camarasa instilled in Rodolfo Franco, Gregorio López Naguil and Héctor Balsadúa, among others, an enthusiasm for the art of scenography; from the 1920s on, these artists would be recognized as the most important Argentine set designers (Gutiérrez and Viñuales 2000: 53).

Evidence of renewal started to emerge as Franco and Balsadúa began to apply new concepts at the Colón and Odeón theatres, such as the idea that all props must have their intrinsic significance converted into a symbolic purpose. Franco brought unprecedented color palettes and luminosity into Argentine operatic stage design, and became renowned for his vertical compositions of multi-level settings (Trastoy and Lima 2006: 228–9). From 1934, the undergraduate course in scenography of the Escuela Superior de Bellas Artes in Buenos Aires established a national standard for the art and craft

Figure 40.2 Oscar Navarro's design for *Fuenteovejuna*. Playwright Lope de Vega, director and costume designer Pedro Orthous, Teatro Experimental de la Universidad de Chile. Teatro Municipal de Santiago (Chile), 1952. (Photo: René Combeau.)

of set design. The school fostered designers such as Germén Gelpi, Mario Vanarelli and Saulo Benavente, who sought a synthetic scenographic language more invested in allegorical detail than in realistic reproductions. In the course of the same decade, with the founding of experimental theatres such as Teatro del Pueblo, new dramatic models with tragic or timeless themes became the norm. This new dramaturgy, typified by the work of playwrights such as Roberto Arlt and Defilippis Novoa, created a more general and symbolic human image, which made way for poetic anti-realistic sets (Neglia 1974: 58–63). Imbued with the spirit of its time, scenography would also demand new forms capable of expressing the audiences' changing sensibility in the era of radio, aviation, and cinema (Bragaglia 1930: 95).

The creation of the Facultad de Artes at the Universidad de Chile in 1929 also contributed to moving the country's scenography gradually away from academic painting and sculpture. Within a decade the concept of *theatrical decor* would be permanently rejected, just as the European artistic movements had proposed. Four set designers from the university theatre movement stand out: Ricardo Moreno, Héctor Del Campo (considered a pioneer in modern Chilean scenography and strongly influenced by cubist art), Oscar Navarro and Guillermo Núñez (both clearly attracted to European symbolism and expressionism, the latter having developed an artistic language with a predilection for lively colors, see Figure 40.2) (Del Campo 1999: 74–7).

In Brazil, fine artist and art critic Tomás Santa Rosa, who would become a seminal figure in the country's modern scenography, was never able to study abroad as he had intended. His focus, however, was not European art, but North America's modern theatrical production. In his application letter for a Guggenheim Foundation scholarship[3] – which he was denied – the artist expressed his interest in studying with Norman Bel Geddes and Jo Mielziner. The application evidenced his knowledge of the most current innovations and experimentation in American scenography at the time[4] (Drago 2014: 10–11).

Political events in Europe, particularly the Spanish Civil War and World War Two, sent numerous European artists and theatre companies into exile, many of whom emigrated to the southern countries of the "new world," bringing with them new aesthetics that resulted in a process of artistic exchange. Such a confluence of artists would prove to be decisive for the integration of Latin American theatre into the new Western scenographic landscape. Spanish set designer Vicente Peralta was one of those artists who immigrated to America and worked at Teatro Colón in Buenos Aires before settling in Santiago, Chile. In 1938 the Spanish designer Santiago Ontañon[5] also immigrated to Chile, bringing new concepts of scenic design, costume, lighting, and theatrical make up (Del Campo 1999: 74–5).

By the 1920s the Tarazona Brothers from Catalonia had already arrived in Mexico, bringing with them scenographic concepts – applied especially at the Teatro Principal – including kinetic effects such as boats in movement, fires, earthquakes, and flying machines (Recchia 1996: 5). Although still representing a late illusionistic style, the brothers' work exercised a strong influence on Mexican theatrical production, bringing new scenographic concepts they had developed in the New York theatre.[6] Until the middle of the previous decade, Mexican sets still belonged to an antiquated school, and were, according to critics, "very affected, very detailed, copies of nature, veritable color photographs"[7] (Rufo 1921 in Moyssén 1999: 508).

The Teatro Ulises, also founded in the 1920s and considered a landmark in the development of Mexico's modern theatre, attracted intellectuals (who later founded the company Los Contemporáneos) such as the painters Julio Castellanos González, Roberto Montenegro Nervo, and Manuel Rodríguez Lozano, who brought his cold and austere palette to Jean Cocteau's *Orpheus* and to *La Madrugada del Panadero*, Halffter's ballet (Villaurrutia 2015). Their small experimental theatre sought to replace the nationalist themes and the culturally fashionable advocacy of revolutionary ideals with a more universal worldview, following the new principles arising in Europe. With the founding of the Teatro de Orientación in 1932, an even more drastic change would occur in terms of form, dimensions, and concepts in scenography as well as in the topology of the stage.

Mexico's modern scenography was also influenced by the work of José Clemente Orozco and Diego Rivera, who designed sets by incorporating the model established by Diaghilev's Ballets Russes: converting their personal pictorial languages onto large backdrops.[8] Towards the end of his life, Orozco discovered that the theatre could be an excellent means of addressing a large and heterogeneous audience, affecting them with the stark contrast of his palette. He designed Mexican-inspired sets for ballets such as the *Obertura republicana* (1943), always preserving the characteristics of his painting – blacks, grays, and whites alternating with bloody, vivid colors. Rivera rarely lent his talents to the theatre but, when he did, he also followed his own style, transforming stages with his earthy tones. Within the modern dance movement (1940–65), other painters helped in professionalizing Mexican scenography and further developing the craft in the country. Among the most important was Carlos González, considered the father of modern Mexican scenic design, who was responsible for the transition from painted flats to abstract three-dimensional scenography (Recchia 1996: 6–7). He created the first constructivist Mexican set (for *Lázaro rió*, directed by Julio Bracho). Also of note were Augustín Lazo, Fernández Ledesma – the first set designer in the country to utilize revolving stages and photographic and cinematic projections (Recchia 1996: 8–9) – and, a few decades later, Julio Prieto Posadas, the great master of an entire generation of set designers (Villaurrutia 2015).

In the Brazilian theatre, the reality was rather different from that found in Europe: there were no rigid hierarchies in productions, no dedication to the rehearsal process, and no defined staging concepts. Lighting was always executed by the theatre's electrician and the country lacked schools for technical and artistic education. The revue theatre[9] and comedies of manners were commercially profitable and therefore took precedence (Figure 40.3) (Souza 2013: 1–2). These comedies improvised box sets by re-using scenic pieces the companies had on hand. Meanwhile, in the revue theatre, famous for its exuberant allegories and lavish finales, sets were painted on paper, cut, and layered on the stage. Among the most well-known designers in this period of the Brazilian theatre – all highly skilled painters – were Oscar Lopes, Angelo Lazary, and the Portuguese Hipólito Collomb (Drago 2014: 68–9). After World War Two, however, the "importing" of European professionals, who brought the ideas of foreign avant-gardes to the Brazilian scene, became increasingly frequent, focused on an intellectually elite theatre. Thus, a new theatre was born, in contrast to the local commercial productions.

In 1941, protesting the Nazi cultural program under German occupation, Louis Jouvet left France along with 25 actors and technicians (and 34 tons of luggage) for a South American tour. Initially scheduled to last three months, the tour was extended

Figure 40.3 Brazilian revue play *Guerra ao mosquito* (*War Against Mosquitoes*). Playwrights Luiz Peixoto and Marques Porto, direction Olavo de Barros. Teatro Carlos Gomes, Rio de Janeiro, 1929. (Cedoc/Funarte Collection.)

to almost four years,[10] traveling over 67,000 kilometers through 11 Latin American countries. The famous French actor and director was known for his role in transforming his country's theatre; therefore, his arrival in Rio de Janeiro was highly anticipated by a young generation that would soon incorporate his ideas into the transformation of the Brazilian theatre. Following their great success in Brazil, Uruguay, and Argentina, and given the continuing German occupation of France, their run was extended with financial support from several South American countries. New participants, war refugees, and even local artists temporarily joined the company. In Rio de Janeiro, Jouvet recruited Brazilian painters and designers to work with him[11] (Pontes 2000: 114–26). In this sense his influence, which had already been visible in approaches to staging, also became the basis for a new era in Brazilian scenography.

This new era was launched, primarily, through the work of amateur companies devoted to renewing staging techniques and the repertoire. The first initiatives were developed by the company Os Comediantes, composed of artists and intellectuals interested in modern dramaturgy who were inspired by the company Teatro Brasileiro do Estudante, led by Pascoal Carlos Magno, one of the first Brazilian theatre artists to be concerned with a production's organic unity, imbuing scenography and lighting with dramatic importance (Souza 2013: 3). Among the members was the aforementioned Tomás Santa Rosa. His set design for the play *O vestido de noiva* (*The Wedding Dress*, by young playwright Nelson Rodrigues), staged by Polish director Zbigniew Ziembinski,[12] divided the stage into three simultaneous temporal areas (past, present, and future), and offered a kind of symbolic imagery then unknown to Brazilian audiences. The production which, according to scholars, is considered a landmark of the modern Brazilian theatre, encouraged visual artists and architects to expand their activities to set design as well (Souza 2013: 10). This partnership between a Polish and a Brazilian artist opened doors to other foreign companies, directors, and designers that soon arrived in Brazil, including Polish director Zygmnt Turkow,[13] Belgian director and set designer Maurice Vaneau, and Italian set designers Aldo Calvo,[14] Bassano Vaccarini,[15] Gianni Ratto,[16] Ruggero Jacobbi, and others connected to the Teatro Brasileiro de Comédia (TBC) company (Echevarría and Pupo-Walker 1996: 280). This migratory process assured a new level of quality for modern realistic productions. In order to meet the demands of international professionals, an efficient infrastructure for technical production was created for the first time in the country. Therefore, the hierarchical leveling of the set design, in relation to other components of the theatrical production, was one of TBC's major contributions to Brazilian scenography (Kosovski 1992: 303–6).

Alternative stages

To think about the modern theatre is to think also about the transformations of scenic space and, in this context, it is important to note the development of the arena theatre. While in Europe the rupture with the proscenium stage was an ideological enterprise rooted in historical and political questions, in Latin America the same event was a fitting response to the actual necessities of theatrical production (economic, aesthetic, and political), and had a startling effect on the audience (Kosovski 1992: 312).

In 1953 director José Renato, influenced by Theatre '47 – the first professional theatre in the United States to employ an arena stage – founded the Teatro de Arena, one of the most important Brazilian political theatres. Because of economic pressures within the Brazilian cultural sector, it became tempting to produce simplified shows

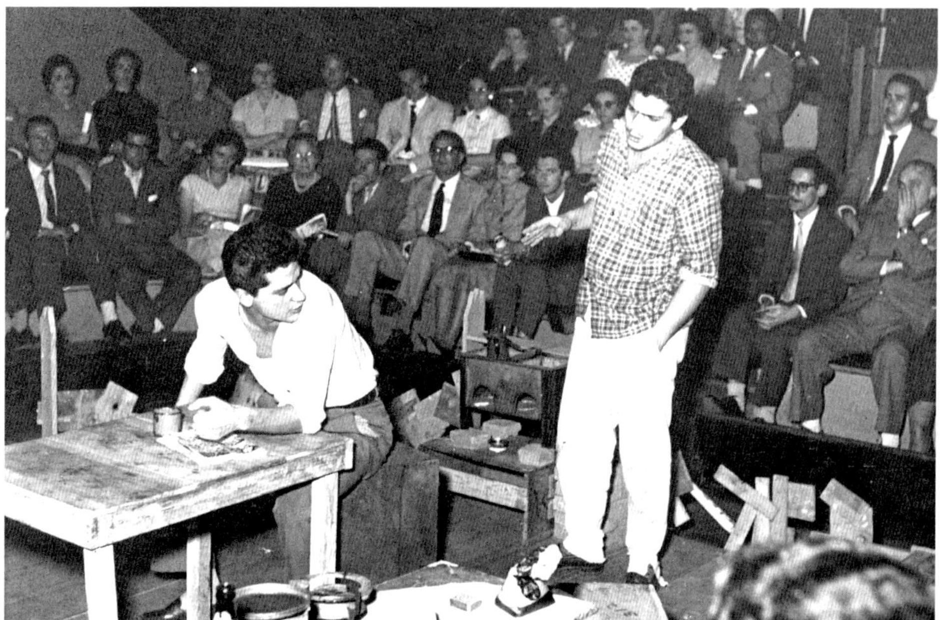

Figure 40.4 *Eles não usam black-tie* (*They Don't Wear Black-Tie*). Playwright Gianfrancesco Guarnieri, direction José Renato. Teatro de Arena, Rio de Janeiro, 1959. Pictured: Oduvaldo Viana Filho and Francisco de Assis. (Photo: Carlos Kerr; Cedoc/Funarte Collection.)

with reduced scenographic costs (Porto and Nunes 2007: 8) (Figure 40.4). In 1959 set designer Flávio Império[17] joined the company, developing an aesthetic quite different from the realism that had characterized the company in its early years. Artistic director Augusto Boal, who had then been formulating his *Joker System*,[18] attributed to Império the creation of *joker scenography*: given the poverty of both the theatre and the country, it utilized left-over materials for the creation of props (Katz and Hamburger 1999: 274).

Experiments with theatre-in-the-round had already been taking place in Cuba and Puerto Rico since 1949, reflecting the direct connections between Caribbean countries and the United States. Meanwhile, in Argentina, Nuevo Teatro explored the effects of the arena stage in the early 1950s with the production of *Mother Courage* by Alejandra Boero and Pedro Asquini. In Uruguay, Teatro Circular was founded as a result of the experiments of director Eduardo Malet and set designer Hugo Mazza, both of whom had worked with such spaces in amateur productions (Muguercia 2013: 226–8). In Peru, high rental costs for scarce theatre spaces led experimental companies to produce shows in available spaces, generally in arena or semi-arena formats (Díaz 1985: 76).

During his visit to Brazil in 1936, the architect Le Corbusier gave a series of lectures on modern architecture.[19] In one of them, while acknowledging his lack of expertise in regard to theatre, he nonetheless discussed the conception of an ideal theatrical building for the city of Rio de Janeiro and mentioned his recent experience at a festival in the city of Recife, when he witnessed the natural theatricality of its inhabitants. The architect realized that the city did not require theatre buildings for dramatic expression: simple platform stages would suffice for the people to express themselves at all times in everyday, natural ways, crossing the border between representation and event.

In 1953 *Antígona en Creole*, adapted by Félix Morriseau-Leroy from the tragedies of Aeschylus and Euripides, was staged outdoors in the hills on the periphery of Port-aux-Prince, Haiti. Occupying areas of extreme poverty, the production, which employed Creole language and voodoo rituals, was a milestone in the appreciation of both religion and popular language for Haitian intellectuals. In 1957 the show *La muerte de Atahualpa* in Peru was performed in a public space and guided the spectators along a path lined by torches towards a site of Incan ruins for a performance in front of an authentic pre-Columbian palace (Muguercia 2013: 225–6). Latin America, freed from its own centuries-old history of Italianate staging, revealed itself open to varied spatial experiences that emphasized the audience's participatory nature.

Revolution, coups, and scenographic experiences

The 1950s represented a period of consolidation for modern staging in several Latin American countries, which gradually began to act more vigorously in the search for their own cultural identities. The Cuban Revolution of 1959 was a crucial political factor in fomenting this change. Cuba was initiating a process of transformation in all segments of society, including the artistic-cultural sphere. In the first two years of the revolutionary government, Cuban intellectuals waged an intense debate over the role of the arts in the country. While some defended an official aesthetic focused on Soviet-inspired socialist realism, others searched for more experimental and universal artistic concepts. The cultural policies established by Castro in 1961,[20] however, prescribed the artists' steady commitment to national and popular traditions, against the pressures of North America's imperialism (Miskulin 2002: 78–89).

A similar approach echoed throughout all of Latin America, challenging the colonial heritage while incorporating and transforming local traditions. As early as 1928, Brazilian poet Oswald de Andrade had already coined the term *cultural anthropophagy*[21] for such phenomena. Thus the idea of Latin culture as a "peripheral culture" was contested by a growing number of artists, who formalized their ideologies in new theatrical identities by basing their aesthetic research on their own socio-cultural conditions (Milaré 1998: 8).

From the 1960s until the mid-1980s, during the many military dictatorships that plagued Latin America,[22] theatre became a strong critical tool against the arbitrary censorship of democratic liberties that gradually came to dominate the continent's cultural landscape. Paradoxically, the value of scenography – visual aesthetics and the new-found flexibility in the playing space – actually strengthened during this period. There are several examples in which the scenographic language eloquently expressed political engagement, be it through its alliance to popular voices and traditions, or as a scathing critique of the bourgeois layer of society and its representations on the stage. In this context, the visual aspect of theatre became more complex – at times a quietly subtle metaphor – expressing what was not possible through the written text.

While military coups spread below the equator, events that shocked the world, such as May 1968 in Paris and the reaction of American youth to the Vietnam War, provided new material for Latin American companies and opened new perspectives for the theatrical creative process. Two approaches began to emerge: one being the theatre of political engagement that had been growing in Latin America since the 1960s, fueled by Brecht's theories; and the other being a theatre of psychedelic aesthetics, closer to Artaudian principles, with its hallucinogenic sensorial experiences rooted in the sounds of the Beat culture, jazz and rock 'n' roll. These distinct creative processes, however, had one element in common: the search for a national and popular theatre. Such an approach was necessary to remedy the lack of national artistic expression relating to the themes and issues of marginalized people and places.

The first edition of the Prague Quadrennial of Theatre Design and Architecture (PQ)[23] declared in its catalogue that the end of the 1960s meant, for Europe, a break from old, locally autonomous cycles. At the same time, Latin American and Eastern countries, formerly considered peripheral, increasingly engaged in dialogue with European centers[24] (Ptácková and Jindra 1967: 24–6). At the International University Festival at Nancy in 1966, the Brazilian production of *Morte e vida Severina* (*The Death and Life of a Severino*), a long poem by João Cabral de Melo Neto,[25] won jury and popular awards. Directed by Silnei Siqueira, with set design by Armando Ferrara and songs by Chico Buarque de Hollanda, the production was the first by TUCA (Theatre of the Catholic University of São Paulo), whose objective was to take the political movement to impoverished urban areas. Due to financial constraints, the set was conceived solely as the relationship between lighting and the actors' bodies. Wearing simple white costumes, the actors' shadows were projected onto the background, thereby creating a *human set*. This innovation derived precisely from economic necessity (Silva 2014: 6–7). Thus began the exploration of the bare stage: theatre centered on the actor's work and the text, which would, gradually, formulate a dramatic language based on the emptiness of the playing space (Guimarães 1998: 10–11).

A clear sign of the expanding relevance of scenography could be seen in the increasing number of specialized schools in Argentina, from which came artists with audacious and experimental productions such as Gastón Breyer, Federico Padilla, Guillermo De La Torre, Maria de la Concepción Ramírez, Maria Julia Bertotto, and Jorge Sarudiansky. In Cuba, many young artists were assigned to the theatre to supply the demands of the new cultural policy. In addition to highlighting the importance of older set designers, such as Maria Elena Molinet and Rubén Vigón, the first Cuban exhibit at PQ, in 1971, attempted to reflect the effort of new creators, searching for new artistic languages and technical means. Thus, Eduardo Arrocha, Manuel Barreiro, Julio Castaño, Salvador Fernandez, and Jesus Ruiz, among many others, imbued with the revolutionary spirit, compensated for "the time lost in the capitalist period." Artists such as Ramon Aguirre, Modesta Hernandez, Maria De Las Casas, Isabel Lopez, Humberto Orsini, and Guillermo Zabaleta represented Venezuela. Uruguay, in its first attendance at PQ, also celebrated the assimilation of new forms and methods in its theatrical production, promoting set designers Jorge Carrozzino and Carmen Prieto, who exercised considerable influence in the country's theatre (Jindra 1971: 119–34, 407–14, 399–405).

Set designer Helio Eichbauer, who represented the counterculture movement in Brazil, returned to the country in 1966 after studying in Prague with renowned designer Josef Svoboda and working at Teatro Studio in Havana where he collaborated with director Vicente Revuelta. Eichbauer garnered national visibility for conceiving the set for *O rei da vela* (*The Candle King*) (Figure 40.5), one of the iconic works of the Tropicália movement,[26] directed by José Celso Martinez Corrêa at the Teatro Oficina. In the production, with its vigorous critique of capitalism and the Brazilian economic elites, the design mingled opera references with elements of the popular revue and mass culture, making use of stark tropical colors and eroticism, in a Brechtian set with a revolving stage, large screens, and the theatrical mechanics exposed (Sá 2008: 120–1).

Figure 40.5 Helio Eichbauer's design mockup for *O rei da vela* (*The Candle King*). Playwright Oswald de Andrade, direction José Celso Martinez Corrêa. Teatro Oficina, São Paulo, 1967. (Courtesy of Helio Eichbauer.)

In opposition to persecutions, imprisonment, and torture promulgated by the military regime, which intensified in Brazil in 1969, a prolific outpouring of new drama emerged, critical of the contemporary situation, created by writers such as Paulo Pontes, Oduvaldo Vianna Filho, and Gianfrancesco Guarnieri, all of whom were repeatedly censored. In this context, many of the most influential personalities of the theatre world, such as Eugène Ionesco, Jean Genet, and Joseph Chaikin, visited the country, enlivening the debate on theatrical innovation. The American company The Living Theatre, upon being invited to visit Brazil in 1971, intended to create new work collectively with actors and directors from Teatro Oficina and from the Argentine Grupo Lobo, confirming once more the search for an intercultural dialogue (Schoenbach 1971: 76–7).[27]

Producers also became a source of creative energy, attempting to overcome the period of political adversity. Renowned actress and producer Ruth Escobar developed large productions exploring relevant contemporary themes, arguably on a scale never again seen on Brazilian stages. One of these productions was the emblematic *Automobile Graveyard* (1968), written by Fernando Arrabal and directed by Víctor Garcia, that placed the audience on swivel chairs on the lower level, as well as on ramps that ran along the walls of an immense playing space, suggesting a garage. The action took place on the ramps, on a suspended platform in the middle of the space, and over carcasses of old cars hung from metal beams (Schoenbach 1971: 71).

García's theatre was presented to the world as a theatre of image, emotion, and sensations. His staging, suspended in time, used visuals as a starting point and tended

Figure 40.6 O *balcão* (*The Balcony*). Playwright Jean Genet, direction Victor Garcia, design Wladimir Pereira Cardoso and Victor Garcia. Teatro Ruth Escobar, São Paulo, 1970.

to dehumanize the actors and transform them into stage objects (Navarro 1988). For his staging of Genet's *The Balcony* in São Paulo in 1969 (a production Genet actually saw in 1970), he created, in conjunction with Wladimir Pereira Cardoso, a vertical playing space that provided a complex system of spatial and interpersonal relationships (Figure 40.6). The stage consisted of a helical ramp whose floor was made of a metallic grate through which light would shine, reflected by an immense parabolic mirror placed five meters below the level of the theatre's original stage; the audience was distributed between overlapping circular balconies made of the same metallic grid. In addition, five single elevators and two cranes were built to serve the scenes (Fernandes 1985: 85–6). Ultimately, Garcia was an important representative of a new movement toward a multiform theatre that would remove audiences from their passivity and transform them into active participants in a festive rite (Bablet 1975: 350).

Brazilian street theatre, with Amir Haddad, artistic director of *Tá na Rua*, as its greatest representative, marked the definitive return of theatre to urban spaces and an appreciation for improvisation in both the dramaturgical as well as the visual spheres – the latter primarily by the use of costumes and props. According to Haddad, the round space of public plazas offered freedom, a place where everyone was equal. In a space where social hierarchies were minimalized, one could propose a utopia of

Figure 40.7 *Na selva das cidades* (*In the Jungle of Cities*). Playwright Bertolt Brecht, direction José Celso Martinez Corrêa, design Lina Bo Bardi. Teatro João Caetano, Rio de Janeiro (Brazil), 1969. Pictured: Liana Duval, Renato Borghi, and Carlos Gregório. Bardi's scenography combined trash with work rubble; everything was destroyed at each re-enactment and the smell of garbage permeated the theatre. (Cedoc/Funarte Collection.)

collective harmony. For him, it was necessary to recover a theatre whose story had not been told: one that involved all other forms of theatrical expression found off the stage (Kosovski 1992).

The internationalization of scenographic practices led to frequent aesthetic similarities between the productions of countries geographically distant (Bablet 1975: 284–6). In an effort to keep up with the times, scenography increasingly turned to multimedia techniques, which proved successful with audiences. While imperialist ideas commonly dominated mass media, the theatre proved successful at recovering artistic approaches capable of communicating with spectators about political and social circumstances and local issues (Jindra 1975: 2–3). Despite the stifling of popular culture by the military dictatorships, scenographic innovation provided strategies of political liberation. By violating the "sacred" proscenium structure and expanding the stage into public streets and squares, theatre integrated with everyday spaces, as well as with urban and popular cultures, thus disseminating ideas through theatrical means.

Festivals as a stage for encounters

In spite of the numerous affinities among Latin American theatre movements, it was still easier to learn about European or North American avant-garde experiments than about those occurring in neighboring countries (Reyes 1988: 42–3). A fruitful communication between these countries only started to be established through meetings, touring companies, classes and workshops, and exchanges, as well as input from politically exiled theatre artists escaping persecution by military dictatorships. Exchanges increased at the end of the 1960s with festivals and meetings in Havana, Puerto Rico, Caracas, and Mexico City; road shows in Panama, Guatemala, and Costa Rica; and the Hispanic theatre festival in New York in the 1980s (Reyes 1988: 43). At the Festival de Manizales in Colombia Latin American theatre companies seemed to embark on an adventure of self-discovery. It was crucial to collectively define what kind of theatre such a historical moment demanded: a theatre that would serve an elite sheltered in cultural ghettos, or a theatre that would involve the masses and abandon conventional cultural facilities? A theatre that would integrate global values with the local? Or a theatre radically inspired by its pre-Colombian forefathers? Which theatre, after all, could supply the demands of Latin America's cultural and racial mosaic? (See Giménez 1988: 60.)

Welcoming new materials and staging technologies

The beginning of the 1970s witnessed the emergence of a Latin American theatrical aesthetic based on exploring alternative materials and focused primarily on creative solutions. The process of searching for new scenic spaces and for political ideologies that aligned with the performing arts resulted in designs that compensated for economic precariousness with a multiplicity of visual and technical solutions. The most notable among these included the presence of exposed structures; the rejection of decorative scenery and props; the use of materials in their original form; the use of reflective materials to amplify the physical space; and the first effects of graphic or photographic projections.

In the 1971 edition of PQ, Helio Eichbauer represented two countries with his design project for *Álbum de família* (*Family Album*) (Figure 40.8), the first staging of a Nelson Rodrigues' play to be presented outside of Brazil (in Venezuela), directed by Martim Gonçalves.

Figure 40.8 *Álbum de família* (*Family Album*). Playwright Nelson Rodrigues, direction Martim Gonçalves, design Helio Eichbauer. Caracas (Venezuela), 1968. (Photo: Miro Anton; courtesy Helio Eichbauer.)

Figure 40.9 *Macunaíma*. Playwright Mário de Andrade, dramaturgy Centro de Pesquisa de Teatro (CPT) and Jacques Thieriot, direction Antunes Filho, design Naum Alves de Souza. Theatro São Padro, São Paulo (Brazil), 1978. (Courtesy of Centro de Pesquisa de Teatro.)

The designer created an abstract and kinetic set that allowed the actors to interact with scenes shot on film and projected on the stage (Sá 2008: 120–1). Eichbauer, who received a Gold Medal at the PQ for the exhibition of his work, was possibly the first Brazilian set designer to experiment with new imaging technologies in effective dialogue with the dramatic scene. Meanwhile, Naum Alves de Souza's design for *Macunaíma* (Figure 40.9), a Brazilian production directed by Antunes Filho in 1978 that garnered international acclaim, represented the birth of a new Brazilian scenic language, based on a sequence of minimalist images made by scenic frames, with meticulously selected elements that created a dense narrative force.

The work of Luiz Carlos Ripper was also emblematic. His partnership with director Rubens Corrêa at Teatro Ipanema in Rio de Janeiro radically deconstructed the proscenium theatre for the productions of *Hoje é dia de rock* (1971; *Today is Rock Day*) and *A China é Azul* (1972; *China is Blue*), and he pioneered the use of organic materials for the setting of *Avatar* (1974), one of the first theatrical performances to occupy a gallery in Rio de Janeiro's Museum of Modern Art (Figure 40.10). For that production he created a triangular arena stage, formed by a wooden mandala that rested over real rocks and greenery, in place of the traditional scenographic simulacrum. For Ripper, the energetic power of the materials also constituted the dramatic scene (Kosovski and Pinheiro 2013: 10).

The Teatro de la Basura, a popular theatre movement that originated in Honduras in the 1980s, was a reaction to the country's political violence. Founded by Candelario Reyes, it was intended to be a theatrical tool to foster self-awareness in the peasant population to improve their social situation.[28] According to Reyes, the country suffered a horrendous foreign dependency and regarded its own culture as trash while favoring imported models. To develop a national theatre from material waste – hence the name

Figure 40.10 *Avatar*. Playwright Paulo Afonso Grisolli, direction and design Luiz Carlos Ripper. Sala Corpo e Som, Museu de Arte Moderna, Rio de Janeiro (Brazil), 1974. Pictured: Isabel Ribeiro. (Cedoc/Funarte Collection.)

basura – would imbue it with literal meaning: while they lacked common theatrical resources, there was an abundance of raw material for their productions. In the Teatro de la Basura, words were only developed at the end of the process, as a complement to the playful experimentation around the garbage with which they manufactured their set. Thus external signs influenced the actors in the same way poverty acted on human beings. Trash was not an object but the subject, often the protagonist of the action. The result was a visual theatre, with a semiotic conversation between space, image, scenic action, and time (Stone and Cohen 1995: 83–7).

Collective processes, scenography, and the playing space

In the 1980s the development of theatrical languages based on processes of collective creation became common throughout much of Latin America, although, in some countries such as Argentina, there were basically no such productions at that time (Rizk 1983: 80). In Colombia, such theatrical principles had been solidified a decade earlier with the founding of the Nuevo Teatro movement in partnership with Santiago García,[29] founder of La Candelaria theatre company. This movement was based on the construction of a national dramaturgy, the search for a popular aesthetic awareness, and on the idea that theatre is an act of collective creation that can promote social change. It was a cry for an ethical theatrical aesthetic, committed to the spectator's reality. The collective work of La Candelaria also encompassed all sound and visual elements (Esquivel 2014: 6, 64, 174). These new languages were studied and cultivated during the *I Taller Internacional del Nuevo Teatro* (First International Workshop of New Theatre) in Cuba in 1983, which gathered representatives from 25 countries. At the end of the event, the group of artists reported on some characteristics of this new theatre: the new (controversial) spatial and emotional relationship with the audience, the new means of collective devised production, and the research on the plurality of theatrical languages (Rizk 1983: 73, 77).

After the popular dismantling promoted in Chile by the military coup of 1973, independent groups started to reorganize the country's theatrical geography. Despite vigorous censorship a new collaborative method emerged, devoid of traditional sets and costumes, and focused, with a critical and sarcastic tone, on subjects related to everyday life. These plays dramatized the day-to-day relationships of the protagonists with salespeople, factory workers, mechanics, etc., and dramaturgical material was often developed through observation in the community. This collective effort allowed for a dramatic creation that went beyond the written text, in a deep connection with what the performing space could offer (Piña 1992: 79–80).

The clear goal of surpassing the boundaries of realism was a defining element of Chile's theatre aesthetics in the 1980s. Companies opted for theatrical models that subverted the traditional concepts of dramatic theatre. Lighting, the physical spaces, the imagery, music, the juxtaposition of scenographic elements, and the multiple styles of character development converged, thus becoming resources as important as the spoken text. Young creators offered complex theatrical models that were non-linear, more visual than auditory. Director Ramón Griffero, for instance, developed productions in order to create a sense of terror in the audience by sensitizing multiple levels of perception (Piña 1992: 81–2). The Teatro Popular ICTUS company, founded in 1956 in Santiago, explored the influence of the performing space on the staging process. The company's method, mainly based on the physical relationships between actors and objects, tried to provide audiences with a collection of clues that were relevant to the creative process, by the arrangement of scenery, objects and costumes (Genovese 1991: 41–2).

In terms of theatre architecture, Lina Bo Bardi and Edson Elito's design for the reconstruction of the Brazilian Teatro Oficina in 1983 was of seminal importance, though, for financial reasons, this construction took about 10 years to complete. The new theatre allowed for multiple staging configurations and, according to the architect, the project included a theatre with no stage – a place for community rituals, not unlike a church (Lima 2009: 127). In that space, the spectator would be continuously aware of the external world; a long glass wall allowed the outside world to enter into the theatre, which, in turn, was designed as an alley for the staging of processions; multiple video projections open the space in infinite dimensions.

Aesthetics post-dictatorship

Gradually the military regimes lost authority in the face of the opposition movements fighting for democracy, freedom, amnesty, and human rights. But, with the process of political opening and the awaited freedom of speech, a period of severe economic crisis arose. In some countries, such as Paraguay, it took a particularly heavy toll. Throughout the 1990s the financial struggle, along with increasing disunity within the artistic communities of opposition, led to the dissolution of established theatre companies and artistic movements that were of great importance to the country's theatrical arts. Set designers, lacking resources, had to deal with the theatres' inadequate infrastructure (Chamorro 1998: 69–70). Carlos dos Santos, an advocate for the post-dictatorship restoration of scenographic arts in Paraguay, used the empty space of the stage as a starting point for his creative process and designed his sets by collaborating with the actors and directors in order to explore the dramatic circumstances.

In the 1980s Uruguay's theatre underwent a conceptual paradigm shift. In its first phase, which pre-dated the end of the military dictatorship in 1984, politically engaged theatre pieces were conceived, new companies and theatre spaces were created, and there was a growth of new audiences. Marked by the return of previously exiled artists and technicians, the second phase saw significant changes in the methods of representation, the ideology of theatre pieces and, consequently, the social and political contexts in which spectators lived. Thus, Uruguay's theatre would embrace questions pertaining to post-modernity – its theories of rupture, narrative deconstruction, fragmentation, and juxtaposition of dramatic elements. After the country's political opening, the exploration of the inner worlds of acting became common, with powerful images of the subconscious, merging internal and external space, emotions, thoughts and images (Mirza 1992: 181–9). At that time, set designer Osvaldo Reyno was recognized for his approach to integrating the visual and performing arts (Abbondanza 1998: 32–3).

The first reactions to the realistic theatre that took place in Argentina, stimulated by the coup of 1976, began to appear with the end of the dictatorship in 1983. From this moment much of the theatre community began to work with a common goal: to expose the historical horror and to preserve memories of the past, in addition to denouncing remaining vestiges of the regime (Fukelman 2013). Several works of theatre broke with the realist model through semantic ambiguity and self-referential scenography. The dominant approach became spatial simultaneity and the fragmentation of perception (Pellettieri 1991: 117–25). While set designer Tito Egurza explored the dissonance between a production's dramatic expression and its visual appearance, Daniela Taiana, early in the following decade, reinforced such rupture by converting industrial materials into unique visual and organizing elements (Cosentino 1998: 16–17; Boero 1998: 15).

In the 1980s and 1990s Brazilian scenography was defined by great visual spectacles and productive partnerships between designers and directors or theatre companies, while embracing post-modernist practices: the cool minimalist aesthetics of Daniela and Gerald Thomas; the use of popular language by José de Anchieta, with the company Ornitorrinco; the experimentalism of Fernando Mello da Costa, searching for new spatial and material solutions with director Bia Lessa; the scenographic research of J. C. Serroni with Antunes Filho that mixed industrial and artisanal materials; the global and functional vision of José Dias' scenography (Serroni 2013: 58–65); the constant metamorphosis of scenography in the creative processes of the Companhia dos Atores; and the search for semantically charged public spaces that could withstand scenographic interventions – a form of site-specific work – led by Marcos Pedroso in collaboration with director Antônio Araújo, within the company Teatro da Vertigem (Figure 40.11). This group is one the great pioneers in contemporary theatre's use of urban spaces, public or otherwise; their daring productions made history when, throughout the 1990s, they were staged in a church, a hospital, and a decommissioned women's prison.

As a result of such paradigmatic ruptures and the variety of scenographic forms developed over the last decades of the twentieth century, old scenic approaches both interacted with, and competed against, new technologies employed in more costly productions (Serroni 1998: 5). In order to overcome technological barriers, many designers

Figure 40.11 *O livro de Jó* (*The Book of Job*). Playwright Luís Alberto Abreu, direction Antônio Araújo, set design Marcos Pedroso, costume design Fábio Namatame, lighting design Guilherme Bonfanti. Teatro da Vertigem Company, Humberto Primo Hospital, São Paulo (Brazil), 1995. (Photo: Lenise Pinheiro.)

commonly relied on strong creative concepts. Hence, in 1998, São Paulo hosted the exhibition "Espaço da Cena Latino-Americana" (Latin American Scenic Space), an event that celebrated theatre's festive atmosphere, praising the simplicity of its scenographic solutions and materials. The exhibition demonstrated that over the previous 40 years, Latin American theatre had embodied "the spirit of time," developing artistic methods that recovered, transformed, and valued traditional elements while adapting itself to economic realities and global artistic trends (Milaré 1998: 9).

As Latin American scenography entered the third millennium – increasingly recognized by spectators and scholars – it was expanding the exchange among artistic forms and genres, and even seeking to erase the borders between them. Despite all the historical differences and material poverty among the countries of Latin America in the twentieth century, the theatre persevered, transforming adversity into creative power and revealing aesthetic forms and concepts that could, ultimately, reflect its many worlds.

Notes

1 In the Lutgardita theatre the curtains were decorated with themes inspired by the Tikal circular stone, and the lateral columns, which reproduce the stelae of Quiriguá in large scale, are also highlighted (Viñuales 2013).

2 Argentina's scenographic production remained, until then, restricted to realist-illusionist aesthetics: mimetic pictorial reproductions in predominantly dark colors, and furniture organization that related to the piece's social necessities and environment rather than artistic concerns. Occasionally, scenery was also designed by prominent painters who were not, however, sufficiently familiar with the specifics of theatrical production (Hainaux 1956: 7).

3 The Guggenheim Foundation gave Brazilians the opportunity to study in New York for the first time in 1940.

4 Mielziner's influence on Santa Rosa's work was evident in the scenographic arrangement for his production of *Death of a Salesman* (1951) (Drago 2014: 155).

5 Part of the so-called Generation of '27, Ontañon was the commissioned set designer for Garcia Lorca's *Blood Wedding*. During the Spanish Civil War, he supported the Republican cause and, while in exile, lived in Uruguay, Peru, Argentina, and Chile.

6 In New York, the Tarazona Brothers worked on at least three Broadway productions: *The Land of Joy* (1917) – when critics compared their work to that of Josef Urban (Bordman and Norton 2010: 376) – *A Night in Spain* (1917) and *Frivolities of 1920* (1920).

7 "*Muy relamidas, muy detalladas, copias del natural, verdaderas fotografías a colores.*"

8 Orozco and Rivera worked a few times in partnership with Roberto Galván, known as one of Mexico's first set designers, and who was responsible for executing the paintings.

9 The revue theatre was a popular genre of great vitality in the early twentieth century, in which musical numbers were used to express social and political critique through comedy.

10 Due to the blockade of the Atlantic, many theatre and ballet companies touring South America extended their tours indefinitely, circulating among the great Latin American capitals.

11 Among them was Brazil-based Portuguese artist Eduardo Anahory who was responsible, in 1945, for the set design for *Rain*, based on Somerset Maugham's novel, for the company Dulcina-Odilon. His technological innovations that made it rain on stage generated a great response (Drago 2014: 71).

12 War refugee Ziembinski (who arrived in Rio de Janeiro a day before Jouvet's debut in the city) was a key player in this renovation process, considered by many to be the first Brazilian director.

13 Turkow arrived in Brazil in 1941 and acted with the company Os Comediantes and with the dramatic circle of the Brazilian-Israeli Sholem Aleichem Library, in Rio de Janeiro, where he partnered, in 1945, with painter Lasar Segall for the set and costume designs for a production of *Dos groise gevins* (*The Big Win*) (Fabel 2013: 1–3).

14 Calvo headed TBC's technical department, where he implemented workshops on scenography, carpentry, and scenic construction. In 1952 he also became resident set designer for film production company Vera Cruz.

15 Vaccarini, part of the Milan Futurist Group, was already an esteemed artist in Italy.
16 Italian director and scenographer who contributed the most to the development of the Brazilian scene, Ratto was one of the founders of Milan's *Piccolo Teatro*, along with Giorgio Strehler and Paolo Grassi, and also vice-director of Milan's *Teatro Scala*.
17 Império was one of the Brazilian set designers responsible for the transition from a decorative style to a non-illusionist scenography. His work showcases a plurality of artistic languages.
18 The principal goal of Boal's *Joker System* was the production's analytical presentation: in order to distance the actors from characters, role-switching was introduced, employing striking physical characteristics that allowed the audience to understand the swift changes (Schoenbach 1971: 75).
19 This story was narrated by the architect at the conference "Spontaneous Theatre," part of the first session of *Centre D'études Philosophiques et Techniques du Théâtre* about the relationships between the theatrical place and the present and future dramaturgy, at the University of Paris in 1948 (Le Corbusier 2011).
20 Recorded in his speech *Palabras a los intelectuales*, available online at: www.cuba.cu/gobierno/discursos/1961/esp/f300661e.html
21 In his *Cannibalist Manifesto*, Oswald de Andrade related many references to the Brazilian native culture and, ironically (in modern vanguard fashion), preached against the intellectual elite that copied European models in detriment of the local culture. He proposed, in the end, a revision of Western traditions, connecting regional expressions to the contemporary culture. "*Tupi or not tupi, that is the question*" (Andrade 1928).
22 In reaction to the Cold War and the international advance of communism, the United States supported military coups against democracy in over half of Latin America's nations. In 1954 Guatemala suffered the fall of president Jacobo Arbenz. In the same year Paraguay's Chief of Staff, general Alfredo Stroessner, led a coup against the president Federico Chávez, assuming the country's presidency. Between 1964 and 1973 Argentina, Brazil, Bolivia, Chile, Peru, the Dominican Republic, and Uruguay, also suffered coup d'états and were ruled by dictatorial military governments.
23 Founded in 1967 and now known today as the Prague Quadrennial of Performance Design and Space.
24 The existence of PQ itself, which became an important platform for the exchange of information between scenic designers from all over the world, was originated by an interaction between Europe and Latin America, established by the presence of Czech set designers at the São Paulo Biennial, especially in 1961 (Convênio 1969).
25 Translated into English by Elizabeth Bishop.
26 Tropicália (or Tropicalism) was a Brazilian musical movement of the late 1960s that spread into other cultural-artistic spheres. It sought to fuse traditional aspects of the national culture with universal popular aesthetic innovations, promoting syncretism between heterogeneous styles.
27 In August 1971 Julian Beck, Judith Malina, and 11 other members of the group, having been arrested for possession of marijuana and incarcerated for three months, were expelled from Brazil by order of President Médici (Schoenbach 1971: 77).
28 Despite sharing common methods with Augusto Boal's Theatre of the Oppressed, Reyes, in his cultural and geographical isolation, denies international influences on his method (Stone and Cohen 1995: 83).
29 Garcia, in 1959, received a scholarship to study in Europe for two years. He went to Prague, where he worked with Otomar Krejča and Josef Svoboda at the Lanterna Magika theatre, and held a six-month internship at the Berliner Ensemble in Germany (Esquivel 2014: 29).

References

Abbondanza, Jorge 1998. "Osvaldo Reyno." In *Espaço da Cena Latino-Americana*. São Paulo: SESC São Paulo.

Andrade, Oswald de 1928. "O manifesto antropófago." *Revista de Antropofagia*, Ano I, Num. I.

Bablet, Denis 1975. *Les révolutions scéniques du XXe siècle*. Paris: Société Internationale d'Art/XX siècle.

Boero, Alejandra 1998. "Daniela Tayana." In *ESPAÇO da Cena Latino-Americana*. São Paulo: SESC São Paulo.
Bordman, Gerald and Richard Norton 2010. *American Musical Theatre – A Chronicle*. New York: Oxford University Press.
Bragaglia, Anton Giulio 1930. *El nuevo teatro argentino*. Buenos Aires: Hipótesis.
Carranza, Luis E. 2010. *Architecture as Revolution: Episodes in the History of Modern Mexico* Austin: University of Texas Press.
Chamorro, Tito 1998. "Uma leitura do teatro paraguaio sob o fascismo e a ditadura." In *ESPAÇO da Cena Latino-Americana*. São Paulo: SESC São Paulo.
Convênio 1969. Convênio entre a Fundação Bienal de S. Paulo, Brasil, e a Praské Quadrienale de Praga – República Socialista da Tchecoslováquia. Rio de Janeiro: 8 July 1969. Available online at: http://services.pq.cz/res/data/184/018859.pdf.
Cosentino, Olga 1998. "Tito Egurza." In *ESPAÇO da Cena Latino-Americana*. São Paulo: SESC São Paulo.
Del Campo, Edith 1999. "Presencia Española en el desarrollo de la escenografía chilena." *Teatro*, [S.l.], n. 6: 74–7. Available online at: www.revistateatro.uchile.cl/index.php/TR/article/view/20700/21867 (accessed 23 November 2015).
Díaz, Grégor 1985. "El teatro en Lima: Lima es el Perú." *Latin American Theatre Review*, 19 (1): 73–6. Available online at: http://hdl.handle.net/1808/2721.
Drago, Niuxa Dias 2014. *A cenografia de Santa Rosa: espaço e modernidade*. Rio de Janeiro: Rio Books.
Echevarría, Roberto González and Enrique Pupo-Walker (Eds) 1996. *The Cambridge History of Latin American Literature*, Vol. 3. Cambridge: Cambridge University Press.
Escudero, Maria 1988. "La Mama Negra de Ecuador." In *Escenarios de dos mundos: inventario teatral de Iberoamérica. Volume 1: Argentina, Bolivia, Brasil, Colombia, Costa Rica*. Madrid: Centro de Documentación Teatral.
Esquivel, Catalina 2014. *Teatro La Candelaria: memoria y presente del teatro colombiano*. Tese de doutoramento. Facultad de Filosofía y Letras /Universidad Autónoma de Barcelona.
Fabel, Nachman 2013. "Lasar Segal e Zygmunt Turkow: dos Groisse Gevins (a Sorte Grande)." *Cadernos de Língua e Literatura Hebraica* 11. Available online at: www.revistas.usp.br/cllh/article/view/83506/86454.
Fernandes, Rofran 1985. *Teatro Ruth Escobar: 20 anos de resistência*. São Paulo: Global Editora.
Fukelman, María 2013. "El teatro independiente en los primeros años de Postdictadura." *La revista del CCC* 17. Available online at: www.centrocultural.coop/revista/articulo/386/. ISSN 1851-3263.
Genovese, Carlos 1991. "El espacio escénico y su influencia modificadora de la puesta en escena: una experiencia del Teatro ICTUS de Chile." *Latin American Theatre Review*, 25, (1): 41–50. Available online at: http://hdl.handle.net/1808/2997.
Giménez, Carlos 1988. "Festivales, ¿Para qué?, ¿Para quiénes?" In *Escenarios de dos mundos: inventario teatral de Iberoamérica. Volume 1: Argentina, Bolivia, Brasil, Colombia, Costa Rica*. Madrid: Centro de Documentación Teatral.
Guimarães, Carmelinda 1998. "Por um espaço latino-americano." In *Espaço da Cena Latino-Americana*. São Paulo: SESC São Paulo.
Gutiérrez, Ramón and Rodrigo Gutiérrez Viñuales 2000. "Fuentes prehispánicas para la conformación de un arte nuevo en América." In "Arte Prehispánico: creación, desarrollo y persistencia." *Temas de la Academia*, Buenos Aires, Academia Nacional de Bellas Artes: 49–67.
Hainaux, René 1956. *Stage Design Throughout the World since 1935*. New York: Theatre Arts Books.
Heliodora, Bárbara 1988. "Escuelas de samba y teatro: los carnavales de Rio de Janeiro." In *Escenarios de dos mundos: inventario teatral de Iberoamérica. Volume 1: Argentina, Bolivia, Brasil, Colombia, Costa Rica*. Madrid: Centro de Documentación Teatral.
Jindra, Vladimir (Ed.) 1971. *PQ 71: Prague Quadrennial of Theatre Design and Architecture 1971* (catalogue). Prague: Theatre Institute.
Jindra, Vladimir (Ed.) 1975. *PQ 75: Prague Quadrennial of Theatre Design and Architecture 1975* (catalogue). Prague: Theatre Institute.
Katz, Renina and Amélia Hamburger 1999. *Flávio Império*. São Paulo: EDUSP.

Kosovski, Lidia 1992. *Teatro e encenação: um olhar sobre o palco*. Dissertação de Mestrado. Rio de Janeiro: Escola de Comunicação/Universidade Federal do Rio de Janeiro.
Kosovski, Lidia and Claudia Pinheiro 2013. *A mão livre de Luiz Carlos Ripper*. Rio de Janeiro: Dois Um Produções.
Le Corbusier 2011. "El teatro espontâneo." In *Laboratori d'arquitectura teatral. Recull de publicacions 2008–2011*, edited by Antoni Ramon, Guillem Aloy and Ekain Olaizola. LATe.0101. Available online at: http://espaciosescenicos.org/LATe-Laboratori-Arquitectura-teatral-i-ATe-Arxiu-d-arquitectura.
L'Exposition universelle de 1867 illustrée: publication autorisée par la Commission Impériale. Paris: Bureaux d'Abonnements, 1867. Available online at: https://archive.org/details/lexpositionunive01expo.
Lima, Evelyn Furquim Werneck 2009. "Histórias de uma arquitetura ética: espaços teatrais de Lina Bo Bardi." *ArtCultura: Revista de História, Cultura e Arte*. Universidade Federal de Uberlândia, Vol. 11. Num. 19: 119–36. Available online at: www.artcultura.inhis.ufu.br/PDF19/e_lima_19.pdf.
Milaré, Sebastião 1998. "Territórios utópicos." In *Espaço da Cena Latino-Americana*. São Paulo: SESC São Paulo.
Mirza, Roger 1992. "El sistema teatral uruguayo de la última década. ¿Un cambio de paradigma?" *Latin American Theatre Review*, Volume 25, Number 2: 181–90. Available online at: http://hdl.handle.net/1808/3246.
Miskulin, Sílvia Cezar 2002. "A política cultural no início da Revolução Cubana: o caso do suplemento cultural *Lunes de Revolución*." Revista Outubro 06. Available online at: http://outubrorevista.com.br/a-politica-cultural-no-inicio-da-revolucao-cubana-o-caso-do-suplemento-cultural-lunes-de-revolucion/.
Morillejo, Joaquín Muñoz 1923. *Escenografía española*. Madrid: Real Academia de Bellas Artes de San Fernando.
Moyssén, Xavier 1999. *La crítica de arte en México 1896–1921. Estudios y documentos II (1914–1921)*. Tomo II. Universidad Nacional Autónoma de México; Instituto de Investigaciones Estéticas.
Muguercia, Magaly 2013. "Teatro como 'acontecimento' na América Latina dos anos 50 e 60." *Sala Preta*, Vol. 13, num. 2: 224–35. Available online at: www.revistas.usp.br/salapreta/article/view/69093/71539.
Navarro, Felipe 1988. "Victor García, un teatro mítico." In *Escenarios de dos mundos: inventario teatral de Iberoamérica. Volume 1: Argentina, Bolivia, Brasil, Colombia, Costa Rica*. Madrid: Centro de Documentación Teatral.
Neglia, Erminio G. 1974. "Una recapitulación de la renovación teatral en Hispanoamerica." *Latin American Theatre Review*, Volume 8, Number 1: 57–66. Available online at: http://hdl.handle.net/1808/2295.
Pellettieri, Osvaldo 1991. "La puesta en escena argentina de los '80: realismo, estilización y parodia." *Latin American Theatre Review*, Volume 24, Number 2: 117–31. Available online at: http://hdl.handle.net/1808/2977.
Piña, Juan Andrés 1992. "Teatro chileno en la década del 80." *Latin American Theatre Review*, Volume 25, Number 2: 79–86. Available online at: https://journals.ku.edu/index.php/latr/article/view/923/898.
Pontes, Heloisa 2000. "Louis Jouvet e o nascimento da crítica e do teatro modernos no Brasil." *Novos Estudos* – CEBRAP, Num. 58: 113–29. Available online at: http://novosestudos.org.br/v1/files/uploads/contents/92/20080627_louis_jouvet2.pdf.
Porto, Joyce Teixeira and Nunes, Marisa (organisers) 2007. *Teatro de Arena*. São Paulo: Centro Cultural São Paulo. Available online at: www.centrocultural.sp.gov.br/cadernos/lightbox/lightbox/pdfs/Teatro%20de%20Arena.pdf.
Ptácková, Vera and Jindra, Vladimir 1967. *PQ 67: Prague Quadrennial of Theatre Design and Architecture 1967* (catalogue).
Recchia, Giovanna 1996. "La escenografía mexicana del siglo XX." *Educación Artística – Separata de teatro*. Ano 4. Num. 13.
Reyes, Carlos José 1988. "Fulgor y límites de la creación colectiva." In *Escenarios de dos mundos: inventario teatral de Iberoamérica. Volume 1: Argentina, Bolivia, Brasil, Colombia, Costa Rica*. Madrid: Centro de Documentación Teatral.

Rizk, Beatriz J. 1983. "I Taller Internacional del Nuevo Teatro (Cuba, 1983)." *Latin American Theatre Review*, Volume 16, Number 2: 73–80. Available online at: http://hdl.handle.net/1808/2629.
Rufo 1921. "Nuestros escenógrafos." *El Universal Ilustrado*. Num. 205, 7 de abril: 12–13.
Sá, Luiz Henrique 2008. *Histórias de cenografia e design: a experiência de Helio Eichbauer*. Dissertação de mestrado. Rio de Janeiro: Universidade do Estado do Rio de Janeiro/Escola Superior de Desenho Industrial.
Schoenbach, Peter J. 1971. "Rio and São Paulo Theatres in 1970: Foreign Dramaturgy." *Latin American Theatre Review*. Vol. 5, Num. 1: 69–80. Available online at: https://journals.ku.edu/index.php/latr/article/view/126.
Serroni, J. C. 1998. "Espaço da cena latino-americana." In *Espaço da Cena Latino-Americana*. São Paulo: SESC São Paulo.
Serroni, J. C. 2013. *Cenografia brasileira: notas de um cenógrafo*. São Paulo: Edições SESC SP.
Silva, Carla Fernanda da 2014. *Morte e vida Severina na ditadura militar: o anarquista Roberto Freire e o teatro como resistência*. Anais do XV Encontro Estadual de História "1964–2014: Memórias, Testemunhos e Estado." UFSC: Florianópolis. Available online at: www.encontro2014.sc.anpuh.org/resources/anais/31/1403622754_ARQUIVO_CarlaFernandadaSilva-MorteeVidaSeverinanaDitaduraMilitar-artigofinal.pdf.
Souza, Camila Maria Bueno 2013. "A produção de *Vestido de Noiva*: a construção de um marco simbólico e do mito de Ziembinski como 'pai do Moderno Teatro Brasileiro.'" Anais do XXVII Simpósio Nacional de História. ANPUH-Brasil: Natal. Available online at: www.snh2013.anpuh.org/resources/anais/27/1371232105_ARQUIVO_ANPUH-2013.Artigo2.3.pdf.
Stone, Kenton V. and Cohen, Deborah J. 1995. "El Teatro de la Basura: la búsqueda de una identidad cultural." *Latin American Theatre Review* , Volume 29, Number 1: 83–92. Available online at: https://journals.ku.edu/index.php/latr/article/view/1082/1057.
Trastoy, Beatriz and Lima, Perla Zayas de 2006. *Lenguajes escénicos*. Buenos Aires: Prometeo Libros.
Villaurrutia, Xavier 2015. *Obras. Poesía/Teatro/Prosas Varias/Crítica*. México, D.F.: Fondo de Cultura Económica.
Viñuales, Rodrigo Gutiérrez 2013. "O neo pré-hispanismo na arquitetura. Auge e decadência de um estilo decorativo – 1921/19." *Arquitextos*, ano 04, num. 041.05. São Paulo: Vitruvius. Available online at: www.vitruvius.com.br/revistas/read/arquitextos/04.041/648/pt_BR.
Wilde, Maritza 1988. "Las Diabladas de Oruro en Bolivia." In *Escenarios de dos mundos: inventario teatral de Iberoamérica. Volume 1: Argentina, Bolivia, Brasil, Colombia, Costa Rica*. Madrid: Centro de Documentación Teatral.

41
DESIGN IN THE UNITED STATES AND CANADA

Arnold Aronson

According to the standard narrative, the birth of US stage design[1] occurred in January 1915 with Robert Edmond Jones' design for Anatole France's *The Man Who Married a Dumb Wife*, directed by Granville Barker at Wallack's Theatre in New York, as part of a double bill with Shaw's *Androcles and the Lion*. Jones' setting, done in shades of black, white, and gray – seemingly influenced by Adolphe Appia and Edward Gordon Craig – used simple geometric shapes, creating the impression of a wood-block print, and a feeling at once vaguely Japanese and medieval. This was a revelation for Broadway audiences more familiar with standard box sets, or scenes created by painted backdrops and stock scenery, the sort of scenery typified, in the derisive words of critic and producer Kenneth Macgowan, by "large-sized colored cut-outs such as ornament Christmas extravaganzas . . . [and] landscapes and elaborately paneled rooms after the manner of bad mid-century oil-paintings in spasmodic three dimensions" (Macgowan 1914: 418).

But the revolutionary approach to design that would become known as the New Stagecraft[2] was already well underway in the so-called Art Theatres and the Little Theatre Movement – the small independent theatres arising across the country that served as a conduit for new drama from Europe, and ultimately for the new American drama spearheaded by Eugene O'Neill and Susan Glaspell. In actuality, a truer date for the emergence of American design might be 1911 when Viennese designer Joseph Urban arrived at the Boston Opera Company where he was to design their 1912 season. Whatever the precise starting date, what is being commemorated is the emergence of a European approach in which the design was an interpretive signifying element within the overall conceptual framework of the production: the design not merely as indexical sign conveying information about time and place, but as an integral artistic component with a point of view that commented on the dramatic text and contributed to the emotional and intellectual response of the audience. Until this point, design in the US and Canada was the domain of the scene painter, stage manager, and producer and was intended primarily to indicate time and place. But with the shift toward design as a conscious effort to create an artistic environment, the technician or artisan needed to give way to artists who would contribute to the production at a level equal to the other creative personnel: the designer. As composer Deems Taylor said of Urban in a posthumous appreciation, "He revolutionized the scene designer's position in the American theatrical world. He was the first to make clear that the designing of stage sets is an art, and that the man who designs them is an artist – or should be" (Taylor 1934: 290). Or, as Robert Edmond Jones would write in his essay, "To a Young Stage Designer," "In the last analysis the designing of stage scenery is not the problem of an architect or a painter or a sculptor or even a musician, but of a poet" (Jones 1941: 77).

The term "scenography" may not have been in common use in the early twentieth century, but Urban used the German term *inszenierung* to describe the total integration of all the creative elements. He explained in a 1913 interview,

> The new art of the theatre is more than a matter of scenery; it concerns the entire production. The scenery is vain unless it fits the play or the playing or unless they fit it. The new art is a fusion of the pictorial with the dramatic. It demands not only new designers of scenery, but new stage managers who understand how to train actors in speech, gesture and movement, harmonizing with the scenery.
>
> *(Urban 1913)*

Urban and Jones introduced new elements into American design. From Urban came a dynamic and unprecedented use of color in combination with a new understanding of stage lighting. Employing a pointillist technique, similar to that of Postimpressionist painter Georges Seurat, Urban understood that color on the stage (as opposed to on an artist's canvas) is a result of the particular combination of paint pigments and stage lighting – red pigment, for instance, becomes visible only under red light or under the red part of the spectrum within "white" light. Thus, instead of covering a canvas with flat expanses of paint as had been the practice of most scene painters, Urban took a semi-dry brush and spattered the canvas. His skies, for example, utilized several shades of blue spattered over each other, then further spattered with red, green, and silver. In the scene shop, under work lights, the painting looked dull, but under stage light employed with subtlety the differing flecks of color were picked up and reflected and Urban could create anything from dawn to moonlight. He also introduced the use of "portals" – proscenium-like frames set within the stage behind the actual proscenium. They had the practical effect of narrowing the sometimes massive openings of many opera house stages to more manageable proportions. (See Aronson 2001.)

Robert Edmond Jones, on the other hand, brought the ideas of Appia into the American theatre. His work tended to be more monochromatic – though often with distinctive and powerful splashes of color – simplified, and atmospheric. Working with director Arthur Hopkins on several Shakespeare productions he stripped the stage of much of its detail, creating instead a stage that was scenically spare, enhanced by a few emblematic set pieces. Their 1921 production of *Macbeth* was exemplary. Creating a dark void on a deep stage he used a few scenic elements such as skewed Gothic arches that could be placed in different configurations creating an almost abstract environment. In several scenes the stage was dominated by three large silver masks hanging above that represented the witches. As Hopkins explained, "To us it is not a play of Scotland or warring Kings or of any time or place or people. It is a play of all times and all people. We care nothing of how Inverness may have looked" (Hopkins 1921). While Jones may have stripped the stage of excessive scenery and replaced detailed realism with suggestion and emblematic images, his costumes were often elaborate and colorful, and, like Appia, light played a dynamic and essential role in transforming space. Lee Simonson, working at first with the Theatre Guild and later on Broadway and at the

Figure 41.1 Joseph Urban, *The Garden of Paradise*, Queen's bower, 1914. This was Urban's first design for Broadway. (Joseph Urban Archive, Rare Book and Manuscript Library, Columbia University.)

Metropolitan Opera, also brought these New Stagecraft approaches to the theatre as did a host of other designers.

But the American theatre could never quite relinquish its attachment to naturalistic techniques. Even in productions that employed New Stagecraft scenography, the texts and the acting style often remained resolutely entrenched in psychological realism. This was the challenge facing another significant figure in the history of American design, Boris Aronson.[3] The Ukrainian-born designer studied with Alexandra Exter in Moscow and was steeped in Russian Constructivism. Arriving in the US in 1923, he introduced Constructivism to the American theatre with his first designs at the Unser Theater in the Bronx. But his early work was largely limited to the then robust Yiddish Theatre, and it had little immediate impact within the larger New York theatre world.[4] Even as he moved into more commercial theatre, as a primary designer for the Group Theatre in the 1930s, for instance, his work was circumscribed by an American penchant for naturalism. One of his most famous sets of the period was for Clifford Odets' *Awake and Sing* (1935), for which Aronson created a highly detailed Bronx tenement apartment that showed no traces of his Constructivist style. Similarly, Norman Bel Geddes, another major figure of the period, designed futuristic theatres that were never built, and models for epic productions such as Dante's *Divine Comedy* that were never produced. Geddes' Broadway productions were, as they were for Aronson, suffused in American naturalism such as his New York City streetscape for Sidney Kingsley's *Dead End* (1935) that included a pool of water in the orchestra pit representing the East River that the actors actually dove into. Geddes' greatest impact would be in the realm of industrial rather than theatrical design.

American scenography, much as American dramaturgy, absorbed the vocabulary of European innovation, but little of the theoretical underpinnings. The dominance of the commercial theatre, which ultimately subsumed the more experimental Little Theatre movement, inhibited the impetus for rapid or fundamental change. Appia and Craig may have provided a foundation for the New Stagecraft, and elements of Expressionism found their way into American scenography of the period – more as style than concept – but the radical Russian and Soviet experiments, Piscator's investigations of still and moving projections, the Bauhaus project of form and mechanization, Brechtian alienation and dialectics, and the multiplicity of European avant-garde styles were mostly absent from the American stage of the interwar years. Even the innovations that did find their way onto the stage co-existed with older forms that were more familiar to audiences of bourgeois theatre. For every instance of the New Stagecraft there could be found an example of kitchen-sink naturalism.

After the Second World War a new generation of dramatists emerged, and many plays moved away from the hard-edged realism of prior decades. Best described as poetic realism, and embodied largely in the plays of Tennessee Williams as well as Arthur Miller's *Death of a Salesman*, it was typified by heightened poetic language, a cinematic structure, and fluid movement between dream and reality, past and present. Even the ostensibly naturalistic dramas of William Inge in the 1950s had an almost ethereal aspect to them as they explored the emotional lives of their characters. With Edward Albee emerging in the late fifties, an American brand of absurdist drama entered the mainstream. All these plays demanded a scenography capable not merely of establishing place but of conveying mood, suggesting inner states of mind and accommodating dreamlike transformations – a scenography that could create a unified framework for a sometimes nonlinear narrative or even alogical structure. This was also the so-called golden age of the musical theatre. Like the dramas, musicals such as *Oklahoma!* and *South Pacific* in the 1940s, and continuing in the 1950s with *Guys and Dolls*, *West Side Story*, and *Gypsy*, among many others, required nuanced creation of mood and tone, while demanding complex yet seamless visual and physical transformations between scenes. Because movies could create an unsurpassed literal reality, theatre design moved more toward the suggestive, the fragmentary, the poetic, and the frankly theatrical. Further contributing to a movement away from literal and illusionistic design was modern dance, which demanded a sophisticated approach to lighting – as did the new scenography of drama and musicals – and thus the art of lighting design came into its own during this period. Beginning in the 1930s, Jean Rosenthal (who designed for Martha Graham, Orson Welles, and several landmark Broadway musicals) and Abe Feder (who was also an innovator in the development of architectural lighting), essentially invented a new scenographic art, and the role of lighting designer thus emerged in the US long before it did elsewhere in the world.

Subsequent generations of lighting designers, including Thomas Skelton, Jules Fisher (who in addition to hundreds of plays and musicals also designed rock concerts), and, notably, Jennifer Tipton, took the art to new levels. Tipton's ability to sculpt space, particularly in dance productions, made her an obvious heir to Appia. But she was also crucial in moving lighting design away from the dependence on saturated color that typified much musical theatre, reintroducing white light onto the stage in new ways. Though comfortable in the worlds of opera and Broadway, she could create incredibly nuanced lighting with a bare minimum of instruments as she did in the Off Broadway productions of Richard Nelson's "Apple Family" cycle at the Public Theater. With the

Wooster Group her use of industrial lighting equipment meshed perfectly with industrial and technological design of their creations.

From a scenographic point of view, poetic realism was typically painterly in style, capable of evoking dream states and possessing elements of fantasy. It lacked the hard edges and, most important, the completion, of realistic design – it tended toward the fragmentary, skeletal, and ethereal. In the US it was most closely associated with Jo Mielziner, Oliver Smith, and some of the work of Donald Oenslager. Perhaps first recognized in Mielziner's design for Maxwell Anderson's *Winterset* (1935), with its backdrop of the Brooklyn Bridge soaring over the scene and disappearing into the mist, it emerged in full force in the 1940s, particularly in Mielziner's designs for Williams' *The Glass Menagerie* and *A Streetcar Named Desire*, and Miller's *Death of a Salesman*, all of which employed scrim to create a hazy dream-like quality while allowing for more fluid and cinematic scene changes. Writing about *The Glass* Menagerie, Mielziner declared,

> My use of translucent and transparent scenic interior walls was not just another trick. It was a true reflection of the contemporary playwright's interest in – and at times obsession with – the exploration of the inner man. Williams was writing not only a memory play but a play of influences that were not confined within the walls of a room.
>
> *(Mielziner 1965: 124)*

In *Salesman*, scrims allowed for a continuous oscillation between past and present, most notably toggling between the leafy suburbia of Willy Loman's memory and the present-day environment with the house hemmed in by apartment buildings. Mielziner also brought these qualities and techniques – including atmospheric innovations in lighting design and projection – to the musical theatre, notably in productions such as *Carousel* (1945), *South Pacific* (1949), and *Guys and Dolls* (1950). His use of skeletal scenic elements – suggesting place without solidity while allowing it to be seen within a larger visual and spatial context – became a significant motif in American design. Mielziner's designs made an indelible impact on American theatre; in some cases, particularly with *Death of a Salesman*, his designs were so integrally bound up in the texts and so closely identified with the productions that it took decades for later generations of designers to overcome those visual motifs. To a large extent, when one looks at the visual record of American theatre in the 1940s and 1950s, one is looking at Jo Mielziner.[5]

The atmospheric and evocative tone of poetic realism differed in various ways from the spare and emblematic New Stagecraft, but both approaches utilized light to sculpt space. In fact, light was probably the key scenographic element in both genres.

Oliver Smith may have established the new painterly mode of the era – a style that owed something to Russian-born Eugene Berman. Smith's iconic 1942 backdrop for the ballet *Rodeo* created a surreal landscape of skeletal fences in distorted perspective against a sky and ground of unreal colors. Ballet's need for open space for the dancers provided a particularly rich environment for painted emblematic scenery. Smith's equally iconic design for *Fall River Legend* in 1948 suggested a confluence of the fragmentary, open-stage designs of the New Stagecraft, particularly those of Lee Simonson, with the surreal landscape of *Rodeo*. The towering louvered shutters and fragmented trusses together with the suggestion of a room with eerily isolated chairs established a scenographic motif that would persist for decades. Smith served as Co-Director of the American Ballet Theatre from 1945 to 1980. He is also known for his designs for several of the most notable musicals of the 1950s and 1960s including *My Fair Lady*, *West Side Story*, *The Sound of Music*, and *Hello, Dolly!* (the first with lighting by Feder, the rest with lighting by Rosenthal), and here too his influence was not limited to pictorial style but to his use of modular units that allowed a rapid, virtually choreographic movement of scenery – a technique that was equally influential for years to come, particularly with designers of musicals, notably Robin Wagner who even applied this technique to complex non-musicals such as *Angels in America* (1993).[6]

Oenslager was stylistically more eclectic than some of his contemporaries. Adapting to the perceived needs of each play, he could range from detailed, three-dimensional naturalism to lyrical, painterly decor. In his position as head of design at Yale University, where he taught from 1925 to 1971, he trained several generations of stage designers and thus his belief in suiting the design to the needs of the play rather than in developing a personal style, and a concomitant belief that the design should *not* be the dominant element in a production, therefore contributed to an American approach to design that was less adventurous and less stylistically unique than most of the European scenography of the same era.

Throughout this period, Boris Aronson would continue to be a significant force, though never – at the time – finding the critical acclaim or financial success of Mielziner or Smith. He designed plays by Tennessee Williams (*The Rose Tattoo*), Arthur Miller (*The Crucible*, *A View from the Bridge*, and *The Price*) and William Inge (*Bus Stop*), always conveying the requisite sense of reality while subtly infusing his work with non-realistic elements. Within the theatre world Aronson was considered a brilliant and versatile designer, but it was not until he teamed up with producer and director Harold Prince on a string of major musicals, starting with *Fiddler on the Roof* in 1964 – a design suffused with the fantastical painterly imagery of Marc Chagall – and continuing with *Cabaret*, *Company*, *Follies*, and *A Little Night Music*, that he was able to find a way finally to fuse the emblematic and sculptural approaches he had been struggling to use since arriving from the Soviet Union with the commercial world of Broadway theatre. Nonetheless, Aronson was largely responsible for introducing Constructivism, Cubism, collage (in the musical *Do Re Mi*), the fantastical, and other non-objective art movements into the American theatre, and this work provided an important counterpoint to the poetic realism of Mielziner.

Shanghai-born Ming Cho Lee came to the US in 1949 to attend college, essentially stumbled into set design as an undergraduate, and wound up assisting both Mielziner and Aronson in the 1950s. Lee had studied Chinese watercolor painting as a teenager and Mielziner helped him adapt his painterly style to the demands of set design; he also inspired a use of skeletal structures. From Aronson came a sculptural and emblematic approach to design as well as a use of collage; and from his observation of contemporary German opera design – particularly the work of Wieland Wagner – and a rejection of the decorative that derived in part from his study of Brecht and Brecht's designers, Lee radically transformed American design in the 1960s. In moving American scenography away from the painterly and imagistic, Lee moved it toward the emblematic. Instead of creating a decor that referenced a particular location or environment within the experiential world, Lee sought out a dominant visual motif that was more metonymy than synecdoche. The design might place the viewer in ancient Greece, as in his landmark production of *Electra* (1964) with the New York Shakespeare Festival, or medieval England as with *Richard III* (1966), also at the Shakespeare Festival, but not within an identifiable architectural structure or scenic background.[7] Furthermore, the textures,

Figure 41.2 Ming Cho Lee, model for *Electra* at the New York Shakespeare Festival Delacorte Theater in Central Park, 1964. This design is often considered a turning point in the history of American scenography, moving from the poetic realism and painterly styles to the sculptural and emblematic. (Courtesy of Ming Cho Lee.)

materials, and colors of this emblematic design created layers of scenographic meaning that shaped spectator response in ways that few previous American designers had done.

Partly because of both the limitations and the demands of the theatres in which his style evolved – the Peabody Institute at Johns Hopkins University and in particular the outdoor Delacorte Theater in New York's Central Park that was the home of the New York Shakespeare Festival – Lee emphasized, more than almost any of his contemporaries, the unit set. Lee did not invent the unit set – it was a staple of much of the New Stagecraft – but he took a somewhat different approach. Especially at the Delacorte he created a framework, usually a pipework structure, on which emblematic scenic units could be hung and which could support raised playing levels. As this evolved, the pipework structure itself – scaffolding – began to emerge as the dominant scenic element. Not only did it create a flexible environment for staging, but the combination of the metal with the functional form gave it a sense of modernity and essentially introduced the industrial esthetic onto the American stage. Lee's approach evolved from the emblematic into scenic collage, created either through sculptural elements or later through photographic images – the pipework structures being an ideal framework on which to mount the array of images that would comprise these collage designs. This was most apparent in his design for the original production of the rock musical *Hair* (1967) that opened the Public Theater, the permanent home of the New York Shakespeare Festival. Lee also turned to other industrial materials ranging from erosion cloth to mylar to create his sets. The scaffolding also contributed to another element that typified Lee's work throughout his career: a sense of verticality that was virtually unknown previously in American theatre. Lee understood the stage as a cubic volume in which each dimension was equally important.

Before his second season at the New York Shakespeare Festival Lee visited the Stratford Shakespeare Festival in Ontario, Canada, founded in 1953, with a stage conceived by artistic director Tyrone Guthrie and set and costume designer Tanya Moiseiwitsch. This would have an effect on the redesign of the Delacorte and a broader influence on the evolution of the thrust stage in general. The Guthrie-Moiseiwitsch creation was a five-sided stepped stage made of natural wood, within an intimate theatre that employed vomitoria to allow for entrances and exits from beneath the auditorium. It was intended to provide the fluidity of the Shakespearean stage, but physically was closer in spirit to the ancient Greek theatre. Guthrie and Moiseiwitsch went on to design the stage for the Guthrie Theater in Minneapolis that opened in 1963. Thrust stages are ubiquitous today, but were rare at the time. The Shakespeare Festival in Ontario was among the first in North America to explore scenographic and staging techniques for the stage whose openness required a generally more sculptural, emblematic, and fragmentary approach to design. The work of British designers Tanya Moiseiwitsch and Desmond Heeley, at Stratford, Ontario, and Minneapolis, along with Lee's work at the Delacorte, was crucial in establishing the vocabulary of thrust design. Many of the facilities built as part of the explosion of new theatres and performing arts centers across the US and Canada in the 1960s and 1970s included thrust stages as either their mainstage or as secondary "experimental" spaces. Other British designers, notably Leslie Hurry, Brian Jackson, Daphne Dare, and Ann Curtis working at Stratford helped lay the foundation for the development of Canadian scenography (see Silver 1996). The establishment of the Canada Council/Conseil des Arts du Canada in 1957, in response to the Massey-Lévesque Commission report of 1951, paved the way for a series of regional theatres which were also crucial in developing Canadian design. (See also Rewa 2004.)

Theatres-in-the-round or arena stages were also being tried, though in far fewer numbers. The Penthouse Theatre at the University of Washington in Seattle (1940) is generally considered the first, followed by Margo Jones' Theater '47 in Dallas. The most successful was the Arena Stage in Washington DC founded in 1950 by Tom and Zelda Fichandler and Edward Mangum. Ming Cho Lee began an ongoing relationship with the Arena Stage in 1967. Until this time design for such theatres was typically limited

Figure 41.3 Festival stage at the Stratford, Ontario, Shakespeare Festival designed by Tanya Moiseiwitsch. (Photo: Terry Manzo; courtesy of the Stratford Festival Archives.)

to a few pieces of furniture or nearly bare stages so as not to obstruct sightlines; there was little established practice or scenic vocabulary. Lee proved to be an innovator in the creation of more complex and sophisticated design for such theatres that utilized the entire cubic volume of the stage space.

Ultimately, Lee was the catalyst who transformed American design. Through him one can trace a direct link to the scenographic work of the early twentieth century: from Adolphe Appia and Edward Gordon Craig through Robert Edmond Jones to Jo Mielziner; from Russian directors Vsevolod Meyerhold and Alexander Tairov via Alexandra Exter to Boris Aronson to Lee. It was Ming Cho Lee who brought together most of the techniques and vocabulary of the 1940s and 1950s – particularly the sculptural approaches of Aronson and Isamu Noguchi, the sculptor who was a primary designer for choreographer Martha Graham, the use of textures employed by Rouben Ter-Arutunian, and of course the poetic realism of his mentor Jo Mielziner (further influenced by the painting of Ben Shahn and Eugene Berman). Lee was also a conduit for the anti-decorative aesthetic of Bertolt Brecht and the conceptual approach that typified the work of many German opera designers of the period. Throughout the 1960s, with his work at the New York Shakespeare Festival, the New York City Opera, the Joffrey Ballet, and Arena Stage in Washington, as well as a host of other opera companies and theatres, Lee fomented a kind of revolution in stage design that foregrounded the use of new materials, highly textured elements, collage, his signature use of scaffolding, and an emblematic and conceptual approach to design. All of this was reinforced by his role as an educator, first at New York University's School of the Arts, and then as head of design at the Yale School of Drama over more than 40 years. Throughout the 1970s and 1980s, and to an extent up to the present day, Lee's influence could be seen and felt in every corner of American theatre, dance, and opera.

Alternative spaces

Aspects of virtually all the stylistic motifs of the first half of the twentieth century can still be found in today's mainstream theatre. However, in addition to the innovations of Ming Cho Lee, other forces contributed to radical changes in the design and architecture of theatre in the post-World War Two era. All the previous developments assumed a basic theatrical structure: the stage. The majority of mainstream theatres, whether Broadway or regional, use some variant of the end stage or thrust. But in the 1950s the very nature of the stage and the theatre building were increasingly questioned.

The emergence of Off Broadway had some effect on these developments. Notably, the original Circle in the Square theatre in a former nightclub in the Greenwich Village neighborhood of New York created an elongated thrust that radically altered the traditional relationship of the spectator to the stage. The Living Theatre in the 1950s pioneered the use of non-traditional spaces, beginning with the living room of Judith Malina and Julian Beck's apartment for their earliest ventures, and a converted storefront, before transforming a former department store into an early version of a performing arts center. Happenings – Allan Kaprow's *18 Happenings in 6 Parts* in 1959 is generally considered the original example – often were done in art galleries or other non-theatre spaces as well as found and site-specific environments, and they frequently fragmented the audience into smaller groups or enfolded them within constructed environments. Happenings drew inspiration from Dada, from Artaud's scenic and spatial proposals for his Theatre of Cruelty, and the compositional methodologies of John Cage. While Happenings, at least initially, were created by visual artists and performed primarily for art world audiences, the aesthetics and practices seeped into the world of theatre. In particular, the fragmentation of space and the concomitant elimination of the "fourth wall," and with it the deconstruction of a unitary and cohesive audience point of view, all encouraged a re-evaluation of scenographic practice. The use of pedestrian and quotidian objects and an often homemade quality also contributed to a new aesthetic, an approach complemented by the consciously crude techniques of the New American Cinema.

The early Off-Off Broadway companies worked in converted storefronts, repurposed industrial lofts and garages, churches, and other non-theatre spaces. Often working on minimal to almost non-existent budgets, scenery ranged from bare makeshift stages to fragmentary settings – both realistic and conceptual – with materials scavenged from streets, garbage dumps, and second-hand shops. Among the first such theatres was Caffe Cino, which had a miniscule (8 ft by 8 ft) raised stage against one wall, surrounded by tables for customers. Sets were simple – pieces of furniture or other objects, draped fabrics, and the occasional painted flat leaning against the back wall. Much was achieved by lighting, particularly by a self-taught designer, Johnny Dodd. As described by Stephen J. Bottoms, Dodd's "great skill lay in conjuring dramatic atmospheres using the limited resources available to him: one show might use a single, naked bulb; another might involve Dodd 'playing' the simple control desk as if it were an organ in order to create colorful, shifting moods for more abstract pieces" (Bottoms 2004: 46). A similar aesthetic was developed in Canada with the more politically oriented Toronto Workshop Productions (TWP) founded by George Luscombe in 1959 in a basement space accommodating some 60 spectators.

In 1968 Richard Schechner, drawing upon the work of Polish director Jerzy Grotowski, aspects of the historical avant-garde, Happenings, and medieval staging practices, developed a non-frontal audience-encompassing staging methodology he termed "environmental theatre." Most forms of conventional staging – whether end-stage, thrust, or arena – are frontal in that the spectators are all focused on a single stage directly "in front" of them and can apprehend the total production from that position. In environmental theatre, according to Schechner, "all the space is used for performance; all the space is used for audience" (Schechner 1968: 48; see also Aronson 1981). In other words, the entire theatrical space – the space that had traditionally been divided between performers and audience, stage and auditorium – was now potentially available as a fluid and transformable space for everyone involved in the theatrical act, performer and spectator alike. Not all productions embraced this totality, though some, like the Living Theatre's *Paradise Now* (1968) and several productions by Schechner's Performance Group, beginning with *Dionysus in 69* (1968), certainly did. Many productions, however, fragmented the stage, surrounded the audience, incorporated the elements of the existing environment, or totally transformed existing spaces through a totalizing scenography. In such cases, the audience was physically as well as psychologically implicated and embedded within the performance even if they did not necessarily move about or come in direct contact with performers. At the Performing Garage, home of the Performance Group, the primary scenic elements were often wooden scaffolds along the walls of the theatre that served as audience seating platforms as well as stages. Performers would climb onto parts of the scaffolding, asking spectators to move or simply standing in their midst. Spectators were encouraged to move about the space at certain times. Other theatre companies that had to perform in more traditional (i.e. proscenium) spaces would abandon the stage for the auditorium or invite the audience onto the stage.

The avant-garde and experimental companies that employed environmental scenography often saw political implications in this approach. By challenging traditional modes of behavior and apprehension they sought to alter the perception of daily life and thus lead the spectators toward an alternative understanding of the world. Implicit in this was a belief – or perhaps a utopian hope – that it would lead to political or social action. So, in a sense, it was functioning as a Brechtian device, even though it often implicated the spectator deep within the world of the play. The apparent elimination of the so-called "fourth wall" and the disruption of conventional relations between performer and spectator could be disconcerting or liberating. But the breakdown of customary boundaries and the reduction of both literal and aesthetic distance could also lead to a violation of acceptable codes of behavior and in some productions, such as *Dionysus* and *Paradise Now*, performers had to deal with unwanted and inappropriate physical contact, as well as more generally disruptive behavior from some spectators.

While Schechner and other creators of environmental theatre had serious artistic, social, and political aims, the superficial aspects of staging were also appealing to more commercial producers who saw in it a gimmick to attract audiences. Productions like *Tony 'n' Tina's Wedding* (1985) engaged the audience as attendees at an Italian-American wedding, while *Tamara*, which premiered in Toronto in 1981, was set in a 10-room nineteenth-century Italian villa in which the spectators could follow performers from room to room. A few Broadway productions, notably a revival of *Candide* (1974), transformed the theatre in order to extend the production into the midst of the auditorium. All of this was a precursor to what would become known in the twenty-first century as immersive theatre. Younger audiences that might not have an extensive experience of live theatre and thus less patience for the relatively static experience of sitting in a darkened auditorium watching actors on a distant stage (especially at expensive Broadway and Off Broadway venues) might be attracted to more physically engaging, unusual, and intimate (though often equally expensive) events such as *Sleep No More* or *Natasha, Pierre, and the Great Comet of 1812* that might also include food and drink as a component of the performance. The productions by Schechner's Performance Group often encouraged spectators to move about the space during the performance, so in theory everyone had a slightly different experience of the play. With immersive productions, notably *Sleep No More* created by the British company Punchdrunk, the audience wandered with some degree of freedom through a highly detailed scenographic environment consisting of multiple rooms spread over several floors so that the experience could be radically different for individual spectators.[8]

Postmodern design

Postmodernism, with its strategies of disruption, juxtaposition, pastiche, the "presence of the past," the melding of high and low art, intentional ugliness and a rejection of what Jean-François Lyotard called a "grand narrative" or metanarrative, defined a scenographic trend in the latter part of the twentieth century, apparent most often in opera design. In a contemporary world seen as a multiplicity of competing, often incongruous and conflicting, elements and images, it was incumbent on the stage to represent this view. Postmodern design was a reflection of an understanding that no single point of view was possible, even within a single image. Postmodern design often foregrounded the ugly and the use of discordance, making the spectator aware of the experience of viewing and, at the same time, being made aware of the whole history, context, and reverberations of an image in the contemporary world. Richard Foreman, describing his own work, declared, "The imagery that I was dealing with was not making pretty pictures, it was a dialectical examination of the problematics of seeing" (quoted in Schechner 1987: 126). I have defined postmodern design as

> the juxtaposition of seemingly incongruous elements within the unifying structure of the stage frame, the purpose of which is to create a referential network within the mind of the viewer that extends beyond the immediately apparent world of the play. A postmodern design will often make reference to other productions, to other works of art, and to an extra- or non-dramatic world. Unity derives from the very presence of a stage, a theatre, and performers, and, perhaps, the visual style of the designer.
>
> *(Aronson 1991: 5)*

The landmark production of postmodern design in Europe is generally considered Patrice Chéreau's staging of Wagner's *Ring Cycle* at Bayreuth in 1976. In the US it might be dated from John Conklin's design for the *Ring* at the San Francisco Opera in 1983. It was particularly apparent in Conklin's architectural pastiche that represented Valhalla that included a recreation of an eighteenth-century idealistic project by Étienne-Louis Boullée, Leo von Klenze's Königstor, and Gottfried Semper's Dresden Opera House. This had the effect of placing the gods, who are, after all, opera singers, in an opera house over a fort on the actual stage of an opera house. Conklin's work with the now-defunct New York City Opera, the Metropolitan Opera, and for many years at the Glimmerglass Opera Festival, were usually near-textbook examples of postmodernist design with multiple layers of historical, theatrical, pictorial, and architectural references.

In Canada, postmodernist tendencies could be seen particularly in the work of Ken MacDonald and Michael Levine. In the US it typifies the work of Robert Israel, Adrianne Lobel, and especially George Tsypin. Tyspin came to prominence in the 1980s for his work on several theatre and opera productions with director Peter Sellars, notably a production of *Don Giovanni* set in Harlem. Tyspin's work in this period was strongly typified by pastiche. As he noted, "We live in a period in which all the myths and all classical literature is treated . . . as if it is happening right now. That is partially the reason that design seems to be a mix of different languages. In my designs I try to achieve a certain fusion of different elements. It's not just a juxtaposition of different styles" (quoted in Aronson 1991: 10). Tsypin, who trained as an architect in the Soviet Union before emigrating to the US, and who has a parallel career as a sculptor and intermedia artist, approaches space and design with a different set of assumptions and expectations than many, more traditionally trained, scenographers. He explains

> I travel around the world and I imagine the sets I design as fragments, ruins of some fantastic city, the Tower of Babel collapsing, shattering in front of my eyes. I see the memories, shadows of the sets I designed strewn across the landscape as I continue this futile attempt to rebuild this ideal, invisible, transparent nonexistent city, that can only be found by traveling inside yourself: The City of Immortals.
>
> *(Tsypin 2005: 16)*

Tsypin sees himself as more than a set designer. In fact, he has often attempted to fill the role of scenographer. He states:

> I see my role as a designer of opera as equal to that of the composer, conductor, and director. But because of the scale of the space, the demands of today's visual culture, and the structural rigor of the musical score, the role of the artist sometimes transcends all others in making a plastic, emotional poem that creates a direct contact with the music. Sometimes it even goes against the music, but always creates a direct electrical charge between the sculptural space, color, light, and sound. The paradox of designing an opera is that while you have to use existing materials on this Earth (the only ones available), you aim at achieving an emotional impact and creating an atmosphere that is of another world.
>
> *(Tsypin 2005: 16–17)*

The combination of scale and aesthetics that typifies Tsypin's work means that, other than some productions at the Metropolitan Opera such as *Guillaume Tell* and *Die Zauberflöte* and a notoriously troubled Broadway production of *Spiderman: Turn Off the Dark* (2010) directed by Julie Taymor, the majority of his work since the 1990s has been done in Europe.

The stunningly visual theatre of Robert Wilson, whose work is exemplary of what critic Bonnie Marranca termed the "theatre of images" (Marranca 1977), has often been considered another manifestation of postmodernism. But I would argue that the

Figure 41.4 Rehearsal for *Spider-Man: Turn Off the Dark* (2011). Set by George Tsypin, costumes by Eiko Ishoka, lighting by Donald Holder. (Courtesy of George Tsypin.)

strikingly beautiful and painstakingly precise images he creates fall within Lyotard's conception of modernism. The work is generally mesmerizing, often inducing a trance-like state in the audience. The image within the frame of a Wilson production is highly structured and complete and rarely refers overtly to any other work of theatre or art. The almost clinical exactitude of his lighting may seem to be the opposite of the atmospherics of Appia and Craig, but the scale and grandeur of his imagery, particularly in his opera productions and most of his creations since *Einstein on the Beach* (1975), place him well within that tradition and his work can, in fact, be seen as a culmination of the theories of Gordon Craig. Regardless of how they are categorized, Wilson's productions, of both his original creations as well as operas, are among the most recognizable examples of scenography in the world today and he can be offered as an ideal example of a scenographer.

Video and projection

Since at least the 1920s and the work of Erwin Piscator in Germany, the projection of film and still images has been a component of theatrical production. The emergence of video as an art form was greatly influenced by Korean-born artist Nam June Paik whose sculptures, installations, happenings, and performances, especially with other Fluxus artists, in the 1960s and 1970s contributed to the ever-growing fascination with video in the theatre. By the 1970s the televisual image began to appear in more traditional stage productions, although the limitations of technology, particularly the relatively small size of the television monitor through the late twentieth century, restricted its use or effectiveness on large stages. But video, and even cinematic projection in the theatre, more often tended toward a sense of novelty or gimmick. It was a way to suggest that a particular production was partaking of the modern. Rarely did such technology integrate successfully with live production.

The avant-garde theatre troupe, Squat Theatre, founded in Hungary, emigrated to the US in 1977 and immediately began to incorporate film and video into their productions, providing a sort of bridge between the art and theatre worlds. Then, in the 1980s, the Wooster Group, under the direction of Elizabeth LeCompte with the scenographic input of James Clayburgh, began to experiment with video, and their work would have a profound impact on many theatre artists and companies in the US and abroad. In their productions, television monitors – cathode ray tubes that now seem as dated as antique radios – appeared on the stage or hanging above the audience. Because, in the relatively intimate space of the Performing Garage,[9] no spectator was very far from the stage so the images, even on small screens, were legible. The monitors even became performers in their own right, moving back and forth on tracks in the stage floor in *Brace Up!*, for instance. What the Wooster Group realized, before most other theatre artists did, was that the video image had a distinct spatial and visual vocabulary and the way in which to integrate it into the theatrical performance was not to try to make it function as scenery but to put it in conversation with the living human performer and the three-dimensional stage. Most obviously, video could bring pre-recorded images and sequences into a performance. In some Wooster Group productions the video imagery included material that seemed utterly alien to the performance – a Japanese horror film, for example, in juxtaposition to *Brace Up!*, which was based on Chekhov's *Three Sisters*; a home-made porno film in *Route 1 & 9* that incorporated text from *Our Town*. But it could also include recorded sequences of actors who were simultaneously present onstage, creating strange temporal dislocations. In two instances, in revivals of earlier work, they included video of actors who had died in the intervening years. They would also use live video feeds of actors offstage, sometimes leaving the stage center eerily empty except for video images and actors on the periphery. All of this served to bring together multiple temporal and spatial references as well as imagery from other genres and culture. For the Wooster Group the video technology was anything but gimmick, it was a crucial tool for the generation of performance texts, and an integral aspect of the production at least equal to, if not more significant than, the performers and the scenographic elements.

The video explorations of the Wooster Group had a direct effect on companies and performers such as the Builders Association, Collapsable Giraffe, Elevator Repair Service, and Andrew Schneider. Of course the use of video continues to evolve with creators not directly connected to the Wooster Group. It plays a major aesthetic and structural role in the works of director Jay Scheib. In Canada, Montreal-based 4D Art has experimented with holographic imagery onstage. The 3LD Art & Technology Center in New York is devoted to exploring new technologies in service of live performance. Video and digital projection inevitably found its way onto Broadway as well, though the increasingly sophisticated use of technology did not always translate into greater aesthetic sophistication.

Among the more interesting artists exploring video, projection, and technology is Robert Lepage and his Quebec-based company, Ex Machina. Ex Machina has its own studio in which to develop work and experiment with new technologies. This is a luxury

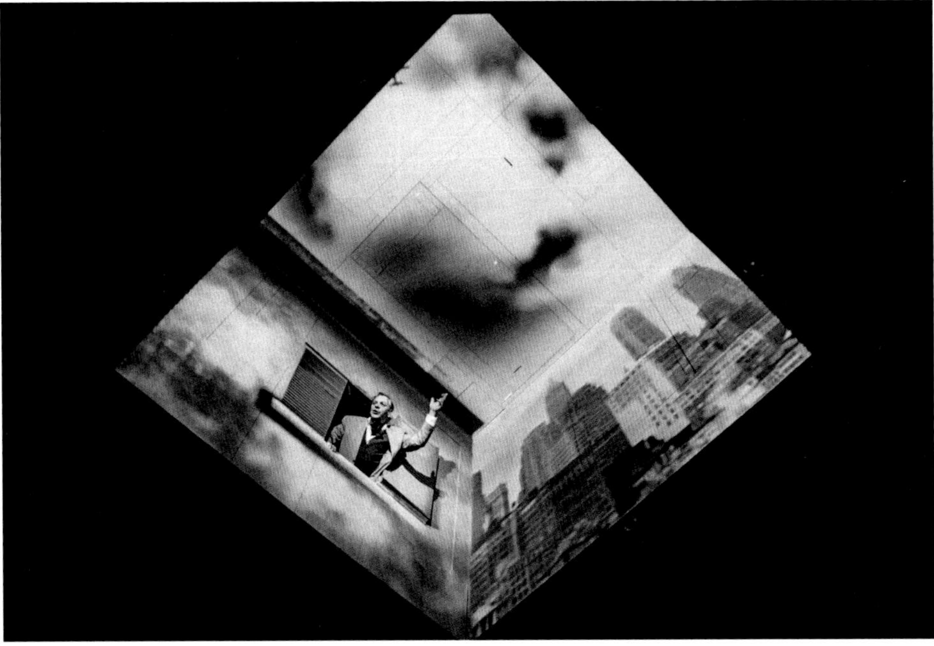

Figure 41.5 *Needles and Opium*, directed by Robert Lepage, set design by Carl Fillion, lighting by Bruno Matte, image design by Lionel Arnould. (©Nicola-Frank Vachon.)

shared by very few theatre artists or companies, at least in North America. Working with a variety of designers, Lepage's productions weave together digital projection, live and recorded video, and kinetic sets often constructed from steel and other industrial and contemporary materials. At their best, as in *Needles and Opium* and *The Seven Streams of the River Ota*, these elements can combine to provide a deep exploration of the human condition. In other cases, such as *Lipsynch*, many critics were more impressed with moment-to-moment imagery than the overall coherence of the nine-hour production. In some cases, such as the rather notorious *Ring* at the Metropolitan Opera, elaborate technology and projection seemed to take precedence over the content.

Design today

Perhaps the only adjective that adequately characterizes twenty-first-century US and Canadian design is eclectic. Within the standard venues presenting opera, musicals, drama, and even more cutting-edge performance, one can encounter virtually every style from naturalism through postmodernism. Projected scenery is supplementing or replacing tangible decor, video can be found in all genres and at every economic level of production, lighting and sound are emerging as dominant elements of scenography, and costumes often incorporate technology. The sheer quantity of lighting instruments and the ability of light to shift and transform with subtlety and nuance might surprise a spectator from half a century ago, as would the amplification and complexity of sound. But the scenery would contain at least some familiar motifs. Certainly echoes

Figure 41.6 *An Octoroon* (2014) by Branden Jacobs-Jenkins. Sets Mimi Lien, Costumes Wade Laboissonniere, lights Matt Frey, sound Matt Tierney, projections Jeff Sugg, wigs and makeup Cookie Jordan. (Photo courtesy of Mimi Lien.)

of poetic realism can be found in many of the more than 100 productions John Lee Beatty has done on Broadway, and in selected work of David Zinn, Marjorie Bradley Kellogg, Ralph Funicello, and Christine Jones, among many others. The emblematic work of Aronson and Lee is carried on in the designs of Santo Loquasto (who also designs costumes). Architectural settings can be seen in the work of Canadian designer Cameron Porteous. Pictorial and theatrical design typify many settings by Tony Walton and David Rockwell. Postmodernism infuses the work of Paul Steinberg and Michael Yeargan in addition to those mentioned above, but Yeargan has also designed neo-realist settings. Kathleen Irwin has created site-specific environments for several productions in Ontario. Mimi Lien has done everything from immersive to architectural to emblematic to the fantasy-on-a-shoestring budget of Taylor Mac's epic *A 24-Decade History of Popular Music*. Yet every one of the designers just cited, as well as dozens of others, have also produced work in a multitude of other styles.

Historically, theatre has been a mass medium that functioned by bringing large numbers of spectators together in a single location. But mass media today tends to be experienced on screens and in isolation. So one response has been to create more intimate and personal forms of theatre. Fiona Templeton created *YOU – The City* in 1988 in which one participant at a time was instructed to go to a location in Times Square in New York City to begin

> a two-hour journey through the public and private places of midtown Manhattan, meeting a series of about 15 individuals, all of whom seemed to know something about you. A church, a peepshow, a playground, an apartment, pushed into the back of a car and driven off alone with even the cabbie in on the inside of your head.
>
> (*YOU* – The City *website*)

Montreal-born Christine Jones, mentioned above, has created Theatre for One, which consists of a mobile black booth described as a

> state-of-the art performance space for one performer and one audience member [for] new work written specifically for one-on-one encounters in this venue. Founded with the belief that heightening the intimate relationship between actor and audience member enhances the transformational impact of a live performance.
>
> (*Theatre for One website*)

Since 2012, The Industry, based in Los Angeles, has been creating new operas such as *Invisible Cities* (2013) produced throughout locations in Union Station with the audience hearing it through wireless headphones, and *Hopscotch* (2015) in which individual audience members were seated in 24 cars, each of which included singers, actors, and musicians, that drove through Los Angeles for 90 minutes as the opera unfolded, stopping at a variety of local sites. As described in a *New York Times* article,

> A limo pulls up, an attendant gestures you inside, and the opera begins. Singers, actors, instrumentalists and dancers – a total of 128 performers are involved in the production – transform the city around you as you are driven around, occasionally changing cars, going for a stroll in a park or being guided

> through a building. Enter a vehicle and encounter a cellist; step out of a car and watch a saxophone quartet play in the hills of Griffith Park. The opera's 24 vignettes take place along three distinct routes – all running simultaneously – so each experience of the piece remains just a partial snapshot of the opera's elusive whole.
>
> (*Robin 2015*)

A larger, collective audience, gathered at a temporary auditorium, could watch a live stream of the event.

But perhaps at some point in the future, historians looking at the scenography of today will ignore the more traditional forms of theatre and look instead at spectacle as embodied in entertainment centers such as Las Vegas or Disneyworld, at arena rock concerts, and sporting events in large stadiums. Las Vegas has long been the home of extravagant cabaret shows, typified by flamboyant costumes and special effects, but in more recent decades many of the hotels have become scenographic spectacles in themselves, often as simulacra of a global pastiche of architectural monuments. The shows reach for ever-more boundary-pushing experiences from Cirque du Soleil in its permanent David Rockwell-designed theatre, to *Le Rêve*, an aquatic spectacle at the Wynn Resort that allows qualified audience members to watch from underwater while wearing diving gear (see Tabački 2015) – a peculiar variant on the personalized theatres discussed above.

But it is the concert and sporting events that recall the collective mass entertainments of the past. Given the sheer size of the venues – arenas typically with seating for 18,000–20,000 and stadiums upwards of 80,000 – all intimacy is lost and for much

Figure 41.7 *Invisible Cities* produced by The Industry at Union Station in Los Angeles, 2013. (Photo: Dana Ross.)

of the audience the performers and athletes are little more than miniscule figures. In these venues massive video screens display a constantly changing array of images from close-ups of performers to digitally-created light shows. It is a gargantuan version – perhaps perversion – of the spatio-temporal dislocation created by video in the Wooster Group productions. The audience, all experiencing a performative event in a single time and place, are largely focused *not* on the source of the performance but on digital enhancements of the event which, at least in the case of sporting events, include instant replays that allow movement through time, as well as images of the audience, thereby turning spectators into an aspect of the scenography. There is a scenography of the performance space – the atmosphere, sounds, smells, and sense of space – and a visual scenography on digital screens that provides the content and shapes the emotional rhythm of the event.

We are in a world of the large and the small, the intimate and the impersonal, the live and the digital. The one thing that most of these performance scenographies have in common is that there is seldom stasis. It is a sensorial field that is constantly changing.

Notes

1 The focus of this chapter is, admittedly, on US design, especially in the first half of the twentieth century. Prior to the 1950s Canadian theatre was largely dominated by touring or packaged productions from the US and UK. As designer Phillip Silver has noted, "Canadian stage design does not have an overt national 'character' or 'look'" (Silver 1996: 134), though something similar might be said of US design. For an overview of the development of Canadian scenography see Silver 1996 and David 1996.
2 See Chapter 33 in this volume by David Bisaha.
3 No relation to author.
4 The best study of Boris Aronson's work is Frank Rich's *The Theatre Art of Boris Aronson* (1987).
5 For a thorough overview of his work see Henderson 2001.
6 Typical of the eclecticism of so many US designers, Wagner also designed the set for *A Chorus Line* (1975), one of finest examples of minimalist design for a musical ever seen on Broadway.
7 For a detailed examination of Lee's work see Aronson 2015.
8 See Chapter 24 in this volume by W. B. Worthen.
9 The Wooster Group emerged out of the Performance Group in the mid-1970s and ultimately took over the theatre.

References

Aronson, Arnold 1981. *The History and Theory of Environmental Scenography*. Ann Arbor, MI: UMI Research Press.

Aronson, Arnold 1991. "Postmodern Design." *Theatre Journal* 43 (1): 1–13.

Aronson, Arnold 2001. *Architect of Dreams: The Theatrical Vision of Joseph Urban*. New York: Miriam & Ira D. Wallach Art Gallery.

Aronson, Arnold 2015. *Ming Cho Lee: A Life in Design*. New York: Theatre Communications Group.

Bottoms, Stephen J. 2004. *Playing Underground: A Critical History of the 1960s Off-Off-Broadway Movement*. Ann Arbor: University of Michigan Press.

David, Gilbert 1996. "Design – Quebec." In *The World Encyclopedia of Contemporary Theatre*, Volume 2: Americas, edited by Don Rubin, 136–7. London: Routledge.

Henderson, Mary C. 2001. *Mielziner: Master of Modern Stage Design*. New York: Watson-Guptill.

Hopkins, Arthur 1921. "The Approaching Macbeth." *New York Times*, February 6: 90.

Jones, Robert Edmond 1941. *The Dramatic Imagination: Reflections and Speculations on the Art of the Theatre*. New York: Duell, Sloan and Pearce.

Macgowan, Kenneth 1914. "The New Stage-Craft in America." *Century Magazine* 87 (January): 418–21.

Marranca, Bonnie 1977. *The Theatre of Images*. New York: Drama Book Specialists.
Mielziner, Jo 1965. *Designing for the Theatre: A Memoir and a Portfolio*. New York: Bramhall House.
Rewa, Natalie 2004. *Scenography in Canada: Selected Designers*. Toronto: University of Toronto Press.
Rich, Frank 1987. *The Theatre Art of Boris Aronson*. New York: Alfred A. Knopf.
Robin, William 2015. "'Hopscotch' Takes Opera into the Streets." *New York Times*, October 30.
Schechner, Richard 1968. "6 Axioms for Environmental Theatre." *The Drama Review* 12 (3): 41–64.
Schechner, Richard 1987. "Richard Foreman on Richard Foreman: An Interview." *The Drama Review* 31 (4): 125–35.
Silver, Phillip 1996. "Design" [Canada]. In *The World Encyclopedia of Contemporary Theatre*, Volume 2: Americas, edited by Don Rubin, 134–6. London: Routledge.
Tabački, Nebojša 2015. "Diving into the Abyss: Scenography for Contemporary Aquatic Theatres." *Theatre and Performance Design* 1 (1–2): 64–78.
Taylor, Deems 1934. "The Scenic Art of Joseph Urban: His Protean Work in the Theatre." *Architecture* 69 (May): 275–90.
Theatre for One. Available online at: www.theatreforone.com/ (accessed 12 December 2016).
Tsypin, George 2005. *George Tsypin Opera Factory: Building in the Black Void*. New York: Princeton Architectural Press.
Urban, Joseph 1913. From the *Sunday Leader*. Typed manuscript in the Joseph Urban Collection (box 34, file 5), Rare Books and Manuscript Library, Columbia University.
YOU – The City. Available online at: www.fionatempleton.org/you-the%20city.htm (accessed 15 December 2016).

42

SPATIAL OSCILLATIONS IN THE AMERICAN AVANT-GARDE

Stephen Bottoms

The twentieth century saw a huge range of experiments with theatrical form but, scenographically speaking – as Bonnie Marranca has observed – avant-garde practice in the West was consistently notable for "its embrace of performance *space*, and rejection of *setting*" (quoted in Chaudhuri 1994: 27). Often dispensing with scenic apparatus altogether, or else integrating it almost seamlessly with the architectural aspects of a performance venue, experimental practitioners sought to articulate and explore space itself as a primary concern of the theatrical event. More specifically, the post-war American avant-garde – on which this chapter focuses – can be read as oscillating productively between treatments of space as *environment*, on the one hand, and as *landscape*, on the other. Should the spectator be surrounded and encompassed (environmentally) by the theatrical event? Or should she be permitted to sit separate and undisturbed, while being presented with a dispersed pictorial plane (a landscape) across which the eye can range freely?

At root, perhaps, these are both the same question. For as Allan Kaprow observed of the vast flat canvases across which Jackson Pollock had dripped and hurled paint, in the immediate post-war heyday of abstract expressionism, they had "ceased to become paintings and became environments . . . the entire painting comes out at us (we are participants rather than observers), right into the room" (Kaprow [1958] 1993: 6). Pollock's paintings, difficult for the eye to command or comprehend as whole, were (are) best appreciated up close, as the viewer attempts to track splashes and drips across a spatial field that stretches beyond the parameters of peripheral vision. In a Pollock painting, Kaprow observed, the *edge* of the canvas becomes an irrelevance. For him, the next logical step was for the artwork to stretch itself out all the way around the walls, ceiling, floor of a space – encompassing the observer, and indeed whatever else was caught within this extended frame. "Pollock left us at the point where we must become . . . dazzled by the space and objects of our everyday life" (ibid.: 7). In this insight lay the genesis of Happenings, a species of mixed-media performance which – during the early 1960s – profoundly altered conceptions of what a theatrical event could consist of. In Kaprow's *18 Happenings in 6 Parts*, for example (New York, 1959), which gave the genre its name, audiences were moved between three sub-compartments of a long narrow loft space, the Reuben Gallery, which had been divided by translucent plastic walls – ensuring a close, sweaty atmosphere. Within this tripartite environment, they witnessed a series of performed actions involving everyday objects (the repeated squeezing of juice out of oranges, for instance), that were visually, aurally, and texturally engaging but involved no sense of characterization or narrative. Kaprow staged the work so that spectators were constantly aware of the event stretching beyond the reach of their own sensory range: one might glimpse distorted figures or colors through the plastic walls; overhear layered rhythmic sounds from elsewhere in the room; and see bodies march in and out of one's immediate space. Happenings staged not dramatic stories but encounters in and through encompassing space.

Happenings drew on many cross-medial influences (not just Pollock but John Cage, Antonin Artaud, the Bauhaus, etc.), and their own impact also proved diverse, informing everything from the emergence of performance art to the protest-based "guerrilla theatre" of the later 1960s. Witness, for example, the attempt of Abbie Hoffman's Yippies to encircle and "levitate" the Pentagon – a spatial joke of epic confrontational proportions. Some theatre practice of the period also sought to hybridize the legacy of happenings with the traditions of dramatic narrative. Richard Schechner's Performance Group, for example, began devising *Dionysus in 69* – a contemporary version of Euripides' *The Bacchae* – in 1967, and the next year Schechner published "Six Axioms for Environmental Theater," (in which he acknowledged an immediate debt to Kaprow's 1966 book *Assemblages, Environments and Happenings*).[1] "The first scenic principle," for Schechner, "is to create and use whole spaces, spaces within spaces, spaces which contain, or envelop, or relate, or touch all the areas where the audience is and/or the performers perform" (Schechner 1995: 2). He put these principles into operation by acquiring a disused garage space on New York's Wooster Street, inside which Jerry Rojo and happenings specialist Michael Kirby built a series of multi-leveled wooden structures that could operate as areas for both spectators and performers to sit or stand. The action of *Dionysus in 69* took place not only in the cleared central area of the space, but in and around these structures – with performers often engaging in small-scale close-up encounters with individual audience members.

The relevance of this approach to *The Bacchae* is evident enough, since the play's narrative involves the reintroduction of Dionysian rites into the too-orderly community of Thebes. In Schechner's version, the audience itself became a part of this destabilized "community": "[o]nce fixed seating and the automatic bifurcation of space are no longer preset, entirely new relationships are possible. Body contact can occur between performers and spectators . . . a sense of shared experience can be engendered" (Schechner 1995: xxix). Such contact famously extended to an orgiastic "group grope" sequence – also a feature of the Living Theatre's similarly anarchic *Paradise Now* (1968). For other practitioners of the period though, this extreme, physicalized "sharing" of theatre space implied not communitarianism but a dishonest imposition of power *over* spectators. "Those events that play amidst the people are playing a sleight-of-hand trick," wrote former Living Theatre associate Lawrence Kornfeld in 1968: "they are trying to convince us that they are not separate from us, [like] a grown-up coming into the midst of children and playing with them as if there were no differences in age" (quoted in Bottoms 2004: 242). Since performers necessarily know more about what is going on in a piece than uninitiated audiences, the only way to respect spectatorial independence was, for Kornfeld, to maintain a spatial distinction between staging and seating. This did not mean, however, an uncomplicated return to the proscenium.

In 1963 Kornfeld had flagged an alternative trajectory for post-happenings theatre with his production of Gertrude Stein's 1913 playlet *What Happened* at Judson Memorial Church in Greenwich Village. Judson had become a haven for experimental arts practice of all sorts – from film to happenings to post-modern dance – thanks not least to its various flexible open spaces, including a basement gymnasium and a main sanctuary lit by large windows, from which the pews had been removed. As director of the Judson Poets' Theater from its inception in 1961, Kornfeld had already staged plays in a wide variety of spatial configurations. For *What Happened*, however, he created a very wide, very shallow proscenium space, across the full width of the sanctuary. Closely-seated spectators had to turn their heads to see across the full width of the space, as if allowing their eyes to range across a landscape. This was Kornfeld's first attempt to realize Stein's call for a "landscape theatre": "I felt that if a play was exactly like a landscape, then there would be no difficulty about the emotion of the person looking on at the play being behind or ahead of the play," Stein had written, "because the landscape does not have to make an acquaintance" (Stein 1985: 122). Stein's plays tend to resist any simple sense of linear narrative: instead, their use of circling, repetitive language offers a non-linear temporal framework within which non-narrative-based stage actions can be juxtaposed in counterpoint or complementarity. For *What Happened*, Kornfeld collaborated with five female dancer-choreographers from the Judson Dance Theater, three male singers, and composer-pianist Al Carmines (Judson's associate pastor), to create a theatrical landscape of music and movement, with multiple simultaneous focal points. Spectators had to make their own choices as to which performers to follow with the eye because, as one reviewer noted, "they are everywhere, filling the stage with life and movement" (Alan Marlowe, quoted in Bottoms 2004: 152). In the most celebrated sequence of this often-revived production, Carmines' piano was pushed by the performers from upstage left to downstage right – playfully emphasizing the sheer horizontal width of the stage – even as they continued to sing and dance.

By the 1970s, with a pendulum swing away from environmental communalism, avant-garde theatre had become preoccupied with this more formalist, Steinian, landscape staging approach. Robert Wilson and Richard Foreman, auteur directors who have both staged versions of Stein's texts as well as their own creations, each developed distinctive takes on such distributed frontality, while operating on rather different scales. Wilson's orientation toward large-scale operatic spectacle was apparent even in his earliest work, staged for pennies in downtown New York, and, by the time he made his most celebrated work, *Einstein on the Beach*, in 1976 – in collaboration with minimalist composer Philip Glass – he had attracted financial backing capable of touring the piece around European opera houses before its American premiere at the Metropolitan Opera House. With a playing time of around five hours, *Einstein* was relatively modest compared with, say, his 12-hour *The Life and Times of Joseph Stalin* (1973), but in both cases the demands made on spectators' attention were mitigated by the invitation to come and go from the auditorium at will. Released from the traditional position of "captive audience," spectators really were free to treat the performance as a landscape to be looked at, or not, as the mood took them. Wilson, moreover, pushed a *pictorial* sense of landscape by emphasizing the theatre's horizontal planes. In the first scene of *Einstein on the Beach*, for example, an obviously two-dimensional, cut-out steam train takes upwards of 30 minutes to move gradually leftward across the very back of the stage. A child (the young Einstein?) stands high on a similarly flattened-looking scaffold structure at mid-stage right; while an adult at extreme downstage left mimes rapid chalk equations. The movement of a dancer (originally the former Judson choreographer Lucinda Childs), marking out a repetitive back-and-forth diagonal across the central stage area, is the only element that connects across these horizontal planes. In the following scene a courtroom interior spans the full width of the stage, but the entire stage-left half of this image is gradually replaced by a jailhouse – with prison bars hanging across the proscenium plane – even as the court proceedings continue to the right. Wherever one is seated in the auditorium, one becomes aware that this bifurcated image can only be fully resolved, pictorially-speaking, when viewed from dead center. It is as if Wilson is teasing spectators with the theatrical impossibility of pictorial "perspective."

Richard Foreman's work, developing during the same period, adopted a more intimate, domestic scale than Wilson – populating his stages with dispersed pieces of furniture, lamps, rugs, and so forth, like deconstructed living spaces (just as his texts, culled from daily notebooks, tended to narrate, cut up and deconstruct Foreman's own lived experiences). Foreman's theatre space throughout the first half of the 1970s was a long narrow Soho loft, but rather than treating this "found" space as an immersive environment, as Kaprow had done, he instead located the audience at its far end, looking down the full 80-foot length of a telescoped proscenium stage. Thus, in contrast to Wilson's exploitation of the horizontal width of the pictorial space, Foreman developed "landscape" practice initially predicated on *depth* of field. His signature use of long taut strings cutting across space at different angles (perhaps suggesting a perversely jumbled take on the perspectival guidelines of Renaissance draftsmanship) was developed as a strategy for articulating this unorthodox playing space: "I found I could add compositional tension to the stage by criss-crossing it with lines of string, which lent the space a shivering, hovering quality" (quoted in Aronson 1997: 164). These strings (sometimes painted black in places, to create the impression of dotted lines in space) were as likely to be anchored to items of furniture as to the edge of the theatre frame, and could be pushed or pulled into alternative angles by the intervention of actors' bodies.

Foreman also became interested, however, in extending the trajectories of his tunnel-like space *beyond* the proscenium threshold. As if turning the perspectival gaze back on the audience, he would periodically dazzle spectators with stage lights directed straight at them, or instruct his actors to pick out, and stare at, individual audience members. This "almost aggressive frontality," as Arnold Aronson puts it (Aronson 1997: 162), persisted in Foreman's theatre long after he left that Broadway loft space, and was maintained, for example, in the much shallower space he occupied at St Mark's Church in the East Village during the 1990s.

Confrontation across the proscenium also became a defining characteristic of Elizabeth LeCompte's work with the Wooster Group, a collective that initially gestated within the womb of Schechner's Performance Group in the 1970s, before taking control of the Performing Garage when the parent company dissolved in 1980. Deliberately abandoning the legacy of "environmental theatre," the Wooster Group took the architectural structures characteristic of Schechner's staging and turned them into landscaping elements that overtly emphasized the proscenium divide. For example, the primary staging element of their mid-1980s piece *L.S.D. (. . . just the high points . . .)* was a long table, stretched across the full width of the stage, which was scattered with microphones so as to evoke memories of Congressional enquiries such as the McCarthy hearings of the 1940s–1950s. This table sat on top of a platform structure (itself long and tabular), which had a linear trench cut into it, running along in front of the table. Performers could thus, variously, be seated at, or stand behind, the table; be seated on the forward part of the platform, as if beneath the table; or be standing in the trench at floor level, cut-off at waist height by the platform. In every instance, the actors insistently faced forward, toward the audience, while being dispersed across the visual field.

To evoke the acid trip of the title, LeCompte kept her entire cast on stage throughout and orchestrated a kind of minutely choreographed chaos, a multiple-focus "be-in" combining elements of dramatic text (including a high-speed rendering of sections from Arthur Miller's *The Crucible*), manic dance sequences, live electric guitar, the playing of LP records, and so forth. As in the Wooster Group's other work, television images were also used as an integral part of the composition – with small, bulky TV sets facing out across the proscenium to further emphasize the frontal orientation. While unremarkable now, such onstage use of video was a provocative gesture when LeCompte first incorporated it. "People said that if you put a television in the theatre, everyone will watch the TV," she recalls. "And this fascinated me. Why, if you bring people to the theatre, would they watch the TV image?" (LeCompte 1987). Her inclusion of screens as a given element in the Wooster Group's theatrical landscape further confirmed the avant-garde's resistance to the traditional singular focal point of Western drama – and invited spectators to negotiate their own seduction by, or resistance to, the onscreen image.

It was perhaps inevitable, though, that such deliberately chaotic cluttering of the stage spectacle would start to produce its own pendular counter-swing. In the late 1980s director Lin Hixson – who had made her name producing large-scale cinematic performance spectacles in Los Angeles (think Wilson, fused with Wooster, transposed to an outdoor landscape) – relocated to Chicago with the explicit intention of forming a small-scale collective that might explore ways to strip back down to basics. Goat Island, founded in 1987, drew inspiration from the Wooster Group's approach to collaging "found" sources as the textual basis for their work, but also resurrected the notion of a more three-dimensional "environmental" staging. Working out of a church gymnasium, just as the Judson dancers had in the 1960s, the company developed a bare-stage aesthetic in which the performers' bodies (often engaged in extended, repetitive, "found movement" sequences reminiscent of postmodern dance) were viewed by an audience located on several sides of the action – with a different seating configuration being designed for each new piece. This was not the immersive environmentalism of Schechner, since the spatial distinction between spectators and performers was always rigidly observed, but if a sweating body suddenly hurled itself to the floor an inch from your feet, you knew this was a moment that only you were experiencing quite so intimately. If you watched the same performance again from a different angle and perspective, you would likely have a very different viewing experience – with your attention now perhaps being drawn to other bodies, closer to.

A primary concern for Goat Island was to sculpt space three-dimensionally and, in attempting this, they drew inspiration as much from architecture as from dance and theatre. The floor-plan for *It's an Earthquake in My Heart* (2001) began as an invocation of the Chevrolet logo – that is, with a long rectangular performance area surrounded on four sides by seating, but skewed at an angle on the short ends, and with two "pit stop" areas cutting into the audience on the longer sides. During the piece's evolution, performer Bryan Saner explains, this spatial layout "was afflicted with oblique angles after being struck by the lightning bolt design of Daniel Liebeskind's Jewish Memorial Museum in Berlin" (Saner 2007: 38). Cracked open along its diagonal length, the space acquired two exit points that led to peripheral performance areas only partially visible to most audience members. To experience the performance was to be acutely aware of one's placement in space; of the fact that one's personal field of vision could not encompass the entirety of the performance. "Perhaps we should be comfortable with not seeing everything," Saner observes. "After all, the beginning of knowledge is not knowing" (Saner 2007: 37).

This is an apt quotation, perhaps, from which to begin to draw this short chapter to a close. The limits of space, and of my own knowledge, prevent any more comprehensive account than I have already sketched, and the selection of practitioners here is inevitably partial. Indeed, I have not even attempted to step outside the theatre space itself, to explore the rich range of performance practices that have developed "site specifically" in real-world spaces in recent decades. Even so, these trajectories can often be traced back to the experiments I have outlined here. Mike Pearson, for example, author of the book *Site Specific Performance* (2010) (see "Site-Specific Theatre" in this volume, pp. 295) and a key international pioneer of such work, developed his 1980s work with the Welsh collective Brith Gof around a spatial model not dissimilar to that developed by Schechner in the Performing Garage. Within the "host" of a found location, Pearson and scenographer Clifford McLucas would create a temporary "ghost" structure from scaffolding or other materials, which responded to the architectural affordances of the environment while adding new levels and staging possibilities. Brith Gof's work was simply on a far larger scale than Schechner's: *Gododdin* (1988), for example, took over the entire floor space of a disused car factory in Cardiff, to stage a kind of defiant memorial to Welsh industrial decline.

In closing, I want to develop slightly further on this theme of international exchange, while also underlining my initial point about the oscillating interdependence between the spatial concepts of "landscape" and "environment." Two contrasting examples will suffice here. The first example is Squat Theatre's *Andy Warhol's Lost Love*, as performed in 1978 in a New York storefront on West 23rd Street, near the Chelsea Hotel. Squat was a collective of expatriate Hungarians, defectors from behind the Iron Curtain, whose work celebrated their new home while viewing it from a foreigner's estranged perspective. For this piece, the paying audience was seated at the back of the space, looking toward an interior stage area and then, beyond that, out through a plate-glass window looking out onto the street. Framed in this rectangle was a "landscape theatre" of actual New York night life – as backdrop to a show about a blonde-wigged Warhol and his Chelsea Girls. Conversely, though, for the non-paying passers-by peering through the window (of which there were many), the peep-show view of semi-nude performers, being watched by rows of serious-looking people at the far end of the store, would have been glimpsed as a feature within a wider environment – another passing peculiarity in the city that never sleeps. The relevance of both perspectives to a play about Warhol should not need underlining.

My second, more recent example brings us back to Robert Wilson, who has long worked internationally. For the Cultural Olympiad of the London 2012 Olympics, Wilson devised a participatory environmental installation at the Holkham Hall estate, on England's Norfolk coast. *Walking* was just what its title indicated, a pedestrian route mapped around the contrasting environs of the estate's nature reserve – "hedgerow-enclosed fields, woodlands, sandy hillocks and, finally, a beach" (Owen 2013: 568). There was no Einstein on this beach, however. Indeed some theatre critics bemoaned *Walking*'s distinct lack of performers of any sort – other than the walkers themselves (who, inevitably, became figures pictured in the scopic field of those following them around the route). Wilson had installed certain architectural elements to punctuate the walk but, as Louise Owen notes, these functioned simply as framing devices, designed "to prepare and enable participants to apprehend the variegated qualities of the . . . landscape" (Owen 2013: 570). Wilson apparently wanted to *stage* nature – to have walkers look, through an aesthetic lens, at what was already present in this place. "*Walking* was not actually about 'walking' as such," Owen observes, "but rather an interrogation of the relation between physical movement, landscape and the gaze" (Owen 2013: 571). That is, even as the extensive journey made demands on the walker's body and heightened one's attention to the immediate, material realities of the lived *environment* ("the ground now a slick mess of umber-colored mud"), the walk seemed structured so as to present the *landscape* as a series of framed, pictorial vistas. Owen describes feeling as if her body had become "a 'camera dolly', facilitating a linear, 'tracking-shot'-style absorption of the landscape through the eyes" (ibid.).

This last remark points rather aptly towards the unresolved creative tension between landscape and environment perspectives in so many avant-garde explorations of space and scenography. Is the spectator encompassed by the action, reminded of her physical placement in space? Or is she permitted the empowered position of a roving disembodied eye, scanning a theatrical landscape (whether interior or exterior, horizontally wide or longitudinally deep)? Or is it a bit of both, at the same time? The phenomenological experience of space – as Kaprow, Kornfeld, Hixson, Wilson, and others know and show – is more both/and than either/or.

Note

1 Schechner's "Six Axioms," first published in *The Drama Review* 12.3 (1968), appeared in revised form in the expanded edition of his book *Environmental Theater* (Schechner 1995: xx–xlv).

References

Aronson, Arnold 1997. "Richard Foreman as Scenographer." *Theatre Forum* (Winter-Spring): 161–70.

Bottoms, Stephen J. 2004. *Playing Underground: A Critical History of the 1960s Off-Off-Broadway Movement*. Ann Arbor: University of Michigan Press.

Chaudhuri, Una 1994. "'There Must Be a Lot of Fish in That Lake': Toward an Ecological Theater." *Theater* 25 (1): 23–31.

Kaprow, Allan [1958] 1993. "The Legacy of Jackson Pollock." In *Allan Kaprow: Essays on the Blurring of Art and Life*, edited by Jeff Kelley. Berkeley and Los Angeles: University of California Press.

LeCompte, Elizabeth 1987. Interviewed for *The South Bank Show* (ITV). Available online at: http://ubu.com/film/wooster.html (accessed 7 March 2016).

Owen, Louise 2013. "Robert Wilson, *Walking* (Holkham Estate, 2012)." *Contemporary Theatre Review* 23 (4): 568–73.

Saner, Bryan 2007. "Alternative Spaces and Vision." In *Small Acts of Repair: Performance, Ecology and Goat Island*, edited by Stephen Bottoms and Matthew Goulish. London and New York: Routledge.

Shank, Ted 1982. *American Alternative Theatre*. London and Basingstoke: Macmillan.

Schechner, Richard 1995. *Environmental Theater* (Rev. ed.). New York: Applause Theatre Books.

Stein, Gertrude 1985. *Lectures in America*. Boston, MA: Beacon Press.

43
CONTEMPORARY CHINESE OPERA DESIGN
The pursuit of cultural awareness

Yi Tianfu

Translated by Hongyi Tian

At the 2015 Prague Quadrennial of Performance Design and Space (PQ15), Chinese scenic designer Gao Guangjian was awarded the Gold Medal for Performance Design for his work on the Beijing opera *Throughout the Empire All Hearts Turned to Him* (National Center for the Performing Arts, Beijing, 2012); his fellow designer Liu Xinglin won the Honorary Award for Performance Design for his design for the Kunqu opera *The Peony Pavilion* (Beijing Northern Kunqu Opera Theatre, 2014). This was the first time Chinese scenic designers received awards at the Quadrennial. The two award-winning designs made it clear that contemporary Chinese opera design is entering a period of artistic and conceptual change. Contemporary Chinese scenic designers are simultaneously drawing upon and transforming classical artistic elements, employing abstract and uncomplicated approaches.

The Chinese works seen at PQ15 demonstrated a cultural awareness shared among many contemporary Chinese opera scenic designers. These artists are examining the elements and symbols within their own culture, while retaining the cultural identity and the spiritual values of Chinese art. Therefore, it is paramount to discuss and analyze the aesthetics in contemporary Chinese opera scenic design, even more so in an increasingly complex and globalized artistic context.

The stage reconstruction of traditional Chinese architectural elements

The designs for contemporary Chinese opera are no longer mere representations of a particular locale in a specific environment, nor are they abstract interpretations of the traditional stage concept of "One Table, Two Chairs." Rather, they are creative approaches, consciously drawing on related art forms, while at the same time taking into account the inherent meanings of the work's text and style, always conscious of the artistic taste of contemporary audiences. A typical approach has been to draw on the aesthetics of traditional Chinese gardens. Employing the cultural elements of the Chinese garden, scenic designers are free to omit, exaggerate, and transform these elements, creating a poetic stage picture and space configuration. Incorporating as much from the shapes, patterns, textures, colors, and lines in traditional Chinese architecture

Figure 43.1 Liu Xinglin's design for *The Peony Pavilion*. (chinatheatre.org.)

as possible, designers reconstruct the stage of Chinese opera in a complex and intriguing manner in accordance with contemporary visual styles, thus conveying a unique and elegant sense of Chinese art. At the same time, recent Chinese opera design has taken inspiration from Western structuralism and minimalism. It has the potential to become a language of scenic design that is at once distinctively Eastern yet at the same time universal.

The deconstruction and re-conception of the Hui- and Suzhou-style gardens can be frequently seen in contemporary Chinese opera performances, creating an abundance of visual messages. Liu Xinglin's design for the Kunqu opera *The Peony Pavilion* may be a perfect example (Figure 43.1). For this sixteenth-century classic opera, the designer constructed a dream-like realm that was anything but the realistic presentation of the world, by incorporating elements from traditional Chinese gardens.

Placed against an empty white backdrop, the half Taihu stone and the half pavilion, along with the garden and bridge, created a theatrical space that blurred the boundary between dream and reality. Moreover, the white backdrop served as an amplifier of all the elements, infusing the entire stage with a sense of simplicity seen in traditional Chinese paintings. In the Kunqu opera *The Moon-Worship Pavilion* (also known as *The Baiyue Pavilion*), designed by Xu Guofeng for the Shanghai Youth Beijing Opera and Kunqu Opera Company (2012) (Figure 43.2), the use of the color white was even simpler and purer – a white backdrop was used as the cyclorama, and a white carpet, the same width as the cyclorama, was placed on the floor. The "sky" and the "earth" seem to be connected like a huge canvas on which one can paint with no constraint. Ingeniously drawing on various elements of the Hui-style architecture, Xu created a stunning visual reconstruction on stage, fully demonstrating the flowing beauty of contemporary Chinese opera.

Much like a *Gongbi* piece in Chinese painting, scenic designs for both *The Peony Pavilion* and *The Moon-Worship Pavilion* employ images from classical art such as architecture, gardens, and natural landscapes, integrating them into poetic spatial configurations with distinct Eastern characteristics. But it is done with a bold re-interpretation

Figure 43.2 *The Moon-Worship Pavilion* designed by Xu Guofeng (2012). (Courtesy of Xu Guofeng.)

of these elements approached with contemporary simplicity, making them cross-cultural presentations that are more accessible to a global audience. In the process these adaptations of the visual language – the fusion of traditional Chinese art and contemporary visual art – make critical contributions to the revitalization of traditional Chinese opera.

The deconstruction of traditional Chinese art elements

The concept of "One Table, Two Chairs," the fundamental scenic unit of traditional Chinese opera, represents hundreds of years of artistic development, symbolizing the soul of the art form, at the same time providing contemporary artists with enduring inspirations. But scenic design in contemporary Chinese opera is no longer confined by such realistic principles as "typicality" and adherence to life. Instead, it experiments with the implications and concepts of symbolism and expressionism.

The exaggeration of the "One Table, Two Chairs" concept in the Beijing opera *Throughout the Empire All Hearts Turned to Him* is a particularly successful example of this trend. The three white drop curtains, confined by the black curtains, form a box-shaped space. Three sets of "One Table, Two Chairs" in different scales can be revealed from within the white curtains and can be arranged as needed to form a layered structure in the space, thus creating an impression of large pillars in a palace, medium pavilions in a garden, and the small, standard set pieces in the performance. This re-imagination and expansion of the "One Table, Two Chairs" concept is indeed an innovative device both in terms of functionality and visual expression. Further, projections of Chinese ink-wash painting make it possible for the table and chairs to be converted into various pavilions, corridors, and halls, transforming them from purely functional set pieces into a critical part of the stage landscape as a whole. Through this structural method, the designer has inventively exaggerated the "One Table, Two Chairs" concept, effectively conveying traditional opera elements within a contemporary space.

In the white space of my own design for the Beijing opera *Su Qin* at the Shenyang Beijing Opera Company (2014) (Figure 43.3), the reconstruction of various images,

Figure 43.3 *Su Qin* at the Shenyang Beijing Opera Company, designed by Yi Tianfu (2014). (Courtesy of Yi Tianfu.)

including buildings, streets, mountains, and rivers, were presented on stage using the three-dimensional visual effect of a two-dimensional Chinese painting. A mountain, an ocean wave, and a few slabs of rock are sufficient to translate the spatial configuration in Chinese painting into the three-dimensional expression on stage, highlighting the inherent poetic sentiment in Chinese culture. In Chinese painting there is a theory of conveying the philosophical notion of "Tao" with the portrayal of natural landscape. To put it in terms of the spatial configuration in Chinese opera, the natural landscape serves as a background of the characters' lives; it also functions as a unique language that assists the storytelling in general. While drawing on the spatial configurations of Chinese painting, contemporary scenic design in Chinese opera is breaking free from the confines of traditional notions of stage space and mere functionality.

Both the tree branch in *Su Qin* and the re-imagined "One Table, Two Chairs" structure in *Throughout the Empire All Hearts Turned to Him* masterfully combine the landscape elements with the pictographic quality of Chinese painting, creating an intense visual image in a simple frame. This innovative employment of traditional art elements in a white space has provided Chinese opera with a visual language possessing the characteristics of contemporary visual art. Reconstructing traditional art elements and expressing the mystic aspect of Chinese culture, contemporary scenic design in Chinese operas can be deemed revolutionary. It has changed not only the long-held realistic principles in Chinese scenic design, but also changed the abstract principle so heavily centered on the "One Table, Two Chairs" concept, creatively bringing forth a new aesthetic that features the synthesis of different art forms.

Minimalism in scenic design

Contemporary Chinese opera has been particularly successful in drawing on minimalism from the West. Stylistically, minimalism advocates for functionality and opposes formality. Currently there are quite a few Chinese scenic designers who, like other

Figure 43.4 *Xu Guangqi and Matteo Ricci*, designed by Yi Tianfu (2013). (Courtesy of Yi Tianfu.)

minimalist artists, use as few shapes, objects, and materials as possible to gain control of the stage space, thus starting a trend in contemporary scenic design.

With traditional Chinese art elements as the primary content, minimalism is able to present the audience with a new way to navigate the space and appreciate the actions. Minimalist design in Chinese opera, frequently featuring an open black or white space as an empty environment for minimal scenic elements, makes actors the focus on the stage, and the narrative and rules inherent in the text will be able to mitigate the often blurry and even controversial qualities in minimal designs.

In the Beijing opera *Xu Guangqi and Matteo Ricci*, written by playwright and theatre theorist Sun Huizhu (William) and performed on the Shanghai Theatre Academy tour to the Piccolo Theatre in Milan, Italy, in July 2013, also employing my designs, the color white can be seen as the overall theme of the performing space (Figure 43.4).

The few rich ink lines in the background bring the audience into an enchanting land of Chinese painting. At times the ink lines form crisscross patterns to express various images including mountains, gardens, and government offices, creating a space that is distinctively Chinese. Such patterns and images are much more than simple imitations or random collages; they are, rather, an artful blending of spirit and environment facilitated by the scenic designer. Together, the colors black and white can therefore be seen as the artistic vision of Chinese opera conveyed in a contemporary approach. This fascinating interplay of black and white also reflects the Chinese philosophical belief that one should have a clear idea of what's right but remain as an observer. It brings out the profoundness of the objects on stage, while conveying the intangible quality of the space of Chinese opera.

In my design for the Hebei Bangzi opera *The Sacrifice* at the Hebei Vocational Academy of the Arts (2016) (Figure 43.5), the stage space of the prison scene is also constructed in the style of minimalism. Different from *Xu Guangqi and Matteo Ricci*, the scenic design in this production features more projections to explore the elusive nature of the piece. It incorporates puppets and projected images and videos, visualizing the social environment and the characters' absurd struggles. Made of black polypropylene fiber, the prison is a closed horseshoe-shaped structure, whose very existence is a sight of beauty and

Figure 43.5 *The Sacrifice* at the Hebei Vocational Academy of the Arts (2016), designed by Yi Tianfu. (Courtesy of Yi Tianfu.)

simplicity. The projected images, for example the moss-covered wall, not only detail the interior of the prison, but also serve as a visual metaphor that symbolizes the horrifying underworld. Shaped like the Chinese character "回," the prison corridors have no exits and seem to go nowhere, materializing the palpable desperation in a cold and rough way. Further, *The Sacrifice* goes one step ahead of many traditional pieces in that it employs a series of collaged images to present the externalized psychology of the characters, instead of merely representing the particular locations. Images such as the interrogation room, the Red Army soldier, and the wolves in a deserted land, are all given truthful presentations on stage. For example, when the character Yang Kaihui misses her child, we see an extremely vivid combination of videos and still images of ferocious wolves. In a split second, the entire stage is transformed from a dingy prison to a bleak wasteland. When the suffocating terror of the prison is greatly intensified with images such as skulls, vultures, and shadow puppets, the audience is compelled to have empathy for Yang who fearlessly defends her ideals. At the same time, they feel urged to relate their own life to the status quo of society. When in the final scene Yang Kaihui, in her deafening monologue, declares that "Everyone should have ideals. Do you believe that? I do!" the audience cannot help but ask themselves the same fundamental question. This highly interactive and immersive experience establishes connections between the artists, the audience, and the art, proving the power and efficacy of contemporary art.

Minimalism has shown a path worth exploring for scenic design in Chinese opera, inspiring us to experiment with new possibilities. The minimalist notion of "Less is more" has intrinsic connections with the concept of "Simplicity is better than complexity" in traditional Chinese aesthetics. Minimalism inspires imagination and contemplation, and has taken deep root in the overall vision of contemporary art as a style. In the same vein, the minimalistic approach in Chinese opera scenic design brings exciting possibilities to the ancient art form.

Installation art in scenic design

In recent years designers have been incorporating elements of installation art in their works to explore innovative possibilities of scenic design. Putting its emphasis on the concept of "the field" in installation art, this new approach in Chinese opera scenic design employs creative materials and technologies, highlighting the structuralized stage space as a whole. For instance, in the Beijing opera *The Red Cliffs*, a joint production of the China Beijing Opera Company and the Beijing Opera Company (2016), designed by Gao Guangjian, there is a rain of arrows that are lined up in three rows from front to back, creating an exaggerated stage image and visual effect. This highly symbolized presentation of the arrows effectively constructs a field in the performance, which is commonly seen in contemporary installation art.

Scenic design in Chinese opera actively embraces the opportunity to collaborate with a variety of art forms, materials, and digital media, ready to incorporate elements from painting, sculpture, and installation art, among others. Fascinating stage expressions are thus made possible as different art forms and materials interweave to create a new artistic language. For example, in the Kunqu opera *Dream of the Emerald Land*, designed by Tan Hua (Shanghai Theatre Academy at the China Kunqu Opera Festival, Suzhou, October 2015) (Figure 43.6), the entire stage is covered with white cloth, with a pond that spans the width of the stage. At the bottom of the pond is a sound-generating device, which is connected to the soundboard. The board then transmits drum signals to the device in the pond, making it vibrate and thus creating a magical sight of drops of water dancing on the pond surface. Reflections of characters are shattered and restored as the sound of drums is cued on and off. The blurry nature of the stage image is joined by the mesmerizing synergy between the actors and their reflections in the water, tremendously

Figure 43.6 *Dream of the Emerald Land*, designed by Tan Hua (2015). (Courtesy of Tan Hua.)

Figure 43.7 *King Lear*, produced by the Hangzhou Yue Opera Company (2016), designed by Yi Tianfu. (Courtesy of Yi Tianfu.)

reinforcing the theme of cycle and retribution in the performance. At the same time, the water in the pond is also given characteristics of "the field" in installation art.

In my design for the Yue opera *King Lear*, produced by the Hangzhou Yue Opera Company (2016) (Figure 43.7), and adapted by Sun Huizhu (William) and Fei Chunfang (Faye), the material language of the space consists of a 10-meter by 12-meter white carpet at center stage, a white cloud and a dark cloud floating above, and a few movable rocks on the carpet. Considering the nature of Yue opera, this design brings interesting challenges to the performance.

To begin with, the rocks on the carpet and the clouds symbolize the kingdom of King Lear. The space configuration of the throne, the rocks, and the clouds make it possible to suggest multiple locations. The white cloud serves as a projection screen so key narrative information can be seen on it. Hidden within the dark cloud is a device that can produce lightning effects. In the scene where a storm rages with full force, lightning can be seen in the dark sky, the rocks weep tears of blood, crying at Lear's misfortune. We are not only watching the performance of the actors, but also feeling the vivid psychology of Lear revealed by the material language on stage. Emphasizing the interaction between the actors and the scenic pieces, this design stands closer to the genre of installation art rather than the given circumstance in the theatre. Bearing similar tragic qualities as Shakespeare's *King Lear*, the rocks, clouds, and lightning lead the audience into a magical land of installation. As pointed out in *La Lecture de l'Art*, an intriguing piece of installation art should be constructed with "materials that belong to a homogeneous symbol system" (Chalumeau 2005: 204). From a semiotic perspective, it is clear that the rocks, clouds, and lightning are effective visual interpretations of King Lear's tragic situation.

As the above mentioned examples suggest, scenic design in Chinese opera has become more than representation of a particular situation; rather, it strengthens visually the theatricality of the space and the quality of installation pieces. Further, set pieces and props in these designs have transformed the stage into a field, where the realistic quality is not the sole purpose. Such designs may seem to have deviated from the particular space suggested in the plot, but they are in line with the overarching theme of the performance.

Conclusion

Contemporary Chinese opera design is at the forefront of Chinese scenography. On the one hand, it embraces boldly re-imagined elements in traditional Chinese art. On the other hand, it actively draws on new ideas in Western art, incorporating installation art, media art, and earth art, appealing to a diverse group of audience members. These innovations signify the valuable explorations by designers, going beyond traditional scenographic limits. The artistic concepts of scenic design in Chinese opera have managed to catch up with the development of contemporary and post-modern art worldwide. However, it remains a question worth pondering for the designers as to how to facilitate further and deeper fusion of traditional Chinese art and contemporary Western art, instead of mechanically assembling elements from both.

Reference

Chalumeau, Jean Luc 2005. *Jiedu Yishu* (*La Lecture de L'Art*), translated by Liu Fang and Wu Qiwen. Beijing: Culture and Arts Press.

44
POSTMODERN DESIGN FOR OPERA

Ewa Kara

First and foremost, opera has always been a visual and highly passionate social spectacle. In this regard, contemporary stage design for opera is no different than it was in Monteverdi's Venice or Wagner's Bayreuth. What has changed are the specific historical conditions and the institutional, economic, social, and artistic frameworks in which opera takes place. Today, opera tends to capture the spectators' attention with theatrically stunning, visually remarkable, and unforgettable designs rather than presenting the audience with a conventionally pleasing aesthetic of picturesque landscapes or splendid interior spaces. Opera's new scenography is daring, deeply embedded in contemporary visual culture and aesthetics, and making increasingly potent use of recent technological developments. It is based on strategic concepts that imagistically and emblematically articulate tensions, subtexts, and inner conflicts embedded in operatic works, while reflecting the fragmentation, transience, and instability of modern reality in numerous ways. Broadly speaking, in postmodern scenography, which has become a key mode for innovation since the 1970s, directors and designers closely collaborate, overtly challenging conventions and rules, using a wide range of strategies in the visual, dramaturgical and critical reimagining of operatic works and in deconstructing opera as a medium.

A majority of contemporary innovative opera stagings can still be described as postmodern design. Arnold Aronson has defined postmodernism in stage design as "the juxtaposition of contrasting and contradictory images, very conscious quotations of historical references, anachronistic uses of images from contemporary culture, and a disruption of aesthetically pleasing and unified designs" that emphatically reject standard interpretations and grand narratives (Aronson 1991: 9). The image is the catalyst, the prime force that organizes, instructs, and drives postmodern design. This new mode parallels the collapse of the hegemony of the text in the theatre and signals broader developments in our culture and intellectual discourses: a "pictorial turn" (Mitchell 1994: 11). The emphasis on images has redefined the relationship between visuality and performance, "of the ocular to the action" (Kennedy 2001: 266). Visual imagery in operatic staging is now more than just a mesmerizing effect or an entertaining element. As it is created with strategic and formal complexity, the image becomes a communicative tool. However, the image "is more than a product of perception. It is created as the result of a personal or collective symbolization. Everything that occurs within vision or before the inner eye, can be thus clarified an image or transformed into an image," as Hans Belting elucidates on its new function (Belting 2001: 11).[1]

This preoccupation with the image engenders scenography with a strong pictorial quality that requires framing; hence the preference among postmodern designers and producers for the proscenium theatres. The proscenium, as Aronson suggests, keeps the audience at a distance generating a dissociating effect; the spectator in this case is "a viewer, not a participant" (Aronson 2005: 26). Yet, the new cultural emphasis on an event-based, site-specific, immersive, interactive and participatory performance has recently transpired in scenography for opera as well, driving it towards another shift in the language of scenographic practice. In the culture that demands the individual's participation and fetishizes the recipient, the spectator is no longer a passive viewer but becomes a co-creator; as Thea Brejzek suggests, "scenography transforms the maker, the viewer, and the setting into co-authors and witnesses" (Brejzek 2012: 19). Combining the pleasure of seeing and the prerequisite of spectacle, postmodern scenography for opera still continues to fetishize images, feeding into and molding spectator's desires, consequently threatening with thorough commodification. Despite this apprehension, in the new millennium opera has institutionalized postmodern design, in particular its aesthetic strand of *cool beauty*, which is a formalist type of beauty that combines abstraction and high fashion with striking effects, a mixing of theatricality and spectacle. Significantly this moment occurred after the peak of postmodernism.

In opera the earliest examples of postmodern design can be dated to the early 1970s in Germany and Italy; in the 1980s it slowly spreads elsewhere, but the biggest opera houses remained largely off-limits to new, more radical approaches to design.[2] Preferring ahistorical or present-day associations, postmodernism seized opera in the 1990s, aesthetically transforming operatic stages across the globe and decisively departing from the traditional operatic décor. Although the mode obviously had precursors and genealogical forebears, nonetheless it could be said that this moment marks a key shift in operatic design: the moment where design comes to the fore in mainstream operatic productions. Finally, on a global scale, design for opera stopped simply being an ancillary element of the operatic spectacle that quickly settles into half-perceived background.

Postmodern design of the 1970s and 1980s played with various styles and conventions, emphasizing simplicity and theatricality, but opera never fully relinquished historical reference or the picturesque. However, postmodern design of the 1990s that might be called *high* postmodernism was a distinctly new style that moved away from history. It continues, I would argue, broadly speaking, in two main stylistic vocabularies and energies: first, a visual asceticism, redolent of a kind of *cool beauty* and, second, a fascination with mass culture resulting in a productive encounter with the vernacular, in a wide variety of forms. Nevertheless, this particular aesthetic turn, while important, cannot eclipse other changes and developments, related but not identical, within twenty-first-century design for opera, which I address in the last part of this chapter. In looking at the very latest developments in operatic scenography, I focus in particular on technological developments, such as the use of video projections on a large scale. Finally, I also examine a still more radical move: opera's increasing tendency to leave the opera house in favor of site-specific productions in unorthodox locations, a shift that affects not only design but also spectatorship.

Transformative festivals: Salzburg and Bregenz

The new phase in postmodern opera design cannot be separated from new global infrastructures of opera production and technological advancements that facilitate swift travels and expedite the dissemination of new styles. 1992 saw the first major transatlantic operatic co-production: Robert Wilson's *Parsifal* (Figure 44.1) was presented just a few months apart in Hamburg (December 1991) and Houston (February 1992).

Such co-productions have become increasingly common. This has meant the alleviation of the costs of staging and a faster circulation of new strategies and visual aesthetics. The ease of travel allows not only effortless transfer of productions from one country to the next, from one continent to another, but also enables quick and efficient mobility of artists who live and work elsewhere. The presence of artists from other nations has profoundly challenged and effectively changed the national design schools as, in particular British, but also American and Canadian directors and designers started to work on operas, mostly in German-speaking countries. Germany above all has remained at the forefront of innovation for three main reasons: 1) it has championed a completely different, non-prescriptive directorial approach – *Regietheater/Regieoper*[3] – elsewhere vilified as *Eurotrash* or *producerist* opera, which advocates scenographic autonomy; 2) its theatres and opera houses are well-funded state or city institutions that therefore have almost unprecedented artistic freedom; and 3) the greatest amount of global output in opera is done in German-speaking countries as both theatre and opera are considered the highest cultural capital.

The shift in operatic design is at its most palpable in the transformations of two prestigious Austrian summer festivals: Salzburger and Bregenzer Festspiele. Salzburg received

Figure 44.1 Robert Wilson's production of *Parsifal*. Los Angeles Opera, 2015. (Photo © AJ Weissbard.)

a vigorous overhaul when in 1991 Gerard Mortier took over the festival after the death of Herbert von Karajan. For Mortier, the enemy was clear: the stultifying presence of lingering historicist realism, "Opera cannot successfully compete with cinematographic images as long as operatic imagery is limited to clumsy artistic transposition of reality" (quoted in Namenwirth 2002: 183). With the showcase production of his first season – *La clemenza di Tito* (1992), directed by Ursel and Karl-Ernst Herrmann, a classically minimalist production with fashionable costumes and symbolically compelling but puzzling props[4] – Mortier renounced the ideals of a post-war reconstruction, breaking from the aggrandizement and luxury, complacency and predictability, elaborate crowd scenes, schematic conventions, and standard repertoire that had characterized von Karajan's festival. The list of invited collaborators was impressive. Among others, Mortier brought in such artists as Eduardo Arroyo, Achim Freyer, George Tsypin, Anna Viebrock, Herbert Wernicke, Robert Wilson, and Reinhard von der Thannen. A new era of operatic performance in Salzburg was marked by visually daring and conceptually challenging productions, often surrounded by controversy, forever changing the standards of opera management.

Another key marker in the shifting of the dominant paradigms in operatic scenography transpired in the other great Austrian summer opera festival: in Bregenz, where hundreds of thousand spectators come to watch crowd-pleasing grand operas on a floating stage at Lake Constance.[5] This still largely populist event saw a distinct change in visual style in the early 1990s, just as in Salzburg. Director David Pountney's groundbreaking *Nabucco* (1993) already signaled a new phase. Stefanos Lazaridis' scenography for this production consisted of two aesthetically disparate colossal walls that were visually astonishing, ingeniously effective and impressive, in particular as each of the walls had been erected from the floor. Pountney has noted that Lazaridis' designs on the

Figure 44.2 *Un ballo in maschera* at the Bregenz Festival (1999) designed by Antony McDonald. (Photo: © Karl Forster.)

lake "completely changed the stylistic direction of the festival" (Pountney 2010: 812).[6] His scenography in general was notable for its groundbreaking unconventionality, poetic imagination, boldness of vision, and theatricality.

A still more spectacular phase started at Bregenz at the turn of the millennium with a particularly audacious design for Verdi's *Un ballo in maschera* (1999): an enormous skeleton turning over pages of a gigantic book of life floating in the lake (Figure 44.2). The creator of this striking image was another designer from the British design school, Antony McDonald, who co-directed it alongside Richard Jones. They repeated their success with a spectacular *La bohéme* (2001) that featured a Parisian café submerged in water. McDonald's epic and technically ambitious scenography was simultaneously technically captivating and visually mesmerizing. Since the advent of this style, the trend of drawing in a huge audience has continued at Bregenz with such imagistically bold designs as Johannes Leiacker's *Tosca* (2007) and Paul Brown's *Aida* (2009). The current most celebrated British female designer – Es Devlin – known for her multi-tier and kinetically sophisticated sets as well as high-profile pop music concerts, designed a dramatically emblematic set for *Carmen* (2017).

From conceptual to post-conceptual scenography

Postmodern scenography has been notorious for its dynamic proliferation of scenographic practices and a wide range of styles; hence, contemporary stage design for opera is likewise highly diverse, but certain strategies reappear frequently. Postmodern designers are habitual users of composite images, direct quotations, metaphors, irony, pastiche, travesty, and mixed chronologies that redirect the audience towards parallel narratives, opposing viewpoints, and ambiguous meanings. It has meant the return of symbolism, vernacular, wit, an expressive potential of decoration, and an emphasis on aesthetic pleasure that were previously repressed. The common denominator is a disjunction that is a hallmark of postmodern design. Postmodern scenography precisely denotes the variety of strategies used by designers, but the term has become an umbrella label for many designs created for almost a half of a century. Critics have used postmodern design as a catchall phrase to brand or categorize non-traditional and unconventional designs, or, as Philip Auslander argues, "to identify new developments in aesthetic genres with well-established conventions" (Auslander 2004: 98). Therefore, it seems useful to add Christopher Balme's (2006) two categories of scenographic strategies – *conceptual* or image-based scenography closely linked to the text, and *post-conceptual* in which complex visual strategies provoke narratives that move beyond the original text – that would allow for differentiation of approaches within postmodern opera design.

Conceptual scenography, according to Balme, is deeply rooted in the text (in opera: in score and libretto), resulting in images that have a close relationship to the content, or, alternatively, the text frames the scenic imagery (Balme 2006: 57). It originated as a counter-movement to anti-pictorial designs of Wieland Wagner.[7] This approach has become a privileged alternative in the German theatre since the end of 1960s, and is emblematic for the theatre of images and characteristic of an old style of *Regietheater*. Balme connects it to the reign of structuralism and semiotics in theatrical theories, although postmodernism, in fact, has decentered and complicated the traditionally dominant place of text and narrative in favor of powerful visuality.[8] In the 1970s vaguely poetic and metaphorical images were acceptable, but more concrete and dramaturgically intense imagery often caused scandals, as did Andreas Reinhardt's set for Ruth

Berghaus's *Il barbiere di Siviglia* (Munich, 1974), one of the key examples of early postmodern design in opera. Reinhardt devised a colossal female torso – a fragmented "brick" sculpture, conceived as a symbol of entrapped femininity – that dominated the stage. The public found it shockingly indecent, especially when during the serenade Count Almaviva climbed the battlement and ostentatiously caressed the statue's pubis. Reinhardt's audacious scenographic concept was both concrete and symbolic but central to the staging itself, allowing the image to direct the interpretation. Such radicalism in opera, however, was rather rare. The images employed in operatic productions slowly moved from spectacular, theatrically conspicuous but visually arresting and simple symbolism, towards images that visually interpreted the work.

The landmark production of early postmodern design and the key example of conceptual scenography is the centennial *Der Ring des Nibelungen* (Bayreuth, 1976), directed by Patrice Chéreau with his team that included Richard Peduzzi (set designer), Jacques Schmidt (costume designer), and André Diot (lighting designer). The extremely influential staging evidenced the postmodern return to figuration as it boldly rejected Wieland Wagner's symbolic abstractionism and conventional mythology.[9] Instead, Peduzzi's scenography suggested a modern world, which diachronically bridged Wagner's era with our own time through anachronistic use of the setting's elements, props, and costumes. *Das Rheingold* was set on a hydroelectric dam with Rhine maidens dressed as nineteenth-century prostitutes; similarly in *Siegfried* the prominent element was a steam-powered hydraulic forge that visually embedded the human drama within the Industrial Revolution instead of mythic times, widely popularizing a strategy of placing the action of the opera in the composer's time. Peduzzi borrowed the final image for *Die Walküre* from *Island of the Dead*, Arnold Böcklin's symbolist painting, while in *Götterdämmerung* Gunther and Siegfried wore tuxedos that indicated thoroughly compound historical periods. This fusion of hybrid imagery and mixed styles is what Foucault described as "an intentional uncertainty as far as time and place are concerned, an extreme diffusion of the elements of reality" (Foucault [1980] 1998: 238). In addition, Peduzzi's sets exhibited strong tendencies toward visual classicism and monumentalism that were distinctive of Italian design, in particular for Giorgio Strehler's productions at La Scala.[10] In the same way, Peduzzi used simple, monumental architecture that supported restrained and elegant imagery. The final effect is sometimes described as anti-romantic in its approach but in fact it triggered a return to Romanticism and theatrical realism attributable to the picturesque visions suggested by the scenographic team.

Postmodernism that favors more concept-oriented imagery became a norm in operatic houses of the German-speaking countries when designers such as Achim Freyer, Axel Manthey, and Erich Wonder rejected traditional forms of operatic scenography and allowed their visual concepts to define the production more effectively. Ruth Berghaus's stagings of Richard Wagner's operas in Frankfurt were particularly significant in the development of postmodern design. Her collaboration with the painter Axel Manthey for *Parsifal* (1982) and the *Ring* (1985–7) decisively differed from recent reinterpretations of Wagner in their radical approach that mixed a variety of painterly, sculptural, symbolic and abstract aesthetics with a post-Brechtian use of estrangement. The result was poetic and playful but often bewildering as images, were far removed from any notions of stage realism. As Elaine Kelly argues, they "presented on stage a kaleidoscope of elusive and often contradictory details, offering their audiences a theatrical experience that encoded the irony, alienation, and fragmentation of late modernity" (Kelly 2014: 194). Here, it was not an object in space but an image in the center and its immateriality that provoked anxiety and discomfort.

Strategies of updating

Unlike traditional operatic scenery that suggests reality on a grand scale, postmodern design does not conform to the audience's expectation. The innovative designs sought to defamiliarize and desentimentalize the past visually in addition to displacing the staging practices in producing canonic works.[11] Initially designers started to move the settings beyond the historical location indicated in the libretto, first to other historical places, but different geographically. For example, when Luciano Damiani chose to use Northern Italian architecture instead of Spanish in Otto Schenk's *Don Giovanni* (Vienna, 1967), he was loudly booed.[12] The next effective step, as in the Chéreau/Peduzzi *Ring*, was to place the action within the period of the opera's composition, often to emphasize staging practices that were typical at that time, an approach particularly useful in the revivals of Baroque opera.

In fact, the Baroque revival was a significant factor in postmodern design practices. Since they were unencumbered with long stage performance history, these operas provided a stimulating opportunity for producers and designers. The renaissance of Early Music has been accompanied by the idea of historically informed performance, which centers on "practices and attitudes that directly rely on documentary sources from the time of the work to inform interpretative decisions about the acoustic, conceptual, and (in the case of opera) visual environment in which a work was originally created" (Hunter 2014: 606). As the vitality of this approach to operatic music was demonstrated in the late 1980s (*Atys*, Paris, 1987), only a few attempts at historically informed performance have exhibited creativity in recreating the authentic experience of seventeenth-century theatre. Specifically, Benjamin Lazar's candlelit staging of *Cadmus et Hermione* (Paris, 2008) with painted and cut-out sets (Adeline Caron) and historical costumes (Alain Blanchot) was "created anew within the conventions and constraints of the historical information, rather than being copied from particular originals" (Hunter 2014: 620). On a completely different spectrum lie productions that use historically informed music while updating opera.

The core shift in opera staging has been and continues to be updating the action to a contemporary time frame. This approach became a fad in the 1980s, but is now a standard alternative. Philip Gossett calls this type of approach a stylistically displaced staging, in which "a story is moved either temporally or spatially, but the subject, characters, situation, and action are basically unchanged" (Gossett 2006: 477). Although upsetting to some spectators, the unusual visual transposition can be easily accepted, as happened, for instance, with Jonathan Miller's popular "mobster" *Rigoletto* (London, 1982) that was set in Manhattan's Little Italy in the 1950s instead of the sixteenth-century Mantua. However, because Miller and his usual design team – Patrick Robertson and Rosemary Vercoe – did not attempt to deconstruct the opera, the sets – though intentionally provocative – remained traditionally representative. Such displaced productions are still recurrent but, except for visual novelty and updated aesthetics, they are ultimately visually conventional.

In contrast, Peter Sellars' staging of Handel's *Theodora* (Glyndebourne, 1996) was intentionally provocative. The oratorio was controversially updated, moving the action from fourth-century Antioch to an American state that permits capital punishment by lethal injection, to which Theodora and Didymus, the dissenting citizens, are subjected in a military hospital after refusing to recant their beliefs. Musicologist scholarship usually calls this type of production a "radical staging" since the operatic text becomes "a sheer, unprescriptive stimulus to the free play of theatrical imagination" (Gossett 2006: 447; Savage 1994: 282). Maria Shevtsova, a theatre scholar, discussing Sellars' Mozart/Da Ponte trilogy (1986–9), calls this type of updating strategy "radical recasting," since Sellars "does not update operas, but reshapes their thematics while retaining their musical structures" (Shevtsova 2005: 256). These intentional but seemingly quotidian adaptations to the contemporary vernacular world become a "radical disruption of pleasing aesthetic synergy," which, as Aronson assures us, "is a cornerstone of postmodern design" (Aronson 2005: 18). If the costumes, props, and other artifacts clearly defined the contemporary spatio-temporal settings, the actual stage space was mysteriously emblematic. Designer George Tsypin created five mobile sculptures resembling broken glass bottles (inspired by the Roman artifacts), each 10 meters tall.[13] It was simple and evocative, abstract and emotional at the same time. Tsypin's solution allowed Sellars to capitalize on an imaginative and ambiguous reading of the set and thus to place restriction on his tendency for topical interpretation and sensationalism of political statement embedded in his radical recasting while maintaining the oratorio's contemporary relevance that demonstrated the stage-worthiness of a long-forgotten masterpiece.

Similarly Hans Neuenfels, assisted frequently by Reinhard von der Thannen, has been shocking audiences with his provocative re-imaginings of the Italian and German canon, deconstructing the operas' implicit themes and subtexts. For example, a highly eroticized and gender-blurring *Cosí fan tutte* (Salzburg, 2000), or *Idomeneo* (Berlin, 2003) with its controversial use of decapitated heads of gods staged as a visual protest "against any form of organized religion or its founders" (Ziolkowski 2009: 3). Von der Thannen usually provides functional but neutral sets – black, gray, or white – which he populates with bizarre props and outlandish costumes: bees (*Nabucco*, Berlin, 2000), bulls (*Don Giovanni*, Stuttgart, 2002), or rats (*Lohengrin*, Bayreuth, 2010), that are frequently symbolic and color-coded, or in fantastically bold colors. He translates topical issues that fascinate Neuenfels into quite physical but absolutely unexpected metaphors, which are "both very funny and entertaining as well as frightening and threatening" (Risi 2013: 355). However, there seems to be a gap between Tsypin's *Theodora* and Von der Thannen's designs for Neuenfels that Balme's concept of post-conceptual scenography can illuminate as the dystopian imaginations are recast in parody of Aesopian imagery.

Post-conceptual scenography and the vernacular

One key aspect of this new strategy, emerging out of the complex genealogies I have outlined so far, is that post-conceptual scenography is primarily figurative and far less linguistically controlled since it tends to abdicate an overarching concept, in particular one of linguistically mediated meaning (Balme 2006: 52). Instead, it favors a multitextual equality of meanings where text, music, and images exist in parallel, allowing an associative functioning of imagery that is, on the one hand, quite concrete, but on the other, ambiguous. Balme connects this new approach with the arrival of the "*junge wilde*" (young wild) British and American designers and directors at the Bayerische Staatsoper in Munich in the early 1990s. The most notorious is Richard Jones' *Giulio*

Cesare in Egitto (1994), designed by Nigel Lowery, with vivid imagery that included a gigantic T-Rex, great white sharks, and a ladder. These images became symbols of the new approach in operatic scenography that emphasizes vernacular references, self-aware pastiche and intertextuality, resulting in "inventive, irreverent, even farcical theatricality that endorsed the genius of the works in brand-new ways" (Sutcliffe 2005: 334). The source of this new strategy Balme traces back to Robert Wilson's theatre that rejects any kind of a single controlling concept in favor of multiple elements running parallel to each other and all equally important (Balme 2006: 58). This lack of an overarching concept supplemented with the dominance of more associatively functioning imagery fosters a *mise-en-scène* that is absolutely unique in its concreteness and anything but unequivocal in its function (Balme 2006: 64). However, Von der Thannen's imagery references a world beyond the text that exhibits a tendency to undermine and disintegrate the opera. In the communicative transaction the pictorial interpretation depends on the spectator's aptitude. Consequently, by situating image production and reception within the changing social and cultural spheres, the responsibility of creating meaning is transferred to the spectator, fostering symbolic and metaphoric equivocality, ambiguous multiplicity, and indeterminacy of meanings.

A post-conceptual whimsical style is typical for Nigel Lowery, who, as Sutcliffe asserts, is "the most individual and original scenic artist the UK has produced" (Sutcliffe 2006). He is methodically iconoclastic in his bravado approach to design and employed imagery, purposely employing painted elements, found objects, cardboard boxes, and obviously contemporary costumes to undercut opera's high-art standards. In this his work is starkly reminiscent of Achim Freyer's unique oeuvre with its emphasis on the painterly, the grotesque, and the lowbrow.[14] Lowery's most cerebral design was for Richard Jones' *The Ring* (London, 1994–6): "Denuded of naturalistic scenery and filled with references to pop art, twentieth-century theatre, and fairy tale, the production invented a new vocabulary of shock and wonder for key points in the action" (Ashman 2008: 267). In his own productions – like Handel's *Rinaldo* (Innsbruck, 2002) – he freely borrows imagery from the rich repository of cultural and vernacular references, which include De Chirico, Picasso, and Klee, as well as a plentitude of cinematic allusions. In addition to dinosaurs and sharks, mermaids and Snow Whites, Barbie dolls and Tweety Bird, pirates and crossing guards, adults wearing lederhosen, fins and snorkel mask, mops and urinals, gym suits and pumpkin heads, etc., can be seen on his stage. This imagery can be bewildering, but Lowery is delightful and endlessly inventive, especially when it comes to elements of satire and irony that lend his scenography an unsettling touch and inherently profound meaning.

The vernacular also epitomizes Anna Viebrock's vocabulary, however her scenographic practice differs significantly from standard methods. She developed her highly distinctive style collaborating with Christoph Marthaler (*Kát'a Kabanová*, Salzburg, 1999) and Jossi Wieler (*La sonnambula*, Stuttgart, 2011), co-creating their productions and forming close partnerships. One startling stylistic habit stands out: in almost every production, Viebrock updates opera to her signature period of the 1970s. She is a scavenger of forgotten and abandoned interior architecture: she recreates lost spaces on stage, using remnants of past domestic life but with any idea of homeliness stripped away. As in a time capsule the spectator of *Tristan und Isolde* (Bayreuth, 2005) is back in shabby East Germany with its Formica furniture, strip-lights, and peeling-off wallpaper that help to recreate a simulacrum of familiar places and lost time. Taking the real spaces she transposes them, building on stage monumentally cavernous spaces with soaring, frequently windowless walls, lending the stage a palpable corporeality and presence. This is a hyperrealism on a different level that obscures the distinctions between art and life, between high and low culture. Her aesthetic of banality can be jarring and alienating, especially for critics and the operagoers that expect perfection and picturesque beauty on the operatic stage. Viebrock denies her audiences this form of escapism, and, instead, she provides them with a Kafkaesque space, desolate and with no exit.

Return of abstraction and the international style of *cool beauty*

Recent decades have seen an aesthetic shift in visuality, culminating in a trend within operatic design that could be described as a new international style of *cool beauty*, which combines abstraction and high fashion, mixing stylization and theatricality while aestheticizing them into an impressive spectacle. This is a prominent if not hegemonic trend epitomized by Robert Wilson's aesthetics that powerfully re-introduced simplicity and abstraction in articulating operatic space. What identifies the style of *cool beauty* are austerely articulated spaces with visibly defined geometric elements, isolated bodies and objects that are frequently backlit, saturated colors and strong contrasts, highly luminous environments in which light is used as a dramaturgical tool, stylized gestures and movements. This visual and production style, which induces a sense of dislocation, Aronson identified and criticized as a scenographic phenomenon of "international chic" (Aronson 2005: 82). Originating in the formalist aesthetics of Wilson and Richard Foreman, it resonates philosophically and culturally with two key postmodern concepts: Jameson's pastiche and Baudrillard's simulacrum. It produces non-specific spatio-temporality within an ultra-modern, fictive world of disintegrated coherence, which is "sleek and beautiful, evocative and mysterious, yet ultimately shallow and unknowable and totally unenlightening" (Aronson 2005: 85). Aronson's critical reaction seems to stem from a more wide-ranging mistrust towards visuality and aesthetics of pleasure, while his negative assessment points toward a particular contemporary combination of aestheticization and formalism, leading to important questions about the epistemological weight and political orientation of such abstraction and aestheticism.[15] However, this new style should be seen not only within the larger picture of design for opera but also in the context of a rejuvenation of "residual cultural form" (Williams 1981: 204), and above all Appia's ideas and Wieland Wagner's scenography, with their emphasis on rudimentary representation, symbolism, light, simplicity, and constrained emotions played in abstract open spaces defined by light rather than built scenery. The style of *cool beauty* renews it by giving it a new quality – the allusive and evocative dimension of the images combined with the higher levels of abstraction – while rejecting the dominant historicist paradigm that paradoxically the Chéreau/Peduzzi *Ring* endorsed.

Wilson's scenography stands out for its singularly unified visual orthodoxy. His visual formalism – criticized as having dissipated into an empty aestheticism – offers an alternative approach that allows discovering opera anew. His three productions of canonical operas from 1991 – *Lohengrin*, *Parsifal*, and *Zauberflöte*, created in Switzerland, Germany, and France – in one decisive move reintroduced abstraction, stylization and theatricalization, tearing opera away from realistic and imposing ideas of operatic décor.[16] The basic set arrangement creates an impression that the Wilsonian space is empty and as a rule the stage in his productions remains and connotes – at least at first glance – *emptiness* in its visual conception. Suppressing the space and minimalizing the depth, Wilson refuses to appeal to the spectator's subjective experience with the object, upsetting habituation and familiarity of seeing, forcing the audience to look attentively at it instead of looking into it or through it. He transcends the dominant and familiar forms of pictorial representation. Denying the melodramatic emotionality, projection, identification, and visual excess on stage, as in his quintessential productions of heightened abstract formalism such as *Madama Butterfly* (1993) and *Pelléas et Mélisande* (1997), both premiered in Paris, Wilson creates a new space for music appreciation while continuing to subvert the conventions of operatic staging and posits the opera in a productive discourse. The aesthetic idiom of geometric abstraction affects the spectators' attitudes and revises practices of looking: limiting the amount of visual stimuli compels the spectators to hear music, reshaping the relationships between seeing and hearing.

The specific aesthetic traits of *cool beauty* can also be identified across the map of contemporary design for opera, appearing in heterogeneous variations and hybridizations, yet palpably part of the same development. Wilson's direct influence can be pinpointed in Heiner Müller's apocalyptic staging of *Tristan und Isolde* (Bayreuth, 1993) that subverted the Romantic yearning for death embedded in the text and music. Erich Wonder designed a cubed space with shifting shapes of light projected onto walls and stage floor. Only a few elements differentiated one act from the next: a delineated box downstage for Act I, a labyrinth of straight rows of hundreds of identical breastplates, "standing limbless and headless in military rows as if to symbolize the uncomprehending worldly forces that ensure the pair can never be alone" and always keeping the lovers apart for Act II, and a broad armchair, in which Tristan awaits for Isolde and his death (Kalb 1993: 100). The entire stage and the costumes (Yohji Yamamoto) in Act III were all covered in dust and other post-catastrophic debris. To emphasize the human anguish and alienation, Wonder maintained monochromatic somberness throughout with few color accents. In contrast, Maria Björnson's design for Graham Vick's *Macbeth* (Milan, 1997) juxtaposed strong colors with the pure form of a monolithic hollow cube, which "pivoted on one corner stage center, revolving into different positions for the various scenes," hovering and engulfing the main characters (Clark 1998). Here Björnson employed strong abstraction and symbolism, combining emblematic meaning of colors (blue, red, yellow, green, and white, used both for the set and costume) with a single stage prop that dominates the center of the empty stage. As Franca Cella writes, in *Macbeth* the cube signifies places of action, but also indicates a state of mind, symbolizing the evil, blood, power, eroticism, tragedy, and so on (Cella 2001: 371). Similarly, Herbert Wernicke's production of Strauss' *Elektra* (Munich, 1997) used bold basic colors; his scenography was based on an extraordinary geometry of red and black, with light as a dramaturgical tool. The *coup de theatre* occurred when the colossal black wall of the palace, which had forced the action onto the forestage, started to open and eventually swiveled diagonally revealing a great staircase and the backstage, all suffused in bright red light. Like Wonder and Björnson, Wernicke used various modes of abstraction, swathes and fields of striking color, de-naturalized lighting, and fashionably stylized costumes. These designers were not afraid of symbolism, even an overtly ostensible one.

In a way, this shift in the visuality of contemporary operatic spectacle is at its most striking in its aesthetics. It can also be traced in more subtle ways, above all in the articulation of the space and in the use of images, metaphors, and symbols that are not necessarily embedded in the text. This move towards the anti-referential and anti-pictorialism, which parallels a tendency towards symbol and abstraction, can be traced in the work of such designers as Michael Levine and Paul Steinberg, as well as Wolfgang Gussmann, Boris Kudlička, Rebecca Ringst, Pierre-André Weitz, Martin Zehetgruber, Johannes Leiacker, and Klaus Grünberg, who have created outstanding designs with remarkable spatial solutions that emphasize abstraction. The austere spaces, rigorously articulated, disavowing verisimilitude and defined with distinct light have long been a forte of the Canadian designer Michael Levine. His sets for Monique Wagemakers' *Rigoletto* (1996) and Simon McBurney's *Die Zauberflöte* (2012), both done in Amsterdam, are striking in their simplicity and sophistication as the space for each opera is physically generated by a hydraulic platform, intensely affecting the dramaturgy of action. The most celebrated production for which he created a set is Anthony Minghella's staging of *Madama Butterfly* (London, 2005). Not just in the sensationally spectacular way Levine re-introduced minimalism on the Metropolitan Opera stage, and similarly to Wilson's *Butterfly* he helped to reverse the opera's inherent exoticism. Hyunseon Lee (2014) shows how this staging deliberately recontextualizes *Butterfly* in its postmodern ritualized and dramatized variation. In more recent productions like Francois Girard's *Parsifal* (Lyon, 2012), Levine incorporates into his sets highly mediated surfaces as digital technology becomes more sophisticated and openly toys with images of reality. According to Natalie Rewa, his scenography "insists on the conception of space that includes shifting proportions and potentialities of negative space as aesthetically significant," but it is also an interactive space as it engages the spectator's imagination (Rewa 2004: 133).

The stark minimalist sets that are typical of American designer Paul Steinberg not only provoke the imagination but also directly target the senses. Unlike Levine, Steinberg developed a unique, idiosyncratically individual style that celebrates ornamentation, pattern, and decoration – a whimsical and aesthetically sophisticated treatment of illusion and geometry, particularly palpable in his designs for David Alden's Baroque operas in Munich (*L'incoronazione di Poppea* 1997, *Rodelinda* 2003, and *Orlando* 2005). Steinberg delights in colors: pastel or garish, geometric patterns and textures in surprising and intensified combinations that he uses for illusionistic effects of curving, warping, and tilting planes, typical for op-art (see Figure 44.3). Such treatment of space is daring and disorienting, challenging the spectator's abilities to translate Steinberg's visual clues into spatial articulation. Frequently the vertigo effect shocks the audiences as Steinberg physically contracts the stage space for a greater familiarity and proximity. In his architectural sets, including *Peter Grimes* (2009) and *Billy Budd* (2012), both premiered in London, Steinberg plays with the scale for emotional response, contrasting the monumental with the intimate, spatially signifying internal dynamics and tensions, while constructing a highly emotional environment.

The sets designed by Es Devlin, a widely celebrated and successful female designer, are highly spectacular, but in a way removed from the grandiose historicism of decades before. As she favors architectural and mobile sets, often multi-tier, her designs fill out the entire space like her designs for David McVicar's *Les Troyens* (London, 2012) with a gigantic Constructivist horse made of destroyed weapons and breathing fire and John Fulljames's *Rise and Fall of the City of Mahagonny* (London, 2015) that she built with shipping containers. Devlin is often still literal in her field of reference. This can be seen in her set for Holten's *Don Giovanni* (London, 2013) (Figure 44.4), which extensively uses video mapping, a new projection technique facilitating a dynamic video projection on any surface, not just flat panels or screens. Using this device tool, she devised a two-story

Figure 44.3 *La Calisto*, sets by Paul Steinberg, costumes by Buki Shiff, lighting by Pat Collins at the Bavarian State Opera, directed by David Alden (2005). (Photo: George Mott; courtesy of Paul Steinberg.)

Figure 44.4 *Don Giovanni* designed by Es Devlin at the Royal Opera House, London, 2013. (Bill Cooper/Royal Opera House/ArenaPAL.)

cube, featuring balconies, stairways, and multiple doors. The cube continuously rotates, producing intimate and secretive spaces as it moves. This, it turns out, is Giovanni's private mental space, while also serving as a space of entrapment and confinement. The video projections (Luke Halls) spectacularly stage David Deutsch's myriad of parallel universes as well as the erasure of the physical architecture that Devlin fashioned for Mozart's opera. Devlin's *Giovanni* is a sophisticated example of mainstream opera integrating radically new modes of performance and projection.

New technologies, mediatization, and dematerialization

Embracing technology, operatic stage designers have made use of new media to create virtual background and projected sceneries with greater ease. This involves numerous forms: standard projections on large screens, live camera work, video projections, animations, and mapping. Projections can be relegated to the background, used as a support of the narrative, or to replace physical scenery almost completely. They perform a traditional function of the scenery; most often they remain a supplementary element, or, as Bertolt Brecht would say "a mechanical auxiliary" (Brecht 1965: 151). For example, George Tsypin's monumentally spare set for Andrei Konchalovsky's *War and Peace* (St. Petersburg, 2000) incorporated Elaine McCarthy's continuous projections of clouds, skylines, and a burning city on the cyclorama – neither strictly cinematically crisp nor photorealistic – supplementing Tsypin's dramatic imagery for Prokofiev's opera and assisting the spectator in understanding the narrative. Recently, however – and less positively – projections have been used as a kind of gimmick indicating modernization of the design, with an empty stylistic panache that can only temporarily distract attention from the traditionalism of set and staging. Examples of this have been seen in rather safe productions, like Deborah Warner's *Eugene Onegin* (London, 2011; set Tom Pye, costumes Chloé Obolensky, video designers Finn Ross and Ian William Galloway) or Richard Eyre's *Werther* (New York, 2014; designer Rob Howell, video designer Wendall K. Harrington), which used projections as a veneer of contemporarily sensibility while in fact remaining within a faithful modality in depicting the period in which the opera was composed.

Video projections in opera are not just scenery; they can also be used as a dramaturgical tool. In his *Don Carlos* (Hamburg, 2001; designer Johannes Leiacker), Peter Konwitschny, notorious producer for his post-Brechtian approach, used live video projections as a device for breaking the fourth wall. He staged the auto-da-fé scene during the intermission as a live telecast of breaking news. The multimedia live event, directed by his assistant Vera Nemirova, had contemporary political allusions (the arrival of celebrities, distribution of anti-war pamphlets, and terrorists chased throughout the opera house) and included real news footage mixed with live images from the street, the foyer, and the auditorium with the spectators cast both as witnesses and voyeurs. These approaches deconstructed Verdi's opera and, as Gundula Kreuzer argues, "exploded rather than reduced the score by blurring the boundaries between stage and auditorium, art and life," inside and outside, disrupting the spatiality of the opera house (Kreuzer 2006: 178).

Unlike Konwitschny, Romeo Castellucci used large-scale realistic black-and-white live video-feed projections in his staging of *Orphée et Eurydice* (Brussels, 2014) to heighten the emotions and reinvent the myth into a tangible story. He directly intertwined two separate narratives, that of Gluck's opera and the life story of "Els" (She) – a contemporary

Eurydice. Castellucci told her story initially through text projected on a grey flat curtain, then through the video projections (Vincent Pinckaers), carefully building up dramatic tension and almost eschewing the entire action on the stage. Video allowed Castellucci to play with various realities, breaking down the fourth wall, which he physically materialized, blurred, and destroyed. Scenographically he juxtaposed different spatiality: the empty space of an almost bare stage was contrasted with a mediatized and intangible space of video projection, which later was set in opposition to a hyper-realistic recreation of an idyllic landscape with a naked Eurydice, presenting yet another level of total theatrical illusion. Overlaying various realities and texts Castellucci complicated the relationship between live action, time and space.

In contrast to realistic projections, different aesthetics of visual representation involving drawing and animation, which recent developments allow on a greater scale, more intensely destabilize spatial perception: the space becomes more eerie, transient, and intangible. Already in his *Die Zauberflöte* (Brussels, 2005), featuring black-and-white, back and frontal projections of his drawings, William Kentridge suggested one direction that projections could take. In his reinterpretation Kentridge visually translates the critique of Enlightenment and early colonialism as ambivalence between clarity and obscurity, visibility and invisibility, gravity and antigravity. His broader critique is inseparable from the way he challenges the spatial corporeality of the stage. As one scholar put it, his projections "fragment volumetric spatiality and flex its borders and corners . . . [and] poetically challenge the everyday politics of space" (Donger 2008: 173). Another production of *Die Zauberflöte* (Berlin, 2012), co-directed and developed by the *Regietheater* producer Barrie Kosky and the British theatre group 1927 (Suzanne Andrade and Paul Barritt), took animation to a yet another level, mixing live performance with animatronics. In this production, all physical scenery, as well as all spoken dialogue, was replaced by animated video and title projections.[17] Barritt's black-and-white and colorful designs combined faux-naïve silent-film aesthetics and the 1920s animation style emblematic of Fleischer Studios' improvisatory animation, surreal action and erotic innuendos. With great virtuosity, the live singers and the pantomime were synchronized with the funny and whimsical images, which had an edge of irony and absurdity. Here opera merged with film and digital technologies to an arguably unprecedented degree, removing deep-seated anxieties towards the power of images.

The new technologies can transform the theatrical space into a virtual performative environment and liberate the opera from its own constraints as an elite art form. With the aid of new technologies the constantly shifting images transform opera into an expanded theatrical experience that blurs the boundaries between film, art, theatre, multimedia, and popular culture. This approach is superbly captured by the Catalan theatre group La Fura dels Baus that combines theatricality, acrobatics, and multimedia. Their two main directors Àlex Ollé and Carlus Padrissa collaborate with sculptor Jaume Plensa (*La damnation de Faust*, Salzburg, 1999), designer Alfons Flores (*Le grand macabre*, Brussels, 2009) and video designer Franc Aleu (*Ring*, Valencia, 2007–9) who delivers virtual landscapes within which the action can be performed, or provides suggestively surreal images. Likewise, Robert Lepage's *techno-en-scène* – as theatre director and scholar Aleksandar Dundjerovic (2006) called the Canadian producer and auteur's *mise-en-scène* – is notorious for the use of mixed media. His *La damnation de Faust* (New York, 2008) used interactive video projections (Holder Förterer) that were seamlessly incorporated into Carl Fillion's starkly functional steel-grid structural multi-tier set, multiplying and fragmenting the stage's spatial articulation. For this spectacular production, Boris Firquet employed large-scale images that were at once atmospheric (billowy curtains and underwater images), historic (making use of Eadweard Muybridge's sequential photos of equine motion), and hyper-realistic (an extreme close up of green grass), creating "spaces [that] visually morph, mutate and transform, often with thrilling speed and theatrical impact" (Dixon 2006: 351). Stagings in which the video imagery becomes an organic but visually bold element of scenography transform and extend spatial perceptions. However, as Lepage and La Fura dels Baus promote the transformative power of new technologies in a global circuit of mainstream opera, they also help to establish a new globalized aesthetic.

Opera is leaving the building

Although the neo-avant-garde theatre rediscovered environmental staging and site-specific performance, these approaches were rarely used in opera before 2000. With advanced contemporary technology, "leaving the opera house" has become less of a problem. Site-specificity involves many forms of practice that, as Bertie Ferdman puts it, "abounds with endless possibilities for reinvigorating theatre and performance and pushing at disciplinary boundaries" (Ferdman 2013: 6), even if it may have been seen as overused as it becomes increasingly more popular.[18] Indeed, new venues like abandoned buildings and public spaces sanction spatial reconfigurations and the application of aesthetics drastically different to those the institutionalized space of the opera house can provide, as well as new ways of involving and stimulating spectators, arguably central to keeping and making opera attractive.

Operas are now staged in a variety of alternative spaces: museums, hotels, gardens, churches, pubs, warehouses, prisons, even buses and limousines. These spaces are attractive to theatre artists, not least because of the strong emotional connotations of their uses; inevitably all these unusual sites heightened the spectator's perception. A good example is the work of Ireland's Opera Theatre Company (OTC), which presented a few productions in highly evocative and theatrical settings. In particular, the OTC stagings of Handel's *Tamerlano* (1992), Ullmann's *The Emperor of Atlantis* (2002), and Beethoven's *Fidelio* (2006) acquired unforeseen authenticity and resonant interpretations by being performed in a heritage site of distinct symbolism and context: Kilmainham Gaol, a late eighteenth-century infamous British prison in Dublin, now a museum and a monument to Irish independence. The OTC succeeded not only in connecting directly with the site on many levels, but also placed it "at the heart of a contemporary discourse of dissonant heritage" (Cooke 2014: 94).

While augmenting the genre's multidimensionality, site-specificity moves opera closer to the interactive, immersive idea of postmodern performance with the expanded notion of scenography. In trying to create more immersive operatic performances, the key device is to dissolve the division between the audience and the stage, usually by putting the spectators and performers in the same space. For the community-oriented Birmingham Opera Company (BOC), finding a shared common space is a priority. In 2012, BOC staged the world premiere of *Mittwoch aus Licht*, Stockhausen's third opera from his cycle *Light*. The production, created by the company's founder and artistic director Graham Vick and designer Paul Brown, was staged in the cavernous Argyle Works, an abandoned chemical factory. For the "World Parliament" scene, Brown placed the Ex Cathedra choir in business suits, their faces painted with international flags, on top of yellow stepladders arranged in a grand circle with the audience sitting on foam mats in the middle. For the scene "The Orchestra Finalists," nine musicians performed suspended from the ceiling, while the audience looked up while lying down on the mats. The "Helicopter String Quartet" – performed by the Elysian Quartet – was presented as a video relay of the music played in four different helicopters flying over the city while the audience watched it indoors. Brown's scenographic design, which combined a real space of live performance with the two-dimensional space of video projection, thereby staging the "unstageable" scene, had significant consequences for both aural and ocular receptions that restructured operatic experience and dialectics of perception.

Similarly, The Industry, a company that since 2012 has been challenging the opera scene in Los Angeles, has extracted its productions from its institutionalized context to confront spectators with new ways of looking and listening, while presenting an expanded definition of opera. For Christopher Cerrone's *Invisible Cities* (2013), based on the book by Italo Calvino, the company's founder and artistic director, Yuval Sharon, presented the piece in and around Union Station, the historic train station. As space is a central aspect of the opera, the train station became the perfect site, with its inherent transience and state of distraction, perpetuated homelessness and loneliness. This was particularly vital since Cerrone composed his opera for headphones. In 2015 The Industry presented *Hopscotch*, a mobile opera in 24 cars. The work involved an exploration of an elusively fragmented story; a defamiliarized and disorienting peregrination through secret sites of the city, intimate performances in limousines and from a great distance on rooftops, in parks or five-story inner courtyards where others might watch. The Industry's site-specific productions stand out as a contemporary manifestation of operatic scenographies that defy conventions, use visceral approach and experiential spaces, emphasize sensorial elements, and increase intimacy between performer and audience.

Productions in post-industrial spaces tap into the same ideas but allow designers to restructure the system of operatic communication while sustaining spectacular theatricality. Adaptive reuse of many types of industrial spaces has furnished opera with alternative structures that provide flexibility while creating possibilities to generate and contextualize operatic works within different contexts. These spaces imply an anti-elitist perspective and a democratization of the spectatorship, while having a seductive ambience. However, both discursively and socially, the practice is a problematic one since, on the one hand, it induces urban revitalization and boosts the local economy through tourism, but, on the other, it enables gentrification while domesticating and commodifying the industrial past and its aesthetic (Storm 2014).

Such scenographic adaptations can be dated back at least to Karl-Ernst and Ursul Herrmanns' *Orfeo ed Euridice* (Brussels, 1988) in the Halles de Schaerbeek, a former glass- and steel-covered market hall that was undergoing adaptive renovation. A more recent example is the Ruhrtriennale festival, founded by Gerard Mortier in 2002 in abandoned industrial structures in the Ruhr industrial region of Germany. So far the most illustrious production was David Pountney's staging of Bernd Alois Zimmermann's *Die Soldaten* (2006) in the Jahrhunderthalle, a former gas power station in Bochum. In Robert Innes Hopkins' environment the audience sat on a movable rostrum on tracks that ran along the stage – a 100-meter-long runway erected along the length of the enormous Jahrhunderthalle. Nine times during the performance the audience was brought toward the stage for a close-up and then retreated for a perspectival view on the action.

As the music critic Shirley Apthorp (2006) noted, this was "a knuckle-whitening ride through a thrilling tale . . . physically engaging" that turned the spectators into voyeurs of human demise, although the production represented "a site-specific performance experience that no conventional house could emulate."

Conclusion

At its best, contemporary design for opera is experimental, dynamic and fluid, allusive and open, frequently commenting on the action, adding layers of meaning, contributing to dramatic tension, transforming and extending spatial perceptions. In many cases, contemporary designers strive for an explicit departure from a traditional operatic design and a definite move towards postmodern scenography and collaborative processes of production and design. What could still be called postmodern design has challenged fundamental assumptions about the meaning and purpose of scenography within operatic performance. Finally, opera scenography moves beyond the modernist idea that design should support the text or its interpretation although it still has remained embedded in traditional performance technologies. On the global scale, operatic design has been increasingly freed from the constraints of literal representation, as well as descriptive and narrative functions. This has not been an easy passage: many singers and operagoers, critics and scholars continue to favor traditionally devised productions. Employing new technologies, video projections, live feeds, digital imagery the opera participates in ongoing cultural and technological shifts, while radically changing the conception and range of scenography within performance. As well as changing aesthetics, construed in a narrow sense, technology and the use of unconventional spaces have pioneered new modes of producing opera, as well as new forms of spectatorship. If, initially, site-specific productions were the work of small companies, now even large opera houses seek unusual venues to attract new audiences, identifying alternative spaces for new and old chamber operas, as well as forms of music theatre which call for more intimate spaces or radically different configurations. Not only the look, meaning, and function of operatic stage design has changed, but also the modes of transmission and the very location of the medium.

Notes

1 All translations are mine unless indicated otherwise.
2 One of the first major opera houses to employ a postmodern artist was La Scala (Robert Wilson's *Salome*, 1987). Opéra de Paris shortly followed suit.
3 *Regietheater* as a concept is amorphous and difficult to define since it encompasses a variety of directorial approaches (Risi 2013). The first survey of operatic stagings diverging from the score and libretto was written by Nagler (1980) whose negative assessment has been echoed by critics including Pleasants (1989) and Littlejohn (1992), as well as musicologists such as Donington (1991), Dean (1997), and Taruskin (2009). Notable exceptions: British music critic Sutcliffe (1996) and American theatre and Germanic studies scholar Levin (2007).
4 First presented in Brussels in 1982, the designer Karl-Ernst Herrmann significantly altered the Salzburg revival, advocating new visual theatricality and presenting an aestheticized image of Mozart's world chic and dazzling, minimal and ahistorical, and fashionably conscious.
5 Operas on the lake now attract approximately 200,000 spectators (Wilkinson 2007).
6 For Bregenz Festival Pountney and Lazaridis also created together *Der fliegende Holländer* (1989) and *Fidelio* (1995) on the lake and for the indoor Martinu's *The Greek Passion* (1999).
7 Ashman called this movement an "anti-Appian revolution" as it presented a challenge to both modernist and traditional stage design (Ashman 1992: 42).

8 Closely collaborating with such directors as Peter Zadek. Claus Peymann and Peter Stein, German designers like Herrmann, Freyer, and Wonder, created visually coherent, clearly formulated concepts.
9 Two radically postmodern productions of Wagner's cycle had preceded it: the Kassel *Ring* (1970–4), director Ulrich Melchinger and designer Thomas Richter-Forgach; and the Leipzig *Ring* (1973–6), director Joachim Herz and designer Rudolf Heinrich. The latter is seen as a pivotal staging of *Regietheater* that also marked a return to built sets. For a detailed analysis see Carnegy 2006.
10 Strehler's favorite designers – Ezio Frigerio (*Simon Boccanegra*, 1971) and Luciano Damiani (*Macbeth*, 1975) – created simple sets that retained elements of history, but their designs were allowed to dramatically focus the productions, while comprising of strikingly powerful visual and theatrical imagery.
11 The short-lived *Krolloper* (1927–31) led in the modern reinterpretation of canonized operas, see Carnegy 2006.
12 Influenced by the *commedia dell'arte*, Damiani's design also emphasized comic and ironic aspects of Mozart's opera, typically considered as a work of a serious nature.
13 See Tsypin 2005: 119.
14 For discussion of Freyer's operatic scenography see Kara 2015.
15 This style marks a general shift in contemporary visuality, coinciding with the Digital Revolution. See Foster (2002) and van Laar and Diepeveen (2013).
16 This coincided with the beginning of Wilson's long-term collaboration with the Italian costume designer Frida Parmeggiani, who was responsible for co-authoring his aesthetic style, including *Parsifal* (Hamburg, 1991), *Madama Butterfly* (Paris, 1993), *Pelléas et Mélisande* (Paris, 1997), *Lohengrin* (New York, 1998), Wagner's *Ring* (Zürich, 1999–2000), and *Johannes-Passion* (Paris, 2007).
17 The entire action is set up against a white wall with multiple doors that allow the singers to appear along the vertical and horizontal axes. Set and costumes designed by Esther Bialas.
18 For the purpose of this chapter I excluded the open-air sites as well as on-location-staged operas created as genuine media products, such as *La traviata im Bahnhof* (Zürich, 2008) and *Peter Grimes* on Aldeburgh Beach (2013). For site-specific performance see Kaye 2000, Pearson and Shanks 2001, Tompkins 2012, and Wilkie 2014, on site-specific opera see O'Neill 2009 and Morris 2015.

References

Apthorp, Shirley 2006. "Die Soldaten, Jahrhunderthalle, Bochum, Germany." *FT.com*, 8 October: 1.
Aronson, Arnold 1991. "George Tsypin." *TD&T* 27 (3): 9–19.
Aronson, Arnold 2005. *Looking into the Abyss: Essays on Scenography*. Ann Arbor: University of Michigan Press.
Ashman, Mike 1992. "Producing Wagner." In *Wagner in Performance*, edited by Barry Millington and Stewart Spencer, 29–47. New Haven, CT: Yale University Press.
Ashman, Mike 2008. "Wagner on Stage: Aesthetic, Dramaturgical, and Social Considerations." In *The Cambridge Companion to Wagner*, edited by Thomas S. Grey, 246–75. Cambridge: Cambridge University Press.
Auslander, Philip 2004. "Postmodernism and Performance." In *The Cambridge Companion to Postmodernism*, edited by Steven Connor, 97–114. Cambridge: Cambridge University Press.
Balme, Christopher 2006. "Libretto-Partitur-Bild: Die Münchner Händel-Inszenierungen zwischen Konzept- und Bildtheater." In *OperMachtTheaterBilder: Neue Wirklichkeiten des Regietheaters*, edited by Jürgen Schläder, 51–72. Leipzig: Henschel.
Belting, Hans 2001. *Bild-Anthropologie: Entwürfe für eine Bildwissenschaft*. München: Fink.
Brecht, Bertolt 1965. *The Mother*, translated by Lee Baxandall. New York: Grove.
Brejzek, Thea 2012. "Scenography or: Making Space." In *The Disappearing Stage: Reflections on the 2011 Praque Quadrennial*, edited by Arnold Aronson, 16–23. Prague: Arts and Theatre Institute.
Carnegy, Patrick 2006. *Wagner and the Art of Theatre*. New Haven, CT: Yale University Press.
Cella, Franca 2001. "La conquista della regia." In *Verdi e la Scala*, edited by Francesco Degarda, 251–383. Milano: Rizzoli, Edizioni del Teatro alla Scala.

Clark, Mike 1998. "Milanese Macbeth." *TCI* 32 (7): 10–11.
Cooke, Pat 2014. "Art and Kilmainham Gaol: Negotiation Art's Critical Intervention in the Heritage Site." In *Art and Archeology. Collaborations, Conversations, Criticisms*, edited by Ian Alden Russell and Andrew Cochrane, 83–98. London: Springer Science & Business Media.
Dean, Winton 1997. "Production Style in Handel's Operas." In *The Cambridge Companion to Handel*, edited by Donald Burrows, 249–61. Cambridge: Cambridge University Press.
Dixon, Steve 2006. *Digital Performance: A History of New Media in Theatre, Dance, Performance Art and Installation*. Cambridge: MIT Press.
Donger, Simon 2008. "Gloom/Invisible Walls as Invisible Hands: Scenography as Geo-Pornographic Approach to Designing Space." *Teatro do Mundo* 3: 161–79.
Donington, Robert 1991. *Opera and Its Symbols: The Unity of Words, Music, and Staging*. New Haven, CT: Yale University Press.
Dundjerovic, Aleksandar Sasha 2006. "*Juliette at Zulu Time*: Robert Lepage and the aesthetics of 'techno-en-scene.'" *International Journal of Performance Arts and Digital Media* 2 (1): 69–85.
Ferdman, Bertie 2013. "A New Journey through Other Spaces: Contemporary Performance beyond 'Site-Specific.'" *Theatre* 43 (2): 5–25.
Foster, Hal 2002. *Design and Crime: And Other Diatribes*. London: Verso.
Foucault, Michel [1980] 1998. "The Imagination of the Nineteenth Century." In *Foucault, Aesthetics, Method, and Epistemology*, edited by James D. Faubion, translated by Alex Susteric, Vol. 2, 235–9. New York: The New Press.
Gossett, Philip 2006. *Divas and Scholars: Performing Italian Opera*. Chicago, IL: University of Chicago Press.
Hunter, Mary 2014. "Historically Informed Performance." In *The Oxford Handbook of Opera*, edited by Helen Greenwald, 606–26. Oxford: Oxford University Press.
Kalb, Jonathan 1993. "Twilight of the Avant-Garde." *The Village Voice*, 21 September: 99–100.
Kara, Ewa 2015. "The Disruption of Order: Achim Freyer's Scenography for Opera." *Theatre and Performance Design* 1 (4): 298–320.
Kaye, Nick 2000. *Site-Specific Art: Performance, Place and Documentation*. London and New York: Routledge.
Kelly, Elaine 2014. *Composing the Canon in the German Democratic Republic: Narratives of Nineteenth-Century Music*. New York: Oxford University Press.
Kennedy, Dennis 2001. *Looking at Shakespeare: A Visual History of Twentieth-Century Performance* (2nd ed.). Cambridge: Cambridge University Press.
Kreuzer, Gundula 2006. "Voices from Beyond: Verdi's Don Carlos and the Modern Stage." *Cambridge Opera Journal* 18 (2): 151–79.
Laar, Timothy van, and Leonard Diepeveen 2013. *Artworld Prestige: Arguing Cultural Value*. Oxford: Oxford University Press.
Lee, Hyunseon 2014. "Global Butterfly: Visual Exoticism, or its Reversal, in Silent Film and Opera Performances." In *Opera, Exoticism and Visual Culture*, edited by Hyunseon Lee and Naomi Segal, 131–61. Oxford: Peter Lang.
Levin, David J. 2007. *Unsettling Opera: Staging Mozart, Verdi, Wagner, and Zemlinsky*. Chicago, IL: University of Chicago Press.
Littlejohn, David 1992. *The Ultimate Art: Essays Around and About Opera*. Berkley: University of California Press.
Mitchell, W. J. T. 1994. *Picture Theory: Essays on Verbal and Visual Representation*. Chicago, IL: University of Chicago Press.
Morris, Christopher 2015. "The Mute Stones Sing: *Rigoletto* Live from Mantua." *TDR: The Drama Review* 59 (4): 51–66.
Nagler, A. M. [Alois Maria] 1981. *Misdirection: Opera Production in the Twentieth Century*. Hamden, CT: Archon Books.
Namenwirth, Simon Michael 2002. *Gerard Mortier at the Monnaie: The Interviews*. Brussels: VUB Brussels University Press.
O'Neill, Sinéad 2009. "Getting out of the House: Unorthodox Performance Spaces in Recent British and Irish Productions." *Opera Quarterly* 25 (3–4): 284–98.
Pearson, Mike and Michael Shanks 2001. *Theatre/Archeology*. London: Routledge.
Pleasants, Henry 1989. *Opera in Crisis: Tradition, Present, Future*. New York: Thames & Hudson.

Pountney, David 2010. "Stefanos Lazaridis, 1942–2010." *Opera* 61 (7): 810.
Rewa, Natalie 2004. *Scenography in Canada: Selected Designers*. Toronto: University of Toronto Press.
Risi, Clemens 2013. "Performing Wagner for the Twenty-First Century." *New Theatre Quarterly* 29 (4): 349–59.
Savage, Roger 1994. "The Staging of Opera." In *The Oxford Illustrated History of Opera*, edited by Roger Parker, 235–85. Oxford: Oxford University Press.
Shevtsova, Maria 2005. "Peter Sellars." In *Fifty Key Theatre Directors*, edited by Shomit Mitter and Maria Shevtsova, 252–7. London and New York: Routledge.
Storm, Anna 2014. *Post-Industrial Landscape Scars*. New York: Palgrave Macmillan.
Sutcliffe, Tom 1996. *Believing in Opera*. Princeton, NJ: Princeton University Press.
Sutcliffe, Tom 2005. "Technology and Interpretation: Aspects of 'Modernism.'" *The Cambridge Companion to Twentieth-Century Opera*, edited by Mervyn Cooke, 321–40. Cambridge: Cambridge University Press.
Sutcliffe, Tom 2006. "Nigel Lowery's brilliant career – tales of the unexpected." *OperaStageCoach* 1 May. Available online at: www.operastagecoach.co.uk/?page=opera/article&id=20 (accessed 25 January 2016).
Taruskin, Richard 2009. *The Danger of Music and Other Anti-Utopian Essays*. Berkley: University of California Press.
Tsypin, George 2005. *George Tsypin Opera Factory: Building in the Black Void*. New York: Princeton Architectural Press.
Wilkinson, Jane 2007. *Performing the Local and the Global: The Theatre Festivals of Lake Constance*. German Linguistic and Cultural Studies: GLCS, Vol. 22. Oxford: Lang.
Williams, Raymond 1981. *The Sociology of Culture*. Chicago, IL: University of Chicago Press.
Ziolkowski, Theodore 2009. *Scandal on Stage: European Theater as Moral Trial*. Cambridge: Cambridge University Press.

INDEX